National Accounts of OECD Countries

MAIN AGGREGATES

2018/1

OECD

BETTER POLICIES FOR BETTER LIVES

This work is published under the responsibility of the Secretary-General of the OECD. The opinions expressed and arguments employed herein do not necessarily reflect the official views of OECD member countries.

This document, as well as any data and any map included herein, are without prejudice to the status of or sovereignty over any territory, to the delimitation of international frontiers and boundaries and to the name of any territory, city or area.

Please cite this publication as:
OECD (2018), *National Accounts of OECD Countries, Volume 2018 Issue 1: Main Aggregates*, OECD Publishing, Paris.
http://dx.doi.org/10.1787/na_ma_dt-v2018-1-en

ISBN 978-92-64-28974-1 (print)
ISBN 978-92-64-28975-8 (PDF)

Series: National Accounts of OECD Countries
ISSN 2221-4321 (print)
ISSN 2221-433X (online)

The statistical data for Israel are supplied by and under the responsibility of the relevant Israeli authorities. The use of such data by the OECD is without prejudice to the status of the Golan Heights, East Jerusalem and Israeli settlements in the West Bank under the terms of international law.

Table of contents

Conventional signs and abbreviations 9

International comparisons 11
  1. Gross domestic product at current prices and PPPs. 12
  2. Gross domestic product at the price levels and PPPs of year 2010. 13
  3. Gross domestic product per head at current prices and PPPs 14
  4. Gross domestic product per head at the price levels and PPPs of year 2010 15
  5. Gross domestic product per head at current prices and current PPPs, index 16
  6. Gross domestic product per head at the price levels and PPPs of year 2010, index 17
  7. Gross domestic product at current prices and exchange rates 18
  8. Gross domestic product at the price levels and exchange rates of year 2010 19
  9. Gross domestic product at current prices and year 2010 exchange rates. 20
 10. Gross domestic product per head at current prices and exchange rates 21
 11. Gross domestic product per head at the price levels and exchange rates of year 2010 22
 12. Gross domestic product, volume indices. 23
 13. Gross domestic product, price indices 24
 14. Actual individual consumption at current prices and PPPs 25
 15. Actual individual consumption at the price levels and PPPs of year 2010 26
 16. Actual individual consumption per head at current prices and PPPs. 27
 17. Actual individual consumption per head at the price levels and PPPs of year 2010 28
 18. Actual individual consumption per head at current prices and current PPPs, index 29
 19. Actual individual consumption per head at the price levels and PPPs of year 2010, index 30
 20. Actual individual consumption at current prices and exchange rates 31
 21. Actual individual consumption at the price levels and exchange rates of year 2010 32
 22. Actual individual consumption at current prices and year 2010 exchange rates 33
 23. Actual individual consumption per head at current prices and exchange rates. 34
 24. Actual individual consumption per head at the price levels and exchange rates of year 2010 . . . 35
 25. Actual individual consumption, volume indices 36
 26. Actual individual consumption, price indices 37
 27. Exchange rates. 38
 28. Purchasing power parities for gross domestic product 39
 29. Purchasing power parities for actual individual consumption. 40
 30. Population, mid-year estimates 41

Country tables 43

Australia
  1. Gross domestic product, expenditure approach. 44
  2. Gross domestic product, output and income approach 45
  3. Disposable income, saving and net lending / net borrowing 46
  4. Population and employment (persons) and employment (hours worked) by industry 47

Austria

1. Gross domestic product, expenditure approach 48
2. Gross domestic product, output and income approach 49
3. Disposable income, saving and net lending / net borrowing.......................... 50
4. Population and employment (persons) and employment (hours worked) by industry 51

Belgium

1. Gross domestic product, expenditure approach 52
2. Gross domestic product, output and income approach 53
3. Disposable income, saving and net lending / net borrowing.......................... 54
4. Population and employment (persons) and employment (hours worked) by industry 55

Canada

1. Gross domestic product, expenditure approach 56
2. Gross domestic product, output and income approach 57
3. Disposable income, saving and net lending / net borrowing.......................... 58
4. Population and employment (persons) and employment (hours worked) by industry 59

Chile

1. Gross domestic product, expenditure approach 60
2. Gross domestic product, output and income approach 61
3. Disposable income, saving and net lending / net borrowing.......................... 62
4. Population and employment (persons) and employment (hours worked) by industry 63

Czech Republic

1. Gross domestic product, expenditure approach 64
2. Gross domestic product, output and income approach 65
3. Disposable income, saving and net lending / net borrowing.......................... 66
4. Population and employment (persons) and employment (hours worked) by industry 67

Denmark

1. Gross domestic product, expenditure approach 68
2. Gross domestic product, output and income approach 69
3. Disposable income, saving and net lending / net borrowing.......................... 70
4. Population and employment (persons) and employment (hours worked) by industry 71

Estonia

1. Gross domestic product, expenditure approach 72
2. Gross domestic product, output and income approach 73
3. Disposable income, saving and net lending / net borrowing.......................... 74
4. Population and employment (persons) and employment (hours worked) by industry 75

Finland

1. Gross domestic product, expenditure approach 76
2. Gross domestic product, output and income approach 77
3. Disposable income, saving and net lending / net borrowing.......................... 78
4. Population and employment (persons) and employment (hours worked) by industry 79

France

1. Gross domestic product, expenditure approach 80
2. Gross domestic product, output and income approach 81
3. Disposable income, saving and net lending / net borrowing.......................... 82
4. Population and employment (persons) and employment (hours worked) by industry 83

Germany

1. Gross domestic product, expenditure approach 84
2. Gross domestic product, output and income approach 85

3. Disposable income, saving and net lending / net borrowing 86
4. Population and employment (persons) and employment (hours worked) by industry 87

Greece
1. Gross domestic product, expenditure approach. 88
2. Gross domestic product, output and income approach 89
3. Disposable income, saving and net lending / net borrowing 90
4. Population and employment (persons) and employment (hours worked) by industry 91

Hungary
1. Gross domestic product, expenditure approach. 92
2. Gross domestic product, output and income approach 93
3. Disposable income, saving and net lending / net borrowing 94
4. Population and employment (persons) and employment (hours worked) by industry 95

Iceland
1. Gross domestic product, expenditure approach. 96
2. Gross domestic product, output and income approach 97
3. Disposable income, saving and net lending / net borrowing 98
4. Population and employment (persons) and employment (hours worked) by industry 99

Ireland
1. Gross domestic product, expenditure approach. 100
2. Gross domestic product, output and income approach 101
3. Disposable income, saving and net lending / net borrowing 102
4. Population and employment (persons) and employment (hours worked) by industry 103

Israel
1. Gross domestic product, expenditure approach. 104
2. Gross domestic product, output and income approach 105
3. Disposable income, saving and net lending / net borrowing 106
4. Population and employment (persons) and employment (hours worked) by industry 107

Italy
1. Gross domestic product, expenditure approach. 108
2. Gross domestic product, output and income approach 109
3. Disposable income, saving and net lending / net borrowing 110
4. Population and employment (persons) and employment (hours worked) by industry 111

Japan
1. Gross domestic product, expenditure approach. 112
2. Gross domestic product, output and income approach 113
3. Disposable income, saving and net lending / net borrowing 114
4. Population and employment (persons) and employment (hours worked) by industry 115

Korea
1. Gross domestic product, expenditure approach. 116
2. Gross domestic product, output and income approach 117
3. Disposable income, saving and net lending / net borrowing 118
4. Population and employment (persons) and employment (hours worked) by industry 119

Latvia
1. Gross domestic product, expenditure approach. 120
2. Gross domestic product, output and income approach 121
3. Disposable income, saving and net lending / net borrowing 122
4. Population and employment (persons) and employment (hours worked) by industry 123

Luxembourg
1. Gross domestic product, expenditure approach 124
2. Gross domestic product, output and income approach 125
3. Disposable income, saving and net lending / net borrowing 126
4. Population and employment (persons) and employment (hours worked) by industry 127

Mexico
1. Gross domestic product, expenditure approach 128
2. Gross domestic product, output and income approach 129
3. Disposable income, saving and net lending / net borrowing 130
4. Population and employment (persons) and employment (hours worked) by industry 131

Netherlands
1. Gross domestic product, expenditure approach 132
2. Gross domestic product, output and income approach 133
3. Disposable income, saving and net lending / net borrowing 134
4. Population and employment (persons) and employment (hours worked) by industry 135

New Zealand
1. Gross domestic product, expenditure approach 136
2. Gross domestic product, output and income approach 137
3. Disposable income, saving and net lending / net borrowing 138
4. Population and employment (persons) and employment (hours worked) by industry 139

Norway
1. Gross domestic product, expenditure approach 140
2. Gross domestic product, output and income approach 141
3. Disposable income, saving and net lending / net borrowing 142
4. Population and employment (persons) and employment (hours worked) by industry 143

Poland
1. Gross domestic product, expenditure approach 144
2. Gross domestic product, output and income approach 145
3. Disposable income, saving and net lending / net borrowing 146
4. Population and employment (persons) and employment (hours worked) by industry 147

Portugal
1. Gross domestic product, expenditure approach 148
2. Gross domestic product, output and income approach 149
3. Disposable income, saving and net lending / net borrowing 150
4. Population and employment (persons) and employment (hours worked) by industry 151

Slovak Republic
1. Gross domestic product, expenditure approach 152
2. Gross domestic product, output and income approach 153
3. Disposable income, saving and net lending / net borrowing 154
4. Population and employment (persons) and employment (hours worked) by industry 155

Slovenia
1. Gross domestic product, expenditure approach 156
2. Gross domestic product, output and income approach 157
3. Disposable income, saving and net lending / net borrowing 158
4. Population and employment (persons) and employment (hours worked) by industry 159

Spain
1. Gross domestic product, expenditure approach 160
2. Gross domestic product, output and income approach 161

3. Disposable income, saving and net lending / net borrowing 162
4. Population and employment (persons) and employment (hours worked) by industry 163

Sweden
1. Gross domestic product, expenditure approach. 164
2. Gross domestic product, output and income approach 165
3. Disposable income, saving and net lending / net borrowing 166
4. Population and employment (persons) and employment (hours worked) by industry 167

Switzerland
1. Gross domestic product, expenditure approach. 168
2. Gross domestic product, output and income approach 169
3. Disposable income, saving and net lending / net borrowing 170
4. Population and employment (persons) and employment (hours worked) by industry 171

Turkey
1. Gross domestic product, expenditure approach. 172
2. Gross domestic product, output and income approach 173
3. Disposable income, saving and net lending / net borrowing 174
4. Population and employment (persons) and employment (hours worked) by industry 175

United Kingdom
1. Gross domestic product, expenditure approach. 176
2. Gross domestic product, output and income approach 177
3. Disposable income, saving and net lending / net borrowing 178
4. Population and employment (persons) and employment (hours worked) by industry 179

United States
1. Gross domestic product, expenditure approach. 180
2. Gross domestic product, output and income approach 181
3. Disposable income, saving and net lending / net borrowing 182
4. Population and employment (persons) and employment (hours worked) by industry 183

Euro area
1. Gross domestic product, expenditure approach. 184
2. Gross domestic product, output and income approach 185
3. Disposable income, saving and net lending / net borrowing 186
4. Population and employment (persons) and employment (hours worked) by industry 187

Conventional signs and abbreviations

Signs and abbreviations

e	Estimated value
..	Not available
.	Decimal point
Billion	Thousand million
FISIM	Financial Intermediation Services Indirectly Measured
NPISH	Non-Profit Institutions Serving Households

Main country groupings

Euro area: (19 countries) Austria, Belgium, Cyprus,* Estonia, Finland, France, Germany, Greece, Ireland, Italy, Latvia, Lithuania, Luxembourg, Malta, Netherlands, Portugal, Slovak Republic, Slovenia and Spain.

OECD-Total: Australia, Austria, Belgium, Canada, Chile, Czech Republic, Denmark, Estonia, Finland, France, Germany, Greece, Hungary, Iceland, Ireland, Israel,** Italy, Japan, Korea, Latvia, Luxembourg, Mexico, Netherlands, New Zealand, Norway, Poland, Portugal, Slovak Republic, Slovenia, Spain, Sweden, Switzerland, Turkey, United Kingdom and United States.

* *Footnote by Turkey: "The information in this document with reference to 'Cyprus' relates to the southern part of the Island. There is no single authority representing both Turkish and Greek Cypriot people on the Island. Turkey recognises the Turkish Republic of Northern Cyprus (TRNC). Until a lasting and equitable solution is found within the context of the United Nations, Turkey shall preserve its position concerning the 'Cyprus issue'".*

Footnote by all the European Union Member States of the OECD and the European Commission: "The Republic of Cyprus is recognised by all members of the United Nations with the exception of Turkey. The information in this document relates to the area under the effective control of the Government of the Republic of Cyprus".

** *The statistical data for Israel are supplied by and under the responsibility of the relevant Israeli authorities. The use of such data by the OECD is without prejudice to the status of the Golan Heights, East Jerusalem and Israeli settlements in the West Bank under the terms of international law.*

Sources and methods:

System of National Accounts 2008: *http://unstats.un.org/unsd/nationalaccount/sna2008.asp*

Classification

The International Standard Industrial Classification (ISIC) are available online: Rev. 4 at *http://unstats.un.org/unsd/cr/registry/regcst.asp?Cl=27.*

National Accounts of OECD Countries, Volume 2018 Issue 1:
Main Aggregates
© OECD 2018

International comparisons

Table 1. Gross domestic product at current prices and PPPs

Billion USD

	2009	2010	2011	2012	2013	2014	2015	2016
Australia	901.0	942.0	990.6	996.0	1 102.7	1 116.3	1 128.4	1 181.2
Austria	341.4	351.7	373.0	391.6	406.4	417.0	431.1	441.4
Belgium	410.3	436.8	455.7	471.3	486.7	500.2	512.2	526.4
Canada	1 304.5	1 361.1	1 427.5	1 464.6	1 550.3	1 617.6	1 599.8	1 625.4
Chile	273.1	310.4	350.6	374.2	394.3	405.4	402.3	415.4
Czech Republic	288.2	290.1	302.3	305.3	320.5	339.6	353.0	367.2
Denmark	222.8	238.8	247.4	250.5	262.4	270.3	276.6	280.8
Estonia	27.4	28.8	32.6	34.4	36.2	37.5	37.7	39.1
Finland	201.9	208.0	219.2	219.9	224.6	226.5	230.5	238.4
France	2 247.0	2 340.5	2 447.6	2 471.8	2 606.1	2 659.4	2 696.2 p	2 765.5 p
Germany	3 033.3	3 207.8	3 427.1	3 503.7	3 647.8	3 813.7	3 905.5	4 030.4
Greece	337.2	313.4	290.3 p	279.3 p	286.2 p	292.3 p	288.9 p	288.4 p
Hungary	206.9	215.6	227.8	229.1	242.0	251.8	257.4	262.0
Iceland	13.1	12.3	12.6	13.1	13.9	14.6	15.7	17.0
Ireland	188.7	197.4	206.8	213.3	222.3	237.5	322.4	339.5
Israel[1]	205.8	219.8	237.3	250.8	275.1	280.0	300.8	318.4
Italy	2 039.2	2 077.2	2 158.3	2 157.5	2 176.3	2 192.7	2 225.2	2 326.9
Japan	4 250.2	4 482.5	4 573.2	4 746.7	4 967.1	4 986.6	5 176.8	5 369.5
Korea	1 396.4	1 505.3	1 559.4	1 611.3	1 644.8	1 704.5	1 795.9	1 872.1 p
Latvia	36.1	36.9	40.7	43.2	45.6	47.5	48.5	50.1
Luxembourg	40.9	43.4	47.7	48.6	51.9	56.5	58.4	59.6
Mexico	1 637.0	1 743.2	1 911.3	2 012.8	2 064.5	2 171.6	2 170.3	2 266.4 p
Netherlands	728.0	740.1	769.0	782.6	817.8	819.7	839.0	860.7 p
New Zealand	132.1	136.0	143.5	145.4	160.7	167.9	172.0	181.0 e
Norway	267.6	283.7	307.8	328.5	340.6	339.1	320.4	307.8
Poland	734.2	801.5	869.8	907.2	940.3	973.2	1 010.2	1 039.7
Portugal	279.7	289.0	282.7	278.2	291.8	299.0	305.9	316.6 p
Slovak Republic	124.2	134.7	139.5	144.1	151.0	156.7	160.1	165.4
Slovenia	56.0	56.9	59.1	59.5	61.4	63.6	64.9	67.6
Spain	1 501.5	1 488.3	1 499.0	1 496.2	1 520.0	1 566.9	1 617.1 p	1 687.6 p
Sweden	368.6	390.4	413.5	425.8	438.5	451.1	469.3	485.3
Switzerland	400.8	415.7	444.5	462.6	486.2	506.9	527.2	534.9
Turkey	1 104.6	1 261.6	1 443.3	1 539.1	1 690.9	1 851.0	1 944.6	2 007.5
United Kingdom	2 154.1	2 251.8	2 315.8	2 401.9	2 520.8	2 630.2	2 708.0	2 798.1
United States	14 418.7	14 964.4	15 517.9	16 155.3	16 691.5	17 427.6	18 120.7	18 624.5
Euro area	11 688.4	12 052.3	12 557.7	12 708.9	13 150.7	13 509.8	13 868.9	14 332.4
OECD-Total	41 872.7	43 776.8	45 744.3 p	47 215.2 p	49 139.0 p	50 892.1 p	52 493.1 p	54 157.8 e

1. The statistical data for Israel are supplied by and under the responsibility of the relevant Israeli authorities. The use of such data by the OECD is without prejudice to the status of the Golan Heights, East Jerusalem and Israeli settlements in the West Bank under the terms of international law.

Table 2. Gross domestic product at the price levels and PPPs of year 2010

Billion USD

	2009	2010	2011	2012	2013	2014	2015	2016
Australia	919.4	942.0	978.6	1 004.5	1 030.2	1 054.4	1 084.2	1 105.4
Austria	345.3	351.7	361.9	364.4	364.5	367.5	371.5	376.9
Belgium	425.6	437.2	445.1	446.1	447.0	453.1	459.4	466.2
Canada	1 320.4	1 361.1	1 403.9	1 428.4	1 463.7	1 505.6	1 520.6	1 542.1
Chile	294.7	311.9	331.0	348.6	362.7	369.6	378.0	384.0
Czech Republic	283.9	290.4	295.5	293.2	291.7	299.7	315.6	323.8
Denmark	234.6	239.0	242.2	242.8	245.0	249.0	253.0	258.0
Estonia	28.2	28.8	31.0	32.3	32.9	33.9	34.5	35.2
Finland	202.1	208.2	213.5	210.5	208.9	207.6	207.6	212.1
France	2 297.6	2 342.7	2 391.5	2 395.8	2 409.6	2 432.5	2 458.4 p	2 487.6 p
Germany	3 085.0	3 210.8	3 328.3	3 344.7	3 361.1	3 425.9	3 485.7	3 553.4
Greece	331.8	313.7	285.0 p	264.2 p	255.6 p	257.5 p	256.8 p	256.2 p
Hungary	214.3	215.8	219.4	215.7	220.3	229.6	237.3	242.6
Iceland	12.7	12.3	12.5	12.7	13.2	13.5	14.1	15.1
Ireland	194.1	197.6	203.5	203.6	206.9	224.2	281.5	296.0
Israel[1]	208.4	219.9	231.3	236.4	246.3	254.9	261.6	272.0
Italy	2 044.7	2 079.2	2 091.2	2 032.2	1 997.1	1 999.4	2 016.5	2 033.8
Japan	4 302.2	4 482.5	4 477.3	4 544.3	4 635.2	4 652.5	4 715.5	4 759.8
Korea	1 413.5	1 505.3	1 560.7	1 596.5	1 642.7	1 697.6	1 745.0	1 794.3 p
Latvia	38.4	36.9	39.3	40.8	41.8	42.6	43.8	44.8
Luxembourg	41.5	43.5	44.6	44.4	46.1	48.7	50.1	51.7
Mexico	1 658.3	1 743.2	1 807.0	1 872.9	1 898.2	1 952.2	2 016.1	2 074.8 p
Netherlands	730.6	740.8	753.1	745.2	743.8	754.3	771.4	788.4 p
New Zealand	134.7	136.0	139.7	143.2	145.9	150.3 p	155.3 p	160.1 e
Norway	282.0	284.0	286.7	294.5	297.6	303.5	309.5	312.8
Poland	774.4	802.3	841.7	855.3	867.2	895.6	930.1	956.7
Portugal	283.6	289.0	284.0	272.6	269.5	271.9	276.6	281.1 p
Slovak Republic	128.4	134.8	138.6	140.9	143.0	147.0	152.6	157.7
Slovenia	56.2	56.9	57.3	55.8	55.1	56.8	58.1	59.9
Spain	1 489.5	1 489.8	1 474.9	1 431.7	1 407.3	1 426.7	1 475.7 p	1 524.0 p
Sweden	368.7	390.8	401.2	400.0	405.0	415.5	434.3	448.4
Switzerland	403.9	416.1	423.1	427.4	435.3	445.9	451.4	457.6
Turkey	1 164.0	1 262.8	1 403.1	1 470.3	1 595.2	1 677.6	1 779.7	1 836.4
United Kingdom	2 216.4	2 253.9	2 286.7	2 320.5	2 368.2	2 440.5	2 497.8	2 543.7
United States	14 594.8	14 964.4	15 204.0	15 542.2	15 802.9	16 208.9	16 672.7	16 920.3
Euro area	11 806.4	12 052.3	12 245.8	12 137.3	12 108.1	12 269.9	12 524.0	12 750.8
OECD-Total	42 510.2	43 776.8	44 670.3 p	45 257.3 p	45 936.7 p	46 941.6 p	48 147.6 p	49 009.5 e

1. The statistical data for Israel are supplied by and under the responsibility of the relevant Israeli authorities. The use of such data by the OECD is without prejudice to the status of the Golan Heights, East Jerusalem and Israeli settlements in the West Bank under the terms of international law.

Table 3. Gross domestic product per head at current prices and PPPs

USD

	2009	2010	2011	2012	2013	2014	2015	2016
Australia	40 897	42 166	43 583	43 082	47 003	46 921	46 761	48 178
Austria	40 928	42 059	44 469	46 478	47 937	48 801	49 959	50 503
Belgium	38 004	40 089	41 450	42 585	43 746	44 743	45 577	46 607
Canada	38 791	40 027	41 565	42 145	44 098	45 508	44 627	44 793
Chile	16 132	18 159	20 303	21 447	22 353	22 727	22 294	22 727 e
Czech Republic	27 469	27 582	28 796	29 051	30 496	32 265	33 479	34 753
Denmark	40 333	43 047	44 408	44 809	46 743	47 905	48 688	49 021
Estonia	20 481	21 573	24 501	25 973	27 450	28 511	28 735	29 741
Finland	37 823	38 775	40 683	40 620	41 293	41 463	42 064	43 378
France	34 753	36 022	37 485	37 671	39 515	40 117	40 489 p	41 364 p
Germany	37 689	39 955	42 693	43 564	45 232	47 092	47 811	48 943
Greece	30 360	28 176	26 141 p	25 284 p	26 098 p	26 839 p	26 697 p	26 746 p
Hungary	20 648	21 556	22 841	23 094	24 463	25 525	26 157	26 701
Iceland	41 105	38 540	39 624	40 698	42 817	44 511	47 446	50 666
Ireland	41 579	43 302	45 176	46 469	48 297	51 468	69 459	72 485
Israel[1]	27 511	28 839	30 569	31 721	34 144	34 101	35 902	37 270
Italy	34 228	34 719	35 935	35 757	35 885	36 071	36 640	38 380
Japan	33 196	35 008	35 775	37 214	39 008	39 183	40 727	42 293
Korea	28 320	30 377	31 228	32 097	32 616	33 587	35 204	36 532 p
Latvia	16 866	17 578	19 782	21 260	22 675	23 802	24 513	25 590
Luxembourg	82 192	85 598	91 814	91 527	95 246	101 275	102 554	102 019
Mexico	14 506	15 257	16 522	17 195	17 437	18 140 e	17 935 e	18 535 e
Netherlands	44 049	44 552	46 067	46 716	48 679	48 612	49 551 p	50 551 p
New Zealand	30 591	31 177	32 667	32 912	36 024	37 036	37 206	38 346 e
Norway	55 424	58 025	62 146	65 442	67 051	66 018	61 713	58 792
Poland	19 077	20 809	22 576	23 542	24 423	25 288	26 271	27 058
Portugal	26 464	27 335	26 780	26 454	27 899	28 747	29 532	30 658 p
Slovak Republic	22 922	24 809	25 836	26 654	27 900	28 928	29 530	30 460
Slovenia	27 444	27 763	28 805	28 906	29 803	30 857	31 472	32 730
Spain	32 382	31 964	32 073	31 993	32 623	33 728 p	34 846 p	36 318 p
Sweden	39 646	41 628	43 755	44 725	45 673	46 524	47 891	48 905
Switzerland	51 555	52 911	56 184	57 850	60 109	61 902	63 648	63 889 p
Turkey	15 330	17 281	19 517	20 549 e	22 314 e	24 159 e	25 112 e	25 655 e
United Kingdom	34 599	35 880	36 593	37 703	39 322	40 717	41 592	42 622
United States	46 930	48 303	49 719	51 388	52 726	54 651	56 420	57 591
Euro area	34 983	35 988	37 405	37 759	38 988	39 966	40 905	42 118
OECD-Total	33 971	35 292	36 656 p	37 617 e	38 936 e	40 090 e	41 111 e	42 162 e

1. The statistical data for Israel are supplied by and under the responsibility of the relevant Israeli authorities. The use of such data by the OECD is without prejudice to the status of the Golan Heights, East Jerusalem and Israeli settlements in the West Bank under the terms of international law.

Table 4. Gross domestic product per head at the price levels and PPPs of year 2010

USD

	2009	2010	2011	2012	2013	2014	2015	2016
Australia	41 733	42 166	43 058	43 451	43 911	44 319	44 931	45 087
Austria	41 397	42 059	43 146	43 245	42 996	43 014	43 053	43 126
Belgium	39 418	40 128	40 485	40 309	40 183	40 526	40 883	41 273
Canada	39 265	40 027	40 879	41 104	41 636	42 357	42 418	42 499
Chile	17 410	18 249	19 169	19 978	20 562	20 724	20 946	21 007 e
Czech Republic	27 061	27 608	28 154	27 895	27 756	28 472	29 932	30 643
Denmark	42 480	43 088	43 484	43 419	43 652	44 123	44 524	45 026
Estonia	21 079	21 594	23 297	24 383	24 950	25 757	26 238	26 726
Finland	37 857	38 812	39 626	38 875	38 403	37 996	37 887	38 591
France	35 536	36 057	36 626	36 513	36 536	36 694	36 919 p	37 208 p
Germany	38 331	39 993	41 462	41 587	41 677	42 305	42 730 p	43 109
Greece	29 876	28 203	25 665 p	23 920 p	23 313 p	23 643 p	23 730 p	23 754 p
Hungary	21 382	21 576	21 997	21 748	22 265	23 269	24 119	24 716
Iceland	39 832	38 540	39 174	39 480	40 787	41 194	42 509	45 038
Ireland	42 729	43 302	44 426	44 316	44 928	48 533	60 577	63 131
Israel[1]	27 857	28 849	29 797	29 897	30 578	31 040	31 228	31 833
Italy	34 320	34 752	34 818	33 680	32 931	32 891	33 204	33 546
Japan	33 602	35 008	35 025	35 627	36 402	36 559	37 098	37 490
Korea	28 666	30 377	31 254	31 803	32 575	33 453	34 206	35 014 e
Latvia	17 934	17 595	19 067	20 082	20 763	21 346	22 169	22 867
Luxembourg	83 234	85 680	85 845	83 599	84 457	87 252	88 003	88 429
Mexico	14 694	15 257	15 621	16 000	16 033	16 308 e	16 661 e	16 969 e
Netherlands	44 207	44 595	45 117	44 482	44 271	44 732	45 557 p	46 262 p
New Zealand	31 203	31 176	31 797	32 408	32 708	33 160 p	33 603 p	33 917 e
Norway	58 398	58 081	57 887	58 681	58 582	59 076	59 613	59 746
Poland	20 103	20 809	21 848	22 195	22 523	23 273	24 186	24 897
Portugal	26 838	27 335	26 901	25 922	25 770	26 141	26 702	27 220 p
Slovak Republic	23 694	24 833	25 684	26 070	26 426	27 125	28 149	29 040
Slovenia	27 546	27 790	27 915	27 118	26 775	27 543	28 144	29 012
Spain	32 125	31 995	31 557	30 614	30 203	30 711 p	31 798 p	32 796 p
Sweden	39 650	41 668	42 456	42 023	42 185	42 857	44 323	45 186
Switzerland	51 955	52 962	53 472	53 440	53 807	54 457	54 501	54 656 p
Turkey	16 155	17 298	18 974	19 631 e	21 052 e	21 896 e	22 982 e	23 469 e
United Kingdom	35 599	35 914	36 133	36 426	36 941	37 780	38 362	38 747
United States	47 503	48 303	48 713	49 438	49 919	50 829	51 912	52 322
Euro area	35 336	35 988	36 476	36 060	35 897	36 298	36 939	37 470
OECD-Total	34 488	35 292	35 796 p	36 057 e	36 399 e	36 978 e	37 708 e	38 154 e

1. The statistical data for Israel are supplied by and under the responsibility of the relevant Israeli authorities. The use of such data by the OECD is without prejudice to the status of the Golan Heights, East Jerusalem and Israeli settlements in the West Bank under the terms of international law.

Table 5. Gross domestic product per head at current prices and current PPPs, index

OECD=100

	2009	2010	2011	2012	2013	2014	2015	2016
Australia	120.4	119.5	118.9 p	114.5 e	120.7 e	117.0 e	113.7 e	114.3 e
Austria	120.5	119.2	121.3 p	123.6 e	123.1 e	121.7 e	121.5 e	119.8 e
Belgium	111.9	113.6	113.1 p	113.2 e	112.4 e	111.6 e	110.9 e	110.5 e
Canada	114.2	113.4	113.4 p	112.0 e	113.3 e	113.5 e	108.6 e	106.2 e
Chile	47.5	51.5	55.4 p	57.0 e	57.4 e	56.7 e	54.2 e	53.9 e
Czech Republic	80.9	78.2	78.6 p	77.2 e	78.3 e	80.5 e	81.4 e	82.4 e
Denmark	118.7	122.0	121.1 p	119.1 e	120.1 e	119.5 e	118.4 e	116.3 e
Estonia	60.3	61.1	66.8 p	69.0 e	70.5 e	71.1 e	69.9 e	70.5 e
Finland	111.3	109.9	111.0 p	108.0 e	106.1 e	103.4 e	102.3 e	102.9 e
France	102.3	102.1	102.3 p	100.1 e	101.5 e	100.1 e	98.5 e	98.1 e
Germany	110.9	113.2	116.5 p	115.8 e	116.2 e	117.5 e	116.3 e	116.1 e
Greece	89.4	79.8	71.3 p	67.2 e	67.0 e	66.9 e	64.9 e	63.4 e
Hungary	60.8	61.1	62.3 p	61.4 e	62.8 e	63.7 e	63.6 e	63.3 e
Iceland	121.0	109.2	108.1 p	108.2 e	110.0 e	111.0 e	115.4 e	120.2 e
Ireland	122.4	122.7	123.2 p	123.5 e	124.0 e	128.4 e	169.0 e	171.9 e
Israel[1]	81.0	81.7	83.4 p	84.3 e	87.7 e	85.1 e	87.3 e	88.4 e
Italy	100.8	98.4	98.0 p	95.1 e	92.2 e	90.0 e	89.1 e	91.0 e
Japan	97.7	99.2	97.6 p	98.9 e	100.2 e	97.7 e	99.1 e	100.3 e
Korea	83.4	86.1	85.2 p	85.3 e	83.8 e	83.8 e	85.6 e	86.6 e
Latvia	49.6	49.8	54.0 p	56.5 e	58.2 e	59.4 e	59.6 e	60.7 e
Luxembourg	241.9	242.5	250.5 p	243.3 e	244.6 e	252.6 e	249.5 e	242.0 e
Mexico	42.7	43.2	45.1 p	45.7 e	44.8 e	45.2 e	43.6 e	44.0 e
Netherlands	129.7	126.2	125.7 p	124.2 e	125.0 e	121.3 e	120.5 e	119.9 e
New Zealand	90.1	88.3	89.1 p	87.5 e	92.5 e	92.4 e	90.5 e	91.0 e
Norway	163.2	164.4	169.5 p	174.0 e	172.2 e	164.7 e	150.1 e	139.4 e
Poland	56.2	59.0	61.6 p	62.6 e	62.7 e	63.1 e	63.9 e	64.2 e
Portugal	77.9	77.5	73.1 p	70.3 e	71.7 e	71.7 e	71.8 e	72.7 e
Slovak Republic	67.5	70.3	70.5 p	70.9 e	71.7 e	72.2 e	71.8 e	72.2 e
Slovenia	80.8	78.7	78.6 p	76.8 e	76.5 e	77.0 e	76.6 e	77.6 e
Spain	95.3	90.6	87.5 p	85.0 e	83.8 e	84.1 e	84.8 e	86.1 e
Sweden	116.7	118.0	119.4 p	118.9 e	117.3 e	116.0 e	116.5 e	116.0 e
Switzerland	151.8	149.9	153.3 p	153.8 e	154.4 e	154.4 e	154.8 e	151.5 e
Turkey	45.1	49.0	53.2 p	54.6 e	57.3 e	60.3 e	61.1 e	60.8 e
United Kingdom	101.8	101.7	99.8 p	100.2 e	101.0 e	101.6 e	101.2 e	101.1 e
United States	138.1	136.9	135.6 p	136.6 e	135.4 e	136.3 e	137.2 e	136.6 e
Euro area	103.0	102.0	102.0 p	100.4 e	100.1 e	99.7 e	99.5 e	99.9 e
OECD-Total	100.0	100.0	100.0 p	100.0 e	100.0 e	100.0 e	100.0 e	100.0 e

1. The statistical data for Israel are supplied by and under the responsibility of the relevant Israeli authorities. The use of such data by the OECD is without prejudice to the status of the Golan Heights, East Jerusalem and Israeli settlements in the West Bank under the terms of international law.

Table 6. Gross domestic product per head at the price levels and PPPs of year 2010, index

OECD=100

	2009	2010	2011	2012	2013	2014	2015	2016
Australia	121.0	119.5	120.3 p	120.5 e	120.6 e	119.9 e	119.2 e	118.2 e
Austria	120.0	119.2	120.5 p	119.9 e	118.1 e	116.3 e	114.2 e	113.0 e
Belgium	114.2	113.6	113.0 p	111.7 e	110.3 e	109.5 e	108.3 e	108.1 e
Canada	113.9	113.4	114.2 p	114.0 e	114.4 e	114.5 e	112.5 e	111.4 e
Chile	50.2	51.5	53.3 p	55.1 e	56.2 e	55.8 e	55.3 e	54.8 e
Czech Republic	78.4	78.2	78.6 p	77.3 e	76.2 e	76.9 e	79.3 e	80.2 e
Denmark	123.1	122.0	121.4 p	120.3 e	119.8 e	119.2 e	118.0 e	117.9 e
Estonia	61.1	61.1	65.0 p	67.6 e	68.5 e	69.6 e	69.5 e	70.0 e
Finland	109.7	109.9	110.6 p	107.7 e	105.4 e	102.7 e	100.5 e	101.1 e
France	102.9	102.1	102.2 p	101.2 e	100.3 e	99.1 e	97.8 e	97.4 e
Germany	111.0	113.2	115.7 p	115.2 e	114.4 e	114.3 e	113.1 e	113.0 e
Greece	86.5	79.8	71.6 p	66.3 e	64.0 e	63.9 e	62.9 e	62.2 e
Hungary	61.9	61.1	61.4 p	60.3 e	61.1 e	62.9 e	63.9 e	64.7 e
Iceland	115.5	109.2	109.4 p	109.5 e	112.1 e	111.4 e	112.7 e	118.0 e
Ireland	123.9	122.7	124.1 p	122.9 e	123.4 e	131.2 e	160.6 e	165.5 e
Israel[1]	80.7	81.7	83.2 p	82.9 e	84.0 e	83.9 e	82.8 e	83.4 e
Italy	99.4	98.4	97.2 p	93.3 e	90.4 e	88.9 e	88.1 e	87.9 e
Japan	97.4	99.2	97.8 p	98.8 e	100.0 e	98.9 e	98.4 e	98.3 e
Korea	83.1	86.1	87.3 p	88.2 e	89.5 e	90.5 e	90.7 e	91.8 e
Latvia	52.0	49.8	53.2 p	55.6 e	57.0 e	57.7 e	58.8 e	59.9 e
Luxembourg	241.1	242.5	239.6 p	231.6 e	231.8 e	235.7 e	233.2 e	231.5 e
Mexico	42.6	43.2	43.6 p	44.4 e	44.0 e	44.1 e	44.2 e	44.5 e
Netherlands	128.1	126.2	125.9 p	123.2 e	121.5 e	120.9 e	120.7 e	121.3 e
New Zealand	90.5	88.3	88.8 p	89.9 e	89.9 e	89.7 e	89.1 e	88.9 e
Norway	169.2	164.4	161.6 p	162.6 e	160.8 e	159.6 e	157.9 e	156.4 e
Poland	58.3	59.0	61.0 p	61.6 e	61.9 e	62.9 e	64.1 e	65.3 e
Portugal	77.8	77.5	75.1 p	71.8 e	70.7 e	70.6 e	70.8 e	71.3 e
Slovak Republic	68.6	70.3	71.7 p	72.2 e	72.5 e	73.3 e	74.6 e	76.0 e
Slovenia	79.8	78.7	77.9 p	75.1 e	73.5 e	74.4 e	74.6 e	76.0 e
Spain	93.1	90.6	88.1 p	84.8 e	82.9 e	83.0 e	84.2 e	85.9 e
Sweden	114.9	118.0	118.5 p	116.4 e	115.8 e	115.8 e	117.4 e	118.3 e
Switzerland	150.5	149.9	149.2 p	148.1 e	147.7 e	147.1 e	144.4 e	143.1 e
Turkey	46.8	49.0	53.0 p	54.4 e	57.8 e	59.2 e	60.9 e	61.5 e
United Kingdom	103.1	101.7	100.8 p	100.9 e	101.4 e	102.1 e	101.6 e	101.6 e
United States	137.7	136.9	136.1 p	137.1 e	137.1 e	137.5 e	137.7 e	137.1 e
Euro area	102.5	102.0	101.9 p	100.0 e	98.6 e	98.2 e	98.0 e	98.2 e
OECD-Total	100.0	100.0	100.0 p	100.0 e	100.0 e	100.0 e	100.0 e	100.0 e

1. The statistical data for Israel are supplied by and under the responsibility of the relevant Israeli authorities. The use of such data by the OECD is without prejudice to the status of the Golan Heights, East Jerusalem and Israeli settlements in the West Bank under the terms of international law.

Table 7. Gross domestic product at current prices and exchange rates

Billion USD

	2009	2010	2011	2012	2013	2014	2015	2016
Australia	1 013.2	1 297.3	1 543.9	1 588.2	1 540.6	1 461.6	1 246.8	1 304.4
Austria	400.1	391.9	431.1	409.4	430.1	441.9	382.1	390.8
Belgium	484.5	483.5	527.0	497.9	520.9	531.1	455.2	468.0
Canada	1 371.2	1 613.5	1 788.6	1 824.3	1 842.6	1 799.3	1 559.6	1 535.8
Chile	172.4	218.5	252.3	267.1	278.4	261.0	242.5	247.0
Czech Republic	206.2	207.5	227.9	207.4	209.4	207.8	186.8	195.3
Denmark	321.2	322.0	344.0	327.1	343.6	353.0	301.3	306.9
Estonia	19.7	19.5	23.2	23.0	25.1	26.2	22.6	23.3
Finland	251.5	247.8	273.7	256.7	270.0	272.6	232.5	238.7
France	2 693.7	2 646.8	2 862.7	2 681.4	2 808.5	2 849.3	2 433.6 p	2 465.5 p
Germany	3 417.8	3 417.1	3 757.7	3 544.0	3 752.5	3 890.6	3 375.6	3 477.8
Greece	330.0	299.4	287.8 p	245.7 p	239.9 p	237.0 p	195.5 p	192.7 p
Hungary	130.6	130.9	140.8	127.9	135.2	140.1	122.9	125.8
Iceland	12.9	13.3	14.7	14.3	15.5	17.3	16.9	20.3
Ireland	236.3	222.0	239.0	225.6	239.4	258.1	290.6	304.8
Israel[1]	207.4	233.6	261.6	257.3	292.5	308.4	299.1	317.7
Italy	2 185.0	2 125.1	2 276.3	2 072.8	2 130.5	2 151.7	1 832.9	1 859.4
Japan	5 231.4	5 700.1	6 157.5	6 203.2	5 155.7	4 850.4	4 395.0	4 949.3
Korea	901.9	1 094.5	1 202.5	1 222.8	1 305.6	1 411.3	1 382.8	1 411.0 p
Latvia	26.2	23.8	28.5	28.1	30.3	31.3	27.0	27.6
Luxembourg	51.4	53.2	60.0	56.7	61.7	66.3	57.8	58.6
Mexico	900.0	1 057.8	1 180.5	1 201.1	1 274.4	1 314.4	1 169.6	1 076.9 p
Netherlands	857.9	836.4	893.8	828.9	866.7	879.6	758.0	777.2 p
New Zealand	121.3	146.6	168.5	176.2	190.5	200.7	175.6	185.0 e
Norway	386.6	429.1	498.8	510.2	523.5	499.3	386.7	371.1
Poland	439.8	479.3	528.8	500.4	524.2	545.2	477.4	471.4
Portugal	243.7	238.3	244.9	216.4	226.1	229.6	199.4	205.2 p
Slovak Republic	88.9	89.5	98.2	93.4	98.5	100.9	87.5	89.8
Slovenia	50.2	48.0	51.3	46.4	48.1	49.9	43.1	44.7
Spain	1 499.0	1 431.6	1 488.1	1 336.0	1 361.9	1 376.9	1 197.8 p	1 237.3 p
Sweden	429.7	488.4	563.1	543.9	578.7	573.8	497.9	514.5
Switzerland	541.5	583.8	699.6	668.0	688.5	709.2	679.3	668.7
Turkey	644.7	771.9	832.5	874.0	950.6	934.2	859.8	863.7
United Kingdom	2 382.8	2 441.2	2 619.7	2 662.1	2 739.8	3 022.8	2 885.6	2 650.9
United States	14 418.7	14 964.4	15 517.9	16 155.3	16 691.5	17 427.6	18 120.7	18 624.5
Euro area	12 907.7	12 645.1	13 623.1	12 639.7	13 190.8	13 476.4	11 662.0	11 934.1
OECD-Total	42 669.4	44 767.4	48 086.5 p	47 893.1 p	48 391.1 p	49 430.7 p	46 597.2 p	47 701.4 e

1. The statistical data for Israel are supplied by and under the responsibility of the relevant Israeli authorities. The use of such data by the OECD is without prejudice to the status of the Golan Heights, East Jerusalem and Israeli settlements in the West Bank under the terms of international law.

Table 8. Gross domestic product at the price levels and exchange rates of year 2010

Billion USD

	2009	2010	2011	2012	2013	2014	2015	2016
Australia	1 266.2	1 297.3	1 347.7	1 383.3	1 418.7	1 452.1	1 493.1	1 522.4
Austria	384.8	391.9	403.3	406.1	406.2	409.6	414.0	420.0
Belgium	470.6	483.5	492.2	493.4	494.4	501.1	508.1	515.6
Canada	1 565.2	1 613.5	1 664.1	1 693.2	1 735.1	1 784.6	1 802.5	1 828.0
Chile	206.5	218.5	231.9	244.2	254.1	259.0	264.8	269.0
Czech Republic	202.9	207.5	211.2	209.5	208.5	214.1	225.5	231.3
Denmark	316.1	322.0	326.3	327.0	330.1	335.4	340.8	347.5
Estonia	19.1	19.5	21.0	21.9	22.3	23.0	23.3	23.8
Finland	240.6	247.8	254.2	250.5	248.6	247.1	247.4	252.7
France	2 595.8	2 646.8	2 701.9	2 706.8	2 722.4	2 748.2	2 777.5 p	2 810.5 p
Germany	3 283.1	3 417.1	3 542.2	3 559.6	3 577.0	3 646.0	3 709.6	3 781.7
Greece	316.7	299.4	272.0 p	252.2 p	244.0 p	245.8 p	245.1 p	244.5 p
Hungary	130.0	130.9	133.1	130.9	133.7	139.3	144.0	147.2
Iceland	13.8	13.3	13.6	13.8	14.3	14.6	15.3	16.4
Ireland	218.0	222.0	228.6	228.7	232.4	251.8	316.1	332.4
Israel[1]	221.5	233.6	245.8	251.2	261.8	270.9	278.0	289.0
Italy	2 089.8	2 125.1	2 137.3	2 077.1	2 041.2	2 043.5	2 062.9	2 080.6
Japan	5 470.8	5 700.1	5 693.5	5 778.6	5 894.2	5 916.3	5 996.4	6 052.7
Korea	1 027.7	1 094.5	1 134.8	1 160.8	1 194.4	1 234.3	1 268.8	1 304.7 p
Latvia	24.7	23.8	25.3	26.3	26.9	27.4	28.3	28.9
Luxembourg	50.7	53.2	54.6	54.4	56.4	59.6	61.3	63.2
Mexico	1 006.3	1 057.8	1 096.5	1 136.5	1 151.9	1 184.7	1 223.4	1 259.0 p
Netherlands	824.8	836.4	850.3	841.3	839.7	851.6	870.9	890.1 p
New Zealand	145.2	146.6	150.5	154.3	157.2	162.0 p	167.4 p	172.5 e
Norway	426.2	429.1	433.3	445.1	449.7	458.6	467.7	472.8
Poland	462.6	479.3	503.4	511.5	518.6	535.6	556.2	572.1
Portugal	233.9	238.3	233.9	224.5	222.0	224.0	228.1	231.7 p
Slovak Republic	85.2	89.5	92.0	93.5	94.9	97.6	101.3	104.7
Slovenia	47.4	48.0	48.3	47.0	46.5	47.9	49.0	50.5
Spain	1 431.4	1 431.6	1 417.3	1 375.8	1 352.4	1 371.0	1 418.1 p	1 464.5 p
Sweden	460.8	488.4	501.4	500.0	506.2	519.3	542.8	560.4
Switzerland	566.8	583.8	593.7	599.6	610.7	625.7	633.4	642.1
Turkey	711.5	771.9	857.7	898.7	975.1	1 025.4	1 087.8	1 122.5
United Kingdom	2 400.5	2 441.2	2 476.6	2 513.3	2 564.9	2 643.2	2 705.3	2 757.6
United States	14 594.8	14 964.4	15 204.0	15 542.2	15 802.9	16 208.9	16 672.7	16 920.3
Euro area	12 387.1	12 645.1	12 848.1	12 734.2	12 703.6	12 873.4	13 140.0	13 378.0
OECD-Total	43 530.0	44 767.4	45 593.6 p	46 147.6 p	46 814.6 p	47 803.3 p	48 981.5 p	49 823.1 e

1. The statistical data for Israel are supplied by and under the responsibility of the relevant Israeli authorities. The use of such data by the OECD is without prejudice to the status of the Golan Heights, East Jerusalem and Israeli settlements in the West Bank under the terms of international law.

Table 9. Gross domestic product at current prices and year 2010 exchange rates

Billion USD

	2009	2010	2011	2012	2013	2014	2015	2016
Australia	1 191.6	1 297.3	1 373.0	1 407.0	1 463.8	1 487.3	1 522.3	1 609.6
Austria	381.5	391.9	410.7	422.0	429.0	441.1	456.3	467.9
Belgium	461.9	483.5	502.1	513.2	519.6	530.2	543.6	560.3
Canada	1 521.5	1 613.5	1 718.1	1 769.4	1 842.0	1 931.9	1 936.5	1 975.9
Chile	189.5	218.5	239.1	254.7	270.2	291.7	310.9	327.7
Czech Republic	205.8	207.5	211.2	212.6	214.6	225.9	240.6	249.9
Denmark	306.2	322.0	328.4	336.9	343.1	352.3	360.4	367.3
Estonia	18.7	19.5	22.1	23.8	25.1	26.2	27.0	28.0
Finland	239.8	247.8	260.7	264.6	269.3	272.1	277.6	285.8
France	2 568.1	2 646.8	2 727.4	2 764.0	2 801.5	2 844.3	2 906.1 p	2 952.0 p
Germany	3 258.5	3 417.1	3 580.1	3 653.1	3 743.1	3 883.8	4 031.1	4 164.1
Greece	314.6	299.4	274.2 p	253.2 p	239.3 p	236.6 p	233.5 p	230.7 p
Hungary	127.1	130.9	136.1	138.4	145.5	156.7	165.1	170.3
Iceland	13.1	13.3	14.0	14.6	15.5	16.5	18.3	20.0
Ireland	225.3	222.0	227.7	232.5	238.8	257.6	347.0	365.0
Israel[1]	218.1	233.6	250.4	265.3	282.5	295.1	310.9	326.4
Italy	2 083.2	2 125.1	2 168.7	2 136.6	2 125.2	2 148.0	2 188.8	2 226.3
Japan	5 576.5	5 700.1	5 598.2	5 638.6	5 732.2	5 854.1	6 060.5	6 134.0
Korea	996.2	1 094.5	1 152.8	1 191.5	1 236.5	1 285.5	1 353.0	1 416.4 p
Latvia	24.9	23.8	26.9	29.0	30.2	31.3	32.2	33.0
Luxembourg	49.0	53.2	57.2	58.4	61.6	66.2	69.0	70.2
Mexico	962.5	1 057.8	1 160.6	1 251.8	1 288.2	1 382.7	1 467.0	1 590.7 p
Netherlands	817.9	836.4	851.5	854.5	864.5	878.1	905.2	930.6 p
New Zealand	140.0	146.6	153.7	156.7	167.4	174.3	181.4	191.5 e
Norway	402.2	429.1	462.6	491.1	508.9	520.6	515.9	515.7
Poland	455.1	479.3	519.6	540.4	549.5	570.3	596.8	616.4
Portugal	232.4	238.3	233.3	223.0	225.5	229.2	238.1	245.7 p
Slovak Republic	84.8	89.5	93.5	96.3	98.2	100.8	104.5	107.5
Slovenia	47.9	48.0	48.9	47.8	48.0	49.8	51.4	53.5
Spain	1 429.1	1 431.6	1 417.7	1 377.2	1 358.5	1 374.5	1 430.4 p	1 481.4 p
Sweden	456.3	488.4	507.3	511.2	523.1	546.2	582.7	611.1
Switzerland	565.0	583.8	595.7	600.6	611.9	623.0	626.8	631.9
Turkey	664.9	771.9	927.9	1 044.5	1 204.2	1 360.4	1 556.1	1 735.7
United Kingdom	2 363.4	2 441.2	2 526.4	2 604.0	2 708.0	2 838.6	2 918.4	3 033.6
United States	14 418.7	14 964.4	15 517.9	16 155.3	16 691.5	17 427.6	18 120.7	18 624.5
Euro area	12 305.9	12 645.1	12 979.2	13 028.9	13 157.9	13 453.0	13 926.5	14 289.0
OECD-Total	43 011.2	44 767.4	46 295.7 p	47 534.0 p	48 875.8 p	50 710.8 p	52 686.1 p	54 350.6 e

1. The statistical data for Israel are supplied by and under the responsibility of the relevant Israeli authorities. The use of such data by the OECD is without prejudice to the status of the Golan Heights, East Jerusalem and Israeli settlements in the West Bank under the terms of international law.

Table 10. Gross domestic product per head at current prices and exchange rates

USD

	2009	2010	2011	2012	2013	2014	2015	2016
Australia	45 987	58 069	67 931	68 701	65 665	61 433	51 669	53 203
Austria	47 971	46 871	51 394	48 589	50 732	51 719	44 274	44 715
Belgium	44 880	44 378	47 936	44 984	46 825	47 502	40 505	41 430
Canada	40 773	47 447	52 082	52 497	52 414	50 620	43 506	42 323
Chile	10 184	12 785	14 609	15 308	15 782	14 633	13 440	13 515 e
Czech Republic	19 652	19 727	21 716	19 733	19 923	19 746	17 721	18 486
Denmark	58 165	58 049	61 760	58 513	61 212	62 554	53 027	53 569
Estonia	14 720	14 627	17 425	17 389	19 040	19 931	17 183	17 735
Finland	47 104	46 202	50 790	47 415	49 638	49 906	42 417	43 433
France	41 662	40 737	43 843	40 866	42 584	42 982	36 545 p	36 876 p
Germany	42 466	42 563	46 810	44 065	46 531	48 042	41 324	42 232
Greece	29 709	26 918	25 916 p	22 243 p	21 875 p	21 761 p	18 071 p	17 869 p
Hungary	13 030	13 092	14 118	12 888	13 668	14 201	12 489	12 820
Iceland	40 552	41 857	46 184	44 565	48 018	52 813	51 156	60 434
Ireland	52 058	48 676	52 220	49 142	52 020	55 928	62 603	65 085
Israel[1]	27 722	30 654	33 701	32 539	36 307	37 556	35 704	37 192
Italy	36 675	35 519	37 900	34 353	35 130	35 397	30 180	30 669
Japan	40 859	44 517	48 169	48 633	40 490	38 114	34 576	38 983
Korea	18 292	22 087	24 080	24 359	25 890	27 811	27 105	27 535 p
Latvia	12 219	11 331	13 827	13 830	15 029	15 713	13 641	14 072
Luxembourg	103 102	104 844	115 521	106 638	113 216	118 797	101 483	100 375
Mexico	7 975	9 258	10 205	10 261	10 764	10 980 e	9 666 e	8 807 e
Netherlands	51 911	50 349	53 541	49 483	51 588	52 164	44 767 p	45 649 p
New Zealand	28 101	33 597	38 348	39 881	42 718	44 265	37 976	39 189 e
Norway	80 062	87 775	100 713	101 660	103 052	97 204	74 487	70 870
Poland	11 428	12 444	13 726	12 985	13 616	14 166	12 413	12 267
Portugal	23 063	22 539	23 196	20 577	21 619	22 077	19 253	19 872 p
Slovak Republic	16 416	16 483	18 188	17 279	18 193	18 630	16 137	16 530
Slovenia	24 608	23 435	24 985	22 537	23 363	24 205	20 875	21 655
Spain	32 329	30 746	31 840	28 568	29 229	29 640 p	25 810 p	26 626 p
Sweden	46 207	52 076	59 593	57 134	60 283	59 180	50 812	51 845
Switzerland	69 649	74 314	88 416	83 538	85 112	86 606	82 016	79 875 p
Turkey	8 947	10 573	11 258	11 669 e	12 545 e	12 192 e	11 103 e	11 038 e
United Kingdom	38 271	38 898	41 395	41 788	42 739	46 795	44 318	40 380
United States	46 930	48 303	49 719	51 388	52 726	54 651	56 420	57 591
Euro area	38 632	37 758	40 579	37 553	39 107	39 867	34 396	35 070
OECD-Total	34 617	36 091	38 533 p	38 157 e	38 343 e	38 939 e	36 494 e	37 136 e

1. The statistical data for Israel are supplied by and under the responsibility of the relevant Israeli authorities. The use of such data by the OECD is without prejudice to the status of the Golan Heights, East Jerusalem and Israeli settlements in the West Bank under the terms of international law.

Table 11. Gross domestic product per head at the price levels and exchange rates of year 2010

USD

	2009	2010	2011	2012	2013	2014	2015	2016
Australia	57 472	58 069	59 298	59 839	60 472	61 034	61 877	62 091
Austria	46 134	46 871	48 083	48 193	47 916	47 936	47 979	48 061
Belgium	43 593	44 378	44 774	44 579	44 440	44 818	45 213	45 645
Canada	46 544	47 447	48 457	48 724	49 355	50 209	50 281	50 377
Chile	12 197	12 785	13 430	13 996	14 405	14 519	14 674	14 717 e
Czech Republic	19 336	19 727	20 117	19 933	19 833	20 345	21 388	21 896
Denmark	57 230	58 049	58 582	58 494	58 808	59 443	59 983	60 660
Estonia	14 278	14 627	15 781	16 517	16 900	17 447	17 773	18 104
Finland	45 066	46 202	47 171	46 277	45 715	45 231	45 144	45 983
France	40 149	40 737	41 380	41 253	41 278	41 457	41 711 p	42 037 p
Germany	40 793	42 563	44 125	44 259	44 355	45 022	45 412	45 923
Greece	28 515	26 918	24 495 p	22 830 p	22 251 p	22 566 p	22 649 p	22 671 p
Hungary	12 974	13 092	13 348	13 196	13 510	14 119	14 635	14 997
Iceland	43 260	41 857	42 545	42 878	44 297	44 739	46 168	48 914
Ireland	48 032	48 676	49 939	49 815	50 504	54 555	68 094	70 966
Israel[1]	29 601	30 654	31 662	31 768	32 492	32 983	33 183	33 826
Italy	35 077	35 519	35 586	34 423	33 657	33 616	33 969	34 318
Japan	42 729	44 517	44 539	45 304	46 290	46 489	47 175	47 674
Korea	20 843	22 087	22 725	23 124	23 685	24 323	24 871	25 459 p
Latvia	11 550	11 331	12 280	12 933	13 385	13 760	14 291	14 741
Luxembourg	101 851	104 844	105 046	102 298	103 348	106 768	107 687	108 208
Mexico	8 917	9 258	9 479	9 709	9 729	9 896 e	10 110 e	10 297 e
Netherlands	49 910	50 349	50 938	50 222	49 983	50 503	51 435 p	52 281 p
New Zealand	33 626	33 597	34 266	34 924	35 248	35 734 p	36 212 p	36 551 e
Norway	88 255	87 775	87 483	88 682	88 532	89 279	90 091	90 291
Poland	12 022	12 444	13 066	13 273	13 469	13 918	14 464	14 889
Portugal	22 129	22 539	22 159	21 353	21 228	21 533	22 017	22 444 p
Slovak Republic	15 727	16 483	17 047	17 304	17 540	18 004	18 684	19 275
Slovenia	23 229	23 435	23 541	22 869	22 579	23 226	23 734	24 465
Spain	30 871	30 746	30 326	29 419	29 025	29 513 p	30 557 p	31 516 p
Sweden	49 554	52 076	53 062	52 520	52 723	53 562	55 395	56 473
Switzerland	72 900	74 314	75 030	74 984	75 500	76 411	76 472	76 691 p
Turkey	9 875	10 573	11 598	11 999 e	12 868 e	13 384 e	14 048 e	14 345 e
United Kingdom	38 556	38 898	39 135	39 453	40 010	40 919	41 549	42 006
United States	47 503	48 303	48 713	49 438	49 919	50 829	51 912	52 322
Euro area	37 074	37 758	38 270	37 834	37 663	38 083	38 755	39 313
OECD-Total	35 315	36 091	36 536 p	36 767 e	37 094 e	37 657 e	38 361 e	38 787 e

1. The statistical data for Israel are supplied by and under the responsibility of the relevant Israeli authorities. The use of such data by the OECD is without prejudice to the status of the Golan Heights, East Jerusalem and Israeli settlements in the West Bank under the terms of international law.

Table 12. Gross domestic product, volume indices

Year 2010=100

	2009	2010	2011	2012	2013	2014	2015	2016
Australia	97.6	100.0	103.9	106.6	109.4	111.9	115.1	117.4
Austria	98.2	100.0	102.9	103.6	103.6	104.5	105.6	107.2
Belgium	97.3	100.0	101.8	102.0	102.2	103.6	105.1	106.6
Canada	97.0	100.0	103.1	104.9	107.5	110.6	111.7	113.3
Chile	94.5	100.0	106.1	111.8	116.3	118.5	121.2	123.1
Czech Republic	97.8	100.0	101.8	101.0	100.5	103.2	108.7	111.5
Denmark	98.2	100.0	101.3	101.6	102.5	104.2	105.8	107.9
Estonia	97.8	100.0	107.6	112.2	114.4	117.7	119.7	122.2
Finland	97.1	100.0	102.6	101.1	100.3	99.7	99.8	102.0
France	98.1	100.0	102.1	102.3	102.9	103.8	104.9 p	106.2 p
Germany	96.1	100.0	103.7	104.2	104.7	106.7	108.6	110.7
Greece	105.8	100.0	90.9 p	84.2 p	81.5 p	82.1 p	81.9 p	81.7 p
Hungary	99.3	100.0	101.7	100.0	102.1	106.4	110.0	112.4
Iceland	103.7	100.0	102.0	103.3	107.8	110.0	114.7	123.3
Ireland	98.2	100.0	103.0	103.0	104.7	113.4	142.4	149.7
Israel[1]	94.8	100.0	105.2	107.5	112.0	115.9	119.0	123.7
Italy	98.3	100.0	100.6	97.7	96.1	96.2	97.1	97.9
Japan	96.0	100.0	99.9	101.4	103.4	103.8	105.2	106.2
Korea	93.9	100.0	103.7	106.1	109.1	112.8	115.9	119.2 p
Latvia	104.1	100.0	106.4	110.7	113.4	115.5	118.9	121.5
Luxembourg	95.4	100.0	102.5	102.2	105.9	112.0	115.2	118.8
Mexico	95.1	100.0	103.7	107.4	108.9	112.0	115.7	119.0 p
Netherlands	98.6	100.0	101.7	100.6	100.4	101.8	104.1	106.4 p
New Zealand	99.1	100.0	102.7	105.3	107.2	110.5 p	114.2 p	117.7 e
Norway	99.3	100.0	101.0	103.7	104.8	106.9	109.0	110.2
Poland	96.5	100.0	105.0	106.7	108.2	111.7	116.0	119.4
Portugal	98.1	100.0	98.2	94.2	93.2	94.0	95.7	97.2 p
Slovak Republic	95.2	100.0	102.8	104.5	106.1	109.0	113.2	117.0
Slovenia	98.8	100.0	100.6	98.0	96.9	99.7	102.0	105.2
Spain	100.0	100.0	99.0	96.1	94.5	95.8	99.1 p	102.3 p
Sweden	94.3	100.0	102.7	102.4	103.6	106.3	111.1	114.7
Switzerland	97.1	100.0	101.7	102.7	104.6	107.2	108.5	110.0
Turkey	92.2	100.0	111.1	116.4	126.3	132.8	140.9	145.4
United Kingdom	98.3	100.0	101.5	103.0	105.1	108.3	110.8	113.0
United States	97.5	100.0	101.6	103.9	105.6	108.3	111.4	113.1
Euro area	98.0	100.0	101.6	100.7	100.5	101.8	103.9	105.8
OECD-Total	97.2	100.0	101.8 p	103.1 p	104.6 p	106.8 p	109.4 p	111.3 e

1. The statistical data for Israel are supplied by and under the responsibility of the relevant Israeli authorities. The use of such data by the OECD is without prejudice to the status of the Golan Heights, East Jerusalem and Israeli settlements in the West Bank under the terms of international law.

Table 13. Gross domestic product, price indices

Year 2010=100

	2009	2010	2011	2012	2013	2014	2015	2016
Australia	94.1	100.0	101.9	101.7	103.2	102.4	102.0	105.7
Austria	99.1	100.0	101.8	103.9	105.6	107.7	110.2	111.4
Belgium	98.2	100.0	102.0	104.0	105.1	105.8	107.0	108.7
Canada	97.2	100.0	103.2	104.5	106.2	108.3	107.4	108.1
Chile	91.8	100.0	103.1	104.3	106.3	112.7	117.4	121.8
Czech Republic	101.4	100.0	100.0	101.5	102.9	105.5	106.7	108.0
Denmark	96.9	100.0	100.6	103.0	103.9	105.0	105.8	105.7
Estonia	98.3	100.0	105.3	108.6	112.4	114.1	115.5	117.4
Finland	99.7	100.0	102.6	105.6	108.3	110.1	112.2	113.1
France	98.9	100.0	100.9	102.1	102.9	103.5	104.6 p	105.0 p
Germany	99.2	100.0	101.1	102.6	104.6	106.5	108.7	110.1
Greece	99.3	100.0	100.8 p	100.4 p	98.1 p	96.3 p	95.3 p	94.4 p
Hungary	97.7	100.0	102.3	105.7	108.8	112.5	114.6	115.7
Iceland	94.8	100.0	103.0	106.4	108.3	112.8	119.6	122.1
Ireland	103.3	100.0	99.6	101.7	102.7	102.3	109.8	109.8
Israel[1]	98.5	100.0	101.9	105.6	107.9	109.0	111.9	112.9
Italy	99.7	100.0	101.5	102.9	104.1	105.1	106.1	107.0
Japan	101.9	100.0	98.3	97.6	97.3	98.9	101.1	101.3
Korea	96.9	100.0	101.6	102.6	103.5	104.1	106.6	108.6 p
Latvia	100.8	100.0	106.4	110.2	112.1	114.0	114.0	114.3
Luxembourg	96.5	100.0	104.8	107.5	109.3	111.1	112.5	111.1
Mexico	95.7	100.0	105.8	110.1	111.8	116.7	119.9	126.3 p
Netherlands	99.2	100.0	100.1	101.6	103.0	103.1	103.9	104.5 p
New Zealand	96.4	100.0	102.1	101.6	106.5	107.6 p	108.4 p	111.0 e
Norway	94.4	100.0	106.8	110.3	113.1	113.5	110.3	109.1
Poland	98.4	100.0	103.2	105.7	106.0	106.5	107.3	107.7
Portugal	99.4	100.0	99.7	99.3	101.6	102.3	104.4	106.0 p
Slovak Republic	99.5	100.0	101.6	102.9	103.5	103.3	103.1	102.7
Slovenia	101.0	100.0	101.1	101.6	103.2	104.0	105.0	106.0
Spain	99.8	100.0	100.0	100.1	100.5	100.3	100.9 p	101.2 p
Sweden	99.0	100.0	101.2	102.3	103.3	105.2	107.3	109.1
Switzerland	99.7	100.0	100.3	100.2	100.2	99.6	99.0	98.4
Turkey	93.4	100.0	108.2	116.2	123.5	132.7	143.0	154.6
United Kingdom	98.5	100.0	102.0	103.6	105.6	107.4	107.9	110.0
United States	98.8	100.0	102.1	103.9	105.6	107.5	108.7	110.1
Euro area	99.3	100.0	101.0	102.3	103.6	104.5	106.0	106.8
OECD-Total	98.8	100.0	101.5 p	103.0 p	104.4 p	106.1 p	107.6 p	109.1 e

1. The statistical data for Israel are supplied by and under the responsibility of the relevant Israeli authorities. The use of such data by the OECD is without prejudice to the status of the Golan Heights, East Jerusalem and Israeli settlements in the West Bank under the terms of international law.

Table 14. Actual individual consumption at current prices and PPPs

Billion USD

	2009	2010	2011	2012	2013	2014	2015	2016
Australia	584.5	617.7	652.5	671.1	721.3	745.2	765.3	772.1
Austria	220.8	229.9	238.3	249.0	259.3	263.2	268.5	275.7
Belgium	263.0	281.1	291.5	303.8	316.8	324.8	328.7	336.4
Canada	877.3 e	924.1 e	960.9	987.0	1 024.3	1 069.4	1 082.5	1 110.8
Chile	184.2 e	203.2 e	227.9 e	249.4 e	270.6	279.0	279.4	290.6 e
Czech Republic	173.9	180.0	183.2	186.9	198.2	206.7	210.2	217.6
Denmark	141.4	149.2	152.3	156.7	162.4	164.8	168.1	170.7
Estonia	17.5	18.3	19.5	21.1	22.2	22.9	23.7	25.0
Finland	131.0	138.2	145.5	151.0	154.7	157.6	160.8	165.9
France	1 594.3	1 674.6	1 720.9	1 767.2	1 860.0	1 881.3	1 896.8 p	1 957.0 p
Germany	2 097.4	2 198.9	2 297.2	2 393.0	2 468.1	2 530.9	2 565.8	2 657.0
Greece	257.5	244.7	227.5 p	216.5 p	218.1 p	220.8 p	218.1 p	219.0 p
Hungary	134.6	140.8	147.0	150.4	154.1	155.9	158.0	162.6
Iceland	8.4	8.1	8.4	8.9	9.1	9.4	9.6	9.9
Ireland	102.5	106.5	105.2	107.6	108.8	109.9	113.8	119.5
Israel[1]	137.4	146.3	158.1	167.7	171.8	173.2	183.6	195.8
Italy	1 411.2	1 500.8	1 519.1	1 510.0	1 507.9	1 497.1	1 511.9	1 575.3
Japan	2 938.8	3 064.1	3 160.2	3 322.9	3 615.2	3 586.0	3 630.3	3 696.4
Korea	813.6	864.2	914.9	955.0	958.3	968.1	1 005.3	895.0 p
Latvia	24.5	26.6	27.8	29.9	32.0	32.6	33.1	34.7
Luxembourg	16.2	16.1	16.9	17.9	19.2	19.5	19.7	20.3
Mexico	1 171.3	1 242.9	1 344.8	1 417.0	1 484.4	1 536.4	1 555.9	1 635.0 p
Netherlands	455.3	450.8	458.9	470.6	482.0	482.7	488.2	498.3 p
New Zealand	93.4	97.1	102.1	105.4	111.5	115.9	118.6	124.4 e
Norway	142.0	148.2	152.7	160.5	170.6	175.6	179.4	184.0
Poland	546.0	605.8	651.0	690.6	706.0	717.4	732.2	756.1
Portugal	201.4	210.4	204.1	201.2	210.0	213.9	217.4	223.4 p
Slovak Republic	85.3	93.1	94.4	97.8	101.2	104.3	106.2	108.9
Slovenia	36.0	37.7	38.8	39.4	39.2	39.6	40.1	41.5
Spain	962.0	973.4	975.3	984.5	993.0	1 023.4	1 058.5 p	1 096.3 p
Sweden	238.5	246.3	255.7	265.9	269.1	275.9	280.7	288.9
Switzerland	227.6	230.5	236.6	248.0	262.3	270.5	277.6 p	283.4 p
Turkey	719.3 e	835.3 e	957.0 e	1 013.0 e	1 096.8 e	1 175.6 e	1 234.6 e	1 277.2 e
United Kingdom	1 622.1	1 678.9	1 709.9	1 783.8	1 831.2	1 882.3	1 923.9	2 014.4
United States	10 826.1	11 200.3	11 692.8	12 063.2	12 396.8	12 933.1	13 387.2	13 867.2 e
Euro area	7 947.9	8 274.9	8 459.0	8 642.0	8 877.4	9 012.8	9 142.7	9 448.9
OECD-Total	29 456.4 e	30 784.0 e	32 048.9 e	33 164.0 e	34 406.1 e	35 365.1 e	36 233.4 e	37 306.4 e

1. The statistical data for Israel are supplied by and under the responsibility of the relevant Israeli authorities. The use of such data by the OECD is without prejudice to the status of the Golan Heights, East Jerusalem and Israeli settlements in the West Bank under the terms of international law.

Table 15. Actual individual consumption at the price levels and PPPs of year 2010

Billion USD

	2009	2010	2011	2012	2013	2014	2015	2016
Australia	594.7	617.7	635.5	645.2	659.7	678.0	698.5	715.8
Austria	227.8	229.9	232.6	233.9	234.4	235.5	237.0	241.1
Belgium	274.2	281.1	282.9	285.2	286.9	289.9	292.8	297.1
Canada	893.3 e	924.1 e	945.2 e	960.7 e	978.1 e	999.7 e	1 019.9 e	1 043.3 e
Chile	185.7 e	203.2 e	218.5 e	231.6 e	242.0 e	248.8 e	255.1 e	261.6 e
Czech Republic	178.3	180.0	179.6	177.5	179.0	182.4	188.2	194.4
Denmark	147.2	149.2	149.6	150.3	150.9	153.4	155.7	158.3
Estonia	18.5	18.3	18.8	19.6	20.2	20.8	21.8	22.7
Finland	134.9	138.2	141.5	142.1	141.6	142.3	144.5	146.9
France	1 643.9	1 674.6	1 685.1	1 688.5	1 700.3	1 719.0	1 743.7 p	1 779.7 p
Germany	2 185.3	2 198.9	2 228.0	2 255.3	2 272.4	2 300.5	2 348.2	2 403.9
Greece	260.6	244.7	222.2 p	203.8 p	196.2 p	195.8 p	195.1 p	194.9 p
Hungary	144.8	140.8	141.7	138.4	139.1	142.5	147.2	152.8
Iceland	8.2 e	8.1 e	8.2 e	8.3 e	8.4 e	8.6 e	9.0 e	9.3 e
Ireland	106.3	106.5	103.8	102.4	102.3	105.0	109.0	112.8
Israel[1]	139.9	146.3	151.7	156.3	162.2	169.1	175.7	185.7
Italy	1 484.6	1 500.8	1 496.9	1 445.4	1 415.1	1 420.0	1 442.7	1 459.8
Japan	2 992.3	3 064.1	3 071.6	3 138.3	3 209.0	3 190.1	3 202.0	3 213.4
Korea	828.4 e	864.2 e	892.1 e	911.5 e	930.4 e	950.1 e	972.3 e	858.2 e
Latvia	26.1	26.6	27.5	28.3	29.6	30.1	30.9	32.0
Luxembourg	15.9	16.1	16.2	16.7	17.2	17.5	18.0	18.5
Mexico	1 202.5	1 242.9	1 285.3	1 314.5	1 337.7	1 364.5	1 406.3	1 455.6 p
Netherlands	448.5	450.8	452.7	447.8	443.4	445.0	451.9	458.6 p
New Zealand	95.1	97.1	100.0	102.0	105.3	108.5 p	111.4 p	116.1 e
Norway	143.3	148.2	151.0	155.6	159.2	162.3	166.0	168.8
Poland	589.9	605.8	621.6	625.7	629.8	646.4	666.0	690.2
Portugal	206.5	210.4	202.2	191.9	190.0	192.7	195.5	199.3
Slovak Republic	92.5	93.1	92.0	91.8	91.6	95.2	97.7	100.1
Slovenia	37.3	37.7	37.8	36.9	35.5	36.0	36.9	38.3
Spain	971.4	973.4	952.1	916.7	889.1	..	..	..
Sweden	239.0	246.3	249.8	251.4	255.1	260.1	268.1	274.8
Switzerland	226.6	230.5	232.3	237.8	243.9	247.4	252.1 p	256.1 p
Turkey	759.2 e	835.3 e	930.1 e	961.8 e	1 037.7 e	1 069.2 e	1 126.1 e	1 172.0 e
United Kingdom	1 666.1	1 678.9	1 671.5	1 699.4	1 729.9	1 769.4	1 813.0	1 861.7
United States	11 023.1	11 200.3	11 409.4	11 565.3	11 723.7	12 041.6	12 421.0	12 722.3 e
Euro area	8 205.8	8 274.9	8 276.2	8 195.8	8 158.1	8 234.5	8 385.4	8 554.9
OECD-Total	30 193.0 e	30 784.0 e	31 241.0 e	31 543.2 e	31 951.6 e	32 531.9 e	33 338.8 e	33 965.9 e

1. The statistical data for Israel are supplied by and under the responsibility of the relevant Israeli authorities. The use of such data by the OECD is without prejudice to the status of the Golan Heights, East Jerusalem and Israeli settlements in the West Bank under the terms of international law.

Table 16. Actual individual consumption per head at current prices and PPPs

USD

	2009	2010	2011	2012	2013	2014	2015	2016
Australia	26 529	27 651	28 711	29 031	30 743	31 322	31 715	31 491
Austria	26 464	27 494	28 409	29 549	30 591	30 809	31 110	31 541
Belgium	24 364	25 799	26 518	27 447	28 478	29 050	29 248	29 782
Canada	26 088 e	27 175 e	27 981	28 404	29 137	30 087	30 196	30 613
Chile	10 881 e	11 887 e	13 197 e	14 295 e	15 341	15 645	15 482	15 897 e
Czech Republic	16 578	17 117	17 451	17 782	18 855	19 639	19 942	20 598
Denmark	25 606	26 898	27 336	28 034	28 929	29 210	29 592	29 794
Estonia	13 104	13 691	14 700	15 893	16 810	17 421	18 083	19 032
Finland	24 533	25 760	26 995	27 895	28 450	28 848	29 342	30 190
France	24 658	25 773	26 356	26 933	28 201	28 380	28 484 p	29 271 p
Germany	26 061	27 389	28 616	29 754	30 604	31 253	31 411	32 265
Greece	23 188	21 999	20 483 p	19 603 p	19 887 p	20 269 p	20 153 p	20 307 p
Hungary	13 432	14 084	14 744	15 162	15 579	15 805	16 055	16 566
Iceland	26 403	25 409	26 395	27 716	27 977	28 802	29 155	29 648
Ireland	22 572	23 366	22 986	23 431	23 645	23 809	24 503	25 518
Israel[1]	18 370	19 192	20 366	21 213	21 323	21 085	21 913	22 916
Italy	23 686	25 085	25 293	25 026	24 863	24 628	24 895	25 983
Japan	22 954	23 930	24 722	26 051	28 392	28 178	28 560	29 115
Korea	16 499	17 440	18 321	19 025	19 004	19 077	19 706	17 466 p
Latvia	11 439	12 687	13 527	14 691	15 895	16 340	16 752	17 716
Luxembourg	32 571	31 653	32 594	33 755	35 230	34 969	34 605	34 822
Mexico	10 379	10 878	11 625	12 106	12 537	12 834 e	12 858 e	13 372 e
Netherlands	27 549	27 135	27 491	28 093	28 689	28 626	28 832 p	29 264 p
New Zealand	21 633	22 248	23 236	23 862	24 996	25 572	25 652	26 358 e
Norway	29 402	30 306	30 820	31 986	33 584	34 190	34 556	35 145
Poland	14 189	15 729	16 899	17 922	18 336	18 641	19 041	19 675
Portugal	19 059	19 900	19 330	19 135	20 078	20 568	20 984	21 636 p
Slovak Republic	15 738	17 146	17 485	18 094	18 687	19 240	19 578	20 052
Slovenia	17 634	18 419	18 904	19 145	19 017	19 215	19 430	20 101
Spain	20 747	20 905	20 868	21 051	21 313	22 029 p	22 809 p	23 593 p
Sweden	25 653	26 264	27 062	27 935	28 025	28 455	28 647	29 113
Switzerland	29 278	29 336	29 897	31 013	32 423	33 029	33 512 p	33 853 p
Turkey	9 983 e	11 442 e	12 941 e	13 524 e	14 474 e	15 344 e	15 942 e	16 323 e
United Kingdom	26 054	26 752	27 019	28 001	28 565	29 139	29 548	30 684
United States	35 237	36 153	37 463	38 372	39 160	40 557	41 682	42 881 e
Euro area	23 788	24 709	25 196	25 676	26 319	26 662	26 966	27 767
OECD-Total	23 898 e	24 818 e	25 682 e	26 422 e	27 262 e	27 859 e	28 377 e	29 043 e

1. The statistical data for Israel are supplied by and under the responsibility of the relevant Israeli authorities. The use of such data by the OECD is without prejudice to the status of the Golan Heights, East Jerusalem and Israeli settlements in the West Bank under the terms of international law.

Table 17. Actual individual consumption per head at the price levels and PPPs of year 2010

USD

	2009	2010	2011	2012	2013	2014	2015	2016
Australia	26 994	27 651	27 962	27 911	28 121	28 497	28 946	29 196
Austria	27 311	27 494	27 734	27 760	27 647	27 560	27 468	27 590
Belgium	25 400	25 799	25 729	25 771	25 790	25 928	26 051	26 308
Canada	26 562 e	27 175 e	27 523 e	27 645 e	27 821 e	28 124 e	28 449 e	28 753 e
Chile	10 969 e	11 887 e	12 654 e	13 270 e	13 718 e	13 949 e	14 139 e	14 311 e
Czech Republic	16 995	17 117	17 115	16 893	17 028	17 333	17 851	18 395
Denmark	26 647	26 898	26 855	26 876	26 885	27 178	27 401	27 625
Estonia	13 861	13 691	14 172	14 777	15 303	15 839	16 575	17 216
Finland	25 261	25 760	26 263	26 242	26 034	26 058	26 372	26 727
France	25 425	25 773	25 808	25 733	25 781	25 932	26 186 p	26 620 p
Germany	27 152	27 389	27 755	28 042	28 178	28 407	28 747	29 191
Greece	23 462	21 999	20 006 p	18 453 p	17 891 p	17 979 p	18 031 p	18 070 p
Hungary	14 444	14 084	14 209	13 953	14 059	14 439	14 965	15 571
Iceland	25 777 e	25 409 e	25 684 e	25 783 e	25 820 e	26 377 e	27 057 e	27 752 e
Ireland	23 422	23 366	22 684	22 312	22 239	22 756	23 479	24 077
Israel[1]	18 704	19 192	19 544	19 768	20 137	20 588	20 971	21 738
Italy	24 919	25 085	24 924	23 954	23 334	23 360	23 755	24 078
Japan	23 371	23 930	24 028	24 604	25 202	25 068	25 191	25 311
Korea	16 800 e	17 440 e	17 864 e	18 157 e	18 449 e	18 723 e	19 059 e	16 746 e
Latvia	12 191	12 687	13 341	13 917	14 727	15 107	15 631	16 354
Luxembourg	32 003	31 653	31 231	31 420	31 467	31 405	31 582	31 593
Mexico	10 655	10 878	11 110	11 230	11 299	11 398 e	11 622 e	11 904 e
Netherlands	27 140	27 135	27 118	26 733	26 391	26 387	26 691 p	26 933 p
New Zealand	22 026	22 248	22 764	23 079	23 599	23 928 p	24 089 p	24 599 e
Norway	29 680	30 306	30 479	31 002	31 338	31 598	31 970	32 248
Poland	15 329	15 729	16 141	16 244	16 365	16 795	17 318	17 960
Portugal	19 543	19 900	19 156	18 254	18 170	18 526	18 877	19 305 p
Slovak Republic	17 072	17 146	17 038	16 977	16 931	17 574	18 021	18 439
Slovenia	18 272	18 419	18 411	17 952	17 231	17 472	17 862	18 552
Spain	20 950	20 905	20 372	19 602	19 081	..	..	
Sweden	25 701	26 264	26 439	26 405	26 569	26 827	27 359	27 696
Switzerland	29 152	29 336	29 358	29 741	30 152	30 217	30 441 p	30 588 p
Turkey	10 537 e	11 442 e	12 577 e	12 841 e	13 695 e	13 955 e	14 541 e	14 978 e
United Kingdom	26 760	26 752	26 412	26 676	26 984	27 391	27 846	28 360
United States	35 878	36 153	36 555	36 788	37 034	37 761	38 674	39 340 e
Euro area	24 560	24 709	24 652	24 350	24 187	24 360	24 732	25 140
OECD-Total	24 495 e	24 818 e	25 034 e	25 131 e	25 317 e	25 627 e	26 110 e	26 442 e

1. The statistical data for Israel are supplied by and under the responsibility of the relevant Israeli authorities. The use of such data by the OECD is without prejudice to the status of the Golan Heights, East Jerusalem and Israeli settlements in the West Bank under the terms of international law.

Table 18. Actual individual consumption per head at current prices and current PPPs, index

OECD=100

	2009	2010	2011	2012	2013	2014	2015	2016
Australia	111.0 e	111.4 e	111.8 e	109.9 e	112.8 e	112.4 e	111.8 e	108.4 e
Austria	110.7 e	110.8 e	110.6 e	111.8 e	112.2 e	110.6 e	109.6 e	108.6 e
Belgium	102.0 e	104.0 e	103.3 e	103.9 e	104.5 e	104.3 e	103.1 e	102.5 e
Canada	109.2 e	109.5 e	109.0 e	107.5 e	106.9 e	108.0 e	106.4 e	105.4 e
Chile	45.5 e	47.9 e	51.4 e	54.1 e	56.3 e	56.2 e	54.6 e	54.7 e
Czech Republic	69.4 e	69.0 e	67.9 e	67.3 e	69.2 e	70.5 e	70.3 e	70.9 e
Denmark	107.1 e	108.4 e	106.4 e	106.1 e	106.1 e	104.9 e	104.3 e	102.6 e
Estonia	54.8 e	55.2 e	57.2 e	60.1 e	61.7 e	62.5 e	63.7 e	65.5 e
Finland	102.7 e	103.8 e	105.1 e	105.6 e	104.4 e	103.6 e	103.4 e	103.9 e
France	103.2 e	103.9 e	102.6 e	101.9 e	103.4 e	101.9 e	100.4 e	100.8 e
Germany	109.1 e	110.4 e	111.4 e	112.6 e	112.3 e	112.2 e	110.7 e	111.1 e
Greece	97.0 e	88.6 e	79.8 e	74.2 e	72.9 e	72.8 e	71.0 e	69.9 e
Hungary	56.2 e	56.8 e	57.4 e	57.4 e	57.1 e	56.7 e	56.6 e	57.0 e
Iceland	110.5 e	102.4 e	102.8 e	104.9 e	102.6 e	103.4 e	102.7 e	102.1 e
Ireland	94.5 e	94.1 e	89.5 e	88.7 e	86.7 e	85.5 e	86.3 e	87.9 e
Israel[1]	76.9 e	77.3 e	79.3 e	80.3 e	78.2 e	75.7 e	77.2 e	78.9 e
Italy	99.1 e	101.1 e	98.5 e	94.7 e	91.2 e	88.4 e	87.7 e	89.5 e
Japan	96.1 e	96.4 e	96.3 e	98.6 e	104.1 e	101.1 e	100.6 e	100.2 e
Korea	69.0 e	70.3 e	71.3 e	72.0 e	69.7 e	68.5 e	69.4 e	60.1 e
Latvia	47.9 e	51.1 e	52.7 e	55.6 e	58.3 e	58.7 e	59.0 e	61.0 e
Luxembourg	136.3 e	127.5 e	126.9 e	127.8 e	129.2 e	125.5 e	121.9 e	119.9 e
Mexico	43.4 e	43.8 e	45.3 e	45.8 e	46.0 e	46.1 e	45.3 e	46.0 e
Netherlands	115.3 e	109.3 e	107.0 e	106.3 e	105.2 e	102.8 e	101.6 e	100.8 e
New Zealand	90.5 e	89.6 e	90.5 e	90.3 e	91.7 e	91.8 e	90.4 e	90.8 e
Norway	123.0 e	122.1 e	120.0 e	121.1 e	123.2 e	122.7 e	121.8 e	121.0 e
Poland	59.4 e	63.4 e	65.8 e	67.8 e	67.3 e	66.9 e	67.1 e	67.7 e
Portugal	79.8 e	80.2 e	75.3 e	72.4 e	73.6 e	73.8 e	73.9 e	74.5 e
Slovak Republic	65.9 e	69.1 e	68.1 e	68.5 e	68.5 e	69.1 e	69.0 e	69.0 e
Slovenia	73.8 e	74.2 e	73.6 e	72.5 e	69.8 e	69.0 e	68.5 e	69.2 e
Spain	86.8 e	84.2 e	81.3 e	79.7 e	78.2 e	79.1 e	80.4 e	81.2 e
Sweden	107.3 e	105.8 e	105.4 e	105.7 e	102.8 e	102.1 e	101.0 e	100.2 e
Switzerland	122.5 e	118.2 e	116.4 e	117.4 e	118.9 e	118.6 e	118.1 e	116.6 e
Turkey	41.8 e	46.1 e	50.4 e	51.2 e	53.1 e	55.1 e	56.2 e	56.2 e
United Kingdom	109.0 e	107.8 e	105.2 e	106.0 e	104.8 e	104.6 e	104.1 e	105.7 e
United States	147.4 e	145.7 e	145.9 e	145.2 e	143.6 e	145.6 e	146.9 e	147.6 e
Euro area	99.5 e	99.6 e	98.1 e	97.2 e	96.5 e	95.7 e	95.0 e	95.6 e
OECD-Total	100.0 e	100.0 e	100.0 e	100.0 e	100.0 e	100.0 e	100.0 e	100.0 e

1. The statistical data for Israel are supplied by and under the responsibility of the relevant Israeli authorities. The use of such data by the OECD is without prejudice to the status of the Golan Heights, East Jerusalem and Israeli settlements in the West Bank under the terms of international law.

Table 19. Actual individual consumption per head at the price levels and PPPs of year 2010, index

OECD=100

	2009	2010	2011	2012	2013	2014	2015	2016
Australia	110.2 e	111.4 e	111.7 e	111.1 e	111.1 e	111.2 e	110.9 e	110.4 e
Austria	111.5 e	110.8 e	110.8 e	110.5 e	109.2 e	107.5 e	105.2 e	104.3 e
Belgium	103.7 e	104.0 e	102.8 e	102.6 e	101.9 e	101.2 e	99.8 e	99.5 e
Canada	108.4 e	109.5 e	109.9 e	110.0 e	109.9 e	109.7 e	109.0 e	108.7 e
Chile	44.8 e	47.9 e	50.5 e	52.8 e	54.2 e	54.4 e	54.2 e	54.1 e
Czech Republic	69.4 e	69.0 e	68.4 e	67.3 e	67.3 e	67.6 e	68.4 e	69.6 e
Denmark	108.8 e	108.4 e	107.3 e	107.0 e	106.2 e	106.1 e	104.9 e	104.5 e
Estonia	56.6 e	55.2 e	56.6 e	58.8 e	60.5 e	61.8 e	63.5 e	65.1 e
Finland	103.1 e	103.8 e	105.0 e	104.5 e	102.9 e	101.7 e	101.0 e	101.1 e
France	103.8 e	103.9 e	103.1 e	102.4 e	101.9 e	101.2 e	100.3 e	100.7 e
Germany	110.8 e	110.4 e	110.9 e	111.6 e	111.3 e	110.8 e	110.1 e	110.4 e
Greece	95.8 e	88.6 e	80.0 e	73.5 e	70.7 e	70.2 e	69.1 e	68.3 e
Hungary	59.0 e	56.8 e	56.8 e	55.5 e	55.6 e	56.3 e	57.3 e	58.9 e
Iceland	105.2 e	102.4 e	102.6 e	102.6 e	102.0 e	102.9 e	103.6 e	105.0 e
Ireland	95.6 e	94.1 e	90.6 e	88.8 e	87.8 e	88.8 e	89.9 e	91.1 e
Israel[1]	76.4 e	77.3 e	78.1 e	78.7 e	79.6 e	80.3 e	80.3 e	82.2 e
Italy	101.7 e	101.1 e	99.6 e	95.4 e	92.2 e	91.2 e	91.0 e	91.1 e
Japan	95.4 e	96.4 e	95.9 e	97.8 e	99.5 e	97.8 e	96.5 e	95.7 e
Korea	68.6 e	70.3 e	71.4 e	72.3 e	72.9 e	73.1 e	73.0 e	63.3 e
Latvia	49.8 e	51.1 e	53.3 e	55.4 e	58.2 e	59.0 e	59.9 e	61.8 e
Luxembourg	130.7 e	127.5 e	124.8 e	125.1 e	124.3 e	122.5 e	121.0 e	119.5 e
Mexico	43.5 e	43.8 e	44.4 e	44.7 e	44.6 e	44.5 e	44.5 e	45.0 e
Netherlands	110.8 e	109.3 e	108.4 e	106.4 e	104.3 e	103.0 e	102.2 e	101.9 e
New Zealand	89.9 e	89.6 e	90.9 e	91.8 e	93.2 e	93.4 e	92.3 e	93.0 e
Norway	121.2 e	122.1 e	121.8 e	123.4 e	123.8 e	123.3 e	122.4 e	122.0 e
Poland	62.6 e	63.4 e	64.5 e	64.6 e	64.6 e	65.5 e	66.3 e	67.9 e
Portugal	79.8 e	80.2 e	76.6 e	72.7 e	71.8 e	72.3 e	72.3 e	73.0 e
Slovak Republic	69.7 e	69.1 e	68.1 e	67.6 e	66.9 e	68.6 e	69.0 e	69.7 e
Slovenia	74.6 e	74.2 e	73.6 e	71.5 e	68.1 e	68.2 e	68.4 e	70.2 e
Spain	85.5 e	84.2 e	81.4 e	78.0 e	75.4 e	..	..	
Sweden	104.9 e	105.8 e	105.7 e	105.1 e	105.0 e	104.7 e	104.8 e	104.7 e
Switzerland	119.0 e	118.2 e	117.3 e	118.4 e	119.2 e	117.9 e	116.6 e	115.7 e
Turkey	43.0 e	46.1 e	50.3 e	51.1 e	54.1 e	54.5 e	55.7 e	56.6 e
United Kingdom	109.2 e	107.8 e	105.6 e	106.2 e	106.6 e	106.9 e	106.6 e	107.2 e
United States	146.5 e	145.7 e	146.0 e	146.4 e	146.3 e	147.3 e	148.1 e	148.8 e
Euro area	100.3 e	99.6 e	98.5 e	96.9 e	95.5 e	95.1 e	94.7 e	95.1 e
OECD-Total	100.0 e	100.0 e	100.0 e	100.0 e	100.0 e	100.0 e	100.0 e	100.0 e

1. The statistical data for Israel are supplied by and under the responsibility of the relevant Israeli authorities. The use of such data by the OECD is without prejudice to the status of the Golan Heights, East Jerusalem and Israeli settlements in the West Bank under the terms of international law.

Table 20. Actual individual consumption at current prices and exchange rates

Billion USD

	2009	2010	2011	2012	2013	2014	2015	2016
Australia	683.1	854.0	1 013.1	1 057.0	1 030.2	1 002.4	872.2	892.4
Austria	264.0	258.4	282.5	268.8	283.8	290.5	248.6	255.2
Belgium	325.2	323.8	352.9	336.0	352.6	357.7	303.7	311.9
Canada	972.0 e	1 131.3 e	1 234.7	1 260.8	1 268.3	1 230.6	1 098.8	1 095.1
Chile	112.1 e	140.6 e	166.4 e	180.6 e	192.1	181.8	171.3	175.8 e
Czech Republic	121.9	123.3	135.9	124.0	125.8	121.8	106.5	111.6
Denmark	218.0	214.9	228.9	217.6	226.8	231.2	197.0	201.4
Estonia	12.9	12.4	14.2	14.1	15.5	16.2	14.2	15.0
Finland	172.5	171.1	190.4	182.4	192.4	195.8	167.0	169.9
France	1 928.5	1 893.7	2 032.0	1 904.4	1 994.8	2 017.3	1 714.4 p	1 743.9 p
Germany	2 386.4	2 332.5	2 529.0	2 400.3	2 537.4	2 597.0	2 232.4	2 296.4
Greece	262.4	240.3	232.4 p	197.4 p	192.0 p	187.0 p	153.3 p	151.3 p
Hungary	85.0	83.2	89.2	81.9	84.0	84.3	73.1	75.7
Iceland	8.8	8.9	9.9	9.8	10.5	11.8	11.1	12.9
Ireland	144.8	134.5	138.9	128.6	134.4	138.8	121.0	126.0
Israel[1]	140.4	159.5	178.4	174.5	197.3	208.6	199.2	212.7
Italy	1 590.1	1 551.0	1 660.5	1 513.6	1 545.9	1 552.8	1 320.3	1 336.6
Japan	3 653.4	3 939.1	4 320.2	4 390.2	3 664.3	3 421.1	3 015.8	3 352.0
Korea	533.6	628.2	701.5	720.0	764.5	821.5	790.3	688.0 p
Latvia	18.3	17.2	19.9	19.4	21.1	21.8	18.6	19.4
Luxembourg	22.9	22.6	24.8	24.2	26.0	26.8	23.1	23.6
Mexico	644.4	751.2	832.7	847.0	925.4	945.6	838.8	770.0 p
Netherlands	537.4	521.0	556.9	519.3	540.6	546.1	464.1	471.8 p
New Zealand	85.8	103.0	119.1	125.5	132.4	139.2	121.2	127.4 e
Norway	219.8	242.1	271.8	274.6	285.8	279.0	229.1	230.0
Poland	315.0	344.1	376.8	356.6	371.3	381.1	326.1	322.1
Portugal	186.7	184.0	187.4	165.0	170.7	173.9	148.6	152.7 p
Slovak Republic	61.8	59.9	64.5	61.5	64.3	66.7	57.3	58.5
Slovenia	33.4	32.7	35.0	32.0	32.2	32.6	27.8	28.9
Spain	1 020.4	988.6	1 034.7	935.7	946.6	958.9	827.3 p	847.9 p
Sweden	283.8	315.6	362.9	354.0	379.0	372.6	317.2	326.6
Switzerland	325.6	347.0	411.2	395.3	408.1	418.1	403.2 p	399.0 p
Turkey	435.8 e	527.8 e	566.5 e	589.4 e	636.2 e	614.4 e	561.5 e	562.3 e
United Kingdom	1 896.5	1 926.0	2 050.1	2 092.4	2 148.7	2 351.7	2 249.2	2 068.4
United States	10 826.1	11 200.3	11 692.8	12 063.2	12 396.8	12 933.1	13 387.2	13 867.2 e
Euro area	9 022.4	8 796.3	9 414.3	8 758.8	9 108.8	9 239.7	7 893.7	8 062.7
OECD-Total	30 528.6 e	31 783.8 e	34 118.1 e	34 017.2 e	34 297.8 e	34 929.9 e	32 810.5 e	33 499.6 e

1. The statistical data for Israel are supplied by and under the responsibility of the relevant Israeli authorities. The use of such data by the OECD is without prejudice to the status of the Golan Heights, East Jerusalem and Israeli settlements in the West Bank under the terms of international law.

Table 21. Actual individual consumption at the price levels and exchange rates of year 2010

Billion USD

	2009	2010	2011	2012	2013	2014	2015	2016
Australia	822.2	854.0	878.6	892.0	912.1	937.3	965.6	989.6
Austria	256.1	258.4	261.5	262.9	263.4	264.7	266.4	271.0
Belgium	315.8	323.8	325.9	328.7	330.6	333.8	337.2	342.2
Canada	1 093.5 e	1 131.3 e	1 157.1 e	1 176.1 e	1 197.3 e	1 223.8 e	1 248.5 e	1 277.2 e
Chile	128.4 e	140.6 e	151.1 e	160.2 e	167.4 e	172.1 e	176.5 e	181.0 e
Czech Republic	122.2	123.3	123.1	121.7	122.7	125.0	129.0	133.2
Denmark	212.0	214.9	215.6	216.5	217.5	220.9	224.3	228.0
Estonia	12.6	12.4	12.8	13.3	13.7	14.2	14.8	15.4
Finland	167.1	171.1	175.4	176.1	175.5	176.3	179.0	181.9
France	1 859.0	1 893.7	1 906.5	1 910.3	1 923.7	1 944.0	1 971.9 p	2 012.6 p
Germany	2 318.1	2 332.5	2 364.5	2 393.4	2 411.6	2 440.3	2 490.9	2 549.9
Greece	255.9	240.3	218.3 p	200.3 p	192.8 p	192.3 p	191.6 p	191.4 p
Hungary	85.5	83.2	83.7	81.8	82.2	84.1	87.0	90.3
Iceland	9.1 e	8.9 e	9.1 e	9.2 e	9.3 e	9.6 e	9.9 e	10.3 e
Ireland	134.2	134.5	131.1	129.3	129.2	132.6	137.6	142.4
Israel[1]	152.6	159.5	165.6	170.6	177.1	184.3	191.5	202.5
Italy	1 534.3	1 551.0	1 547.7	1 494.4	1 463.1	1 467.5	1 490.9	1 508.6
Japan	3 846.8	3 939.1	3 946.5	4 032.3	4 123.1	4 101.1	4 116.4	4 131.1
Korea	602.2 e	628.2 e	648.5 e	662.6 e	676.3 e	690.7 e	706.8 e	623.8 e
Latvia	16.9	17.2	17.8	18.3	19.2	19.5	20.0	20.7
Luxembourg	22.4	22.6	22.8	23.5	24.1	24.6	25.3	25.9
Mexico	726.8	751.2	776.8	794.5	808.5	824.7	850.0	879.7 p
Netherlands	518.4	521.0	523.4	517.8	512.7	514.3	522.3	530.0 p
New Zealand	100.9	103.0	106.1	108.2	111.7	115.1 p	118.1 p	123.2 e
Norway	234.2	242.1	246.8	254.4	260.3	265.2	271.2	275.9
Poland	335.0	344.1	353.2	355.5	357.8	367.1	378.2	392.0
Portugal	180.6	184.0	176.9	167.9	166.2	168.5	171.0	174.3
Slovak Republic	59.5	59.9	59.2	59.1	59.0	61.3	62.9	64.4
Slovenia	32.4	32.7	32.8	32.1	30.8	31.3	32.0	33.2
Spain	986.5	988.6	967.4	931.0	902.9	..	..	
Sweden	306.2	315.6	320.3	322.2	327.0	333.3	343.5	352.1
Switzerland	341.3	347.0	349.9	358.3	367.4	372.6	379.6 p	385.6 p
Turkey	479.7 e	527.8 e	587.9 e	608.0 e	656.0 e	675.6 e	711.5 e	740.6 e
United Kingdom	1 911.3	1 926.0	1 918.4	1 950.4	1 985.3	2 029.8	2 079.9	2 135.7
United States	11 023.1	11 200.3	11 409.4	11 565.3	11 723.7	12 041.6	12 421.0	12 722.3 e
Euro area	8 722.9	8 796.3	8 797.6	8 712.2	8 672.2	8 753.3	8 913.7	9 093.9
OECD-Total	31 219.3 e	31 783.8 e	32 191.6 e	32 497.0 e	32 907.6 e	33 495.8 e	34 305.7 e	34 954.0 e

1. The statistical data for Israel are supplied by and under the responsibility of the relevant Israeli authorities. The use of such data by the OECD is without prejudice to the status of the Golan Heights, East Jerusalem and Israeli settlements in the West Bank under the terms of international law.

Table 22. Actual individual consumption at current prices and year 2010 exchange rates

Billion USD

	2009	2010	2011	2012	2013	2014	2015	2016
Australia	803.4	854.0	900.9	936.5	978.9	1 020.1	1 065.0	1 101.2
Austria	251.7	258.4	269.2	277.1	283.1	290.0	296.9	305.6
Belgium	310.1	323.8	336.2	346.3	351.7	357.1	362.7	373.5
Canada	1 078.5 e	1 131.3 e	1 186.0	1 222.9	1 267.8	1 321.4	1 364.3	1 408.9
Chile	123.3 e	140.6 e	157.8 e	172.1 e	186.4	203.2	219.6	233.2 e
Czech Republic	121.7	123.3	125.9	127.1	129.0	132.4	137.2	142.8
Denmark	207.8	214.9	218.5	224.2	226.5	230.7	235.7	241.0
Estonia	12.3	12.4	13.5	14.6	15.5	16.2	17.0	18.0
Finland	164.4	171.1	181.4	188.0	191.9	195.5	199.4	203.5
France	1 838.6	1 893.7	1 936.0	1 963.1	1 989.8	2 013.7	2 047.3 p	2 088.0 p
Germany	2 275.1	2 332.5	2 474.0	2 474.2	2 531.0	2 592.5	2 665.8	2 749.6
Greece	250.2	240.3	221.5 p	203.4 p	191.5 p	186.7 p	183.1 p	181.2 p
Hungary	82.7	83.2	86.2	88.7	90.3	94.3	98.2	102.5
Iceland	8.9	8.9	9.4	10.1	10.5	11.2	12.0	12.7
Ireland	138.1	134.5	132.3	132.5	134.1	138.5	144.5	150.9
Israel[1]	147.7	159.5	170.8	180.0	190.5	199.6	207.1	218.5
Italy	1 516.0	1 551.0	1 582.1	1 560.2	1 542.0	1 550.1	1 576.7	1 600.4
Japan	3 894.4	3 939.1	3 927.8	3 990.6	4 074.0	4 129.0	4 158.6	4 154.4
Korea	589.3	628.2	672.5	701.6	724.1	748.2	773.3	690.6 p
Latvia	17.4	17.2	18.8	20.0	21.1	21.7	22.2	23.2
Luxembourg	21.9	22.6	23.6	24.9	26.0	26.7	27.5	28.3
Mexico	689.2	751.2	818.7	882.8	935.3	994.7	1 052.1	1 137.3 p
Netherlands	512.3	521.0	530.6	535.3	539.3	545.2	554.3	564.9 p
New Zealand	99.0	103.0	108.6	111.6	116.3	120.9	125.2	131.9 e
Norway	228.7	242.1	252.1	264.3	277.8	290.9	305.7	319.7
Poland	326.0	344.1	370.2	385.1	389.1	398.7	407.6	421.2
Portugal	178.0	184.0	178.5	170.1	170.3	173.6	177.5	182.8 p
Slovak Republic	58.9	59.9	61.4	63.4	64.2	66.6	68.4	70.0
Slovenia	31.9	32.7	33.3	32.9	32.2	32.6	33.2	34.6
Spain	972.8	988.6	985.8	964.5	944.2	957.2	988.0 p	1 015.3 p
Sweden	301.4	315.6	326.9	332.8	342.5	354.7	371.3	388.0
Switzerland	339.8	347.0	350.2	355.4	362.7	367.3	372.1 p	377.0 p
Turkey	449.5 e	527.8 e	631.3 e	704.3 e	806.0 e	894.8 e	1 016.2 e	1 129.9 e
United Kingdom	1 881.1	1 926.0	1 977.1	2 046.7	2 123.8	2 208.4	2 274.8	2 367.1
United States	10 826.1	11 200.3	11 692.8	12 063.2	12 396.8	12 933.1	13 387.2	13 867.2 e
Euro area	8 601.7	8 796.3	8 969.3	9 028.5	9 086.0	9 223.6	9 426.5	9 653.7
OECD-Total	30 747.6 e	31 783.8 e	32 897.4 e	33 770.6 e	34 656.1 e	35 817.6 e	36 947.5 e	38 034.7 e

1. The statistical data for Israel are supplied by and under the responsibility of the relevant Israeli authorities. The use of such data by the OECD is without prejudice to the status of the Golan Heights, East Jerusalem and Israeli settlements in the West Bank under the terms of international law.

Table 23. Actual individual consumption per head at current prices and exchange rates

USD

	2009	2010	2011	2012	2013	2014	2015	2016
Australia	31 006	38 227	44 573	45 725	43 914	42 135	36 147	36 397
Austria	31 645	30 903	33 678	31 901	33 476	34 004	28 809	29 205
Belgium	30 124	29 713	32 097	30 356	31 694	31 995	27 026	27 617
Canada	28 903 e	33 268 e	35 953	36 282	36 077	34 623	30 651	30 178
Chile	6 624 e	8 223 e	9 639 e	10 347 e	10 888	10 194	9 495	9 618 e
Czech Republic	11 618	11 728	12 949	11 796	11 973	11 571	10 102	10 559
Denmark	39 476	38 744	41 103	38 928	40 402	40 970	34 679	35 149
Estonia	9 634	9 311	10 644	10 650	11 777	12 314	10 840	11 402
Finland	32 302	31 908	35 345	33 695	35 375	35 852	30 463	30 926
France	29 827	29 146	31 121	29 025	30 245	30 431	25 746 p	26 083 p
Germany	29 651	29 053	31 504	29 845	31 463	32 069	27 328	27 886
Greece	23 624	21 607	20 932 p	17 868 p	17 506 p	17 170 p	14 168 p	14 031 p
Hungary	8 476	8 318	8 944	8 259	8 486	8 542	7 430	7 711
Iceland	27 415	28 128	31 189	30 684	32 566	35 935	33 511	38 317
Ireland	31 903	29 497	30 336	28 010	29 205	30 070	26 062	26 911
Israel[1]	18 765	20 926	22 986	22 069	24 486	25 400	23 781	24 896
Italy	26 690	25 923	27 648	25 085	25 490	25 544	21 741	22 047
Japan	28 535	30 764	33 796	34 419	28 777	26 882	23 726	26 402
Korea	10 821	12 677	14 047	14 343	15 161	16 188	15 492	13 425 p
Latvia	8 521	8 208	9 667	9 522	10 491	10 910	9 396	9 901
Luxembourg	46 058	44 478	47 741	45 474	47 723	47 994	40 493	40 465
Mexico	5 711	6 575	7 198	7 236	7 816	7 899 e	6 932 e	6 297 e
Netherlands	32 516	31 362	33 360	31 000	32 179	32 385	27 412 p	27 712 p
New Zealand	19 873	23 600	27 110	28 414	29 676	30 698	26 207	26 993 e
Norway	45 511	49 519	54 881	54 717	56 258	54 312	44 135	43 934
Poland	8 186	8 933	9 779	9 254	9 642	9 902	8 479	8 383
Portugal	17 665	17 401	17 747	15 692	16 323	16 716	14 348	14 784 p
Slovak Republic	11 398	11 035	11 946	11 376	11 882	12 319	10 562	10 768
Slovenia	16 369	15 983	17 040	15 541	15 651	15 829	13 475	13 986
Spain	22 007	21 231	22 138	20 007	20 316	20 642 p	17 827 p	18 248 p
Sweden	30 522	33 652	38 404	37 192	39 478	38 429	32 375	32 913
Switzerland	41 886	44 173	51 971	49 428	50 453	51 063	48 680 p	47 653 p
Turkey	6 049 e	7 230 e	7 660 e	7 869 e	8 397 e	8 019 e	7 250 e	7 186 e
United Kingdom	30 461	30 689	32 395	32 845	33 518	36 406	34 544	31 507
United States	35 237	36 153	37 463	38 372	39 160	40 557	41 682	42 881 e
Euro area	27 003	26 266	28 042	26 023	27 005	27 333	23 282	23 694
OECD-Total	24 767 e	25 624 e	27 340 e	27 102 e	27 176 e	27 516 e	25 696 e	26 079 e

1. The statistical data for Israel are supplied by and under the responsibility of the relevant Israeli authorities. The use of such data by the OECD is without prejudice to the status of the Golan Heights, East Jerusalem and Israeli settlements in the West Bank under the terms of international law.

Table 24. Actual individual consumption per head at the price levels and exchange rates of year 2010

USD

	2009	2010	2011	2012	2013	2014	2015	2016
Australia	37 319	38 227	38 657	38 587	38 877	39 396	40 017	40 362
Austria	30 698	30 903	31 173	31 202	31 075	30 977	30 874	31 011
Belgium	29 252	29 713	29 645	29 694	29 716	29 861	30 003	30 298
Canada	32 517 e	33 268 e	33 694 e	33 843 e	34 058 e	34 429 e	34 827 e	35 199 e
Chile	7 588 e	8 223 e	8 753 e	9 180 e	9 490 e	9 650 e	9 781 e	9 900 e
Czech Republic	11 644	11 728	11 732	11 580	11 672	11 876	12 231	12 604
Denmark	38 382	38 744	38 700	38 730	38 743	39 147	39 468	39 791
Estonia	9 427	9 311	9 642	10 054	10 412	10 771	11 272	11 708
Finland	31 290	31 908	32 546	32 521	32 263	32 278	32 666	33 106
France	28 752	29 146	29 198	29 114	29 168	29 325	29 613 p	30 103 p
Germany	28 802	29 053	29 455	29 759	29 903	30 133	30 493	30 965
Greece	23 044	21 607	19 659 p	18 133 p	17 580 p	17 659 p	17 709 p	17 748 p
Hungary	8 530	8 318	8 396	8 244	8 307	8 528	8 838	9 196
Iceland	28 536 e	28 128 e	28 433 e	28 543 e	28 583 e	29 200 e	29 953 e	30 722 e
Ireland	29 568	29 497	28 636	28 167	28 074	28 727	29 640	30 394
Israel[1]	20 394	20 926	21 331	21 575	21 977	22 448	22 866	23 701
Italy	25 752	25 923	25 769	24 766	24 126	24 141	24 550	24 883
Japan	30 045	30 764	30 873	31 613	32 380	32 226	32 384	32 538
Korea	12 212 e	12 677 e	12 986 e	13 199 e	13 411 e	13 610 e	13 855 e	12 174 e
Latvia	7 888	8 208	8 632	9 005	9 528	9 775	10 113	10 581
Luxembourg	44 970	44 478	43 905	44 171	44 237	44 129	44 378	44 394
Mexico	6 440	6 575	6 715	6 787	6 829	6 889 e	7 025 e	7 195 e
Netherlands	31 367	31 362	31 357	30 911	30 516	30 497	30 849 p	31 129 p
New Zealand	23 364	23 600	24 148	24 482	25 034	25 382 p	25 553 p	26 093 e
Norway	48 498	49 519	49 826	50 681	51 231	51 632	52 240	52 693
Poland	8 706	8 933	9 167	9 225	9 294	9 538	9 835	10 200
Portugal	17 089	17 401	16 758	15 969	15 895	16 199	16 506	16 880 p
Slovak Republic	10 987	11 035	10 970	10 931	10 902	11 310	11 598	11 867
Slovenia	15 855	15 983	15 983	15 584	14 959	15 161	15 499	16 098
Spain	21 277	21 231	20 699	19 907	19 379	..	..	..
Sweden	32 931	33 652	33 892	33 849	34 059	34 374	35 055	35 487
Switzerland	43 894	44 173	44 225	44 803	45 422	45 499	45 836 p	46 058 p
Turkey	6 658 e	7 230 e	7 951 e	8 118 e	8 657 e	8 817 e	9 188 e	9 464 e
United Kingdom	30 698	30 689	30 313	30 616	30 970	31 422	31 944	32 533
United States	35 878	36 153	36 555	36 788	37 034	37 761	38 674	39 340 e
Euro area	26 107	26 266	26 205	25 884	25 711	25 895	26 290	26 724
OECD-Total	25 328 e	25 624 e	25 796 e	25 891 e	26 075 e	26 386 e	26 867 e	27 212 e

1. The statistical data for Israel are supplied by and under the responsibility of the relevant Israeli authorities. The use of such data by the OECD is without prejudice to the status of the Golan Heights, East Jerusalem and Israeli settlements in the West Bank under the terms of international law.

Table 25. Actual individual consumption, volume indices

Year 2005=100

	2009	2010	2011	2012	2013	2014	2015	2016
Australia	96.3	100.0	102.9	104.5	106.8	109.8	113.1	115.9
Austria	99.1	100.0	101.2	101.8	102.0	102.4	103.1	104.9
Belgium	97.5	100.0	100.7	101.5	102.1	103.1	104.1	105.7
Canada	96.7 e	100.0 e	102.3 e	104.0 e	105.8 e	108.2 e	110.4 e	112.9 e
Chile	91.4 e	100.0 e	107.5 e	114.0 e	119.1 e	122.4 e	125.6 e	128.7 e
Czech Republic	99.0	100.0	99.8	98.7	99.5	101.3	104.5	108.0
Denmark	98.6	100.0	100.3	100.8	101.2	102.8	104.3	106.1
Estonia	101.4	100.0	103.3	107.3	110.7	114.2	119.3	124.1
Finland	97.6	100.0	102.5	102.9	102.5	103.0	104.6	106.3
France	98.2	100.0	100.7	100.9	101.6	102.7	104.1 p	106.3 p
Germany	99.4	100.0	101.4	102.6	103.4	104.6	106.8	109.3
Greece	106.5	100.0	90.8 p	83.3 p	80.2 p	80.0 p	79.7 p	79.6 p
Hungary	102.8	100.0	100.7	98.3	98.8	101.2	104.5	108.5
Iceland	101.8 e	100.0 e	101.4 e	102.3 e	103.5 e	106.9 e	110.8 e	115.2 e
Ireland	99.8	100.0	97.5	96.1	96.1	98.6	102.3	105.9
Israel[1]	95.7	100.0	103.8	107.0	111.0	115.6	120.1	127.0
Italy	98.9	100.0	99.8	96.3	94.3	94.6	96.1	97.3
Japan	97.7	100.0	100.2	102.4	104.7	104.1	104.5	104.9
Korea	95.9 e	100.0 e	103.2 e	105.5 e	107.7 e	109.9 e	112.5 e	99.3 e
Latvia	98.1	100.0	103.2	106.4	111.4	113.2	116.2	120.4
Luxembourg	99.2	100.0	101.0	104.0	106.9	109.1	111.9	114.9
Mexico	96.7	100.0	103.4	105.8	107.6	109.8	113.2	117.1 p
Netherlands	99.5	100.0	100.5	99.4	98.4	98.7	100.3	101.7 p
New Zealand	98.0	100.0	103.0	105.0	108.4	111.8 p	114.7 p	119.6 e
Norway	96.7	100.0	101.9	105.1	107.5	109.6	112.0	114.0
Poland	97.4	100.0	102.6	103.3	104.0	106.7	109.9	113.9
Portugal	98.2	100.0	96.2	91.3	90.3	91.6	92.9	94.7
Slovak Republic	99.3	100.0	98.8	98.6	98.5	102.3	105.0	107.6
Slovenia	98.9	100.0	100.2	97.9	94.1	95.5	97.7	101.5
Spain	99.8	100.0	97.9	94.2	91.3	..	..	
Sweden	97.0	100.0	101.5	102.1	103.6	105.6	108.8	111.6
Switzerland	98.3	100.0	100.8	103.2	105.9	107.4	109.4 p	111.1 p
Turkey	90.9 e	100.0 e	111.4 e	115.2 e	124.3 e	128.0 e	134.8 e	140.3 e
United Kingdom	99.2	100.0	99.6	101.3	103.1	105.4	108.0	110.9
United States	98.4	100.0	101.9	103.3	104.7	107.5	110.9	113.6 e
Euro area	99.2	100.0	100.0	99.0	98.6	99.5	101.3	103.4
OECD-Total	98.2 e	100.0 e	101.3 e	102.2 e	103.5 e	105.4 e	107.9 e	110.0 e

1. The statistical data for Israel are supplied by and under the responsibility of the relevant Israeli authorities. The use of such data by the OECD is without prejudice to the status of the Golan Heights, East Jerusalem and Israeli settlements in the West Bank under the terms of international law.

Table 26. Actual individual consumption, price indices

Year 2005=100

	2009	2010	2011	2012	2013	2014	2015	2016
Australia	97.7	100.0	102.5	105.0	107.3	108.8	110.3	111.3
Austria	98.3	100.0	102.9	105.4	107.5	109.6	111.4	112.8
Belgium	98.2	100.0	103.2	105.4	106.4	107.0	107.6	109.1
Canada	98.6 e	100.0 e	102.5 e	104.0 e	105.9 e	108.0 e	109.3 e	110.3 e
Chile	96.0 e	100.0 e	104.4 e	107.5 e	111.4 e	118.1 e	124.4 e	128.9 e
Czech Republic	99.6	100.0	102.3	104.4	105.1	105.9	106.4	107.2
Denmark	98.0	100.0	101.4	103.5	104.1	104.4	105.1	105.7
Estonia	97.4	100.0	105.2	109.3	112.9	114.2	114.9	116.7
Finland	98.4	100.0	103.5	106.8	109.4	110.9	111.4	111.8
France	98.9	100.0	101.5	102.8	103.4	103.6	103.8 p	103.7 p
Germany	98.1	100.0	101.9	103.4	105.0	106.2	107.0	107.8
Greece	97.7	100.0	101.4 p	101.6 p	99.3 p	97.1 p	95.5 p	94.7 p
Hungary	96.7	100.0	103.0	108.4	109.9	112.0	112.9	113.5
Iceland	97.2 e	100.0 e	104.0 e	110.0 e	113.9 e	117.6 e	120.7 e	123.3 e
Ireland	102.9	100.0	100.9	102.5	103.8	104.5	105.0	106.0
Israel[1]	96.8	100.0	103.1	105.5	107.6	108.3	108.1	107.9
Italy	98.8	100.0	102.2	104.4	105.4	105.6	105.8	106.1
Japan	101.2	100.0	99.5	99.0	98.8	100.7	101.0	100.6
Korea	97.9 e	100.0 e	103.7 e	105.9 e	107.1 e	108.3 e	109.4 e	110.7 e
Latvia	102.9	100.0	105.8	109.0	109.9	111.5	111.0	112.1
Luxembourg	97.6	100.0	103.6	106.1	107.6	108.6	109.0	109.1
Mexico	94.8	100.0	105.4	111.1	115.7	120.6	123.8	129.3 p
Netherlands	98.8	100.0	101.4	103.4	105.2	106.0	106.1	106.6 p
New Zealand	98.1	100.0	102.4	103.2	104.2	105.0 p	106.0 p	107.1 e
Norway	97.6	100.0	102.1	103.9	106.7	109.7	112.7	115.9
Poland	97.3	100.0	104.8	108.3	108.7	108.6	107.8	107.5
Portugal	98.6	100.0	100.9	101.3	102.4	103.0	103.8	104.9 p
Slovak Republic	98.9	100.0	103.7	107.3	108.7	108.7	108.7	108.6
Slovenia	98.4	100.0	101.6	102.8	104.4	104.2	103.8	104.0
Spain	98.6	100.0	101.9	103.6	104.6	..	..	
Sweden	98.4	100.0	102.1	103.3	104.8	106.4	108.1	110.2
Switzerland	99.6	100.0	100.1	99.2	98.7	98.6	98.0 p	97.8 p
Turkey	93.7 e	100.0 e	107.4 e	115.8 e	122.9 e	132.4 e	142.8 e	152.6 e
United Kingdom	98.4	100.0	103.1	104.9	107.0	108.8	109.4	110.8
United States	98.2	100.0	102.5	104.3	105.7	107.4	107.8	109.0 e
Euro area	98.6	100.0	102.0	103.6	104.8	105.4	105.8	106.2
OECD-Total	98.5 e	100.0 e	102.2 e	103.9 e	105.3 e	106.9 e	107.7 e	108.8 e

1. The statistical data for Israel are supplied by and under the responsibility of the relevant Israeli authorities. The use of such data by the OECD is without prejudice to the status of the Golan Heights, East Jerusalem and Israeli settlements in the West Bank under the terms of international law.

Table 27. Exchange rates

National currency per USD

	2009	2010	2011	2012	2013	2014	2015	2016
Australia	1.2822	1.0902	0.9695	0.9658	1.0358	1.1094	1.3311	1.3452
Austria	0.7198	0.7550	0.7194	0.7783	0.7532	0.7537	0.9017	0.9040
Belgium	0.7198	0.7550	0.7194	0.7783	0.7532	0.7537	0.9017	0.9040
Canada	1.1431	1.0302	0.9895	0.9992	1.0298	1.1061	1.2791	1.3254
Chile	560.86	510.25	483.67	486.47	495.27	570.35	654.12	676.96
Czech Republic	19.063	19.098	17.696	19.578	19.571	20.758	24.599	24.440
Denmark	5.3609	5.6241	5.3687	5.7925	5.6163	5.6125	6.7279	6.7317
Estonia	0.7195	0.7546	0.7194	0.7783	0.7532	0.7537	0.9017	0.9040
Finland	0.7198	0.7550	0.7194	0.7783	0.7532	0.7537	0.9017	0.9040
France	0.7198	0.7550	0.7194	0.7783	0.7532	0.7537	0.9017	0.9040
Germany	0.7198	0.7550	0.7194	0.7783	0.7532	0.7537	0.9017	0.9040
Greece	0.7198	0.7550	0.7194	0.7783	0.7532	0.7537	0.9017	0.9040
Hungary	202.34	207.94	201.06	225.10	223.70	232.60	279.33	281.52
Iceland	123.638	122.242	115.954	125.083	122.179	116.767	131.919	120.812
Ireland	0.7198	0.7550	0.7194	0.7783	0.7532	0.7537	0.9017	0.9040
Israel[1]	3.9323	3.7390	3.5781	3.8559	3.6108	3.5779	3.8868	3.8406
Italy	0.7198	0.7550	0.7194	0.7783	0.7532	0.7537	0.9017	0.9040
Japan	93.57	87.78	79.81	79.79	97.60	105.94	121.04	108.79
Korea	1 276.9	1 156.1	1 108.3	1 126.5	1 094.9	1 053.0	1 131.2	1 160.4
Latvia	0.7193	0.7548	0.7132	0.7781	0.7533	0.7537	0.9017	0.9040
Luxembourg	0.7198	0.7550	0.7194	0.7783	0.7532	0.7537	0.9017	0.9040
Mexico	13.5135	12.6360	12.4233	13.1695	12.7720	13.2925	15.8483	18.6641
Netherlands	0.7198	0.7550	0.7194	0.7783	0.7532	0.7537	0.9017	0.9040
New Zealand	1.6009	1.3878	1.2658	1.2343	1.2194	1.2054	1.4340	1.4365
Norway	6.2883	6.0442	5.6046	5.8175	5.8750	6.3017	8.0642	8.4000
Poland	3.1201	3.0153	2.9628	3.2565	3.1606	3.1545	3.7695	3.9428
Portugal	0.7198	0.7550	0.7194	0.7783	0.7532	0.7537	0.9017	0.9040
Slovak Republic	0.720	0.755	0.719	0.778	0.753	0.754	0.902	0.904
Slovenia	0.7198	0.7550	0.7194	0.7783	0.7532	0.7537	0.9017	0.9040
Spain	0.7198	0.7550	0.7194	0.7783	0.7532	0.7537	0.9017	0.9040
Sweden	7.6538	7.2075	6.4935	6.7750	6.5140	6.8608	8.4348	8.5620
Switzerland	1.0881	1.0429	0.8880	0.9377	0.9269	0.9162	0.9624	0.9854
Turkey	1.5500	1.5028	1.6750	1.7960	1.9038	2.1885	2.7200	3.0201
United Kingdom	0.6419	0.6472	0.6241	0.6330	0.6397	0.6077	0.6545	0.7406
United States	1.0000	1.0000	1.0000	1.0000	1.0000	1.0000	1.0000	1.0000

1. The statistical data for Israel are supplied by and under the responsibility of the relevant Israeli authorities. The use of such data by the OECD is without prejudice to the status of the Golan Heights, East Jerusalem and Israeli settlements in the West Bank under the terms of international law.

Table 28. Purchasing power parities for gross domestic product

National currency per USD

	2009	2010	2011	2012	2013	2014	2015	2016
Australia	1.44	1.50	1.51	1.54	1.45	1.45	1.47	1.49
Austria	0.844	0.841	0.831	0.814	0.797	0.799	0.799	0.800
Belgium	0.850	0.836	0.832	0.822	0.806	0.800	0.801	0.804
Canada	1.20	1.22	1.24	1.24	1.22	1.23	1.25	1.25
Chile	354.06	359.25	348.02	347.23	349.68	367.21	394.34	402.57
Czech Republic	13.6	13.7	13.3	13.3	12.8	12.7	13.0	13.0
Denmark	7.73	7.58	7.47	7.56	7.35	7.33	7.33	7.36
Estonia	0.52	0.51	0.51	0.52	0.52	0.52	0.53	0.54	0.54
Finland	0.896	0.900	0.898	0.908	0.905	0.907	0.909	0.905
France	0.863	0.854	0.841	0.844	0.812	0.808	0.814	0.806
Germany	0.811	0.804	0.789	0.787	0.775	0.769	0.779	0.780
Greece	0.704	0.721	0.713	0.685	0.631	0.611	0.610	0.604
Hungary	127.7	126.3	124.3	125.6	125.0	129.4	133.4	135.2
Iceland	122.0	132.8	135.2	137.0	137.0	138.5	142.2	144.1
Ireland	0.901	0.849	0.832	0.823	0.811	0.819	0.813	0.812
Israel[1]	3.962	3.974	3.945	3.955	3.840	3.940	3.865	3.833
Italy	0.771	0.772	0.759	0.748	0.737	0.740	0.743	0.722
Japan	115	112	107	104	101	103	103	100
Korea	825	841	855	855	869	872	871	875
Latvia	0.521	0.487	0.499	0.506	0.499	0.498	0.502	0.497
Luxembourg	0.903	0.925	0.905	0.907	0.895	0.884	0.892	0.889
Mexico	7.43	7.67	7.67	7.86	7.88	8.05	8.54	8.87
Netherlands	0.85	0.85	0.84	0.82	0.80	0.81	0.81	0.82
New Zealand	1.471	1.496	1.486	1.496	1.446	1.441	1.464	1.468
Norway	9.08	9.14	9.08	9.04	9.03	9.28	9.73	10.13
Poland	1.87	1.80	1.80	1.80	1.76	1.77	1.78	1.79
Portugal	0.627	0.623	0.623	0.605	0.584	0.579	0.588	0.586
Slovak Republic	0.5	0.5	0.5	0.5	0.5	0.5	0.5	0.5
Slovenia	0.65	0.64	0.62	0.61	0.59	0.59	0.60	0.60
Spain	0.719	0.726	0.714	0.695	0.675	0.662	0.668	0.663
Sweden	8.92	9.02	8.84	8.65	8.60	8.73	8.95	9.08
Switzerland	1.47	1.46	1.40	1.35	1.31	1.28	1.24	1.23
Turkey	0.90	0.92	0.97	1.02	1.07	1.10	1.20	1.30
United Kingdom	0.710	0.702	0.706	0.702	0.695	0.698	0.697	0.702
United States	1.00	1.00	1.00	1.00	1.00	1.00	1.00	1.00

1. The statistical data for Israel are supplied by and under the responsibility of the relevant Israeli authorities. The use of such data by the OECD is without prejudice to the status of the Golan Heights, East Jerusalem and Israeli settlements in the West Bank under the terms of international law.

Table 29. Purchasing power parities for actual individual consumption

National currency per USD

	2009	2010	2011	2012	2013	2014	2015	2016
Australia	1.50	1.51	1.51	1.52	1.48	1.49	1.52	1.55
Austria	0.861	0.849	0.853	0.840	0.824	0.832	0.835	0.837
Belgium	0.890	0.870	0.871	0.861	0.838	0.830	0.833	0.838
Canada	1.27	1.26	1.27	1.28	1.28	1.27	1.30	1.31
Chile	341.47	352.98	353.27	352.14	351.50	371.64	401.17	409.58
Czech Republic	13.4	13.1	13.1	13.0	12.4	12.2	12.5	12.5
Denmark	8.26	8.10	8.07	8.04	7.84	7.87	7.88	7.94
Estonia	0.53	0.51	0.52	0.52	0.53	0.53	0.54	0.54
Finland	0.948	0.935	0.942	0.940	0.937	0.937	0.936	0.926
France	0.871	0.854	0.849	0.839	0.808	0.808	0.815	0.806
Germany	0.819	0.801	0.792	0.781	0.774	0.773	0.784	0.781
Greece	0.733	0.742	0.735	0.709	0.663	0.638	0.634	0.625
Hungary	127.7	122.8	122.0	122.6	121.8	125.7	129.3	131.0
Iceland	128.4	135.3	137.0	138.5	142.2	145.7	151.6	156.1
Ireland	1.017	0.953	0.949	0.930	0.930	0.952	0.959	0.953
Israel[1]	4.017	4.077	4.038	4.012	4.146	4.310	4.218	4.172
Italy	0.811	0.780	0.786	0.780	0.772	0.782	0.787	0.767
Japan	116	113	109	105	99	101	101	99
Korea	837	840	850	849	873	894	889	892
Latvia	0.536	0.488	0.510	0.504	0.497	0.503	0.506	0.505
Luxembourg	1.018	1.061	1.054	1.049	1.020	1.034	1.055	1.051
Mexico	7.43	7.64	7.69	7.87	7.96	8.18	8.54	8.79
Netherlands	0.85	0.87	0.87	0.86	0.84	0.85	0.86	0.86
New Zealand	1.47	1.47	1.48	1.47	1.45	1.45	1.47	1.47
Norway	9.73	9.88	9.98	9.95	9.84	10.01	10.30	10.50
Poland	1.80	1.71	1.71	1.68	1.66	1.68	1.68	1.68
Portugal	0.667	0.660	0.660	0.638	0.612	0.613	0.617	0.618
Slovak Republic	0.5	0.5	0.5	0.5	0.5	0.5	0.5	0.5
Slovenia	0.67	0.66	0.65	0.63	0.62	0.62	0.63	0.63
Spain	0.764	0.767	0.763	0.740	0.718	0.706	0.705	0.699
Sweden	9.11	9.24	9.22	9.02	9.18	9.27	9.53	9.68
Switzerland	1.56	1.57	1.54	1.49	1.44	1.42	1.40	1.39
Turkey	0.94	0.95	0.99	1.04	1.10	1.14	1.24	1.33
United Kingdom	0.751	0.742	0.748	0.743	0.751	0.759	0.765	0.761
United States	1.00	1.00	1.00	1.00	1.00	1.00	1.00	1.00

1. The statistical data for Israel are supplied by and under the responsibility of the relevant Israeli authorities. The use of such data by the OECD is without prejudice to the status of the Golan Heights, East Jerusalem and Israeli settlements in the West Bank under the terms of international law.

Table 30. Population, mid-year estimates

Thousands

	2009	2010	2011	2012	2013	2014	2015	2016
Australia	22 032	22 340	22 728	23 117	23 461	23 791	24 130	24 518
Austria	8 341	8 361	8 389	8 426	8 477	8 544	8 630	8 740
Belgium	10 796	10 896	10 994	11 068	11 125	11 180	11 238	11 295
Canada	33 629	34 005	34 343	34 751	35 155	35 545	35 849	36 286
Chile	16 928	17 093	17 267	17 450	17 640	17 836	18 045	18 278 e
Czech Republic	10 491	10 517	10 497	10 509	10 511	10 525	10 543	10 565
Denmark	5 523	5 547	5 570	5 591	5 613	5 643	5 682	5 729
Estonia	1 336	1 333	1 330	1 325	1 320	1 316	1 313	1 316
Finland	5 339	5 363	5 388	5 414	5 439	5 463	5 481	5 495
France	64 655	64 974	65 294	65 615	65 953	66 290	66 590 p	66 858 p
Germany	80 483	80 284	80 275	80 426	80 646	80 983	81 687	82 349
Greece	11 107	11 121	11 105 p	11 045 p	10 965 p	10 892 p	10 821 p	10 784 p
Hungary	10 023	10 000	9 972	9 920	9 893	9 866	9 839	9 814
Iceland	319	318	319	321	324	327	331	335
Ireland	4 539	4 560	4 577	4 590	4 602	4 615	4 642	4 683
Israel[1]	7 482	7 621	7 763	7 907	8 056	8 212	8 377	8 543
Italy	59 578	59 830	60 060	60 339	60 646	60 789	60 731	60 628
Japan	128 034	128 043	127 831	127 552	127 333	127 262	127 110	126 960
Korea	49 308	49 554	49 937	50 200	50 429	50 747	51 015	51 246
Latvia	2 142	2 097	2 059	2 034	2 013	1 994	1 977	1 959
Luxembourg	498	508	519	532	545	558	569	584
Mexico	112 853	114 256	115 683	117 054	118 395	119 713 e	121 005 e	122 273 e
Netherlands	16 526	16 612	16 693	16 752	16 800	16 863	16 932 p	17 026 p
New Zealand	4 318	4 363	4 393	4 418	4 460	4 534	4 623	4 720 e
Norway	4 829	4 889	4 953	5 019	5 080	5 137	5 191	5 236
Poland	38 483	38 517	38 526	38 534	38 502	38 484	38 455	38 427
Portugal	10 568	10 573	10 558	10 515	10 457	10 401	10 358	10 326 p
Slovak Republic	5 418	5 430	5 398	5 406	5 413	5 419	5 422	5 431
Slovenia	2 041.7	2 048.8	2 052.8	2 056.8	2 059.6	2 061.8	2 063.3	2 064.6
Spain	46 368	46 562	46 736	46 766	46 593	46 455 p	46 407 p	46 468 p
Sweden	9 299	9 378	9 449	9 519	9 600	9 696	9 799	9 923
Switzerland	7 775	7 856	7 912	7 997	8 089	8 189	8 282	8 372 p
Turkey	72 050	73 003	73 950	74 899 e	75 774 e	76 619 e	77 440 e	78 247 e
United Kingdom	62 260	62 759	63 285	63 705	64 106	64 597	65 110	65 648
United States	307 240	309 801	312 114	314 377	316 569	318 887	321 173	323 391
Euro area	334 120	334 894	335 722	336 581	337 298	338 036	339 050	340 291
OECD-Total	1 232 611	1 240 414	1 247 920 p	1 255 150 e	1 262 046 e	1 269 434 e	1 276 861 e	1 284 519 e

1. The statistical data for Israel are supplied by and under the responsibility of the relevant Israeli authorities. The use of such data by the OECD is without prejudice to the status of the Golan Heights, East Jerusalem and Israeli settlements in the West Bank under the terms of international law.

Country tables

AUSTRALIA

Table 1. Gross domestic product, expenditure approach

Million AUD, fiscal years

		2009	2010	2011	2012	2013	2014	2015	2016
	AT CURRENT PRICES								
1	**Final consumption expenditure**	**964 760**	**1 026 977**	**1 086 667**	**1 127 228**	**1 177 327**	**1 222 184**	**1 277 395**	**1 322 428**
2	Household[1]	731 012	775 116	817 502	853 570	894 930	929 476	968 070	997 424
3	NPISH's[1]	..	..	..	..	..	..	..	..
4	Government	233 748	251 861	269 165	273 658	282 397	292 708	309 325	325 004
5	Individual	144 873	155 859	164 639	167 323	172 240	182 591	192 973	203 027
6	Collective	88 875	96 002	104 526	106 335	110 157	110 117	116 352	121 977
7	*of which: Actual individual consumption*	875 885	930 975	982 141	1 020 893	1 067 170	1 112 067	1 161 043	1 200 451
8	**Gross capital formation**	**347 715**	**373 554**	**413 861**	**426 565**	**425 284**	**423 889**	**419 805**	**424 279**
9	Gross fixed capital formation, total[2]	350 887	367 161	409 169	425 996	427 501	422 548	418 702	421 155
10	Dwellings	68 571	72 687	69 205	70 064	76 833	87 437	98 720	103 640
11	Other buildings and structures	130 213	142 477	177 356	195 451	194 366	174 360	157 605	151 693
12	Transport equipment	28 951	27 643	26 825	28 730	26 150	27 755	29 333	30 115
13	Other machinery and equipment[3]	44 562	43 691	52 256	45 394	42 106	43 667	43 322	42 655
14	Cultivated assets	3 319	4 981	4 070	4 101	3 456	2 780	3 128	5 293
15	Intangible fixed assets	38 321	41 304	45 678	47 136	46 672	45 177	43 272	44 674
16	Changes in inventories, acquisitions less disposals of valuables	-3 172	6 393	4 692	569	-2 217	1 341	1 103	3 124
17	Changes in inventories	-3 172	6 393	4 692	569	-2 217	1 341	1 103	3 124
18	Acquisitions less disposals of valuables	..	..	..	..	..	..	..	..
19	**External balance of goods and services**	**-13 398**	**13 686**	**-3 729**	**-19 912**	**-6 835**	**-24 669**	**-37 597**	**11 366**
20	Exports of goods and services	257 770	303 673	322 096	306 588	336 322	324 491	319 524	373 236
21	Exports of goods	201 809	247 021	265 747	248 880	273 820	255 524	244 147	291 594
22	Exports of services	55 961	56 652	56 349	57 708	62 502	68 967	75 377	81 642
23	Imports of goods and services	271 168	289 987	325 825	326 500	343 157	349 160	357 121	361 870
24	Imports of goods	210 755	225 028	256 670	251 327	263 785	268 719	271 476	277 899
25	Imports of services	60 413	64 959	69 155	75 173	79 372	80 441	85 645	83 971
26	**Statistical discrepancy**	**0**	**0**	**0**	**0**	**0**	**0**	**0**	**-3 349**
27	**Gross domestic product**	**1 299 079**	**1 414 219**	**1 496 800**	**1 533 882**	**1 595 776**	**1 621 404**	**1 659 604**	**1 754 724**
	AT CONSTANT PRICES, REFERENCE YEAR 2010								
28	**Final consumption expenditure**	**988 923**	**1 026 977**	**1 059 171**	**1 074 155**	**1 097 950**	**1 124 130**	**1 159 336**	**1 189 541**
29	Household[1]	745 410	775 116	798 161	812 283	832 091	851 993	875 763	894 488
30	NPISH's[1]	..	..	..	..	..	..	..	..
31	Government	243 535	251 861	261 010	261 891	265 867	272 145	283 623	295 159
32	Individual	150 939	155 859	159 651	160 128	162 158	169 764	176 939	184 383
33	Collective	92 596	96 002	101 359	101 763	103 709	102 381	106 684	110 776
34	*of which: Actual individual consumption*	896 337	930 975	957 821	972 447	994 306	1 021 774	1 052 692	1 078 821
35	**Gross capital formation**	**354 089**	**373 554**	**417 114**	**424 368**	**413 438**	**404 289**	**390 299**	**391 868**
36	Gross fixed capital formation, total[2]	354 566	367 161	409 589	422 122	414 494	401 030	387 327	387 253
37	Dwellings	70 500	72 687	68 577	68 019	72 223	78 848	86 557	88 729
38	Other buildings and structures	134 096	142 477	176 279	190 283	186 027	164 210	146 563	138 966
39	Transport equipment	28 336	27 643	26 904	29 354	26 175	27 056	27 215	28 262
40	Other machinery and equipment[3]	42 619	43 691	53 133	46 063	40 349	40 799	37 601	37 924
41	Cultivated assets	3 617	4 981	4 111	4 283	3 747	2 964	3 127	4 827
42	Intangible fixed assets	38 015	41 304	45 333	46 561	46 142	45 238	43 894	46 028
43	Changes in inventories, acquisitions less disposals of valuables	..	..	..	..	..	..	..	..
44	Changes in inventories	..	..	..	..	..	..	..	..
45	Acquisitions less disposals of valuables	..	..	..	..	..	..	..	..
46	**External balance of goods and services**	**38 097**	**13 686**	**-5 283**	**10 678**	**38 145**	**59 380**	**85 791**	**93 027**
47	Exports of goods and services	301 083	303 673	317 650	334 497	354 409	378 445	404 426	426 578
48	Exports of goods	243 787	247 021	262 672	279 329	296 236	315 209	335 715	352 016
49	Exports of services	57 122	56 652	54 979	55 203	58 252	63 165	68 344	73 462
50	Imports of goods and services	262 986	289 987	322 934	323 819	316 264	319 065	318 636	333 550
51	Imports of goods	206 425	225 028	253 077	248 991	244 656	250 307	250 720	264 301
52	Imports of services	56 661	64 959	69 857	74 945	71 713	68 954	68 172	69 772
53	**Statistical discrepancy (including chaining residual)**	**-725**	**2**	**-1 742**	**-1 160**	**-2 911**	**-4 815**	**-7 686**	**-14 832**
54	**Gross domestic product**	**1 380 384**	**1 414 219**	**1 469 260**	**1 508 040**	**1 546 621**	**1 582 984**	**1 627 740**	**1 659 604**

Note: Detailed metadata:http://metalinks.oecd.org/nav1/20180308/a53e
1. *Final consumption expenditure of households includes Final consumption expenditure of NPISH's.*
2. *Ownership transfer cost are included in the total but have not been allocated by type of asset and by industry.*
3. Including weapons systems.
Source: Australian Bureau of Statistics (ABS).

AUSTRALIA

Table 2. Gross domestic product, output and income approach
ISIC Rev. 4

Million AUD, fiscal years

		2009	2010	2011	2012	2013	2014	2015	2016
	OUTPUT APPROACH AT CURRENT PRICES								
1	**Total gross value added at basic prices**	**1 209 140**	**1 321 354**	**1 404 131**	**1 437 615**	**1 491 663**	**1 512 687**	**1 542 772**	**1 628 070**
2	Agriculture, forestry and fishing	28 595	32 250	33 809	35 011	35 427	38 471	40 338	48 547
3	Industry, including energy	229 754	269 549	277 583	262 646	278 274	251 825	239 497	273 178
4	Manufacturing	103 965	104 144	105 414	101 365	101 638	102 263	100 696	100 836
5	Construction	95 844	102 998	114 410	121 397	127 335	130 000	129 902	131 258
6	Services	..	..	..	..	..	..	..	..
7	Distrib. trade, repairs; transp.; accommod., food serv. activ.	206 934	220 823	237 155	245 510	246 249	252 686	261 634	263 173
8	Information and communication	41 583	41 522	42 134	42 350	43 024	43 825	44 077	43 858
9	Financial and insurance activities	103 949	111 025	116 835	122 357	127 982	136 900	142 965	150 819
10	Real estate activities	138 350	146 338	159 265	169 683	178 711	185 397	194 199	201 674
11	Prof., scientif., techn. activ.; admin., support service activ.	124 055	135 957	146 550	151 883	154 255	159 927	162 109	178 090
12	Public admin.; compulsory s.s.; education; human health	204 997	224 023	236 111	246 799	257 940	270 494	285 064	295 446
13	Other service activities	35 079	36 869	40 279	39 979	42 466	43 162	42 987	42 028
14	**FISIM (Financial Intermediation Services Indirectly Measured)**	..	..	..	..	..	..	..	..
15	**Gross value added at basic prices, excluding FISIM**	**1 209 140**	**1 321 354**	**1 404 131**	**1 437 615**	**1 491 663**	**1 512 687**	**1 542 772**	**1 628 070**
16	**Taxes less subsidies on products**	**89 939**	**92 865**	**92 669**	**96 267**	**104 113**	**108 717**	**116 832**	**120 482**
17	Taxes on products	..	..	..	..	..	..	..	..
18	Subsidies on products	..	..	..	..	..	..	..	..
19	**Residual item**	**0**	**0**	**0**	**0**	**0**	**0**	**0**	**6 173**
20	**Gross domestic product at market prices**	**1 299 079**	**1 414 219**	**1 496 800**	**1 533 882**	**1 595 776**	**1 621 404**	**1 659 604**	**1 754 724**
	OUTPUT APPROACH AT CONSTANT PRICES (REF. YEAR 2010)								
21	**Total gross value added at basic prices**	**1 289 129**	**1 321 354**	**1 374 949**	**1 412 247**	**1 450 505**	**1 485 522**	**1 526 375**	**1 559 704**
22	Agriculture, forestry and fishing	31 174	32 250	32 564	32 327	32 697	33 137	31 019	36 088
23	Industry, including energy	267 609	269 549	280 050	289 656	301 001	310 851	317 283	316 542
24	Manufacturing	104 410	104 144	105 090	101 706	100 614	99 190	96 847	95 104
25	Construction	100 222	102 998	114 720	119 028	124 280	121 041	119 936	115 006
26	Services	..	..	..	..	..	..	..	..
27	Distrib. trade, repairs; transp.; accommod., food serv. activ.	217 173	220 823	230 487	237 271	237 758	243 945	252 141	259 281
28	Information and communication	40 186	41 522	42 015	41 958	43 677	46 953	50 515	51 783
29	Financial and insurance activities	108 767	111 025	116 651	120 591	123 443	128 359	132 744	137 645
30	Real estate activities	142 750	146 338	150 336	154 458	158 268	160 742	167 670	171 588
31	Prof., scientif., techn. activ.; admin., support service activ.	126 517	135 957	139 954	143 826	146 567	149 840	154 794	161 083
32	Public admin.; compulsory s.s.; education; human health	219 132	224 023	229 863	235 791	244 461	252 039	261 213	269 193
33	Other service activities	36 258	36 869	38 308	37 486	39 001	39 717	40 105	39 515
34	**FISIM (Financial Intermediation Services Indirectly Measured)**	..	..	..	..	..	..	..	..
35	**Gross value added at basic prices, excluding FISIM**	**1 289 129**	**1 321 354**	**1 374 949**	**1 412 247**	**1 450 505**	**1 485 522**	**1 526 375**	**1 559 704**
36	**Taxes less subsidies on products**	**91 225**	**92 865**	**94 310**	**95 754**	**96 050**	**97 440**	**101 243**	**102 504**
37	Taxes on products	..	..	..	..	..	..	..	..
38	Subsidies on products	..	..	..	..	..	..	..	..
39	**Residual item**	**30**	**0**	**0**	**40**	**67**	**22**	**123**	**-2 604**
40	**Gross domestic product at market prices**	**1 380 384**	**1 414 219**	**1 469 260**	**1 508 040**	**1 546 621**	**1 582 984**	**1 627 740**	**1 659 604**
	INCOME APPROACH								
41	**Compensation of employees**	**614 167**	**669 801**	**715 652**	**739 661**	**765 782**	**787 696**	**813 190**	**830 275**
42	Agriculture, forestry and fishing	6 644	7 027	7 278	7 387	7 793	8 243	8 588	8 934
43	Industry, including energy	89 098	94 709	103 584	104 774	105 665	105 166	102 848	99 950
44	Manufacturing	59 175	60 996	63 812	62 814	62 637	62 319	61 767	60 467
45	Construction	49 028	54 447	60 237	64 485	67 218	68 102	68 524	68 542
46	Distrib. trade, repairs; transp.; accommod., food serv. activ.	125 233	134 206	142 576	146 517	148 965	152 291	158 341	160 027
47	Information and communication	13 760	14 353	15 414	15 679	15 988	16 581	17 231	17 918
48	Financial and insurance activities	34 271	37 550	38 350	38 785	40 122	41 798	42 969	44 559
49	Real estate activities	12 557	13 482	13 769	15 408	16 235	16 950	18 678	19 575
50	Prof., scientif., techn. activ.; admin., support service activ.	90 550	101 217	110 432	113 183	118 400	122 301	126 199	130 821
51	Public admin.; compulsory s.s.; education; human health	170 691	188 758	198 126	207 465	217 446	228 182	241 307	251 000
52	Other service activities	22 335	24 052	25 886	25 978	27 950	28 082	28 505	28 948
53	**Wages and salaries**	**550 913**	**601 482**	**642 893**	**664 679**	**686 956**	**705 725**	**727 017**	**740 837**
54	Agriculture, forestry and fishing	5 889	6 194	6 431	6 525	6 873	7 240	7 577	7 867
55	Industry, including energy	80 393	85 526	93 832	94 932	95 614	95 378	93 246	90 480
56	Manufacturing	53 093	54 858	57 449	56 537	56 326	56 194	55 753	54 509
57	Construction	43 892	48 973	54 336	58 196	60 686	61 482	61 777	61 731
58	Distrib. trade, repairs; transp.; accommod., food serv. activ.	113 033	120 965	128 957	132 527	134 588	137 807	143 090	144 427
59	Information and communication	12 527	13 081	14 123	14 397	14 663	15 186	15 788	16 382
60	Financial and insurance activities	31 670	34 682	35 269	35 819	36 855	38 407	39 367	40 772
61	Real estate activities	11 345	12 218	12 458	14 001	14 785	15 416	16 972	17 750
62	Prof., scientif., techn. activ.; admin., support service activ.	81 974	92 152	100 518	102 947	107 548	111 195	114 670	118 691
63	Public admin.; compulsory s.s.; education; human health	150 149	165 989	173 607	182 074	190 150	198 280	208 747	216 619
64	Other service activities	20 041	21 702	23 362	23 461	25 194	25 334	25 783	26 118
65	**Gross operating surplus and mixed income**	**556 871**	**609 542**	**643 328**	**646 226**	**672 247**	**673 481**	**675 025**	**743 499**
66	**Taxes less subsidies on production and imports**	**128 041**	**134 876**	**137 820**	**147 995**	**157 747**	**160 227**	**171 389**	**174 778**
67	Taxes on production and imports	144 778	152 362	156 768	170 617	182 265	182 235	193 862	197 814
68	Subsidies on production and imports	16 737	17 486	18 948	22 622	24 518	22 008	22 473	23 036
69	**Residual item**	**0**	**0**	**0**	**0**	**0**	**0**	**0**	**6 173**
70	**Gross domestic product**	**1 299 079**	**1 414 219**	**1 496 800**	**1 533 882**	**1 595 776**	**1 621 404**	**1 659 604**	**1 754 724**

Note: Detailed metadata:http://metalinks.oecd.org/nav1/20180308/a53e
Source: Australian Bureau of Statistics (ABS).

AUSTRALIA

Table 3. Disposable income, saving and net lending / net borrowing

Million AUD, fiscal years

		2009	2010	2011	2012	2013	2014	2015	2016
	DISPOSABLE INCOME								
1	**Gross domestic product**	1 299 079	1 414 219	1 496 800	1 533 882	1 595 776	1 621 404	1 659 604	1 754 724
2	Net primary incomes from the rest of the world	-50 549	-56 864	-45 604	-38 213	-41 830	-33 450	-37 322	-40 930
3	Primary incomes receivable from the rest of the world	38 515	44 394	47 324	46 583	49 068	53 021	53 737	60 128
4	Primary incomes payable to the rest of the world	89 064	101 258	92 928	84 796	90 898	86 471	91 059	101 058
5	**Gross national income at market prices**	1 248 530	1 357 355	1 451 196	1 495 669	1 553 946	1 587 954	1 622 282	1 707 621
6	Consumption of fixed capital	215 534	225 797	235 662	248 874	266 111	283 709	300 459	309 026
7	**Net national income at market prices**	1 032 996	1 131 558	1 215 534	1 246 795	1 287 835	1 304 245	1 321 823	1 398 595
8	Net current transfers from the rest of the world	-1 300	-2 117	-2 063	-2 278	-2 134	-1 885	-227	-587
9	Current transfers receivable from the rest of the world	7 085	7 653	7 536	7 497	8 114	8 551	8 861	8 909
10	Current transfers payable to the rest of the world	8 385	9 770	9 599	9 775	10 248	10 436	9 088	9 496
11	**Net national disposable income**	1 031 696	1 129 441	1 213 471	1 244 517	1 285 701	1 302 360	1 321 596	1 398 008
	SAVING AND NET LENDING / NET BORROWING								
12	**Net national disposable income**	1 031 696	1 129 441	1 213 471	1 244 517	1 285 701	1 302 360	1 321 596	1 398 008
13	Final consumption expenditures	964 760	1 026 977	1 086 667	1 127 228	1 177 327	1 222 184	1 277 395	1 322 428
14	Adj. for change in net equity of households in pension funds	..	..	..	..	..	..	..	..
15	**Saving, net**	66 936	102 464	126 804	117 289	108 374	80 176	44 201	75 580
16	Net capital transfers from the rest of the world	-280	-287	-383	-359	-399	-531	-695	-580
17	Capital transfers receivable from the rest of the world	0	0	0	0	0	0	0	0
18	Capital transfers payable to the rest of the world	280	287	383	359	399	531	695	580
19	Gross capital formation	347 715	373 554	413 861	426 565	425 284	423 889	419 805	424 279
20	Acquisitions less disposals of non-financial non-produced assets	4	29	25	94	-44	-12	-27	-140
21	Consumption of fixed capital	215 534	225 797	235 662	248 874	266 111	283 709	300 459	309 026
22	**Net lending / net borrowing**	-65 531	-45 614	-51 804	-60 856	-51 153	-60 523	-75 815	-30 589
	REAL DISPOSABLE INCOME								
23	**Gross domestic product at constant prices, reference year 2010**	1 380 384	1 414 219	1 469 260	1 508 040	1 546 621	1 582 984	1 627 740	1 659 604
24	Trading gain or loss	-51 106	0	3 357	-28 753	-41 093	-76 324	-110 587	-68 848
25	**Real gross domestic income**	1 329 278	1 414 219	1 472 617	1 479 288	1 505 528	1 506 660	1 517 153	1 590 756
26	Net real primary incomes from the rest of the world	-51 724	-56 864	-44 867	-36 853	-39 464	-31 083	-34 118	-37 105
27	Real primary incomes receivable from the rest of the world	39 410	44 394	46 559	44 925	46 293	49 269	49 125	54 509
28	Real primary incomes payable to the rest of the world	91 134	101 258	91 427	81 778	85 757	80 352	83 243	91 615
29	**Real gross national income at market prices**	1 277 554	1 357 355	1 427 750	1 442 435	1 466 064	1 475 577	1 483 034	1 548 055
30	Net real current transfers from the rest of the world	-1 330	-2 117	-2 030	-2 197	-2 013	-1 752	-208	-532
31	Real current transfers receivable from the rest of the world	7 250	7 653	7 414	7 230	7 655	7 946	8 100	8 077
32	Real current transfers payable to the rest of the world	8 580	9 770	9 444	9 427	9 668	9 697	8 308	8 609
33	**Real gross national disposable income**	1 276 224	1 355 238	1 425 720	1 440 238	1 464 051	1 473 826	1 482 827	1 547 523
34	Consumption of fixed capital at constant prices	216 358	225 797	236 264	247 457	257 782	266 770	274 437	281 436
35	**Real net national income at market prices**	1 057 010	1 131 558	1 195 895	1 202 419	1 215 003	1 211 946	1 208 365	1 267 905
36	**Real net national disposable income**	1 055 679	1 129 441	1 193 865	1 200 222	1 212 989	1 210 194	1 208 158	1 267 373

Note: Detailed metadata:http://metalinks.oecd.org/nav1/20180308/776b
Source: Australian Bureau of Statistics (ABS).

AUSTRALIA

Table 4. Population and employment (persons) and employment (hours worked) by industry
ISIC Rev. 4

		2009	2010	2011	2012	2013	2014	2015	2016
	POPULATION, THOUSAND PERSONS, NATIONAL CONCEPT								
1	**Total population**	22 031.8	22 340.0	22 728.3	23 117.4	23 460.7	23 791.1	24 130.3	24 517.9
2	Economically active population	11 682.5	11 924.4	12 073.5	..	..	..	..	..
3	Unemployed persons	639.2	602.4	624.5	..	..	..	..	..
4	Total employment	10 957.4	11 196.2	11 390.0	11 485.4	11 546.1	11 767.9	11 971.2	12 205.9
5	Employees	9 697.1	9 945.9	10 202.2	10 315.1	10 356.7	10 545.6	10 741.0	10 960.7
6	Self-employed	1 260.4	1 250.3	1 187.8	1 170.3	1 189.5	1 222.2	1 230.2	1 245.3
	TOTAL EMPLOYMENT, THOUSAND PERSONS, DOMESTIC CONCEPT								
7	Agriculture, forestry and fishing	358.9	319.6	338.7	299.2	326.7	297.3	333.5	..
8	Industry, including energy	1 367.0	1 394.4	1 457.7	1 399.0	1 412.5	1 365.8	1 332.6	..
9	Manufacturing	1 047.7	1 030.0	1 026.9	990.8	1 005.9	998.6	971.5	..
10	Construction	1 001.9	1 030.4	983.1	989.1	1 027.4	1 041.3	1 087.8	..
11	Distrib. trade, repairs; transp.; accommod., food serv. activ.	3 060.6	3 093.2	3 014.5	3 177.1	3 127.3	3 185.0	3 233.3	..
12	Information and communication	353.1	364.8	400.8	382.5	370.5	398.2	389.2	..
13	Financial and insurance activities	388.1	426.8	431.7	423.5	407.0	393.6	432.5	..
14	Real estate activities	145.7	151.9	168.7	150.2	175.2	170.0	174.4	..
15	Prof., scientif., techn. activ.; admin., support service activ.	1 100.9	1 117.6	1 181.5	1 163.2	1 202.0	1 271.1	1 224.0	..
16	Public admin.; compulsory s.s.; education; human health	2 734.0	2 846.0	2 927.5	3 016.0	3 028.6	3 145.3	3 264.0	..
17	Other service activities	447.3	451.5	485.8	485.3	468.8	500.4	499.9	..
18	**Total employment**	10 957.4	11 196.2	11 390.0	11 485.4	11 546.1	11 767.9	11 971.2	..
	EMPLOYEES, THOUSAND PERSONS, DOMESTIC CONCEPT								
19	Agriculture, forestry and fishing	186.7	190.9	209.9	165.7	182.7	164.8	205.3	..
20	Industry, including energy	1 283.9	1 304.6	1 384.2	1 320.4	1 336.5	1 281.6	1 257.6	..
21	Manufacturing	970.7	944.4	961.1	916.9	935.5	918.9	905.2	..
22	Construction	727.7	748.2	735.6	749.6	780.3	789.1	829.8	..
23	Distrib. trade, repairs; transp.; accommod., food serv. activ.	2 785.5	2 833.6	2 764.6	2 946.1	2 908.1	2 955.7	2 997.7	..
24	Information and communication	321.4	336.4	369.0	355.2	340.8	366.0	356.8	..
25	Financial and insurance activities	374.1	408.4	417.9	410.0	393.5	380.9	415.9	..
26	Real estate activities	131.5	136.5	149.2	136.8	159.3	158.4	158.7	..
27	Prof., scientif., techn. activ.; admin., support service activ.	906.0	898.0	976.1	964.2	992.5	1 051.7	1 018.2	..
28	Public admin.; compulsory s.s.; education; human health	2 616.4	2 733.8	2 805.0	2 881.4	2 898.2	2 992.9	3 101.9	..
29	Other service activities	364.0	355.6	390.8	385.6	364.9	404.6	399.0	..
30	**Total employees**	9 697.1	9 945.9	10 202.2	10 315.1	10 356.7	10 545.6	10 740.9	..
	SELF-EMPLOYED, THOUSAND PERSONS, DOMESTIC CONCEPT								
31	Agriculture, forestry and fishing	172.2	128.7	128.8	133.5	144.0	132.5	128.2	..
32	Industry, including energy	83.1	89.8	73.5	78.7	76.0	84.2	75.0	..
33	Manufacturing	77.0	85.5	65.8	73.9	70.4	79.7	66.4	..
34	Construction	274.2	282.3	247.5	239.6	247.1	252.2	258.0	..
35	Distrib. trade, repairs; transp.; accommod., food serv. activ.	275.2	259.6	249.9	231.0	219.3	229.2	235.6	..
36	Information and communication	31.7	28.4	31.8	27.3	29.8	32.2	32.4	..
37	Financial and insurance activities	14.0	18.4	13.8	13.5	13.5	12.7	16.6	..
38	Real estate activities	14.2	15.4	19.4	13.4	16.0	11.6	15.7	..
39	Prof., scientif., techn. activ.; admin., support service activ.	194.9	219.6	205.4	199.0	209.6	219.4	205.8	..
40	Public admin.; compulsory s.s.; education; human health	117.6	112.1	122.5	134.5	130.4	152.4	162.1	..
41	Other service activities	83.3	96.0	95.1	99.7	103.9	95.8	100.9	..
42	**Total self-employed**	1 260.4	1 250.3	1 187.8	1 170.3	1 189.5	1 222.2	1 230.3	..
	TOTAL EMPLOYMENT, MILLION HOURS, DOMESTIC CONCEPT								
43	Industry, including energy	2 749.4	2 807.0	2 981.4	2 822.9	2 819.7	2 744.4	2 613.0	..
44	Distrib. trade, repairs; transp.; accommod., food serv. activ.	5 091.8	5 122.5	4 951.7	5 203.0	5 104.6	5 238.9	5 194.9	..
45	Financial and insurance activities	745.5	792.1	832.1	798.9	779.8	761.3	813.6	..
46	Prof., scientif., techn. activ.; admin., support service activ.	1 976.6	1 940.7	2 089.6	2 098.9	2 167.1	2 270.1	2 165.7	..
47	Public admin.; compulsory s.s.; education; human health	4 460.3	4 573.6	4 773.2	4 847.2	4 938.4	5 146.9	5 237.5	..
48	**Total employment**	19 494.8	19 651.0	20 179.9	20 210.8	20 383.6	20 727.2	20 745.1	..
	EMPLOYEES, MILLION HOURS, DOMESTIC CONCEPT								
49	Industry, including energy	2 601.9	2 635.8	2 841.8	2 675.1	2 682.0	2 583.5	2 479.7	..
50	Distrib. trade, repairs; transp.; accommod., food serv. activ.	4 533.3	4 576.1	4 433.8	4 740.9	4 649.7	4 776.6	4 732.6	..
51	Financial and insurance activities	721.6	763.1	805.1	778.0	756.6	740.8	788.9	..
52	Prof., scientif., techn. activ.; admin., support service activ.	1 652.5	1 591.6	1 767.3	1 787.9	1 835.4	1 917.3	1 849.3	..
53	Public admin.; compulsory s.s.; education; human health	4 291.5	4 412.8	4 604.9	4 632.9	4 736.3	4 919.8	5 007.0	..
54	**Total employees**	17 182.1	17 380.7	18 064.2	18 112.0	18 220.0	18 524.6	18 586.7	..
	SELF-EMPLOYED, MILLION HOURS, DOMESTIC CONCEPT								
55	Industry, including energy	147.5	171.2	139.6	147.8	137.8	160.9	133.3	..
56	Distrib. trade, repairs; transp.; accommod., food serv. activ.	558.5	546.4	517.9	462.1	454.9	462.3	462.3	..
57	Financial and insurance activities	23.9	29.1	27.0	20.9	23.2	20.5	24.7	..
58	Prof., scientif., techn. activ.; admin., support service activ.	324.1	349.1	322.3	311.0	331.7	352.8	316.4	..
59	Public admin.; compulsory s.s.; education; human health	168.8	160.8	168.3	214.4	202.2	227.0	230.5	..
60	**Total self-employed**	2 312.7	2 270.2	2 115.7	2 098.9	2 163.7	2 202.7	2 158.3	..

Note: Detailed metadata:http://metalinks.oecd.org/nav1/20180308/e8c4
Source: Australian Bureau of Statistics (ABS).

AUSTRIA

Table 1. Gross domestic product, expenditure approach

Million EUR (1999 ATS euro)

		2009	2010	2011	2012	2013	2014	2015	2016
	AT CURRENT PRICES								
1	**Final consumption expenditure**	**213 630**	**218 947**	**227 251**	**233 638**	**238 329**	**243 875**	**249 758**	**256 867**
2	Household	148 385	152 497	159 576	164 097	167 274	170 949	173 840	178 529
3	NPISH's	5 666	5 813	5 970	6 254	6 545	6 954	7 485	7 696
4	Government	59 580	60 637	61 705	63 287	64 510	65 972	68 434	70 642
5	Individual	35 964	36 778	37 676	38 857	39 914	41 078	42 831	44 526
6	Collective	23 616	23 859	24 029	24 430	24 596	24 895	25 603	26 116
7	*of which: Actual individual consumption*	190 014	195 088	203 222	209 208	213 734	218 980	224 156	230 751
8	**Gross capital formation**	**65 603**	**66 896**	**74 867**	**76 404**	**76 842**	**78 333**	**81 199**	**85 209**
9	Gross fixed capital formation, total	64 559	63 904	69 691	72 173	74 630	75 429	77 581	81 533
10	Dwellings	12 509	12 817	13 561	13 730	14 038	14 268	14 660	14 972
11	Other buildings and structures	19 143	18 188	19 382	20 892	20 911	21 511	22 201	23 052
12	Transport equipment	5 318	5 616	6 503	6 297	6 341	6 001	6 006	6 959
13	Other machinery and equipment	12 510	11 581	12 846	13 218	13 998	14 367	14 543	15 628
14	Cultivated assets	152	130	125	103	112	125	115	112
15	Intangible fixed assets	11 554	11 850	13 465	13 928	15 510	15 689	16 126	16 577
16	Changes in inventories, acquisitions less disposals of valuables	1 044	2 992	5 175	4 231	2 213	2 903	3 618	3 676
17	Changes in inventories	-663	1 422	2 841	2 476	555	1 511	1 409	1 874
18	Acquisitions less disposals of valuables	1 706	1 570	2 335	1 756	1 658	1 393	2 209	1 802
19	**External balance of goods and services**	**9 657**	**10 370**	**8 667**	**8 907**	**9 122**	**10 891**	**12 839**	**11 859**
20	Exports of goods and services	130 217	151 683	167 310	171 989	173 102	177 854	182 345	184 639
21	Exports of goods	91 435	111 997	123 526	125 801	123 657	126 108	128 747	128 925
22	Exports of services	38 782	39 686	43 784	46 188	49 445	51 746	53 598	55 715
23	Imports of goods and services	120 560	141 313	158 644	163 082	163 980	166 963	169 506	172 780
24	Imports of goods	92 845	111 784	126 381	128 430	124 937	125 196	126 608	128 566
25	Imports of services	27 715	29 530	32 263	34 652	39 043	41 767	42 898	44 214
26	**Statistical discrepancy**	**-846**	**-316**	**-655**	**-296**	**-383**	**-36**	**697**	**-638**
27	**Gross domestic product**	**288 044**	**295 897**	**310 129**	**318 653**	**323 910**	**333 063**	**344 493**	**353 297**
	AT CONSTANT PRICES, REFERENCE YEAR 2010								
28	**Final consumption expenditure**	**217 380**	**218 947**	**221 119**	**221 991**	**222 319**	**223 295**	**225 028**	**228 797**
29	Household	151 010	152 497	154 635	155 325	154 965	155 235	155 731	158 045
30	NPISH's	5 741	5 813	5 804	5 952	6 187	6 392	6 742	6 869
31	Government	60 628	60 637	60 679	60 710	61 171	61 681	62 583	63 918
32	Individual	36 587	36 778	36 999	37 239	37 759	38 222	38 717	39 759
33	Collective	24 041	23 859	23 680	23 470	23 410	23 456	23 864	24 151
34	*of which: Actual individual consumption*	193 339	195 088	197 439	198 516	198 903	199 832	201 164	204 642
35	**Gross capital formation**	**67 015**	**66 896**	**72 786**	**72 275**	**71 744**	**72 025**	**73 433**	**75 988**
36	Gross fixed capital formation, total	65 601	63 904	68 153	68 771	69 847	69 346	70 196	72 766
37	Dwellings	12 734	12 817	13 192	13 013	12 992	12 906	13 043	13 076
38	Other buildings and structures	19 714	18 188	18 681	19 427	18 928	18 983	19 208	19 519
39	Transport equipment	5 452	5 616	6 438	6 123	6 088	5 707	5 658	6 491
40	Other machinery and equipment	12 704	11 581	12 580	12 648	13 303	13 522	13 519	14 400
41	Cultivated assets	165	130	120	96	100	113	111	104
42	Intangible fixed assets	11 447	11 850	13 195	13 326	14 553	14 436	14 580	14 885
43	Changes in inventories, acquisitions less disposals of valuables	..	..	..	..	..	..	..	..
44	Changes in inventories	..	..	..	..	..	..	..	..
45	Acquisitions less disposals of valuables	..	..	..	..	..	..	..	..
46	**External balance of goods and services**	**7 870**	**10 370**	**10 959**	**11 886**	**11 881**	**12 283**	**12 620**	**10 882**
47	Exports of goods and services	134 077	151 683	160 686	162 996	164 040	168 883	174 115	177 450
48	Exports of goods	94 627	111 997	119 041	120 093	119 127	122 588	126 362	128 055
49	Exports of services	39 367	39 686	41 645	42 895	44 858	46 235	47 688	49 261
50	Imports of goods and services	126 207	141 313	149 727	151 110	152 159	156 600	161 495	166 567
51	Imports of goods	97 767	111 784	118 822	118 769	116 448	118 938	123 281	127 250
52	Imports of services	28 383	29 530	30 905	32 363	35 764	37 702	38 285	39 399
53	**Statistical discrepancy (including chaining residual)**	**-1 707**	**-316**	**-319**	**466**	**752**	**1 634**	**1 533**	**1 482**
54	**Gross domestic product**	**290 559**	**295 897**	**304 545**	**306 617**	**306 696**	**309 237**	**312 614**	**317 149**

Note: Detailed metadata:http://metalinks.oecd.org/nav1/20180308/94fa
Source: Österreichische Nationalbank via Eurostat.

AUSTRIA

Table 2. Gross domestic product, output and income approach
ISIC Rev. 4

Million EUR (1999 ATS euro)

		2009	2010	2011	2012	2013	2014	2015	2016
	OUTPUT APPROACH AT CURRENT PRICES								
1	**Total gross value added at basic prices**	**256 671**	**263 633**	**276 404**	**283 548**	**288 624**	**297 147**	**307 293**	**314 693**
2	Agriculture, forestry and fishing	3 303	3 750	4 348	4 297	4 064	4 000	3 829	3 892
3	Industry, including energy	56 838	58 434	61 443	63 655	64 132	65 534	66 937	67 205
4	Manufacturing	47 130	48 759	51 468	53 235	53 431	55 170	57 043	57 259
5	Construction	17 457	17 124	17 477	18 028	18 546	18 939	19 281	20 098
6	Services	..	..	..	..	..	..	..	..
7	Distrib. trade, repairs; transp.; accommod., food serv. activ.	59 536	61 722	64 909	66 079	66 006	68 519	71 566	73 151
8	Information and communication	8 494	8 519	9 217	9 405	9 802	10 369	10 764	11 052
9	Financial and insurance activities	12 124	12 113	12 953	12 255	12 797	12 961	13 564	13 476
10	Real estate activities	23 092	24 051	25 279	26 372	27 737	28 670	29 731	31 000
11	Prof., scientif., techn. activ.; admin., support service activ.	22 490	23 255	24 895	25 989	26 998	27 992	29 131	30 322
12	Public admin.; compulsory s.s.; education; human health	45 818	46 997	47 981	49 382	50 262	51 622	53 694	55 573
13	Other service activities	7 519	7 669	7 903	8 086	8 281	8 541	8 796	8 924
14	**FISIM (Financial Intermediation Services Indirectly Measured)**	..	..	..	..	..	..	..	..
15	**Gross value added at basic prices, excluding FISIM**	**256 671**	**263 633**	**276 404**	**283 548**	**288 624**	**297 147**	**307 293**	**314 693**
16	**Taxes less subsidies on products**	**31 373**	**32 263**	**33 725**	**35 105**	**35 286**	**35 916**	**37 200**	**38 604**
17	Taxes on products	32 047	32 910	34 363	35 744	35 964	36 607	37 841	39 224
18	Subsidies on products	674	647	638	640	678	691	641	620
19	**Residual item**	**0**	**0**	**0**	**0**	**0**	**0**	**0**	**0**
20	**Gross domestic product at market prices**	**288 044**	**295 897**	**310 129**	**318 653**	**323 910**	**333 063**	**344 493**	**353 297**
	OUTPUT APPROACH AT CONSTANT PRICES (REF. YEAR 2010)								
21	**Total gross value added at basic prices**	**258 678**	**263 633**	**272 240**	**273 680**	**274 071**	**276 477**	**279 068**	**282 781**
22	Agriculture, forestry and fishing	3 951	3 750	4 285	3 975	3 856	3 973	3 947	4 052
23	Industry, including energy	55 081	58 434	61 719	63 024	63 749	64 542	64 648	65 497
24	Manufacturing	45 098	48 759	52 285	53 351	53 489	54 842	55 197	55 910
25	Construction	17 812	17 124	16 977	16 883	16 678	16 338	16 134	16 230
26	Services	..	..	..	..	..	..	..	..
27	Distrib. trade, repairs; transp.; accommod., food serv. activ.	60 861	61 722	63 357	62 949	62 074	63 235	64 579	65 452
28	Information and communication	8 735	8 519	9 137	9 067	9 268	9 402	9 493	9 606
29	Financial and insurance activities	12 059	12 113	12 344	12 307	12 006	11 673	12 200	12 231
30	Real estate activities	23 664	24 051	24 828	25 240	25 727	25 978	25 724	26 127
31	Prof., scientif., techn. activ.; admin., support service activ.	22 507	23 255	24 500	25 002	25 470	25 892	26 496	26 994
32	Public admin.; compulsory s.s.; education; human health	46 569	46 997	47 324	47 516	47 551	47 741	48 089	48 903
33	Other service activities	7 602	7 669	7 769	7 747	7 746	7 793	7 837	7 783
34	**FISIM (Financial Intermediation Services Indirectly Measured)**	..	..	..	..	..	..	..	..
35	**Gross value added at basic prices, excluding FISIM**	**258 678**	**263 633**	**272 240**	**273 680**	**274 071**	**276 477**	**279 068**	**282 781**
36	**Taxes less subsidies on products**	**31 883**	**32 263**	**32 305**	**32 926**	**32 622**	**32 761**	**33 538**	**34 359**
37	Taxes on products	32 567	32 910	32 932	33 545	33 264	33 419	34 216	35 024
38	Subsidies on products	684	647	627	618	642	659	679	660
39	**Residual item**	**-2**	**0**	**0**	**11**	**2**	**-1**	**7**	**10**
40	**Gross domestic product at market prices**	**290 559**	**295 897**	**304 545**	**306 617**	**306 696**	**309 237**	**312 614**	**317 149**
	INCOME APPROACH								
41	**Compensation of employees**	**136 194**	**138 878**	**144 318**	**150 324**	**154 509**	**158 789**	**163 818**	**170 090**
42	Agriculture, forestry and fishing	497	516	553	586	613	655	675	691
43	Industry, including energy	29 648	29 881	31 485	33 274	34 097	34 888	35 487	36 784
44	Manufacturing	26 444	26 669	28 149	29 682	30 387	31 117	31 791	32 954
45	Construction	9 380	9 465	9 782	10 175	10 398	10 829	11 129	11 525
46	Distrib. trade, repairs; transp.; accommod., food serv. activ.	31 349	31 885	33 000	34 361	35 360	36 558	37 531	39 057
47	Information and communication	4 548	4 549	4 960	5 304	5 579	5 811	6 072	6 272
48	Financial and insurance activities	7 703	7 848	8 054	8 030	8 217	8 259	8 554	8 746
49	Real estate activities	1 529	1 542	1 604	1 708	1 779	1 788	1 853	1 931
50	Prof., scientif., techn. activ.; admin., support service activ.	11 866	12 420	13 341	14 115	14 943	15 435	16 080	16 975
51	Public admin.; compulsory s.s.; education; human health	35 389	36 395	37 042	38 136	38 786	39 728	41 468	43 042
52	Other service activities	4 285	4 378	4 499	4 636	4 738	4 837	4 969	5 068
53	**Wages and salaries**	**112 345**	**114 606**	**119 035**	**124 040**	**127 380**	**130 766**	**134 981**	**140 289**
54	Agriculture, forestry and fishing	410	425	455	482	503	532	552	566
55	Industry, including energy	24 758	24 896	26 178	27 605	28 157	28 811	29 416	30 508
56	Manufacturing	22 222	22 381	23 625	24 932	25 425	25 981	26 556	27 547
57	Construction	8 004	8 066	8 298	8 641	8 808	9 160	9 404	9 749
58	Distrib. trade, repairs; transp.; accommod., food serv. activ.	25 877	26 312	27 296	28 451	29 288	30 198	31 093	32 383
59	Information and communication	3 725	3 777	4 124	4 396	4 619	4 811	5 033	5 204
60	Financial and insurance activities	6 078	6 226	6 379	6 376	6 544	6 537	6 643	6 865
61	Real estate activities	1 261	1 278	1 320	1 398	1 467	1 463	1 519	1 584
62	Prof., scientif., techn. activ.; admin., support service activ.	9 802	10 279	11 023	11 670	12 369	12 753	13 281	14 029
63	Public admin.; compulsory s.s.; education; human health	28 841	29 681	30 203	31 150	31 673	32 468	33 892	35 165
64	Other service activities	3 588	3 665	3 759	3 870	3 953	4 033	4 148	4 236
65	**Gross operating surplus and mixed income**	**116 331**	**120 207**	**126 617**	**127 489**	**127 755**	**131 838**	**136 145**	**138 069**
66	**Taxes less subsidies on production and imports**	**35 519**	**36 811**	**39 193**	**40 839**	**41 646**	**42 436**	**44 529**	**45 138**
67	Taxes on production and imports	41 483	42 626	44 894	46 779	47 307	48 187	49 804	51 513
68	Subsidies on production and imports	5 965	5 815	5 701	5 940	5 661	5 751	5 274	6 375
69	**Residual item**	**0**	**0**	**0**	**0**	**0**	**0**	**0**	**0**
70	**Gross domestic product**	**288 044**	**295 897**	**310 129**	**318 653**	**323 910**	**333 063**	**344 493**	**353 297**

Note: Detailed metadata:http://metalinks.oecd.org/nav1/20180308/94fa

Source: Österreichische Nationalbank via Eurostat.

AUSTRIA

Table 3. Disposable income, saving and net lending / net borrowing

Million EUR (1999 ATS euro)

		2009	2010	2011	2012	2013	2014	2015	2016
	DISPOSABLE INCOME								
1	**Gross domestic product**	**288 044**	**295 897**	**310 129**	**318 653**	**323 910**	**333 063**	**344 493**	**353 297**
2	Net primary incomes from the rest of the world	-125	2 475	1 046	322	874	439	-2 521	-180
3	Primary incomes receivable from the rest of the world	26 654	30 046	35 464	33 613	21 009	23 018	15 955	27 030
4	Primary incomes payable to the rest of the world	26 778	27 570	34 418	33 292	20 135	22 579	18 477	27 210
5	**Gross national income at market prices**	**287 919**	**298 372**	**311 174**	**318 975**	**324 784**	**333 502**	**341 972**	**353 117**
6	Consumption of fixed capital	50 402	51 796	53 713	56 109	58 089	60 055	61 802	63 578
7	**Net national income at market prices**	**237 517**	**246 576**	**257 462**	**262 866**	**266 695**	**273 447**	**280 170**	**289 539**
8	Net current transfers from the rest of the world	-2 749	-2 989	-3 018	-3 134	-3 909	-3 113	-3 206	-3 688
9	Current transfers receivable from the rest of the world	2 045	2 196	2 424	2 602	2 530	2 636	4 643	4 784
10	Current transfers payable to the rest of the world	4 795	5 185	5 442	5 736	6 439	5 748	7 849	8 472
11	**Net national disposable income**	**234 768**	**243 588**	**254 444**	**259 732**	**262 786**	**270 334**	**276 964**	**285 851**
	SAVING AND NET LENDING / NET BORROWING								
12	**Net national disposable income**	**234 768**	**243 588**	**254 444**	**259 732**	**262 786**	**270 334**	**276 964**	**285 851**
13	Final consumption expenditures	213 630	218 947	227 251	233 638	238 329	243 875	249 758	256 867
14	Adj. for change in net equity of households in pension funds	0	0	0	0	0	0	0	0
15	**Saving, net**	**21 138**	**24 641**	**27 193**	**26 094**	**24 457**	**26 460**	**27 206**	**28 984**
16	Net capital transfers from the rest of the world	79	357	-154	-249	-166	-176	-1 603	-449
17	Capital transfers receivable from the rest of the world	381	612	82	14	109	126	498	672
18	Capital transfers payable to the rest of the world	302	255	235	263	275	302	2 101	1 121
19	Gross capital formation[1]	64 757	66 580	74 211	76 108	76 459	78 297	81 896	84 571
20	Acquisitions less disposals of non-financial non-produced assets	204	180	176	199	230	171	123	144
21	Consumption of fixed capital	50 402	51 796	53 713	56 109	58 089	60 055	61 802	63 578
22	**Net lending / net borrowing**	**6 658**	**10 033**	**6 365**	**5 646**	**5 691**	**7 870**	**5 385**	**7 398**
	REAL DISPOSABLE INCOME								
23	**Gross domestic product at constant prices, reference year 2010**	**290 559**	**295 897**	**304 545**	**306 617**	**306 696**	**309 237**	**312 614**	**317 149**
24	Trading gain or loss	2 808	0	-2 846	-4 179	-4 482	-3 970	-1 952	-2 377
25	**Real gross domestic income**	**293 367**	**295 897**	**301 699**	**302 438**	**302 213**	**305 267**	**310 661**	**314 773**
26	Net real primary incomes from the rest of the world	-127	2 475	1 017	305	815	402	-2 274	-161
27	Real primary incomes receivable from the rest of the world	27 146	30 046	34 500	31 903	19 602	21 097	14 388	24 083
28	Real primary incomes payable to the rest of the world	27 273	27 570	33 482	31 597	18 786	20 695	16 662	24 243
29	**Real gross national income at market prices**	**293 240**	**298 372**	**302 716**	**302 744**	**303 028**	**305 669**	**308 388**	**314 612**
30	Net real current transfers from the rest of the world	-2 800	-2 989	-2 936	-2 975	-3 647	-2 853	-2 891	-3 286
31	Real current transfers receivable from the rest of the world	2 083	2 196	2 358	2 469	2 360	2 416	4 187	4 262
32	Real current transfers payable to the rest of the world	4 883	5 185	5 294	5 444	6 008	5 269	7 078	7 548
33	**Real gross national disposable income**	**290 440**	**295 383**	**299 781**	**299 769**	**299 381**	**302 816**	**305 497**	**311 326**
34	Consumption of fixed capital at constant prices	51 209	51 796	52 664	53 667	54 677	55 639	56 436	57 339
35	**Real net national income at market prices**	**241 907**	**246 576**	**250 464**	**249 490**	**248 830**	**250 626**	**252 655**	**257 967**
36	**Real net national disposable income**	**239 106**	**243 588**	**247 528**	**246 516**	**245 183**	**247 774**	**249 764**	**254 681**

Note: Detailed metadata:http://metalinks.oecd.org/nav1/20180308/d75e
1. Including a statistical discrepancy.
Source: Österreichische Nationalbank via Eurostat.

Table 4. Population and employment (persons) and employment (hours worked) by industry
ISIC Rev. 4

		2009	2010	2011	2012	2013	2014	2015	2016
	POPULATION, THOUSAND PERSONS, NATIONAL CONCEPT								
1	**Total population**	8 341.5	8 361.1	8 388.5	8 426.3	8 477.2	8 543.9	8 629.5	8 739.8
2	Economically active population	..	..	..	..	..	..	..	..
3	Unemployed persons	..	..	..	..	..	..	..	..
4	Total employment[1]	4 051.0	4 074.7	4 127.1	4 158.1	4 156.1	4 178.7	4 201.0	4 249.8
5	Employees[1]	3 478.5	3 502.0	3 555.1	3 594.3	3 598.4	3 613.3	3 649.3	3 699.2
6	Self-employed[1]	572.4	572.7	572.0	563.8	557.7	565.4	551.7	550.6
	TOTAL EMPLOYMENT, THOUSAND PERSONS, DOMESTIC CONCEPT								
7	Agriculture, forestry and fishing	201.6	199.0	195.8	184.9	182.6	188.5	176.6	171.4
8	Industry, including energy	675.8	667.0	676.3	682.9	681.8	681.4	683.6	688.4
9	Manufacturing	621.0	611.9	620.8	626.9	625.2	624.9	627.4	631.7
10	Construction	275.6	276.1	280.7	283.6	280.3	284.0	283.0	286.9
11	Distrib. trade, repairs; transp.; accommod., food serv. activ.	1 095.9	1 101.6	1 118.8	1 129.8	1 133.6	1 145.6	1 155.1	1 169.2
12	Information and communication	96.0	98.1	102.7	104.9	106.9	109.7	110.2	112.9
13	Financial and insurance activities	136.7	135.0	134.1	133.8	131.0	129.7	127.9	128.0
14	Real estate activities	60.8	60.5	61.2	62.0	64.0	63.1	62.8	62.9
15	Prof., scientif., techn. activ.; admin., support service activ.	426.2	440.6	459.5	474.0	482.3	487.5	493.0	506.4
16	Public admin.; compulsory s.s.; education; human health	921.0	939.8	949.6	962.5	969.3	981.0	1 001.7	1 017.0
17	Other service activities	178.1	180.6	183.2	186.6	187.9	189.4	191.7	194.2
18	**Total employment**	4 067.5	4 098.2	4 162.0	4 205.2	4 219.8	4 259.9	4 285.4	4 337.2
	EMPLOYEES, THOUSAND PERSONS, DOMESTIC CONCEPT								
19	Agriculture, forestry and fishing	22.6	23.0	24.4	25.3	25.9	27.3	28.3	28.3
20	Industry, including energy	655.2	647.0	656.5	663.2	662.2	662.2	664.7	669.4
21	Manufacturing	601.5	593.1	602.3	608.6	607.3	607.2	610.1	614.3
22	Construction	252.5	252.3	256.6	259.6	255.8	258.6	257.6	261.2
23	Distrib. trade, repairs; transp.; accommod., food serv. activ.	969.4	973.7	990.7	1 003.9	1 008.5	1 018.5	1 030.8	1 045.6
24	Information and communication	80.4	81.7	86.1	88.5	90.8	93.7	94.6	97.4
25	Financial and insurance activities	123.4	123.2	122.5	121.6	119.4	118.2	116.2	116.4
26	Real estate activities	45.1	45.0	45.6	47.0	49.6	48.7	48.1	48.2
27	Prof., scientif., techn. activ.; admin., support service activ.	333.2	345.9	363.8	374.9	384.0	388.7	393.5	405.3
28	Public admin.; compulsory s.s.; education; human health	873.1	891.2	899.3	910.8	917.8	929.5	949.8	964.2
29	Other service activities	140.2	142.7	144.6	146.5	148.0	149.0	150.1	150.7
30	**Total employees**	3 495.1	3 525.5	3 590.0	3 641.3	3 662.0	3 694.5	3 733.6	3 786.6
	SELF-EMPLOYED, THOUSAND PERSONS, DOMESTIC CONCEPT								
31	Agriculture, forestry and fishing	179.1	176.0	171.3	159.6	156.7	161.1	148.2	143.0
32	Industry, including energy	20.6	20.1	19.8	19.8	19.6	19.3	18.9	19.0
33	Manufacturing	19.5	18.8	18.5	18.2	18.0	17.7	17.4	17.4
34	Construction	23.1	23.8	24.2	24.0	24.5	25.3	25.4	25.8
35	Distrib. trade, repairs; transp.; accommod., food serv. activ.	126.5	127.9	128.1	125.9	125.1	127.0	124.3	123.7
36	Information and communication	15.6	16.4	16.6	16.4	16.1	16.0	15.6	15.5
37	Financial and insurance activities	13.3	11.8	11.7	12.1	11.6	11.5	11.7	11.6
38	Real estate activities	15.6	15.5	15.7	15.0	14.4	14.3	14.7	14.8
39	Prof., scientif., techn. activ.; admin., support service activ.	93.0	94.7	95.8	99.1	98.3	98.8	99.5	101.1
40	Public admin.; compulsory s.s.; education; human health	47.9	48.6	50.3	51.8	51.5	51.5	51.9	52.8
41	Other service activities	37.9	37.9	38.6	40.1	39.9	40.5	41.5	43.5
42	**Total self-employed**	572.5	572.7	572.0	563.8	557.7	565.4	551.7	550.6
	TOTAL EMPLOYMENT, MILLION HOURS, DOMESTIC CONCEPT								
43	Industry, including energy	1 096.1	1 101.9	1 119.4	1 127.5	1 121.6	1 117.9	1 115.2	1 119.7
44	Distrib. trade, repairs; transp.; accommod., food serv. activ.	1 858.3	1 854.4	1 865.2	1 867.0	1 858.9	1 846.5	1 825.0	1 879.3
45	Financial and insurance activities	219.7	219.4	220.5	215.5	212.9	206.7	201.5	209.2
46	Prof., scientif., techn. activ.; admin., support service activ.	713.4	734.3	774.1	790.6	792.3	807.7	807.6	828.5
47	Public admin.; compulsory s.s.; education; human health	1 390.3	1 402.1	1 435.4	1 421.0	1 421.5	1 429.2	1 432.9	1 463.9
48	**Total employment**	6 805.2	6 827.0	6 957.5	6 929.5	6 887.0	6 907.7	6 851.8	6 980.1
	EMPLOYEES, MILLION HOURS, DOMESTIC CONCEPT								
49	Industry, including energy	1 043.7	1 055.1	1 071.0	1 078.8	1 074.3	1 070.1	1 067.0	1 074.0
50	Distrib. trade, repairs; transp.; accommod., food serv. activ.	1 538.3	1 537.7	1 549.1	1 564.2	1 550.5	1 553.8	1 533.8	1 580.2
51	Financial and insurance activities	193.5	195.8	197.4	191.1	189.4	183.9	179.4	185.6
52	Prof., scientif., techn. activ.; admin., support service activ.	519.0	537.9	569.9	582.2	585.8	600.5	603.2	618.8
53	Public admin.; compulsory s.s.; education; human health	1 305.1	1 317.1	1 343.0	1 329.8	1 336.8	1 342.5	1 348.8	1 375.7
54	**Total employees**	5 490.1	5 536.4	5 638.6	5 662.3	5 654.5	5 684.9	5 651.5	5 769.6
	SELF-EMPLOYED, MILLION HOURS, DOMESTIC CONCEPT								
55	Industry, including energy	52.5	46.8	48.4	48.7	47.3	47.8	48.2	45.7
56	Distrib. trade, repairs; transp.; accommod., food serv. activ.	320.1	316.7	316.1	302.8	308.4	292.7	291.2	299.1
57	Financial and insurance activities	26.2	23.6	23.2	24.4	23.5	22.8	22.1	23.7
58	Prof., scientif., techn. activ.; admin., support service activ.	194.4	196.5	204.2	208.3	206.6	207.1	204.3	209.7
59	Public admin.; compulsory s.s.; education; human health	85.2	85.0	92.4	91.3	84.7	86.6	84.1	88.2
60	**Total self-employed**	1 315.2	1 290.5	1 318.9	1 267.1	1 232.4	1 222.8	1 200.3	1 210.6

Note: Detailed metadata:http://metalinks.oecd.org/nav1/20180308/9e8b
1.   Data in terms of jobs instead of persons.
Source: Österreichische Nationalbank via Eurostat.

BELGIUM

Table 1. Gross domestic product, expenditure approach

Million EUR (1999 BEF euro)

		2009	2010	2011	2012	2013	2014	2015	2016
	AT CURRENT PRICES								
1	**Final consumption expenditure**	**265 328**	**275 692**	**286 197**	**295 193**	**300 472**	**304 293**	**308 098**	**316 288**
2	Household	176 979	184 948	191 260	196 018	199 424	201 811	204 739	211 342
3	NPISH's	4 567	4 745	4 810	5 164	4 961	5 078	5 149	5 232
4	Government	83 782	85 999	90 128	94 011	96 087	97 404	98 210	99 714
5	Individual	52 559	54 753	57 777	60 307	61 177	62 725	63 967	65 425
6	Collective	31 223	31 246	32 351	33 704	34 910	34 680	34 243	34 288
7	*of which: Actual individual consumption*	234 105	244 446	253 846	261 489	265 562	269 614	273 855	282 000
8	**Gross capital formation**	**75 561**	**82 849**	**90 948**	**89 918**	**86 995**	**93 458**	**96 760**	**101 135**
9	Gross fixed capital formation, total	78 780	79 661	85 609	87 672	86 944	92 314	95 186	99 154
10	Dwellings	21 430	22 338	22 138	22 854	22 452	23 790	23 980	24 786
11	Other buildings and structures	17 092	16 677	19 704	21 317	21 042	20 846	20 251	20 727
12	Transport equipment	7 200	7 144	7 941	6 745	7 360	8 559	8 599	11 011
13	Other machinery and equipment	15 828	15 288	16 374	16 592	15 760	16 226	16 912	18 517
14	Cultivated assets	170	157	189	203	188	197	191	185
15	Intangible fixed assets	12 654	13 179	14 359	14 929	15 324	17 301	19 583	18 032
16	Changes in inventories, acquisitions less disposals of valuables	-3 219	3 188	5 339	2 246	52	1 144	1 574	1 982
17	Changes in inventories	-3 311	3 087	5 232	2 182	-47	1 107	1 550	1 995
18	Acquisitions less disposals of valuables	92	101	107	64	98	37	24	-13
19	**External balance of goods and services**	**7 892**	**6 560**	**1 962**	**2 390**	**4 873**	**2 537**	**5 578**	**5 625**
20	Exports of goods and services	241 739	279 114	309 486	318 935	320 661	330 737	331 492	350 559
21	Exports of goods	175 662	204 549	233 477	234 928	234 668	236 340	229 922	248 165
22	Exports of services	66 077	74 564	76 009	84 007	85 992	94 397	101 570	102 394
23	Imports of goods and services	233 847	272 554	307 524	316 546	315 788	328 200	325 914	344 934
24	Imports of goods	175 789	206 661	239 184	239 849	237 335	239 419	229 632	247 034
25	Imports of services	58 058	65 893	68 340	76 697	78 452	88 781	96 282	97 901
26	**Statistical discrepancy**	**0**	**0**	**0**	**0**	**0**	**0**	**0**	**0**
27	**Gross domestic product**	**348 781**	**365 101**	**379 106**	**387 500**	**392 340**	**400 288**	**410 435**	**423 048**
	AT CONSTANT PRICES, REFERENCE YEAR 2010								
28	**Final consumption expenditure**	**269 842**	**275 692**	**277 439**	**279 782**	**281 485**	**283 249**	**285 401**	**289 100**
29	Household	180 045	184 948	185 681	186 585	188 264	189 396	191 131	194 342
30	NPISH's	4 650	4 745	4 664	4 872	4 625	4 671	4 673	4 707
31	Government	85 182	85 999	87 060	88 288	88 565	89 150	89 573	90 043
32	Individual	53 754	54 753	55 736	56 686	56 726	57 994	58 762	59 336
33	Collective	31 420	31 246	31 324	31 602	31 838	31 171	30 839	30 739
34	*of which: Actual individual consumption*	238 448	244 446	246 081	248 147	249 613	252 071	254 578	258 392
35	**Gross capital formation**	**81 359**	**82 849**	**88 876**	**86 649**	**83 979**	**90 148**	**93 250**	**97 694**
36	Gross fixed capital formation, total	80 327	79 661	83 022	83 185	81 946	86 833	89 157	92 369
37	Dwellings	21 764	22 338	21 812	21 860	21 130	22 305	22 426	23 118
38	Other buildings and structures	17 720	16 677	18 865	20 191	20 017	19 846	19 562	19 891
39	Transport equipment	7 152	7 144	7 663	6 315	6 872	8 013	7 947	10 158
40	Other machinery and equipment	16 096	15 288	15 977	15 857	14 989	15 312	15 684	17 024
41	Cultivated assets	162	157	178	177	164	184	194	187
42	Intangible fixed assets	12 938	13 179	13 892	14 027	14 132	15 862	17 823	16 254
43	Changes in inventories, acquisitions less disposals of valuables	..	..	..	..	..	..	..	..
44	Changes in inventories		..						
45	Acquisitions less disposals of valuables	93	101	104	61	93	35	23	-12
46	**External balance of goods and services**	**4 350**	**6 560**	**5 385**	**6 112**	**7 766**	**5 170**	**5 349**	**3 022**
47	Exports of goods and services	252 974	279 114	297 864	298 871	301 528	317 160	327 567	352 191
48	Exports of goods	184 245	204 549	223 316	218 466	219 828	227 638	229 962	254 672
49	Exports of services	68 718	74 564	74 549	80 548	81 861	89 751	97 774	97 979
50	Imports of goods and services	248 624	272 554	292 480	292 759	293 761	311 990	322 218	349 169
51	Imports of goods	188 538	206 661	224 115	217 264	216 498	225 032	228 173	253 579
52	Imports of services	60 087	65 893	68 365	75 973	77 884	88 051	95 406	97 083
53	**Statistical discrepancy (including chaining residual)**	**-202**	**0**	**-33**	**-4**	**56**	**-236**	**-356**	**-547**
54	**Gross domestic product**	**355 349**	**365 101**	**371 666**	**372 539**	**373 286**	**378 331**	**383 645**	**389 269**

Note: Detailed metadata:http://metalinks.oecd.org/nav1/20180308/a112
Source: Banque Nationale de Belgique via Eurostat.

Table 2. Gross domestic product, output and income approach
ISIC Rev. 4

Million EUR (1999 BEF euro)

		2009	2010	2011	2012	2013	2014	2015	2016
	OUTPUT APPROACH AT CURRENT PRICES								
1	**Total gross value added at basic prices**	312 596	326 534	339 644	346 698	350 877	358 051	367 472	377 636
2	Agriculture, forestry and fishing	2 265	2 784	2 441	3 040	2 699	2 598	2 804	2 610
3	Industry, including energy	53 592	57 549	58 695	58 206	58 506	59 251	61 829	63 551
4	Manufacturing	44 651	48 069	48 401	48 810	49 065	50 319	52 660	53 859
5	Construction	17 938	18 129	19 456	19 633	19 489	19 562	19 643	20 102
6	Services	..	..	..	..	..	..	..	..
7	Distrib. trade, repairs; transp.; accommod., food serv. activ.	64 195	66 678	68 751	69 282	69 402	70 672	72 659	73 711
8	Information and communication	13 418	13 942	14 316	14 977	14 556	14 559	15 227	15 649
9	Financial and insurance activities	17 851	20 098	21 396	21 896	21 517	21 398	21 974	23 500
10	Real estate activities	28 467	28 796	29 628	30 059	30 008	31 157	31 748	32 277
11	Prof., scientif., techn. activ.; admin., support service activ.	39 179	40 721	43 584	44 645	47 140	49 369	51 444	53 542
12	Public admin.; compulsory s.s.; education; human health	68 689	70 682	73 886	77 239	79 671	81 327	81 888	84 282
13	Other service activities	7 003	7 155	7 491	7 723	7 889	8 158	8 257	8 411
14	**FISIM (Financial Intermediation Services Indirectly Measured)**	..	..	..	..	..	..	..	..
15	Gross value added at basic prices, excluding FISIM	312 596	326 534	339 644	346 698	350 877	358 051	367 472	377 636
16	**Taxes less subsidies on products**	36 185	38 567	39 462	40 802	41 463	42 237	42 964	45 413
17	Taxes on products	38 092	40 912	41 972	42 977	43 548	44 172	45 103	47 468
18	Subsidies on products	1 907	2 345	2 510	2 176	2 084	1 934	2 139	2 055
19	Residual item	0	0	0	0	0	0	0	0
20	**Gross domestic product at market prices**	348 781	365 101	379 106	387 500	392 340	400 288	410 435	423 048
	OUTPUT APPROACH AT CONSTANT PRICES (REF. YEAR 2010)								
21	**Total gross value added at basic prices**	318 367	326 534	333 538	334 188	334 735	339 255	344 614	348 795
22	Agriculture, forestry and fishing	2 581	2 784	2 807	2 786	2 380	2 385	2 725	2 477
23	Industry, including energy	54 261	57 549	58 355	57 442	57 823	60 206	62 212	62 722
24	Manufacturing	45 180	48 069	48 943	48 993	49 798	51 941	53 723	53 911
25	Construction	18 092	18 129	19 219	19 366	19 034	19 185	19 590	19 656
26	Services	..	..	..	..	..	..	..	..
27	Distrib. trade, repairs; transp.; accommod., food serv. activ.	65 290	66 678	67 298	66 689	65 341	65 382	66 607	65 956
28	Information and communication	13 406	13 942	14 273	15 257	15 543	16 054	16 765	17 259
29	Financial and insurance activities	19 155	20 098	21 111	22 015	21 782	19 915	19 679	20 830
30	Real estate activities	28 246	28 796	29 325	29 389	29 200	30 040	29 989	30 171
31	Prof., scientif., techn. activ.; admin., support service activ.	39 703	40 721	42 772	41 329	42 975	44 730	46 167	46 764
32	Public admin.; compulsory s.s.; education; human health	70 490	70 682	71 060	72 392	73 068	73 736	73 568	75 629
33	Other service activities	7 121	7 155	7 367	7 505	7 513	7 484	7 332	7 300
34	**FISIM (Financial Intermediation Services Indirectly Measured)**	..	..	..	..	..	..	..	..
35	Gross value added at basic prices, excluding FISIM	318 367	326 534	333 538	334 188	334 735	339 255	344 614	348 795
36	**Taxes less subsidies on products**	36 981	38 567	38 128	38 348	38 546	39 070	39 039	40 456
37	Taxes on products	38 930	40 912	40 552	40 393	40 484	40 859	40 983	42 287
38	Subsidies on products	1 949	2 345	2 425	2 045	1 938	1 789	1 944	1 831
39	**Residual item**	2	0	0	2	5	5	-9	18
40	**Gross domestic product at market prices**	355 349	365 101	371 666	372 539	373 286	378 331	383 645	389 269
	INCOME APPROACH								
41	**Compensation of employees**	179 623	183 229	191 626	198 306	202 271	204 850	206 542	209 145
42	Agriculture, forestry and fishing	393	411	455	482	500	531	560	572
43	Industry, including energy	32 694	32 808	34 221	35 035	35 352	35 385	34 667	34 669
44	Manufacturing	29 051	29 063	30 227	30 928	31 198	31 161	30 527	30 521
45	Construction	9 292	9 301	9 996	10 222	10 140	10 239	10 099	10 099
46	Distrib. trade, repairs; transp.; accommod., food serv. activ.	38 131	38 972	39 833	41 180	41 515	41 679	42 580	42 499
47	Information and communication	7 133	7 083	7 345	7 549	7 729	7 773	7 932	7 968
48	Financial and insurance activities	9 489	9 306	9 718	9 877	9 968	10 012	9 900	9 728
49	Real estate activities	813	827	866	897	938	939	979	1 010
50	Prof., scientif., techn. activ.; admin., support service activ.	18 614	19 462	20 997	21 783	22 362	23 336	24 335	24 968
51	Public admin.; compulsory s.s.; education; human health	58 490	60 419	63 454	66 291	68 665	69 808	70 319	72 408
52	Other service activities	4 575	4 640	4 743	4 991	5 102	5 147	5 172	5 224
53	**Wages and salaries**	130 245	132 611	138 889	143 361	146 021	148 116	149 104	152 824
54	Agriculture, forestry and fishing	291	305	338	355	371	393	417	434
55	Industry, including energy	23 189	23 357	24 528	25 315	25 557	25 475	25 083	25 477
56	Manufacturing	20 768	20 957	21 988	22 523	22 639	22 491	22 196	22 592
57	Construction	6 752	6 815	7 347	7 513	7 451	7 530	7 438	7 568
58	Distrib. trade, repairs; transp.; accommod., food serv. activ.	28 440	28 851	29 644	30 427	30 676	30 762	31 290	31 830
59	Information and communication	5 123	5 138	5 358	5 484	5 633	5 722	5 884	6 035
60	Financial and insurance activities	6 800	6 702	6 978	7 024	7 147	7 154	7 074	6 987
61	Real estate activities	601	608	637	651	685	685	717	749
62	Prof., scientif., techn. activ.; admin., support service activ.	13 843	14 473	15 697	16 177	16 675	17 581	18 350	19 229
63	Public admin.; compulsory s.s.; education; human health	41 679	42 837	44 740	46 616	47 971	48 916	48 947	50 526
64	Other service activities	3 525	3 527	3 622	3 799	3 857	3 900	3 904	3 990
65	**Gross operating surplus and mixed income**	135 750	147 008	151 953	151 201	151 887	156 524	164 213	171 259
66	**Taxes less subsidies on production and imports**	33 408	34 864	35 527	37 993	38 182	38 915	39 681	42 644
67	Taxes on production and imports	44 735	47 927	49 524	51 944	52 437	53 342	54 435	57 142
68	Subsidies on production and imports	11 327	13 064	13 997	13 951	14 255	14 427	14 754	14 498
69	**Residual item**	0	0	0	0	0	0	0	0
70	**Gross domestic product**	348 781	365 101	379 106	387 500	392 340	400 288	410 435	423 048

Note: Detailed metadata:http://metalinks.oecd.org/nav1/20180308/a112
Source: Banque Nationale de Belgique via Eurostat.

Table 3. Disposable income, saving and net lending / net borrowing

Million EUR (1999 BEF euro)

		2009	2010	2011	2012	2013	2014	2015	2016
	DISPOSABLE INCOME								
1	**Gross domestic product**	**348 781**	**365 101**	**379 106**	**387 500**	**392 340**	**400 288**	**410 435**	**423 048**
2	Net primary incomes from the rest of the world	430	11 508	3 823	9 482	6 468	2 823	-934	2 693
3	Primary incomes receivable from the rest of the world	59 121	63 712	60 296	59 301	52 797	51 242	46 614	49 437
4	Primary incomes payable to the rest of the world	58 691	52 205	56 473	49 819	46 328	48 419	47 548	46 744
5	**Gross national income at market prices**	**349 211**	**376 608**	**382 929**	**396 983**	**398 808**	**403 111**	**409 501**	**425 741**
6	Consumption of fixed capital	67 658	70 287	73 664	76 378	77 406	78 079	79 424	81 089
7	**Net national income at market prices**	**281 553**	**306 321**	**309 265**	**320 605**	**321 402**	**325 032**	**330 077**	**344 652**
8	Net current transfers from the rest of the world	-5 302	-4 551	-4 904	-6 011	-6 763	-6 384	-6 436	-7 910
9	Current transfers receivable from the rest of the world	6 927	8 238	7 991	7 636	7 469	6 895	7 201	7 165
10	Current transfers payable to the rest of the world	12 230	12 789	12 895	13 647	14 232	13 280	13 637	15 075
11	**Net national disposable income**	**276 251**	**301 770**	**304 361**	**314 594**	**314 639**	**318 648**	**323 640**	**336 742**
	SAVING AND NET LENDING / NET BORROWING								
12	**Net national disposable income**	**276 251**	**301 770**	**304 361**	**314 594**	**314 639**	**318 648**	**323 640**	**336 742**
13	Final consumption expenditures	265 328	275 692	286 197	295 193	300 472	304 293	308 098	316 288
14	Adj. for change in net equity of households in pension funds	0	0	0	0	0	0	0	0
15	**Saving, net**	**10 923**	**26 078**	**18 164**	**19 401**	**14 167**	**14 354**	**15 543**	**20 454**
16	Net capital transfers from the rest of the world	-203	-277	-460	2 310	-174	-290	25	-352
17	Capital transfers receivable from the rest of the world	338	207	189	2 778	326	183	278	160
18	Capital transfers payable to the rest of the world	541	484	650	468	500	473	253	512
19	Gross capital formation	75 561	82 849	90 948	89 918	86 995	93 458	96 760	101 135
20	Acquisitions less disposals of non-financial non-produced assets	263	32	-85	-374	88	625	-86	-821
21	Consumption of fixed capital	67 658	70 287	73 664	76 378	77 406	78 079	79 424	81 089
22	**Net lending / net borrowing**	**2 554**	**13 208**	**505**	**8 545**	**4 317**	**-1 940**	**-1 682**	**877**
	REAL DISPOSABLE INCOME								
23	**Gross domestic product at constant prices, reference year 2010**	**355 349**	**365 101**	**371 666**	**372 539**	**373 286**	**378 331**	**383 645**	**389 269**
24	Trading gain or loss	4 008	0	-3 480	-3 850	-3 201	-2 657	51	2 233
25	**Real gross domestic income**	**359 357**	**365 101**	**368 186**	**368 689**	**370 085**	**375 674**	**383 696**	**391 501**
26	Net real primary incomes from the rest of the world	443	11 508	3 713	9 022	6 101	2 650	-874	2 492
27	Real primary incomes receivable from the rest of the world	60 914	63 712	58 559	56 422	49 802	48 091	43 577	45 750
28	Real primary incomes payable to the rest of the world	60 471	52 205	54 846	47 400	43 700	45 442	44 450	43 258
29	**Real gross national income at market prices**	**359 800**	**376 608**	**371 898**	**377 711**	**376 186**	**378 323**	**382 822**	**393 994**
30	Net real current transfers from the rest of the world	-5 463	-4 551	-4 763	-5 719	-6 379	-5 992	-6 017	-7 320
31	Real current transfers receivable from the rest of the world	7 137	8 238	7 761	7 265	7 045	6 471	6 732	6 630
32	Real current transfers payable to the rest of the world	12 600	12 789	12 524	12 984	13 425	12 463	12 748	13 951
33	**Real gross national disposable income**	**354 337**	**372 057**	**367 136**	**371 992**	**369 807**	**372 331**	**376 805**	**386 673**
34	Consumption of fixed capital at constant prices	68 915	70 287	71 425	72 452	72 992	73 398	74 214	75 770
35	**Real net national income at market prices**	**290 091**	**306 321**	**300 356**	**305 041**	**303 171**	**305 045**	**308 572**	**318 951**
36	**Real net national disposable income**	**284 627**	**301 770**	**295 594**	**299 322**	**296 791**	**299 053**	**302 555**	**311 631**

Note: Detailed metadata:http://metalinks.oecd.org/nav1/20180308/44ad
Source: Banque Nationale de Belgique via Eurostat.

Table 4. Population and employment (persons) and employment (hours worked) by industry
ISIC Rev. 4

		2009	2010	2011	2012	2013	2014	2015	2016
	POPULATION, THOUSAND PERSONS, NATIONAL CONCEPT								
1	**Total population**	**10 796.0**	**10 896.0**	**10 994.0**	**11 068.0**	**11 125.0**	**11 180.0**	**11 238.0**	**11 295.0**
2	Economically active population	..	..	..	..	..	..	..	..
3	Unemployed persons	..	..	..	..	..	..	..	..
4	Total employment	4 524.0	4 553.2	4 614.3	4 634.6	4 618.9	4 637.9	4 677.7	4 735.4
5	Employees	3 802.4	3 826.3	3 879.4	3 891.9	3 870.2	3 883.2	3 912.7	3 957.2
6	Self-employed	721.6	726.9	734.9	742.7	748.6	754.8	765.1	778.3
	TOTAL EMPLOYMENT, THOUSAND PERSONS, DOMESTIC CONCEPT								
7	Agriculture, forestry and fishing	67.5	64.2	61.6	60.7	59.7	59.5	60.1	59.8
8	Industry, including energy	611.4	593.8	596.8	589.2	576.7	563.2	551.2	552.1
9	Manufacturing	559.9	541.6	543.1	535.3	523.0	509.6	498.5	499.1
10	Construction	267.8	269.5	274.5	275.9	272.4	268.3	266.9	268.6
11	Distrib. trade, repairs; transp.; accommod., food serv. activ.	996.9	995.3	994.6	990.1	976.5	970.7	977.4	981.8
12	Information and communication	108.0	107.5	109.5	109.9	109.6	110.9	112.0	114.4
13	Financial and insurance activities	132.4	130.1	129.8	128.6	126.8	125.9	124.8	123.2
14	Real estate activities	23.7	24.1	24.5	24.6	24.7	25.1	26.1	27.0
15	Prof., scientif., techn. activ.; admin., support service activ.	737.7	767.9	798.6	812.5	823.6	849.0	879.5	908.3
16	Public admin.; compulsory s.s.; education; human health	1 299.9	1 326.3	1 349.0	1 363.7	1 375.9	1 393.9	1 407.2	1 424.6
17	Other service activities	200.1	195.3	196.4	199.8	194.2	193.5	195.1	198.3
18	**Total employment**	**4 445.5**	**4 474.0**	**4 535.3**	**4 555.0**	**4 540.1**	**4 559.9**	**4 600.4**	**4 658.1**
	EMPLOYEES, THOUSAND PERSONS, DOMESTIC CONCEPT								
19	Agriculture, forestry and fishing	19.4	19.8	20.4	21.1	21.1	21.6	22.7	22.7
20	Industry, including energy	586.0	568.9	571.9	564.6	552.2	538.6	526.0	526.8
21	Manufacturing	534.9	517.0	518.6	511.1	499.0	485.5	474.0	474.5
22	Construction	211.9	212.4	215.2	214.9	210.0	204.7	201.2	200.7
23	Distrib. trade, repairs; transp.; accommod., food serv. activ.	854.1	854.0	856.1	855.9	844.8	841.2	849.5	855.6
24	Information and communication	97.0	95.8	96.8	96.9	96.2	96.9	98.2	100.4
25	Financial and insurance activities	123.4	121.2	121.3	120.3	118.7	118.0	117.2	116.0
26	Real estate activities	19.7	19.8	20.0	20.1	20.1	20.3	21.0	21.5
27	Prof., scientif., techn. activ.; admin., support service activ.	436.7	460.1	482.2	485.8	491.1	512.5	536.4	557.4
28	Public admin.; compulsory s.s.; education; human health	1 225.8	1 250.9	1 272.2	1 285.4	1 296.0	1 311.8	1 322.8	1 337.4
29	Other service activities	149.9	144.2	144.3	147.3	141.2	139.6	140.3	141.3
30	**Total employees**	**3 723.9**	**3 747.1**	**3 800.4**	**3 812.3**	**3 791.5**	**3 805.2**	**3 835.3**	**3 879.8**
	SELF-EMPLOYED, THOUSAND PERSONS, DOMESTIC CONCEPT								
31	Agriculture, forestry and fishing	48.2	44.4	41.2	39.7	38.6	37.9	37.4	37.1
32	Industry, including energy	25.4	25.0	24.9	24.6	24.5	24.6	25.1	25.3
33	Manufacturing	25.0	24.6	24.5	24.2	24.0	24.0	24.5	24.6
34	Construction	55.9	57.1	59.4	61.0	62.3	63.6	65.7	67.9
35	Distrib. trade, repairs; transp.; accommod., food serv. activ.	142.8	141.3	138.5	134.2	131.7	129.5	127.9	126.2
36	Information and communication	11.0	11.7	12.6	13.0	13.3	13.9	13.9	14.0
37	Financial and insurance activities	8.9	8.9	8.5	8.3	8.1	7.9	7.6	7.2
38	Real estate activities	4.0	4.3	4.5	4.4	4.6	4.9	5.1	5.5
39	Prof., scientif., techn. activ.; admin., support service activ.	301.0	307.8	316.5	326.8	332.5	336.5	343.1	350.9
40	Public admin.; compulsory s.s.; education; human health	74.1	75.4	76.8	78.3	80.0	82.1	84.4	87.2
41	Other service activities	50.2	51.1	52.0	52.5	53.0	53.9	54.8	57.0
42	**Total self-employed**	**721.6**	**726.9**	**734.9**	**742.7**	**748.6**	**754.8**	**765.1**	**778.3**
	TOTAL EMPLOYMENT, MILLION HOURS, DOMESTIC CONCEPT								
43	Industry, including energy	932.3	923.5	939.5	926.0	908.2	888.0	872.0	874.1
44	Distrib. trade, repairs; transp.; accommod., food serv. activ.	1 547.2	1 544.2	1 556.6	1 552.4	1 527.0	1 508.9	1 515.1	1 530.3
45	Financial and insurance activities	200.8	195.8	195.8	194.8	192.7	190.9	187.8	185.5
46	Prof., scientif., techn. activ.; admin., support service activ.	1 292.0	1 328.8	1 389.0	1 416.7	1 432.8	1 465.3	1 478.2	1 519.6
47	Public admin.; compulsory s.s.; education; human health	1 815.8	1 846.9	1 878.3	1 907.3	1 922.9	1 939.3	1 948.9	1 966.1
48	**Total employment**	**6 882.1**	**6 916.1**	**7 073.4**	**7 105.4**	**7 073.5**	**7 091.6**	**7 105.8**	**7 200.6**
	EMPLOYEES, MILLION HOURS, DOMESTIC CONCEPT								
49	Industry, including energy	875.0	866.8	881.3	867.3	849.3	829.5	812.6	813.7
50	Distrib. trade, repairs; transp.; accommod., food serv. activ.	1 218.0	1 215.6	1 226.4	1 230.6	1 216.4	1 207.2	1 219.9	1 234.1
51	Financial and insurance activities	181.4	177.2	177.8	176.9	174.8	173.5	171.7	170.3
52	Prof., scientif., techn. activ.; admin., support service activ.	621.1	650.2	685.3	690.9	695.9	721.8	752.8	784.5
53	Public admin.; compulsory s.s.; education; human health	1 673.3	1 702.8	1 731.2	1 754.9	1 764.7	1 779.1	1 785.5	1 798.7
54	**Total employees**	**5 290.6**	**5 320.8**	**5 434.9**	**5 454.2**	**5 416.7**	**5 425.8**	**5 456.7**	**5 524.1**
	SELF-EMPLOYED, MILLION HOURS, DOMESTIC CONCEPT								
55	Industry, including energy	57.3	56.7	58.2	58.7	58.9	58.5	59.5	60.4
56	Distrib. trade, repairs; transp.; accommod., food serv. activ.	329.2	328.6	330.2	321.9	310.6	301.7	295.2	296.2
57	Financial and insurance activities	19.4	18.6	18.0	17.9	17.9	17.5	16.2	15.2
58	Prof., scientif., techn. activ.; admin., support service activ.	671.0	678.6	703.6	725.8	736.9	743.4	725.4	735.1
59	Public admin.; compulsory s.s.; education; human health	142.6	144.1	147.1	152.4	158.2	160.2	163.4	167.4
60	**Total self-employed**	**1 591.6**	**1 595.3**	**1 638.5**	**1 651.1**	**1 656.8**	**1 665.8**	**1 649.2**	**1 676.5**

Note: Detailed metadata:http://metalinks.oecd.org/nav1/20180308/038c
Source: Banque Nationale de Belgique via Eurostat.

CANADA

Table 1. Gross domestic product, expenditure approach

Million CAD

		2009	2010	2011	2012	2013	2014	2015	2016
	AT CURRENT PRICES								
1	**Final consumption expenditure**	**1 246 307**	**1 304 141**	**1 363 718**	**1 405 369**	**1 455 081**	**1 514 179**	**1 563 236**	**1 613 915**
2	Household	878 202	923 451	963 911	995 046	1 034 804	1 083 056	1 117 690	1 154 829
3	NPISH's	22 968	22 899	24 666	25 553	26 429	26 826	28 535	29 492
4	Government	345 137	357 791	375 141	384 770	393 848	404 297	417 011	429 594
5	Individual	209 884 e	219 043 e	233 215	239 201	244 844	251 340	259 244	267 067
6	Collective	135 253 e	138 748 e	141 926	145 569	149 004	152 957	157 767	162 527
7	*of which: Actual individual consumption*	1 111 054 e	1 165 393 e	1 221 792	1 259 800	1 306 077	1 361 222	1 405 469	1 451 388
8	**Gross capital formation**	**345 057**	**391 221**	**428 462**	**454 381**	**473 806**	**496 105**	**479 928**	**471 932**
9	Gross fixed capital formation, total	350 517	390 875	417 091	447 559	460 101	486 542	475 988	472 419
10	Dwellings	103 633	114 776	119 714	129 692	131 422	138 071	146 758	157 102
11	Other buildings and structures	120 039	145 441	159 534	175 913	187 725	200 818	180 313	170 572
12	Transport equipment	13 478	14 515	15 287	16 403	16 469	17 319	17 350	16 677
13	Other machinery and equipment	42 371	42 947	45 613	46 818	45 710	48 118	50 133	48 039
14	Cultivated assets	..	..	..	..	..	..	..	..
15	Intangible fixed assets	47 594	51 821	54 719	56 219	56 723	59 061	57 315	56 022
16	Changes in inventories, acquisitions less disposals of valuables	-5 460	346	11 371	6 822	13 705	9 563	3 940	-487
17	Changes in inventories	-5 460	346	11 371	6 822	13 705	9 563	3 940	-487
18	Acquisitions less disposals of valuables	..	..	..	..	..	..	..	..
19	**External balance of goods and services**	**-23 146**	**-31 860**	**-21 228**	**-35 908**	**-31 247**	**-19 580**	**-49 310**	**-49 185**
20	Exports of goods and services	445 692	483 214	540 970	550 736	572 359	627 641	628 955	630 353
21	Exports of goods	367 211	403 968	456 613	461 512	479 224	529 334	524 972	521 469
22	Exports of services	78 481	79 246	84 357	89 224	93 135	98 307	103 983	108 884
23	Imports of goods and services	468 838	515 074	562 198	586 644	603 606	647 221	678 265	679 538
24	Imports of goods	373 985	413 670	456 045	474 800	487 370	524 661	548 707	547 341
25	Imports of services	94 853	101 404	106 153	111 844	116 236	122 560	129 558	132 197
26	**Statistical discrepancy**	**-853**	**-1 372**	**-1 031**	**-1 034**	**-109**	**-521**	**1 057**	**-1 156**
27	**Gross domestic product**	**1 567 365**	**1 662 130**	**1 769 921**	**1 822 808**	**1 897 531**	**1 990 183**	**1 994 911**	**2 035 506**
	AT CONSTANT PRICES, REFERENCE YEAR 2010								
28	**Final consumption expenditure**	**1 263 629**	**1 304 141**	**1 330 506**	**1 351 518**	**1 374 161**	**1 402 333**	**1 430 536**	**1 463 106**
29	Household	890 501	923 451	943 713	961 798	986 608	1 013 301	1 034 560	1 059 006
30	NPISH's	23 214	22 899	24 324	24 775	25 434	25 228	26 450	26 316
31	Government	349 913	357 791	362 480	365 007	362 440	364 328	370 118	378 414
32	Individual	..	..	..	..	..	..	..	..
33	Collective	..	..	..	..	..	..	..	..
34	*of which: Actual individual consumption*	1 126 496 e	1 165 393 e	1 192 036 e	1 211 527 e	1 233 443 e	1 260 675 e	1 286 162 e	1 315 766 e
35	**Gross capital formation**	**348 252**	**391 221**	**422 416**	**437 339**	**452 378**	**456 283**	**429 724**	**413 163**
36	Gross fixed capital formation, total	350 528	390 875	409 002	428 997	434 503	444 805	421 921	409 465
37	Dwellings	106 581	114 776	116 306	122 975	122 858	125 896	130 594	134 923
38	Other buildings and structures	123 460	145 441	153 679	164 351	171 772	178 457	159 221	149 145
39	Transport equipment	12 457	14 515	15 683	16 587	16 871	17 625	17 258	16 972
40	Other machinery and equipment	39 691	42 947	45 904	45 896	43 626	42 900	39 986	37 182
41	Cultivated assets	..	..	..	..	..	..	..	..
42	Intangible fixed assets	47 950	51 821	53 874	54 244	53 393	53 634	50 436	47 727
43	Changes in inventories, acquisitions less disposals of valuables	..		..	..	..	..	..	..
44	Changes in inventories	..	..	..	..	..	..	..	..
45	Acquisitions less disposals of valuables	..	..	..	..	..	..	..	..
46	**External balance of goods and services**	**387**	**-31 860**	**-37 578**	**-43 745**	**-39 115**	**-20 474**	**-5 118**	**6 540**
47	Exports of goods and services	453 103	483 214	506 209	519 585	533 510	565 111	584 737	590 576
48	Exports of goods	372 696	403 968	424 150	434 635	447 377	473 579	490 212	492 526
49	Exports of services	80 438	79 246	82 079	84 989	86 171	91 507	94 511	97 825
50	Imports of goods and services	452 716	515 074	543 787	563 330	572 624	585 585	589 855	584 036
51	Imports of goods	362 856	413 670	438 075	452 285	461 315	472 042	473 843	467 705
52	Imports of services	89 850	101 404	105 683	111 128	111 366	113 591	116 104	116 462
53	**Statistical discrepancy (including chaining residual)**	**143**	**-1 372**	**-1 003**	**-847**	**11**	**337**	**1 738**	**330**
54	**Gross domestic product**	**1 612 411**	**1 662 130**	**1 714 341**	**1 744 264**	**1 787 435**	**1 838 480**	**1 856 881**	**1 883 139**

Note: Detailed metadata:http://metalinks.oecd.org/nav1/20180308/ccca
Source: Statistics Canada.

CANADA

Table 2. Gross domestic product, output and income approach
ISIC Rev. 4

Million CAD

		2009	2010	2011	2012	2013	2014	2015	2016
	OUTPUT APPROACH AT CURRENT PRICES								
1	**Total gross value added at basic prices**	**1 465 150**	**1 555 133**	**1 658 213**	**1 706 036**	**1 777 213**	**1 863 041**	**1 861 812**	**1 896 063**
2	Agriculture, forestry and fishing	21 566	22 134	28 419	30 027	32 738	28 356	..	..
3	Industry, including energy	293 146	328 571	365 409	357 811	370 334	398 395	..	..
4	Manufacturing	162 894	172 042	182 251	189 188	188 791	194 629	..	..
5	Construction	105 680	115 436	121 696	134 959	142 311	149 566	..	..
6	Services	..	..	..	..	..	..	..	..
7	Distrib. trade, repairs; transp.; accommod., food serv. activ.	253 034	265 101	277 638	289 004	301 350	316 337	..	..
8	Information and communication	68 105	70 415	73 967	76 633	78 603	82 373	..	..
9	Financial and insurance activities	104 946	110 940	117 138	116 353	123 286	131 446	..	..
10	Real estate activities	172 632	180 325	188 042	197 061	205 903	215 181	..	..
11	Prof., scientif., techn. activ.; admin., support service activ.	111 628	117 100	123 769	130 525	134 765	141 464	..	..
12	Public admin.; compulsory s.s.; education; human health	301 556	312 035	327 954	338 300	351 821	362 235	..	..
13	Other service activities	32 858	33 076	34 182	35 363	36 101	37 688	..	..
14	**FISIM (Financial Intermediation Services Indirectly Measured)**	..	..	..	..	..	..	..	..
15	**Gross value added at basic prices, excluding FISIM**	**1 465 150**	**1 555 133**	**1 658 213**	**1 706 036**	**1 777 213**	**1 863 041**	**1 861 812**	**1 896 063**
16	**Taxes less subsidies on products**	**102 215**	**106 998**	**111 709**	**116 772**	**120 319**	**127 139**	**133 099**	**139 443**
17	Taxes on products	112 629	119 673	125 665	129 212	132 793	139 522	145 521	151 244
18	Subsidies on products	10 414	12 675	13 956	12 440	12 474	12 383	12 422	11 801
19	**Residual item**	**0**	**0**	**0**	**0**	**0**	**0**	..	..
20	**Gross domestic product at market prices**	**1 567 365**	**1 662 131**	**1 769 922**	**1 822 808**	**1 897 532**	**1 990 180**	**1 994 911**	**2 035 506**
	OUTPUT APPROACH AT CONSTANT PRICES (REF. YEAR 2010)								
21	**Total gross value added at basic prices**	**1 502 393**	**1 555 133**	**1 606 416**	**1 637 049**	**1 678 415**	**1 726 660**	**1 743 422**	**1 767 252**
22	Agriculture, forestry and fishing	21 890	22 134	23 052	23 292	27 440	25 223	26 190	27 210
23	Industry, including energy	310 043	328 571	344 714	344 981	351 084	368 521	365 371	365 679
24	Manufacturing	164 203	172 042	178 399	181 192	180 667	185 824	186 306	187 203
25	Construction	106 661	115 436	119 949	129 454	135 086	138 657	132 332	128 014
26	Services	..	..	..	..	..	..	..	..
27	Distrib. trade, repairs; transp.; accommod., food serv. activ.	254 630	265 101	275 228	280 445	291 342	301 463	307 659	313 990
28	Information and communication	69 277	70 415	72 306	72 771	73 715	77 191	78 687	81 143
29	Financial and insurance activities	109 218	110 940	114 464	116 338	120 925	123 150	128 878	133 946
30	Real estate activities	174 705	180 325	185 610	191 198	196 819	202 414	209 279	216 323
31	Prof., scientif., techn. activ.; admin., support service activ.	116 067	117 100	121 007	125 943	127 327	132 148	132 145	131 262
32	Public admin.; compulsory s.s.; education; human health	305 674	312 035	316 756	319 286	320 300	322 716	327 332	333 937
33	Other service activities	34 172	33 076	33 257	33 518	34 217	35 557	36 073	36 311
34	**FISIM (Financial Intermediation Services Indirectly Measured)**	..	..	..	..	..	..	..	..
35	**Gross value added at basic prices, excluding FISIM**	**1 502 393**	**1 555 133**	**1 606 416**	**1 637 049**	**1 678 415**	**1 726 660**	**1 743 422**	**1 767 252**
36	**Taxes less subsidies on products**	..	..	..	..	..	..	..	..
37	Taxes on products	..	..	..	..	..	..	..	..
38	Subsidies on products	..	..	..	..	..	..	..	..
39	**Residual item**	..	..	..	..	..	..	..	..
40	**Gross domestic product at market prices**	**1 612 412**	**1 662 131**	**1 714 342**	**1 744 266**	**1 787 436**	**1 838 481**	**1 856 882**	**1 883 140**
	INCOME APPROACH								
41	**Compensation of employees**	**812 073**	**837 683**	**883 045**	**923 413**	**961 179**	**998 463**	**1 026 914**	**1 044 005**
42	Agriculture, forestry and fishing	..	..	..	..	..	..	..	..
43	Industry, including energy	..	..	..	..	..	..	..	..
44	Manufacturing	..	..	..	..	..	..	..	..
45	Construction	..	..	..	..	..	..	..	..
46	Distrib. trade, repairs; transp.; accommod., food serv. activ.	..	..	..	..	..	..	..	..
47	Information and communication	..	..	..	..	..	..	..	..
48	Financial and insurance activities	..	..	..	..	..	..	..	..
49	Real estate activities	..	..	..	..	..	..	..	..
50	Prof., scientif., techn. activ.; admin., support service activ.	..	..	..	..	..	..	..	..
51	Public admin.; compulsory s.s.; education; human health	..	..	..	..	..	..	..	..
52	Other service activities	..	..	..	..	..	..	..	..
53	**Wages and salaries**	**705 172**	**727 616**	**766 670**	**799 649**	**828 737**	**861 053**	**884 410**	**896 899**
54	Agriculture, forestry and fishing	7 311	7 462	7 969	8 263	8 613	8 745	9 192	9 536
55	Industry, including energy	115 327	119 151	127 183	132 426	133 909	138 455	137 240	134 619
56	Manufacturing	80 850	82 164	85 426	87 786	87 559	90 328	92 182	92 430
57	Construction	53 442	57 261	61 453	68 114	72 671	76 652	77 149	75 991
58	Distrib. trade, repairs; transp.; accommod., food serv. activ.	149 865	153 311	161 200	169 461	175 855	183 453	190 551	192 947
59	Information and communication	18 300	18 759	19 718	20 567	20 555	20 772	21 089	22 399
60	Financial and insurance activities	56 370	58 502	61 542	62 440	65 483	69 377	73 372	75 914
61	Real estate activities	11 545	11 982	12 604	12 789	13 412	14 209	15 028	15 548
62	Prof., scientif., techn. activ.; admin., support service activ.	73 722	75 762	80 014	83 707	87 559	91 967	95 186	96 352
63	Public admin.; compulsory s.s.; education; human health	190 833	196 183	204 102	209 571	216 883	221 925	228 863	236 402
64	Other service activities	28 454	29 241	30 882	32 308	33 794	35 496	36 738	37 188
65	**Gross operating surplus and mixed income**	**582 571**	**644 112**	**700 156**	**705 186**	**734 622**	**779 739**	**748 103**	**760 394**
66	**Taxes less subsidies on production and imports**	**171 868**	**178 963**	**185 689**	**193 175**	**201 620**	**211 459**	**220 952**	**229 950**
67	Taxes on production and imports	187 969	197 523	205 821	212 452	219 449	229 441	239 333	247 775
68	Subsidies on production and imports	16 101	18 560	20 132	19 277	17 829	17 982	18 381	17 825
69	**Residual item**	**853**	**1 372**	**1 031**	**1 034**	**110**	**522**	**-1 058**	**1 157**
70	**Gross domestic product**	**1 567 365**	**1 662 130**	**1 769 921**	**1 822 808**	**1 897 531**	**1 990 183**	**1 994 911**	**2 035 506**

Note: Detailed metadata:http://metalinks.oecd.org/nav1/20180308/ccca
Source: Statistics Canada.

CANADA

Table 3. Disposable income, saving and net lending / net borrowing

Million CAD

		2009	2010	2011	2012	2013	2014	2015	2016
	DISPOSABLE INCOME								
1	**Gross domestic product**	**1 567 365**	**1 662 130**	**1 769 921**	**1 822 808**	**1 897 531**	**1 990 183**	**1 994 911**	**2 035 506**
2	Net primary incomes from the rest of the world	-27 056	-32 928	-33 509	-32 422	-28 972	-32 235	-30 649	-26 896
3	Primary incomes receivable from the rest of the world	40 724	41 318	42 846	45 305	49 726	55 575	60 818	66 519
4	Primary incomes payable to the rest of the world	67 780	74 246	76 355	77 727	78 698	87 810	91 467	93 415
5	**Gross national income at market prices**	**1 540 309**	**1 629 202**	**1 736 412**	**1 790 386**	**1 868 559**	**1 957 948**	**1 964 262**	**2 008 610**
6	Consumption of fixed capital	268 289	269 097	280 060	294 108	308 976	323 208	341 184	352 116
7	**Net national income at market prices**	**1 272 020**	**1 360 105**	**1 456 352**	**1 496 278**	**1 559 583**	**1 634 740**	**1 623 078**	**1 656 494**
8	Net current transfers from the rest of the world	-3 482	-3 966	-3 628	-4 198	-4 048	-3 443	-3 977	-3 511
9	Current transfers receivable from the rest of the world	9 052	9 020	9 410	8 922	9 691	10 681	10 927	11 853
10	Current transfers payable to the rest of the world	12 534	12 986	13 038	13 120	13 739	14 124	14 904	15 364
11	**Net national disposable income**	**1 268 538**	**1 356 139**	**1 452 724**	**1 492 080**	**1 555 537**	**1 631 297**	**1 619 101**	**1 652 983**
	SAVING AND NET LENDING / NET BORROWING								
12	**Net national disposable income**	**1 268 538**	**1 356 139**	**1 452 724**	**1 492 080**	**1 555 537**	**1 631 297**	**1 619 101**	**1 652 983**
13	Final consumption expenditures	1 246 307	1 304 141	1 363 718	1 405 369	1 455 081	1 514 179	1 563 236	1 613 915
14	Adj. for change in net equity of households in pension funds	38 057	38 076	46 937	47 452	44 876	46 439	44 300	42 395
15	**Saving, net**	**22 231**	**51 998**	**89 006**	**86 711**	**100 456**	**117 118**	**55 865**	**39 068**
16	Net capital transfers from the rest of the world	-816	-123	-63	-274	-105	-164	-103	-91
17	Capital transfers receivable from the rest of the world	-227	260	272	284	300	316	332	280
18	Capital transfers payable to the rest of the world	589	383	335	558	405	480	435	371
19	Gross capital formation	345 057	391 221	423 827	454 381	473 806	495 540	479 928	471 932
20	Acquisitions less disposals of non-financial non-produced assets	..	..	..	..	..	..	..	..
21	Consumption of fixed capital	268 289	269 097	280 060	294 108	308 976	323 208	341 184	352 116
22	**Net lending / net borrowing**	**-56 206**	**-71 621**	**-55 855**	**-74 870**	**-64 589**	**-55 900**	**-81 924**	**-81 996**
	REAL DISPOSABLE INCOME								
23	**Gross domestic product at constant prices, reference year 2010**	**1 612 411**	**1 662 130**	**1 714 341**	**1 744 264**	**1 787 435**	**1 838 480**	**1 856 881**	**1 883 139**
24	Trading gain or loss	-24 946 e	0 e	16 809 e	8 994 e	9 341 e	1 524 e	-40 764 e	-52 798 e
25	**Real gross domestic income**	**1 587 465 e**	**1 662 130 e**	**1 731 151 e**	**1 753 259 e**	**1 796 776 e**	**1 840 004 e**	**1 816 116 e**	**1 830 341 e**
26	Net real primary incomes from the rest of the world	-27 403 e	-32 928 e	-32 775 e	-31 185 e	-27 434 e	-29 803 e	-27 902 e	-24 185 e
27	Real primary incomes receivable from the rest of the world	41 246 e	41 318 e	41 907 e	43 576 e	47 086 e	51 381 e	55 367 e	59 814 e
28	Real primary incomes payable to the rest of the world	68 649 e	74 246 e	74 682 e	74 761 e	74 519 e	81 184 e	83 269 e	83 999 e
29	**Real gross national income at market prices**	**1 560 062 e**	**1 629 202 e**	**1 698 376 e**	**1 722 074 e**	**1 769 343 e**	**1 810 201 e**	**1 788 214 e**	**1 806 156 e**
30	Net real current transfers from the rest of the world	-11 059 e	-3 966 e	-1 906 e	-9 616 e	-3 826 e	-5 172 e	-3 480 e	-653 e
31	Real current transfers receivable from the rest of the world	9 168 e	9 020 e	9 204 e	8 582 e	9 176 e	9 875 e	9 948 e	10 658 e
32	Real current transfers payable to the rest of the world	20 227 e	12 986 e	11 110 e	18 198 e	13 003 e	15 047 e	13 427 e	11 311 e
33	**Real gross national disposable income**	**1 556 535 e**	**1 625 236 e**	**1 694 827 e**	**1 718 036 e**	**1 765 510 e**	**1 807 018 e**	**1 784 593 e**	**1 802 998 e**
34	Consumption of fixed capital at constant prices	..	..	..	..	..	..	..	..
35	**Real net national income at market prices**	**1 288 333 e**	**1 360 105 e**	**1 424 450 e**	**1 439 187 e**	**1 476 773 e**	**1 511 382 e**	**1 477 609 e**	**1 489 530 e**
36	**Real net national disposable income**	**1 284 806 e**	**1 356 139 e**	**1 420 902 e**	**1 435 150 e**	**1 472 941 e**	**1 508 199 e**	**1 473 988 e**	**1 486 373 e**

Note: Detailed metadata:http://metalinks.oecd.org/nav1/20180308/81f2
Source: Statistics Canada.

Table 4. Population and employment (persons) and employment (hours worked) by industry
ISIC Rev. 4

		2009	2010	2011	2012	2013	2014	2015	2016
	POPULATION, THOUSAND PERSONS, NATIONAL CONCEPT								
1	**Total population**	**33 628.6**	**34 005.3**	**34 342.8**	**34 750.5**	**35 155.5**	**35 544.6**	**35 848.6**	**36 286.4**
2	Economically active population	..	..	..	..	..	..	..	..
3	Unemployed persons	..	..	..	..	..	..	..	..
4	Total employment	16 501.3	16 753.4	16 995.6	17 179.4	17 394.1	17 509.4	17 685.4	17 815.0
5	Employees	15 116.8	15 374.0	15 630.4	15 826.5	16 032.2	16 146.6	16 332.5	16 454.2
6	Self-employed	1 384.5	1 379.4	1 365.2	1 352.9	1 361.9	1 362.8	1 353.0	1 360.7
	TOTAL EMPLOYMENT, THOUSAND PERSONS, DOMESTIC CONCEPT								
7	Agriculture, forestry and fishing	308.3	300.6	309.6	295.3	308.9	298.1	284.1	290.0
8	Industry, including energy	2 084.9	2 097.9	2 138.1	2 149.3	2 121.8	2 107.7	2 102.9	2 065.1
9	Manufacturing	1 727.5	1 730.0	1 743.6	1 741.1	1 704.8	1 684.8	1 698.1	1 680.1
10	Construction	1 133.4	1 214.5	1 253.4	1 353.5	1 395.3	1 425.3	1 393.4	1 391.6
11	Distrib. trade, repairs; transp.; accommod., food serv. activ.	4 811.1	4 886.5	4 959.9	5 048.5	5 094.3	5 142.1	5 246.8	5 284.2
12	Information and communication	556.7	567.3	583.9	581.7	601.6	606.9	632.9	654.4
13	Financial and insurance activities	1 025.5	1 051.5	1 084.7	1 048.1	1 085.9	1 098.1	1 083.3	1 086.7
14	Real estate activities	264.1	271.0	279.9	285.9	275.5	278.2	285.6	290.0
15	Prof., scientif., techn. activ.; admin., support service activ.	1 774.0	1 807.5	1 823.7	1 845.4	1 865.3	1 891.5	1 900.2	1 944.3
16	Public admin.; compulsory s.s.; education; human health	4 058.9	4 136.0	4 179.5	4 190.0	4 248.1	4 256.4	4 343.2	4 414.6
17	Other service activities	968.8	965.3	959.7	966.5	1 007.1	1 001.9	1 006.1	1 049.6
18	**Total employment**	**16 985.7**	**17 298.1**	**17 572.3**	**17 764.1**	**18 003.7**	**18 106.3**	**18 278.5**	**18 470.6**
	EMPLOYEES, THOUSAND PERSONS, DOMESTIC CONCEPT								
19	Agriculture, forestry and fishing	144.6	147.1	155.7	151.3	156.5	160.4	153.9	162.7
20	Industry, including energy	1 999.2	2 016.6	2 065.0	2 075.9	2 050.7	2 036.3	2 034.5	1 996.2
21	Manufacturing	1 648.9	1 655.8	1 676.5	1 674.3	1 640.2	1 619.9	1 635.3	1 616.3
22	Construction	923.6	1 006.5	1 049.2	1 144.7	1 191.1	1 224.5	1 189.8	1 188.6
23	Distrib. trade, repairs; transp.; accommod., food serv. activ.	4 549.2	4 621.7	4 706.5	4 801.3	4 840.1	4 880.1	4 984.9	5 025.6
24	Information and communication	494.3	505.2	525.4	525.9	541.6	549.6	575.2	593.2
25	Financial and insurance activities	972.7	999.3	1 030.6	992.6	1 031.5	1 046.7	1 028.9	1 033.3
26	Real estate activities	192.5	198.3	201.9	206.1	197.3	203.4	207.4	211.0
27	Prof., scientif., techn. activ.; admin., support service activ.	1 424.9	1 449.0	1 460.4	1 490.5	1 509.0	1 524.7	1 540.6	1 578.4
28	Public admin.; compulsory s.s.; education; human health	3 841.3	3 909.7	3 956.2	3 962.7	4 013.0	4 027.3	4 101.2	4 166.6
29	Other service activities	807.3	803.7	801.0	809.5	837.9	841.9	850.1	880.3
30	**Total employees**	**15 349.6**	**15 657.0**	**15 952.0**	**16 160.4**	**16 368.7**	**16 494.9**	**16 666.6**	**16 835.7**
	SELF-EMPLOYED, THOUSAND PERSONS, DOMESTIC CONCEPT								
31	Agriculture, forestry and fishing	163.7	153.6	153.9	144.1	152.4	137.8	130.2	127.3
32	Industry, including energy	85.7	81.3	73.1	73.3	71.1	71.4	68.4	68.9
33	Manufacturing	78.6	74.2	67.1	66.8	64.5	65.0	62.8	63.8
34	Construction	209.8	208.0	204.2	208.8	204.2	200.8	203.6	203.1
35	Distrib. trade, repairs; transp.; accommod., food serv. activ.	261.9	264.8	253.4	247.3	254.2	262.0	261.9	258.7
36	Information and communication	62.3	62.2	58.5	55.7	60.0	57.4	57.8	61.2
37	Financial and insurance activities	52.9	52.2	54.1	55.5	54.4	51.4	54.4	53.5
38	Real estate activities	71.6	72.7	78.0	79.8	78.2	74.8	78.2	79.0
39	Prof., scientif., techn. activ.; admin., support service activ.	349.1	358.5	363.3	354.9	356.3	366.8	359.5	366.0
40	Public admin.; compulsory s.s.; education; human health	217.6	226.3	223.4	227.3	235.0	229.1	242.0	248.1
41	Other service activities	161.6	161.6	158.6	157.0	169.2	160.0	156.0	169.3
42	**Total self-employed**	**1 636.0**	**1 641.1**	**1 620.4**	**1 603.7**	**1 635.0**	**1 611.4**	**1 611.9**	**1 634.9**
	TOTAL EMPLOYMENT, MILLION HOURS, DOMESTIC CONCEPT								
43	Industry, including energy	3 934.7	4 028.9	4 114.9	4 160.5	4 114.3	4 089.6	4 060.4	3 978.0
44	Distrib. trade, repairs; transp.; accommod., food serv. activ.	7 954.7	8 062.3	8 162.5	8 340.1	8 413.7	8 489.1	8 689.5	8 741.1
45	Financial and insurance activities	1 748.3	1 782.6	1 834.1	1 805.0	1 867.1	1 878.9	1 861.7	1 884.8
46	Prof., scientif., techn. activ.; admin., support service activ.	3 033.3	3 078.3	3 101.9	3 159.2	3 184.5	3 195.2	3 244.6	3 290.0
47	Public admin.; compulsory s.s.; education; human health	6 409.6	6 528.8	6 556.3	6 614.5	6 641.6	6 648.6	6 815.9	6 939.3
48	**Total employment**	**28 893.6**	**29 459.1**	**29 866.0**	**30 421.8**	**30 739.8**	**30 846.7**	**31 202.7**	**31 454.8**
	EMPLOYEES, MILLION HOURS, DOMESTIC CONCEPT								
49	Industry, including energy	3 792.6	3 894.7	3 995.4	4 037.0	3 994.9	3 968.3	3 947.1	3 862.7
50	Distrib. trade, repairs; transp.; accommod., food serv. activ.	7 451.4	7 553.6	7 695.2	7 886.5	7 936.6	7 995.6	8 195.8	8 272.5
51	Financial and insurance activities	1 659.6	1 697.8	1 747.3	1 712.2	1 776.8	1 795.9	1 772.6	1 798.6
52	Prof., scientif., techn. activ.; admin., support service activ.	2 524.8	2 567.7	2 587.3	2 659.9	2 680.5	2 705.9	2 754.4	2 801.2
53	Public admin.; compulsory s.s.; education; human health	6 053.9	6 170.9	6 210.9	6 264.9	6 278.9	6 298.1	6 453.4	6 562.1
54	**Total employees**	**26 142.1**	**26 731.9**	**27 218.5**	**27 791.1**	**28 057.6**	**28 246.3**	**28 592.9**	**28 849.5**
	SELF-EMPLOYED, MILLION HOURS, DOMESTIC CONCEPT								
55	Industry, including energy	142.2	134.2	119.5	123.5	119.4	121.3	113.3	115.3
56	Distrib. trade, repairs; transp.; accommod., food serv. activ.	503.3	508.7	467.3	453.6	477.0	493.5	493.7	468.7
57	Financial and insurance activities	88.7	84.7	86.7	92.7	90.3	83.0	89.1	86.2
58	Prof., scientif., techn. activ.; admin., support service activ.	508.5	510.6	514.7	499.2	504.1	489.2	490.2	488.9
59	Public admin.; compulsory s.s.; education; human health	355.7	357.9	345.4	349.6	362.7	350.5	362.5	377.2
60	**Total self-employed**	**2 751.5**	**2 727.2**	**2 647.5**	**2 630.7**	**2 682.2**	**2 600.4**	**2 609.8**	**2 605.3**

Note: Detailed metadata:http://metalinks.oecd.org/nav1/20180308/4c13
Source: Statistics Canada.

CHILE

Table 1. Gross domestic product, expenditure approach

Million CLP

		2009	2010	2011	2012	2013	2014	2015	2016
	AT CURRENT PRICES								
1	**Final consumption expenditure**	68 838 063	78 539 423	87 891 950	95 613 553	103 336 792	112 815 464	121 782 172	129 722 595
2	Household	..	..	..	..	85 293 183	92 674 673	..	..
3	NPISH's					1 083 704	1 060 819		
4	Government	12 005 433	13 502 289	14 535 180	15 496 038	16 959 906	19 079 972	20 912 109	22 643 154
5	Individual	6 061 088 e	6 682 584 e	7 145 127 e	7 720 642 e	8 743 506	9 967 808	11 200 911	11 931 231 e
6	Collective	5 976 845 e	6 761 178 e	7 329 555 e	7 721 367 e	8 216 400	9 112 164	9 711 198	..
7	*of which: Actual individual consumption*	62 893 717 e	71 719 718 e	80 501 897 e	87 838 157 e	95 120 393	103 703 300	112 070 974	119 010 672 e
8	**Gross capital formation**	20 360 570	25 803 077	30 065 675	34 370 342	35 331 564	34 582 344	37 029 582	36 099 389
9	Gross fixed capital formation, total	21 716 921	24 035 476	28 207 442	32 325 359	34 199 263	35 444 691	37 481 694	38 737 411
10	Dwellings[1]	..	..	..	..	..	..	..	..
11	Other buildings and structures[1]	14 693 792	15 154 664	17 295 417	19 755 789	21 492 422	22 338 449	24 045 943	24 688 620
12	Transport equipment	..	..	..	..	..	..	..	..
13	Other machinery and equipment	..	..	..	..	..	..	..	..
14	Cultivated assets[1]	..	..	..	..	..	..	..	..
15	Intangible fixed assets	..	..	..	..	..	..	..	..
16	Changes in inventories, acquisitions less disposals of valuables	-1 356 351	1 767 601	1 858 233	2 044 983	1 132 301	-862 347	-452 112	-2 638 022
17	Changes in inventories	-1 356 351	1 767 601	1 858 233	2 044 983	1 132 301	-862 347	-452 112	-2 638 022
18	Acquisitions less disposals of valuables	..	..	..	..	..	..	..	..
19	**External balance of goods and services**	7 487 724	7 166 111	4 048 466	-36 553	-792 140	1 457 539	-174 948	1 405 463
20	Exports of goods and services	35 813 375	42 089 051	46 071 888	44 340 449	44 395 415	49 212 855	47 080 506	47 599 327
21	Exports of goods	30 898 533 e	36 268 890 e	39 522 896 e	37 989 505 e	37 976 347	42 811 030	40 522 905	41 001 989
22	Exports of services	5 012 855 e	6 050 088 e	6 719 299 e	6 352 639 e	6 419 068	6 401 825	6 557 601	6 597 338
23	Imports of goods and services	28 325 650	34 922 940	42 023 422	44 377 001	45 187 555	47 755 316	47 255 454	46 193 864
24	Imports of goods	23 733 013 e	29 865 587 e	36 074 493 e	38 780 848 e	39 153 596	41 419 393	40 790 395	39 650 805
25	Imports of services	4 676 262 e	5 126 876 e	6 070 070 e	5 548 298 e	6 033 960	6 335 923	6 465 059	6 543 058
26	**Statistical discrepancy**							..	..
27	**Gross domestic product**	96 686 357	111 508 611	122 006 090	129 947 342	137 876 216	148 855 347	158 636 806	167 227 448
	AT CONSTANT PRICES, REFERENCE YEAR 2010								
28	**Final consumption expenditure**	71 735 070	78 539 423	84 203 487	88 972 520	92 794 653	95 537 327	97 857 411	100 640 334
29	Household	..	..	..	..	..	..	..	..
30	NPISH's								
31	Government	13 014 376	13 502 289	13 833 256	14 346 566	14 755 056	15 406 099	16 101 806	16 928 642
32	Individual	..	..	..	..	..	..	..	..
33	Collective	..	..	..	..	..	..	..	..
34	*of which: Actual individual consumption*	65 540 561 e	71 719 718 e	77 123 564 e	81 737 179 e	85 416 468 e	87 820 727 e	90 054 030 e	92 329 896 e
35	**Gross capital formation**	20 253 343	25 803 077	29 958 444	33 471 668	34 033 636	30 610 452	30 785 003	29 416 218
36	Gross fixed capital formation, total	21 245 923	24 035 476	27 916 926	31 066 858	32 096 123	30 544 727	30 313 840	30 064 505
37	Dwellings[1]	..	..	..	..	..	..	..	..
38	Other buildings and structures[1]	14 608 617	15 154 664	16 732 652	18 099 145	19 146 976	18 604 661	19 105 351	18 894 878
39	Transport equipment	..	..	..	..	..	..	..	..
40	Other machinery and equipment	..	..	..	..	..	..	..	..
41	Cultivated assets[1]	..	..	..	..	..	..	..	..
42	Intangible fixed assets	..	..	..	..	..	..	..	..
43	Changes in inventories, acquisitions less disposals of valuables	..	..	..	..	..	..	..	..
44	Changes in inventories	..	..	..	..	..	..	..	..
45	Acquisitions less disposals of valuables	..	..	..	..	..	..	..	..
46	**External balance of goods and services**	13 366 545	7 166 111	4 160 881	2 233 446	2 852 796	5 856 192	6 123 896	6 700 080
47	Exports of goods and services	41 158 671	42 089 051	44 385 489	44 542 758	45 997 845	46 157 195	45 324 246	45 268 338
48	Exports of goods	36 406 801 e	36 268 890 e	37 773 750 e	38 562 993 e	40 117 824 e	40 813 526 e	40 097 478 e	39 983 740 e
49	Exports of services	5 113 998 e	6 050 088 e	6 859 244 e	6 185 807 e	6 107 557 e	5 627 286 e	5 506 862 e	5 554 621 e
50	Imports of goods and services	27 792 125	34 922 940	40 224 608	42 309 312	43 145 049	40 301 003	39 200 350	38 568 258
51	Imports of goods	23 230 378 e	29 865 587 e	34 384 619 e	36 754 519 e	37 322 229 e	34 923 217 e	34 091 298 e	33 570 554 e
52	Imports of services	4 645 406 e	5 126 876 e	5 920 856 e	5 607 739 e	5 884 604 e	5 434 083 e	5 161 716 e	5 050 814 e
53	**Statistical discrepancy (including chaining residual)**	-3 287	0	0	-61 672	-24 402	128 757	342 756	499 348
54	**Gross domestic product**	105 351 672	111 508 611	118 322 811	124 615 962	129 656 683	132 132 728	135 109 066	137 255 979

Note: Detailed metadata:http://metalinks.oecd.org/nav1/20180308/33de
1. *Other buildings and structures* and *Cultivated assets* are included in *Dwellings*.
Source: Central Bank of Chile.

CHILE

Table 2. Gross domestic product, output and income approach
ISIC Rev. 4

Million CLP

		2009	2010	2011	2012	2013	2014	2015	2016
	OUTPUT APPROACH AT CURRENT PRICES								
1	**Total gross value added at basic prices**	89 081 664	102 687 538	112 074 642	118 873 358	126 187 233	136 169 824	144 830 643	152 915 561
2	Agriculture, forestry and fishing	3 617 212	4 032 028	4 479 096	4 294 475	4 662 792	5 831 447	6 247 319	6 576 212
3	Industry, including energy	26 674 025	33 129 088	35 169 717	33 845 393	34 013 463	36 497 765	36 539 750	36 844 767
4	Manufacturing	10 863 341	12 012 289	13 434 738	14 041 414	15 325 681	16 610 700	18 103 188	18 357 835
5	Construction	6 624 926	6 674 016	7 168 010	8 438 326	8 995 309	9 413 094	10 404 697	11 009 660
6	Services	..	..	..	..	..	..	..	..
7	Distrib. trade, repairs; transp.; accommod., food serv. activ.	13 696 846	16 444 128	17 751 273	20 163 731	21 567 047	23 580 283	25 424 003	27 482 138
8	Information and communication	3 142 874	3 663 300	3 960 164	4 192 058	4 309 022	4 421 118	4 725 444	4 922 328
9	Financial and insurance activities	4 980 533	5 223 277	5 925 233	6 119 530	6 897 538	6 948 688	7 520 967	8 161 112
10	Real estate activities	6 274 063	7 084 456	8 002 165	8 853 564	9 805 197	10 709 726	11 958 278	12 947 997
11	Prof., scientif., techn. activ.; admin., support service activ.	9 599 492	10 291 992	12 039 953	13 705 281	14 727 501	15 539 793	16 757 119	17 335 684
12	Public admin.; compulsory s.s.; education; human health	14 471 691	16 145 251	17 579 032	19 261 000	21 209 364	23 227 910	25 253 066	27 635 663
13	Other service activities	..	..	..	..	..	..	..	..
14	FISIM (Financial Intermediation Services Indirectly Measured)	..	..	..	..	..	..	..	..
15	Gross value added at basic prices, excluding FISIM	89 081 664	102 687 538	112 074 642	118 873 358	126 187 233	136 169 824	144 830 643	152 915 561
16	**Taxes less subsidies on products**	7 604 693	8 821 073	9 931 448	11 073 984	11 688 983	12 685 524	13 806 164	14 311 886
17	Taxes on products	7 604 693	8 821 073	9 931 448	11 073 984	11 688 983	12 685 524	13 806 164	14 311 886
18	Subsidies on products	..	..	..	..	..	..	..	..
19	**Residual item**	..	..	..	..	..	..	..	..
20	**Gross domestic product at market prices**	96 686 357	111 508 611	122 006 090	129 947 342	137 876 216	148 855 347	158 636 806	167 227 448
	OUTPUT APPROACH AT CONSTANT PRICES (REF. YEAR 2010)								
21	**Total gross value added at basic prices**	97 604 051	102 687 538	108 690 286	114 276 954	118 862 872	121 132 068	123 934 416	125 906 859
22	Agriculture, forestry and fishing	3 996 475	4 032 028	4 489 844	4 350 364	4 369 840	4 372 548	4 623 179	4 787 880
23	Industry, including energy	31 971 405	33 129 088	33 617 705	35 053 160	36 562 117	37 032 307	37 186 413	36 667 622
24	Manufacturing	11 632 141	12 012 289	12 959 638	13 391 317	13 663 454	13 622 383	13 646 561	13 519 612
25	Construction	6 569 752	6 674 016	7 030 688	7 535 105	7 912 934	7 765 752	8 070 107	8 270 914
26	Services	..	..	..	..	..	..	..	..
27	Distrib. trade, repairs; transp.; accommod., food serv. activ.	14 652 205	16 444 128	18 326 678	19 578 905	20 810 257	21 405 608	21 997 273	22 641 231
28	Information and communication	3 207 257	3 663 300	3 826 454	4 030 587	4 116 907	4 218 588	4 475 268	4 612 075
29	Financial and insurance activities	4 897 772	5 223 277	5 748 746	6 272 370	6 701 178	6 908 861	7 280 137	7 551 309
30	Real estate activities	6 906 742	7 084 456	7 411 858	7 643 679	7 930 007	8 263 304	8 448 147	8 673 199
31	Prof., scientif., techn. activ.; admin., support service activ.	9 898 243	10 291 992	11 189 213	11 842 598	12 092 987	12 173 921	12 323 845	12 104 612
32	Public admin.; compulsory s.s.; education; human health	15 564 317	16 145 251	17 049 098	17 986 514	18 428 563	19 026 497	19 493 439	20 376 513
33	Other service activities	..	..	..	..	..	..	..	..
34	FISIM (Financial Intermediation Services Indirectly Measured)	..	..	..	..	..	..	..	..
35	Gross value added at basic prices, excluding FISIM	97 604 051	102 687 538	108 690 286	114 276 954	118 862 872	121 132 068	123 934 416	125 906 859
36	**Taxes less subsidies on products**	7 786 059	8 821 073	9 632 526	10 339 027	10 792 776	10 999 592	11 175 422	11 350 072
37	Taxes on products	7 786 059	8 821 073	9 632 526	10 339 027	10 792 776	10 999 592	11 175 422	11 350 072
38	Subsidies on products	..	..	..	..	..	..	..	..
39	**Residual item**	-38 438	0	0	-20	1 034	1 068	-772	-952
40	**Gross domestic product at market prices**	105 351 672	111 508 611	118 322 811	124 615 962	129 656 683	132 132 728	135 109 066	137 255 979
	INCOME APPROACH								
41	**Compensation of employees**	..	..	..	..	52 887 073	56 981 835	61 112 726	..
42	Agriculture, forestry and fishing					1 652 305	1 781 778	2 047 332	
43	Industry, including energy	..	..	..	..	7 907 105	8 297 364	8 524 292	
44	Manufacturing					4 910 620	5 129 007	5 350 974	
45	Construction				..	5 085 809	5 341 462	5 717 131	
46	Distrib. trade, repairs; transp.; accommod., food serv. activ.					10 321 685	11 282 817	..	
47	Information and communication					1 507 442	1 584 201	..	
48	Financial and insurance activities				..	2 859 139	3 115 937	..	
49	Real estate activities				..	378 526	424 773	..	
50	Prof., scientif., techn. activ.; admin., support service activ.					6 476 641	6 807 572	..	
51	Public admin.; compulsory s.s.; education; human health					14 478 216	16 029 528	..	
52	Other service activities				..	2 220 203	2 316 403	..	
53	**Wages and salaries**	..	..	..	..	..	..	..	..
54	Agriculture, forestry and fishing					..	..		
55	Industry, including energy					..	..		
56	Manufacturing					..	..		
57	Construction					..	..		
58	Distrib. trade, repairs; transp.; accommod., food serv. activ.					..	..		
59	Information and communication					..	..		
60	Financial and insurance activities					..	..		
61	Real estate activities								
62	Prof., scientif., techn. activ.; admin., support service activ.					..	..		
63	Public admin.; compulsory s.s.; education; human health								
64	Other service activities				..	..	..		
65	**Gross operating surplus and mixed income**	..	..	..	..	70 217 563	75 719 120	79 952 563	..
66	**Taxes less subsidies on production and imports**	..	..	..	..	14 771 579	16 154 392	17 571 517	..
67	Taxes on production and imports					..	..	..	
68	Subsidies on production and imports					..	..	..	
69	**Residual item**								..
70	**Gross domestic product**	96 686 357	111 508 611	122 006 090	129 947 342	137 876 216	148 855 347	158 636 806	..

Note: Detailed metadata:http://metalinks.oecd.org/nav1/20180308/33de
Source: Central Bank of Chile.

Table 3. Disposable income, saving and net lending / net borrowing

Million CLP

		2009	2010	2011	2012	2013	2014	2015	2016
	DISPOSABLE INCOME								
1	**Gross domestic product**	96 686 357	111 508 611	122 006 090	129 947 342	137 876 216	148 855 347	158 636 806	..
2	Net primary incomes from the rest of the world	-6 655 338	-7 920 018	-7 464 323	-6 244 848	-6 117 684	-5 302 779	-4 270 809	..
3	Primary incomes receivable from the rest of the world	3 220 911	4 443 756	3 776 815	4 032 578	4 854 071	5 910 077	5 683 800	..
4	Primary incomes payable to the rest of the world	9 876 249	12 363 773	11 241 138	10 277 427	10 971 755	11 212 856	9 954 609	..
5	**Gross national income at market prices**	90 031 018	103 588 593	114 541 768	123 702 494	131 758 532	143 552 568	154 365 997	..
6	Consumption of fixed capital	..	..	..	..	..	..	..	..
7	**Net national income at market prices**	90 031 018	103 588 593	114 541 768	123 702 494	131 758 532	143 552 568	154 365 997	..
8	Net current transfers from the rest of the world	911 130	2 310 003	1 425 054	1 057 970	1 163 656	1 274 779	1 296 425	..
9	Current transfers receivable from the rest of the world	1 410 232	2 909 355	2 100 394	1 902 992	2 087 260	2 319 542	2 494 486	..
10	Current transfers payable to the rest of the world	499 102	599 352	675 339	845 022	923 605	1 044 763	1 198 062	..
11	**Net national disposable income**	90 942 148	105 898 596	115 966 822	124 760 464	132 922 187	144 827 347	155 662 422	..
	SAVING AND NET LENDING / NET BORROWING								
12	**Net national disposable income**	90 942 148	105 898 596	115 966 822	124 760 464	132 922 187	144 827 347	155 662 422	..
13	Final consumption expenditures	68 838 063	78 539 423	87 891 950	95 613 553	103 336 792	112 815 464	121 782 172	..
14	Adj. for change in net equity of households in pension funds	..	..	..	..	..	..	..	..
15	**Saving, net**	22 104 085	27 359 173	28 074 872	29 146 911	29 585 395	32 011 884	33 880 250	..
16	Net capital transfers from the rest of the world	8 051	3 238 655	5 774	5 697	5 610	5 845	437 261	..
17	Capital transfers receivable from the rest of the world	..	..	..	..	..	..	..	..
18	Capital transfers payable to the rest of the world	..	..	..	..	..	..	..	..
19	Gross capital formation	20 360 570	25 803 077	30 065 675	34 370 342	35 331 564	34 582 344	37 029 582	..
20	Acquisitions less disposals of non-financial non-produced assets	..	..	..	..	..	..	..	..
21	Consumption of fixed capital	..	..	..	..	..	..	..	..
22	**Net lending / net borrowing**	1 751 567	4 794 751	-1 985 029	-5 217 734	-5 740 558	-2 564 616	-2 712 072	..
	REAL DISPOSABLE INCOME								
23	**Gross domestic product at constant prices, reference year 2010**	105 351 672	111 508 611	118 322 811	124 615 962	129 656 683	132 132 728	135 109 066	137 255 979
24	Trading gain or loss	-5 768 568 e	0 e	-242 688 e	-2 258 350 e	-3 578 137 e	-4 537 185 e	-6 387 424 e	..
25	**Real gross domestic income**	99 583 104 e	111 508 611 e	118 080 123 e	122 357 611 e	126 078 546 e	127 595 543 e	128 721 642 e	..
26	Net real primary incomes from the rest of the world	-6 854 734 e	-7 920 018 e	-7 224 132 e	-5 880 111 e	-5 594 212 e	-4 545 426 e	-3 465 435 e	..
27	Real primary incomes receivable from the rest of the world	3 317 410 e	4 443 756 e	3 655 283 e	3 797 051 e	4 438 722 e	5 065 988 e	4 611 969 e	..
28	Real primary incomes payable to the rest of the world	10 172 144 e	12 363 773 e	10 879 415 e	9 677 161 e	10 032 934 e	9 611 414 e	8 077 404 e	..
29	**Real gross national income at market prices**	92 728 370 e	103 588 593 e	110 855 991 e	116 477 501 e	120 484 334 e	123 050 117 e	125 256 206 e	..
30	Net real current transfers from the rest of the world	938 427 e	2 310 003 e	1 379 198 e	996 178 e	1 064 085 e	1 092 713 e	1 051 950 e	..
31	Real current transfers receivable from the rest of the world	1 452 482 e	2 909 355 e	2 032 806 e	1 791 846 e	1 908 659 e	1 988 261 e	2 024 085 e	..
32	Real current transfers payable to the rest of the world	514 055 e	599 352 e	653 608 e	795 667 e	844 574 e	895 548 e	972 135 e	..
33	**Real gross national disposable income**	93 666 797 e	105 898 596 e	112 235 189 e	117 473 679 e	121 548 419 e	124 142 830 e	126 308 156 e	..
34	Consumption of fixed capital at constant prices	..	..	..	..	..	..	..	..
35	**Real net national income at market prices**	92 728 370 e	103 588 593 e	110 855 991 e	116 477 501 e	120 484 334 e	123 050 117 e	125 256 206 e	..
36	**Real net national disposable income**	93 666 797 e	105 898 596 e	112 235 189 e	117 473 679 e	121 548 419 e	124 142 830 e	126 308 156 e	..

Note: Detailed metadata:http://metalinks.oecd.org/nav1/20180308/7e64
Source: Central Bank of Chile.

Table 4. Population and employment (persons) and employment (hours worked) by industry
ISIC Rev. 4

		2009	2010	2011	2012	2013	2014	2015	2016
	POPULATION, THOUSAND PERSONS, NATIONAL CONCEPT								
1	**Total population**	**16 927.8**	**17 093.3**	**17 267.3**	**17 450.0**	**17 639.7**	**17 836.2**	**18 044.7**	**18 278.0 e**
2	Economically active population	7 299.4	7 762.6	8 060.9	8 150.0	8 277.3	8 442.7	8 559.6	..
3	Unemployed persons	707.2	632.0	573.8	524.2	491.0	539.5	531.8	..
4	Total employment	6 592.2	7 130.6	7 487.1	7 625.8	7 786.3	7 903.2	8 027.8	..
5	Employees	5 060.0	5 680.5	5 957.7	6 128.6	6 245.8	6 295.8	6 398.1	..
6	Self-employed	1 532.2	1 450.1	1 529.4	1 497.2	1 540.5	1 607.4	1 629.6	..
	TOTAL EMPLOYMENT, THOUSAND PERSONS, DOMESTIC CONCEPT								
7	Agriculture, forestry and fishing	..	..	..	..	728.3	727.3	737.0	..
8	Industry, including energy	..	..	..	..	1 213.1	1 216.1	1 211.9	..
9	Manufacturing	..	..	..	..	886.2	893.7	896.0	..
10	Construction	..	..	..	..	673.4	667.2	691.7	..
11	Distrib. trade, repairs; transp.; accommod., food serv. activ.	..	..	..	..	2 307.0	2 311.6	2 373.4	..
12	Information and communication	..	..	..	..	143.4	151.1	137.2	..
13	Financial and insurance activities	..	..	..	..	173.3	171.3	172.6	..
14	Real estate activities	..	..	..	..	62.6	66.1	66.0	..
15	Prof., scientif., techn. activ.; admin., support service activ.	..	..	..	..	399.7	436.4	420.6	..
16	Public admin.; compulsory s.s.; education; human health	..	..	..	..	1 380.2	1 464.3	1 545.6	..
17	Other service activities	..	..	..	..	705.5	691.8	671.6	..
18	**Total employment**	**6 496.6**	**6 927.8**	**7 266.7**	**7 375.1**	**7 786.3 |**	**7 903.2**	**8 027.8**	**..**
	EMPLOYEES, THOUSAND PERSONS, DOMESTIC CONCEPT								
19	Agriculture, forestry and fishing	..	..	..	..	526.3	524.8	541.7	..
20	Industry, including energy	..	..	..	..	1 035.6	1 015.5	1 010.1	..
21	Manufacturing	..	..	..	..	719.6	703.7	705.3	..
22	Construction	..	..	..	..	530.4	515.0	521.1	..
23	Distrib. trade, repairs; transp.; accommod., food serv. activ.	..	..	..	..	1 666.4	1 662.0	1 715.4	..
24	Information and communication	..	..	..	..	130.5	139.4	126.7	..
25	Financial and insurance activities	..	..	..	..	167.3	166.7	168.8	..
26	Real estate activities	..	..	..	..	55.4	57.4	54.3	..
27	Prof., scientif., techn. activ.; admin., support service activ.	..	..	..	..	283.4	280.4	275.1	..
28	Public admin.; compulsory s.s.; education; human health	..	..	..	..	1 339.2	1 398.8	1 462.3	..
29	Other service activities	..	..	..	..	511.2	535.8	522.5	..
30	**Total employees**	**..**	**5 483.4**	**5 743.8**	**5 882.5**	**6 245.8 |**	**6 295.8**	**6 398.1**	**..**
	SELF-EMPLOYED, THOUSAND PERSONS, DOMESTIC CONCEPT								
31	Agriculture, forestry and fishing	..	..	..	..	202.0	202.5	195.3	..
32	Industry, including energy	..	..	..	..	177.4	200.6	201.8	..
33	Manufacturing	..	..	..	..	166.6	190.0	190.7	..
34	Construction	..	..	..	..	143.0	152.2	170.6	..
35	Distrib. trade, repairs; transp.; accommod., food serv. activ.	..	..	..	..	640.6	649.6	658.0	..
36	Information and communication	..	..	..	..	12.9	11.7	10.4	..
37	Financial and insurance activities	..	..	..	..	5.9	4.6	3.8	..
38	Real estate activities	..	..	..	..	7.2	8.7	11.7	..
39	Prof., scientif., techn. activ.; admin., support service activ.	..	..	..	..	116.3	156.0	145.5	..
40	Public admin.; compulsory s.s.; education; human health	..	..	..	..	41.0	65.5	83.3	..
41	Other service activities	..	..	..	..	194.3	156.0	149.2	..
42	**Total self-employed**	**..**	**1 444.5**	**1 522.9**	**1 492.6**	**1 540.5 |**	**1 607.4**	**1 629.6**	**..**
	TOTAL EMPLOYMENT, MILLION HOURS, DOMESTIC CONCEPT								
43	Industry, including energy	..	..	..	..	..	..	..	..
44	Distrib. trade, repairs; transp.; accommod., food serv. activ.	..	..	..	..	..	..	..	..
45	Financial and insurance activities	..	..	..	..	..	..	..	..
46	Prof., scientif., techn. activ.; admin., support service activ.	..	..	..	..	..	..	..	..
47	Public admin.; compulsory s.s.; education; human health	..	..	..	..	..	..	..	..
48	**Total employment**	**..**	**..**	**..**	**..**	**..**	**..**	**..**	**..**
	EMPLOYEES, MILLION HOURS, DOMESTIC CONCEPT								
49	Industry, including energy	..	..	..	..	..	..	..	..
50	Distrib. trade, repairs; transp.; accommod., food serv. activ.	..	..	..	..	..	..	..	..
51	Financial and insurance activities	..	..	..	..	..	..	..	..
52	Prof., scientif., techn. activ.; admin., support service activ.	..	..	..	..	..	..	..	..
53	Public admin.; compulsory s.s.; education; human health	..	..	..	..	..	..	..	..
54	**Total employees**	**..**	**..**	**..**	**..**	**..**	**..**	**..**	**..**
	SELF-EMPLOYED, MILLION HOURS, DOMESTIC CONCEPT								
55	Industry, including energy	..	..	..	..	..	..	..	..
56	Distrib. trade, repairs; transp.; accommod., food serv. activ.	..	..	..	..	..	..	..	..
57	Financial and insurance activities	..	..	..	..	..	..	..	..
58	Prof., scientif., techn. activ.; admin., support service activ.	..	..	..	..	..	..	..	..
59	Public admin.; compulsory s.s.; education; human health	..	..	..	..	..	..	..	..
60	**Total self-employed**	**..**	**..**	**..**	**..**	**..**	**..**	**..**	**..**

Note: Detailed metadata:http://metalinks.oecd.org/nav1/20180308/9889
Source: Central Bank of Chile.

CZECH REPUBLIC

Table 1. Gross domestic product, expenditure approach

Million CZK

		2009	2010	2011	2012	2013	2014	2015	2016
	AT CURRENT PRICES								
1	**Final consumption expenditure**	**2 735 997**	**2 765 219**	**2 791 888**	**2 801 813**	**2 851 036**	**2 922 816**	**3 035 307**	**3 158 777**
2	Household	1 883 654	1 912 766	1 951 963	1 970 389	1 996 648	2 044 283	2 125 028	2 213 886
3	NPISH's	27 044	27 140	26 764	27 346	28 384	29 378	27 149	27 760
4	Government	825 299	825 313	813 161	804 078	826 004	849 155	883 130	917 131
5	Individual	412 889	415 709	426 611	429 178	437 805	454 282	467 721	484 765
6	Collective	412 410	409 604	386 550	374 900	388 199	394 873	415 409	432 366
7	*of which: Actual individual consumption*	2 323 587	2 355 615	2 405 338	2 426 913	2 462 837	2 527 943	2 619 898	2 726 411
8	**Gross capital formation**	**1 042 076**	**1 074 727**	**1 087 401**	**1 063 114**	**1 010 887**	**1 116 425**	**1 284 787**	**1 257 260**
9	Gross fixed capital formation, total	1 063 294	1 066 185	1 067 017	1 051 943	1 027 089	1 084 075	1 216 306	1 191 539
10	Dwellings	148 149	160 459	148 039	149 389	133 017	144 939	164 331	174 919
11	Other buildings and structures	349 374	330 571	321 310	304 377	293 878	289 958	318 224	284 736
12	Transport equipment	105 599	112 221	105 401	97 032	106 055	112 398	117 035	133 093
13	Other machinery and equipment	258 751	266 319	280 788	277 472	270 845	302 619	339 776	317 055
14	Cultivated assets	3 878	3 622	3 604	2 034	2 915	3 362	3 359	3 411
15	Intangible fixed assets	130 989	118 975	132 449	147 559	146 393	153 461	177 604	185 087
16	Changes in inventories, acquisitions less disposals of valuables	-21 218	8 542	20 384	11 171	-16 202	32 350	68 481	65 721
17	Changes in inventories	-25 083	5 001	16 736	5 161	-21 957	26 535	62 955	60 086
18	Acquisitions less disposals of valuables	3 865	3 541	3 648	6 010	5 755	5 815	5 526	5 635
19	**External balance of goods and services**	**152 336**	**122 518**	**154 466**	**194 985**	**236 205**	**274 548**	**275 689**	**357 203**
20	Exports of goods and services	2 306 533	2 616 396	2 876 356	3 092 438	3 150 270	3 560 847	3 724 850	3 796 688
21	Exports of goods	1 916 601	2 198 394	2 440 415	2 624 117	2 681 419	3 039 813	3 153 079	3 203 235
22	Exports of services	389 932	418 002	435 941	468 321	468 851	521 034	571 771	593 453
23	Imports of goods and services	2 154 197	2 493 878	2 721 890	2 897 453	2 914 065	3 286 299	3 449 161	3 439 485
24	Imports of goods	1 846 169	2 153 658	2 362 118	2 500 318	2 514 444	2 819 864	2 965 375	2 955 332
25	Imports of services	308 028	340 220	359 772	397 135	399 621	466 435	483 786	484 153
26	**Statistical discrepancy**	**0**	**0**	**0**	**0**	**0**	**0**	**0**	**0**
27	**Gross domestic product**	**3 930 409**	**3 962 464**	**4 033 755**	**4 059 912**	**4 098 128**	**4 313 789**	**4 595 783**	**4 773 240**
	AT CONSTANT PRICES, REFERENCE YEAR 2010								
28	**Final consumption expenditure**	**2 741 341**	**2 765 219**	**2 743 834**	**2 704 547**	**2 734 118**	**2 777 475**	**2 865 773**	**2 955 606**
29	Household	1 892 272	1 912 766	1 918 031	1 893 966	1 902 780	1 936 368	2 009 768	2 082 681
30	NPISH's	27 459	27 140	26 781	27 278	28 377	29 532	28 644	29 096
31	Government	821 586	825 313	799 022	783 319	803 156	811 723	827 316	843 826
32	Individual	413 452	415 709	407 006	402 970	411 756	421 112	424 342	431 595
33	Collective	408 129	409 604	392 016	380 099	391 257	390 112	402 785	412 120
34	*of which: Actual individual consumption*	2 333 182	2 355 615	2 351 818	2 324 222	2 343 019	2 387 114	2 462 742	2 543 131
35	**Gross capital formation**	**1 031 068**	**1 074 727**	**1 093 873**	**1 050 686**	**997 152**	**1 082 516**	**1 222 858**	**1 195 067**
36	Gross fixed capital formation, total	1 052 018	1 066 185	1 075 395	1 042 149	1 016 155	1 056 049	1 163 662	1 136 909
37	Dwellings	145 509	160 459	150 933	155 070	143 195	157 777	193 289	210 782
38	Other buildings and structures	347 015	330 571	319 848	302 200	291 273	282 019	291 443	252 347
39	Transport equipment	99 768	112 221	108 254	91 915	99 932	103 894	113 634	130 847
40	Other machinery and equipment	258 783	266 319	285 464	275 753	266 526	287 855	310 392	290 115
41	Cultivated assets	4 197	3 622	3 001	1 645	2 279	2 544	2 773	2 931
42	Intangible fixed assets	133 073	118 975	130 628	141 488	135 757	142 228	162 458	167 596
43	Changes in inventories, acquisitions less disposals of valuables	..	..	..	..	..	..	..	..
44	Changes in inventories	..	..	..	..	..	..	..	..
45	Acquisitions less disposals of valuables	..	..	..	..	..	..	..	..
46	**External balance of goods and services**	**107 677**	**122 518**	**195 203**	**246 603**	**250 396**	**233 675**	**224 714**	**272 843**
47	Exports of goods and services	2 281 787	2 616 396	2 856 208	2 978 430	2 983 998	3 242 125	3 437 211	3 593 066
48	Exports of goods	1 896 364	2 198 394	2 421 530	2 522 792	2 538 141	2 772 417	2 916 586	3 051 407
49	Exports of services	385 400	418 002	434 678	455 649	445 741	469 517	520 152	541 207
50	Imports of goods and services	2 174 110	2 493 878	2 661 005	2 731 827	2 733 602	3 008 450	3 212 497	3 320 223
51	Imports of goods	1 874 945	2 153 658	2 295 986	2 341 401	2 354 109	2 589 040	2 775 910	2 878 765
52	Imports of services	299 052	340 220	365 019	391 113	379 602	419 557	436 972	442 199
53	**Statistical discrepancy (including chaining residual)**	**-5 703**	**0**	**0**	**-1 183**	**-363**	**-4 266**	**-6 829**	**-5 318**
54	**Gross domestic product**	**3 874 383**	**3 962 464**	**4 032 910**	**4 000 653**	**3 981 303**	**4 089 400**	**4 306 516**	**4 418 198**

Note: Detailed metadata:http://metalinks.oecd.org/nav1/20180308/5eeb
Source: Czech Statistical Office via Eurostat.

Table 2. Gross domestic product, output and income approach
ISIC Rev. 4

Million CZK

		2009	2010	2011	2012	2013	2014	2015	2016
	OUTPUT APPROACH AT CURRENT PRICES								
1	**Total gross value added at basic prices**	**3 554 148**	**3 583 122**	**3 640 335**	**3 648 512**	**3 668 332**	**3 898 599**	**4 135 579**	**4 292 397**
2	Agriculture, forestry and fishing	64 549	60 210	86 632	95 396	98 504	106 720	102 390	105 308
3	Industry, including energy	1 067 588	1 071 791	1 122 892	1 132 814	1 135 373	1 262 666	1 329 933	1 379 763
4	Manufacturing	812 444	840 039	889 814	902 251	911 016	1 043 300	1 108 858	1 162 392
5	Construction	239 153	246 085	224 714	213 612	210 879	214 628	232 259	234 341
6	Services	..	..	..	..	..	..	..	..
7	Distrib. trade, repairs; transp.; accommod., food serv. activ.	646 335	668 153	662 448	666 399	658 940	694 386	764 214	799 843
8	Information and communication	188 903	183 851	187 848	186 241	184 493	195 666	212 187	220 588
9	Financial and insurance activities	158 919	169 072	168 816	164 197	170 694	168 093	177 087	181 421
10	Real estate activities	321 487	322 291	320 048	319 377	321 564	333 741	348 276	360 797
11	Prof., scientif., techn. activ.; admin., support service activ.	243 788	237 102	238 413	237 032	246 524	253 363	271 677	285 440
12	Public admin.; compulsory s.s.; education; human health	541 783	543 448	543 625	550 579	559 227	583 938	606 243	631 304
13	Other service activities	81 643	81 119	84 899	82 865	82 134	85 398	91 313	93 592
14	**FISIM (Financial Intermediation Services Indirectly Measured)**	..	..	..	..	..	..	..	..
15	Gross value added at basic prices, excluding FISIM	3 554 148	3 583 122	3 640 335	3 648 512	3 668 332	3 898 599	4 135 579	4 292 397
16	**Taxes less subsidies on products**	**376 261**	**379 342**	**393 420**	**411 400**	**429 796**	**415 190**	**460 204**	**480 843**
17	Taxes on products	414 592	427 869	464 120	485 181	507 076	496 861	546 676	576 514
18	Subsidies on products	38 331	48 527	70 700	73 781	77 280	81 671	86 472	95 671
19	**Residual item**	**0**	**0**	**0**	**0**	**0**	**0**	**0**	**0**
20	**Gross domestic product at market prices**	**3 930 409**	**3 962 464**	**4 033 755**	**4 059 912**	**4 098 128**	**4 313 789**	**4 595 783**	**4 773 240**
	OUTPUT APPROACH AT CONSTANT PRICES (REF. YEAR 2010)								
21	**Total gross value added at basic prices**	**3 484 260**	**3 583 122**	**3 655 028**	**3 624 215**	**3 606 414**	**3 729 050**	**3 905 248**	**4 004 236**
22	Agriculture, forestry and fishing	71 771	60 210	61 372	63 900	67 368	67 368	71 078	77 731
23	Industry, including energy	1 006 859	1 071 791	1 142 177	1 110 025	1 060 103	1 114 496	1 160 548	1 219 103
24	Manufacturing	754 972	840 039	924 958	895 200	870 703	924 555	972 674	1 040 898
25	Construction	236 651	246 085	229 718	222 536	225 395	229 821	238 827	233 195
26	Services	..	..	..	..	..	..	..	..
27	Distrib. trade, repairs; transp.; accommod., food serv. activ.	641 571	668 153	672 679	672 016	668 290	690 941	743 824	746 036
28	Information and communication	184 402	183 851	187 263	182 843	188 944	204 999	224 865	229 220
29	Financial and insurance activities	168 638	169 072	173 576	174 368	190 465	187 786	197 716	211 180
30	Real estate activities	319 110	322 291	328 681	334 140	340 642	351 481	360 387	360 638
31	Prof., scientif., techn. activ.; admin., support service activ.	238 726	237 102	241 694	244 324	251 613	254 750	273 299	282 279
32	Public admin.; compulsory s.s.; education; human health	537 105	543 448	533 143	534 736	537 242	541 343	544 700	550 346
33	Other service activities	82 852	81 119	84 725	83 887	82 943	84 171	90 305	90 033
34	**FISIM (Financial Intermediation Services Indirectly Measured)**	..	..	..	..	..	..	..	..
35	Gross value added at basic prices, excluding FISIM	3 484 260	3 583 122	3 655 028	3 624 215	3 606 414	3 729 050	3 905 248	4 004 236
36	**Taxes less subsidies on products**	**391 291**	**379 342**	**377 882**	**376 369**	**374 799**	**363 051**	**402 243**	**414 792**
37	Taxes on products	438 658	427 869	432 826	424 947	418 976	408 773	447 080	461 032
38	Subsidies on products	46 943	48 527	54 944	49 602	46 173	46 844	47 843	49 339
39	**Residual item**	**-1 168**	**0**	**0**	**69**	**90**	**-2 701**	**-975**	**-830**
40	**Gross domestic product at market prices**	**3 874 383**	**3 962 464**	**4 032 910**	**4 000 653**	**3 981 303**	**4 089 400**	**4 306 516**	**4 418 198**
	INCOME APPROACH								
41	**Compensation of employees**	**1 568 402**	**1 591 106**	**1 626 392**	**1 664 701**	**1 676 183**	**1 734 660**	**1 821 089**	**1 928 612**
42	Agriculture, forestry and fishing	35 733	33 314	34 492	36 113	37 390	38 683	38 650	39 563
43	Industry, including energy	464 988	466 804	499 390	513 820	517 171	540 243	573 478	606 029
44	Manufacturing	406 708	409 204	437 150	450 215	454 084	476 514	510 592	542 776
45	Construction	102 209	102 366	98 866	95 828	88 993	86 820	89 992	92 469
46	Distrib. trade, repairs; transp.; accommod., food serv. activ.	318 350	328 027	334 722	337 266	337 534	346 584	365 290	391 392
47	Information and communication	72 005	71 847	71 991	74 892	77 572	82 153	86 397	92 949
48	Financial and insurance activities	52 174	53 243	56 253	61 096	59 301	62 133	60 749	63 265
49	Real estate activities	17 254	17 466	16 125	18 347	19 647	19 268	19 590	20 885
50	Prof., scientif., techn. activ.; admin., support service activ.	114 353	120 372	118 168	122 638	124 271	127 749	135 630	144 320
51	Public admin.; compulsory s.s.; education; human health	357 859	362 873	360 497	368 239	376 697	392 343	410 680	434 865
52	Other service activities	33 477	34 794	35 888	36 462	37 607	38 684	40 633	42 875
53	**Wages and salaries**	**1 201 811**	**1 211 077**	**1 236 804**	**1 268 726**	**1 274 608**	**1 320 787**	**1 384 461**	**1 464 310**
54	Agriculture, forestry and fishing	27 582	25 502	26 393	27 966	28 898	29 777	29 803	30 530
55	Industry, including energy	352 886	352 253	378 119	389 061	390 655	408 984	433 387	459 608
56	Manufacturing	310 258	309 546	331 967	341 626	343 830	361 186	386 232	411 991
57	Construction	79 822	79 317	75 979	74 234	69 182	67 382	69 587	70 918
58	Distrib. trade, repairs; transp.; accommod., food serv. activ.	247 137	252 815	257 077	260 535	260 285	267 708	281 420	299 247
59	Information and communication	55 295	54 728	55 043	57 348	58 956	62 386	65 751	70 292
60	Financial and insurance activities	39 759	40 397	42 142	46 341	44 797	47 234	45 809	47 987
61	Real estate activities	13 319	13 356	12 214	14 056	15 003	14 715	14 984	15 966
62	Prof., scientif., techn. activ.; admin., support service activ.	87 952	91 457	89 911	93 578	94 393	97 142	103 163	109 797
63	Public admin.; compulsory s.s.; education; human health	272 112	274 498	272 323	277 509	283 513	295 469	308 966	326 717
64	Other service activities	25 947	26 754	27 603	28 098	28 926	29 990	31 591	33 248
65	**Gross operating surplus and mixed income**	**2 024 035**	**2 020 881**	**2 038 281**	**2 009 824**	**2 020 192**	**2 197 703**	**2 340 637**	**2 389 996**
66	**Taxes less subsidies on production and imports**	**337 972**	**350 477**	**369 082**	**385 387**	**401 753**	**381 426**	**434 057**	**454 632**
67	Taxes on production and imports	430 632	448 009	488 313	508 196	527 830	518 181	570 653	601 429
68	Subsidies on production and imports	92 660	97 532	119 231	122 809	126 077	136 755	136 596	146 797
69	**Residual item**	..	..	..	..	..	..	..	..
70	**Gross domestic product**	**3 930 409**	**3 962 464**	**4 033 755**	**4 059 912**	**4 098 128**	**4 313 789**	**4 595 783**	**4 773 240**

Note: Detailed metadata:http://metalinks.oecd.org/nav1/20180308/1783
Source: Czech Statistical Office via Eurostat.

CZECH REPUBLIC

Table 3. Disposable income, saving and net lending / net borrowing

Million CZK

		2009	2010	2011	2012	2013	2014	2015	2016
	DISPOSABLE INCOME								
1	**Gross domestic product**	3 930 409	3 962 464	4 033 755	4 059 912	4 098 128	4 313 789	4 595 783	4 773 240
2	Net primary incomes from the rest of the world	-277 012	-292 552	-305 473	-251 570	-244 607	-291 511	-310 421	-305 477
3	Primary incomes receivable from the rest of the world	117 295	118 164	128 688	155 760	142 004	162 937	184 369	195 183
4	Primary incomes payable to the rest of the world	394 307	410 716	434 161	407 330	386 611	454 448	494 790	500 660
5	**Gross national income at market prices**	3 653 397	3 669 912	3 728 282	3 808 342	3 853 521	4 022 278	4 285 362	4 467 763
6	Consumption of fixed capital	840 987	849 695	863 985	879 573	906 134	938 874	968 777	995 355
7	**Net national income at market prices**	2 812 410	2 820 217	2 864 297	2 928 769	2 947 387	3 083 404	3 316 585	3 472 408
8	Net current transfers from the rest of the world	-27 954	..	..	..	..	-36 647	-36 866	-58 021
9	Current transfers receivable from the rest of the world	42 143	..	..	..	..	62 246	71 137	57 216
10	Current transfers payable to the rest of the world	70 097	..	..	..	..	98 893	108 003	115 237
11	**Net national disposable income**	2 784 456	2 789 827	2 828 681	2 894 434	2 911 306	3 046 757	3 279 719	3 414 387
	SAVING AND NET LENDING / NET BORROWING								
12	**Net national disposable income**	2 784 456	2 789 827	2 828 681	2 894 434	2 911 306	3 046 757	3 279 719	3 414 387
13	Final consumption expenditures	2 735 997	2 765 219	2 791 888	2 801 813	2 851 036	2 922 816	3 035 307	3 158 777
14	Adj. for change in net equity of households in pension funds	0	0	0	0	0	0	0	0
15	**Saving, net**	48 459	24 608	36 793	92 621	60 270	123 941	244 412	255 610
16	Net capital transfers from the rest of the world	65 076	69 204	70 419	45 116	85 219	72 906	128 205	26 355
17	Capital transfers receivable from the rest of the world	65 859	72 929	71 171	60 943	91 582	81 396	134 365	30 942
18	Capital transfers payable to the rest of the world	783	3 725	752	15 827	6 363	8 490	6 160	4 587
19	Gross capital formation	1 042 076	1 074 727	1 087 401	1 063 114	1 010 887	1 116 425	1 284 787	1 257 260
20	Acquisitions less disposals of non-financial non-produced assets	-15 205	-8 051	-112	3 185	-4 412	-1 990	-830	-1 291
21	Consumption of fixed capital	840 987	849 695	863 985	879 573	906 134	938 874	968 777	995 355
22	**Net lending / net borrowing**	-72 349	-123 169	-116 092	-48 989	45 148	21 286	57 437	21 351
	REAL DISPOSABLE INCOME								
23	**Gross domestic product at constant prices, reference year 2010**	3 865 766	3 953 651	4 023 940	3 991 755	3 972 448	4 080 305	4 296 938	4 408 371
24	Trading gain or loss	49 810	0	-42 393	-46 591	-11 318	42 240	41 605	67 144
25	**Real gross domestic income**	3 924 193	3 962 464	3 990 517	3 945 164	3 961 130	4 122 545	4 348 121	4 485 342
26	Net real primary incomes from the rest of the world	-276 574	-292 552	-302 199	-244 460	-236 430	-278 587	-293 693	-287 052
27	Real primary incomes receivable from the rest of the world	117 109	118 164	127 309	151 358	137 257	155 713	174 434	183 411
28	Real primary incomes payable to the rest of the world	393 683	410 716	429 507	395 817	373 687	434 301	468 126	470 463
29	**Real gross national income at market prices**	3 647 619	3 669 912	3 688 319	3 700 704	3 724 700	3 843 957	4 054 428	4 198 290
30	Net real current transfers from the rest of the world	-27 910	..	..	..	..	-35 022	-34 879	-54 521
31	Real current transfers receivable from the rest of the world	42 076	..	..	..	..	59 486	67 303	53 765
32	Real current transfers payable to the rest of the world	69 986	..	..	..	..	94 509	102 183	108 286
33	**Real gross national disposable income**	3 619 709	..	..	..	..	3 808 935	4 019 549	4 143 768
34	Consumption of fixed capital at constant prices	828 105	849 695	870 735	891 174	910 700	925 322	935 474	942 003
35	**Real net national income at market prices**	2 807 962	2 820 217	2 833 595	2 845 991	2 848 857	2 946 707	3 137 857	3 262 969
36	**Real net national disposable income**	2 780 052	2 789 827	2 798 360	2 812 626	2 813 982	2 911 684	3 102 978	3 208 448

Note: Detailed metadata:http://metalinks.oecd.org/nav1/20180308/9a70
Source: Czech Statistical Office via Eurostat.

CZECH REPUBLIC

Table 4. Population and employment (persons) and employment (hours worked) by industry
ISIC Rev. 4

		2009	2010	2011	2012	2013	2014	2015	2016
	POPULATION, THOUSAND PERSONS, NATIONAL CONCEPT								
1	**Total population**	10 491.5	10 517.2	10 496.7	10 509.3	10 510.7	10 524.8	10 542.9	10 565.3
2	Economically active population	..	..	..	..	..	..	..	..
3	Unemployed persons	..	..	..	..	..	..	..	..
4	Total employment	4 996.7	4 986.7	4 992.3	5 011.8	5 036.6	5 094.5	5 167.1	5 232.8
5	Employees	4 222.7	4 180.8	4 179.0	4 202.5	4 251.5	4 319.4	4 403.6	4 457.7
6	Self-employed	774.0	805.8	813.3	809.3	785.1	775.1	763.5	775.1
	TOTAL EMPLOYMENT, THOUSAND PERSONS, DOMESTIC CONCEPT								
7	Agriculture, forestry and fishing	167.9	159.1	162.9	165.4	167.1	165.5	163.3	162.3
8	Industry, including energy	1 422.6	1 378.8	1 423.9	1 436.6	1 434.0	1 453.9	1 500.7	1 523.8
9	Manufacturing	1 292.8	1 252.4	1 297.6	1 310.5	1 308.4	1 325.3	1 371.9	1 396.5
10	Construction	463.7	471.5	447.3	441.5	431.1	411.5	409.6	408.1
11	Distrib. trade, repairs; transp.; accommod., food serv. activ.	1 243.1	1 242.3	1 237.4	1 230.9	1 235.9	1 232.6	1 242.9	1 257.3
12	Information and communication	133.6	129.9	124.5	126.8	129.1	133.3	136.3	140.9
13	Financial and insurance activities	90.4	87.8	89.0	94.6	95.6	97.4	95.0	96.1
14	Real estate activities	101.8	103.2	89.8	95.1	95.6	95.5	95.2	97.9
15	Prof., scientif., techn. activ.; admin., support service activ.	422.8	419.5	405.2	414.2	422.0	431.7	441.8	455.5
16	Public admin.; compulsory s.s.; education; human health	897.8	896.1	889.3	879.5	890.4	904.8	913.7	921.7
17	Other service activities	166.2	169.1	174.2	180.0	180.0	182.7	183.4	185.0
18	**Total employment**	5 110.1	5 057.2	5 043.4	5 064.6	5 080.9	5 109.0	5 181.9	5 248.5
	EMPLOYEES, THOUSAND PERSONS, DOMESTIC CONCEPT								
19	Agriculture, forestry and fishing	128.5	113.2	114.3	115.7	118.3	117.5	115.4	113.7
20	Industry, including energy	1 304.6	1 251.2	1 294.4	1 305.5	1 305.0	1 323.1	1 368.9	1 394.3
21	Manufacturing	1 178.0	1 129.2	1 173.2	1 183.9	1 184.2	1 200.0	1 246.4	1 273.2
22	Construction	322.5	317.4	292.5	288.9	283.2	273.2	272.7	267.4
23	Distrib. trade, repairs; transp.; accommod., food serv. activ.	1 026.0	1 020.3	1 002.0	1 009.4	1 023.0	1 026.5	1 050.3	1 062.8
24	Information and communication	116.2	112.0	108.7	109.8	111.8	115.1	117.7	121.5
25	Financial and insurance activities	73.1	73.7	74.3	78.0	77.2	78.2	77.0	77.4
26	Real estate activities	69.1	67.6	59.3	64.5	68.6	66.8	65.8	66.6
27	Prof., scientif., techn. activ.; admin., support service activ.	315.9	316.4	308.0	315.3	324.9	333.2	342.6	349.8
28	Public admin.; compulsory s.s.; education; human health	865.7	866.1	861.7	851.7	864.8	879.3	887.3	898.0
29	Other service activities	114.4	113.2	115.0	116.3	119.1	120.9	120.7	121.9
30	**Total employees**	4 336.1	4 251.4	4 230.2	4 255.3	4 295.9	4 333.9	4 418.4	4 473.4
	SELF-EMPLOYED, THOUSAND PERSONS, DOMESTIC CONCEPT								
31	Agriculture, forestry and fishing	39.4	45.9	48.6	49.7	48.8	48.1	47.9	48.6
32	Industry, including energy	118.1	127.5	129.5	131.1	129.0	130.8	131.8	129.4
33	Manufacturing	114.8	123.3	124.4	126.6	124.2	125.4	125.6	123.3
34	Construction	141.2	154.1	154.8	152.6	148.0	138.3	136.9	140.6
35	Distrib. trade, repairs; transp.; accommod., food serv. activ.	217.1	221.9	235.4	221.5	212.9	206.0	192.6	194.5
36	Information and communication	17.4	17.8	15.8	17.1	17.3	18.2	18.6	19.5
37	Financial and insurance activities	17.3	14.1	14.7	16.6	18.4	19.1	18.0	18.6
38	Real estate activities	32.6	35.6	30.5	30.5	27.0	28.8	29.4	31.3
39	Prof., scientif., techn. activ.; admin., support service activ.	106.9	103.0	97.2	98.8	97.2	98.5	99.2	105.8
40	Public admin.; compulsory s.s.; education; human health	32.2	30.0	27.6	27.7	25.6	25.5	26.4	23.7
41	Other service activities	51.8	55.9	59.2	63.6	60.9	61.8	62.7	63.1
42	**Total self-employed**	774.0	805.8	813.3	809.3	785.1	775.1	763.5	775.1
	TOTAL EMPLOYMENT, MILLION HOURS, DOMESTIC CONCEPT								
43	Industry, including energy	2 409.2	2 418.5	2 489.8	2 487.6	2 474.9	2 515.3	2 577.8	2 639.7
44	Distrib. trade, repairs; transp.; accommod., food serv. activ.	2 302.6	2 299.3	2 310.8	2 251.1	2 247.9	2 256.8	2 248.2	2 322.2
45	Financial and insurance activities	156.8	153.8	157.6	163.9	165.0	166.2	158.5	159.3
46	Prof., scientif., techn. activ.; admin., support service activ.	745.5	738.0	710.2	716.3	725.3	743.7	741.4	786.1
47	Public admin.; compulsory s.s.; education; human health	1 517.1	1 528.0	1 528.5	1 493.0	1 493.7	1 553.7	1 552.9	1 573.1
48	**Total employment**	9 089.7	9 100.5	9 106.6	8 995.4	8 957.7	9 077.3	9 100.3	9 334.0
	EMPLOYEES, MILLION HOURS, DOMESTIC CONCEPT								
49	Industry, including energy	2 152.2	2 132.6	2 211.3	2 218.0	2 214.3	2 246.4	2 308.6	2 361.2
50	Distrib. trade, repairs; transp.; accommod., food serv. activ.	1 803.2	1 799.6	1 784.8	1 784.2	1 817.6	1 834.6	1 851.8	1 911.3
51	Financial and insurance activities	125.7	128.2	131.0	134.8	132.0	132.8	128.1	128.1
52	Prof., scientif., techn. activ.; admin., support service activ.	541.7	546.9	532.1	544.1	557.2	569.7	569.8	587.6
53	Public admin.; compulsory s.s.; education; human health	1 460.0	1 472.0	1 475.9	1 444.9	1 452.8	1 513.2	1 511.1	1 533.7
54	**Total employees**	7 407.0	7 360.6	7 360.3	7 355.2	7 406.2	7 526.4	7 576.0	7 738.1
	SELF-EMPLOYED, MILLION HOURS, DOMESTIC CONCEPT								
55	Industry, including energy	257.0	285.9	278.5	269.7	260.6	268.9	269.3	278.6
56	Distrib. trade, repairs; transp.; accommod., food serv. activ.	499.5	499.7	526.0	466.8	430.3	422.2	396.4	410.9
57	Financial and insurance activities	31.1	25.6	26.5	29.1	33.0	33.4	30.4	31.2
58	Prof., scientif., techn. activ.; admin., support service activ.	203.9	191.1	178.1	172.2	168.1	174.0	171.7	198.5
59	Public admin.; compulsory s.s.; education; human health	57.1	56.0	52.5	48.1	40.9	40.5	41.8	39.4
60	**Total self-employed**	1 682.7	1 739.9	1 746.2	1 640.2	1 551.5	1 550.9	1 524.3	1 595.9

Note: Detailed metadata:http://metalinks.oecd.org/nav1/20180308/08e2
Source: Czech Statistical Office via Eurostat.

DENMARK

Table 1. Gross domestic product, expenditure approach

Million DKK

		2009	2010	2011	2012	2013	2014	2015	2016
	AT CURRENT PRICES								
1	**Final consumption expenditure**	**1 315 968**	**1 357 797**	**1 375 510**	**1 412 034**	**1 422 205**	**1 445 193**	**1 474 494**	**1 504 610**
2	Household	807 917	834 283	855 735	879 669	890 590	904 523	925 483	950 676
3	NPISH's	26 970	27 940	29 164	30 731	29 754	29 813	29 845	29 177
4	Government	481 081	495 575	490 610	501 635	501 861	510 856	519 166	524 757
5	Individual	333 908	346 466	344 236	350 327	353 291	363 228	370 364	375 710
6	Collective	147 172	149 109	146 374	151 308	148 569	147 629	148 802	149 047
7	*of which:* Actual individual consumption	1 168 795	1 208 688	1 229 136	1 260 726	1 273 635	1 297 564	1 325 692	1 355 563
8	**Gross capital formation**	**328 729**	**327 344**	**353 247**	**368 889**	**379 969**	**398 036**	**404 794**	**433 385**
9	Gross fixed capital formation, total	347 337	328 025	335 356	355 838	367 650	379 664	394 843	421 691
10	Dwellings	71 972	66 871	79 695	77 186	71 327	76 473	84 109	92 262
11	Other buildings and structures	79 892	74 913	78 980	83 404	87 613	89 448	89 658	94 717
12	Transport equipment	41 480	36 160	26 883	32 060	34 152	44 689	44 891	45 716
13	Other machinery and equipment	50 631	43 148	41 942	51 164	62 252	51 789	54 652	57 214
14	Cultivated assets	122	-53	-147	2	-60	-77	29	-71
15	Intangible fixed assets	88 681	91 528	89 668	92 317	93 562	99 455	102 797	112 939
16	Changes in inventories, acquisitions less disposals of valuables	-18 609	-682	17 891	13 051	12 319	18 373	9 951	11 694
17	Changes in inventories	-21 276	-3 184	14 759	9 561	8 577	14 987	6 697	8 630
18	Acquisitions less disposals of valuables	2 667	2 502	3 132	3 490	3 742	3 386	3 254	3 063
19	**External balance of goods and services**	**77 447**	**125 785**	**118 097**	**114 079**	**127 503**	**137 936**	**147 820**	**127 968**
20	Exports of goods and services	811 578	914 933	993 979	1 035 249	1 058 019	1 081 976	1 128 604	1 107 027
21	Exports of goods	505 862	568 345	632 457	644 498	656 441	669 802	695 295	700 667
22	Exports of services	305 716	346 587	361 523	390 752	401 579	412 175	433 308	406 360
23	Imports of goods and services	734 132	789 148	875 882	921 170	930 516	944 041	980 783	979 060
24	Imports of goods	437 128	478 944	542 347	562 532	570 670	580 543	589 058	584 513
25	Imports of services	297 003	310 204	333 535	358 638	359 846	363 497	391 725	394 546
26	**Statistical discrepancy**	**0**	**0**	**0**	**0**	**0**	**0**	**0**	**0**
27	**Gross domestic product**	**1 722 143**	**1 810 926**	**1 846 854**	**1 895 002**	**1 929 677**	**1 981 165**	**2 027 108**	**2 065 962**
	AT CONSTANT PRICES, REFERENCE YEAR 2010								
28	**Final consumption expenditure**	**1 343 243**	**1 357 797**	**1 357 064**	**1 365 205**	**1 367 181**	**1 384 585**	**1 403 892**	**1 423 987**
29	Household	827 809	834 283	835 598	838 729	842 222	850 587	864 666	884 220
30	NPISH's	27 709	27 940	29 002	30 322	29 218	28 768	28 511	27 269
31	Government	487 752	495 575	492 464	496 195	495 701	505 299	510 686	512 138
32	Individual	336 779	346 466	347 722	348 771	351 623	363 329	368 312	370 563
33	Collective	151 047	149 109	144 742	147 391	144 114	142 130	142 577	141 824
34	*of which:* Actual individual consumption	1 192 218	1 208 688	1 212 321	1 217 819	1 223 043	1 242 392	1 261 242	1 282 069
35	**Gross capital formation**	**329 277**	**327 344**	**345 198**	**353 120**	**365 093**	**380 755**	**384 364**	**407 412**
36	Gross fixed capital formation, total	348 026	328 025	329 300	341 593	350 928	361 846	372 910	395 190
37	Dwellings	73 370	66 871	77 439	73 209	67 502	72 114	78 031	83 605
38	Other buildings and structures	81 870	74 913	75 651	78 511	82 691	84 246	84 377	87 182
39	Transport equipment	40 718	36 160	27 733	32 718	34 830	46 990	43 735	44 046
40	Other machinery and equipment	48 666	43 148	41 580	48 561	58 093	47 293	51 822	54 924
41	Cultivated assets	131	-53	-140	3	-115	-152	24	-64
42	Intangible fixed assets	89 213	91 528	87 754	88 502	88 895	93 684	97 271	107 786
43	Changes in inventories, acquisitions less disposals of valuables	..	..	..	..	..	..	..	..
44	Changes in inventories	..	..	..	..	..	..	..	..
45	Acquisitions less disposals of valuables	2 787	2 502	2 845	2 977	3 219	2 965	2 718	2 661
46	**External balance of goods and services**	**103 897**	**125 785**	**132 872**	**121 301**	**124 482**	**121 591**	**128 984**	**123 338**
47	Exports of goods and services	888 801	914 933	980 761	992 159	1 008 147	1 039 690	1 064 098	1 094 319
48	Exports of goods	533 564	568 345	601 371	597 862	611 983	632 434	646 488	661 096
49	Exports of services	357 238	346 587	379 390	395 386	396 863	407 898	418 305	434 082
50	Imports of goods and services	784 904	789 148	847 889	870 858	883 665	918 099	935 114	970 981
51	Imports of goods	458 209	478 944	505 186	510 871	528 290	548 127	554 437	566 080
52	Imports of services	327 647	310 204	342 703	360 811	355 144	369 781	380 781	405 324
53	**Statistical discrepancy (including chaining residual)**	**1 249**	**0**	**0**	**-336**	**-299**	**-411**	**-411**	**-260**
54	**Gross domestic product**	**1 777 666**	**1 810 926**	**1 835 134**	**1 839 290**	**1 856 457**	**1 886 520**	**1 916 829**	**1 954 477**

Note: Detailed metadata:http://metalinks.oecd.org/nav1/20180308/0605
Source: Statistics Denmark via Eurostat.

DENMARK

Table 2. Gross domestic product, output and income approach
ISIC Rev. 4

Million DKK

		2009	2010	2011	2012	2013	2014	2015	2016
	OUTPUT APPROACH AT CURRENT PRICES								
1	**Total gross value added at basic prices**	**1 484 941**	**1 562 743**	**1 593 742**	**1 636 086**	**1 669 456**	**1 718 979**	**1 759 217**	**1 789 317**
2	Agriculture, forestry and fishing	14 356	21 766	24 233	31 357	25 127	27 389	16 275	16 544
3	Industry, including energy	267 371	287 848	300 293	312 011	311 466	313 454	316 837	333 213
4	Manufacturing	191 245	198 005	203 954	216 675	227 310	234 970	251 544	274 147
5	Construction	76 199	68 993	73 782	74 530	75 662	78 519	81 943	86 961
6	Services	..	..	..	..	..	..	..	..
7	Distrib. trade, repairs; transp.; accommod., food serv. activ.	277 017	304 452	309 281	314 410	336 369	354 546	366 345	355 233
8	Information and communication	72 573	74 119	73 519	73 193	78 298	77 455	83 046	81 975
9	Financial and insurance activities	93 102	96 659	94 140	102 419	98 822	102 909	107 691	105 799
10	Real estate activities	145 697	155 198	164 389	164 887	168 068	176 017	179 643	185 802
11	Prof., scientif., techn. activ.; admin., support service activ.	123 550	124 531	126 634	128 236	137 477	143 099	153 233	163 582
12	Public admin.; compulsory s.s.; education; human health	362 129	375 160	371 652	378 874	381 396	388 259	395 310	399 049
13	Other service activities	52 946	54 017	55 820	56 169	56 770	57 332	58 893	61 159
14	**FISIM (Financial Intermediation Services Indirectly Measured)**	..	..	..	..	..	..	..	..
15	Gross value added at basic prices, excluding FISIM	1 484 941	1 562 743	1 593 742	1 636 086	1 669 456	1 718 979	1 759 217	1 789 317
16	**Taxes less subsidies on products**	**237 202**	**248 183**	**253 111**	**258 916**	**260 221**	**262 186**	**267 892**	**276 645**
17	Taxes on products	249 923	260 028	265 569	272 919	275 178	278 457	285 677	294 157
18	Subsidies on products	12 721	11 845	12 457	14 003	14 957	16 271	17 786	17 512
19	**Residual item**	0	0	0	0	0	0	0	0
20	**Gross domestic product at market prices**	**1 722 143**	**1 810 926**	**1 846 854**	**1 895 002**	**1 929 677**	**1 981 165**	**2 027 108**	**2 065 962**
	OUTPUT APPROACH AT CONSTANT PRICES (REF. YEAR 2010)								
21	**Total gross value added at basic prices**	**1 534 518**	**1 562 743**	**1 586 910**	**1 590 374**	**1 604 992**	**1 629 814**	**1 653 883**	**1 681 895**
22	Agriculture, forestry and fishing	16 715	21 766	19 430	21 654	20 652	24 183	22 240	21 981
23	Industry, including energy	278 186	287 848	295 322	299 562	293 538	293 149	290 017	300 465
24	Manufacturing	190 787	198 005	210 380	218 967	225 068	228 090	230 152	242 545
25	Construction	78 688	68 993	71 361	73 019	74 463	76 621	78 936	81 734
26	Services	..	..	..	..	..	..	..	..
27	Distrib. trade, repairs; transp.; accommod., food serv. activ.	291 201	304 452	315 476	311 239	321 340	324 384	333 997	338 513
28	Information and communication	70 682	74 119	76 197	77 675	85 201	86 066	95 151	104 584
29	Financial and insurance activities	100 237	96 659	91 264	90 370	88 884	88 271	87 452	83 386
30	Real estate activities	150 318	155 198	159 923	157 497	155 051	159 364	159 459	161 146
31	Prof., scientif., techn. activ.; admin., support service activ.	125 464	124 531	126 558	126 648	134 543	138 067	143 097	148 849
32	Public admin.; compulsory s.s.; education; human health	367 838	375 160	377 450	377 519	377 166	386 320	391 549	391 093
33	Other service activities	54 797	54 017	53 930	54 571	55 154	54 095	54 342	54 238
34	**FISIM (Financial Intermediation Services Indirectly Measured)**	..	..	..	..	..	..	..	..
35	Gross value added at basic prices, excluding FISIM	1 534 518	1 562 743	1 586 910	1 590 374	1 604 992	1 629 814	1 653 883	1 681 895
36	**Taxes less subsidies on products**	**243 151**	**248 183**	**248 224**	**248 914**	**251 461**	**256 708**	**263 017**	**272 852**
37	Taxes on products	254 262	260 028	259 822	260 445	263 457	268 772	273 720	281 077
38	Subsidies on products	11 178	11 845	11 598	11 535	11 954	12 051	11 075	9 618
39	**Residual item**	**-3**	**0**	**0**	**2**	**4**	**-2**	**-71**	**-270**
40	**Gross domestic product at market prices**	**1 777 666**	**1 810 926**	**1 835 134**	**1 839 290**	**1 856 457**	**1 886 520**	**1 916 829**	**1 954 477**
	INCOME APPROACH								
41	**Compensation of employees**	**945 677**	**953 668**	**966 474**	**977 516**	**993 804**	**1 018 240**	**1 049 250**	**1 080 730**
42	Agriculture, forestry and fishing	8 192	8 776	8 903	9 047	9 346	9 572	9 747	10 033
43	Industry, including energy	139 156	134 055	137 641	138 386	137 163	141 045	145 848	152 420
44	Manufacturing	125 585	120 844	124 074	123 973	123 708	127 028	131 671	137 440
45	Construction	58 239	54 349	55 858	56 314	55 714	58 279	61 932	66 709
46	Distrib. trade, repairs; transp.; accommod., food serv. activ.	200 029	201 286	207 121	209 524	211 424	216 193	222 871	230 106
47	Information and communication	46 007	46 900	46 231	46 021	46 064	46 799	48 904	51 476
48	Financial and insurance activities	50 534	49 958	50 856	49 762	49 890	50 210	52 392	52 351
49	Real estate activities	12 057	12 549	12 831	13 058	13 308	13 615	14 250	14 654
50	Prof., scientif., techn. activ.; admin., support service activ.	88 894	90 802	94 298	97 664	103 598	108 268	113 720	120 693
51	Public admin.; compulsory s.s.; education; human health	306 675	317 901	314 763	319 248	328 935	335 635	340 513	342 746
52	Other service activities	35 895	37 092	37 972	38 492	38 362	38 623	39 072	39 543
53	**Wages and salaries**	**867 106**	**874 694**	**888 416**	**901 198**	**915 367**	**943 504**	**970 771**	**998 893**
54	Agriculture, forestry and fishing	7 640	8 205	8 363	8 554	8 802	9 038	9 203	9 443
55	Industry, including energy	130 026	125 506	129 294	130 508	130 549	135 851	140 154	145 752
56	Manufacturing	117 865	113 468	116 892	117 287	118 282	123 004	127 160	132 052
57	Construction	54 861	51 256	52 841	53 478	53 361	56 448	59 862	64 048
58	Distrib. trade, repairs; transp.; accommod., food serv. activ.	188 951	190 308	196 431	199 386	202 974	209 686	215 705	221 846
59	Information and communication	43 232	44 291	43 840	43 789	44 170	45 375	47 363	49 640
60	Financial and insurance activities	42 860	42 059	42 348	41 818	41 585	41 195	42 755	42 347
61	Real estate activities	11 349	11 868	12 166	12 428	12 775	13 211	13 786	14 148
62	Prof., scientif., techn. activ.; admin., support service activ.	83 396	85 753	89 196	92 720	98 947	104 457	109 380	115 592
63	Public admin.; compulsory s.s.; education; human health	271 785	281 427	279 041	283 126	287 089	292 698	296 625	299 683
64	Other service activities	33 005	34 023	34 896	35 391	35 115	35 546	35 939	36 394
65	**Gross operating surplus and mixed income**	**537 745**	**604 779**	**622 462**	**653 335**	**664 641**	**686 632**	**692 801**	**689 153**
66	**Taxes less subsidies on production and imports**	**238 720**	**252 479**	**257 918**	**264 152**	**271 232**	**276 293**	**285 058**	**296 080**
67	Taxes on production and imports	284 466	296 570	304 180	312 445	320 016	324 789	333 376	341 515
68	Subsidies on production and imports	45 746	44 091	46 262	48 293	48 784	48 496	48 318	45 436
69	**Residual item**	0	0	0	0	0	0	0	0
70	**Gross domestic product**	**1 722 143**	**1 810 926**	**1 846 854**	**1 895 002**	**1 929 677**	**1 981 165**	**2 027 108**	**2 065 962**

Note: Detailed metadata:http://metalinks.oecd.org/nav1/20180308/0605
Source: Statistics Denmark via Eurostat.

DENMARK

Table 3. Disposable income, saving and net lending / net borrowing

Million DKK

		2009	2010	2011	2012	2013	2014	2015	2016
	DISPOSABLE INCOME								
1	**Gross domestic product**	1 722 143	1 810 926	1 846 854	1 895 002	1 929 677	1 981 165	2 027 108	2 065 962
2	Net primary incomes from the rest of the world	17 185	29 620	38 945	42 791	61 099	72 064	63 286	52 186
3	Primary incomes receivable from the rest of the world	135 387	146 833	163 308	152 170	178 437	186 705	192 727	177 907
4	Primary incomes payable to the rest of the world	118 202	117 213	124 363	109 379	117 338	114 641	129 441	125 721
5	**Gross national income at market prices**	1 739 327	1 840 547	1 885 798	1 937 793	1 990 777	2 053 229	2 090 395	2 118 148
6	Consumption of fixed capital	313 401	320 684	324 119	332 471	333 835	334 195	336 741	343 124
7	**Net national income at market prices**	1 425 926	1 519 863	1 561 679	1 605 322	1 656 942	1 719 034	1 753 654	1 775 024
8	Net current transfers from the rest of the world	-34 951	-36 558	-35 416	-37 835	-38 881	-33 194	-32 423	-28 891
9	Current transfers receivable from the rest of the world	15 183	13 768	15 818	17 566	20 139	21 762	24 541	24 572
10	Current transfers payable to the rest of the world	50 134	50 326	51 234	55 401	59 020	54 956	56 964	53 463
11	**Net national disposable income**	1 390 975	1 483 304	1 526 264	1 567 487	1 618 061	1 685 840	1 721 232	1 746 132
	SAVING AND NET LENDING / NET BORROWING								
12	**Net national disposable income**	1 390 975	1 483 304	1 526 264	1 567 487	1 618 061	1 685 840	1 721 232	1 746 132
13	Final consumption expenditures	1 315 968	1 357 797	1 375 510	1 412 034	1 422 205	1 445 193	1 474 494	1 504 610
14	Adj. for change in net equity of households in pension funds	0	0	0	0	0	0	0	0
15	**Saving, net**	75 008	125 507	150 754	155 453	195 857	240 648	246 737	241 522
16	Net capital transfers from the rest of the world	-476	395	5 261	345	-45	-4 124	-7 490	-47
17	Capital transfers receivable from the rest of the world	815	903	5 820	866	1 149	1 049	1 009	901
18	Capital transfers payable to the rest of the world	1 291	508	559	521	1 194	5 173	8 499	948
19	Gross capital formation	328 729	327 344	353 242	368 889	379 969	398 036	404 794	433 385
20	Acquisitions less disposals of non-financial non-produced assets	-197	-75	-508	-108	546	12	-334	-178
21	Consumption of fixed capital	313 401	320 684	324 119	332 471	333 835	334 195	336 741	343 124
22	**Net lending / net borrowing**	59 401	119 317	127 395	119 488	149 132	172 671	171 528	151 392
	REAL DISPOSABLE INCOME								
23	**Gross domestic product at constant prices, reference year 2010**	1 777 666	1 810 926	1 835 134	1 839 290	1 856 457	1 886 520	1 916 829	1 954 477
24	Trading gain or loss	-26 302	0	-16 585	-10 849	-1 480	11 080	12 238	-1 955
25	**Real gross domestic income**	1 751 364	1 810 926	1 818 549	1 828 441	1 854 977	1 897 600	1 929 067	1 952 522
26	Net real primary incomes from the rest of the world	17 477	29 620	38 348	41 288	58 734	69 024	60 225	49 321
27	Real primary incomes receivable from the rest of the world	137 684	146 833	160 805	146 825	171 530	178 830	183 406	168 138
28	Real primary incomes payable to the rest of the world	120 208	117 213	122 457	105 537	112 796	109 805	123 181	118 818
29	**Real gross national income at market prices**	1 768 839	1 840 547	1 856 896	1 869 729	1 913 712	1 966 625	1 989 293	2 001 842
30	Net real current transfers from the rest of the world	-35 544	-36 558	-34 873	-36 506	-37 376	-31 794	-30 855	-27 305
31	Real current transfers receivable from the rest of the world	15 441	13 768	15 576	16 949	19 359	20 844	23 354	23 223
32	Real current transfers payable to the rest of the world	50 985	50 326	50 449	53 455	56 735	52 638	54 209	50 527
33	**Real gross national disposable income**	1 733 295	1 803 989	1 822 023	1 833 223	1 876 336	1 934 831	1 958 438	1 974 538
34	Consumption of fixed capital at constant prices	316 561	320 684	318 397	318 594	318 123	317 487	318 708	322 737
35	**Real net national income at market prices**	1 450 121	1 519 863	1 537 745	1 548 936	1 592 800	1 646 526	1 668 839	1 677 559
36	**Real net national disposable income**	1 414 577	1 483 304	1 502 872	1 512 430	1 555 424	1 614 732	1 637 985	1 650 254

Note: Detailed metadata:http://metalinks.oecd.org/nav1/20180308/b382
Source: Statistics Denmark via Eurostat.

Table 4. Population and employment (persons) and employment (hours worked) by industry
ISIC Rev. 4

		2009	2010	2011	2012	2013	2014	2015	2016
	POPULATION, THOUSAND PERSONS, NATIONAL CONCEPT								
1	**Total population**	5 523.0	5 547.0	5 570.0	5 591.0	5 613.0	5 643.0	5 682.0	5 729.0
2	Economically active population	..	..	..	..	..	..	..	..
3	Unemployed persons	..	..	..	..	..	..	..	..
4	Total employment	2 813.0	2 747.0	2 747.0	2 730.0	2 732.0	2 757.0	2 792.0	2 841.0
5	Employees	2 625.0	2 563.0	2 563.0	2 548.0	2 552.0	2 578.0	2 614.0	2 662.0
6	Self-employed	189.0	184.0	184.0	181.0	180.0	179.0	178.0	179.0
	TOTAL EMPLOYMENT, THOUSAND PERSONS, DOMESTIC CONCEPT								
7	Agriculture, forestry and fishing	72.0	71.0	70.0	69.0	69.0	69.0	68.0	68.0
8	Industry, including energy	346.0	316.0	315.0	311.0	303.0	306.0	309.0	315.0
9	Manufacturing	317.0	289.0	289.0	283.0	278.0	280.0	284.0	289.0
10	Construction	184.0	168.0	167.0	165.0	163.0	167.0	173.0	180.0
11	Distrib. trade, repairs; transp.; accommod., food serv. activ.	707.0	691.0	705.0	702.0	705.0	712.0	722.0	739.0
12	Information and communication	99.0	98.0	96.0	96.0	97.0	98.0	101.0	104.0
13	Financial and insurance activities	90.0	83.0	83.0	80.0	77.0	78.0	78.0	79.0
14	Real estate activities	41.0	44.0	45.0	44.0	45.0	45.0	45.0	46.0
15	Prof., scientif., techn. activ.; admin., support service activ.	270.0	261.0	262.0	266.0	276.0	284.0	294.0	306.0
16	Public admin.; compulsory s.s.; education; human health	895.0	904.0	889.0	881.0	881.0	884.0	886.0	887.0
17	Other service activities	150.0	152.0	154.0	152.0	151.0	152.0	151.0	154.0
18	**Total employment**	2 854.0	2 788.0	2 787.0	2 767.0	2 766.0	2 794.0	2 829.0	2 877.0
	EMPLOYEES, THOUSAND PERSONS, DOMESTIC CONCEPT								
19	Agriculture, forestry and fishing	37.0	38.0	38.0	38.0	38.0	39.0	39.0	39.0
20	Industry, including energy	338.0	307.0	307.0	303.0	295.0	298.0	302.0	308.0
21	Manufacturing	309.0	281.0	281.0	276.0	271.0	273.0	276.0	282.0
22	Construction	163.0	148.0	149.0	148.0	145.0	150.0	155.0	162.0
23	Distrib. trade, repairs; transp.; accommod., food serv. activ.	657.0	645.0	659.0	658.0	663.0	671.0	683.0	699.0
24	Information and communication	93.0	91.0	89.0	88.0	89.0	89.0	93.0	96.0
25	Financial and insurance activities	90.0	83.0	83.0	80.0	77.0	78.0	78.0	79.0
26	Real estate activities	35.0	36.0	37.0	37.0	37.0	37.0	38.0	39.0
27	Prof., scientif., techn. activ.; admin., support service activ.	239.0	230.0	231.0	235.0	243.0	250.0	260.0	272.0
28	Public admin.; compulsory s.s.; education; human health	880.0	889.0	873.0	864.0	865.0	867.0	869.0	869.0
29	Other service activities	134.0	136.0	138.0	136.0	134.0	135.0	133.0	135.0
30	**Total employees**	2 666.0	2 604.0	2 603.0	2 585.0	2 587.0	2 614.0	2 651.0	2 698.0
	SELF-EMPLOYED, THOUSAND PERSONS, DOMESTIC CONCEPT								
31	Agriculture, forestry and fishing	35.0	33.0	32.0	31.0	31.0	30.0	29.0	29.0
32	Industry, including energy	9.0	8.0	8.0	8.0	8.0	8.0	8.0	8.0
33	Manufacturing	8.0	8.0	7.0	7.0	7.0	7.0	7.0	7.0
34	Construction	21.0	19.0	18.0	18.0	17.0	17.0	17.0	17.0
35	Distrib. trade, repairs; transp.; accommod., food serv. activ.	50.0	47.0	47.0	45.0	42.0	41.0	40.0	39.0
36	Information and communication	7.0	7.0	8.0	8.0	8.0	9.0	9.0	8.0
37	Financial and insurance activities	0.0	0.0	0.0	0.0	0.0	0.0	0.0	0.0
38	Real estate activities	6.0	8.0	8.0	8.0	8.0	7.0	7.0	7.0
39	Prof., scientif., techn. activ.; admin., support service activ.	30.0	31.0	31.0	32.0	33.0	33.0	34.0	34.0
40	Public admin.; compulsory s.s.; education; human health	15.0	15.0	16.0	16.0	16.0	16.0	17.0	17.0
41	Other service activities	16.0	16.0	16.0	16.0	17.0	17.0	18.0	19.0
42	**Total self-employed**	189.0	184.0	184.0	181.0	180.0	179.0	178.0	179.0
	TOTAL EMPLOYMENT, MILLION HOURS, DOMESTIC CONCEPT								
43	Industry, including energy	526.3	489.7	500.3	489.9	476.1	478.2	483.8	494.5
44	Distrib. trade, repairs; transp.; accommod., food serv. activ.	942.6	920.9	950.3	930.5	935.5	933.7	948.0	960.5
45	Financial and insurance activities	135.4	125.7	124.8	120.3	116.6	115.6	118.3	119.1
46	Prof., scientif., techn. activ.; admin., support service activ.	382.8	383.3	391.7	394.9	412.6	419.8	435.3	452.7
47	Public admin.; compulsory s.s.; education; human health	1 244.4	1 249.6	1 235.7	1 214.8	1 220.8	1 214.7	1 208.6	1 208.3
48	**Total employment**	4 044.7	3 965.2	4 004.3	3 938.1	3 943.9	3 951.1	3 995.3	4 053.6
	EMPLOYEES, MILLION HOURS, DOMESTIC CONCEPT								
49	Industry, including energy	511.3	474.9	485.6	475.5	461.7	463.7	469.2	480.3
50	Distrib. trade, repairs; transp.; accommod., food serv. activ.	856.0	840.3	868.3	854.1	861.7	863.0	875.4	889.9
51	Financial and insurance activities	135.4	125.7	124.8	120.3	116.6	115.6	118.3	119.1
52	Prof., scientif., techn. activ.; admin., support service activ.	328.7	327.6	334.8	337.9	353.9	359.7	374.2	392.0
53	Public admin.; compulsory s.s.; education; human health	1 219.9	1 224.5	1 210.4	1 189.5	1 195.2	1 188.9	1 181.8	1 180.7
54	**Total employees**	3 712.7	3 642.7	3 677.6	3 622.1	3 628.4	3 636.3	3 675.6	3 738.9
	SELF-EMPLOYED, MILLION HOURS, DOMESTIC CONCEPT								
55	Industry, including energy	15.0	14.8	14.7	14.4	14.5	14.4	14.6	14.2
56	Distrib. trade, repairs; transp.; accommod., food serv. activ.	86.6	80.6	82.0	76.4	73.8	70.8	72.6	70.6
57	Financial and insurance activities	0.0	0.0	0.0	0.0	0.0	0.0	0.0	0.0
58	Prof., scientif., techn. activ.; admin., support service activ.	54.1	55.6	56.8	56.9	58.7	60.1	61.1	60.7
59	Public admin.; compulsory s.s.; education; human health	24.5	25.0	25.3	25.3	25.6	25.8	26.7	27.5
60	**Total self-employed**	332.0	322.5	326.7	316.0	315.5	314.8	319.7	314.7

Note: Detailed metadata:http://metalinks.oecd.org/nav1/20180308/c713
Source: Statistics Denmark via Eurostat.

Table 1. Gross domestic product, expenditure approach

Million EUR (2011 EEK euro)

		2009	2010	2011	2012	2013	2014	2015	2016
	AT CURRENT PRICES								
1	**Final consumption expenditure**	**10 533**	**10 650**	**11 528**	**12 439**	**13 306**	**13 934**	**14 688**	**15 503**
2	Household	7 346	7 480	8 195	8 885	9 457	9 813	10 232	10 771
3	NPISH's	206	209	232	255	281	305	334	362
4	Government	2 981	2 961	3 101	3 300	3 568	3 815	4 122	4 370
5	Individual	1 707	1 679	1 754	1 844	1 972	2 094	2 271	2 431
6	Collective	1 274	1 283	1 347	1 455	1 596	1 722	1 851	1 939
7	*of which: Actual individual consumption*	9 258	9 367	10 181	10 984	11 710	12 212	12 837	13 564
8	**Gross capital formation**	**2 930**	**3 131**	**4 185**	**5 217**	**5 094**	**5 357**	**5 075**	**5 115**
9	Gross fixed capital formation, total	3 215	3 125	4 367	5 127	5 253	4 829	4 807	4 712
10	Dwellings	440	392	453	517	648	776	886	1 016
11	Other buildings and structures	1 483	1 313	1 953	2 241	2 199	1 720	1 735	1 368
12	Transport equipment	224	303	572	743	684	552	403	465
13	Other machinery and equipment	585	560	748	861	893	1 132	1 056	984
14	Cultivated assets	22	19	23	15	27	14	26	15
15	Intangible fixed assets	287	303	367	445	473	410	479	536
16	Changes in inventories, acquisitions less disposals of valuables	-285	6	-182	90	-159	528	268	402
17	Changes in inventories	-287	4	-185	85	-164	525	267	402
18	Acquisitions less disposals of valuables	2	3	3	5	5	4	1	1
19	**External balance of goods and services**	**702**	**935**	**955**	**278**	**532**	**559**	**814**	**814**
20	Exports of goods and services	8 601	11 049	14 424	15 422	15 960	16 321	15 995	16 664
21	Exports of goods	5 295	7 482	10 384	10 749	10 968	10 998	10 757	11 168
22	Exports of services	3 306	3 567	4 040	4 673	4 992	5 323	5 237	5 496
23	Imports of goods and services	7 900	10 113	13 469	15 144	15 428	15 762	15 180	15 849
24	Imports of goods	6 021	7 887	10 735	12 030	11 893	12 089	11 612	11 958
25	Imports of services	1 879	2 226	2 734	3 114	3 535	3 673	3 568	3 892
26	**Statistical discrepancy**	**-18**	**0**	**0**	**0**	**0**	**-84**	**-229**	**-334**
27	**Gross domestic product**	**14 146**	**14 717**	**16 668**	**17 935**	**18 932**	**19 766**	**20 348**	**21 098**
	AT CONSTANT PRICES, REFERENCE YEAR 2010								
28	**Final consumption expenditure**	**10 785**	**10 650**	**10 972**	**11 413**	**11 785**	**12 157**	**12 673**	**13 144**
29	Household	7 603	7 480	7 750	8 081	8 350	8 616	8 996	9 383
30	NPISH's	211	209	223	236	257	281	309	333
31	Government	2 972	2 961	2 999	3 095	3 178	3 259	3 368	3 434
32	Individual	1 688	1 679	1 702	1 735	1 765	1 797	1 865	1 912
33	Collective	1 284	1 283	1 297	1 359	1 413	1 462	1 503	1 522
34	*of which: Actual individual consumption*	9 501	9 367	9 675	10 054	10 372	10 695	11 171	11 625
35	**Gross capital formation**	**2 936**	**3 131**	**4 013**	**4 842**	**4 676**	**4 904**	**4 544**	**4 617**
36	Gross fixed capital formation, total	3 210	3 125	4 199	4 734	4 804	4 385	4 257	4 208
37	Dwellings	432	392	430	469	558	668	758	876
38	Other buildings and structures	1 454	1 313	1 856	2 021	1 963	1 505	1 480	1 192
39	Transport equipment	227	303	550	699	644	518	369	417
40	Other machinery and equipment	595	560	730	798	829	1 058	973	911
41	Cultivated assets	25	19	21	14	22	12	21	13
42	Intangible fixed assets	293	303	359	417	431	365	394	436
43	Changes in inventories, acquisitions less disposals of valuables	..	..	..	..	..	..	..	..
44	Changes in inventories	..	..	..	..	..	..	..	..
45	Acquisitions less disposals of valuables	2	3	2	4	4	3	1	0
46	**External balance of goods and services**	**564**	**935**	**853**	**267**	**379**	**237**	**408**	**255**
47	Exports of goods and services	8 907	11 049	13 719	14 380	14 777	15 147	15 048	15 663
48	Exports of goods	5 548	7 482	9 923	10 194	10 472	10 682	10 651	11 065
49	Exports of services	3 342	3 567	3 796	4 183	4 301	4 455	4 393	4 591
50	Imports of goods and services	8 343	10 113	12 867	14 113	14 398	14 909	14 639	15 409
51	Imports of goods	6 401	7 887	10 189	11 150	11 102	11 483	11 264	11 727
52	Imports of services	1 939	2 226	2 678	2 965	3 303	3 435	3 383	3 687
53	**Statistical discrepancy (including chaining residual)**	**106**	**0**	**-2**	**-5**	**-4**	**26**	**-12**	**-39**
54	**Gross domestic product**	**14 391**	**14 717**	**15 835**	**16 517**	**16 836**	**17 323**	**17 613**	**17 977**

Note: Detailed metadata:http://metalinks.oecd.org/nav1/20180308/5874
Source: Statistical Office of Estonia via Eurostat.

Table 2. Gross domestic product, output and income approach
ISIC Rev. 4

Million EUR (2011 EEK euro)

		2009	2010	2011	2012	2013	2014	2015	2016
	OUTPUT APPROACH AT CURRENT PRICES								
1	**Total gross value added at basic prices**	12 281	12 874	14 616	15 676	16 591	17 202	17 610	18 118
2	Agriculture, forestry and fishing	300	411	567	573	566	602	552	465
3	Industry, including energy	2 439	2 839	3 265	3 355	3 613	3 825	3 790	3 788
4	Manufacturing	1 735	2 020	2 422	2 494	2 581	2 781	2 815	2 853
5	Construction	869	763	1 001	1 152	1 156	1 102	1 098	1 090
6	Services	..	..	..	..	..	..	..	..
7	Distrib. trade, repairs; transp.; accommod., food serv. activ.	2 594	2 862	3 302	3 624	3 837	3 874	3 833	3 995
8	Information and communication	677	681	737	804	845	911	964	1 057
9	Financial and insurance activities	540	524	564	608	598	634	696	715
10	Real estate activities	1 301	1 262	1 416	1 541	1 654	1 723	1 841	1 859
11	Prof., scientif., techn. activ.; admin., support service activ.	1 118	1 157	1 293	1 405	1 495	1 515	1 587	1 690
12	Public admin.; compulsory s.s.; education; human health	2 146	2 083	2 153	2 259	2 437	2 600	2 804	2 973
13	Other service activities	296	293	317	355	390	416	445	486
14	**FISIM (Financial Intermediation Services Indirectly Measured)**	..	..	..	..	..	..	..	..
15	**Gross value added at basic prices, excluding FISIM**	12 281	12 874	14 616	15 676	16 591	17 202	17 610	18 118
16	**Taxes less subsidies on products**	1 865	1 842	2 051	2 259	2 341	2 564	2 737	2 980
17	Taxes on products	1 965	1 935	2 151	2 366	2 417	2 622	2 811	3 044
18	Subsidies on products	100	93	99	107	76	58	74	64
19	**Residual item**	0	0	0	0	0	0	0	0
20	**Gross domestic product at market prices**	14 146	14 717	16 668	17 935	18 932	19 766	20 348	21 098
	OUTPUT APPROACH AT CONSTANT PRICES (REF. YEAR 2010)								
21	**Total gross value added at basic prices**	12 427	12 874	13 877	14 432	14 692	14 993	15 160	15 393
22	Agriculture, forestry and fishing	373	411	466	494	472	529	548	459
23	Industry, including energy	2 452	2 839	3 158	3 180	3 306	3 573	3 655	3 632
24	Manufacturing	1 701	2 020	2 317	2 345	2 417	2 558	2 609	2 604
25	Construction	792	763	962	1 048	1 000	941	905	917
26	Services	..	..	..	..	..	..	..	..
27	Distrib. trade, repairs; transp.; accommod., food serv. activ.	2 676	2 862	3 097	3 193	3 243	3 236	3 182	3 345
28	Information and communication	699	681	732	816	861	931	956	1 066
29	Financial and insurance activities	615	524	487	544	537	557	609	590
30	Real estate activities	1 286	1 262	1 329	1 371	1 407	1 370	1 413	1 385
31	Prof., scientif., techn. activ.; admin., support service activ.	1 129	1 157	1 249	1 332	1 389	1 375	1 399	1 470
32	Public admin.; compulsory s.s.; education; human health	2 108	2 083	2 091	2 123	2 138	2 150	2 166	2 179
33	Other service activities	295	293	306	327	343	350	357	374
34	**FISIM (Financial Intermediation Services Indirectly Measured)**	..	..	..	..	..	..	..	..
35	**Gross value added at basic prices, excluding FISIM**	12 427	12 874	13 877	14 432	14 692	14 993	15 160	15 393
36	**Taxes less subsidies on products**	1 971	1 842	1 958	2 085	2 145	2 335	2 461	2 596
37	Taxes on products	2 071	1 935	2 049	2 177	2 214	2 387	2 533	2 660
38	Subsidies on products	100	93	91	93	71	54	73	65
39	**Residual item**	-7	0	0	0	0	-5	-8	-12
40	**Gross domestic product at market prices**	14 391	14 717	15 835	16 517	16 836	17 323	17 613	17 977
	INCOME APPROACH								
41	**Compensation of employees**	7 142	6 959	7 458	8 144	8 613	9 250	9 822	10 411
42	Agriculture, forestry and fishing	153	159	174	188	201	207	211	223
43	Industry, including energy	1 412	1 441	1 592	1 757	1 855	1 995	2 105	2 154
44	Manufacturing	1 180	1 199	1 333	1 480	1 570	1 710	1 833	1 875
45	Construction	597	536	605	693	701	674	658	708
46	Distrib. trade, repairs; transp.; accommod., food serv. activ.	1 600	1 557	1 663	1 851	1 957	2 156	2 316	2 435
47	Information and communication	337	327	349	405	444	465	508	602
48	Financial and insurance activities	244	217	232	235	243	253	274	303
49	Real estate activities	122	108	111	120	126	142	156	163
50	Prof., scientif., techn. activ.; admin., support service activ.	665	690	741	818	859	927	952	1 030
51	Public admin.; compulsory s.s.; education; human health	1 787	1 710	1 767	1 833	1 972	2 145	2 326	2 465
52	Other service activities	224	215	226	244	257	287	315	328
53	**Wages and salaries**	5 265	5 155	5 546	6 087	6 425	6 892	7 298	7 724
54	Agriculture, forestry and fishing	116	120	131	141	150	155	158	171
55	Industry, including energy	1 046	1 078	1 193	1 324	1 391	1 496	1 577	1 612
56	Manufacturing	875	899	1 001	1 116	1 178	1 284	1 375	1 405
57	Construction	458	417	474	540	542	516	509	544
58	Distrib. trade, repairs; transp.; accommod., food serv. activ.	1 208	1 184	1 268	1 417	1 493	1 645	1 764	1 858
59	Information and communication	255	247	262	305	338	352	384	454
60	Financial and insurance activities	180	160	172	179	181	188	205	223
61	Real estate activities	91	81	84	91	97	108	118	123
62	Prof., scientif., techn. activ.; admin., support service activ.	505	526	565	626	657	711	725	786
63	Public admin.; compulsory s.s.; education; human health	1 239	1 180	1 227	1 281	1 385	1 505	1 621	1 709
64	Other service activities	168	161	170	184	193	216	237	246
65	**Gross operating surplus and mixed income**	5 177	6 023	7 264	7 641	8 080	8 005	7 835	7 780
66	**Taxes less subsidies on production and imports**	1 827	1 735	1 946	2 150	2 239	2 511	2 691	2 907
67	Taxes on production and imports	2 075	2 044	2 271	2 496	2 554	2 780	2 962	3 204
68	Subsidies on production and imports	248	309	325	345	314	269	271	297
69	**Residual item**	0	0	0	0	0	0	0	0
70	**Gross domestic product**	14 146	14 717	16 668	17 935	18 932	19 766	20 348	21 098

Note: Detailed metadata:http://metalinks.oecd.org/nav1/20180308/5874
Source: Statistical Office of Estonia via Eurostat.

Table 3. Disposable income, saving and net lending / net borrowing

Million EUR (2011 EEK euro)

		2009	2010	2011	2012	2013	2014	2015	2016
	DISPOSABLE INCOME								
1	**Gross domestic product**	**14 146**	**14 717**	**16 668**	**17 935**	**18 932**	**19 766**	**20 348**	**21 098**
2	Net primary incomes from the rest of the world	-430	-780	-835	-723	-437	-527	-428	-411
3	Primary incomes receivable from the rest of the world	747	843	1 025	1 003	1 182	1 124	990	1 107
4	Primary incomes payable to the rest of the world	1 177	1 623	1 860	1 726	1 618	1 652	1 418	1 518
5	**Gross national income at market prices**	**13 715**	**13 936**	**15 832**	**17 212**	**18 496**	**19 239**	**19 920**	**20 687**
6	Consumption of fixed capital	2 383	2 391	2 470	2 707	2 973	3 122	3 281	3 347
7	**Net national income at market prices**	**11 332**	**11 545**	**13 363**	**14 504**	**15 523**	**16 117**	**16 639**	**17 340**
8	Net current transfers from the rest of the world	88	101	127	97	3	20	10	-2
9	Current transfers receivable from the rest of the world	321	388	424	436	430	446	472	499
10	Current transfers payable to the rest of the world	232	286	297	339	427	426	462	501
11	**Net national disposable income**	**11 421**	**11 646**	**13 489**	**14 601**	**15 526**	**16 136**	**16 649**	**17 338**
	SAVING AND NET LENDING / NET BORROWING								
12	**Net national disposable income**	**11 421**	**11 646**	**13 489**	**14 601**	**15 526**	**16 136**	**16 649**	**17 338**
13	Final consumption expenditures	10 533	10 650	11 528	12 440	13 306	13 934	14 688	15 503
14	Adj. for change in net equity of households in pension funds	0	0	0	0	0	0	0	0
15	**Saving, net**	**888**	**996**	**1 961**	**2 162**	**2 220**	**2 202**	**1 962**	**1 835**
16	Net capital transfers from the rest of the world	483	374	468	588	577	319	351	226
17	Capital transfers receivable from the rest of the world	485	380	473	593	583	330	364	229
18	Capital transfers payable to the rest of the world	2	6	5	5	6	11	13	3
19	Gross capital formation	2 930	3 131	4 185	5 217	5 094	5 357	5 075	5 115
20	Acquisitions less disposals of non-financial non-produced assets	0	-135	-189	-20	86	104	-73	0
21	Consumption of fixed capital	2 383	2 391	2 470	2 707	2 973	3 122	3 281	3 347
22	**Net lending / net borrowing**[1]	**843**	**765**	**904**	**260**	**590**	**267**	**821**	**626**
	REAL DISPOSABLE INCOME								
23	**Gross domestic product at constant prices, reference year 2010**	**14 391**	**14 717**	**15 835**	**16 517**	**16 836**	**17 323**	**17 613**	**17 977**
24	Trading gain or loss	22	0	61	-9	100	154	130	217
25	**Real gross domestic income**	**14 414**	**14 717**	**15 895**	**16 507**	**16 936**	**17 477**	**17 743**	**18 194**
26	Net real primary incomes from the rest of the world	-439	-780	-796	-666	-391	-466	-373	-355
27	Real primary incomes receivable from the rest of the world	761	843	978	923	1 057	994	863	954
28	Real primary incomes payable to the rest of the world	1 200	1 623	1 774	1 588	1 448	1 460	1 236	1 309
29	**Real gross national income at market prices**	**13 975**	**13 936**	**15 099**	**15 842**	**16 546**	**17 011**	**17 370**	**17 839**
30	Net real current transfers from the rest of the world	90	101	121	89	2	17	9	-2
31	Real current transfers receivable from the rest of the world	327	388	404	401	384	394	412	430
32	Real current transfers payable to the rest of the world	237	286	283	312	382	376	403	432
33	**Real gross national disposable income**	**14 065**	**14 038**	**15 220**	**15 931**	**16 548**	**17 028**	**17 379**	**17 837**
34	Consumption of fixed capital at constant prices	2 369	2 391	2 459	2 647	2 805	2 928	3 023	3 110
35	**Real net national income at market prices**	**11 547**	**11 545**	**12 743**	**13 350**	**13 886**	**14 250**	**14 509**	**14 953**
36	**Real net national disposable income**	**11 637**	**11 646**	**12 864**	**13 439**	**13 889**	**14 267**	**14 518**	**14 951**

Note: Detailed metadata:http://metalinks.oecd.org/nav1/20180308/a4a5
1.   Including a statistical discrepancy.
Source: Statistical Office of Estonia via Eurostat.

Table 4. Population and employment (persons) and employment (hours worked) by industry
ISIC Rev. 4

		2009	2010	2011	2012	2013	2014	2015	2016
	POPULATION, THOUSAND PERSONS, NATIONAL CONCEPT								
1	**Total population**	**1 335.7**	**1 333.3**	**1 329.7**	**1 325.2**	**1 320.2**	**1 315.8**	**1 313.3**	**1 315.9**
2	Economically active population	..	..	..	..	..	..	..	..
3	Unemployed persons	..	..	..	..	..	..	..	..
4	Total employment	596.1	570.2	605.5	618.7	624.1	627.7	643.4	647.3
5	Employees	546.6	522.1	552.9	564.2	567.3	570.7	583.5	586.3
6	Self-employed	49.5	48.1	52.6	54.5	56.8	56.9	59.9	61.0
	TOTAL EMPLOYMENT, THOUSAND PERSONS, DOMESTIC CONCEPT								
7	Agriculture, forestry and fishing	22.5	22.8	25.7	26.5	24.9	22.6	24.3	24.5
8	Industry, including energy	126.6	121.8	135.0	129.7	128.6	126.6	131.5	131.0
9	Manufacturing	110.5	104.3	117.4	112.6	114.0	111.4	117.9	118.7
10	Construction	49.8	36.8	45.9	47.1	47.2	48.0	51.9	45.6
11	Distrib. trade, repairs; transp.; accommod., food serv. activ.	146.7	138.1	143.6	143.4	145.3	153.4	151.9	156.5
12	Information and communication	14.6	12.7	16.7	18.2	19.6	22.0	26.3	27.6
13	Financial and insurance activities	11.4	9.4	10.2	10.6	10.2	8.2	9.4	10.9
14	Real estate activities	9.0	10.2	10.7	10.8	11.6	11.3	10.3	11.7
15	Prof., scientif., techn. activ.; admin., support service activ.	37.2	39.0	40.1	42.8	47.6	44.0	43.0	45.1
16	Public admin.; compulsory s.s.; education; human health	133.7	131.5	132.2	139.0	137.6	140.9	143.8	138.7
17	Other service activities	25.1	25.8	23.9	25.4	28.3	28.5	30.5	33.1
18	**Total employment**	**576.6**	**548.1**	**584.0**	**593.5**	**600.9**	**605.5**	**622.9**	**624.7**
	EMPLOYEES, THOUSAND PERSONS, DOMESTIC CONCEPT								
19	Agriculture, forestry and fishing	16.3	16.3	17.3	19.6	18.9	16.9	18.1	17.6
20	Industry, including energy	122.0	117.1	130.8	125.4	123.5	121.1	125.6	124.3
21	Manufacturing	106.3	99.6	113.2	108.5	109.1	106.1	112.2	112.2
22	Construction	43.7	31.8	38.4	39.1	39.1	40.8	43.9	36.2
23	Distrib. trade, repairs; transp.; accommod., food serv. activ.	131.8	124.7	129.7	127.7	131.0	137.7	135.1	141.6
24	Information and communication	13.3	11.2	15.1	15.5	16.5	19.6	23.7	24.0
25	Financial and insurance activities	11.3	9.4	9.9	10.2	9.6	7.9	9.2	10.7
26	Real estate activities	7.7	8.4	9.0	10.0	10.5	10.0	8.3	9.4
27	Prof., scientif., techn. activ.; admin., support service activ.	30.4	32.0	33.2	35.1	38.4	34.6	36.1	38.9
28	Public admin.; compulsory s.s.; education; human health	131.6	129.2	129.9	136.4	134.9	138.8	141.1	135.9
29	Other service activities	19.8	20.9	19.4	20.7	22.2	22.0	23.5	26.6
30	**Total employees**	**527.9**	**501.0**	**532.7**	**539.7**	**544.6**	**549.4**	**564.6**	**565.2**
	SELF-EMPLOYED, THOUSAND PERSONS, DOMESTIC CONCEPT								
31	Agriculture, forestry and fishing	6.2	6.5	8.4	6.9	6.0	5.7	6.2	6.9
32	Industry, including energy	4.6	4.7	4.2	4.3	5.1	5.5	5.9	6.7
33	Manufacturing	4.2	4.7	4.2	4.1	4.9	5.3	5.7	6.5
34	Construction	6.1	5.0	7.5	8.0	8.1	7.2	8.0	9.4
35	Distrib. trade, repairs; transp.; accommod., food serv. activ.	14.9	13.4	13.9	15.7	14.3	15.7	16.8	14.9
36	Information and communication	..	..	..	..	3.1	2.4	2.6	3.6
37	Financial and insurance activities	..	..	..	..	..	..	..	..
38	Real estate activities	..	..	..	..	1.1	1.3	2.0	2.3
39	Prof., scientif., techn. activ.; admin., support service activ.	6.8	7.0	6.9	7.7	9.2	9.4	6.9	6.2
40	Public admin.; compulsory s.s.; education; human health	2.1	2.3	2.3	2.6	2.7	2.1	2.7	2.8
41	Other service activities	5.3	4.9	4.5	4.7	6.1	6.5	7.0	6.5
42	**Total self-employed**	**48.7**	**47.1**	**51.3**	**53.8**	**56.3**	**56.1**	**58.3**	**59.5**
	TOTAL EMPLOYMENT, MILLION HOURS, DOMESTIC CONCEPT								
43	Industry, including energy	227.7	232.4	263.3	249.7	243.7	240.1	249.2	252.6
44	Distrib. trade, repairs; transp.; accommod., food serv. activ.	279.0	270.2	286.3	279.6	280.3	292.2	288.3	298.9
45	Financial and insurance activities	21.1	17.7	20.7	19.7	18.9	14.5	16.6	19.7
46	Prof., scientif., techn. activ.; admin., support service activ.	65.5	70.9	74.1	79.6	86.6	79.6	79.3	83.0
47	Public admin.; compulsory s.s.; education; human health	237.6	233.4	238.0	247.4	247.1	253.3	249.7	243.8
48	**Total employment**	**1 056.4**	**1 027.5**	**1 120.6**	**1 119.2**	**1 121.2**	**1 125.9**	**1 153.4**	**1 158.9**
	EMPLOYEES, MILLION HOURS, DOMESTIC CONCEPT								
49	Industry, including energy	219.5	223.5	255.2	241.2	233.5	229.7	237.5	239.5
50	Distrib. trade, repairs; transp.; accommod., food serv. activ.	248.3	240.6	257.1	248.2	253.5	262.4	256.4	268.6
51	Financial and insurance activities	21.0	17.7	20.1	18.8	17.6	14.0	16.2	19.2
52	Prof., scientif., techn. activ.; admin., support service activ.	52.6	57.3	60.6	63.7	68.8	62.4	66.9	69.8
53	Public admin.; compulsory s.s.; education; human health	234.2	229.5	233.5	243.2	242.2	250.0	245.8	239.1
54	**Total employees**	**963.2**	**935.0**	**1 017.0**	**1 012.5**	**1 013.9**	**1 020.3**	**1 048.4**	**1 044.0**
	SELF-EMPLOYED, MILLION HOURS, DOMESTIC CONCEPT								
55	Industry, including energy	8.2	8.9	8.2	8.6	10.2	10.4	11.6	13.2
56	Distrib. trade, repairs; transp.; accommod., food serv. activ.	30.7	29.6	29.2	31.4	26.9	29.8	32.0	30.2
57	Financial and insurance activities	..	..	..	..	..	..	..	..
58	Prof., scientif., techn. activ.; admin., support service activ.	13.0	13.6	13.5	15.9	17.7	17.2	12.4	13.2
59	Public admin.; compulsory s.s.; education; human health	3.4	3.9	4.5	4.2	4.9	3.3	3.9	4.8
60	**Total self-employed**	**93.2**	**92.5**	**103.6**	**106.6**	**107.3**	**105.6**	**105.0**	**114.9**

Note: Detailed metadata:http://metalinks.oecd.org/nav1/20180308/bdec
Source: Statistical Office of Estonia via Eurostat.

FINLAND

Table 1. Gross domestic product, expenditure approach

Million EUR (1999 FIM euro)

		2009	2010	2011	2012	2013	2014	2015	2016
	AT CURRENT PRICES								
1	**Final consumption expenditure**	**139 052**	**144 253**	**152 262**	**157 790**	**161 588**	**164 346**	**167 057**	**170 772**
2	Household	90 383	94 466	100 464	103 735	105 890	108 064	110 422	113 462
3	NPISH's	4 829	5 087	5 307	5 373	5 387	5 571	5 494	5 605
4	Government	43 840	44 700	46 491	48 682	50 311	50 711	51 141	51 705
5	Individual	28 929	29 662	31 229	32 872	33 636	33 975	34 616	34 572
6	Collective	14 911	15 038	15 262	15 810	16 675	16 736	16 525	17 133
7	*of which: Actual individual consumption*	124 141	129 215	137 000	141 980	144 913	147 610	150 532	153 639
8	**Gross capital formation**	**38 428**	**40 479**	**46 282**	**45 007**	**43 550**	**43 039**	**43 853**	**47 249**
9	Gross fixed capital formation, total	41 187	40 933	43 779	44 610	43 083	42 235	42 713	46 549
10	Dwellings	9 475	11 341	12 358	12 559	12 111	11 393	11 704	13 277
11	Other buildings and structures	12 721	11 563	12 507	12 296	12 207	12 138	12 211	13 589
12	Transport equipment	2 253	2 177	2 146	2 328	2 185	1 888	1 946	2 210
13	Other machinery and equipment	6 104	5 000	5 942	6 839	6 269	6 377	6 607	7 355
14	Cultivated assets	51	51	45	40	40	40	37	30
15	Intangible fixed assets	9 589	9 867	9 711	9 464	9 310	9 376	8 991	8 830
16	Changes in inventories, acquisitions less disposals of valuables	-2 759	-454	2 503	397	467	804	1 140	700
17	Changes in inventories	-2 826	-520	2 434	328	398	743	1 072	632
18	Acquisitions less disposals of valuables	67	66	69	69	69	61	68	68
19	**External balance of goods and services**	**3 640**	**2 368**	**-1 675**	**-2 883**	**-1 800**	**-1 911**	**-989**	**-2 526**
20	Exports of goods and services	65 661	72 366	77 093	78 881	78 924	76 482	76 493	76 834
21	Exports of goods	45 627	51 470	55 655	56 561	56 728	56 447	53 267	52 957
22	Exports of services	20 034	20 896	21 438	22 320	22 196	20 035	23 226	23 877
23	Imports of goods and services	62 021	69 998	78 768	81 764	80 724	78 393	77 482	79 360
24	Imports of goods	41 791	49 221	57 269	57 272	56 572	55 009	51 490	52 715
25	Imports of services	20 230	20 777	21 499	24 492	24 152	23 384	25 992	26 645
26	**Statistical discrepancy**	**-91**	**0**	**0**	**-121**	**0**	**0**	**-317**	**278**
27	**Gross domestic product**	**181 029**	**187 100**	**196 869**	**199 793**	**203 338**	**205 474**	**209 604**	**215 773**
	AT CONSTANT PRICES, REFERENCE YEAR 2010								
28	**Final consumption expenditure**	**141 337**	**144 253**	**147 114**	**147 682**	**147 723**	**148 267**	**150 136**	**152 809**
29	Household	91 623	94 466	97 369	97 735	97 347	97 939	99 818	101 644
30	NPISH's	4 969	5 087	5 101	5 080	5 002	5 190	5 088	5 140
31	Government	44 752	44 700	44 644	44 867	45 364	45 137	45 233	46 027
32	Individual	29 547	29 662	29 941	30 122	30 140	30 002	30 272	30 589
33	Collective	15 205	15 038	14 703	14 744	15 228	15 139	14 960	15 445
34	*of which: Actual individual consumption*	126 133	129 215	132 411	132 938	132 493	133 127	135 174	137 363
35	**Gross capital formation**	**37 700**	**40 479**	**45 004**	**42 134**	**40 087**	**39 375**	**39 968**	**42 480**
36	Gross fixed capital formation, total	40 489	40 933	42 610	41 782	39 719	38 695	38 967	41 868
37	Dwellings	9 142	11 341	11 944	11 526	10 916	10 201	10 407	11 513
38	Other buildings and structures	12 271	11 563	12 136	11 328	11 060	10 948	11 063	12 141
39	Transport equipment	2 270	2 177	2 121	2 230	2 102	1 808	1 839	2 079
40	Other machinery and equipment	6 120	5 000	5 807	6 572	5 952	6 027	6 198	6 874
41	Cultivated assets	51	51	43	40	37	38	35	29
42	Intangible fixed assets	9 768	9 867	9 444	8 943	8 609	8 566	8 125	7 860
43	Changes in inventories, acquisitions less disposals of valuables	..	..	..	..	..	..	..	..
44	Changes in inventories	..	..	..	..	..	..	..	..
45	Acquisitions less disposals of valuables	70	66	67	67	64	57	63	60
46	**External balance of goods and services**	**2 429**	**2 368**	**-419**	**-715**	**-226**	**-1 305**	**-3 035**	**-5 496**
47	Exports of goods and services	68 155	72 366	73 803	74 718	75 553	73 494	74 177	75 904
48	Exports of goods	47 805	51 470	52 961	53 455	54 581	54 802	52 667	53 852
49	Exports of services	20 329	20 896	20 842	21 267	20 973	18 723	21 442	21 979
50	Imports of goods and services	65 726	69 998	74 222	75 433	75 779	74 799	77 212	81 400
51	Imports of goods	44 920	49 221	53 327	52 270	52 987	52 863	52 900	56 555
52	Imports of services	20 746	20 777	20 895	23 247	22 857	21 994	24 337	24 941
53	**Statistical discrepancy (including chaining residual)**	**198**	**0**	**211**	**72**	**155**	**216**	**-264**	**1 001**
54	**Gross domestic product**	**181 664**	**187 100**	**191 910**	**189 173**	**187 739**	**186 553**	**186 805**	**190 794**

Note: Detailed metadata:http://metalinks.oecd.org/nav1/20180308/b17d
Source: Statistics Finland via Eurostat.

FINLAND

Table 2. Gross domestic product, output and income approach
ISIC Rev. 4

Million EUR (1999 FIM euro)

		2009	2010	2011	2012	2013	2014	2015	2016
	OUTPUT APPROACH AT CURRENT PRICES								
1	**Total gross value added at basic prices**	158 348	163 620	170 454	172 417	175 002	176 987	180 818	185 649
2	Agriculture, forestry and fishing	4 028	4 468	4 649	4 713	5 222	4 934	4 665	4 991
3	Industry, including energy	35 893	38 495	38 340	35 286	35 983	36 313	37 341	37 613
4	Manufacturing	30 292	31 948	32 164	29 067	29 641	29 908	31 024	31 366
5	Construction	10 724	10 548	10 905	11 336	11 300	11 081	11 552	12 786
6	Services	..	..	..	..	..	..	..	..
7	Distrib. trade, repairs; transp.; accommod., food serv. activ.	25 898	26 394	28 260	29 350	28 888	28 504	28 772	29 234
8	Information and communication	8 039	8 168	8 593	8 961	9 253	9 825	10 304	10 711
9	Financial and insurance activities	4 563	4 234	4 565	4 635	4 332	5 230	5 204	5 240
10	Real estate activities	17 789	18 325	19 414	20 079	20 967	21 663	22 814	23 886
11	Prof., scientif., techn. activ.; admin., support service activ.	12 536	12 947	13 914	14 523	14 735	14 832	15 080	15 837
12	Public admin.; compulsory s.s.; education; human health	33 992	34 964	36 523	38 142	38 839	39 054	39 449	39 524
13	Other service activities	4 886	5 077	5 291	5 392	5 483	5 551	5 637	5 827
14	**FISIM (Financial Intermediation Services Indirectly Measured)**	..	..	..	..	..	..	..	..
15	**Gross value added at basic prices, excluding FISIM**	158 348	163 620	170 454	172 417	175 002	176 987	180 818	185 649
16	**Taxes less subsidies on products**	22 681	23 480	26 415	27 376	28 336	28 487	28 786	30 124
17	Taxes on products	23 334	24 176	27 123	28 111	29 104	29 259	29 625	30 970
18	Subsidies on products	653	696	708	735	768	772	839	846
19	**Residual item**	0	0	0	0	0	0	0	0
20	**Gross domestic product at market prices**	181 029	187 100	196 869	199 793	203 338	205 474	209 604	215 773
	OUTPUT APPROACH AT CONSTANT PRICES (REF. YEAR 2010)								
21	**Total gross value added at basic prices**	158 790	163 620	166 820	163 585	162 131	161 130	161 368	164 333
22	Agriculture, forestry and fishing	4 444	4 468	4 663	4 547	4 925	4 843	4 838	4 988
23	Industry, including energy	35 911	38 495	38 276	35 029	35 023	34 939	34 352	34 749
24	Manufacturing	29 670	31 948	31 912	28 258	28 497	28 239	27 868	28 385
25	Construction	9 602	10 548	10 671	10 102	9 897	9 543	9 856	10 411
26	Services	..	..	..	..	..	..	..	..
27	Distrib. trade, repairs; transp.; accommod., food serv. activ.	25 620	26 394	27 451	27 942	26 959	26 403	26 324	26 783
28	Information and communication	7 849	8 168	8 740	9 258	9 518	9 969	10 303	10 546
29	Financial and insurance activities	4 154	4 234	4 211	4 116	3 731	4 123	4 132	4 116
30	Real estate activities	18 526	18 325	19 076	19 006	19 040	19 061	19 255	19 604
31	Prof., scientif., techn. activ.; admin., support service activ.	12 833	12 947	13 591	13 752	13 546	13 342	13 409	13 903
32	Public admin.; compulsory s.s.; education; human health	35 019	34 964	34 964	34 739	34 557	34 077	34 004	34 256
33	Other service activities	4 982	5 077	5 177	5 054	4 969	4 913	4 955	5 051
34	**FISIM (Financial Intermediation Services Indirectly Measured)**	..	..	..	..	..	..	..	..
35	**Gross value added at basic prices, excluding FISIM**	158 790	163 620	166 820	163 585	162 131	161 130	161 368	164 333
36	**Taxes less subsidies on products**	22 875	23 480	25 090	25 562	25 578	25 393	25 408	26 427
37	Taxes on products	23 545	24 176	25 791	26 284	26 323	26 153	26 199	27 222
38	Subsidies on products	670	696	701	722	747	764	798	801
39	**Residual item**	-1	0	0	26	30	30	29	34
40	**Gross domestic product at market prices**	181 664	187 100	191 910	189 173	187 739	186 553	186 805	190 794
	INCOME APPROACH								
41	**Compensation of employees**	90 940	92 404	96 828	100 288	101 169	101 413	102 518	104 355
42	Agriculture, forestry and fishing	1 038	1 125	1 121	1 163	1 169	1 175	1 167	1 094
43	Industry, including energy	18 508	18 036	18 787	19 214	18 670	18 448	18 599	18 775
44	Manufacturing	17 052	16 561	17 216	17 543	16 994	16 785	16 935	16 968
45	Construction	6 892	7 179	7 616	7 820	7 893	7 780	8 010	8 484
46	Distrib. trade, repairs; transp.; accommod., food serv. activ.	16 992	16 837	17 716	18 411	18 639	18 682	18 647	19 029
47	Information and communication	4 647	4 714	4 982	5 149	5 459	5 474	5 696	5 878
48	Financial and insurance activities	2 595	2 628	2 768	2 830	2 897	2 833	2 910	2 981
49	Real estate activities	895	874	901	934	929	930	975	1 023
50	Prof., scientif., techn. activ.; admin., support service activ.	8 648	9 191	9 822	10 294	10 445	10 765	10 809	11 394
51	Public admin.; compulsory s.s.; education; human health	27 393	28 332	29 503	30 775	31 293	31 443	31 756	31 642
52	Other service activities	3 332	3 488	3 612	3 698	3 775	3 883	3 949	4 055
53	**Wages and salaries**	73 342	75 133	78 580	81 283	81 968	82 254	83 095	84 451
54	Agriculture, forestry and fishing	846	905	905	939	954	939	931	861
55	Industry, including energy	15 047	14 838	15 391	15 727	15 309	15 183	15 272	15 372
56	Manufacturing	13 868	13 623	14 102	14 361	13 933	13 815	13 912	13 877
57	Construction	5 610	5 913	6 253	6 425	6 492	6 402	6 584	6 973
58	Distrib. trade, repairs; transp.; accommod., food serv. activ.	13 874	13 972	14 650	15 178	15 322	15 436	15 359	15 623
59	Information and communication	3 803	3 897	4 099	4 232	4 504	4 518	4 691	4 813
60	Financial and insurance activities	2 115	2 175	2 295	2 321	2 386	2 325	2 390	2 442
61	Real estate activities	741	735	749	776	774	774	812	852
62	Prof., scientif., techn. activ.; admin., support service activ.	7 108	7 556	8 071	8 443	8 573	8 853	8 896	9 359
63	Public admin.; compulsory s.s.; education; human health	21 544	22 357	23 282	24 287	24 640	24 734	25 008	24 924
64	Other service activities	2 654	2 785	2 885	2 955	3 014	3 090	3 152	3 232
65	**Gross operating surplus and mixed income**	69 867	73 752	76 166	74 698	76 180	77 880	80 754	83 510
66	**Taxes less subsidies on production and imports**	20 222	20 944	23 875	24 807	25 989	26 181	26 332	27 908
67	Taxes on production and imports	23 531	24 378	27 371	28 320	29 473	29 727	29 913	31 360
68	Subsidies on production and imports	3 309	3 434	3 496	3 513	3 484	3 546	3 581	3 452
69	**Residual item**	0	0	0	0	0	0	0	0
70	**Gross domestic product**	181 029	187 100	196 869	199 793	203 338	205 474	209 604	215 773

Note: Detailed metadata:http://metalinks.oecd.org/nav1/20180308/b17d

Source: Statistics Finland via Eurostat.

Table 3. Disposable income, saving and net lending / net borrowing

Million EUR (1999 FIM euro)

		2009	2010	2011	2012	2013	2014	2015	2016
	DISPOSABLE INCOME								
1	**Gross domestic product**	181 029	187 100	196 869	199 793	203 338	205 474	209 604	215 773
2	Net primary incomes from the rest of the world	2 321	2 535	892	1 043	696	1 868	1 868	1 702
3	Primary incomes receivable from the rest of the world	12 330	15 005	15 284	15 358	14 287	16 809	15 458	17 281
4	Primary incomes payable to the rest of the world	10 009	12 470	14 392	14 315	13 591	14 941	13 590	15 579
5	**Gross national income at market prices**	183 350	189 635	197 761	200 836	204 034	207 342	211 472	217 475
6	Consumption of fixed capital	35 395	35 339	36 581	38 266	39 064	39 443	39 715	40 304
7	**Net national income at market prices**	147 955	154 296	161 180	162 570	164 970	167 899	171 757	177 171
8	Net current transfers from the rest of the world	-2 273	-2 212	-2 099	-1 927	-2 698	-2 646	-2 590	-2 491
9	Current transfers receivable from the rest of the world	890	1 001	1 415	1 643	1 230	1 187	1 068	1 134
10	Current transfers payable to the rest of the world	3 163	3 213	3 514	3 570	3 928	3 833	3 658	3 625
11	**Net national disposable income**	145 682	152 084	159 081	160 643	162 272	165 253	169 167	174 680
	SAVING AND NET LENDING / NET BORROWING								
12	**Net national disposable income**	145 682	152 084	159 081	160 643	162 272	165 253	169 167	174 680
13	Final consumption expenditures	139 052	144 253	152 262	157 790	161 588	164 346	167 057	170 772
14	Adj. for change in net equity of households in pension funds	0	0	0	0	0	0	0	0
15	**Saving, net**	6 630	7 831	6 819	2 853	684	907	2 110	3 908
16	Net capital transfers from the rest of the world	144	173	196	201	219	172	146	63
17	Capital transfers receivable from the rest of the world	160	178	206	208	233	188	154	87
18	Capital transfers payable to the rest of the world	16	5	10	7	14	16	8	24
19	Gross capital formation	38 337	40 479	46 282	44 886	43 550	43 039	43 536	47 527
20	Acquisitions less disposals of non-financial non-produced assets	-18	-18	-12	-12	-12	-12	-12	-12
21	Consumption of fixed capital	35 395	35 339	36 581	38 266	39 064	39 443	39 715	40 304
22	**Net lending / net borrowing**	3 850	2 882	-2 674	-3 554	-3 571	-2 505	-1 553	-3 240
	REAL DISPOSABLE INCOME								
23	**Gross domestic product at constant prices, reference year 2010**	181 664	187 100	191 910	189 173	187 739	186 553	186 805	190 794
24	Trading gain or loss	897	0	-1 413	-2 153	-1 562	-620	2 142	2 482
25	**Real gross domestic income**	182 561	187 100	190 497	187 020	186 177	185 933	188 947	193 276
26	Net real primary incomes from the rest of the world	2 341	2 535	863	976	637	1 690	1 684	1 525
27	Real primary incomes receivable from the rest of the world	12 434	15 005	14 789	14 376	13 081	15 210	13 935	15 479
28	Real primary incomes payable to the rest of the world	10 094	12 470	13 926	13 400	12 444	13 520	12 251	13 955
29	**Real gross national income at market prices**	184 901	189 635	191 360	187 996	186 815	187 624	190 630	194 800
30	Net real current transfers from the rest of the world	-2 292	-2 212	-2 031	-1 804	-2 470	-2 394	-2 335	-2 231
31	Real current transfers receivable from the rest of the world	898	1 001	1 369	1 538	1 126	1 074	963	1 016
32	Real current transfers payable to the rest of the world	3 190	3 213	3 400	3 342	3 596	3 468	3 297	3 247
33	**Real gross national disposable income**	182 609	187 423	189 329	186 192	184 344	185 229	188 296	192 569
34	Consumption of fixed capital at constant prices	35 021	35 339	35 571	35 986	36 117	36 188	36 218	36 232
35	**Real net national income at market prices**	149 207	154 296	155 963	152 176	151 047	151 932	154 830	158 698
36	**Real net national disposable income**	146 915	152 084	153 932	150 373	148 577	149 537	152 495	156 467

Note: Detailed metadata:http://metalinks.oecd.org/nav1/20180308/63ad
Source: Statistics Finland via Eurostat.

Table 4. Population and employment (persons) and employment (hours worked) by industry
ISIC Rev. 4

		2009	2010	2011	2012	2013	2014	2015	2016
	POPULATION, THOUSAND PERSONS, NATIONAL CONCEPT								
1	**Total population**	**5 338.9**	**5 363.4**	**5 388.3**	**5 414.0**	**5 439.0**	**5 462.5**	**5 480.5**	**5 495.3**
2	Economically active population	..	..	..	..	..	..	..	..
3	Unemployed persons	..	..	..	..	..	..	..	..
4	Total employment	2 501.0	2 483.8	2 515.5	2 537.6	2 519.6	2 507.5	2 504.1	2 510.4
5	Employees	2 202.0	2 188.7	2 214.0	2 231.4	2 221.1	2 205.3	2 197.5	2 208.2
6	Self-employed	299.0	295.1	301.5	306.2	298.5	302.2	306.6	302.2
	TOTAL EMPLOYMENT, THOUSAND PERSONS, DOMESTIC CONCEPT								
7	Agriculture, forestry and fishing	121.3	119.7	115.4	114.8	112.4	111.4	108.3	98.5
8	Industry, including energy	415.0	396.4	400.7	400.3	386.0	375.7	369.8	365.3
9	Manufacturing	383.0	364.8	368.8	367.6	353.5	343.6	338.3	333.3
10	Construction	186.5	188.6	193.6	193.0	190.4	188.0	191.3	200.4
11	Distrib. trade, repairs; transp.; accommod., food serv. activ.	537.5	525.4	529.4	537.8	533.0	531.6	526.8	526.3
12	Information and communication	93.7	93.5	94.6	95.9	98.8	98.4	100.0	100.6
13	Financial and insurance activities	46.3	46.6	47.4	47.0	46.4	44.8	45.0	45.0
14	Real estate activities	24.3	24.4	24.0	24.2	23.8	23.5	24.8	25.2
15	Prof., scientif., techn. activ.; admin., support service activ.	253.7	261.0	270.9	277.0	277.2	284.5	283.8	294.8
16	Public admin.; compulsory s.s.; education; human health	701.9	704.3	712.6	717.0	719.0	713.7	716.8	714.0
17	Other service activities	120.8	123.9	126.9	130.6	132.6	135.9	137.5	140.3
18	**Total employment**	**2 501.0**	**2 483.8**	**2 515.5**	**2 537.6**	**2 519.6**	**2 507.5**	**2 504.1**	**2 510.4**
	EMPLOYEES, THOUSAND PERSONS, DOMESTIC CONCEPT								
19	Agriculture, forestry and fishing	40.4	41.6	40.1	41.4	42.4	40.8	39.8	36.1
20	Industry, including energy	394.0	375.8	375.0	376.2	363.3	355.4	349.7	345.3
21	Manufacturing	363.2	345.4	344.5	344.8	332.2	324.7	319.6	314.7
22	Construction	153.8	156.1	160.4	159.6	157.0	154.1	157.0	163.7
23	Distrib. trade, repairs; transp.; accommod., food serv. activ.	466.9	455.3	458.5	466.5	465.6	461.9	455.8	457.5
24	Information and communication	86.3	85.8	87.3	88.4	91.2	90.6	91.7	93.1
25	Financial and insurance activities	45.1	45.2	45.9	45.5	44.9	43.3	43.5	43.5
26	Real estate activities	20.7	20.4	20.4	20.6	20.4	20.1	21.0	21.6
27	Prof., scientif., techn. activ.; admin., support service activ.	208.3	216.9	228.2	231.7	232.3	238.5	235.5	244.7
28	Public admin.; compulsory s.s.; education; human health	681.3	684.5	691.3	694.7	695.7	690.2	691.9	689.3
29	Other service activities	105.2	107.1	106.9	106.8	108.3	110.4	111.6	113.4
30	**Total employees**	**2 202.0**	**2 188.7**	**2 214.0**	**2 231.4**	**2 221.1**	**2 205.3**	**2 197.5**	**2 208.2**
	SELF-EMPLOYED, THOUSAND PERSONS, DOMESTIC CONCEPT								
31	Agriculture, forestry and fishing	80.9	78.1	75.3	73.4	70.0	70.6	68.5	62.4
32	Industry, including energy	21.0	20.6	25.7	24.1	22.7	20.3	20.1	20.0
33	Manufacturing	19.8	19.4	24.3	22.8	21.3	18.9	18.7	18.6
34	Construction	32.7	32.5	33.2	33.4	33.4	33.9	34.3	36.7
35	Distrib. trade, repairs; transp.; accommod., food serv. activ.	70.6	70.1	70.9	71.3	67.4	69.7	71.0	68.8
36	Information and communication	7.4	7.7	7.3	7.5	7.6	7.8	8.3	7.5
37	Financial and insurance activities	1.2	1.4	1.5	1.5	1.5	1.5	1.5	1.5
38	Real estate activities	3.6	4.0	3.6	3.6	3.4	3.4	3.8	3.6
39	Prof., scientif., techn. activ.; admin., support service activ.	45.4	44.1	42.7	45.3	44.9	46.0	48.3	50.1
40	Public admin.; compulsory s.s.; education; human health	20.6	19.8	21.3	22.3	23.3	23.5	24.9	24.7
41	Other service activities	15.6	16.8	20.0	23.8	24.3	25.5	25.9	26.9
42	**Total self-employed**	**299.0**	**295.1**	**301.5**	**306.2**	**298.5**	**302.2**	**306.6**	**302.2**
	TOTAL EMPLOYMENT, MILLION HOURS, DOMESTIC CONCEPT								
43	Industry, including energy	647.6	630.6	640.4	635.0	605.8	586.8	577.4	571.8
44	Distrib. trade, repairs; transp.; accommod., food serv. activ.	909.8	892.4	879.0	885.5	874.7	871.3	863.2	864.4
45	Financial and insurance activities	74.2	74.1	74.1	73.3	72.7	70.3	70.9	71.7
46	Prof., scientif., techn. activ.; admin., support service activ.	404.2	409.3	427.6	430.6	428.1	439.3	438.5	456.0
47	Public admin.; compulsory s.s.; education; human health	1 083.8	1 089.8	1 103.9	1 108.5	1 112.1	1 103.2	1 106.9	1 101.7
48	**Total employment**	**4 153.3**	**4 142.4**	**4 181.9**	**4 187.7**	**4 131.1**	**4 103.1**	**4 099.7**	**4 103.9**
	EMPLOYEES, MILLION HOURS, DOMESTIC CONCEPT								
49	Industry, including energy	602.4	588.3	596.6	590.8	567.2	553.0	543.8	538.2
50	Distrib. trade, repairs; transp.; accommod., food serv. activ.	750.3	732.9	740.6	744.5	741.6	734.2	724.0	729.0
51	Financial and insurance activities	72.2	71.8	71.7	70.9	70.3	67.9	68.5	69.3
52	Prof., scientif., techn. activ.; admin., support service activ.	321.5	335.3	349.0	352.2	351.0	359.4	355.1	369.5
53	Public admin.; compulsory s.s.; education; human health	1 047.6	1 054.7	1 063.2	1 067.5	1 068.8	1 059.5	1 061.2	1 057.2
54	**Total employees**	**3 472.0**	**3 473.5**	**3 518.5**	**3 522.6**	**3 495.3**	**3 464.6**	**3 452.9**	**3 476.0**
	SELF-EMPLOYED, MILLION HOURS, DOMESTIC CONCEPT								
55	Industry, including energy	45.2	42.3	43.8	44.2	38.6	33.8	33.6	33.6
56	Distrib. trade, repairs; transp.; accommod., food serv. activ.	159.5	159.5	138.4	141.0	133.1	137.1	139.2	135.4
57	Financial and insurance activities	2.0	2.3	2.4	2.4	2.4	2.4	2.4	2.4
58	Prof., scientif., techn. activ.; admin., support service activ.	82.7	74.0	78.6	78.4	77.1	79.9	83.4	86.5
59	Public admin.; compulsory s.s.; education; human health	36.2	35.1	40.7	41.0	43.3	43.7	45.7	44.5
60	**Total self-employed**	**681.3**	**668.9**	**663.4**	**665.1**	**635.8**	**638.5**	**646.8**	**627.9**

Note: Detailed metadata:http://metalinks.oecd.org/nav1/20180308/e9fa
Source: Statistics Finland via Eurostat.

Table 1. Gross domestic product, expenditure approach

Million EUR (1999 FRF euro)

		2009	2010	2011	2012	2013	2014	2015	2016
	AT CURRENT PRICES								
1	**Final consumption expenditure**	**1 553 540**	**1 598 200**	**1 634 071**	**1 659 313**	**1 683 217**	**1 701 788**	**1 727 373 p**	**1 759 625 p**
2	Household	1 051 463	1 082 394	1 106 881	1 119 646	1 132 231	1 141 496	1 160 572 p	1 186 093 p
3	NPISH's	38 143	39 623	41 048	42 083	43 362	44 615	45 920 p	46 790 p
4	Government	463 934	476 183	486 142	497 584	507 624	515 677	520 881 p	526 742 p
5	Individual	298 600	307 824	313 816	320 490	326 788	334 360	339 313 p	343 647 p
6	Collective	165 334	168 359	172 326	177 094	180 836	181 317	181 568 p	183 095 p
7	*of which: Actual individual consumption*	1 388 206	1 429 841	1 461 745	1 482 219	1 502 381	1 520 471	1 545 805 p	1 576 530 p
8	**Gross capital formation**	**413 100**	**437 892**	**477 972**	**472 626**	**471 862**	**488 207**	**499 936 p**	**512 647 p**
9	Gross fixed capital formation, total	427 320	441 067	461 566	469 106	466 668	469 072	473 219 p	489 359 p
10	Dwellings	121 318	125 811	131 289	130 376	129 780	129 845	128 967 p	133 392 p
11	Other buildings and structures	124 133	122 627	130 792	132 227	130 980	128 625	124 848 p	124 432 p
12	Transport equipment	24 457	26 899	29 724	28 965	28 149	30 360	33 548 p	35 802 p
13	Other machinery and equipment	57 680	61 152	60 563	63 670	62 000	61 166	61 566 p	65 465 p
14	Cultivated assets	830	843	819	1 029	1 210	1 311	1 269 p	1 244 p
15	Intangible fixed assets	90 966	95 031	99 587	103 442	106 218	108 815	112 846 p	118 375 p
16	Changes in inventories, acquisitions less disposals of valuables	-14 220	-3 175	16 406	3 520	5 194	19 135	26 717 p	23 288 p
17	Changes in inventories	-14 739	-3 856	15 729	2 804	4 537	18 225	26 114 p	23 335 p
18	Acquisitions less disposals of valuables	519	681	677	716	657	910	603 p	-47 p
19	**External balance of goods and services**	**-27 623**	**-37 611**	**-52 759**	**-45 010**	**-39 823**	**-42 386**	**-33 066 p**	**-43 415 p**
20	Exports of goods and services	466 753	520 469	572 553	595 230	605 134	620 855	651 088 p	652 178 p
21	Exports of goods	346 794	390 583	427 402	440 063	443 174	445 843	466 365 p	467 089 p
22	Exports of services	119 959	129 886	145 151	155 167	161 960	175 012	184 723 p	185 089 p
23	Imports of goods and services	494 376	558 080	625 312	640 240	644 957	663 241	684 154 p	695 593 p
24	Imports of goods	377 959	431 221	486 688	492 296	485 220	485 456	492 829 p	495 845 p
25	Imports of services	116 417	126 859	138 624	147 944	159 737	177 785	191 325 p	199 748 p
26	**Statistical discrepancy**	**0**	**0**	**0**	**0**	**0**	**0**	**0 p**	**0 p**
27	**Gross domestic product**	**1 939 017**	**1 998 481**	**2 059 284**	**2 086 929**	**2 115 256**	**2 147 609**	**2 194 243 p**	**2 228 857 p**
	AT CONSTANT PRICES, REFERENCE YEAR 2010								
28	**Final consumption expenditure**	**1 571 927**	**1 598 200**	**1 608 458**	**1 613 692**	**1 626 365**	**1 641 569**	**1 663 556 p**	**1 695 432 p**
29	Household	1 063 917	1 082 394	1 087 130	1 084 402	1 089 531	1 097 195	1 112 550 p	1 137 589 p
30	NPISH's	37 837	39 623	40 217	40 486	40 911	41 973	42 879 p	43 301 p
31	Government	470 198	476 183	481 111	488 850	496 017	502 509	508 216 p	514 585 p
32	Individual	301 888	307 824	312 119	317 557	322 152	328 799	333 641 p	338 879 p
33	Collective	168 324	168 359	168 992	171 298	173 870	173 774	174 668 p	175 823 p
34	*of which: Actual individual consumption*	1 403 621	1 429 841	1 439 466	1 442 386	1 452 481	1 467 789	1 488 894 p	1 519 617 p
35	**Gross capital formation**	**423 647**	**437 892**	**468 474**	**456 757**	**457 907**	**472 736**	**484 112 p**	**493 549 p**
36	Gross fixed capital formation, total	432 075	441 067	450 180	451 222	447 587	447 733	452 173 p	465 045 p
37	Dwellings	123 209	125 811	126 901	124 117	123 644	121 260	119 741 p	122 904 p
38	Other buildings and structures	126 421	122 627	126 020	124 448	122 829	121 079	119 588 p	118 977 p
39	Transport equipment	24 434	26 899	28 874	27 945	27 184	28 665	31 090 p	33 060 p
40	Other machinery and equipment	58 247	61 152	60 076	62 335	60 370	59 579	59 522 p	63 200 p
41	Cultivated assets	843	843	766	885	1 011	1 114	1 089 p	1 093 p
42	Intangible fixed assets	91 409	95 031	98 338	101 643	103 435	105 690	109 254 p	113 247 p
43	Changes in inventories, acquisitions less disposals of valuables	..	..	..	..	..	..	..	..
44	Changes in inventories	..	..	..	..	..	..	..	..
45	Acquisitions less disposals of valuables	..	..	..	..	..	..	..	..
46	**External balance of goods and services**	**-35 212**	**-37 611**	**-36 898**	**-26 698**	**-28 455**	**-38 523**	**-49 619 p**	**-66 511 p**
47	Exports of goods and services	477 424	520 469	556 273	570 399	581 288	600 541	626 159 p	637 730 p
48	Exports of goods	354 048	390 583	412 001	417 777	422 861	429 575	446 101 p	457 062 p
49	Exports of services	123 408	129 886	144 272	152 767	158 682	171 425	180 568 p	181 127 p
50	Imports of goods and services	512 636	558 080	593 171	597 097	609 743	639 064	675 778 p	704 241 p
51	Imports of goods	394 748	431 221	456 066	452 767	454 538	467 162	490 993 p	511 553 p
52	Imports of services	117 847	126 859	137 105	144 680	156 057	173 192	186 187 p	194 146 p
53	**Statistical discrepancy (including chaining residual)**	**-407**	**0**	**0**	**10**	**-279**	**-766**	**-883 p**	**-397 p**
54	**Gross domestic product**	**1 959 955**	**1 998 481**	**2 040 034**	**2 043 761**	**2 055 538**	**2 075 016**	**2 097 166 p**	**2 122 073 p**

Note: Detailed metadata:http://metalinks.oecd.org/nav1/20180308/e917

Source: Institut National de la Statistique et des Etudes Economiques (INSEE) via Eurostat.

FRANCE

Table 2. Gross domestic product, output and income approach
ISIC Rev. 4

Million EUR (1999 FRF euro)

		2009	2010	2011	2012	2013	2014	2015	2016
	OUTPUT APPROACH AT CURRENT PRICES								
1	**Total gross value added at basic prices**	1 752 722	1 800 982	1 849 498	1 873 450	1 897 908	1 925 074	1 963 342 p	1 992 345 p
2	Agriculture, forestry and fishing	25 669	32 092	34 044	34 078	30 882	33 458	34 647 p	32 689 p
3	Industry, including energy	241 546	243 780	254 065	258 467	263 767	267 166	278 030 p	279 973 p
4	Manufacturing	201 691	202 620	210 379	212 245	215 361	217 640	226 313 p	226 737 p
5	Construction	109 755	109 247	112 731	110 445	112 759	110 903	107 501 p	109 593 p
6	Services	..	..	..	..	..	..	..	..
7	Distrib. trade, repairs; transp.; accommod., food serv. activ.	317 373	322 391	328 763	333 591	335 064	338 289	344 511 p	350 580 p
8	Information and communication	92 329	93 018	94 189	94 172	93 791	95 029	98 329 p	103 648 p
9	Financial and insurance activities	69 261	81 796	78 971	79 347	83 951	86 923	87 966 p	82 071 p
10	Real estate activities	229 279	230 483	235 771	240 716	243 084	246 856	253 038 p	259 147 p
11	Prof., scientif., techn. activ.; admin., support service activ.	218 484	227 712	239 052	240 147	241 597	246 432	253 404 p	262 521 p
12	Public admin.; compulsory s.s.; education; human health	395 784	405 702	416 899	426 353	435 622	442 099	446 711 p	452 113 p
13	Other service activities	53 240	54 761	55 014	56 134	57 392	57 920	59 207 p	60 009 p
14	**FISIM (Financial Intermediation Services Indirectly Measured)**	..	..	..	..	..	..	..	..
15	Gross value added at basic prices, excluding FISIM	1 752 722	1 800 982	1 849 498	1 873 450	1 897 908	1 925 074	1 963 342 p	1 992 345 p
16	**Taxes less subsidies on products**	186 295	197 499	209 786	213 479	217 348	222 535	230 901 p	236 513 p
17	Taxes on products	203 123	213 185	225 453	230 251	234 627	240 446	249 981 p	256 717 p
18	Subsidies on products	16 828	15 686	15 667	16 772	17 279	17 911	19 080 p	20 204 p
19	**Residual item**	0	0	0	0	0	0	0 p	-1 p
20	**Gross domestic product at market prices**	1 939 017	1 998 481	2 059 284	2 086 929	2 115 256	2 147 609	2 194 243 p	2 228 857 p
	OUTPUT APPROACH AT CONSTANT PRICES (REF. YEAR 2010)								
21	**Total gross value added at basic prices**	1 769 818	1 800 982	1 839 021	1 846 727	1 858 169	1 878 632	1 895 079 p	1 915 183 p
22	Agriculture, forestry and fishing	33 209	32 092	33 342	30 467	29 884	34 278	34 470 p	31 113 p
23	Industry, including energy	239 157	243 780	250 452	251 861	254 354	255 995	259 528 p	263 313 p
24	Manufacturing	197 772	202 620	210 602	209 754	210 060	213 831	216 197 p	219 449 p
25	Construction	111 849	109 247	107 098	101 453	101 913	99 184	97 281 p	97 383 p
26	Services	..	..	..	..	..	..	..	..
27	Distrib. trade, repairs; transp.; accommod., food serv. activ.	314 133	322 391	332 557	333 698	333 964	336 828	340 032 p	346 556 p
28	Information and communication	89 587	93 018	98 787	103 102	102 576	106 660	109 965 p	113 026 p
29	Financial and insurance activities	81 450	81 796	87 107	88 928	88 943	90 074	90 973 p	89 522 p
30	Real estate activities	226 774	230 483	229 182	232 605	236 396	239 218	241 553 p	243 838 p
31	Prof., scientif., techn. activ.; admin., support service activ.	219 311	227 712	235 316	234 462	235 252	238 518	241 621 p	246 548 p
32	Public admin.; compulsory s.s.; education; human health	401 906	405 702	411 324	416 996	421 553	425 445	427 107 p	430 984 p
33	Other service activities	53 182	54 761	53 856	53 759	53 770	53 511	54 189 p	54 625 p
34	**FISIM (Financial Intermediation Services Indirectly Measured)**	..	..	..	..	..	..	..	..
35	Gross value added at basic prices, excluding FISIM	1 769 818	1 800 982	1 839 021	1 846 727	1 858 169	1 878 632	1 895 079 p	1 915 183 p
36	**Taxes less subsidies on products**	190 099	197 499	201 014	197 192	197 578	196 800	202 169 p	206 750 p
37	Taxes on products	205 413	213 185	216 442	213 001	213 658	212 385	218 086 p	222 754 p
38	Subsidies on products	15 292	15 686	15 428	15 826	16 102	15 597	15 930 p	16 030 p
39	**Residual item**	38	0	-1	-158	-209	-416	-82 p	140 p
40	**Gross domestic product at market prices**	1 959 955	1 998 481	2 040 034	2 043 761	2 055 538	2 075 016	2 097 166 p	2 122 073 p
	INCOME APPROACH								
41	**Compensation of employees**	1 013 013	1 040 212	1 068 929	1 092 356	1 107 702	1 126 700	1 139 847 p	1 159 670 p
42	Agriculture, forestry and fishing	8 136	8 439	8 600	9 061	9 533	9 737	9 689 p	9 945 p
43	Industry, including energy	146 108	147 558	150 355	152 891	153 919	155 417	155 608 p	156 403 p
44	Manufacturing	128 695	129 494	131 740	133 378	133 907	135 219	134 976 p	135 623 p
45	Construction	67 327	67 353	68 719	69 022	69 966	69 862	68 018 p	67 918 p
46	Distrib. trade, repairs; transp.; accommod., food serv. activ.	204 527	210 438	214 948	219 929	221 202	224 650	227 496 p	232 538 p
47	Information and communication	49 344	50 834	52 387	54 133	54 825	56 078	57 759 p	59 620 p
48	Financial and insurance activities	45 709	46 839	47 309	49 140	48 757	49 550	50 572 p	51 178 p
49	Real estate activities	13 890	14 174	14 813	14 877	15 133	15 089	14 916 p	15 607 p
50	Prof., scientif., techn. activ.; admin., support service activ.	142 742	150 035	159 173	162 803	166 040	170 678	175 976 p	183 261 p
51	Public admin.; compulsory s.s.; education; human health	295 923	303 613	311 000	318 225	325 114	331 611	335 257 p	338 190 p
52	Other service activities	39 307	40 929	41 625	42 275	43 213	44 028	44 556 p	45 006 p
53	**Wages and salaries**	746 658	768 018	784 783	800 407	808 911	820 071	831 446 p	847 814 p
54	Agriculture, forestry and fishing	5 911	6 137	6 246	6 494	6 696	6 803	6 852 p	7 056 p
55	Industry, including energy	106 602	107 602	108 817	110 106	110 379	111 042	111 363 p	112 235 p
56	Manufacturing	95 416	95 936	96 828	97 815	97 854	98 448	98 534 p	99 289 p
57	Construction	53 780	54 243	55 060	55 365	55 968	55 635	54 256 p	54 286 p
58	Distrib. trade, repairs; transp.; accommod., food serv. activ.	157 197	162 090	164 190	167 850	168 188	170 215	172 983 p	177 255 p
59	Information and communication	36 545	37 924	38 721	39 986	40 383	41 150	42 400 p	43 900 p
60	Financial and insurance activities	32 299	33 185	33 450	34 540	34 304	34 518	35 118 p	35 656 p
61	Real estate activities	10 852	11 096	11 531	11 553	11 726	11 676	11 515 p	12 074 p
62	Prof., scientif., techn. activ.; admin., support service activ.	108 684	114 650	120 999	123 719	125 972	129 159	134 028 p	139 873 p
63	Public admin.; compulsory s.s.; education; human health	204 464	209 475	213 715	218 210	221 998	226 056	228 658 p	230 762 p
64	Other service activities	30 324	31 616	32 054	32 584	33 297	33 817	34 274 p	34 718 p
65	**Gross operating surplus and mixed income**	678 528	708 464	721 230	718 004	721 733	737 330	769 386 p	777 364 p
66	**Taxes less subsidies on production and imports**	247 476	249 805	269 125	276 569	285 823	283 578	285 010 p	291 824 p
67	Taxes on production and imports	290 999	295 146	312 820	321 719	330 843	339 117	349 616 p	357 689 p
68	Subsidies on production and imports	43 523	45 341	43 695	45 150	45 020	55 539	64 606 p	65 865 p
69	**Residual item**	0	0	0	0	-1	1	0 p	0 p
70	**Gross domestic product**	1 939 017	1 998 481	2 059 284	2 086 929	2 115 257	2 147 609	2 194 243 p	2 228 858 p

Note: Detailed metadata:http://metalinks.oecd.org/nav1/20180308/e917

Source: Institut National de la Statistique et des Etudes Economiques (INSEE) via Eurostat.

Table 3. Disposable income, saving and net lending / net borrowing

Million EUR (1999 FRF euro)

		2009	2010	2011	2012	2013	2014	2015	2016
	DISPOSABLE INCOME								
1	**Gross domestic product**	1 939 017	1 998 481	2 059 284	2 086 929	2 115 257	2 147 609	2 194 243 p	2 228 858 p
2	Net primary incomes from the rest of the world	34 630	40 794	47 419	29 599	29 492	30 824	33 242 p	35 464 p
3	Primary incomes receivable from the rest of the world	151 061	158 232	167 292	157 270	147 425	146 331	148 298 p	146 232 p
4	Primary incomes payable to the rest of the world	116 431	117 438	119 873	127 671	117 933	115 507	115 056 p	110 768 p
5	**Gross national income at market prices**	1 973 647	2 039 275	2 106 703	2 116 528	2 144 749	2 178 433	2 227 485 p	2 264 322 p
6	Consumption of fixed capital	345 930	354 182	367 245	376 622	381 626	387 640	392 702 p	401 593 p
7	**Net national income at market prices**	1 627 717	1 685 093	1 739 458	1 739 906	1 763 123	1 790 793	1 834 783 p	1 862 729 p
8	Net current transfers from the rest of the world	-38 159	-38 115	-40 638	-45 756	-50 085	-53 450	-49 281 p	-49 881 p
9	Current transfers receivable from the rest of the world	17 256	18 644	20 061	19 682	19 866	19 604	21 856 p	23 779 p
10	Current transfers payable to the rest of the world	55 415	56 759	60 699	65 438	69 951	73 054	71 137 p	73 660 p
11	**Net national disposable income**	1 589 558	1 646 978	1 698 820	1 694 150	1 713 038	1 737 343	1 785 501 p	1 812 848 p
	SAVING AND NET LENDING / NET BORROWING								
12	**Net national disposable income**	1 589 558	1 646 978	1 698 820	1 694 150	1 713 038	1 737 343	1 785 501 p	1 812 848 p
13	Final consumption expenditures	1 553 540	1 598 200	1 634 071	1 659 313	1 683 217	1 701 788	1 727 373 p	1 759 625 p
14	Adj. for change in net equity of households in pension funds	0	0	0	0	0	0	0	0
15	**Saving, net**	36 018	48 778	64 749	34 837	29 821	35 555	58 128 p	53 223 p
16	Net capital transfers from the rest of the world	318	115	-168	-3 431	470	-1 070	-1 184 p	1 716 p
17	Capital transfers receivable from the rest of the world	1 038	1 200	1 126	1 086	1 371	1 250	1 807 p	2 572 p
18	Capital transfers payable to the rest of the world	720	1 085	1 294	4 517	901	2 320	2 991 p	856 p
19	Gross capital formation	413 100	437 892	477 972	472 626	471 862	488 207	499 936 p	512 648 p
20	Acquisitions less disposals of non-financial non-produced assets	0	0	0	0	0	0	0	0
21	Consumption of fixed capital	345 930	354 182	367 245	376 622	381 626	387 640	392 702 p	401 593 p
22	**Net lending / net borrowing**	-30 834	-34 817	-46 146	-64 598	-59 945	-66 082	-50 290 p	-56 116 p
	REAL DISPOSABLE INCOME								
23	**Gross domestic product at constant prices, reference year 2010**	1 959 955	1 998 481	2 040 034	2 043 761	2 055 538	2 075 016	2 097 166 p	2 122 073 p
24	Trading gain or loss	7 662	0	-14 984	-17 068	-9 835	-1 723	18 512 p	24 976 p
25	**Real gross domestic income**	1 967 617	1 998 481	2 025 050	2 026 693	2 045 703	2 073 293	2 115 678 p	2 147 049 p
26	Net real primary incomes from the rest of the world	35 141	40 794	46 631	28 745	28 522	29 757	32 052 p	34 162 p
27	Real primary incomes receivable from the rest of the world	153 289	158 232	164 511	152 731	142 577	141 267	142 988 p	140 865 p
28	Real primary incomes payable to the rest of the world	118 148	117 438	117 880	123 986	114 055	111 510	110 936 p	106 702 p
29	**Real gross national income at market prices**	2 002 757	2 039 275	2 071 681	2 055 438	2 074 226	2 103 050	2 147 729 p	2 181 211 p
30	Net real current transfers from the rest of the world	-38 722	-38 115	-39 962	-44 435	-48 438	-51 600	-47 516 p	-48 050 p
31	Real current transfers receivable from the rest of the world	17 511	18 644	19 728	19 114	19 213	18 926	21 073 p	22 906 p
32	Real current transfers payable to the rest of the world	56 232	56 759	59 690	63 549	67 651	70 526	68 590 p	70 956 p
33	**Real gross national disposable income**	1 964 036	2 001 160	2 031 718	2 011 003	2 025 787	2 051 450	2 100 212 p	2 133 161 p
34	Consumption of fixed capital at constant prices	349 831	354 182	358 878	363 364	367 075	371 210	376 246 p	382 432 p
35	**Real net national income at market prices**	1 651 725	1 685 093	1 710 541	1 689 687	1 705 148	1 728 824	1 769 088 p	1 794 359 p
36	**Real net national disposable income**	1 613 003	1 646 978	1 670 578	1 645 251	1 656 710	1 677 224	1 721 571 p	1 746 309 p

Note: Detailed metadata:http://metalinks.oecd.org/nav1/20180308/1d62
Source: Institut National de la Statistique et des Etudes Economiques (INSEE) via Eurostat.

Table 4. Population and employment (persons) and employment (hours worked) by industry
ISIC Rev. 4

		2009	2010	2011	2012	2013	2014	2015	2016
	POPULATION, THOUSAND PERSONS, NATIONAL CONCEPT								
1	**Total population**	64 655.0	64 974.0	65 294.0	65 615.0	65 953.0	66 290.0	66 590.0 p	66 858.0 p
2	Economically active population	..	..	..	..	..	..	..	..
3	Unemployed persons	..	..	..	..	..	..	..	..
4	Total employment	27 220.0	27 257.0	27 476.0	27 570.0	27 648.0	27 781.0	27 851.0 p	28 040.0 p
5	Employees	24 775.0	24 747.0	24 867.0	24 873.0	24 844.0	24 924.0	25 002.0 p	25 196.0 p
6	Self-employed	2 444.0	2 511.0	2 608.0	2 698.0	2 804.0	2 857.0	2 849.0 p	2 844.0 p
	TOTAL EMPLOYMENT, THOUSAND PERSONS, DOMESTIC CONCEPT								
7	Agriculture, forestry and fishing	777.0	761.0	756.0	754.0	752.0	750.0	746.0 p	743.0 p
8	Industry, including energy	3 189.0	3 066.0	3 041.0	3 027.0	3 006.0	2 991.0	2 963.0 p	2 933.0 p
9	Manufacturing	2 893.0	2 764.0	2 738.0	2 720.0	2 696.0	2 682.0	2 653.0 p	2 626.0 p
10	Construction	1 869.0	1 843.0	1 841.0	1 834.0	1 832.0	1 818.0	1 767.0 p	1 743.0 p
11	Distrib. trade, repairs; transp.; accommod., food serv. activ.	6 028.0	6 080.0	6 121.0	6 164.0	6 126.0	6 119.0	6 146.0 p	6 212.0 p
12	Information and communication	779.0	774.0	784.0	802.0	809.0	808.0	816.0 p	832.0 p
13	Financial and insurance activities	767.0	768.0	777.0	783.0	783.0	784.0	789.0 p	792.0 p
14	Real estate activities	347.0	345.0	355.0	354.0	355.0	343.0	343.0 p	346.0 p
15	Prof., scientif., techn. activ.; admin., support service activ.	3 586.0	3 667.0	3 824.0	3 844.0	3 866.0	3 936.0	3 996.0 p	4 115.0 p
16	Public admin.; compulsory s.s.; education; human health	8 028.0	8 060.0	8 066.0	8 080.0	8 166.0	8 255.0	8 298.0 p	8 313.0 p
17	Other service activities	1 489.0	1 523.0	1 534.0	1 544.0	1 557.0	1 568.0	1 570.0 p	1 583.0 p
18	**Total employment**	26 859.0	26 888.0	27 099.0	27 185.0	27 252.0	27 373.0	27 434.0 p	27 612.0 p
	EMPLOYEES, THOUSAND PERSONS, DOMESTIC CONCEPT								
19	Agriculture, forestry and fishing	328.0	321.0	322.0	325.0	326.0	332.0	337.0 p	341.0 p
20	Industry, including energy	3 056.0	2 932.0	2 904.0	2 886.0	2 861.0	2 842.0	2 816.0 p	2 788.0 p
21	Manufacturing	2 765.0	2 635.0	2 607.0	2 587.0	2 558.0	2 541.0	2 514.0 p	2 489.0 p
22	Construction	1 583.0	1 548.0	1 533.0	1 515.0	1 499.0	1 480.0	1 436.0 p	1 417.0 p
23	Distrib. trade, repairs; transp.; accommod., food serv. activ.	5 404.0	5 448.0	5 470.0	5 492.0	5 433.0	5 419.0	5 452.0 p	5 515.0 p
24	Information and communication	739.0	731.0	735.0	749.0	751.0	748.0	756.0 p	772.0 p
25	Financial and insurance activities	740.0	741.0	748.0	754.0	753.0	753.0	758.0 p	761.0 p
26	Real estate activities	318.0	315.0	324.0	321.0	320.0	309.0	309.0 p	312.0 p
27	Prof., scientif., techn. activ.; admin., support service activ.	3 304.0	3 366.0	3 490.0	3 485.0	3 486.0	3 544.0	3 605.0 p	3 722.0 p
28	Public admin.; compulsory s.s.; education; human health	7 636.0	7 644.0	7 639.0	7 639.0	7 697.0	7 763.0	7 787.0 p	7 800.0 p
29	Other service activities	1 325.0	1 350.0	1 344.0	1 341.0	1 341.0	1 347.0	1 350.0 p	1 362.0 p
30	**Total employees**	24 433.0	24 396.0	24 509.0	24 507.0	24 468.0	24 537.0	24 606.0 p	24 790.0 p
	SELF-EMPLOYED, THOUSAND PERSONS, DOMESTIC CONCEPT								
31	Agriculture, forestry and fishing	449.0	440.0	434.0	429.0	426.0	419.0	409.0 p	402.0 p
32	Industry, including energy	133.0	134.0	137.0	140.0	145.0	149.0	147.0 p	145.0 p
33	Manufacturing	128.0	129.0	131.0	133.0	137.0	141.0	139.0 p	137.0 p
34	Construction	286.0	295.0	308.0	319.0	333.0	338.0	331.0 p	327.0 p
35	Distrib. trade, repairs; transp.; accommod., food serv. activ.	624.0	632.0	651.0	671.0	693.0	700.0	693.0 p	696.0 p
36	Information and communication	40.0	43.0	49.0	53.0	58.0	60.0	60.0 p	60.0 p
37	Financial and insurance activities	27.0	27.0	28.0	29.0	30.0	31.0	31.0 p	31.0 p
38	Real estate activities	29.0	30.0	32.0	33.0	34.0	34.0	34.0 p	34.0 p
39	Prof., scientif., techn. activ.; admin., support service activ.	282.0	301.0	335.0	359.0	381.0	392.0	391.0 p	393.0 p
40	Public admin.; compulsory s.s.; education; human health	392.0	416.0	428.0	441.0	468.0	492.0	511.0 p	513.0 p
41	Other service activities	164.0	173.0	189.0	203.0	216.0	221.0	220.0 p	221.0 p
42	**Total self-employed**	2 426.0	2 492.0	2 589.0	2 678.0	2 784.0	2 836.0	2 828.0 p	2 822.0 p
	TOTAL EMPLOYMENT, MILLION HOURS, DOMESTIC CONCEPT								
43	Industry, including energy	4 929.4	4 820.7	4 820.4	4 784.0	4 707.8	4 687.5	4 669.6 p	4 610.4 p
44	Distrib. trade, repairs; transp.; accommod., food serv. activ.	9 359.7	9 463.0	9 563.1	9 586.6	9 482.4	9 417.3	9 421.2 p	9 428.1 p
45	Financial and insurance activities	1 192.8	1 203.2	1 227.6	1 242.4	1 234.1	1 232.7	1 256.0 p	1 257.1 p
46	Prof., scientif., techn. activ.; admin., support service activ.	5 465.3	5 645.0	5 892.0	5 901.9	5 882.7	5 975.9	6 102.5 p	6 275.2 p
47	Public admin.; compulsory s.s.; education; human health	11 116.8	11 173.5	11 252.7	11 231.8	11 217.5	11 343.0	11 376.2 p	11 386.0 p
48	**Total employment**	40 859.9	41 083.5	41 586.3	41 562.9	41 256.1	41 305.5	41 409.2 p	41 493.3 p
	EMPLOYEES, MILLION HOURS, DOMESTIC CONCEPT								
49	Industry, including energy	4 615.9	4 503.9	4 497.0	4 453.7	4 372.1	4 343.6	4 322.9 p	4 270.1 p
50	Distrib. trade, repairs; transp.; accommod., food serv. activ.	7 888.3	7 979.9	8 042.3	8 036.9	7 901.0	7 832.3	7 900.6 p	7 919.3 p
51	Financial and insurance activities	1 138.3	1 150.3	1 170.4	1 182.8	1 171.7	1 170.4	1 190.3 p	1 191.4 p
52	Prof., scientif., techn. activ.; admin., support service activ.	4 868.5	5 014.0	5 202.0	5 165.9	5 118.8	5 196.0	5 324.5 p	5 496.0 p
53	Public admin.; compulsory s.s.; education; human health	10 370.9	10 384.6	10 437.0	10 407.0	10 378.5	10 470.9	10 466.5 p	10 480.4 p
54	**Total employees**	35 236.7	35 363.9	35 700.2	35 563.4	35 190.4	35 213.1	35 356.9 p	35 511.8 p
	SELF-EMPLOYED, MILLION HOURS, DOMESTIC CONCEPT								
55	Industry, including energy	313.5	316.8	323.4	330.4	335.6	343.9	346.7 p	340.2 p
56	Distrib. trade, repairs; transp.; accommod., food serv. activ.	1 471.4	1 483.1	1 520.8	1 549.7	1 581.4	1 585.1	1 520.6 p	1 508.8 p
57	Financial and insurance activities	54.5	52.8	57.2	59.7	62.4	62.3	65.7 p	65.7 p
58	Prof., scientif., techn. activ.; admin., support service activ.	596.8	631.0	690.0	736.0	763.9	779.9	778.0 p	779.2 p
59	Public admin.; compulsory s.s.; education; human health	746.0	788.8	815.7	824.8	839.0	872.1	909.6 p	905.6 p
60	**Total self-employed**	5 623.3	5 719.7	5 886.1	5 999.5	6 065.7	6 092.5	6 052.3 p	5 981.5 p

Note: Detailed metadata:http://metalinks.oecd.org/nav1/20180308/d579
Source: Institut National de la Statistique et des Etudes Economiques (INSEE) via Eurostat.

GERMANY

Table 1. Gross domestic product, expenditure approach

Million EUR (1999 DEM euro)

		2009	2010	2011	2012	2013	2014	2015	2016
	AT CURRENT PRICES								
1	**Final consumption expenditure**	**1 894 248**	**1 939 610**	**2 001 224**	**2 057 742**	**2 106 353**	**2 157 121**	**2 217 532**	**2 289 840**
2	Household	1 375 161	1 406 989	1 454 007	1 494 689	1 512 625	1 540 580	1 577 215	1 619 138
3	NPISH's	37 880	39 285	41 526	43 340	50 875	52 606	53 254	55 256
4	Government	481 207	493 336	505 691	519 713	542 853	563 935	587 063	615 446
5	Individual	304 769	314 878	323 721	330 134	347 536	364 278	382 356	401 654
6	Collective	176 438	178 458	181 970	189 579	195 317	199 657	204 707	213 792
7	*of which: Actual individual consumption*	1 717 810	1 761 152	1 819 254	1 868 163	1 911 036	1 957 464	2 012 825	2 076 048
8	**Gross capital formation**	**444 510**	**506 347**	**569 751**	**532 531**	**551 462**	**572 336**	**582 812**	**603 591**
9	Gross fixed capital formation, total	471 421	501 449	547 821	554 746	556 752	586 555	604 285	630 034
10	Dwellings	126 066	133 266	150 704	160 243	163 622	172 722	174 831	185 485
11	Other buildings and structures	100 725	103 856	113 524	112 763	113 542	116 995	116 150	119 015
12	Transport equipment	43 860	56 865	56 582	51 299	50 757	55 910	56 569	56 660
13	Other machinery and equipment	..	..	..	..	..	..	..	..
14	Cultivated assets	300	302	294	339	560	460	382	397
15	Intangible fixed assets	86 162	88 116	94 980	97 580	98 981	104 679	112 144	119 300
16	Changes in inventories, acquisitions less disposals of valuables	-26 911	4 898	21 930	-22 215	-5 290	-14 219	-21 473	-26 443
17	Changes in inventories	-28 842	2 629	19 073	-25 007	-8 201	-16 617	-24 055	-29 353
18	Acquisitions less disposals of valuables	1 931	2 269	2 857	2 792	2 911	2 398	2 582	2 910
19	**External balance of goods and services**	**121 522**	**134 103**	**132 145**	**167 987**	**168 425**	**203 013**	**243 306**	**250 619**
20	Exports of goods and services	930 040	1 090 085	1 211 489	1 268 318	1 283 053	1 340 265	1 426 706	1 450 012
21	Exports of goods	770 393	918 340	1 030 111	1 071 424	1 077 420	1 115 751	1 179 210	1 194 439
22	Exports of services	159 647	171 745	181 378	196 894	205 633	224 514	247 496	255 573
23	Imports of goods and services	808 518	955 982	1 079 344	1 100 331	1 114 628	1 137 252	1 183 400	1 199 393
24	Imports of goods	629 218	757 196	866 676	871 038	867 569	887 392	918 147	922 376
25	Imports of services	179 300	198 786	212 668	229 293	247 059	249 860	265 253	277 017
26	**Statistical discrepancy**	**0**	**0**	**0**	**0**	**0**	**0**	**0**	**0**
27	**Gross domestic product**	**2 460 280**	**2 580 060**	**2 703 120**	**2 758 260**	**2 826 240**	**2 932 470**	**3 043 650**	**3 144 050**
	AT CONSTANT PRICES, REFERENCE YEAR 2010								
28	**Final consumption expenditure**	**1 927 972**	**1 939 610**	**1 963 661**	**1 988 682**	**2 004 587**	**2 026 892**	**2 067 624**	**2 119 218**
29	Household	1 401 924	1 406 989	1 425 702	1 444 274	1 447 370	1 461 017	1 487 047	1 517 578
30	NPISH's	39 018	39 285	40 086	41 190	47 150	47 735	47 684	48 894
31	Government	487 021	493 336	497 973	503 203	510 011	517 904	532 704	552 240
32	Individual	309 431	314 878	319 538	321 585	326 214	333 582	345 673	358 331
33	Collective	177 584	178 458	178 404	181 599	183 794	184 311	187 006	193 895
34	*of which: Actual individual consumption*	1 750 233	1 761 152	1 785 280	1 807 118	1 820 855	1 842 517	1 880 734	1 925 291
35	**Gross capital formation**	**448 117**	**506 347**	**553 387**	**507 765**	**515 360**	**526 246**	**527 462**	**538 753**
36	Gross fixed capital formation, total	475 825	501 449	537 403	533 893	527 173	546 880	555 305	572 304
37	Dwellings	127 762	133 266	146 579	151 550	150 404	155 135	154 082	160 306
38	Other buildings and structures	102 080	103 856	109 848	106 203	104 406	105 445	102 786	103 596
39	Transport equipment	44 218	56 865	56 012	50 354	49 780	54 607	55 034	54 789
40	Other machinery and equipment	..	..	..	..	..	..	..	..
41	Cultivated assets	311	302	296	297	299	172	157	157
42	Intangible fixed assets	87 129	88 116	92 839	93 870	94 302	98 285	103 713	109 440
43	Changes in inventories, acquisitions less disposals of valuables	..	..	..	..	..	..	..	..
44	Changes in inventories	..	..	..	..	..	..	..	..
45	Acquisitions less disposals of valuables	1 972	2 269	2 786	2 689	2 777	2 272	2 436	2 745
46	**External balance of goods and services**	**104 658**	**134 103**	**157 252**	**191 278**	**181 698**	**201 166**	**207 760**	**198 393**
47	Exports of goods and services	951 753	1 090 085	1 180 344	1 213 701	1 234 521	1 291 751	1 359 336	1 395 091
48	Exports of goods	789 038	918 340	999 338	1 023 490	1 035 979	1 078 774	1 130 477	1 156 374
49	Exports of services	162 746	171 745	181 088	190 293	198 640	213 187	229 005	238 726
50	Imports of goods and services	847 096	955 982	1 023 092	1 022 423	1 052 823	1 090 584	1 151 576	1 196 698
51	Imports of goods	663 077	757 196	816 787	805 202	822 163	859 948	909 771	944 072
52	Imports of services	183 798	198 786	206 320	217 492	231 188	231 208	242 579	253 253
53	**Statistical discrepancy (including chaining residual)**	**-1 825**	**0**	**190**	**-76**	**-838**	**-1 381**	**-1 933**	**-1 011**
54	**Gross domestic product**	**2 478 922**	**2 580 060**	**2 674 490**	**2 687 649**	**2 700 807**	**2 752 924**	**2 800 913**	**2 855 352**

Note: Detailed metadata:http://metalinks.oecd.org/nav1/20180308/824f
Source: Statistisches Bundesamt (Destatis) via Eurostat.

GERMANY

Table 2. Gross domestic product, output and income approach
ISIC Rev. 4

Million EUR (1999 DEM euro)

		2009	2010	2011	2012	2013	2014	2015	2016
	OUTPUT APPROACH AT CURRENT PRICES								
1	**Total gross value added at basic prices**	**2 207 236**	**2 321 695**	**2 428 078**	**2 478 596**	**2 542 656**	**2 639 816**	**2 740 226**	**2 831 942**
2	Agriculture, forestry and fishing	16 248	16 700	19 967	19 388	24 840	20 226	16 899	17 392
3	Industry, including energy	522 487	600 439	635 684	650 111	652 498	684 476	711 692	728 603
4	Manufacturing	439 843	515 175	556 004	563 279	570 445	603 863	631 954	648 788
5	Construction	91 295	99 843	106 503	110 962	113 037	119 089	124 889	134 940
6	Services	..	..	..	..	..	..	..	..
7	Distrib. trade, repairs; transp.; accommod., food serv. activ.	373 250	370 497	386 990	386 919	395 406	418 615	440 517	454 045
8	Information and communication	104 580	103 345	112 130	116 418	119 927	124 873	129 065	134 257
9	Financial and insurance activities	104 790	106 292	101 652	108 418	108 461	109 353	111 524	111 469
10	Real estate activities	266 222	267 279	281 645	278 631	289 902	290 582	299 492	308 912
11	Prof., scientif., techn. activ.; admin., support service activ.	233 342	246 332	255 925	264 606	275 906	289 012	301 304	312 608
12	Public admin.; compulsory s.s.; education; human health	399 793	414 351	428 936	442 779	458 440	476 344	493 369	514 582
13	Other service activities	95 229	96 617	98 646	100 364	104 239	107 246	111 475	115 134
14	FISIM (Financial Intermediation Services Indirectly Measured)	..	..	..	..	..	..	..	..
15	**Gross value added at basic prices, excluding FISIM**	**2 207 236**	**2 321 695**	**2 428 078**	**2 478 596**	**2 542 656**	**2 639 816**	**2 740 226**	**2 831 942**
16	**Taxes less subsidies on products**	**253 044**	**258 365**	**275 042**	**279 664**	**283 584**	**292 654**	**303 424**	**312 108**
17	Taxes on products	263 780	266 327	282 030	286 129	290 337	299 408	310 987	319 328
18	Subsidies on products	10 736	7 962	6 988	6 465	6 753	6 754	7 563	7 220
19	**Residual item**	**0**	**0**	**0**	**0**	**0**	**0**	**0**	**0**
20	**Gross domestic product at market prices**	**2 460 280**	**2 580 060**	**2 703 120**	**2 758 260**	**2 826 240**	**2 932 470**	**3 043 650**	**3 144 050**
	OUTPUT APPROACH AT CONSTANT PRICES (REF. YEAR 2010)								
21	**Total gross value added at basic prices**	**2 226 970**	**2 321 695**	**2 404 347**	**2 418 278**	**2 431 047**	**2 477 016**	**2 515 324**	**2 563 151**
22	Agriculture, forestry and fishing	22 084	16 700	14 977	14 850	15 615	13 737	15 913	15 822
23	Industry, including energy	519 260	600 439	632 983	631 362	628 840	662 464	676 995	689 604
24	Manufacturing	435 065	515 175	559 068	546 601	546 652	578 387	589 515	602 137
25	Construction	92 804	99 843	103 617	102 449	99 913	102 718	102 738	104 735
26	Services	..	..	..	..	..	..	..	..
27	Distrib. trade, repairs; transp.; accommod., food serv. activ.	376 647	370 497	385 020	396 209	392 542	399 248	401 989	411 437
28	Information and communication	103 128	103 345	114 827	119 653	123 580	129 419	132 788	136 395
29	Financial and insurance activities	103 656	106 292	106 696	107 674	117 463	111 670	110 841	114 200
30	Real estate activities	270 593	267 279	276 634	271 475	278 986	275 591	276 099	277 676
31	Prof., scientif., techn. activ.; admin., support service activ.	237 095	246 332	252 072	255 028	255 298	261 358	266 211	271 039
32	Public admin.; compulsory s.s.; education; human health	407 058	414 351	421 022	423 881	423 757	426 823	436 270	446 049
33	Other service activities	97 293	96 617	96 598	96 086	95 516	95 264	95 931	96 820
34	FISIM (Financial Intermediation Services Indirectly Measured)	..	..	..	..	..	..	..	..
35	**Gross value added at basic prices, excluding FISIM**	**2 226 970**	**2 321 695**	**2 404 347**	**2 418 278**	**2 431 047**	**2 477 016**	**2 515 324**	**2 563 151**
36	**Taxes less subsidies on products**	**251 725**	**258 365**	**269 966**	**269 371**	**269 733**	**275 779**	**285 674**	**292 159**
37	Taxes on products	263 078	266 327	276 767	275 702	276 128	282 200	292 028	297 913
38	Subsidies on products	11 665	7 962	6 808	6 336	6 403	6 416	6 354	5 845
39	**Residual item**	**227**	**0**	**177**	**0**	**27**	**129**	**-85**	**42**
40	**Gross domestic product at market prices**	**2 478 922**	**2 580 060**	**2 674 490**	**2 687 649**	**2 700 807**	**2 752 924**	**2 800 913**	**2 855 352**
	INCOME APPROACH								
41	**Compensation of employees**	**1 245 663**	**1 281 963**	**1 337 273**	**1 388 832**	**1 427 407**	**1 482 753**	**1 540 222**	**1 598 200**
42	Agriculture, forestry and fishing	6 048	6 095	6 613	6 789	7 102	7 417	7 684	7 928
43	Industry, including energy	339 502	348 877	366 552	379 144	393 052	405 367	417 908	427 530
44	Manufacturing	309 957	319 461	336 384	347 707	360 682	373 669	385 005	394 440
45	Construction	64 223	65 593	68 614	71 084	71 306	73 863	76 325	78 955
46	Distrib. trade, repairs; transp.; accommod., food serv. activ.	225 711	230 544	238 600	248 771	254 078	263 022	272 620	285 849
47	Information and communication	53 565	53 917	56 633	60 136	61 442	65 355	68 312	71 361
48	Financial and insurance activities	62 477	61 909	63 882	65 478	67 114	69 234	69 548	70 871
49	Real estate activities	10 764	10 907	11 272	11 708	11 638	12 233	12 726	13 605
50	Prof., scientif., techn. activ.; admin., support service activ.	115 705	124 654	135 314	144 597	147 078	156 011	167 068	172 847
51	Public admin.; compulsory s.s.; education; human health	316 343	327 257	335 865	345 989	358 428	372 582	388 249	406 991
52	Other service activities	51 325	52 210	53 928	55 136	56 169	57 669	59 782	62 263
53	**Wages and salaries**	**1 008 327**	**1 037 105**	**1 086 105**	**1 130 504**	**1 164 763**	**1 210 196**	**1 258 501**	**1 309 010**
54	Agriculture, forestry and fishing	5 038	5 076	5 504	5 661	5 929	6 194	6 426	6 631
55	Industry, including energy	274 261	282 101	300 302	313 212	323 675	334 629	344 498	351 925
56	Manufacturing	251 457	258 746	276 173	288 348	297 705	308 264	318 070	325 020
57	Construction	53 283	54 421	57 020	59 230	59 480	61 666	63 696	66 026
58	Distrib. trade, repairs; transp.; accommod., food serv. activ.	188 344	191 977	200 008	208 335	213 115	221 138	230 064	239 446
59	Information and communication	43 920	43 907	46 078	48 751	50 191	53 195	55 642	58 859
60	Financial and insurance activities	49 114	49 355	50 146	51 511	52 720	53 868	54 507	55 138
61	Real estate activities	8 870	9 013	9 349	9 595	9 777	10 139	10 663	11 292
62	Prof., scientif., techn. activ.; admin., support service activ.	94 691	101 476	109 653	116 403	120 531	127 312	136 613	144 875
63	Public admin.; compulsory s.s.; education; human health	247 973	256 394	263 196	271 955	282 511	294 018	306 665	322 699
64	Other service activities	42 805	43 385	44 849	45 851	46 834	48 037	49 727	52 119
65	**Gross operating surplus and mixed income**	**973 897**	**1 051 627**	**1 099 183**	**1 094 336**	**1 119 985**	**1 161 918**	**1 202 291**	**1 237 563**
66	**Taxes less subsidies on production and imports**	**240 720**	**246 470**	**266 664**	**275 092**	**278 848**	**287 799**	**301 137**	**308 287**
67	Taxes on production and imports	279 473	281 784	299 745	305 208	310 107	319 527	332 799	341 656
68	Subsidies on production and imports	38 753	35 314	33 081	30 116	31 259	31 728	31 662	33 369
69	**Residual item**	**0**	**0**	**0**	**0**	**0**	**0**	**0**	**0**
70	**Gross domestic product**	**2 460 280**	**2 580 060**	**2 703 120**	**2 758 260**	**2 826 240**	**2 932 470**	**3 043 650**	**3 144 050**

Note: Detailed metadata:http://metalinks.oecd.org/nav1/20180308/824f
Source: Statistisches Bundesamt (Destatis) via Eurostat.

GERMANY

Table 3. Disposable income, saving and net lending / net borrowing

Million EUR (1999 DEM euro)

		2009	2010	2011	2012	2013	2014	2015	2016
	DISPOSABLE INCOME								
1	**Gross domestic product**	**2 460 280**	**2 580 060**	**2 703 120**	**2 758 260**	**2 826 240**	**2 932 470**	**3 043 650**	**3 144 050**
2	Net primary incomes from the rest of the world	55 275	50 832	68 213	64 687	63 897	57 905	56 135	53 142
3	Primary incomes receivable from the rest of the world	183 688	199 923	219 523	203 519	190 027	188 655	191 155	188 095
4	Primary incomes payable to the rest of the world	128 413	149 091	151 310	138 832	126 130	130 750	135 020	134 953
5	**Gross national income at market prices**	**2 515 555**	**2 630 892**	**2 771 333**	**2 822 947**	**2 890 137**	**2 990 375**	**3 099 785**	**3 197 192**
6	Consumption of fixed capital	450 794	459 725	475 539	492 278	506 192	520 625	536 120	552 291
7	**Net national income at market prices**	**2 064 761**	**2 171 167**	**2 295 794**	**2 330 669**	**2 383 945**	**2 469 750**	**2 563 665**	**2 644 901**
8	Net current transfers from the rest of the world	-32 245	-36 766	-33 098	-35 688	-42 651	-36 726	-37 543	-35 879
9	Current transfers receivable from the rest of the world	41 933	44 116	51 659	54 271	60 629	62 930	70 528	72 062
10	Current transfers payable to the rest of the world	74 178	80 882	84 757	89 959	103 280	99 656	108 071	107 941
11	**Net national disposable income**	**2 032 516**	**2 134 401**	**2 262 696**	**2 294 981**	**2 341 294**	**2 433 024**	**2 526 122**	**2 609 022**
	SAVING AND NET LENDING / NET BORROWING								
12	**Net national disposable income**	**2 032 516**	**2 134 401**	**2 262 696**	**2 294 981**	**2 341 294**	**2 433 024**	**2 526 122**	**2 609 022**
13	Final consumption expenditures	1 894 248	1 939 610	2 001 224	2 057 742	2 106 353	2 157 121	2 217 532	2 289 840
14	Adj. for change in net equity of households in pension funds	0	0	0	0	0	0	0	0
15	**Saving, net**	**138 268**	**194 791**	**261 472**	**237 239**	**234 941**	**275 903**	**308 590**	**319 182**
16	Net capital transfers from the rest of the world	-1 886	-448	-5 712	-3 555	-3 729	-2 773	-3 396	-4 436
17	Capital transfers receivable from the rest of the world	4 332	3 845	4 252	4 911	4 966	5 123	4 561	5 115
18	Capital transfers payable to the rest of the world	6 218	4 293	9 964	8 466	8 695	7 896	7 957	9 551
19	Gross capital formation	444 510	506 347	569 751	532 531	551 462	572 336	582 812	603 591
20	Acquisitions less disposals of non-financial non-produced assets	-32	-2 303	-1 148	-1 744	-1 105	-2 896	-2 379	-3 324
21	Consumption of fixed capital	450 794	459 725	475 539	492 278	506 192	520 625	536 120	552 291
22	**Net lending / net borrowing**	**142 698**	**150 024**	**162 696**	**195 175**	**187 047**	**224 315**	**260 881**	**266 770**
	REAL DISPOSABLE INCOME								
23	**Gross domestic product at constant prices, reference year 2010**	**2 478 922**	**2 580 060**	**2 674 490**	**2 687 649**	**2 700 807**	**2 752 924**	**2 800 913**	**2 855 352**
24	Trading gain or loss	20 105	0	-28 002	-29 664	-21 561	-10 286	19 156	32 238
25	**Real gross domestic income**	**2 499 027**	**2 580 060**	**2 646 489**	**2 657 984**	**2 679 246**	**2 742 638**	**2 820 069**	**2 887 590**
26	Net real primary incomes from the rest of the world	56 146	50 832	66 784	62 335	60 574	54 157	52 011	48 807
27	Real primary incomes receivable from the rest of the world	186 581	199 923	214 924	196 120	180 144	176 443	177 113	172 752
28	Real primary incomes payable to the rest of the world	130 435	149 091	148 140	133 785	119 570	122 286	125 102	123 945
29	**Real gross national income at market prices**	**2 555 172**	**2 630 892**	**2 713 272**	**2 720 320**	**2 739 820**	**2 796 795**	**2 872 081**	**2 936 397**
30	Net real current transfers from the rest of the world	-32 753	-36 766	-32 405	-34 391	-40 433	-34 349	-34 785	-32 952
31	Real current transfers receivable from the rest of the world	42 593	44 116	50 577	52 298	57 476	58 856	65 347	66 184
32	Real current transfers payable to the rest of the world	75 346	80 882	82 981	86 689	97 908	93 205	100 132	99 136
33	**Real gross national disposable income**	**2 522 420**	**2 594 126**	**2 680 868**	**2 685 929**	**2 699 387**	**2 762 446**	**2 837 296**	**2 903 445**
34	Consumption of fixed capital at constant prices	454 760	459 725	466 391	473 747	479 861	486 067	493 469	501 928
35	**Real net national income at market prices**	**2 097 279**	**2 171 167**	**2 247 696**	**2 245 938**	**2 259 955**	**2 309 872**	**2 375 343**	**2 429 157**
36	**Real net national disposable income**	**2 064 526**	**2 134 401**	**2 215 292**	**2 211 548**	**2 219 522**	**2 275 524**	**2 340 558**	**2 396 204**

Note: Detailed metadata:http://metalinks.oecd.org/nav1/20180308/36e7
Source: Statistisches Bundesamt (Destatis) via Eurostat.

Table 4. Population and employment (persons) and employment (hours worked) by industry
ISIC Rev. 4

		2009	2010	2011	2012	2013	2014	2015	2016
	POPULATION, THOUSAND PERSONS, NATIONAL CONCEPT								
1	**Total population**	**80 483.0**	**80 284.0**	**80 275.0**	**80 426.0**	**80 646.0**	**80 983.0**	**81 687.0**	**82 349.0**
2	Economically active population[1]	..	..	..	..	..	..	..	..
3	Unemployed persons[1]	..	..	..	..	..	..	..	..
4	Total employment	40 845.0	40 983.0	41 534.0	42 006.0	42 257.0	42 608.0	42 990.0	43 544.0
5	Employees	36 360.0	36 496.0	36 971.0	37 446.0	37 791.0	38 196.0	38 631.0	39 211.0
6	Self-employed	4 485.0	4 487.0	4 563.0	4 560.0	4 466.0	4 412.0	4 359.0	4 333.0
	TOTAL EMPLOYMENT, THOUSAND PERSONS, DOMESTIC CONCEPT								
7	Agriculture, forestry and fishing	667.0	661.0	670.0	667.0	641.0	649.0	637.0	619.0
8	Industry, including energy	7 844.0	7 705.0	7 854.0	7 994.0	8 022.0	8 069.0	8 092.0	8 108.0
9	Manufacturing	7 277.0	7 138.0	7 285.0	7 418.0	7 442.0	7 487.0	7 518.0	7 539.0
10	Construction	2 312.0	2 331.0	2 376.0	2 412.0	2 427.0	2 436.0	2 427.0	2 450.0
11	Distrib. trade, repairs; transp.; accommod., food serv. activ.	9 481.0	9 476.0	9 619.0	9 710.0	9 761.0	9 801.0	9 846.0	9 976.0
12	Information and communication	1 189.0	1 162.0	1 176.0	1 203.0	1 218.0	1 230.0	1 218.0	1 240.0
13	Financial and insurance activities	1 225.0	1 214.0	1 201.0	1 201.0	1 194.0	1 188.0	1 187.0	1 179.0
14	Real estate activities	464.0	463.0	463.0	467.0	460.0	463.0	467.0	468.0
15	Prof., scientif., techn. activ.; admin., support service activ.	4 967.0	5 172.0	5 372.0	5 471.0	5 545.0	5 634.0	5 769.0	5 903.0
16	Public admin.; compulsory s.s.; education; human health	9 761.0	9 915.0	9 910.0	10 009.0	10 107.0	10 280.0	10 486.0	10 735.0
17	Other service activities	2 982.0	2 921.0	2 936.0	2 927.0	2 944.0	2 922.0	2 940.0	2 960.0
18	**Total employment**	**40 892.0**	**41 020.0**	**41 577.0**	**42 061.0**	**42 319.0**	**42 672.0**	**43 069.0**	**43 638.0**
	EMPLOYEES, THOUSAND PERSONS, DOMESTIC CONCEPT								
19	Agriculture, forestry and fishing	311.0	309.0	320.0	327.0	332.0	343.0	350.0	349.0
20	Industry, including energy	7 544.0	7 416.0	7 568.0	7 708.0	7 744.0	7 795.0	7 825.0	7 841.0
21	Manufacturing	6 985.0	6 857.0	7 007.0	7 140.0	7 172.0	7 222.0	7 259.0	7 280.0
22	Construction	1 828.0	1 843.0	1 874.0	1 899.0	1 909.0	1 924.0	1 934.0	1 964.0
23	Distrib. trade, repairs; transp.; accommod., food serv. activ.	8 346.0	8 355.0	8 502.0	8 607.0	8 674.0	8 743.0	8 815.0	8 943.0
24	Information and communication	1 046.0	1 018.0	1 029.0	1 050.0	1 075.0	1 090.0	1 082.0	1 108.0
25	Financial and insurance activities	1 069.0	1 061.0	1 050.0	1 052.0	1 050.0	1 043.0	1 039.0	1 026.0
26	Real estate activities	394.0	393.0	392.0	396.0	400.0	407.0	409.0	414.0
27	Prof., scientif. activ.; admin., support service activ.	4 174.0	4 371.0	4 530.0	4 633.0	4 695.0	4 796.0	4 928.0	5 072.0
28	Public admin.; compulsory s.s.; education; human health	9 166.0	9 313.0	9 286.0	9 385.0	9 501.0	9 655.0	9 841.0	10 081.0
29	Other service activities	2 529.0	2 454.0	2 463.0	2 444.0	2 473.0	2 464.0	2 487.0	2 507.0
30	**Total employees**	**36 407.0**	**36 533.0**	**37 014.0**	**37 501.0**	**37 853.0**	**38 260.0**	**38 710.0**	**39 305.0**
	SELF-EMPLOYED, THOUSAND PERSONS, DOMESTIC CONCEPT								
31	Agriculture, forestry and fishing	356.0	352.0	350.0	340.0	309.0	306.0	287.0	270.0
32	Industry, including energy	300.0	289.0	286.0	286.0	278.0	274.0	267.0	267.0
33	Manufacturing	292.0	281.0	278.0	278.0	270.0	265.0	259.0	259.0
34	Construction	484.0	488.0	502.0	513.0	518.0	512.0	493.0	486.0
35	Distrib. trade, repairs; transp.; accommod., food serv. activ.	1 135.0	1 121.0	1 117.0	1 103.0	1 087.0	1 058.0	1 031.0	1 033.0
36	Information and communication	143.0	144.0	147.0	153.0	143.0	140.0	136.0	132.0
37	Financial and insurance activities	156.0	153.0	151.0	149.0	144.0	145.0	148.0	153.0
38	Real estate activities	70.0	70.0	71.0	71.0	60.0	56.0	58.0	54.0
39	Prof., scientif. activ.; admin., support service activ.	793.0	801.0	842.0	838.0	850.0	838.0	841.0	831.0
40	Public admin.; compulsory s.s.; education; human health	595.0	602.0	624.0	624.0	606.0	625.0	645.0	654.0
41	Other service activities	453.0	467.0	473.0	483.0	471.0	458.0	453.0	453.0
42	**Total self-employed**	**4 485.0**	**4 487.0**	**4 563.0**	**4 560.0**	**4 466.0**	**4 412.0**	**4 359.0**	**4 333.0**
	TOTAL EMPLOYMENT, MILLION HOURS, DOMESTIC CONCEPT								
43	Industry, including energy	10 896.0	11 111.0	11 501.0	11 511.0	11 593.0	11 748.0	11 825.0	11 744.0
44	Distrib. trade, repairs; transp.; accommod., food serv. activ.	13 143.0	13 150.0	13 281.0	13 183.0	13 100.0	13 150.0	13 192.0	13 269.0
45	Financial and insurance activities	1 828.0	1 814.0	1 804.0	1 787.0	1 769.0	1 768.0	1 769.0	1 756.0
46	Prof., scientif., techn. activ.; admin., support service activ.	6 734.0	7 052.0	7 368.0	7 366.0	7 390.0	7 516.0	7 683.0	7 822.0
47	Public admin.; compulsory s.s.; education; human health	12 897.0	13 260.0	13 269.0	13 329.0	13 332.0	13 655.0	13 972.0	14 187.0
48	**Total employment**	**56 133.0**	**57 013.0**	**57 909.0**	**57 835.0**	**57 668.0**	**58 336.0**	**58 923.0**	**59 286.0**
	EMPLOYEES, MILLION HOURS, DOMESTIC CONCEPT								
49	Industry, including energy	10 243.0	10 476.0	10 881.0	10 893.0	11 000.0	11 170.0	11 256.0	11 182.0
50	Distrib. trade, repairs; transp.; accommod., food serv. activ.	10 575.0	10 630.0	10 790.0	10 766.0	10 749.0	10 858.0	10 958.0	11 046.0
51	Financial and insurance activities	1 487.0	1 480.0	1 478.0	1 474.0	1 472.0	1 473.0	1 467.0	1 444.0
52	Prof., scientif., techn. activ.; admin., support service activ.	5 139.0	5 441.0	5 683.0	5 730.0	5 752.0	5 913.0	6 069.0	6 222.0
53	Public admin.; compulsory s.s.; education; human health	11 874.0	12 228.0	12 205.0	12 285.0	12 330.0	12 626.0	12 906.0	13 114.0
54	**Total employees**	**46 937.0**	**47 845.0**	**48 665.0**	**48 776.0**	**48 890.0**	**49 713.0**	**50 381.0**	**50 801.0**
	SELF-EMPLOYED, MILLION HOURS, DOMESTIC CONCEPT								
55	Industry, including energy	652.0	635.0	620.0	618.0	593.0	578.0	569.0	562.0
56	Distrib. trade, repairs; transp.; accommod., food serv. activ.	2 568.0	2 520.0	2 492.0	2 417.0	2 351.0	2 292.0	2 234.0	2 223.0
57	Financial and insurance activities	341.0	334.0	326.0	313.0	296.0	295.0	302.0	312.0
58	Prof., scientif., techn. activ.; admin., support service activ.	1 595.0	1 611.0	1 685.0	1 636.0	1 638.0	1 603.0	1 614.0	1 601.0
59	Public admin.; compulsory s.s.; education; human health	1 023.0	1 032.0	1 064.0	1 044.0	1 003.0	1 029.0	1 066.0	1 073.0
60	**Total self-employed**	**9 196.0**	**9 167.0**	**9 244.0**	**9 059.0**	**8 778.0**	**8 623.0**	**8 543.0**	**8 484.0**

Note: Detailed metadata:http://metalinks.oecd.org/nav1/20180308/334d

1. Since May 2007, the source of unemployment data is the labour force survey. Data have been recalculated over the whole period and thus they appear different from the results published earlier.

Source: Statistisches Bundesamt (Destatis) via Eurostat.

GREECE

Table 1. Gross domestic product, expenditure approach

Million EUR (2001 GRD euro)

		2009	2010	2011	2012	2013	2014	2015	2016
	AT CURRENT PRICES								
1	**Final consumption expenditure**	**217 205**	**206 992**	**189 782 p**	**175 232 p**	**164 777 p**	**161 670 p**	**158 909 p**	**156 975 p**
2	Household	157 389	152 038	139 855 p	128 866 p	122 909 p	120 500 p	118 013 p	116 821 p
3	NPISH's	4 449	4 765	4 823 p	4 801 p	4 944 p	4 941 p	4 956 p	4 915 p
4	Government	55 367	50 188	45 104 p	41 564 p	36 924 p	36 230 p	35 940 p	35 239 p
5	Individual	27 042	24 630	22 534 p	19 929 p	16 723 p	15 522 p	15 269 p	15 052 p
6	Collective	28 325	25 558	22 570 p	21 635 p	20 201 p	20 708 p	20 671 p	20 187 p
7	*of which: Actual individual consumption*	188 880	181 434	167 212 p	153 597 p	144 576 p	140 962 p	138 238 p	136 788 p
8	**Gross capital formation**	**43 559**	**38 534**	**31 271 p**	**24 480 p**	**20 958 p**	**21 280 p**	**17 312 p**	**18 482 p**
9	Gross fixed capital formation, total	49 387	39 698	31 607 p	24 140 p	21 963 p	20 624 p	20 309 p	20 458 p
10	Dwellings	15 538	11 205	9 567 p	5 903 p	4 020 p	1 815 p	1 310 p	1 127 p
11	Other buildings and structures	11 494	8 849	7 114 p	7 977 p	7 935 p	6 806 p	6 070 p	7 544 p
12	Transport equipment	8 216	7 406	5 639 p	2 104 p	2 524 p	3 501 p	3 018 p	2 772 p
13	Other machinery and equipment	7 122	5 664	4 115 p	3 558 p	3 183 p	3 947 p	4 775 p	4 252 p
14	Cultivated assets	129	76	105 p	105 p	88 p	94 p	69 p	84 p
15	Intangible fixed assets	3 920	4 193	3 351 p	2 873 p	2 954 p	2 884 p	3 112 p	3 155 p
16	Changes in inventories, acquisitions less disposals of valuables	-5 828	-1 164	-336 p	340 p	-1 005 p	655 p	-2 997 p	-1 976 p
17	Changes in inventories	-5 955	-1 443	-394 p	339 p	-996 p	632 p	-3 018 p	-1 980 p
18	Acquisitions less disposals of valuables	127	279	58 p	1 p	-9 p	24 p	21 p	4 p
19	**External balance of goods and services**	**-23 230**	**-19 495**	**-14 024 p**	**-8 508 p**	**-5 081 p**	**-4 294 p**	**91 p**	**-1 258 p**
20	Exports of goods and services	45 089	49 958	52 866 p	54 845 p	54 835 p	57 837 p	55 931 p	53 059 p
21	Exports of goods	20 227	23 433	26 833 p	29 932 p	29 828 p	30 090 p	28 833 p	28 254 p
22	Exports of services	24 862	26 525	26 033 p	24 913 p	25 007 p	27 746 p	27 098 p	24 804 p
23	Imports of goods and services	68 319	69 452	66 889 p	63 353 p	59 915 p	62 130 p	55 840 p	54 317 p
24	Imports of goods	53 941	53 743	52 716 p	50 815 p	47 582 p	49 333 p	44 945 p	44 727 p
25	Imports of services	14 377	15 709	14 173 p	12 538 p	12 333 p	12 797 p	10 895 p	9 591 p
26	**Statistical discrepancy**	..	..	..	..	..	..	..	..
27	**Gross domestic product**	**237 534**	**226 031**	**207 029 p**	**191 204 p**	**180 654 p**	**178 656 p**	**176 312 p**	**174 199 p**
	AT CONSTANT PRICES, REFERENCE YEAR 2010								
28	**Final consumption expenditure**	**220 016**	**206 992**	**188 183 p**	**173 990 p**	**167 919 p**	**168 218 p**	**168 079 p**	**167 491 p**
29	Household	163 077	152 038	136 783 p	125 422 p	121 891 p	122 607 p	121 949 p	121 882 p
30	NPISH's	4 657	4 765	4 735 p	4 744 p	4 936 p	5 010 p	5 078 p	5 113 p
31	Government	52 371	50 188	46 665 p	43 865 p	41 036 p	40 477 p	40 975 p	40 376 p
32	Individual	25 579	24 630	23 314 p	21 032 p	18 585 p	17 341 p	17 408 p	17 246 p
33	Collective	26 792	25 558	23 351 p	22 833 p	22 451 p	23 136 p	23 567 p	23 130 p
34	*of which: Actual individual consumption*	193 254	181 434	164 832 p	151 216 p	145 553 p	145 228 p	144 692 p	144 511 p
35	**Gross capital formation**	**43 186**	**38 534**	**30 124 p**	**22 892 p**	**20 622 p**	**21 994 p**	**20 006 p**	**21 491 p**
36	Gross fixed capital formation, total	49 220	39 698	31 561 p	24 158 p	22 122 p	21 087 p	21 014 p	21 345 p
37	Dwellings	15 175	11 205	9 573 p	5 944 p	4 094 p	1 911 p	1 418 p	1 240 p
38	Other buildings and structures	11 225	8 849	7 119 p	8 032 p	8 080 p	7 168 p	6 572 p	8 302 p
39	Transport equipment	8 390	7 406	5 688 p	2 128 p	2 544 p	3 511 p	3 027 p	2 763 p
40	Other machinery and equipment	7 306	5 664	4 102 p	3 551 p	3 175 p	3 935 p	4 743 p	4 238 p
41	Cultivated assets	130	76	105 p	106 p	89 p	100 p	70 p	87 p
42	Intangible fixed assets	3 980	4 193	3 264 p	2 768 p	2 862 p	2 825 p	3 099 p	3 165 p
43	Changes in inventories, acquisitions less disposals of valuables	..	..	..	..	..	..	..	..
44	Changes in inventories	..	..	..	..	..	..	..	..
45	Acquisitions less disposals of valuables	..	..	..	..	..	..	..	..
46	**External balance of goods and services**	**-24 278**	**-19 495**	**-12 919 p**	**-6 610 p**	**-4 478 p**	**-4 785 p**	**-3 318 p**	**-4 509 p**
47	Exports of goods and services	47 642	49 958	49 972 p	50 558 p	51 322 p	55 299 p	57 008 p	55 971 p
48	Exports of goods	21 753	23 433	24 654 p	26 275 p	26 695 p	27 795 p	30 080 p	31 200 p
49	Exports of services	25 869	26 525	25 317 p	24 205 p	24 545 p	27 509 p	26 830 p	24 759 p
50	Imports of goods and services	71 920	69 452	62 890 p	57 167 p	55 800 p	60 084 p	60 327 p	60 480 p
51	Imports of goods	57 169	53 743	49 080 p	45 091 p	43 782 p	47 369 p	49 041 p	50 477 p
52	Imports of services	14 795	15 709	13 810 p	12 054 p	12 016 p	12 698 p	11 220 p	10 011 p
53	**Statistical discrepancy (including chaining residual)**	**209**	**0**	**0 p**	**122 p**	**160 p**	**159 p**	**279 p**	**121 p**
54	**Gross domestic product**	**239 133**	**226 031**	**205 389 p**	**190 395 p**	**184 223 p**	**185 586 p**	**185 046 p**	**184 594 p**

Note: Detailed metadata:http://metalinks.oecd.org/nav1/20180308/158e
Source: Hellenic Statistical Authority (ELSTAT) via Eurostat.

GREECE

Table 2. Gross domestic product, output and income approach
ISIC Rev. 4

Million EUR (2001 GRD euro)

		2009	2010	2011	2012	2013	2014	2015	2016
	OUTPUT APPROACH AT CURRENT PRICES								
1	**Total gross value added at basic prices**	**212 391**	**199 644**	**181 909 p**	**168 979 p**	**160 237 p**	**157 913 p**	**155 707 p**	**151 818 p**
2	Agriculture, forestry and fishing	6 663	6 519	6 109 p	6 191 p	5 794 p	6 070 p	6 608 p	6 022 p
3	Industry, including energy	25 825	22 368	22 016 p	21 571 p	21 791 p	21 493 p	21 047 p	20 971 p
4	Manufacturing	18 146	16 356	16 175 p	15 377 p	15 251 p	15 019 p	14 659 p	14 981 p
5	Construction	10 550	8 888	6 310 p	5 821 p	4 701 p	3 783 p	3 277 p	3 824 p
6	Services	..	..	..	..	..	..	..	..
7	Distrib. trade, repairs; transp.; accommod., food serv. activ.	51 420	49 399	44 313 p	37 677 p	36 344 p	37 678 p	37 285 p	35 292 p
8	Information and communication	8 568	7 683	6 355 p	5 518 p	5 749 p	5 518 p	5 304 p	5 198 p
9	Financial and insurance activities	9 775	9 623	8 652 p	8 396 p	8 293 p	7 513 p	7 238 p	7 024 p
10	Real estate activities	29 544	33 515	31 367 p	32 324 p	30 331 p	28 867 p	27 921 p	27 157 p
11	Prof., scientif., techn. activ.; admin., support service activ.	13 463	10 593	9 570 p	8 683 p	7 649 p	7 600 p	7 971 p	7 770 p
12	Public admin.; compulsory s.s.; education; human health	46 716	43 238	40 403 p	35 920 p	32 859 p	32 933 p	32 418 p	32 020 p
13	Other service activities	9 868	7 820	6 815 p	6 879 p	6 726 p	6 459 p	6 637 p	6 539 p
14	**FISIM (Financial Intermediation Services Indirectly Measured)**	..	..	..	..	..	..	..	..
15	**Gross value added at basic prices, excluding FISIM**	212 391	199 644	181 909 p	168 979 p	160 237 p	157 913 p	155 707 p	151 818 p
16	**Taxes less subsidies on products**	**25 143**	**26 388**	**25 120 p**	**22 225 p**	**20 418 p**	**20 743 p**	**20 605 p**	**22 382 p**
17	Taxes on products	25 674	26 920	25 788 p	23 315 p	22 263 p	22 235 p	22 248 p	24 128 p
18	Subsidies on products	531	532	668 p	1 090 p	1 845 p	1 492 p	1 643 p	1 746 p
19	**Residual item**	..	..	..	..	..	..	..	0 p
20	**Gross domestic product at market prices**	**237 534**	**226 031**	**207 029 p**	**191 204 p**	**180 654 p**	**178 656 p**	**176 312 p**	**174 199 p**
	OUTPUT APPROACH AT CONSTANT PRICES (REF. YEAR 2010)								
21	**Total gross value added at basic prices**	**211 682**	**199 644**	**181 672 p**	**169 968 p**	**165 455 p**	**166 219 p**	**165 462 p**	**163 418 p**
22	Agriculture, forestry and fishing	6 228	6 519	6 378 p	7 063 p	6 572 p	7 128 p	6 924 p	6 318 p
23	Industry, including energy	26 390	22 368	21 338 p	19 975 p	19 732 p	18 935 p	19 097 p	20 121 p
24	Manufacturing	18 878	16 356	15 289 p	14 150 p	14 078 p	13 783 p	14 193 p	15 404 p
25	Construction	9 793	8 888	6 536 p	6 159 p	5 027 p	4 370 p	4 095 p	5 091 p
26	Services	..	..	..	..	..	..	..	..
27	Distrib. trade, repairs; transp.; accommod., food serv. activ.	51 919	49 399	43 816 p	36 995 p	35 735 p	37 423 p	36 375 p	34 156 p
28	Information and communication	8 908	7 683	6 264 p	5 532 p	5 910 p	5 518 p	5 215 p	5 057 p
29	Financial and insurance activities	10 382	9 623	8 251 p	7 837 p	7 921 p	7 404 p	7 382 p	7 271 p
30	Real estate activities	30 249	33 515	31 138 p	32 823 p	33 159 p	34 292 p	34 752 p	34 731 p
31	Prof., scientif., techn. activ.; admin., support service activ.	13 523	10 593	9 512 p	8 737 p	7 614 p	7 378 p	7 703 p	7 528 p
32	Public admin.; compulsory s.s.; education; human health	44 254	43 238	41 717 p	37 911 p	36 642 p	36 977 p	36 893 p	36 404 p
33	Other service activities	10 183	7 820	6 724 p	6 956 p	7 039 p	6 881 p	7 140 p	7 033 p
34	**FISIM (Financial Intermediation Services Indirectly Measured)**	..	..	..	..	..	..	..	..
35	**Gross value added at basic prices, excluding FISIM**	211 682	199 644	181 672 p	169 968 p	165 455 p	166 219 p	165 462 p	163 418 p
36	**Taxes less subsidies on products**	**27 408**	**26 388**	**23 717 p**	**20 512 p**	**18 933 p**	**19 486 p**	**19 673 p**	**21 098 p**
37	Taxes on products	27 947	26 920	24 387 p	21 496 p	20 509 p	20 670 p	21 021 p	22 656 p
38	Subsidies on products	539	532	669 p	1 008 p	1 600 p	1 234 p	1 382 p	1 582 p
39	**Residual item**	**44**	**0**	**0 p**	**-85 p**	**-165 p**	**-119 p**	**-89 p**	**78 p**
40	**Gross domestic product at market prices**	**239 134**	**226 031**	**205 389 p**	**190 395 p**	**184 223 p**	**185 586 p**	**185 046 p**	**184 594 p**
	INCOME APPROACH								
41	**Compensation of employees**	**84 875**	**82 130**	**73 259 p**	**66 080 p**	**59 715 p**	**59 196 p**	**58 390 p**	**58 384 p**
42	Agriculture, forestry and fishing	970	967	924 p	862 p	816 p	788 p	764 p	741 p
43	Industry, including energy	11 541	11 358	10 426 p	8 678 p	7 880 p	7 865 p	7 734 p	7 630 p
44	Manufacturing	8 925	8 885	8 111 p	6 726 p	5 960 p	5 688 p	5 660 p	5 517 p
45	Construction	4 175	3 332	2 650 p	1 946 p	1 681 p	1 380 p	1 154 p	1 192 p
46	Distrib. trade, repairs; transp.; accommod., food serv. activ.	19 563	20 380	17 769 p	16 013 p	13 762 p	14 074 p	13 770 p	13 979 p
47	Information and communication	2 756	3 173	2 595 p	2 345 p	2 292 p	2 000 p	1 913 p	1 782 p
48	Financial and insurance activities	5 833	5 059	4 853 p	4 209 p	3 825 p	3 503 p	3 302 p	3 595 p
49	Real estate activities	118	95	67 p	72 p	64 p	83 p	97 p	96 p
50	Prof., scientif., techn. activ.; admin., support service activ.	4 197	5 338	4 432 p	3 926 p	3 498 p	3 525 p	3 489 p	3 245 p
51	Public admin.; compulsory s.s.; education; human health	30 702	27 992	25 974 p	24 182 p	21 882 p	22 082 p	21 839 p	21 859 p
52	Other service activities	5 020	4 437	3 570 p	3 847 p	4 015 p	3 896 p	4 327 p	4 264 p
53	**Wages and salaries**	**67 044**	**63 836**	**56 510 p**	**50 048 p**	**44 738 p**	**44 719 p**	**44 109 p**	**44 092 p**
54	Agriculture, forestry and fishing	896	830	791 p	736 p	696 p	671 p	649 p	628 p
55	Industry, including energy	9 676	9 266	8 736 p	7 142 p	6 468 p	6 362 p	6 363 p	6 247 p
56	Manufacturing	7 383	7 136	6 727 p	5 444 p	4 810 p	4 657 p	4 674 p	4 524 p
57	Construction	3 243	2 542	2 056 p	1 508 p	1 300 p	1 079 p	920 p	964 p
58	Distrib. trade, repairs; transp.; accommod., food serv. activ.	15 630	15 797	14 090 p	12 782 p	10 968 p	11 395 p	11 173 p	11 342 p
59	Information and communication	2 095	2 266	1 641 p	1 545 p	1 503 p	1 407 p	1 286 p	1 213 p
60	Financial and insurance activities	4 053	3 651	3 306 p	2 994 p	2 468 p	2 507 p	2 414 p	2 552 p
61	Real estate activities	98	73	54 p	58 p	51 p	65 p	73 p	73 p
62	Prof., scientif., techn. activ.; admin., support service activ.	3 290	4 243	3 556 p	3 071 p	2 779 p	2 848 p	2 841 p	2 617 p
63	Public admin.; compulsory s.s.; education; human health	23 869	21 586	19 425 p	17 044 p	15 285 p	15 241 p	14 903 p	15 013 p
64	Other service activities	4 195	3 583	2 855 p	3 169 p	3 220 p	3 145 p	3 487 p	3 443 p
65	**Gross operating surplus and mixed income**	**128 365**	**118 529**	**110 117 p**	**103 539 p**	**100 081 p**	**96 044 p**	**93 792 p**	**90 037 p**
66	**Taxes less subsidies on production and imports**	**24 295**	**25 372**	**23 652 p**	**21 585 p**	**20 858 p**	**23 416 p**	**24 130 p**	**25 778 p**
67	Taxes on production and imports	28 080	28 734	28 151 p	26 024 p	25 593 p	27 789 p	28 436 p	30 204 p
68	Subsidies on production and imports	3 786	3 362	4 499 p	4 439 p	4 735 p	4 374 p	4 306 p	4 425 p
69	**Residual item**	..	..	..	..	..	..	..	..
70	**Gross domestic product**	**237 534**	**226 031**	**207 029 p**	**191 204 p**	**180 654 p**	**178 656 p**	**176 312 p**	**174 199 p**

Note: Detailed metadata:http://metalinks.oecd.org/nav1/20180308/8216
Source: Hellenic Statistical Authority (ELSTAT) via Eurostat.

GREECE

Table 3. Disposable income, saving and net lending / net borrowing

Million EUR (2001 GRD euro)

		2009	2010	2011	2012	2013	2014	2015	2016
	DISPOSABLE INCOME								
1	**Gross domestic product**	237 534 p	226 032 p	207 029 p	191 204 p	180 655 p	178 657 p	176 312 p	174 199 p
2	Net primary incomes from the rest of the world	-5 273 p	-4 630 p	-5 652 p	1 268 p	-218 p	1 210 p	798 p	924 p
3	Primary incomes receivable from the rest of the world	7 935 p	7 075 p	6 219 p	6 720 p	6 219 p	7 768 p	6 943 p	6 275 p
4	Primary incomes payable to the rest of the world	13 208 p	11 705 p	11 871 p	5 452 p	6 437 p	6 558 p	6 144 p	5 351 p
5	**Gross national income at market prices**	232 261 p	221 401 p	201 376 p	192 473 p	180 437 p	179 867 p	177 111 p	175 123 p
6	Consumption of fixed capital	37 682 p	37 913 p	36 937 p	37 027 p	34 973 p	32 029 p	30 849 p	30 083 p
7	**Net national income at market prices**	194 580 p	183 488 p	164 440 p	155 446 p	145 464 p	147 837 p	146 261 p	145 039 p
8	Net current transfers from the rest of the world	-1 218 p	-1 506 p	-1 629 p	-856 p	1 319 p	-629 p	-811 p	-852 p
9	Current transfers receivable from the rest of the world	2 673 p	2 391 p	1 907 p	2 079 p	4 296 p	2 230 p	1 769 p	1 609 p
10	Current transfers payable to the rest of the world	3 891 p	3 897 p	3 536 p	2 935 p	2 977 p	2 859 p	2 580 p	2 461 p
11	**Net national disposable income**	193 362 p	181 983 p	162 811 p	154 590 p	146 783 p	147 208 p	145 450 p	144 187 p
	SAVING AND NET LENDING / NET BORROWING								
12	**Net national disposable income**	193 362 p	181 983 p	162 811 p	154 590 p	146 783 p	147 208 p	145 450 p	144 187 p
13	Final consumption expenditures	217 205 p	206 992 p	189 782 p	175 232 p	164 777 p	161 670 p	158 909 p	156 976 p
14	Adj. for change in net equity of households in pension funds	..	..	..	..	..	..	..	..
15	**Saving, net**	-23 843 p	-25 009 p	-26 971 p	-20 642 p	-17 994 p	-14 461 p	-13 459 p	-12 789 p
16	Net capital transfers from the rest of the world	2 269 p	3 907 p	4 038 p	3 548 p	4 434 p	3 674 p	4 430 p	2 956 p
17	Capital transfers receivable from the rest of the world	2 545 p	4 143 p	4 231 p	3 705 p	5 126 p	3 815 p	4 526 p	3 012 p
18	Capital transfers payable to the rest of the world	276 p	236 p	193 p	157 p	692 p	142 p	96 p	55 p
19	Gross capital formation	43 559 p	38 534 p	31 271 p	24 480 p	20 958 p	21 280 p	17 312 p	18 482 p
20	Acquisitions less disposals of non-financial non-produced assets	-86 p	-13 p	-9 p	51 p	170 p	188 p	269 p	115 p
21	Consumption of fixed capital	37 682 p	37 913 p	36 937 p	37 027 p	34 973 p	32 029 p	30 849 p	30 083 p
22	**Net lending / net borrowing**	-27 365 p	-21 711 p	-17 258 p	-4 598 p	286 p	-226 p	4 239 p	1 653 p
	REAL DISPOSABLE INCOME								
23	**Gross domestic product at constant prices, reference year 2010**	239 133	226 032	205 389	190 395	184 223	185 586	185 046	184 594
24	Trading gain or loss	659 p	0 p	-931 p	-2 019 p	-1 033 p	6 p	2 968 p	2 746 p
25	**Real gross domestic income**	239 791 p	226 032 p	204 458 p	188 376 p	183 191 p	185 593 p	188 014 p	187 340 p
26	Net real primary incomes from the rest of the world	-5 323 p	-4 630 p	-5 582 p	1 249 p	-222 p	1 257 p	851 p	993 p
27	Real primary incomes receivable from the rest of the world	8 011 p	7 075 p	6 142 p	6 621 p	6 306 p	8 070 p	7 404 p	6 748 p
28	Real primary incomes payable to the rest of the world	13 333 p	11 705 p	11 724 p	5 372 p	6 528 p	6 813 p	6 552 p	5 755 p
29	**Real gross national income at market prices**	234 469 p	221 401 p	198 876 p	189 625 p	182 970 p	186 849 p	188 865 p	188 333 p
30	Net real current transfers from the rest of the world	-1 229 p	-1 506 p	-1 609 p	-843 p	1 338 p	-653 p	-865 p	-917 p
31	Real current transfers receivable from the rest of the world	2 698 p	2 391 p	1 883 p	2 049 p	4 356 p	2 316 p	1 887 p	1 730 p
32	Real current transfers payable to the rest of the world	3 928 p	3 897 p	3 492 p	2 892 p	3 018 p	2 970 p	2 751 p	2 647 p
33	**Real gross national disposable income**	233 239 p	219 896 p	197 267 p	188 782 p	184 307 p	186 196 p	188 000 p	187 417 p
34	Consumption of fixed capital at constant prices	37 930 p	37 913 p	36 599 p	36 498 p	34 264 p	31 942 p	31 242 p	30 744 p
35	**Real net national income at market prices**	196 429 p	183 488 p	162 398 p	153 146 p	147 506 p	153 577 p	155 968 p	155 981 p
36	**Real net national disposable income**	195 199 p	181 983 p	160 789 p	152 303 p	148 843 p	152 923 p	155 104 p	155 064 p

Note: Detailed metadata:http://metalinks.oecd.org/nav1/20180308/7348
Source: Hellenic Statistical Authority (ELSTAT) via Eurostat.

Table 4. Population and employment (persons) and employment (hours worked) by industry
ISIC Rev. 4

		2009	2010	2011	2012	2013	2014	2015	2016
	POPULATION, THOUSAND PERSONS, NATIONAL CONCEPT								
1	**Total population**	**11 107.0**	**11 121.4**	**11 105.0 p**	**11 045.0 p**	**10 965.2 p**	**10 892.4 p**	**10 821.0 p**	**10 783.7 p**
2	Economically active population	..	..	..	..	..	..	..	..
3	Unemployed persons	..	..	..	..	..	..	..	..
4	Total employment	4 829.0	4 705.5	4 381.8 p	4 105.2 p	3 997.7 p	4 034.8 p	4 064.0 p	4 083.0 p
5	Employees	3 190.8	3 150.0	2 919.8 p	2 715.7 p	2 652.5 p	2 683.0 p	2 709.2 p	2 733.0 p
6	Self-employed	1 638.2	1 555.5	1 462.1 p	1 389.5 p	1 345.2 p	1 351.8 p	1 354.8 p	1 350.0 p
	TOTAL EMPLOYMENT, THOUSAND PERSONS, DOMESTIC CONCEPT								
7	Agriculture, forestry and fishing	543.0	535.0	499.5 p	490.8 p	488.5 p	490.4 p	473.1 p	461.8 p
8	Industry, including energy	538.5	494.0	452.2 p	414.9 p	389.9 p	380.2 p	382.6 p	377.9 p
9	Manufacturing	475.6	430.6	391.7 p	359.2 p	336.4 p	326.3 p	330.0 p	324.2 p
10	Construction	368.8	313.6	241.2 p	206.8 p	202.9 p	205.4 p	196.6 p	199.2 p
11	Distrib. trade, repairs; transp.; accommod., food serv. activ.	1 527.4	1 489.8	1 401.9 p	1 302.9 p	1 262.9 p	1 301.3 p	1 335.8 p	1 358.2 p
12	Information and communication	87.1	89.5	84.8 p	83.5 p	85.9 p	83.5 p	80.8 p	84.0 p
13	Financial and insurance activities	107.4	101.8	99.4 p	96.4 p	91.7 p	83.1 p	79.8 p	81.1 p
14	Real estate activities	9.7	11.2	9.2 p	8.6 p	8.2 p	8.9 p	9.1 p	9.2 p
15	Prof., scientif., techn. activ.; admin., support service activ.	348.1	346.3	330.8 p	324.0 p	315.5 p	331.1 p	343.8 p	347.1 p
16	Public admin.; compulsory s.s.; education; human health	977.6	984.1	945.0 p	890.0 p	871.2 p	866.8 p	875.7 p	886.9 p
17	Other service activities	321.4	340.1	317.9 p	287.3 p	281.1 p	284.2 p	286.7 p	277.6 p
18	**Total employment**	**4 829.0**	**4 705.5**	**4 381.8 p**	**4 105.2 p**	**3 997.7 p**	**4 034.8 p**	**4 064.0 p**	**4 083.0 p**
	EMPLOYEES, THOUSAND PERSONS, DOMESTIC CONCEPT								
19	Agriculture, forestry and fishing	82.8	105.1	97.5 p	96.0 p	95.2 p	96.0 p	92.2 p	89.4 p
20	Industry, including energy	419.0	392.3	358.5 p	337.6 p	323.4 p	318.3 p	320.9 p	315.9 p
21	Manufacturing	359.0	332.0	300.8 p	284.6 p	271.3 p	265.7 p	269.6 p	263.7 p
22	Construction	247.8	196.5	140.8 p	108.3 p	101.8 p	104.1 p	97.0 p	101.0 p
23	Distrib. trade, repairs; transp.; accommod., food serv. activ.	908.1	911.0	856.5 p	785.0 p	769.9 p	796.3 p	816.7 p	832.2 p
24	Information and communication	74.1	76.8	70.9 p	70.5 p	73.4 p	70.8 p	68.9 p	70.9 p
25	Financial and insurance activities	96.4	90.7	87.4 p	83.9 p	79.5 p	71.8 p	69.9 p	72.1 p
26	Real estate activities	5.3	5.7	2.9 p	3.5 p	3.9 p	4.7 p	4.8 p	4.8 p
27	Prof., scientif., techn. activ.; admin., support service activ.	196.7	184.5	172.4 p	171.8 p	168.3 p	184.4 p	196.9 p	200.4 p
28	Public admin.; compulsory s.s.; education; human health	913.8	917.2	881.6 p	832.7 p	813.5 p	806.4 p	814.8 p	824.4 p
29	Other service activities	246.7	270.1	251.2 p	226.5 p	223.8 p	226.3 p	227.1 p	221.9 p
30	**Total employees**	**3 190.8**	**3 150.0**	**2 919.8 p**	**2 715.7 p**	**2 652.5 p**	**2 683.0 p**	**2 709.2 p**	**2 733.0 p**
	SELF-EMPLOYED, THOUSAND PERSONS, DOMESTIC CONCEPT								
31	Agriculture, forestry and fishing	460.1	429.9	401.9 p	394.8 p	393.4 p	394.4 p	380.8 p	372.4 p
32	Industry, including energy	119.5	101.7	93.7 p	77.3 p	66.5 p	61.9 p	61.7 p	61.9 p
33	Manufacturing	116.6	98.7	90.9 p	74.6 p	65.1 p	60.6 p	60.5 p	60.5 p
34	Construction	121.1	117.2	100.3 p	98.5 p	101.1 p	101.3 p	99.6 p	98.3 p
35	Distrib. trade, repairs; transp.; accommod., food serv. activ.	619.2	578.8	545.4 p	517.9 p	493.0 p	504.9 p	519.1 p	526.0 p
36	Information and communication	13.0	12.7	14.0 p	13.1 p	12.5 p	12.7 p	11.8 p	13.1 p
37	Financial and insurance activities	11.0	11.1	11.9 p	12.6 p	12.2 p	11.3 p	9.9 p	8.9 p
38	Real estate activities	4.4	5.5	6.4 p	5.1 p	4.3 p	4.2 p	4.3 p	4.3 p
39	Prof., scientif., techn. activ.; admin., support service activ.	151.4	161.8	158.4 p	152.2 p	147.2 p	142.7 p	146.9 p	146.8 p
40	Public admin.; compulsory s.s.; education; human health	63.8	66.9	63.3 p	57.2 p	57.7 p	60.5 p	60.9 p	62.5 p
41	Other service activities	74.7	70.0	66.7 p	60.8 p	57.3 p	57.9 p	59.7 p	55.8 p
42	**Total self-employed**	**1 638.2**	**1 555.5**	**1 462.1 p**	**1 389.5 p**	**1 345.2 p**	**1 351.8 p**	**1 354.8 p**	**1 350.0 p**
	TOTAL EMPLOYMENT, MILLION HOURS, DOMESTIC CONCEPT								
43	Industry, including energy	1 139.3	1 039.0	945.9 p	866.7 p	812.5 p	787.2 p	783.2 p	786.5 p
44	Distrib. trade, repairs; transp.; accommod., food serv. activ.	3 437.0	3 288.7	3 160.1 p	2 967.0 p	2 909.9 p	2 915.3 p	2 977.3 p	3 008.0 p
45	Financial and insurance activities	225.3	207.3	194.2 p	197.7 p	184.9 p	167.6 p	159.3 p	168.2 p
46	Prof., scientif., techn. activ.; admin., support service activ.	728.7	716.7	700.4 p	691.1 p	638.0 p	678.8 p	730.5 p	714.0 p
47	Public admin.; compulsory s.s.; education; human health	1 797.1	1 681.8	1 637.7 p	1 571.6 p	1 558.3 p	1 527.7 p	1 545.1 p	1 554.5 p
48	**Total employment**	**10 050.2**	**9 503.0**	**8 928.8 p**	**8 437.8 p**	**8 232.2 p**	**8 153.9 p**	**8 254.6 p**	**8 288.9 p**
	EMPLOYEES, MILLION HOURS, DOMESTIC CONCEPT								
49	Industry, including energy	872.0	796.8	736.4 p	691.7 p	656.8 p	639.5 p	638.9 p	637.6 p
50	Distrib. trade, repairs; transp.; accommod., food serv. activ.	1 957.6	1 893.9	1 796.2 p	1 645.4 p	1 619.0 p	1 612.5 p	1 642.7 p	1 680.0 p
51	Financial and insurance activities	200.8	181.0	167.2 p	167.4 p	156.9 p	144.7 p	137.3 p	145.8 p
52	Prof., scientif., techn. activ.; admin., support service activ.	380.5	361.4	340.1 p	341.3 p	308.7 p	367.6 p	393.5 p	388.7 p
53	Public admin.; compulsory s.s.; education; human health	1 690.9	1 592.9	1 517.9 p	1 457.1 p	1 448.0 p	1 420.0 p	1 425.9 p	1 440.3 p
54	**Total employees**	**6 491.4**	**6 130.2**	**5 668.9 p**	**5 286.9 p**	**5 138.7 p**	**5 119.2 p**	**5 146.7 p**	**5 224.1 p**
	SELF-EMPLOYED, MILLION HOURS, DOMESTIC CONCEPT								
55	Industry, including energy	267.4	242.2	209.4 p	175.0 p	155.7 p	147.8 p	144.3 p	149.0 p
56	Distrib. trade, repairs; transp.; accommod., food serv. activ.	1 479.4	1 394.8	1 363.9 p	1 321.6 p	1 290.9 p	1 302.8 p	1 334.6 p	1 327.9 p
57	Financial and insurance activities	24.5	26.3	27.0 p	30.2 p	28.0 p	22.9 p	22.0 p	22.5 p
58	Prof., scientif., techn. activ.; admin., support service activ.	348.3	355.3	360.2 p	349.7 p	329.4 p	311.2 p	337.0 p	325.3 p
59	Public admin.; compulsory s.s.; education; human health	106.2	88.8	119.8 p	114.4 p	110.3 p	107.7 p	119.2 p	114.2 p
60	**Total self-employed**	**3 558.8**	**3 372.8**	**3 260.0 p**	**3 150.9 p**	**3 093.5 p**	**3 034.8 p**	**3 108.0 p**	**3 064.9 p**

Note: Detailed metadata:http://metalinks.oecd.org/nav1/20180308/1990
Source: Hellenic Statistical Authority (ELSTAT) via Eurostat.

HUNGARY

Table 1. Gross domestic product, expenditure approach

Million HUF

		2009	2010	2011	2012	2013	2014	2015	2016
	AT CURRENT PRICES								
1	**Final consumption expenditure**	**19 993 662**	**20 155 203**	**20 787 579**	**21 257 738**	**21 770 859**	**22 910 741**	**23 788 970**	**24 844 404**
2	Household	13 763 873	13 885 374	14 497 047	15 028 373	15 310 967	15 874 174	16 377 060	17 019 808
3	NPISH's	407 835	414 970	443 958	473 421	510 920	532 032	584 226	649 827
4	Government	5 821 954	5 854 859	5 846 574	5 755 944	5 948 972	6 504 535	6 827 684	7 174 769
5	Individual	3 018 090	2 996 136	2 990 614	2 941 422	2 957 956	3 197 246	3 459 645	3 635 184
6	Collective	2 803 864	2 858 723	2 855 960	2 814 522	2 991 016	3 307 289	3 368 039	3 539 585
7	*of which: Actual individual consumption*	17 189 798	17 296 480	17 931 619	18 443 216	18 779 843	19 603 452	20 420 931	21 304 819
8	**Gross capital formation**	**5 363 545**	**5 624 809**	**5 790 183**	**5 599 317**	**6 366 463**	**7 600 016**	**7 494 266**	**7 005 186**
9	Gross fixed capital formation, total	5 999 618	5 511 170	5 568 681	5 547 667	6 308 229	7 223 420	7 524 883	6 811 662
10	Dwellings	1 094 294	842 035	627 821	581 239	557 246	631 437	757 392	856 751
11	Other buildings and structures	2 030 929	1 911 715	1 976 584	1 870 654	2 286 668	2 588 403	2 743 507	1 879 973
12	Transport equipment	459 878	434 277	453 424	500 021	569 974	818 128	877 374	871 966
13	Other machinery and equipment	1 626 766	1 582 113	1 753 509	1 660 509	1 728 055	2 031 734	1 971 900	2 043 840
14	Cultivated assets	47 916	51 356	54 254	50 383	42 889	52 471	51 109	48 596
15	Intangible fixed assets	739 835	689 674	703 089	735 111	951 251	927 785	915 657	923 441
16	Changes in inventories, acquisitions less disposals of valuables	-636 073	113 639	221 502	51 650	58 234	376 596	-30 617	193 524
17	Changes in inventories	-666 555	82 297	187 842	21 190	24 004	334 481	-76 759	151 328
18	Acquisitions less disposals of valuables	30 482	31 342	33 660	30 460	34 230	42 115	46 142	42 196
19	**External balance of goods and services**	**1 067 397**	**1 444 587**	**1 727 176**	**1 924 009**	**2 109 755**	**2 080 956**	**3 040 874**	**3 570 730**
20	Exports of goods and services	19 662 653	22 277 737	24 553 129	24 868 399	25 909 435	28 568 063	30 964 666	31 714 233
21	Exports of goods	15 909 028	18 205 575	20 042 133	20 232 168	20 862 346	22 786 269	24 676 415	24 969 010
22	Exports of services	3 753 625	4 072 162	4 510 996	4 636 231	5 047 089	5 781 794	6 288 251	6 745 223
23	Imports of goods and services	18 595 256	20 833 150	22 825 953	22 944 390	23 799 680	26 487 107	27 923 792	28 143 503
24	Imports of goods	15 189 792	17 511 625	19 248 178	19 388 133	19 869 420	22 128 525	23 309 037	23 503 260
25	Imports of services	3 405 464	3 321 525	3 577 775	3 556 257	3 930 260	4 358 582	4 614 755	4 640 243
26	**Statistical discrepancy**	..	..	..	..	..	..	..	..
27	**Gross domestic product**	**26 424 604**	**27 224 599**	**28 304 938**	**28 781 064**	**30 247 077**	**32 591 713**	**34 324 110**	**35 420 320**
	AT CONSTANT PRICES, REFERENCE YEAR 2010								
28	**Final consumption expenditure**	**20 568 964**	**20 155 203**	**20 268 951**	**19 856 393**	**20 110 691**	**20 794 661**	**21 398 526**	**22 110 511**
29	Household	14 274 516	13 885 374	13 983 887	13 654 256	13 676 137	14 056 925	14 555 998	15 164 995
30	NPISH's	419 520	414 970	418 151	421 661	430 915	439 150	465 416	505 217
31	Government	5 877 619	5 854 859	5 866 913	5 781 503	6 020 334	6 328 343	6 396 352	6 449 164
32	Individual	3 084 137	2 996 136	3 007 020	2 930 406	2 985 222	2 996 191	3 054 164	3 087 531
33	Collective	2 795 343	2 858 723	2 859 892	2 850 962	3 036 080	3 333 992	3 342 095	3 360 529
34	*of which: Actual individual consumption*	17 778 184	17 296 480	17 409 060	17 006 933	17 089 457	17 496 169	18 082 791	18 767 236
35	**Gross capital formation**	**5 376 169**	**5 624 809**	**5 429 109**	**5 056 976**	**5 351 582**	**6 019 584**	**5 789 910**	**5 575 881**
36	Gross fixed capital formation, total	6 088 095	5 511 170	5 437 622	5 276 835	5 796 341	6 509 447	6 635 871	5 933 464
37	Dwellings	1 117 553	842 035	611 250	550 997	518 035	574 769	671 295	736 079
38	Other buildings and structures	2 067 422	1 911 715	1 928 681	1 776 313	2 069 330	2 284 652	2 356 415	1 597 742
39	Transport equipment	470 180	434 277	438 667	486 897	529 655	715 035	759 424	745 543
40	Other machinery and equipment	1 630 011	1 582 113	1 706 675	1 572 990	1 571 935	1 869 840	1 815 956	1 881 617
41	Cultivated assets	50 165	51 356	52 191	47 266	39 637	47 614	47 314	47 147
42	Intangible fixed assets	755 006	689 674	700 158	694 331	902 388	842 717	778 020	760 296
43	Changes in inventories, acquisitions less disposals of valuables	..	..	..	..	..	..	..	..
44	Changes in inventories	..	..	..	..	..	..	..	..
45	Acquisitions less disposals of valuables	..	..	..	..	..	..	..	..
46	**External balance of goods and services**	**1 102 518**	**1 444 587**	**1 978 988**	**2 311 135**	**2 338 604**	**2 137 940**	**2 820 967**	**3 048 508**
47	Exports of goods and services	20 015 302	22 277 737	23 736 027	23 310 212	24 285 190	26 492 180	28 745 791	29 734 728
48	Exports of goods	16 163 572	18 205 575	19 401 871	19 023 224	19 631 782	21 192 357	22 965 208	23 481 437
49	Exports of services	3 853 759	4 072 162	4 334 157	4 286 758	4 650 060	5 291 494	5 771 069	6 239 653
50	Imports of goods and services	18 912 784	20 833 150	21 757 039	20 999 076	21 946 586	24 354 240	25 924 823	26 686 220
51	Imports of goods	15 450 300	17 511 625	18 330 738	17 710 090	18 311 984	20 377 789	21 704 364	22 429 357
52	Imports of services	3 462 277	3 321 525	3 426 301	3 288 886	3 636 951	3 978 825	4 223 095	4 261 084
53	**Statistical discrepancy (including chaining residual)**	**-7 568**	**0**	**1**	**-2 405**	**-8 143**	**15 552**	**-66 281**	**-129 080**
54	**Gross domestic product**	**27 040 083**	**27 224 599**	**27 677 049**	**27 222 099**	**27 792 734**	**28 967 736**	**29 943 122**	**30 605 819**

Note: Detailed metadata:http://metalinks.oecd.org/nav1/20180308/cb48
Source: Hungarian Central Statistical Office via Eurostat.

Table 2. Gross domestic product, output and income approach
ISIC Rev. 4

Million HUF

		2009	2010	2011	2012	2013	2014	2015	2016
	OUTPUT APPROACH AT CURRENT PRICES								
1	**Total gross value added at basic prices**	**22 458 995**	**23 054 029**	**24 058 485**	**24 191 258**	**25 519 375**	**27 493 971**	**28 823 388**	**29 943 368**
2	Agriculture, forestry and fishing	783 602	812 897	1 105 409	1 106 623	1 165 124	1 292 435	1 273 487	1 317 182
3	Industry, including energy	5 535 962	5 926 876	6 202 591	6 337 164	6 585 962	7 238 040	7 946 270	8 020 290
4	Manufacturing	4 529 798	4 960 511	5 274 199	5 378 521	5 717 337	6 363 437	7 044 812	7 050 011
5	Construction	1 090 692	968 016	987 039	933 800	1 029 316	1 172 046	1 195 284	1 112 621
6	Services	..						..	
7	Distrib. trade, repairs; transp.; accommod., food serv. activ.	3 938 898	4 048 652	4 315 870	4 294 895	4 739 395	5 084 165	5 305 602	5 487 068
8	Information and communication	1 259 969	1 240 624	1 268 318	1 280 990	1 354 319	1 430 355	1 420 529	1 497 007
9	Financial and insurance activities	1 130 405	1 140 872	1 143 638	1 100 155	1 019 934	1 049 285	1 025 753	1 039 166
10	Real estate activities	2 021 798	2 094 542	2 123 562	2 135 998	2 210 276	2 273 511	2 309 643	2 430 827
11	Prof., scientif., techn. activ.; admin., support service activ.	1 974 270	2 061 683	2 162 541	2 172 907	2 313 317	2 463 890	2 557 097	2 778 659
12	Public admin.; compulsory s.s.; education; human health	4 059 442	4 079 007	4 056 126	4 133 722	4 360 048	4 685 337	4 950 870	5 373 949
13	Other service activities	663 957	680 860	693 391	695 004	741 684	804 907	838 853	886 599
14	**FISIM (Financial Intermediation Services Indirectly Measured)**	..	..	..	..	..	..	..	..
15	**Gross value added at basic prices, excluding FISIM**	**22 458 995**	**23 054 029**	**24 058 485**	**24 191 258**	**25 519 375**	**27 493 971**	**28 823 388**	**29 943 368**
16	**Taxes less subsidies on products**	**3 965 609**	**4 170 570**	**4 246 453**	**4 589 806**	**4 727 702**	**5 097 742**	**5 500 722**	**5 476 952**
17	Taxes on products	4 093 905	4 344 256	4 464 378	4 846 118	5 004 158	5 396 637	5 800 997	5 855 495
18	Subsidies on products	128 296	173 686	217 925	256 312	276 456	298 895	300 275	378 543
19	**Residual item**	**0**	**0**	**0**	**0**	**0**	**0**	**0**	**0**
20	**Gross domestic product at market prices**	**26 424 604**	**27 224 599**	**28 304 938**	**28 781 064**	**30 247 077**	**32 591 713**	**34 324 110**	**35 420 320**
	OUTPUT APPROACH AT CONSTANT PRICES (REF. YEAR 2010)								
21	**Total gross value added at basic prices**	**22 888 663**	**23 054 029**	**23 473 830**	**23 066 522**	**23 703 919**	**24 759 588**	**25 587 954**	**26 194 495**
22	Agriculture, forestry and fishing	1 044 021	812 897	938 146	741 628	850 672	998 529	957 562	1 051 939
23	Industry, including energy	5 498 340	5 926 876	5 948 450	5 823 125	5 674 392	6 003 403	6 548 295	6 614 878
24	Manufacturing	4 487 464	4 960 511	5 006 241	4 937 191	4 833 835	5 146 125	5 652 669	5 657 209
25	Construction	1 073 243	968 016	994 653	931 368	988 137	1 093 606	1 121 054	1 003 534
26	Services	..						..	
27	Distrib. trade, repairs; transp.; accommod., food serv. activ.	4 054 483	4 048 652	4 134 942	4 137 544	4 354 625	4 505 346	4 650 654	4 777 624
28	Information and communication	1 227 251	1 240 624	1 280 651	1 295 576	1 351 872	1 411 365	1 430 343	1 511 330
29	Financial and insurance activities	1 207 586	1 140 872	1 081 792	1 046 999	994 144	961 436	976 235	980 129
30	Real estate activities	2 119 776	2 094 542	2 125 346	2 089 299	2 100 924	2 137 701	2 138 405	2 204 695
31	Prof., scientif., techn. activ.; admin., support service activ.	2 022 963	2 061 683	2 123 744	2 141 291	2 230 091	2 352 221	2 418 926	2 600 972
32	Public admin.; compulsory s.s.; education; human health	4 033 207	4 079 007	4 147 963	4 147 955	4 211 796	4 487 307	4 530 641	4 617 567
33	Other service activities	674 993	680 860	698 150	680 621	693 204	734 995	740 863	762 653
34	**FISIM (Financial Intermediation Services Indirectly Measured)**	..	..	..	..	..	..	..	..
35	**Gross value added at basic prices, excluding FISIM**	**22 888 663**	**23 054 029**	**23 473 830**	**23 066 522**	**23 703 919**	**24 759 588**	**25 587 954**	**26 194 495**
36	**Taxes less subsidies on products**	**4 151 669**	**4 170 570**	**4 203 220**	**4 155 889**	**4 096 886**	**4 220 151**	**4 367 145**	**4 427 818**
37	Taxes on products	4 284 419	4 344 256	4 420 922	4 391 778	4 346 293	4 481 319	4 631 770	4 705 888
38	Subsidies on products	133 099	173 686	217 703	236 071	249 862	261 810	264 979	279 458
39	**Residual item**	**-248**	**0**	**-1**	**-311**	**-8 071**	**-12 002**	**-11 976**	**-16 493**
40	**Gross domestic product at market prices**	**27 040 083**	**27 224 599**	**27 677 049**	**27 222 099**	**27 792 734**	**28 967 736**	**29 943 122**	**30 605 819**
	INCOME APPROACH								
41	**Compensation of employees**	**11 903 418**	**11 978 900**	**12 413 727**	**12 643 782**	**13 146 972**	**13 941 141**	**14 128 508**	**15 111 619**
42	Agriculture, forestry and fishing	258 436	262 650	286 924	310 912	325 836	364 202	326 587	338 867
43	Industry, including energy	2 656 727	2 727 740	2 938 061	3 016 784	3 060 042	3 273 535	3 376 036	3 614 828
44	Manufacturing	2 294 054	2 346 588	2 554 381	2 627 388	2 674 123	2 865 928	2 972 741	3 198 300
45	Construction	579 990	543 751	568 981	561 885	575 734	589 881	524 251	542 287
46	Distrib. trade, repairs; transp.; accommod., food serv. activ.	2 640 786	2 629 442	2 772 480	2 796 195	2 903 994	2 946 104	2 966 027	3 143 213
47	Information and communication	565 175	562 908	598 405	629 486	668 651	718 959	700 624	745 191
48	Financial and insurance activities	536 481	549 143	512 103	531 537	531 114	542 645	554 195	572 699
49	Real estate activities	169 024	163 778	161 438	152 841	157 665	167 889	155 802	165 393
50	Prof., scientif., techn. activ.; admin., support service activ.	1 127 551	1 215 677	1 283 712	1 323 407	1 390 673	1 492 262	1 467 988	1 579 418
51	Public admin.; compulsory s.s.; education; human health	3 019 116	2 979 250	2 926 956	2 950 159	3 144 163	3 438 624	3 650 113	3 968 212
52	Other service activities	350 132	344 562	364 666	370 576	389 099	407 040	406 885	441 510
53	**Wages and salaries**	**9 355 407**	**9 733 270**	**10 060 932**	**10 329 193**	**10 780 981**	**11 364 137**	**11 384 049**	**12 238 482**
54	Agriculture, forestry and fishing	211 320	220 521	240 712	262 477	276 842	309 212	271 515	285 291
55	Industry, including energy	2 063 529	2 197 773	2 349 078	2 413 202	2 466 575	2 607 175	2 666 510	2 873 582
56	Manufacturing	1 797 098	1 908 568	2 059 043	2 120 953	2 173 506	2 299 020	2 361 254	2 552 639
57	Construction	482 013	467 579	490 684	485 213	499 607	507 126	437 398	451 920
58	Distrib. trade, repairs; transp.; accommod., food serv. activ.	2 114 055	2 180 984	2 290 413	2 317 558	2 415 830	2 412 542	2 409 852	2 577 139
59	Information and communication	448 671	468 477	494 909	515 394	547 860	584 028	563 174	602 239
60	Financial and insurance activities	397 870	423 045	403 303	415 982	416 424	421 879	431 213	450 776
61	Real estate activities	137 806	139 233	136 852	129 693	133 477	140 450	126 923	135 727
62	Prof., scientif., techn. activ.; admin., support service activ.	937 028	1 037 584	1 087 995	1 126 703	1 179 127	1 258 829	1 210 254	1 310 659
63	Public admin.; compulsory s.s.; education; human health	2 281 280	2 310 932	2 265 061	2 355 683	2 519 759	2 781 017	2 932 903	3 186 747
64	Other service activities	281 835	287 143	301 924	307 288	325 479	341 879	334 307	364 401
65	**Gross operating surplus and mixed income**	**10 761 798**	**11 077 469**	**11 720 178**	**11 582 835**	**12 360 257**	**13 524 590**	**14 633 515**	**14 760 994**
66	**Taxes less subsidies on production and imports**	**3 759 388**	**4 168 230**	**4 171 033**	**4 554 447**	**4 739 848**	**5 125 982**	**5 562 087**	**5 547 707**
67	Taxes on production and imports	4 341 368	4 771 930	4 918 500	5 360 822	5 592 369	6 015 992	6 463 528	6 489 004
68	Subsidies on production and imports	581 980	603 700	747 467	806 375	852 521	890 010	901 441	941 297
69	**Residual item**	**0**	**0**	**0**	**0**	**0**	**0**	**0**	**0**
70	**Gross domestic product**	**26 424 604**	**27 224 599**	**28 304 938**	**28 781 064**	**30 247 077**	**32 591 713**	**34 324 110**	**35 420 320**

Note: Detailed metadata:http://metalinks.oecd.org/nav1/20180308/cb48
Source: Hungarian Central Statistical Office via Eurostat.

HUNGARY

Table 3. Disposable income, saving and net lending / net borrowing

Million HUF

		2009	2010	2011	2012	2013	2014	2015	2016
	DISPOSABLE INCOME								
1	**Gross domestic product**	26 297 412	27 085 900	28 166 115	28 660 518	30 127 349	32 400 148	33 999 012	..
2	Net primary incomes from the rest of the world	-1 193 575	-1 257 693	-1 307 671	-1 142 593	-788 350	-1 358 188	-1 594 827	..
3	Primary incomes receivable from the rest of the world	3 791 201	4 012 565	3 245 466	3 661 680	3 718 532	3 298 299	3 202 788	..
4	Primary incomes payable to the rest of the world	4 984 776	5 270 258	4 553 137	4 804 273	4 506 882	4 656 487	4 797 615	..
5	**Gross national income at market prices**	25 103 837	25 828 207	26 858 444	27 517 925	29 338 999	31 041 960	32 404 185	..
6	Consumption of fixed capital	4 685 700	4 899 431	5 059 645	5 271 212	5 357 309	5 532 708	5 813 370	..
7	**Net national income at market prices**	20 418 137	20 928 776	21 798 799	22 246 713	23 981 690	25 509 252	26 590 815	..
8	Net current transfers from the rest of the world	-82 165	-114 344	-160 164	-265 596	-177 784	-237 384	-370 221	..
9	Current transfers receivable from the rest of the world	392 837	408 273	417 558	466 883	659 522	635 318	623 379	..
10	Current transfers payable to the rest of the world	475 002	522 617	577 722	732 479	837 306	872 702	993 600	..
11	**Net national disposable income**	20 335 972	20 814 432	21 638 635	21 981 117	23 803 906	25 271 868	26 220 594	..
	SAVING AND NET LENDING / NET BORROWING								
12	**Net national disposable income**	20 335 972	20 814 432	21 638 635	21 981 117	23 803 906	25 271 868	26 220 594	..
13	Final consumption expenditures	19 881 219	20 030 956	20 664 035	21 151 200	21 666 716	22 745 988	23 586 743	..
14	Adj. for change in net equity of households in pension funds	0	0	0	0	0	0	0	..
15	**Saving, net**	454 753	783 476	974 600	829 917	2 137 190	2 525 880	2 633 851	..
16	Net capital transfers from the rest of the world	455 286	558 385	670 409	718 646	1 070 930	1 216 996	1 625 786	..
17	Capital transfers receivable from the rest of the world	479 743	622 796	687 850	773 656	1 134 533	1 249 600	1 703 362	..
18	Capital transfers payable to the rest of the world	24 457	64 411	17 441	55 010	63 603	32 604	77 576	..
19	Gross capital formation	5 348 796	5 610 357	5 774 900	5 585 309	6 350 878	7 405 008	7 382 791	..
20	Acquisitions less disposals of non-financial non-produced assets	-4 050	58 808	7 793	-7 687	-5 449	7 288	33 278	..
21	Consumption of fixed capital	4 685 700	4 899 431	5 059 645	5 271 212	5 357 309	5 532 708	5 813 370	..
22	**Net lending / net borrowing**	250 993	572 127	921 957	1 242 153	2 220 000	1 863 288	2 656 938	..
	REAL DISPOSABLE INCOME								
23	**Gross domestic product at constant prices, reference year 2010**	26 902 324	27 085 900	27 536 045	27 083 413	27 651 140	28 820 157	29 790 573	30 449 894
24	Trading gain or loss	-2 924	0	-302 205	-505 814	-390 299	-308 295	-251 543	..
25	**Real gross domestic income**	26 899 400	27 085 900	27 233 840	26 577 600	27 260 841	28 511 862	29 539 030	..
26	Net real primary incomes from the rest of the world	-1 220 898	-1 257 693	-1 264 388	-1 059 554	-713 341	-1 195 194	-1 385 618	..
27	Real primary incomes receivable from the rest of the world	3 877 987	4 012 565	3 138 044	3 395 565	3 364 727	2 902 476	2 782 647	..
28	Real primary incomes payable to the rest of the world	5 098 885	5 270 258	4 402 432	4 455 120	4 078 069	4 097 670	4 168 265	..
29	**Real gross national income at market prices**	25 678 502	25 828 207	25 969 452	25 518 045	26 547 500	27 316 667	28 153 412	..
30	Net real current transfers from the rest of the world	-84 046	-114 344	-154 863	-246 294	-160 868	-208 896	-321 656	..
31	Real current transfers receivable from the rest of the world	401 830	408 273	403 737	432 952	596 771	559 075	541 604	..
32	Real current transfers payable to the rest of the world	485 876	522 617	558 600	679 246	757 639	767 971	863 260	..
33	**Real gross national disposable income**	25 594 456	25 713 863	25 814 589	25 271 751	26 386 631	27 107 771	27 831 757	..
34	Consumption of fixed capital at constant prices	4 780 064	4 899 431	4 953 943	5 017 142	5 004 959	5 110 454	5 231 259	..
35	**Real net national income at market prices**	20 885 539	20 928 776	21 077 277	20 629 921	21 699 919	22 447 930	23 102 639	..
36	**Real net national disposable income**	20 801 494	20 814 432	20 922 414	20 383 628	21 539 051	22 239 034	22 780 983	..

Note: Detailed metadata:http://metalinks.oecd.org/nav1/20180308/ca8d
Source: Hungarian Central Statistical Office via Eurostat.

Table 4. Population and employment (persons) and employment (hours worked) by industry
ISIC Rev. 4

		2009	2010	2011	2012	2013	2014	2015	2016
	POPULATION, THOUSAND PERSONS, NATIONAL CONCEPT								
1	**Total population**	**10 022.7**	**10 000.0**	**9 971.7**	**9 920.4**	**9 893.1**	**9 866.5**	**9 839.3**	**9 814.0**
2	Economically active population	..	..	..	..	..	..	..	..
3	Unemployed persons	..	..	..	..	..	..	..	..
4	Total employment	3 747.8	3 732.4	3 759.0	3 827.2	3 892.8	4 100.8	4 210.5	4 411.0
5	Employees	3 409.1	3 413.1	3 437.8	3 524.7	3 613.7	3 812.9	3 905.8	4 101.2
6	Self-employed	338.7	319.3	321.2	302.5	279.1	287.9	304.7	309.8
	TOTAL EMPLOYMENT, THOUSAND PERSONS, DOMESTIC CONCEPT								
7	Agriculture, forestry and fishing	284.3	286.9	274.1	284.8	277.7	281.5	270.5	262.5
8	Industry, including energy	915.5	891.3	888.0	881.3	836.5	861.3	854.1	870.4
9	Manufacturing	819.5	795.4	794.5	790.8	754.2	775.8	772.0	787.0
10	Construction	287.0	265.5	259.7	258.7	258.8	267.3	272.4	280.3
11	Distrib. trade, repairs; transp.; accommod., food serv. activ.	964.3	968.9	965.6	985.0	985.3	999.0	1 024.7	1 059.7
12	Information and communication	91.6	95.0	100.1	102.3	110.4	118.6	122.1	132.1
13	Financial and insurance activities	97.0	94.7	93.7	94.7	92.8	92.4	89.5	87.6
14	Real estate activities	72.0	67.7	65.0	60.3	63.2	63.1	65.6	67.3
15	Prof., scientif., techn. activ.; admin., support service activ.	284.9	276.5	312.0	301.8	337.4	419.3	439.0	467.5
16	Public admin.; compulsory s.s.; education; human health	848.9	864.1	849.7	851.4	896.7	941.3	990.7	1 009.1
17	Other service activities	167.4	158.6	161.6	155.4	160.9	169.9	186.9	193.1
18	**Total employment**	**4 012.9**	**3 969.3**	**3 969.4**	**3 975.8**	**4 019.5**	**4 213.6**	**4 315.6**	**4 429.5**
	EMPLOYEES, THOUSAND PERSONS, DOMESTIC CONCEPT								
19	Agriculture, forestry and fishing	123.2	122.2	119.6	119.9	114.4	115.6	115.4	110.4
20	Industry, including energy	887.4	865.0	860.8	855.7	815.4	839.9	832.6	848.6
21	Manufacturing	792.3	770.0	768.4	766.2	733.7	754.9	751.1	765.8
22	Construction	242.7	222.9	214.6	216.5	225.7	233.8	238.8	247.3
23	Distrib. trade, repairs; transp.; accommod., food serv. activ.	861.1	868.7	866.8	887.3	902.9	917.0	944.0	980.8
24	Information and communication	84.4	88.3	93.7	96.2	103.3	110.8	113.2	121.4
25	Financial and insurance activities	82.3	80.3	78.4	80.2	78.9	78.8	76.4	74.9
26	Real estate activities	69.3	66.0	63.2	58.6	61.4	61.2	63.6	65.0
27	Prof., scientif., techn. activ.; admin., support service activ.	254.9	252.0	288.0	279.8	307.3	388.0	408.7	434.9
28	Public admin.; compulsory s.s.; education; human health	834.4	849.9	835.0	836.0	884.8	929.0	977.6	995.3
29	Other service activities	124.6	119.8	123.5	118.0	128.8	136.0	150.3	153.7
30	**Total employees**	**3 564.3**	**3 535.0**	**3 543.6**	**3 548.2**	**3 622.9**	**3 810.0**	**3 920.4**	**4 032.3**
	SELF-EMPLOYED, THOUSAND PERSONS, DOMESTIC CONCEPT								
31	Agriculture, forestry and fishing	161.1	164.7	154.4	164.9	163.3	165.9	155.1	152.1
32	Industry, including energy	28.1	26.3	27.2	25.6	21.0	21.4	21.5	21.8
33	Manufacturing	27.2	25.4	26.1	24.5	20.5	20.9	20.9	21.2
34	Construction	44.2	42.6	45.1	42.2	33.1	33.5	33.6	33.0
35	Distrib. trade, repairs; transp.; accommod., food serv. activ.	103.2	100.3	98.8	97.7	82.4	82.0	80.8	78.9
36	Information and communication	7.3	6.6	6.4	6.1	7.0	7.8	9.0	10.7
37	Financial and insurance activities	14.8	14.4	15.3	14.6	13.8	13.6	13.2	12.7
38	Real estate activities	2.7	1.7	1.8	1.6	1.8	1.9	2.1	2.3
39	Prof., scientif., techn. activ.; admin., support service activ.	30.0	24.6	24.0	22.0	30.1	31.2	30.4	32.6
40	Public admin.; compulsory s.s.; education; human health	14.4	14.1	14.7	15.4	11.8	12.3	13.1	13.8
41	Other service activities	42.8	38.8	38.2	37.5	32.2	34.0	36.6	39.3
42	**Total self-employed**	**448.6**	**434.2**	**425.8**	**427.6**	**396.6**	**403.6**	**395.2**	**397.2**
	TOTAL EMPLOYMENT, MILLION HOURS, DOMESTIC CONCEPT								
43	Industry, including energy	1 768.1	1 575.0	1 567.8	1 538.1	1 462.4	1 508.8	1 504.0	1 527.1
44	Distrib. trade, repairs; transp.; accommod., food serv. activ.	2 002.9	1 724.3	1 714.1	1 719.0	1 708.9	1 740.4	1 767.9	1 831.3
45	Financial and insurance activities	194.9	169.9	166.0	165.7	159.4	157.2	151.4	151.8
46	Prof., scientif., techn. activ.; admin., support service activ.	550.7	485.0	547.1	522.6	580.2	731.2	759.0	814.7
47	Public admin.; compulsory s.s.; education; human health	1 606.3	1 530.0	1 487.8	1 481.1	1 564.0	1 642.1	1 739.8	1 820.1
48	**Total employment**	**7 877.6**	**7 053.3**	**7 025.2**	**6 957.7**	**7 012.3**	**7 380.7**	**7 547.6**	**7 793.3**
	EMPLOYEES, MILLION HOURS, DOMESTIC CONCEPT								
49	Industry, including energy	1 712.0	1 520.7	1 513.0	1 487.9	1 418.8	1 465.8	1 462.0	1 483.5
50	Distrib. trade, repairs; transp.; accommod., food serv. activ.	1 768.1	1 509.1	1 505.4	1 517.6	1 537.0	1 568.4	1 600.8	1 667.6
51	Financial and insurance activities	165.0	138.9	135.7	136.8	134.5	134.4	130.9	128.2
52	Prof., scientif., techn. activ.; admin., support service activ.	498.2	435.6	498.6	480.1	523.5	671.9	701.5	752.3
53	Public admin.; compulsory s.s.; education; human health	1 578.4	1 502.8	1 460.1	1 453.7	1 543.0	1 619.9	1 715.4	1 795.0
54	**Total employees**	**6 976.7**	**6 191.8**	**6 187.6**	**6 128.4**	**6 245.0**	**6 597.0**	**6 779.3**	**7 017.5**
	SELF-EMPLOYED, MILLION HOURS, DOMESTIC CONCEPT								
55	Industry, including energy	56.1	54.3	54.8	50.2	43.6	43.0	42.0	43.7
56	Distrib. trade, repairs; transp.; accommod., food serv. activ.	234.8	215.1	208.7	201.4	171.9	171.9	167.0	163.7
57	Financial and insurance activities	29.9	30.9	30.3	28.8	24.9	22.8	20.4	23.6
58	Prof., scientif., techn. activ.; admin., support service activ.	52.5	49.3	48.5	42.5	56.7	59.3	57.5	62.5
59	Public admin.; compulsory s.s.; education; human health	28.0	27.2	27.7	27.4	21.0	22.2	24.3	25.1
60	**Total self-employed**	**900.9**	**861.5**	**837.6**	**829.3**	**767.3**	**783.7**	**768.3**	**775.8**

Note: Detailed metadata:http://metalinks.oecd.org/nav1/20180308/bb22
Source: Hungarian Central Statistical Office via Eurostat.

ICELAND

Table 1. Gross domestic product, expenditure approach

Million ISK

		2009	2010	2011	2012	2013	2014	2015	2016
	AT CURRENT PRICES								
1	**Final consumption expenditure**	**1 220 219**	**1 237 655**	**1 309 773**	**1 395 165**	**1 457 340**	**1 545 898**	**1 643 376**	**1 768 879**
2	Household	793 309	806 963	856 729	924 392	961 245	1 021 201	1 076 842	1 161 515
3	NPISH's	31 985	31 310	32 619	34 470	36 874	39 847	43 897	50 153
4	Government	394 925	399 381	420 425	436 303	459 221	484 850	522 636	557 211
5	Individual	256 638	255 139	264 309	271 992	290 242	312 728	341 639	365 502
6	Collective	138 287	144 241	156 116	164 311	168 979	172 123	180 997	193 667
7	*of which: Actual individual consumption*	1 081 932	1 093 413	1 153 657	1 230 854	1 288 361	1 373 775	1 462 378	1 552 600
8	**Gross capital formation**	**236 686**	**224 230**	**263 139**	**286 306**	**291 896**	**347 726**	**425 109**	**524 519**
9	Gross fixed capital formation, total	238 807	226 755	261 613	284 506	296 849	345 681	421 620	521 593
10	Dwellings	40 110	35 542	39 966	44 880	50 826	58 812	58 361	80 793
11	Other buildings and structures	115 170	95 850	83 992	80 073	96 892	113 371	140 992	194 457
12	Transport equipment	-733	8 974	23 871	44 387	26 819	43 450	84 187	85 388
13	Other machinery and equipment	46 368	50 704	76 493	76 590	81 870	85 116	85 259	104 517
14	Cultivated assets	3 588	3 763	3 973	3 860	3 705	4 338	4 568	4 822
15	Intangible fixed assets	34 303	31 923	33 318	34 717	36 738	40 595	48 254	51 616
16	Changes in inventories, acquisitions less disposals of valuables	-2 121	-2 525	1 526	1 800	-4 953	2 045	3 489	2 926
17	Changes in inventories	-2 121	-2 525	1 526	1 800	-4 953	2 045	3 489	2 926
18	Acquisitions less disposals of valuables	..	..	..	..	..	..	..	..
19	**External balance of goods and services**	**143 484**	**165 223**	**135 403**	**106 213**	**150 444**	**125 413**	**163 877**	**155 411**
20	Exports of goods and services	791 773	869 551	962 536	1 013 269	1 047 908	1 068 320	1 188 745	1 186 686
21	Exports of goods	459 377	502 089	562 698	576 340	561 036	568 316	614 382	540 233
22	Exports of services	332 395	367 462	399 838	436 929	486 871	500 004	574 363	646 453
23	Imports of goods and services	648 288	704 328	827 133	907 056	897 464	942 907	1 024 868	1 031 275
24	Imports of goods	403 986	438 225	526 252	564 304	553 221	578 635	649 890	641 897
25	Imports of services	244 303	266 103	300 881	342 751	344 243	364 272	374 978	389 378
26	**Statistical discrepancy**	**0**	**0**	**0**	**0**	**0**	**0**	**0**	**0**
27	**Gross domestic product**	**1 600 390**	**1 627 108**	**1 708 315**	**1 787 684**	**1 899 680**	**2 019 038**	**2 232 362**	**2 448 809**
	AT CONSTANT PRICES, REFERENCE YEAR 2010								
28	**Final consumption expenditure**	**1 255 760**	**1 237 655**	**1 258 793**	**1 268 325**	**1 279 779**	**1 315 056**	**1 361 140**	**1 435 043**
29	Household	808 665	806 963	828 732	846 373	853 470	881 588	923 950	991 311
30	NPISH's	32 527	31 310	31 266	30 692	31 007	31 540	31 844	32 447
31	Government	414 849	399 381	398 793	391 473	395 504	402 283	406 195	413 882
32	Individual	..	..	..	..	..	..	..	..
33	Collective	..	..	..	..	..	..	..	..
34	*of which: Actual individual consumption*	1 113 445 e	1 093 413 e	1 108 753 e	1 118 952 e	1 131 388 e	1 168 636 e	1 211 227 e	1 259 581 e
35	**Gross capital formation**	**245 248**	**224 230**	**250 318**	**263 523**	**269 367**	**312 563**	**370 428**	**454 885**
36	Gross fixed capital formation, total	248 211	226 755	252 981	266 319	272 296	315 872	374 354	459 721
37	Dwellings	43 335	35 542	37 448	40 037	44 361	50 909	49 317	63 822
38	Other buildings and structures	121 236	95 850	80 361	72 894	85 643	98 971	118 038	158 313
39	Transport equipment	-743	8 974	23 475	47 002	28 407	46 716	89 379	95 447
40	Other machinery and equipment	45 858	50 704	76 494	72 540	77 250	81 764	81 012	105 174
41	Cultivated assets	3 702	3 763	3 582	3 269	3 071	3 560	3 655	3 792
42	Intangible fixed assets	35 945	31 923	31 623	30 870	31 189	33 101	37 171	36 832
43	Changes in inventories, acquisitions less disposals of valuables	..	..	..	..	..	..	..	..
44	Changes in inventories	..	..	..	..	..	..	..	..
45	Acquisitions less disposals of valuables	..	..	..	..	..	..	..	..
46	**External balance of goods and services**	**186 478**	**165 223**	**147 165**	**144 900**	**206 373**	**160 784**	**135 515**	**115 342**
47	Exports of goods and services	861 067	869 551	899 179	931 535	994 059	1 025 518	1 119 577	1 241 693
48	Exports of goods	525 418	502 089	515 687	533 418	553 309	562 657	581 116	602 561
49	Exports of services	338 724	367 462	383 491	398 154	440 546	461 975	535 282	634 990
50	Imports of goods and services	674 590	704 328	752 015	786 635	787 686	864 734	984 063	1 126 352
51	Imports of goods	426 048	438 225	467 998	478 661	477 435	521 869	619 194	703 877
52	Imports of services	248 762	266 103	284 018	308 643	311 037	343 832	364 793	422 492
53	**Statistical discrepancy (including chaining residual)**	**486**	**0**	**2 774**	**4 188**	**-2 166**	**2 158**	**-171**	**183**
54	**Gross domestic product**	**1 687 971**	**1 627 108**	**1 659 049**	**1 680 935**	**1 753 353**	**1 790 562**	**1 866 912**	**2 005 452**

Note: Detailed metadata:http://metalinks.oecd.org/nav1/20180308/70ff
Source: Statistics Iceland via Eurostat.

ICELAND

Table 2. Gross domestic product, output and income approach
ISIC Rev. 4

Million ISK

		2009	2010	2011	2012	2013	2014	2015	2016
	OUTPUT APPROACH AT CURRENT PRICES								
1	**Total gross value added at basic prices**[1]	**1 426 370**	**1 442 898**	**1 513 697**	**1 573 731**	**1 673 937**	**1 745 606**	**1 940 043**	**2 083 133**
2	Agriculture, forestry and fishing	93 179	106 033	115 649	120 000	114 059	105 846	119 913	116 488
3	Industry, including energy	249 942	292 157	313 849	300 964	313 865	307 027	332 155	315 251
4	Manufacturing	178 044	209 351	220 634	203 975	214 449	216 152	224 671	210 319
5	Construction	67 410	63 440	64 533	72 202	80 704	95 360	105 924	152 417
6	Services	..	..	..	..	..	..	..	..
7	Distrib. trade, repairs; transp.; accommod., food serv. activ.	227 456	234 346	256 895	256 911	286 344	306 898	374 012	439 277
8	Information and communication	56 811	56 408	66 506	66 244	81 265	80 959	93 119	104 219
9	Financial and insurance activities	158 449	124 276	113 111	143 920	131 365	137 532	121 217	114 978
10	Real estate activities	156 458	148 135	145 143	153 185	166 834	180 048	195 303	197 431
11	Prof., scientif., techn. activ.; admin., support service activ.	97 098	101 120	107 126	111 342	121 540	138 684	165 426	196 508
12	Public admin.; compulsory s.s.; education; human health	279 900	276 078	287 298	304 489	329 022	343 939	378 958	386 129
13	Other service activities	39 666	40 905	43 588	44 473	48 940	49 314	54 017	60 434
14	**FISIM (Financial Intermediation Services Indirectly Measured)**	..	..	..	..	..	..	..	..
15	**Gross value added at basic prices, excluding FISIM**[1]	**1 426 370**	**1 442 898**	**1 513 697**	**1 573 731**	**1 673 937**	**1 745 606**	**1 940 043**	**2 083 133**
16	**Taxes less subsidies on products**	**174 020**	**184 209**	**194 618**	**213 954**	**225 743**	**273 432**	**292 319**	..
17	Taxes on products	200 514	210 184	222 448	243 297	255 292	301 409	321 208	..
18	Subsidies on products	26 494	25 974	27 830	29 343	29 549	27 978	28 889	..
19	**Residual item**	**0**	**0**	**0**	**0**	**0**	**0**	**0**	**0**
20	**Gross domestic product at market prices**	**1 600 390**	**1 627 108**	**1 708 315**	**1 787 684**	**1 899 680**	**2 019 038**	**2 232 362**	**2 448 809**
	OUTPUT APPROACH AT CONSTANT PRICES (REF. YEAR 2010)								
21	**Total gross value added at basic prices**[1]	**1 491 331**	**1 442 898**	**1 461 200**	**1 480 685**	**1 529 810**	**1 566 761**	**1 640 248**	..
22	Agriculture, forestry and fishing	120 475	107 517	101 254	112 226	113 968	112 869	118 092	..
23	Industry, including energy	287 570	291 425	307 136	316 838	352 415	362 161	381 884	..
24	Manufacturing	203 542	208 619	225 162	232 490	245 659	252 332	264 918	..
25	Construction	71 635	63 440	61 362	62 255	67 987	74 438	82 184	..
26	Services	..	..	..	..	..	..	..	..
27	Distrib. trade, repairs; transp.; accommod., food serv. activ.	238 964	234 346	247 252	259 443	276 259	297 185	337 545	..
28	Information and communication	58 440	56 408	61 011	65 110	71 304	76 541	81 858	..
29	Financial and insurance activities	139 103	124 276	109 989	90 568	73 681	64 369	54 925	..
30	Real estate activities	136 949	138 394	141 296	143 309	146 058	146 302	147 654	..
31	Prof., scientif., techn. activ.; admin., support service activ.	101 124	101 120	104 954	106 791	111 740	118 161	133 493	..
32	Public admin.; compulsory s.s.; education; human health	286 771	276 078	275 672	271 537	274 333	279 035	281 749	..
33	Other service activities	40 722	40 905	42 037	42 235	44 959	46 211	46 764	..
34	**FISIM (Financial Intermediation Services Indirectly Measured)**	..	..	..	..	..	..	..	..
35	**Gross value added at basic prices, excluding FISIM**[1]	**1 491 331**	**1 442 898**	**1 461 200**	**1 480 685**	**1 529 810**	**1 566 761**	**1 640 248**	..
36	**Taxes less subsidies on products**	..	..	..	..	..	..	..	..
37	Taxes on products	..	..	..	..	..	..	..	..
38	Subsidies on products	..	..	..	..	..	..	..	..
39	**Residual item**	..	..	..	..	..	..	..	..
40	**Gross domestic product at market prices**	**1 687 971**	**1 627 108**	**1 659 049**	**1 680 935**	**1 753 353**	**1 790 562**	**1 866 912**	**2 005 452**
	INCOME APPROACH								
41	**Compensation of employees**	**740 950**	**778 195**	**851 474**	**910 349**	**987 190**	**1 045 345**	**1 155 144**	**1 298 382**
42	Agriculture, forestry and fishing	48 027	56 838	64 243	66 558	66 763	62 360	67 177	..
43	Industry, including energy	108 625	114 174	130 924	142 536	152 122	160 768	171 160	..
44	Manufacturing	91 862	96 681	111 885	122 221	131 301	138 197	150 414	..
45	Construction	43 507	39 535	39 685	42 367	47 932	55 540	61 398	..
46	Distrib. trade, repairs; transp.; accommod., food serv. activ.	150 461	167 818	184 925	195 857	214 936	233 982	270 700	..
47	Information and communication	39 879	41 981	45 665	49 254	54 331	58 559	62 711	..
48	Financial and insurance activities	47 873	50 552	56 156	58 104	66 681	60 540	61 675	..
49	Real estate activities	3 926	4 029	4 856	5 396	6 205	6 204	6 859	..
50	Prof., scientif., techn. activ.; admin., support service activ.	54 075	57 848	65 072	72 398	78 335	89 806	100 986	..
51	Public admin.; compulsory s.s.; education; human health	218 059	217 549	230 270	246 271	265 836	282 256	313 670	..
52	Other service activities	26 517	27 872	29 677	31 608	34 050	35 330	38 808	..
53	**Wages and salaries**	..	..	..	..	..	..	..	..
54	Agriculture, forestry and fishing	..	..	..	..	..	..	..	..
55	Industry, including energy	..	..	..	..	..	..	..	..
56	Manufacturing	..	..	..	..	..	..	..	..
57	Construction	..	..	..	..	..	..	..	..
58	Distrib. trade, repairs; transp.; accommod., food serv. activ.	..	..	..	..	..	..	..	..
59	Information and communication	..	..	..	..	..	..	..	..
60	Financial and insurance activities	..	..	..	..	..	..	..	..
61	Real estate activities	..	..	..	..	..	..	..	..
62	Prof., scientif., techn. activ.; admin., support service activ.	..	..	..	..	..	..	..	..
63	Public admin.; compulsory s.s.; education; human health	..	..	..	..	..	..	..	..
64	Other service activities	..	..	..	..	..	..	..	..
65	**Gross operating surplus and mixed income**	**676 698**	**655 715**	**652 576**	**652 642**	**676 029**	**688 326**	**771 423**	**840 086**
66	**Taxes less subsidies on production and imports**	**182 742**	**193 198**	**204 266**	**224 693**	**236 461**	**285 366**	**305 795**	**310 341**
67	Taxes on production and imports	210 747	220 687	233 266	254 951	267 192	314 514	335 302	344 419
68	Subsidies on production and imports	28 005	27 489	29 001	30 258	30 731	29 148	29 508	34 078
69	**Residual item**	**0**	**0**	**0**	**0**	**0**	**0**	**0**	**0**
70	**Gross domestic product**	**1 600 390**	**1 627 108**	**1 708 315**	**1 787 684**	**1 899 680**	**2 019 038**	**2 232 362**	**2 448 809**

Note: Detailed metadata:http://metalinks.oecd.org/nav1/20180308/70ff

1. Gross value added by industry and total is at factor cost, not at basic prices.

Source: Statistics Iceland via Eurostat.

ICELAND

Table 3. Disposable income, saving and net lending / net borrowing

Million ISK

		2009	2010	2011	2012	2013	2014	2015	2016
	DISPOSABLE INCOME								
1	**Gross domestic product**	1 593 337	1 620 293	1 701 585	1 778 499	1 891 244	2 006 018	2 213 543	..
2	Net primary incomes from the rest of the world	-288 458	-260 895	-211 858	-166 898	-23 430	-32 987	-18 598	..
3	Primary incomes receivable from the rest of the world	105 072	74 690	159 899	109 534	130 378	107 580	111 036	..
4	Primary incomes payable to the rest of the world	393 530	335 585	371 757	276 432	153 808	140 567	129 634	..
5	**Gross national income at market prices**	1 304 879	1 359 398	1 489 727	1 611 600	1 867 814	1 973 027	..	..
6	Consumption of fixed capital	298 847	293 327	291 636	304 661	308 104	310 355	323 629	..
7	**Net national income at market prices**	1 006 031	1 066 071	1 198 092	1 306 940	1 559 710	1 662 671	..	..
8	Net current transfers from the rest of the world	-8 440	-11 275	-13 190	-9 651	-12 750	-12 581	-35 330	..
9	Current transfers receivable from the rest of the world	6 812	6 366	8 519	13 491	14 077	15 982	16 591	..
10	Current transfers payable to the rest of the world	15 252	17 641	21 709	23 142	26 827	28 563	51 921	..
11	**Net national disposable income**	997 591	1 054 796	1 184 901	1 297 289	1 546 960	1 650 090	..	..
	SAVING AND NET LENDING / NET BORROWING								
12	**Net national disposable income**	997 591	1 054 796	1 184 901	1 297 289	1 546 960	1 650 090	..	..
13	Final consumption expenditures	1 213 166	1 230 545	1 301 213	1 385 980	1 448 902	1 532 801	1 623 487	..
14	Adj. for change in net equity of households in pension funds	0	0	0	0	0	0	..	..
15	**Saving, net**	-215 575	-175 749	-116 311	-88 691	98 058	117 289	..	..
16	Net capital transfers from the rest of the world	-1 387	-1 379	-1 474	-1 244	-1 290	-1 593	-1 476	..
17	Capital transfers receivable from the rest of the world	0	0	0	0	0	0	0	..
18	Capital transfers payable to the rest of the world	1 387	1 379	1 474	1 244	1 290	1 593	1 476	..
19	Gross capital formation	236 686	224 525	264 969	286 306	291 894	347 804	423 440	..
20	Acquisitions less disposals of non-financial non-produced assets	0	0	0	0	0	0	0	..
21	Consumption of fixed capital	298 847	293 327	291 636	304 661	308 104	310 355	323 629	..
22	**Net lending / net borrowing**	-154 801	-108 325	-91 119	-71 580	112 979	78 248	..	..
	REAL DISPOSABLE INCOME								
23	**Gross domestic product at constant prices, reference year 2010**	1 680 901	1 620 293	1 652 100	1 673 895	1 746 009	1 783 062	1 859 092	1 997 052
24	Trading gain or loss	-39 443	0	-19 536	-53 550	-71 030	-60 295	-9 856	..
25	**Real gross domestic income**	1 641 458	1 620 293	1 632 564	1 620 344	1 674 979	1 722 767	1 849 236	..
26	Net real primary incomes from the rest of the world	-297 170	-260 895	-203 264	-152 056	-20 751	-28 329	-15 537	..
27	Real primary incomes receivable from the rest of the world	108 245	74 690	153 413	99 794	115 469	92 390	92 762	..
28	Real primary incomes payable to the rest of the world	405 415	335 585	356 677	251 850	136 220	120 719	108 299	..
29	**Real gross national income at market prices**	1 344 288	1 359 398	1 429 300	1 468 287	1 654 228	1 694 434	..	..
30	Net real current transfers from the rest of the world	-12 429	-11 275	-14 476	-21 769	-22 081	-24 309	-24 549	..
31	Real current transfers receivable from the rest of the world	7 018	6 366	8 173	12 291	12 467	13 725	13 860	..
32	Real current transfers payable to the rest of the world	15 713	17 641	20 828	21 084	23 759	24 530	43 376	..
33	**Real gross national disposable income**	1 335 593	1 348 123	1 416 645	1 459 495	1 642 936	1 683 630	..	..
34	Consumption of fixed capital at constant prices	..	..	..	..	..	..	..	..
35	**Real net national income at market prices**	1 036 415	1 066 071	1 149 493	1 190 719	1 381 356	1 427 901	..	..
36	**Real net national disposable income**	1 027 720	1 054 796	1 136 838	1 181 926	1 370 064	1 417 097	..	..

Note: Detailed metadata:http://metalinks.oecd.org/nav1/20180308/b141
Source: Statistics Iceland via Eurostat.

Table 4. Population and employment (persons) and employment (hours worked) by industry
ISIC Rev. 4

		2009	2010	2011	2012	2013	2014	2015	2016
	POPULATION, THOUSAND PERSONS, NATIONAL CONCEPT								
1	**Total population**	**319.2**	**318.0**	**319.0**	**320.7**	**323.8**	**327.4**	**330.8**	**335.4**
2	Economically active population	..	..	..	..	..	..	..	..
3	Unemployed persons	..	..	..	..	..	..	..	..
4	Total employment	164.4 p	162.3 p	164.2 p	167.2 p	171.3 p	175.4 p	180.4 p	188.7 p
5	Employees	154.4 p	152.5 p	154.1 p	156.8 p	160.9 p	165.0 p	170.2 p	178.6 p
6	Self-employed	10.1 p	9.9 p	10.1 p	10.4 p	10.3 p	10.4 p	10.2 p	10.2 p
	TOTAL EMPLOYMENT, THOUSAND PERSONS, DOMESTIC CONCEPT								
7	Agriculture, forestry and fishing	7.0 p	7.3 p	7.4 p	7.5 p	7.6 p	7.4 p	7.5 p	7.4 p
8	Industry, including energy	22.4 p	22.5 p	23.1 p	23.6 p	24.2 p	24.5 p	24.6 p	25.1 p
9	Manufacturing	19.9 p	20.1 p	20.7 p	21.2 p	21.8 p	22.0 p	22.1 p	22.6 p
10	Construction	10.7 p	9.0 p	8.5 p	8.6 p	9.1 p	9.6 p	10.4 p	11.9 p
11	Distrib. trade, repairs; transp.; accommod., food serv. activ.	37.3 p	37.4 p	38.6 p	40.3 p	41.9 p	43.7 p	46.2 p	50.5 p
12	Information and communication	7.2 p	7.2 p	7.3 p	7.3 p	7.5 p	7.6 p	7.8 p	7.9 p
13	Financial and insurance activities	7.0 p	6.8 p	6.7 p	6.6 p	6.4 p	6.2 p	5.9 p	5.9 p
14	Real estate activities	0.9 p	1.0 p	1.0 p	1.1 p	1.1 p	1.2 p	1.3 p	1.4 p
15	Prof., scientif., techn. activ.; admin., support service activ.	12.2 p	12.1 p	12.6 p	13.3 p	13.8 p	14.4 p	15.4 p	17.4 p
16	Public admin.; compulsory s.s.; education; human health	51.4 p	50.8 p	50.5 p	50.6 p	51.3 p	52.1 p	52.7 p	52.5 p
17	Other service activities	8.3 p	8.3 p	8.4 p	8.4 p	8.4 p	8.6 p	8.7 p	8.7 p
18	**Total employment**	**164.4 p**	**162.3 p**	**164.2 p**	**167.2 p**	**171.3 p**	**175.4 p**	**180.4 p**	**188.7 p**
	EMPLOYEES, THOUSAND PERSONS, DOMESTIC CONCEPT								
19	Agriculture, forestry and fishing	5.5 p	5.6 p	5.6 p	5.7 p	5.7 p	5.6 p	5.6 p	5.5 p
20	Industry, including energy	22.0 p	22.1 p	22.7 p	23.3 p	23.9 p	24.1 p	24.3 p	24.8 p
21	Manufacturing	19.6 p	19.7 p	20.3 p	20.9 p	21.5 p	21.7 p	21.8 p	22.3 p
22	Construction	9.0 p	7.5 p	6.9 p	6.9 p	7.4 p	7.9 p	8.7 p	10.2 p
23	Distrib. trade, repairs; transp.; accommod., food serv. activ.	35.8 p	36.0 p	37.2 p	38.9 p	40.5 p	42.4 p	44.9 p	49.2 p
24	Information and communication	6.9 p	6.8 p	7.0 p	6.9 p	7.1 p	7.2 p	7.4 p	7.6 p
25	Financial and insurance activities	6.9 p	6.7 p	6.7 p	6.6 p	6.4 p	6.1 p	5.9 p	5.9 p
26	Real estate activities	0.9 p	0.9 p	0.9 p	1.0 p	1.1 p	1.2 p	1.2 p	1.3 p
27	Prof., scientif., techn. activ.; admin., support service activ.	10.9 p	10.9 p	11.4 p	12.0 p	12.4 p	13.1 p	14.0 p	16.1 p
28	Public admin.; compulsory s.s.; education; human health	49.8 p	49.2 p	48.8 p	48.8 p	49.6 p	50.4 p	50.9 p	50.7 p
29	Other service activities	6.7 p	6.8 p	6.8 p	6.8 p	6.9 p	7.0 p	7.2 p	7.2 p
30	**Total employees**	**154.4 p**	**152.5 p**	**154.1 p**	**156.8 p**	**160.9 p**	**165.0 p**	**170.2 p**	**178.6 p**
	SELF-EMPLOYED, THOUSAND PERSONS, DOMESTIC CONCEPT								
31	Agriculture, forestry and fishing	1.5 p	1.7 p	1.8 p	1.8 p	1.9 p	1.9 p	1.8 p	1.9 p
32	Industry, including energy	0.4 p	0.3 p	0.3 p	0.4 p	0.3 p	0.3 p	0.3 p	0.3 p
33	Manufacturing	0.4 p	0.3 p	0.3 p	0.3 p	0.3 p	0.3 p	0.3 p	0.3 p
34	Construction	1.7 p	1.5 p	1.6 p	1.7 p	1.7 p	1.7 p	1.6 p	1.7 p
35	Distrib. trade, repairs; transp.; accommod., food serv. activ.	1.4 p	1.4 p	1.4 p	1.4 p	1.4 p	1.4 p	1.3 p	1.3 p
36	Information and communication	0.4 p	0.4 p	0.4 p	0.4 p	0.4 p	0.4 p	0.4 p	0.3 p
37	Financial and insurance activities	0.1 p	0.1 p	0.1 p	0.1 p	0.1 p	0.1 p	0.0	0.0
38	Real estate activities	0.1 p	0.1 p	0.1 p	0.1 p	0.1 p	0.1 p	0.1 p	0.1 p
39	Prof., scientif., techn. activ.; admin., support service activ.	1.3 p	1.2 p	1.3 p	1.3 p	1.3 p	1.4 p	1.3 p	1.3 p
40	Public admin.; compulsory s.s.; education; human health	1.6 p	1.6 p	1.7 p	1.7 p	1.7 p	1.7 p	1.7 p	1.7 p
41	Other service activities	1.6 p	1.5 p	1.6 p	1.6 p	1.6 p	1.6 p	1.5 p	1.5 p
42	**Total self-employed**	**10.1 p**	**9.9 p**	**10.1 p**	**10.4 p**	**10.3 p**	**10.4 p**	**10.2 p**	**10.2 p**
	TOTAL EMPLOYMENT, MILLION HOURS, DOMESTIC CONCEPT								
43	Industry, including energy	35.9 p	36.5 p	38.0 p	38.4 p	39.2 p	39.4 p	39.6 p	40.1 p
44	Distrib. trade, repairs; transp.; accommod., food serv. activ.	52.3 p	52.7 p	54.4 p	56.1 p	58.4 p	60.5 p	64.1 p	69.6 p
45	Financial and insurance activities	12.5 p	12.0 p	12.1 p	12.0 p	11.8 p	11.2 p	10.6 p	10.4 p
46	Prof., scientif., techn. activ.; admin., support service activ.	18.9 p	18.7 p	19.9 p	20.7 p	21.4 p	22.2 p	23.5 p	26.3 p
47	Public admin.; compulsory s.s.; education; human health	82.7 p	80.1 p	79.5 p	77.6 p	78.7 p	79.7 p	81.0 p	80.4 p
48	**Total employment**	**254.7 p**	**250.3 p**	**254.2 p**	**254.8 p**	**260.7 p**	**264.8 p**	**272.3 p**	**281.8 p**
	EMPLOYEES, MILLION HOURS, DOMESTIC CONCEPT								
49	Industry, including energy	35.5 p	36.2 p	37.7 p	38.0 p	38.9 p	39.0 p	39.2 p	39.8 p
50	Distrib. trade, repairs; transp.; accommod., food serv. activ.	50.9 p	51.3 p	53.0 p	54.8 p	57.0 p	59.1 p	62.7 p	68.3 p
51	Financial and insurance activities	12.4 p	12.0 p	12.1 p	11.9 p	11.7 p	11.1 p	10.6 p	10.3 p
52	Prof., scientif., techn. activ.; admin., support service activ.	17.6 p	17.5 p	18.7 p	19.3 p	20.1 p	20.9 p	22.1 p	24.9 p
53	Public admin.; compulsory s.s.; education; human health	80.6 p	78.2 p	77.6 p	75.7 p	76.8 p	77.7 p	79.0 p	78.4 p
54	**Total employees**	**244.5 p**	**240.6 p**	**244.0 p**	**244.3 p**	**250.2 p**	**254.1 p**	**261.7 p**	**271.3 p**
	SELF-EMPLOYED, MILLION HOURS, DOMESTIC CONCEPT								
55	Industry, including energy	0.4 p	0.3 p	0.3 p	0.3 p	0.3 p	0.4 p	0.4 p	0.3 p
56	Distrib. trade, repairs; transp.; accommod., food serv. activ.	1.4 p	1.4 p	1.4 p	1.4 p	1.4 p	1.4 p	1.4 p	1.3 p
57	Financial and insurance activities	0.1 p	0.1 p	0.1 p	0.1 p	0.1 p	0.1 p	0.1 p	0.1 p
58	Prof., scientif., techn. activ.; admin., support service activ.	1.3 p	1.2 p	1.3 p	1.3 p	1.3 p	1.4 p	1.4 p	1.4 p
59	Public admin.; compulsory s.s.; education; human health	2.1 p	1.9 p	1.9 p	1.9 p	1.9 p	2.0 p	2.0 p	2.0 p
60	**Total self-employed**	**10.2 p**	**9.8 p**	**10.2 p**	**10.5 p**	**10.5 p**	**10.7 p**	**10.6 p**	**10.5 p**

Note: Detailed metadata:http://metalinks.oecd.org/nav1/20180308/582a
Source: Statistics Iceland via Eurostat.

IRELAND

Table 1. Gross domestic product, expenditure approach

Million EUR (1999 IEP euro)

		2009	2010	2011	2012	2013	2014	2015	2016
	AT CURRENT PRICES								
1	**Final consumption expenditure**	**115 443**	**111 302**	**110 579**	**110 542**	**111 254**	**114 779**	**119 674**	**124 968**
2	Household	79 401	77 964	77 443	77 748	78 972	81 571	85 233	88 752
3	NPISH's	1 789	1 824	1 808	1 830	1 826	1 862	2 093	2 095
4	Government	34 253	31 514	31 328	30 964	30 456	31 347	32 347	34 121
5	Individual	23 052	21 764	20 634	20 487	20 424	21 160	21 761	23 093
6	Collective	11 201	9 750	10 694	10 477	10 032	10 186	10 586	11 028
7	*of which:* Actual individual consumption	104 242	101 552	99 885	100 065	101 222	104 593	109 088	113 940
8	**Gross capital formation**	**34 419**	**28 921**	**29 617**	**35 496**	**33 842**	**43 579**	**55 512**	**90 045**
9	Gross fixed capital formation, total	35 876	29 422	28 837	34 542	33 610	40 422	53 291	87 694
10	Dwellings	7 926	5 037	4 024	3 218	3 524	4 499	4 880	5 762
11	Other buildings and structures	9 149	6 184	5 317	6 145	7 308	8 077	9 284	11 932
12	Transport equipment	7 285	6 875	7 419	10 178	7 568	9 557	9 093	14 008
13	Other machinery and equipment	1 822	1 580	1 871	1 734	3 498	4 659	4 816	3 551
14	Cultivated assets	-44	-55	19	83	-20	1	128	35
15	Intangible fixed assets	8 571	8 645	8 200	11 442	9 884	11 857	22 841	49 433
16	Changes in inventories, acquisitions less disposals of valuables	-1 457	-502	780	954	232	3 157	2 221	2 351
17	Changes in inventories	-1 446	-507	784	961	236	3 159	2 225	2 348
18	Acquisitions less disposals of valuables	-11	5	-4	-7	-3	-1	-4	2
19	**External balance of goods and services**	**22 922**	**27 872**	**32 160**	**30 146**	**33 870**	**34 603**	**86 730**	**60 643**
20	Exports of goods and services	158 596	172 797	177 303	187 658	191 185	219 786	326 610	335 041
21	Exports of goods	97 273	103 255	100 578	101 869	98 733	114 460	200 327	194 070
22	Exports of services	61 323	69 542	76 725	85 789	92 452	105 326	126 283	140 971
23	Imports of goods and services	135 674	144 925	145 143	157 512	157 315	185 184	239 880	274 398
24	Imports of goods	58 523	61 967	59 321	64 973	64 226	73 730	86 933	88 219
25	Imports of services	77 151	82 958	85 822	92 538	93 089	111 453	152 947	186 179
26	**Statistical discrepancy**	**-2 687**	**-512**	**-417**	**-623**	**1 332**	**1 576**	**121**	**-89**
27	**Gross domestic product**	**170 097**	**167 583**	**171 939**	**175 561**	**180 298**	**194 537**	**262 037**	**275 567**
	AT CONSTANT PRICES, REFERENCE YEAR 2010								
28	**Final consumption expenditure**	**112 450**	**111 302**	**109 470**	**107 751**	**107 291**	**110 119**	**114 145**	**118 387**
29	Household	77 325	77 964	76 732	75 943	75 845	77 589	80 661	83 350
30	NPISH's	1 774	1 824	1 793	1 668	1 606	1 489	1 719	1 657
31	Government	33 349	31 514	30 944	30 141	29 845	31 070	31 743	33 394
32	Individual	22 231	21 764	20 438	20 009	20 099	21 049	21 497	22 487
33	Collective	11 143	9 750	10 506	10 133	9 750	10 027	10 249	10 907
34	*of which:* Actual individual consumption	101 336	101 552	98 964	97 620	97 545	100 098	103 907	107 496
35	**Gross capital formation**	**33 297**	**28 921**	**30 216**	**35 291**	**33 271**	**42 215**	**52 334**	**83 298**
36	Gross fixed capital formation, total	34 627	29 422	29 444	34 325	32 963	38 953	49 931	80 308
37	Dwellings	7 510	5 037	4 103	3 261	3 472	4 163	4 369	4 966
38	Other buildings and structures	8 415	6 184	5 424	6 149	7 109	7 477	8 137	9 843
39	Transport equipment	7 161	6 875	7 539	10 209	7 501	9 458	8 875	13 551
40	Other machinery and equipment	1 849	1 580	1 922	1 799	3 660	4 625	4 634	3 677
41	Cultivated assets	-44	-55	17	66	-16	2	242	79
42	Intangible fixed assets	8 472	8 645	8 459	11 238	9 647	11 804	22 222	46 921
43	Changes in inventories, acquisitions less disposals of valuables	..	..	..	..	..	..	..	..
44	Changes in inventories	..	..	..	..	..	..	..	..
45	Acquisitions less disposals of valuables	-11	5	-5	-6	-3	-1	-3	2
46	**External balance of goods and services**	**19 042**	**27 872**	**29 432**	**28 522**	**32 724**	**36 783**	**72 773**	**49 946**
47	Exports of goods and services	163 378	172 797	178 250	181 067	186 583	213 508	295 477	309 107
48	Exports of goods	100 766	103 255	102 598	100 345	99 993	116 297	185 128	186 803
49	Exports of services	62 655	69 542	75 651	80 592	86 299	97 024	112 349	124 140
50	Imports of goods and services	144 336	144 925	148 817	152 544	153 859	176 725	222 705	259 161
51	Imports of goods	65 726	61 967	64 126	67 859	69 431	75 781	87 739	94 902
52	Imports of services	78 967	82 958	84 691	84 870	84 735	100 670	133 680	161 798
53	**Statistical discrepancy (including chaining residual)**	**-171**	**-512**	**3 468**	**1 086**	**2 193**	**976**	**-576**	**-683**
54	**Gross domestic product**	**164 617**	**167 583**	**172 586**	**172 650**	**175 479**	**190 094**	**238 677**	**250 948**

Note: Detailed metadata:http://metalinks.oecd.org/nav1/20180308/4272
Source: Central Statistics Office (CSO) of Ireland via Eurostat.

Table 2. Gross domestic product, output and income approach
ISIC Rev. 4

Million EUR (1999 IEP euro)

		2009	2010	2011	2012	2013	2014	2015	2016
	OUTPUT APPROACH AT CURRENT PRICES								
1	**Total gross value added at basic prices**	**152 160**	**151 871**	**156 665**	**159 685**	**165 714**	**178 583**	**243 302**	**255 269**
2	Agriculture, forestry and fishing	942	1 604	2 079	1 741	2 027	2 505	2 340	2 548
3	Industry, including energy	39 225	37 080	41 314	40 774	40 866	43 419	94 454	93 318
4	Manufacturing	34 545	32 758	36 838	35 771	35 768	38 414	89 928	88 566
5	Construction	4 111	2 509	2 595	3 651	4 543	5 775	6 179	7 040
6	Services	..	..	..	..	..	..	..	..
7	Distrib. trade, repairs; transp.; accommod., food serv. activ.	24 493	24 586	25 369	26 134	28 557	28 909	30 669	32 118
8	Information and communication	12 723	13 834	13 777	15 276	16 446	18 921	21 533	24 918
9	Financial and insurance activities	16 037	17 088	15 116	14 519	13 137	14 731	16 393	17 346
10	Real estate activities	8 551	9 995	10 640	11 687	12 442	13 647	14 491	15 756
11	Prof., scientif., techn. activ.; admin., support service activ.	13 070	13 767	14 787	15 300	16 974	19 600	25 213	29 356
12	Public admin.; compulsory s.s.; education; human health	29 424	27 868	27 996	27 733	27 759	27 985	28 978	29 711
13	Other service activities	3 584	3 541	2 990	2 872	2 964	3 091	3 051	3 158
14	**FISIM (Financial Intermediation Services Indirectly Measured)**	..	..	..	..	..	..	..	..
15	Gross value added at basic prices, excluding FISIM	152 160	151 871	156 665	159 685	165 714	178 583	243 302	255 269
16	**Taxes less subsidies on products**	**15 250**	**15 201**	**14 858**	**15 253**	**15 917**	**17 530**	**18 857**	**20 209**
17	Taxes on products	16 499	16 311	15 945	16 341	16 996	18 511	19 768	21 083
18	Subsidies on products	1 249	1 111	1 088	1 089	1 079	981	911	874
19	**Residual item**	**2 687**	**512**	**417**	**623**	**-1 332**	**-1 576**	**-121**	**89**
20	**Gross domestic product at market prices**	**170 097**	**167 583**	**171 939**	**175 561**	**180 298**	**194 537**	**262 037**	**275 567**
	OUTPUT APPROACH AT CONSTANT PRICES (REF. YEAR 2010)								
21	**Total gross value added at basic prices**	**148 497**	**151 871**	**161 269**	**158 944**	**162 210**	**174 216**	**220 262**	**231 575**
22	Agriculture, forestry and fishing	1 643	1 604	1 816	1 542	1 668	2 090	2 194	2 479
23	Industry, including energy	35 612	37 080	43 233	42 578	41 411	44 602	81 540	83 666
24	Manufacturing	31 383	32 758	38 979	38 363	37 057	39 975	77 497	79 597
25	Construction	3 314	2 509	2 157	2 078	2 231	2 360	2 500	2 876
26	Services	..	..	..	..	..	..	..	..
27	Distrib. trade, repairs; transp.; accommod., food serv. activ.	24 709	24 586	24 563	24 425	24 821	26 150	27 766	29 206
28	Information and communication	12 761	13 834	13 829	14 394	15 960	18 483	20 749	22 787
29	Financial and insurance activities	15 945	17 088	18 817	16 833	16 055	17 087	18 445	19 065
30	Real estate activities	10 319	9 995	10 124	10 434	10 790	11 227	11 227	11 340
31	Prof., scientif., techn. activ.; admin., support service activ.	12 812	13 767	14 188	14 192	15 613	17 816	21 728	24 861
32	Public admin.; compulsory s.s.; education; human health	27 700	27 868	29 162	28 709	29 361	29 750	30 888	31 373
33	Other service activities	3 664	3 541	3 380	3 442	3 454	3 574	3 718	4 094
34	**FISIM (Financial Intermediation Services Indirectly Measured)**	..	..	..	..	..	..	..	..
35	Gross value added at basic prices, excluding FISIM	148 497	151 871	161 269	158 944	162 210	174 216	220 262	231 575
36	**Taxes less subsidies on products**	**15 420**	**15 201**	**14 784**	**14 765**	**15 363**	**16 836**	**18 175**	**19 485**
37	Taxes on products	16 588	16 311	15 889	15 855	16 448	17 880	19 150	20 423
38	Subsidies on products	1 165	1 111	1 105	1 089	1 083	1 036	953	906
39	**Residual item**	**700**	**512**	**-3 468**	**-1 060**	**-2 094**	**-958**	**239**	**-113**
40	**Gross domestic product at market prices**	**164 617**	**167 583**	**172 586**	**172 650**	**175 479**	**190 094**	**238 677**	**250 948**
	INCOME APPROACH								
41	**Compensation of employees**	**74 017**	**69 045**	**69 857 |**	**69 607**	**70 798**	**73 243**	**76 808**	**80 945**
42	Agriculture, forestry and fishing	573	620	622 |	624	689	726	669	684
43	Industry, including energy	10 780	10 184	10 570 |	10 402	10 857	11 179	11 895	12 570
44	Manufacturing	8 892	8 542	9 135 |	8 972	9 464	9 774	10 437	11 109
45	Construction	5 565	4 010	3 323 |	3 064	3 173	3 608	4 031	4 687
46	Distrib. trade, repairs; transp.; accommod., food serv. activ.	14 226	13 475	14 122 |	14 305	14 591	15 024	15 773	17 003
47	Information and communication	3 824	3 920	3 568 |	3 922	4 145	4 278	4 768	5 019
48	Financial and insurance activities	6 393	6 354	6 250 |	6 403	6 180	6 226	6 049	6 186
49	Real estate activities	252	231	302 |	304	355	426	470	536
50	Prof., scientif., techn. activ.; admin., support service activ.	5 823	5 229	6 000 |	5 905	6 239	7 004	7 572	8 255
51	Public admin.; compulsory s.s.; education; human health	24 562	23 197	23 654 |	23 230	23 163	23 273	24 054	24 406
52	Other service activities	2 018	1 824	1 446 |	1 447	1 407	1 499	1 526	1 597
53	**Wages and salaries**	**68 719**	**64 112**	**59 486 |**	**59 256**	**59 923**	**62 054**	**65 049**	**68 460**
54	Agriculture, forestry and fishing	525	568	528 |	528	590	624	564	576
55	Industry, including energy	10 058	9 481	8 649 |	8 528	8 748	9 101	9 655	10 149
56	Manufacturing	8 249	7 919	7 562 |	7 440	7 647	8 006	8 478	8 973
57	Construction	5 148	3 704	3 002 |	2 797	2 891	3 266	3 707	4 302
58	Distrib. trade, repairs; transp.; accommod., food serv. activ.	13 109	12 423	12 315 |	12 514	12 828	13 193	13 701	14 822
59	Information and communication	3 511	3 600	2 985 |	3 298	3 376	3 613	3 929	4 125
60	Financial and insurance activities	5 841	5 826	4 745 |	4 718	4 552	4 577	4 646	4 759
61	Real estate activities	231	211	263 |	270	315	369	402	453
62	Prof., scientif., techn. activ.; admin., support service activ.	5 325	4 788	5 215 |	5 177	5 426	6 103	6 496	7 030
63	Public admin.; compulsory s.s.; education; human health	23 110	21 827	20 518 |	20 138	19 972	20 035	20 638	20 867
64	Other service activities	1 862	1 685	1 266 |	1 287	1 227	1 173	1 311	1 378
65	**Gross operating surplus and mixed income**	**78 441**	**83 057**	**87 068**	**90 272**	**94 639**	**104 567**	**165 836**	**173 771**
66	**Taxes less subsidies on production and imports**	**14 952**	**14 970**	**14 596**	**15 059**	**16 193**	**18 304**	**19 514**	**20 763**
67	Taxes on production and imports	18 561	18 292	18 019	18 601	19 549	21 485	22 851	23 916
68	Subsidies on production and imports	3 608	3 322	3 423	3 542	3 356	3 181	3 337	3 153
69	**Residual item**	**2 687**	**512**	**417**	**623**	**-1 332**	**-1 576**	**-121**	**89**
70	**Gross domestic product**	**170 097**	**167 583**	**171 939**	**175 561**	**180 298**	**194 537**	**262 037**	**275 567**

Note: Detailed metadata:http://metalinks.oecd.org/nav1/20180308/4272
Source: Central Statistics Office (CSO) of Ireland via Eurostat.

Table 3. Disposable income, saving and net lending / net borrowing

Million EUR (1999 IEP euro)

		2009	2010	2011	2012	2013	2014	2015	2016
	DISPOSABLE INCOME								
1	**Gross domestic product**	170 097	167 583	171 939	175 561	180 298	194 537	262 038	275 567
2	Net primary incomes from the rest of the world	-27 900	-27 194	-32 331	-32 159	-27 106	-28 671	-54 804	-47 825
3	Primary incomes receivable from the rest of the world	55 654	56 109	57 229	57 641	56 089	62 703	61 954	70 168
4	Primary incomes payable to the rest of the world	83 553	83 303	89 560	89 800	83 195	91 374	116 757	117 994
5	**Gross national income at market prices**	142 199	140 388	139 609	143 402	153 193	165 866	207 234	227 742
6	Consumption of fixed capital	24 091	23 862	23 992	25 650	27 177	29 486	56 781	62 893
7	**Net national income at market prices**	118 108	116 525	115 618	117 752	126 016	136 380	150 452	164 849
8	Net current transfers from the rest of the world	-2 972	-2 704	-2 670	-2 609	-2 922	-2 751	-3 338	-3 627
9	Current transfers receivable from the rest of the world	3 602	3 428	3 679	3 918	3 200	2 924	3 988	4 489
10	Current transfers payable to the rest of the world	6 575	6 132	6 349	6 527	6 122	5 674	7 327	8 116
11	**Net national disposable income**	115 135	113 821	112 948	115 143	123 093	133 630	147 114	161 222
	SAVING AND NET LENDING / NET BORROWING								
12	**Net national disposable income**	115 135	113 821	112 948	115 143	123 093	133 630	147 114	161 222
13	Final consumption expenditures	115 443	111 302	110 579	110 542	111 254	114 779	119 674	124 968
14	Adj. for change in net equity of households in pension funds	0	0	0	0	0	0	0	0
15	**Saving, net**	-308	2 519	2 368	4 601	11 839	18 850	27 440	36 254
16	Net capital transfers from the rest of the world	73	82	364	86	105	136	61	628
17	Capital transfers receivable from the rest of the world	73	82	364	86	105	136	61	628
18	Capital transfers payable to the rest of the world	0	0	0	0	0	0	0	0
19	Gross capital formation	34 419	28 921	29 617	35 496	33 842	43 579	55 512	90 045
20	Acquisitions less disposals of non-financial non-produced assets	59	-9	0	0	1 040	6 904	1 364	5 690
21	Consumption of fixed capital	24 091	23 862	23 992	25 650	27 177	29 486	56 781	62 893
22	**Net lending / net borrowing**	-7 935	-1 937	-2 476	-4 536	2 906	-3 587	27 285	4 129
	REAL DISPOSABLE INCOME								
23	**Gross domestic product at constant prices, reference year 2010**	164 167	167 124	172 113	172 177	174 999	189 573	238 023	250 261
24	Trading gain or loss	834	0	-1 273	-847	-941	-3 234	9 880	7 360
25	**Real gross domestic income**	165 451	167 583	171 313	171 802	174 539	186 859	248 556	258 308
26	Net real primary incomes from the rest of the world	-27 138	-27 194	-32 213	-31 470	-26 240	-27 539	-51 984	-44 830
27	Real primary incomes receivable from the rest of the world	54 134	56 109	57 021	56 407	54 298	60 228	58 766	65 773
28	Real primary incomes payable to the rest of the world	81 271	83 303	89 234	87 877	80 537	87 767	110 750	110 603
29	**Real gross national income at market prices**	138 315	140 388	139 101	140 332	148 299	159 320	196 572	213 478
30	Net real current transfers from the rest of the world	-2 891	-2 704	-2 660	-2 553	-2 829	-2 642	-3 167	-3 400
31	Real current transfers receivable from the rest of the world	3 504	3 428	3 665	3 834	3 098	2 808	3 783	4 208
32	Real current transfers payable to the rest of the world	6 395	6 132	6 326	6 387	5 927	5 450	6 950	7 608
33	**Real gross national disposable income**	135 424	137 684	136 441	137 779	145 470	156 678	193 405	210 077
34	Consumption of fixed capital at constant prices	..	..	..	..	..	..	..	..
35	**Real net national income at market prices**	114 882	116 525	115 196	115 231	121 990	130 998	142 712	154 524
36	**Real net national disposable income**	111 991	113 821	112 536	112 678	119 161	128 356	139 545	151 124

Note: Detailed metadata:http://metalinks.oecd.org/nav1/20180308/665d
Source: Central Statistics Office (CSO) of Ireland via Eurostat.

Table 4. Population and employment (persons) and employment (hours worked) by industry
ISIC Rev. 4

		2009	2010	2011	2012	2013	2014	2015	2016
	POPULATION, THOUSAND PERSONS, NATIONAL CONCEPT								
1	**Total population**	**4 539.1**	**4 559.8**	**4 577.2**	**4 590.2**	**4 601.8**	**4 614.8**	**4 642.2**	**4 683.4**
2	Economically active population	..	..	..	..	..	..	..	..
3	Unemployed persons	..	..	..	..	..	..	..	..
4	Total employment	1 961.7	1 882.5	1 872.6	1 861.7	1 908.5	1 940.4	1 989.5	2 045.5
5	Employees	1 616.2	1 564.1	1 569.2	1 559.0	1 582.6	1 607.9	1 651.3	1 705.4
6	Self-employed	345.5	318.4	303.4	302.6	326.0	332.5	338.2	340.1
	TOTAL EMPLOYMENT, THOUSAND PERSONS, DOMESTIC CONCEPT								
7	Agriculture, forestry and fishing	96.7	85.5	83.1	85.9	107.0	109.3	110.2	113.2
8	Industry, including energy	261.8	247.7	218.1	212.6	218.5	217.1	225.5	234.0
9	Manufacturing	230.2	216.5	195.3	190.5	196.1	195.9	202.9	211.8
10	Construction	159.3	121.9	121.6	115.7	115.9	123.2	139.0	148.8
11	Distrib. trade, repairs; transp.; accommod., food serv. activ.	509.2	501.1	537.5	535.4	550.4	558.8	564.0	582.5
12	Information and communication	74.8	75.7	66.0	69.1	69.5	70.0	71.5	74.5
13	Financial and insurance activities	99.4	93.5	84.2	83.6	81.2	81.3	80.7	79.7
14	Real estate activities	9.6	9.4	12.5	12.6	13.0	13.7	15.0	16.4
15	Prof., scientif., techn. activ.; admin., support service activ.	172.4	163.8	189.2	185.4	191.5	201.7	204.3	209.2
16	Public admin.; compulsory s.s.; education; human health	481.4	488.7	483.3	483.4	483.8	489.2	497.6	502.0
17	Other service activities	97.7	95.6	76.9	77.8	77.5	76.3	81.6	85.2
18	**Total employment**	**1 962.3**	**1 882.7**	**1 872.4**	**1 861.5**	**1 908.3**	**1 940.4**	**1 989.4**	**2 045.4**
	EMPLOYEES, THOUSAND PERSONS, DOMESTIC CONCEPT								
19	Agriculture, forestry and fishing	16.5	16.8	18.3	17.9	23.8	24.5	23.2	24.3
20	Industry, including energy	234.9	226.2	198.7	192.2	197.3	196.0	204.1	211.1
21	Manufacturing	205.8	196.8	178.0	172.7	177.2	176.2	183.6	190.3
22	Construction	100.4	73.7	81.5	76.8	75.4	81.6	91.8	102.1
23	Distrib. trade, repairs; transp.; accommod., food serv. activ.	430.0	422.3	460.9	463.5	478.8	483.9	489.9	511.8
24	Information and communication	65.9	65.5	53.9	57.7	57.3	59.0	61.0	63.0
25	Financial and insurance activities	95.3	89.2	79.8	79.4	76.6	76.3	75.3	75.9
26	Real estate activities	6.3	6.3	8.7	8.9	10.1	10.7	11.3	12.7
27	Prof., scientif., techn. activ.; admin., support service activ.	132.1	125.4	149.7	145.8	148.9	159.8	164.9	168.9
28	Public admin.; compulsory s.s.; education; human health	459.9	466.3	462.4	460.8	461.1	466.3	474.1	479.2
29	Other service activities	75.5	72.6	55.2	55.9	52.9	49.9	55.6	56.2
30	**Total employees**	**1 616.9**	**1 564.3**	**1 569.1**	**1 558.9**	**1 582.3**	**1 607.9**	**1 651.3**	**1 705.4**
	SELF-EMPLOYED, THOUSAND PERSONS, DOMESTIC CONCEPT								
31	Agriculture, forestry and fishing	80.1	68.7	64.8	68.0	83.1	84.8	87.0	88.9
32	Industry, including energy	26.8	21.5	19.3	20.4	21.1	21.1	21.3	22.9
33	Manufacturing	24.4	19.7	17.3	17.8	18.9	19.7	19.3	21.6
34	Construction	59.0	48.2	40.0	38.9	40.5	41.6	47.2	46.6
35	Distrib. trade, repairs; transp.; accommod., food serv. activ.	79.2	78.8	76.7	71.9	71.7	74.8	74.1	70.7
36	Information and communication	8.8	10.2	12.1	11.3	12.1	11.1	10.5	11.4
37	Financial and insurance activities	4.1	4.3	4.4	4.2	4.7	5.0	5.4	3.9
38	Real estate activities	3.4	3.1	3.9	3.7	2.9	2.9	3.7	3.7
39	Prof., scientif., techn. activ.; admin., support service activ.	40.3	38.3	39.4	39.7	42.5	41.9	39.4	40.3
40	Public admin.; compulsory s.s.; education; human health	21.5	22.4	21.0	22.7	22.8	22.9	23.5	22.8
41	Other service activities	22.2	22.9	21.7	21.9	24.6	26.5	26.0	28.9
42	**Total self-employed**	**345.5**	**318.4**	**303.4**	**302.6**	**326.0**	**332.5**	**338.2**	**340.1**
	TOTAL EMPLOYMENT, MILLION HOURS, DOMESTIC CONCEPT								
43	Industry, including energy	515.1	478.9	424.8	416.5	431.6	436.6	453.4	467.0
44	Distrib. trade, repairs; transp.; accommod., food serv. activ.	892.4	872.5	878.0	879.7	901.0	915.2	931.0	954.0
45	Financial and insurance activities	187.2	178.7	150.4	150.2	148.0	149.5	149.2	149.6
46	Prof., scientif., techn. activ.; admin., support service activ.	333.1	321.6	316.5	313.8	326.4	339.9	347.9	360.4
47	Public admin.; compulsory s.s.; education; human health	796.7	810.1	744.3	749.4	752.3	764.4	784.3	784.2
48	**Total employment**	**3 555.3**	**3 391.3**	**3 187.2**	**3 178.5**	**3 281.4**	**3 358.9**	**3 462.6**	**3 556.5**
	EMPLOYEES, MILLION HOURS, DOMESTIC CONCEPT								
49	Industry, including energy	461.1	435.3	385.4	374.2	388.6	393.5	410.8	420.8
50	Distrib. trade, repairs; transp.; accommod., food serv. activ.	726.5	706.8	717.5	730.7	751.0	758.5	778.0	807.9
51	Financial and insurance activities	179.4	170.6	141.0	141.6	138.6	139.7	138.5	141.5
52	Prof., scientif., techn. activ.; admin., support service activ.	253.7	244.7	238.1	238.7	244.3	258.2	270.6	280.9
53	Public admin.; compulsory s.s.; education; human health	761.5	774.7	712.0	713.8	716.1	727.1	745.2	747.7
54	**Total employees**	**2 855.5**	**2 748.2**	**2 576.2**	**2 576.2**	**2 627.8**	**2 687.1**	**2 776.5**	**2 865.8**
	SELF-EMPLOYED, MILLION HOURS, DOMESTIC CONCEPT								
55	Industry, including energy	54.0	43.6	39.4	42.3	43.0	43.1	42.6	46.1
56	Distrib. trade, repairs; transp.; accommod., food serv. activ.	165.9	165.7	160.5	149.0	150.0	156.7	152.9	146.1
57	Financial and insurance activities	7.8	8.1	9.4	8.6	9.4	9.7	10.6	8.1
58	Prof., scientif., techn. activ.; admin., support service activ.	79.5	77.0	78.4	75.1	82.2	81.8	77.3	79.6
59	Public admin.; compulsory s.s.; education; human health	35.1	35.3	32.3	35.7	36.2	37.3	39.0	36.5
60	**Total self-employed**	**699.8**	**643.2**	**611.0**	**602.3**	**653.6**	**671.9**	**686.1**	**690.7**

Note: Detailed metadata:http://metalinks.oecd.org/nav1/20180308/ebd7
Source: Central Statistics Office (CSO) of Ireland via Eurostat.

ISRAEL

Table 1. Gross domestic product, expenditure approach

Million ILS

		2009	2010	2011	2012	2013	2014	2015	2016
	AT CURRENT PRICES								
1	**Final consumption expenditure**	**645 201**	**694 119**	**740 603**	**781 432**	**826 173**	**864 940**	**897 846**	**944 881**
2	Household	447 272	483 639	518 095	541 968	571 491	599 214	619 787	655 010
3	NPISH's	11 891	12 122	13 097	13 995	14 592	15 096	16 276	17 217
4	Government	186 039	198 358	209 411	225 469	240 089	250 631	261 783	272 655
5	Individual	92 930	100 510	107 288	116 915	126 169	132 014	138 270	144 647
6	Collective	93 109	97 848	102 122	108 554	113 920	118 616	123 513	128 008
7	*of which: Actual individual consumption*	552 092	596 271	638 480	672 878	712 253	746 324	774 334	816 874
8	**Gross capital formation**	**148 968**	**161 079**	**190 964**	**210 692**	**210 789**	**222 985**	**229 665**	**249 961**
9	Gross fixed capital formation, total	152 110	164 961	190 423	206 704	213 760	219 276	219 819	247 283
10	Dwellings	43 278	49 964	57 136	63 196	69 279	74 283	75 826	82 166
11	Other buildings and structures	27 758	31 335	36 130	41 471	47 390	44 793	44 353	45 754
12	Transport equipment	13 019	15 291	14 918	14 056	15 145	15 643	13 069	22 497
13	Other machinery and equipment	31 541	31 826	44 030	44 146	38 531	40 790	42 061	48 889
14	Cultivated assets	482	565	464	525	394	448	355	191
15	Intangible fixed assets	36 032	35 980	37 745	43 310	43 020	43 318	44 156	47 786
16	Changes in inventories, acquisitions less disposals of valuables	..	..	..	..	..	..	..	..
17	Changes in inventories	-3 142	-3 883	541	3 988	-2 971	3 710	9 846	2 679
18	Acquisitions less disposals of valuables	..	..	..	..	..	..	..	..
19	**External balance of goods and services**	**21 466**	**18 268**	**4 568**	**-14**	**19 156**	**15 560**	**35 018**	**25 488**
20	Exports of goods and services	271 869	305 636	336 926	357 661	351 347	355 484	363 531	369 361
21	Exports of goods	184 265	212 160	232 201	235 250	225 176	227 073	220 438	215 778
22	Exports of services	87 604	93 476	104 725	122 411	126 171	128 411	143 093	153 583
23	Imports of goods and services	250 403	287 368	332 358	357 675	332 191	339 924	328 513	343 873
24	Imports of goods	180 119	217 182	259 161	271 260	253 516	252 883	233 136	243 940
25	Imports of services	70 284	70 186	73 197	86 415	78 675	87 041	95 377	99 933
26	**Statistical discrepancy**	**0**	**0**	**0**	**0**	**0**	**0**	**0**	**0**
27	**Gross domestic product**	**815 635**	**873 466**	**936 134**	**992 110**	**1 056 119**	**1 103 485**	**1 162 530**	**1 220 331**
	AT CONSTANT PRICES, REFERENCE YEAR 2010								
28	**Final consumption expenditure**	**665 879**	**694 119**	**717 966**	**739 941**	**767 125**	**799 255**	**828 991**	**874 340**
29	Household	460 847	483 639	502 852	517 151	536 487	560 790	582 731	618 589
30	NPISH's	12 037	12 122	12 415	12 592	12 944	13 158	13 848	14 441
31	Government	193 007	198 358	202 699	210 199	217 707	225 390	232 534	241 666
32	Individual	97 661	100 510	103 880	108 109	112 554	115 429	119 733	124 404
33	Collective	95 342	97 848	98 819	102 091	105 144	109 990	112 790	117 253
34	*of which: Actual individual consumption*	570 523	596 271	619 147	637 850	661 986	689 268	716 198	757 106
35	**Gross capital formation**	**147 009**	**161 079**	**185 467**	**197 230**	**197 718**	**205 961**	**210 889**	**227 949**
36	Gross fixed capital formation, total	150 319	164 961	187 008	195 123	202 213	203 733	202 138	226 172
37	Dwellings	44 414	49 964	54 884	58 542	62 195	65 901	66 903	72 322
38	Other buildings and structures	28 644	31 335	34 536	38 046	42 456	39 791	39 350	40 567
39	Transport equipment	11 919	15 291	14 850	13 174	15 431	14 895	12 414	20 433
40	Other machinery and equipment	30 039	31 826	44 496	42 591	38 466	40 444	41 029	48 623
41	Cultivated assets	490	565	432	462	340	399	316	162
42	Intangible fixed assets	34 851	35 980	37 810	42 138	42 883	41 815	41 584	44 003
43	Changes in inventories, acquisitions less disposals of valuables	..	..	..	..	..	..	..	..
44	Changes in inventories	..	..	..	..	..	..	..	..
45	Acquisitions less disposals of valuables	..	..	..	..	..	..	..	..
46	**External balance of goods and services**	**16 017**	**18 268**	**15 594**	**1 710**	**13 160**	**6 518**	**-1 733**	**-24 966**
47	Exports of goods and services	265 367	305 636	334 908	328 301	339 152	345 535	336 309	344 870
48	Exports of goods	182 237	212 160	228 279	213 332	215 682	220 949	208 086	207 551
49	Exports of services	83 048	93 476	106 629	115 342	124 039	125 134	128 767	137 603
50	Imports of goods and services	249 350	287 368	319 314	326 591	325 993	339 016	338 043	369 835
51	Imports of goods	183 138	217 182	244 357	245 655	248 311	253 735	252 096	280 381
52	Imports of services	65 790	70 186	74 957	81 303	77 927	85 588	86 234	90 518
53	**Statistical discrepancy (including chaining residual)**	**-819**	**0**	**0**	**329**	**690**	**997**	**1 200**	**3 195**
54	**Gross domestic product**	**828 086**	**873 466**	**919 027**	**939 210**	**978 692**	**1 012 731**	**1 039 346**	**1 080 519**

Note: Detailed metadata:http://metalinks.oecd.org/nav1/20180308/cf6f

Information on data for Israel: http://dx.doi.org/10.1787/888932315602

Source: Israel Central Bureau of Statistics.

Table 2. Gross domestic product, output and income approach
ISIC Rev. 4

Million ILS

		2009	2010	2011	2012	2013	2014	2015	2016
	OUTPUT APPROACH AT CURRENT PRICES								
1	**Total gross value added at basic prices**	731 356	779 026	836 076	889 700	945 711	984 545	1 041 119	1 093 473
2	Agriculture, forestry and fishing	14 246	13 143	14 301	12 110	12 639	12 630	13 630	14 255
3	Industry, including energy	129 441	137 649	137 219	147 015	153 420	158 094	158 893	164 783
4	Manufacturing	112 899	120 707	123 565	133 747	130 381	133 567	136 889	142 545
5	Construction	35 635	40 709	45 997	51 163	56 169	58 193	59 689	63 081
6	Services	..	..	..	..	..	..	..	..
7	Distrib. trade, repairs; transp.; accommod., food serv. activ.	102 688	116 427	119 037	132 259	138 994	145 037	154 153	161 292
8	Information and communication	69 202	68 797	69 651	78 995	81 889	91 624	107 112	118 014
9	Financial and insurance activities	47 237	46 192	49 294	46 598	52 952	49 521	49 416	50 636
10	Real estate activities	101 203	112 781	128 848	133 533	138 620	149 237	157 508	166 516
11	Prof., scientif., techn. activ.; admin., support service activ.	66 307	69 385	84 076	89 565	101 386	103 036	111 789	115 982
12	Public admin.; compulsory s.s.; education; human health	139 269	147 723	159 345	170 907	181 390	187 535	197 051	206 002
13	Other service activities	26 128	26 220	28 308	27 555	28 250	29 639	31 877	32 911
14	**FISIM (Financial Intermediation Services Indirectly Measured)**	..	..	..	..	..	..	..	..
15	**Gross value added at basic prices, excluding FISIM**	731 356	779 026	836 076	889 700	945 711	984 545	1 041 119	1 093 473
16	**Taxes less subsidies on products**	84 279	94 440	100 057	102 410	110 409	118 940	121 409	126 858
17	Taxes on products	87 854	98 113	104 414	107 156	116 335	125 577	128 277	134 422
18	Subsidies on products	3 575	3 673	4 357	4 746	5 926	6 637	6 868	7 564
19	**Residual item**	..	..	..	..	..	..	..	..
20	**Gross domestic product at market prices**	815 635	873 466	936 133	992 110	1 056 120	1 103 485	1 162 528	1 220 331
	OUTPUT APPROACH AT CONSTANT PRICES (REF. YEAR 2010)								
21	**Total gross value added at basic prices**	741 399	779 026	814 086	830 061	863 543	892 879	920 384	957 900
22	Agriculture, forestry and fishing	14 548	13 143	14 621	14 137	13 774	13 303	12 312	12 812
23	Industry, including energy	120 702	137 649	134 682	132 409	138 079	140 433	141 351	143 879
24	Manufacturing	105 277	120 707	119 953	122 564	121 472	123 734	123 942	125 320
25	Construction	36 424	40 709	44 767	47 430	50 476	50 933	51 106	53 087
26	Services	..	..	..	..	..	..	..	..
27	Distrib. trade, repairs; transp.; accommod., food serv. activ.	107 910	116 427	119 181	121 247	124 278	129 647	135 663	143 455
28	Information and communication	70 074	68 797	67 856	73 262	81 926	88 716	95 506	103 582
29	Financial and insurance activities	45 876	46 192	48 535	44 550	44 191	43 419	43 648	44 130
30	Real estate activities	107 604	112 781	120 042	118 936	123 874	129 636	134 963	138 718
31	Prof., scientif., techn. activ.; admin., support service activ.	65 141	69 385	89 032	104 910	112 726	122 159	128 370	137 217
32	Public admin.; compulsory s.s.; education; human health	147 039	147 723	150 454	151 299	153 269	154 401	156 919	160 428
33	Other service activities	25 317	26 220	29 227	29 806	30 379	31 760	33 305	35 166
34	**FISIM (Financial Intermediation Services Indirectly Measured)**	..	..	..	..	..	..	..	..
35	**Gross value added at basic prices, excluding FISIM**	741 399	779 026	814 086	830 061	863 543	892 879	920 384	957 900
36	**Taxes less subsidies on products**	88 643	94 440	100 135	101 910	106 779	110 539	113 496	118 319
37	Taxes on products	92 090	98 113	104 029	105 873	110 932	114 838	117 910	122 921
38	Subsidies on products	3 448	3 673	3 894	3 964	4 153	4 299	4 414	4 602
39	**Residual item**	60	0	-70	-63	-102	-112	-94	-107
40	**Gross domestic product at market prices**	830 102	873 466	914 151	931 908	970 220	1 003 306	1 033 786	1 076 113
	INCOME APPROACH								
41	**Compensation of employees**	368 858	394 366	423 425	447 430	469 590	486 908	511 871	539 723
42	Agriculture, forestry and fishing	5 543	5 796	6 304	6 548	6 660	6 775	7 038	6 864
43	Industry, including energy	67 701	71 493	75 814	77 957	79 781	81 300	82 781	84 980
44	Manufacturing	60 857	64 163	68 029	69 619	70 999	72 287	73 717	75 781
45	Construction	16 961	18 422	21 069	22 372	23 874	25 109	26 940	28 668
46	Distrib. trade, repairs; transp.; accommod., food serv. activ.	65 237	70 767	76 113	79 207	81 409	85 113	89 999	95 922
47	Information and communication	31 739	33 260	36 077	39 093	40 918	41 917	47 374	52 622
48	Financial and insurance activities	19 852	21 965	23 042	23 491	25 167	26 460	27 218	27 420
49	Real estate activities	2 371	2 707	3 013	3 572	3 545	3 747	3 977	4 512
50	Prof., scientif., techn. activ.; admin., support service activ.	43 272	46 575	49 279	53 355	59 276	62 145	64 962	70 594
51	Public admin.; compulsory s.s.; education; human health	98 795	105 774	112 694	121 389	129 423	134 419	141 069	146 587
52	Other service activities	17 387	17 607	20 021	20 446	19 536	19 923	20 514	21 554
53	**Wages and salaries**	300 567	319 674	343 882	363 565	382 814	397 143	417 348	440 000
54	Agriculture, forestry and fishing	4 349	4 538	4 944	5 285	5 300	5 391	5 600	5 462
55	Industry, including energy	55 588	58 733	62 366	64 483	65 811	67 064	68 286	70 100
56	Manufacturing	50 420	53 202	56 477	58 352	59 226	60 300	61 493	63 215
57	Construction	14 984	16 269	18 629	20 239	21 482	22 593	24 241	25 796
58	Distrib. trade, repairs; transp.; accommod., food serv. activ.	53 730	55 327	59 673	62 209	62 827	65 685	69 456	74 027
59	Information and communication	24 797	25 853	28 206	29 510	31 229	31 991	36 155	40 161
60	Financial and insurance activities	17 777	19 759	20 790	21 388	23 198	24 390	25 089	25 276
61	Real estate activities	2 124	2 436	2 718	2 978	3 123	3 301	3 503	3 974
62	Prof., scientif., techn. activ.; admin., support service activ.	38 749	41 898	44 463	47 749	54 065	56 682	59 251	64 387
63	Public admin.; compulsory s.s.; education; human health	79 234	85 105	91 331	98 534	104 972	109 024	114 418	118 893
64	Other service activities	9 235	9 757	10 761	11 189	10 808	11 022	11 349	11 924
65	**Gross operating surplus and mixed income**	333 898	354 367	380 263	408 538	441 198	459 876	489 042	517 523
66	**Taxes less subsidies on production and imports**	112 879	124 733	132 446	136 141	145 331	156 701	161 616	163 085
67	Taxes on production and imports	117 557	129 495	137 897	142 213	153 218	164 899	169 738	..
68	Subsidies on production and imports	4 678	4 761	5 451	6 071	7 887	8 198	8 122	..
69	**Residual item**	..	..	..	..	..	..	..	..
70	**Gross domestic product**	815 635	873 466	936 134	992 110	1 056 119	1 103 485	1 162 530	1 220 331

Note: Detailed metadata:http://metalinks.oecd.org/nav1/20180308/cf6f
Information on data for Israel: http://dx.doi.org/10.1787/888932315602

Source: Israel Central Bureau of Statistics.

Table 3. Disposable income, saving and net lending / net borrowing

Million ILS

		2009	2010	2011	2012	2013	2014	2015	2016
	DISPOSABLE INCOME								
1	**Gross domestic product**	**815 635**	**873 466**	**936 134**	**992 110**	**1 056 119**	**1 103 485**	**1 162 530**	**1 220 331**
2	Net primary incomes from the rest of the world	-19 780	-16 744	-12 173	-24 290	-20 458	-7 890	-10 072	-14 717
3	Primary incomes receivable from the rest of the world	23 068	25 342	28 379	28 703	27 415	34 030	41 550	39 408
4	Primary incomes payable to the rest of the world	42 848	42 086	40 552	52 993	47 873	41 920	51 622	54 125
5	**Gross national income at market prices**	**795 855**	**856 722**	**923 961**	**967 820**	**1 035 661**	**1 095 595**	**1 152 458**	**1 205 614**
6	Consumption of fixed capital	117 023	118 836	124 899	133 960	138 047	145 180	151 466	157 580
7	**Net national income at market prices**	**678 832**	**737 886**	**799 062**	**833 860**	**897 614**	**950 415**	**1 000 991**	**1 048 034**
8	Net current transfers from the rest of the world	28 236	30 378	30 694	30 465	32 481	35 157	35 201	35 614
9	Current transfers receivable from the rest of the world	37 529	39 732	39 552	39 782	41 685	44 503	46 243	47 120
10	Current transfers payable to the rest of the world	9 293	9 354	8 858	9 316	9 204	9 346	11 042	11 507
11	**Net national disposable income**	**707 068**	**768 264**	**829 757**	**864 325**	**930 095**	**985 573**	**1 036 192**	**1 083 648**
	SAVING AND NET LENDING / NET BORROWING								
12	**Net national disposable income**	**707 068**	**768 264**	**829 757**	**864 325**	**930 095**	**985 573**	**1 036 192**	**1 083 648**
13	Final consumption expenditures	645 201	694 119	740 603	781 432	826 173	864 940	897 846	944 881
14	Adj. for change in net equity of households in pension funds	..	..	..	..	..	..	..	..
15	**Saving, net**	**61 867**	**74 145**	**89 154**	**82 893**	**103 922**	**120 633**	**138 346**	**138 767**
16	Net capital transfers from the rest of the world	4 139	4 379	5 171	3 374	6 699	9 767	8 248	8 348
17	Capital transfers receivable from the rest of the world	4 139	4 379	5 171	3 374	6 699	9 767	8 248	8 348
18	Capital transfers payable to the rest of the world	0	0	0	0	0	0	0	0
19	Gross capital formation	148 968	161 079	190 964	210 692	210 789	222 985	229 665	249 961
20	Acquisitions less disposals of non-financial non-produced assets	..	..	..	..	..	..	..	..
21	Consumption of fixed capital	117 023	118 836	124 899	133 960	138 047	145 180	151 466	157 580
22	**Net lending / net borrowing**	**34 061**	**36 281**	**28 260**	**9 535**	**37 878**	**52 594**	**68 395**	**54 733**
	REAL DISPOSABLE INCOME								
23	**Gross domestic product at constant prices, reference year 2010**	**828 086**	**873 466**	**919 027**	**939 210**	**978 692**	**1 012 731**	**1 039 346**	**1 080 519**
24	Trading gain or loss	6 489 e	0 e	-11 164 e	-2 061 e	3 903 e	6 787 e	32 751 e	45 226 e
25	**Real gross domestic income**	**834 575 e**	**873 466 e**	**907 863 e**	**937 149 e**	**982 595 e**	**1 019 518 e**	**1 072 097 e**	**1 125 745 e**
26	Net real primary incomes from the rest of the world	-20 239 e	-16 744 e	-11 805 e	-22 944 e	-19 034 e	-7 290 e	-9 289 e	-13 576 e
27	Real primary incomes receivable from the rest of the world	23 604 e	25 342 e	27 522 e	27 113 e	25 506 e	31 441 e	38 318 e	36 354 e
28	Real primary incomes payable to the rest of the world	43 843 e	42 086 e	39 327 e	50 057 e	44 540 e	38 730 e	47 606 e	49 930 e
29	**Real gross national income at market prices**	**814 336 e**	**856 722 e**	**896 058 e**	**914 205 e**	**963 561 e**	**1 012 229 e**	**1 062 809 e**	**1 112 169 e**
30	Net real current transfers from the rest of the world	28 891 e	30 378 e	29 767 e	28 778 e	30 220 e	32 482 e	32 462 e	32 853 e
31	Real current transfers receivable from the rest of the world	38 400 e	39 732 e	38 358 e	37 578 e	38 783 e	41 117 e	42 645 e	43 468 e
32	Real current transfers payable to the rest of the world	9 509 e	9 354 e	8 591 e	8 800 e	8 564 e	8 635 e	10 183 e	10 615 e
33	**Real gross national disposable income**	**843 227 e**	**887 100 e**	**925 825 e**	**942 982 e**	**993 781 e**	**1 044 711 e**	**1 095 271 e**	**1 145 022 e**
34	Consumption of fixed capital at constant prices	..	..	..	..	..	..	..	..
35	**Real net national income at market prices**	**694 596 e**	**737 886 e**	**774 931 e**	**787 666 e**	**835 125 e**	**878 096 e**	**923 125 e**	**966 803 e**
36	**Real net national disposable income**	**723 487 e**	**768 264 e**	**804 698 e**	**816 443 e**	**865 345 e**	**910 578 e**	**955 587 e**	**999 656 e**

Note: Detailed metadata:http://metalinks.oecd.org/nav1/20180308/2c63
   Information on data for Israel: http://dx.doi.org/10.1787/888932315602
Source: Israel Central Bureau of Statistics.

Table 4. Population and employment (persons) and employment (hours worked) by industry
ISIC Rev. 4

		2009	2010	2011	2012	2013	2014	2015	2016
	POPULATION, THOUSAND PERSONS, NATIONAL CONCEPT								
1	**Total population**	7 482.1	7 620.8	7 763.1	7 907.2	8 056.0	8 212.1	8 377.1	8 543.4
2	Economically active population	3 255.7	3 326.3	3 416.7	3 606.0	3 677.8	..	..	..
3	Unemployed persons	229.6	205.6	196.6	247.1	228.3	..	..	..
4	Total employment	3 026.0	3 120.7	3 220.0	3 359.0	3 449.5	3 555.8	3 643.8	3 736.8
5	Employees	2 661.2	2 743.4	2 834.3	2 932.6	3 015.1	3 110.6	3 183.3	3 259.5
6	Self-employed	364.8	377.3	385.7	426.4	434.4	445.2	460.5	477.3
	TOTAL EMPLOYMENT, THOUSAND PERSONS, DOMESTIC CONCEPT								
7	Agriculture, forestry and fishing	67.4	64.6	62.4	69.4	75.7	73.6	72.0	73.9
8	Industry, including energy	415.1	419.9	427.9	434.5	437.8	424.1	427.3	432.2
9	Manufacturing	386.0	386.6	394.8	405.4	405.5	392.7	395.2	397.0
10	Construction	211.3	227.5	229.2	233.6	254.4	266.5	277.7	286.5
11	Distrib. trade, repairs; transp.; accommod., food serv. activ.	665.1	691.4	712.4	744.8	759.2	770.2	790.5	814.2
12	Information and communication	160.9	163.3	170.7	166.4	170.2	179.4	186.3	192.7
13	Financial and insurance activities	112.4	118.6	119.9	117.1	121.6	128.9	128.2	128.9
14	Real estate activities	22.0	22.1	22.6	24.6	28.2	29.2	28.1	33.0
15	Prof., scientif., techn. activ.; admin., support service activ.	393.3	406.6	402.9	415.2	431.0	446.6	457.1	475.1
16	Public admin.; compulsory s.s.; education; human health	994.9	1 022.4	1 073.1	1 140.1	1 164.8	1 222.6	1 266.3	1 281.0
17	Other service activities	262.6	267.6	282.7	298.4	298.8	305.2	299.6	307.6
18	**Total employment**	**3 305.7**	**3 404.8**	**3 504.8**	**3 645.0**	**3 742.5**	**3 847.4**	**3 934.1**	**4 026.2**
	EMPLOYEES, THOUSAND PERSONS, DOMESTIC CONCEPT								
19	Agriculture, forestry and fishing	52.8	50.4	48.9	53.3	58.2	56.6	55.7	58.1
20	Industry, including energy	376.7	385.9	411.0	410.3	412.1	411.9	414.8	419.5
21	Manufacturing	347.9	353.3	378.4	381.9	381.1	381.6	383.7	385.7
22	Construction	177.3	192.0	193.2	196.8	215.7	225.2	234.5	238.9
23	Distrib. trade, repairs; transp.; accommod., food serv. activ.	573.0	593.4	610.8	635.9	654.5	666.2	680.8	703.4
24	Information and communication	150.4	151.4	156.3	152.0	155.8	163.3	169.4	175.4
25	Financial and insurance activities	105.8	110.1	111.1	109.5	111.5	118.7	118.5	118.3
26	Real estate activities	13.8	15.0	13.5	14.5	16.9	18.1	18.0	20.5
27	Prof., scientif., techn. activ.; admin., support service activ.	318.0	329.2	325.0	332.6	344.2	348.2	349.9	368.8
28	Public admin.; compulsory s.s.; education; human health	949.6	976.1	1 019.2	1 073.3	1 097.5	1 148.1	1 188.6	1 201.3
29	Other service activities	220.9	221.4	227.4	238.1	238.9	242.9	239.8	240.3
30	**Total employees**	**2 939.1**	**3 025.5**	**3 117.0**	**3 216.5**	**3 305.4**	**3 399.3**	**3 470.5**	**3 545.6**
	SELF-EMPLOYED, THOUSAND PERSONS, DOMESTIC CONCEPT								
31	Agriculture, forestry and fishing	14.5	14.2	13.4	16.1	17.5	17.0	16.3	15.8
32	Industry, including energy	38.4	33.9	16.9	24.2	25.8	12.3	12.5	12.7
33	Manufacturing	38.1	33.3	16.4	23.4	24.5	11.0	11.5	11.3
34	Construction	34.0	35.5	36.1	36.7	38.7	41.3	43.3	47.7
35	Distrib. trade, repairs; transp.; accommod., food serv. activ.	92.1	98.0	101.7	109.0	104.7	104.0	109.7	110.8
36	Information and communication	10.5	11.9	14.5	14.5	14.4	16.1	16.9	17.3
37	Financial and insurance activities	6.6	8.5	8.8	7.6	10.1	10.3	9.8	10.5
38	Real estate activities	8.1	7.1	9.2	10.2	11.3	11.2	10.1	12.5
39	Prof., scientif., techn. activ.; admin., support service activ.	75.4	77.4	77.9	82.6	86.8	98.4	107.2	106.3
40	Public admin.; compulsory s.s.; education; human health	45.3	46.3	53.9	66.9	67.3	74.5	77.6	79.7
41	Other service activities	41.7	46.2	55.4	60.3	59.9	62.2	59.8	67.3
42	**Total self-employed**	**366.6**	**379.3**	**387.8**	**428.5**	**437.1**	**448.1**	**463.6**	**480.6**
	TOTAL EMPLOYMENT, MILLION HOURS, DOMESTIC CONCEPT								
43	Industry, including energy	888.9	895.0	907.2	917.1	909.8	887.1	894.0	906.4
44	Distrib. trade, repairs; transp.; accommod., food serv. activ.	1 356.4	1 406.1	1 434.5	1 468.3	1 483.8	1 478.3	1 526.0	1 611.4
45	Financial and insurance activities	218.2	236.9	235.8	223.7	232.9	246.0	247.3	253.8
46	Prof., scientif., techn. activ.; admin., support service activ.	777.5	802.0	785.8	802.7	825.6	843.4	870.8	911.8
47	Public admin.; compulsory s.s.; education; human health	1 739.2	1 787.5	1 892.8	1 989.8	2 026.8	2 127.5	2 187.0	2 235.9
48	**Total employment**	**6 485.9**	**6 660.6**	**6 823.2**	**6 994.4**	**7 142.7**	**7 287.2**	**7 456.9**	**7 732.7**
	EMPLOYEES, MILLION HOURS, DOMESTIC CONCEPT								
49	Industry, including energy	806.1	821.2	870.4	867.3	857.4	863.1	870.5	882.1
50	Distrib. trade, repairs; transp.; accommod., food serv. activ.	1 146.7	1 181.1	1 206.2	1 219.2	1 250.2	1 252.4	1 287.2	1 363.6
51	Financial and insurance activities	205.0	219.1	217.9	208.0	213.5	225.9	226.6	230.9
52	Prof., scientif., techn. activ.; admin., support service activ.	621.7	644.6	631.2	638.0	659.3	662.2	668.6	706.4
53	Public admin.; compulsory s.s.; education; human health	1 671.1	1 721.6	1 810.8	1 888.3	1 927.6	2 017.8	2 073.0	2 119.7
54	**Total employees**	**5 745.2**	**5 898.6**	**6 059.6**	**6 164.0**	**6 311.1**	**6 461.8**	**6 592.4**	**6 818.3**
	SELF-EMPLOYED, MILLION HOURS, DOMESTIC CONCEPT								
55	Industry, including energy	82.8	73.9	36.8	49.8	52.4	24.0	23.5	24.3
56	Distrib. trade, repairs; transp.; accommod., food serv. activ.	209.7	225.0	228.4	249.1	233.6	225.9	238.8	247.8
57	Financial and insurance activities	13.2	17.9	17.9	15.7	19.4	20.0	20.7	22.9
58	Prof., scientif., techn. activ.; admin., support service activ.	155.7	157.4	154.6	164.7	166.3	181.2	202.2	205.4
59	Public admin.; compulsory s.s.; education; human health	68.1	65.9	81.9	101.5	99.1	109.8	113.9	116.2
60	**Total self-employed**	**740.7**	**762.0**	**763.5**	**830.3**	**831.7**	**825.4**	**864.5**	**914.4**

Note: Detailed metadata:http://metalinks.oecd.org/nav1/20180308/1ca7
    Information on data for Israel: http://dx.doi.org/10.1787/888932315602
Source: Israel Central Bureau of Statistics.

ITALY

Table 1. Gross domestic product, expenditure approach

Million EUR (1999 ITL euro)

		2009	2010	2011	2012	2013	2014	2015	2016
	AT CURRENT PRICES								
1	**Final consumption expenditure**	**1 278 173**	**1 306 580**	**1 328 114**	**1 309 173**	**1 296 296**	**1 299 306**	**1 318 191**	**1 338 926**
2	Household	945 051	970 153	998 377	985 067	971 969	976 780	997 382	1 013 237
3	NPISH's	8 689	8 779	8 819	8 658	8 911	9 216	9 110	9 174
4	Government	324 433	327 648	320 918	315 448	315 416	313 311	311 699	316 515
5	Individual	190 896	192 135	187 329	184 324	183 419	184 387	183 992	185 957
6	Collective	133 537	135 513	133 589	131 124	131 997	128 924	127 707	130 558
7	*of which: Actual individual consumption*	1 144 636	1 171 067	1 194 525	1 178 049	1 164 299	1 170 382	1 190 484	1 208 368
8	**Gross capital formation**	**305 022**	**329 530**	**335 062**	**288 155**	**272 062**	**276 246**	**286 010**	**287 358**
9	Gross fixed capital formation, total	314 360	320 002	321 837	296 166	276 668	271 516	279 802	288 078
10	Dwellings	87 912	89 549	86 203	81 160	77 794	72 551	72 008	74 315
11	Other buildings and structures	83 759	80 058	83 980	75 035	66 040	61 892	61 928	61 105
12	Transport equipment	18 633	18 268	19 292	14 148	10 986	12 121	15 441	19 425
13	Other machinery and equipment	72 367	78 221	78 573	72 101	67 630	69 177	70 175	72 777
14	Cultivated assets	647	677	689	714	712	663	650	624
15	Intangible fixed assets	41 212	41 532	41 290	41 698	42 616	44 303	47 419	47 632
16	Changes in inventories, acquisitions less disposals of valuables	-9 338	9 529	13 225	-8 010	-4 606	4 730	6 208	-720
17	Changes in inventories	-10 893	7 288	10 913	-10 642	-6 418	2 665	4 047	-2 940
18	Acquisitions less disposals of valuables	1 555	2 241	2 312	2 632	1 812	2 065	2 161	2 220
19	**External balance of goods and services**	**-10 317**	**-31 596**	**-25 713**	**15 937**	**36 241**	**46 275**	**48 421**	**54 665**
20	Exports of goods and services	353 530	404 149	442 219	461 174	463 129	475 301	494 564	500 948
21	Exports of goods	284 862	328 625	363 867	377 407	379 080	389 510	405 981	410 008
22	Exports of services	68 668	75 523	78 352	83 767	84 049	85 791	88 583	90 941
23	Imports of goods and services	363 846	435 744	467 932	445 237	426 888	429 026	446 143	446 283
24	Imports of goods	285 287	350 355	382 450	360 579	343 018	342 108	354 876	352 356
25	Imports of services	78 559	85 389	85 482	84 658	83 870	86 918	91 267	93 927
26	**Statistical discrepancy**	**0**	**0**	**0**	**0**	**0**	**0**	**0**	**0**
27	**Gross domestic product**	**1 572 878**	**1 604 515**	**1 637 463**	**1 613 265**	**1 604 599**	**1 621 827**	**1 652 622**	**1 680 948**
	AT CONSTANT PRICES, REFERENCE YEAR 2010								
28	**Final consumption expenditure**	**1 293 138**	**1 306 580**	**1 300 509**	**1 257 228**	**1 232 845**	**1 233 129**	**1 248 920**	**1 264 259**
29	Household	958 535	970 153	970 083	931 832	908 635	910 941	928 297	941 629
30	NPISH's	8 796	8 779	8 732	8 328	8 427	8 508	8 327	8 400
31	Government	325 793	327 648	321 694	317 259	316 281	314 022	312 241	314 031
32	Individual	191 088	192 135	189 757	188 371	188 150	189 098	189 369	189 056
33	Collective	134 704	135 513	131 937	128 919	128 177	125 091	123 111	125 127
34	*of which: Actual individual consumption*	1 158 432	1 171 067	1 168 572	1 128 323	1 104 727	1 108 026	1 125 710	1 139 042
35	**Gross capital formation**	**312 459**	**329 530**	**326 188**	**277 582**	**261 939**	**264 593**	**271 122**	**272 909**
36	Gross fixed capital formation, total	321 759	320 002	313 785	284 720	265 832	259 767	265 227	273 646
37	Dwellings	89 588	89 549	83 361	77 108	73 667	68 533	67 620	69 381
38	Other buildings and structures	86 350	80 058	80 030	71 077	62 669	58 745	58 815	58 592
39	Transport equipment	19 738	18 268	19 189	13 816	10 635	11 623	14 573	18 943
40	Other machinery and equipment	72 592	78 221	77 253	69 082	64 769	65 365	65 409	67 865
41	Cultivated assets	705	677	707	707	736	675	657	636
42	Intangible fixed assets	43 419	41 532	41 241	42 173	43 050	44 643	47 029	47 015
43	Changes in inventories, acquisitions less disposals of valuables	..	..	..	..	..	..	..	..
44	Changes in inventories	..	..	..	..	..	..	..	..
45	Acquisitions less disposals of valuables	1 780	2 241	2 029	2 118	1 456	1 696	1 738	1 776
46	**External balance of goods and services**	**-26 160**	**-31 596**	**-12 931**	**32 232**	**44 793**	**43 969**	**36 392**	**32 354**
47	Exports of goods and services	361 539	404 149	425 107	434 987	438 035	449 943	469 848	481 164
48	Exports of goods	292 068	328 625	349 141	355 273	358 887	369 712	386 741	395 103
49	Exports of services	69 445	75 523	75 966	79 734	79 156	80 246	83 132	86 072
50	Imports of goods and services	387 698	435 744	438 038	402 755	393 242	405 975	433 456	448 810
51	Imports of goods	305 086	350 355	354 413	323 381	314 833	325 962	353 497	366 294
52	Imports of services	82 492	85 389	83 626	79 512	78 587	80 177	80 309	82 910
53	**Statistical discrepancy (including chaining residual)**	**-1 535**	**0**	**0**	**1 234**	**1 595**	**1 233**	**1 178**	**1 457**
54	**Gross domestic product**	**1 577 903**	**1 604 515**	**1 613 767**	**1 568 274**	**1 541 172**	**1 542 924**	**1 557 612**	**1 570 980**

Note: Detailed metadata:http://metalinks.oecd.org/nav1/20180308/19bf
Source: Istituto Centrale di Statistica (ISTAT) via Eurostat.

ITALY

Table 2. Gross domestic product, output and income approach
ISIC Rev. 4

Million EUR (1999 ITL euro)

		2009	2010	2011	2012	2013	2014	2015	2016
	OUTPUT APPROACH AT CURRENT PRICES								
1	**Total gross value added at basic prices**	1 421 651	1 443 247	1 470 334	1 448 021	1 444 106	1 457 859	1 485 226	1 508 204
2	Agriculture, forestry and fishing	28 150	28 417	30 880	31 698	33 614	31 477	33 364	31 815
3	Industry, including energy	259 929	270 579	273 891	267 781	267 973	270 481	279 258	288 751
4	Manufacturing	215 612	228 279	232 205	222 812	222 142	225 653	237 880	246 284
5	Construction	85 055	81 207	82 072	77 886	74 255	70 387	70 710	71 612
6	Services	..	..	..	..	..	..	..	..
7	Distrib. trade, repairs; transp.; accommod., food serv. activ.	286 337	290 228	297 838	291 286	288 775	295 601	304 296	313 315
8	Information and communication	62 556	62 264	61 592	58 108	54 568	53 760	54 648	54 945
9	Financial and insurance activities	73 067	75 910	78 824	77 968	80 669	84 880	83 559	79 128
10	Real estate activities	187 240	188 746	195 793	199 878	201 031	203 588	208 852	212 522
11	Prof., scientif., techn. activ.; admin., support service activ.	132 672	135 963	138 145	136 324	135 565	138 401	141 397	144 377
12	Public admin.; compulsory s.s.; education; human health	251 219	252 869	252 171	249 204	249 398	250 550	250 425	252 564
13	Other service activities	55 427	57 065	59 129	57 889	58 259	58 736	58 717	59 175
14	**FISIM (Financial Intermediation Services Indirectly Measured)**	..	..	..	..	..	..	..	..
15	**Gross value added at basic prices, excluding FISIM**	1 421 651	1 443 247	1 470 334	1 448 021	1 444 106	1 457 859	1 485 226	1 508 204
16	**Taxes less subsidies on products**	151 227	161 268	167 129	165 244	160 493	163 968	167 396	172 744
17	Taxes on products	167 404	179 295	185 337	186 232	183 281	189 973	191 690	198 316
18	Subsidies on products	16 177	18 027	18 208	20 988	22 788	26 005	24 294	25 572
19	**Residual item**	0	0	0	0	0	0	0	0
20	**Gross domestic product at market prices**	1 572 878	1 604 515	1 637 463	1 613 265	1 604 599	1 621 827	1 652 622	1 680 948
	OUTPUT APPROACH AT CONSTANT PRICES (REF. YEAR 2010)								
21	**Total gross value added at basic prices**	1 418 573	1 443 247	1 451 697	1 416 148	1 395 029	1 398 237	1 410 801	1 421 242
22	Agriculture, forestry and fishing	28 314	28 417	28 960	28 210	28 603	27 939	29 222	29 314
23	Industry, including energy	253 812	270 579	273 676	266 606	260 626	259 892	262 781	266 572
24	Manufacturing	209 759	228 279	232 880	224 835	221 287	222 534	228 748	231 446
25	Construction	84 350	81 207	76 979	71 649	68 017	64 171	63 643	63 683
26	Services	..	..	..	..	..	..	..	..
27	Distrib. trade, repairs; transp.; accommod., food serv. activ.	284 097	290 228	294 939	284 642	280 032	283 935	290 143	295 383
28	Information and communication	61 389	62 264	62 263	60 479	59 251	59 774	60 535	60 405
29	Financial and insurance activities	72 028	75 910	77 534	78 948	76 592	76 301	75 643	73 805
30	Real estate activities	191 598	188 746	192 186	191 186	189 889	191 477	194 191	196 084
31	Prof., scientif., techn. activ.; admin., support service activ.	133 802	135 963	134 503	129 092	128 597	129 733	130 918	132 399
32	Public admin.; compulsory s.s.; education; human health	253 401	252 869	252 297	248 955	247 905	249 195	247 878	246 195
33	Other service activities	56 267	57 065	58 361	56 577	55 671	56 320	56 307	57 775
34	**FISIM (Financial Intermediation Services Indirectly Measured)**	..	..	..	..	..	..	..	..
35	**Gross value added at basic prices, excluding FISIM**	1 418 573	1 443 247	1 451 697	1 416 148	1 395 029	1 398 237	1 410 801	1 421 242
36	**Taxes less subsidies on products**	159 371	161 268	162 069	152 222	146 432	145 066	147 136	149 941
37	Taxes on products	177 199	179 295	178 110	166 791	160 576	159 334	161 490	164 887
38	Subsidies on products	17 829	18 027	16 041	14 611	14 155	14 205	14 331	14 827
39	**Residual item**	-41	0	0	-96	-289	-379	-325	-203
40	**Gross domestic product at market prices**	1 577 903	1 604 515	1 613 767	1 568 274	1 541 172	1 542 924	1 557 612	1 570 980
	INCOME APPROACH								
41	**Compensation of employees**	634 815	642 342	651 471	643 066	637 180	639 257	652 580	668 212
42	Agriculture, forestry and fishing	7 703	8 041	8 260	8 283	8 103	8 422	8 783	9 317
43	Industry, including energy	143 637	144 524	148 655	146 815	146 184	146 766	150 095	152 501
44	Manufacturing	130 290	131 023	134 790	132 537	131 848	132 269	135 301	137 460
45	Construction	38 290	37 737	37 581	34 856	31 648	30 062	30 627	30 583
46	Distrib. trade, repairs; transp.; accommod., food serv. activ.	122 515	124 364	127 333	127 204	126 558	127 582	131 943	136 286
47	Information and communication	23 287	23 287	23 340	23 277	23 359	23 262	24 665	25 419
48	Financial and insurance activities	36 102	36 467	36 899	35 943	34 000	34 688	34 961	37 133
49	Real estate activities	2 301	2 357	2 461	2 367	2 227	2 180	2 274	2 461
50	Prof., scientif., techn. activ.; admin., support service activ.	45 951	48 367	50 516	49 903	51 042	52 261	54 948	57 434
51	Public admin.; compulsory s.s.; education; human health	181 903	183 565	182 359	179 268	178 271	177 971	177 904	180 471
52	Other service activities	33 125	33 633	34 068	35 150	35 788	36 062	36 379	36 607
53	**Wages and salaries**	461 819	466 743	473 602	468 152	464 305	466 808	477 784	490 527
54	Agriculture, forestry and fishing	5 983	6 235	6 403	6 404	6 287	6 551	6 807	7 214
55	Industry, including energy	101 944	102 638	105 837	104 748	104 485	105 305	107 826	110 284
56	Manufacturing	92 458	93 044	96 001	94 565	94 241	94 919	97 258	99 510
57	Construction	26 918	26 511	26 535	24 770	22 422	21 402	22 108	22 210
58	Distrib. trade, repairs; transp.; accommod., food serv. activ.	91 712	93 189	95 517	95 452	94 941	95 930	99 649	103 603
59	Information and communication	16 787	16 781	16 904	16 937	16 998	17 002	17 995	18 671
60	Financial and insurance activities	25 565	25 707	25 791	25 465	24 224	24 522	24 879	25 726
61	Real estate activities	1 688	1 726	1 808	1 738	1 634	1 606	1 688	1 842
62	Prof., scientif., techn. activ.; admin., support service activ.	33 984	35 772	37 368	36 988	37 815	38 827	40 872	42 986
63	Public admin.; compulsory s.s.; education; human health	129 421	129 925	128 505	125 923	125 102	124 927	124 876	126 764
64	Other service activities	27 819	28 259	28 933	29 726	30 397	30 737	31 085	31 228
65	**Gross operating surplus and mixed income**	753 277	764 411	781 471	752 344	758 496	768 049	780 417	801 723
66	**Taxes less subsidies on production and imports**	184 787	197 762	204 522	217 855	208 924	214 521	219 626	211 014
67	Taxes on production and imports	213 476	226 085	233 426	248 830	241 713	250 869	252 453	246 134
68	Subsidies on production and imports	28 689	28 323	28 904	30 975	32 789	36 348	32 827	35 120
69	**Residual item**	0	0	0	0	0	0	0	0
70	**Gross domestic product**	1 572 878	1 604 515	1 637 463	1 613 265	1 604 599	1 621 827	1 652 622	1 680 948

Note: Detailed metadata:http://metalinks.oecd.org/nav1/20180308/19bf
Source: Istituto Centrale di Statistica (ISTAT) via Eurostat.

ITALY

Table 3. Disposable income, saving and net lending / net borrowing

Million EUR (1999 ITL euro)

		2009	2010	2011	2012	2013	2014	2015	2016
	DISPOSABLE INCOME								
1	**Gross domestic product**	1 572 878	1 604 515	1 637 463	1 613 265	1 604 599	1 621 827	1 652 153	1 680 523
2	Net primary incomes from the rest of the world	-963	-3 199	-4 317	-2 256	-2 735	61	-8 938	3 771
3	Primary incomes receivable from the rest of the world	66 082	61 117	66 224	59 200	57 830	62 181	53 255	62 914
4	Primary incomes payable to the rest of the world	67 045	64 316	70 541	61 455	60 565	62 120	62 192	59 144
5	**Gross national income at market prices**	1 571 915	1 601 316	1 633 144	1 611 010	1 601 864	1 621 888	1 643 216	1 684 294
6	Consumption of fixed capital	270 527	280 120	289 710	294 926	295 278	296 049	298 437	298 867
7	**Net national income at market prices**	1 301 388	1 321 195	1 343 435	1 316 084	1 306 586	1 325 839	1 344 779	1 385 427
8	Net current transfers from the rest of the world	-18 386	-19 996	-19 253	-19 515	-18 157	-15 929	-14 733	-16 463
9	Current transfers receivable from the rest of the world	14 411	12 110	14 020	13 882	14 171	15 118	15 146	15 604
10	Current transfers payable to the rest of the world	32 797	32 106	33 273	33 397	32 328	31 047	29 879	32 067
11	**Net national disposable income**	1 283 002	1 301 199	1 324 182	1 296 569	1 288 429	1 309 910	1 330 046	1 368 964
	SAVING AND NET LENDING / NET BORROWING								
12	**Net national disposable income**	1 283 002	1 301 199	1 324 182	1 296 569	1 288 429	1 309 910	1 330 046	1 368 964
13	Final consumption expenditures	1 278 173	1 306 580	1 328 114	1 309 173	1 296 296	1 299 306	1 318 313	1 337 750
14	Adj. for change in net equity of households in pension funds	0	0	0	0	0	0	0	0
15	**Saving, net**	4 829	-5 381	-3 932	-12 604	-7 867	10 604	11 733	31 214
16	Net capital transfers from the rest of the world	512	121	1 081	2 123	2 405	3 635	5 094	-933
17	Capital transfers receivable from the rest of the world	1 631	1 487	2 741	3 168	3 653	4 792	6 395	585
18	Capital transfers payable to the rest of the world	1 119	1 366	1 660	1 045	1 248	1 157	1 301	1 518
19	Gross capital formation	305 022	329 530	335 062	288 155	272 062	276 246	285 439	285 847
20	Acquisitions less disposals of non-financial non-produced assets	294	73	48	-1 836	3 141	941	1 184	1 973
21	Consumption of fixed capital	270 527	280 120	289 710	294 926	295 278	296 049	298 437	298 867
22	**Net lending / net borrowing**	-29 449	-54 743	-48 251	-1 874	14 613	33 101	28 641	41 328
	REAL DISPOSABLE INCOME								
23	**Gross domestic product at constant prices, reference year 2010**	1 577 903	1 604 515	1 613 767	1 568 274	1 541 172	1 542 924	1 557 612	1 570 980
24	Trading gain or loss	17 367	0	-12 218	-18 331	-11 996	-1 390	7 662	17 249
25	**Real gross domestic income**	1 595 269	1 604 515	1 601 548	1 549 944	1 529 176	1 541 534	1 565 273	1 588 230
26	Net real primary incomes from the rest of the world	-977	-3 199	-4 222	-2 167	-2 607	58	-8 468	3 564
27	Real primary incomes receivable from the rest of the world	67 022	61 117	64 772	56 876	55 111	59 103	50 454	59 459
28	Real primary incomes payable to the rest of the world	67 999	64 316	68 994	59 043	57 718	59 044	58 922	55 896
29	**Real gross national income at market prices**	1 594 292	1 601 316	1 597 324	1 547 777	1 526 569	1 541 592	1 556 807	1 591 794
30	Net real current transfers from the rest of the world	-18 648	-19 996	-18 831	-18 749	-17 304	-15 141	-13 958	-15 559
31	Real current transfers receivable from the rest of the world	14 616	12 110	13 712	13 337	13 505	14 370	14 350	14 747
32	Real current transfers payable to the rest of the world	33 264	32 106	32 543	32 086	30 808	29 510	28 308	30 306
33	**Real gross national disposable income**	1 575 645	1 581 320	1 578 493	1 529 028	1 509 265	1 526 452	1 542 848	1 576 235
34	Consumption of fixed capital at constant prices	277 922	280 120	282 960	284 046	284 042	283 439	283 154	283 912
35	**Real net national income at market prices**	1 319 914	1 321 195	1 313 969	1 264 427	1 245 170	1 260 200	1 274 063	1 309 340
36	**Real net national disposable income**	1 301 266	1 301 199	1 295 138	1 245 678	1 227 867	1 245 059	1 260 105	1 293 782

Note: Detailed metadata:http://metalinks.oecd.org/nav1/20180308/25dc
Source: Istituto Centrale di Statistica (ISTAT) via Eurostat.

Table 4. Population and employment (persons) and employment (hours worked) by industry
ISIC Rev. 4

		2009	2010	2011	2012	2013	2014	2015	2016
	POPULATION, THOUSAND PERSONS, NATIONAL CONCEPT								
1	**Total population**	**59 578.3**	**59 829.6**	**60 060.0**	**60 339.1**	**60 646.4**	**60 789.1**	**60 730.6**	**60 627.5**
2	Economically active population	..	..	..	..	..	..	..	..
3	Unemployed persons	..	..	..	..	..	..	..	..
4	Total employment	24 569.3	24 406.8	24 458.1	24 384.7	23 576.9	23 848.2	24 003.7	24 318.7
5	Employees	18 203.0	18 002.0	18 063.5	18 040.7	17 436.5	17 695.2	17 898.9	18 247.0
6	Self-employed	6 366.3	6 404.8	6 394.6	6 344.0	6 140.4	6 153.0	6 104.8	6 071.7
	TOTAL EMPLOYMENT, THOUSAND PERSONS, DOMESTIC CONCEPT								
7	Agriculture, forestry and fishing	942.1	959.5	942.2	918.7	892.2	890.6	899.3	926.8
8	Industry, including energy	4 633.3	4 470.2	4 439.9	4 369.6	4 251.1	4 179.2	4 147.5	4 178.6
9	Manufacturing	4 328.3	4 166.2	4 135.3	4 057.2	3 941.0	3 868.1	3 832.8	3 856.5
10	Construction	1 945.3	1 911.9	1 867.6	1 778.5	1 643.1	1 578.0	1 559.1	1 510.0
11	Distrib. trade, repairs; transp.; accommod., food serv. activ.	6 150.3	6 133.1	6 187.9	6 209.7	6 113.8	6 124.8	6 200.7	6 345.6
12	Information and communication	609.1	597.3	595.0	591.3	585.4	577.4	586.6	603.9
13	Financial and insurance activities	699.9	690.3	684.7	681.9	669.7	669.1	669.8	675.0
14	Real estate activities	171.5	177.4	186.9	185.8	179.5	175.4	178.3	187.4
15	Prof., scientif., techn. activ.; admin., support service activ.	2 653.9	2 700.6	2 782.3	2 825.2	2 814.4	2 867.5	2 942.2	3 026.2
16	Public admin.; compulsory s.s.; education; human health	4 666.9	4 636.0	4 632.2	4 595.9	4 578.0	4 614.3	4 644.1	4 693.8
17	Other service activities	2 453.2	2 489.4	2 530.1	2 608.2	2 595.6	2 663.1	2 670.3	2 674.4
18	**Total employment**	**24 925.5**	**24 765.7**	**24 842.7**	**24 764.8**	**24 322.8**	**24 339.4**	**24 497.9**	**24 821.7**
	EMPLOYEES, THOUSAND PERSONS, DOMESTIC CONCEPT								
19	Agriculture, forestry and fishing	416.3	424.1	427.6	433.9	423.6	430.6	437.1	461.1
20	Industry, including energy	4 037.1	3 886.9	3 864.0	3 804.7	3 698.0	3 645.1	3 623.0	3 668.6
21	Manufacturing	3 746.4	3 596.5	3 571.4	3 504.5	3 399.6	3 345.2	3 319.9	3 357.7
22	Construction	1 217.2	1 181.5	1 143.9	1 078.5	978.3	924.1	925.7	920.1
23	Distrib. trade, repairs; transp.; accommod., food serv. activ.	3 912.0	3 900.6	3 954.8	4 000.3	3 928.2	3 944.3	4 045.0	4 185.8
24	Information and communication	476.8	466.9	464.8	466.5	469.3	461.7	472.8	500.9
25	Financial and insurance activities	582.8	571.9	566.8	564.5	554.2	549.7	549.3	550.5
26	Real estate activities	69.0	69.1	71.2	73.0	69.5	68.6	72.4	78.6
27	Prof., scientif., techn. activ.; admin., support service activ.	1 511.4	1 537.1	1 592.9	1 594.2	1 601.6	1 645.4	1 713.0	1 785.1
28	Public admin.; compulsory s.s.; education; human health	4 298.8	4 261.8	4 253.8	4 207.9	4 190.3	4 203.5	4 224.4	4 286.0
29	Other service activities	2 022.0	2 042.2	2 085.7	2 170.5	2 168.2	2 235.7	2 236.3	2 219.9
30	**Total employees**	**18 543.9**	**18 342.1**	**18 425.5**	**18 394.0**	**18 081.2**	**18 108.7**	**18 299.0**	**18 656.6**
	SELF-EMPLOYED, THOUSAND PERSONS, DOMESTIC CONCEPT								
31	Agriculture, forestry and fishing	525.8	535.4	514.6	484.8	468.6	460.0	462.2	465.7
32	Industry, including energy	596.2	583.3	575.9	564.9	553.1	534.1	524.5	510.0
33	Manufacturing	581.9	569.7	563.9	552.7	541.4	522.9	512.9	498.8
34	Construction	727.6	730.4	723.7	700.0	664.8	653.9	633.4	589.9
35	Distrib. trade, repairs; transp.; accommod., food serv. activ.	2 238.3	2 232.5	2 233.1	2 209.4	2 185.6	2 180.5	2 155.7	2 159.8
36	Information and communication	132.3	130.4	130.2	124.8	116.1	115.7	113.8	103.0
37	Financial and insurance activities	117.1	118.4	117.9	117.4	115.5	119.4	120.5	124.5
38	Real estate activities	102.5	108.3	109.6	112.8	110.0	106.8	105.9	108.8
39	Prof., scientif., techn. activ.; admin., support service activ.	1 142.5	1 163.5	1 189.4	1 231.0	1 212.8	1 222.1	1 229.2	1 241.1
40	Public admin.; compulsory s.s.; education; human health	368.1	374.2	378.4	388.0	387.7	410.8	419.7	407.8
41	Other service activities	431.2	447.2	444.4	437.7	427.4	427.4	434.0	454.5
42	**Total self-employed**	**6 381.6**	**6 423.6**	**6 417.2**	**6 370.8**	**6 241.6**	**6 230.7**	**6 198.9**	**6 165.1**
	TOTAL EMPLOYMENT, MILLION HOURS, DOMESTIC CONCEPT								
43	Industry, including energy	7 980.4	7 804.7	7 805.0	7 481.0	7 270.3	7 185.2	7 181.7	7 301.7
44	Distrib. trade, repairs; transp.; accommod., food serv. activ.	12 009.0	11 960.9	12 019.7	11 863.2	11 527.4	11 490.3	11 571.7	11 844.8
45	Financial and insurance activities	1 255.8	1 236.6	1 232.7	1 210.5	1 179.1	1 165.3	1 171.6	1 191.3
46	Prof., scientif., techn. activ.; admin., support service activ.	4 640.4	4 779.8	4 910.2	4 864.8	4 767.3	4 838.4	4 962.4	5 131.6
47	Public admin.; compulsory s.s.; education; human health	6 687.6	6 579.1	6 588.0	6 452.2	6 398.5	6 448.5	6 465.3	6 528.6
48	**Total employment**	**44 259.2**	**44 015.4**	**44 052.5**	**42 946.5**	**41 823.2**	**41 794.1**	**42 087.3**	**42 802.9**
	EMPLOYEES, MILLION HOURS, DOMESTIC CONCEPT								
49	Industry, including energy	6 703.0	6 539.8	6 558.7	6 303.5	6 119.9	6 080.7	6 098.9	6 240.2
50	Distrib. trade, repairs; transp.; accommod., food serv. activ.	6 833.1	6 777.8	6 830.9	6 773.6	6 546.4	6 566.3	6 725.1	6 955.8
51	Financial and insurance activities	993.8	973.1	973.4	963.0	939.2	919.9	923.4	935.3
52	Prof., scientif., techn. activ.; admin., support service activ.	2 342.1	2 414.4	2 504.3	2 439.4	2 421.0	2 469.8	2 585.0	2 728.5
53	Public admin.; compulsory s.s.; education; human health	6 072.3	5 952.2	5 951.0	5 798.6	5 758.6	5 781.5	5 784.8	5 860.9
54	**Total employees**	**29 969.8**	**29 636.3**	**29 756.3**	**29 059.9**	**28 333.0**	**28 353.7**	**28 728.4**	**29 412.9**
	SELF-EMPLOYED, MILLION HOURS, DOMESTIC CONCEPT								
55	Industry, including energy	1 277.4	1 264.9	1 246.3	1 177.5	1 150.4	1 104.5	1 082.7	1 061.5
56	Distrib. trade, repairs; transp.; accommod., food serv. activ.	5 175.9	5 183.0	5 188.8	5 089.6	4 981.0	4 924.0	4 846.6	4 889.0
57	Financial and insurance activities	262.0	263.5	259.3	247.4	239.9	245.3	248.2	256.1
58	Prof., scientif., techn. activ.; admin., support service activ.	2 298.3	2 365.4	2 405.9	2 425.3	2 346.3	2 368.6	2 377.4	2 403.1
59	Public admin.; compulsory s.s.; education; human health	615.3	626.9	636.9	653.6	639.9	667.0	680.5	667.7
60	**Total self-employed**	**14 289.4**	**14 379.1**	**14 296.2**	**13 886.6**	**13 490.2**	**13 440.4**	**13 358.8**	**13 390.0**

Note: Detailed metadata:http://metalinks.oecd.org/nav1/20180308/b1cc
Source: Istituto Centrale di Statistica (ISTAT) via Eurostat.

JAPAN

Table 1. Gross domestic product, expenditure approach

Billion JPY

		2009	2010	2011	2012	2013	2014	2015	2016
	AT CURRENT PRICES								
1	**Final consumption expenditure**	**382 425**	**386 483**	**385 459**	**390 483**	**398 142**	**403 645**	**406 508**	**406 333**
2	Household	280 474	282 865	279 650	283 173	289 446	293 078	293 724	291 942
3	NPISH's	5 839	6 092	6 605	7 069	7 227	7 005	7 486	7 916
4	Government	96 112	97 527	99 205	100 241	101 469	103 562	105 297	106 474
5	Individual	55 537	56 819	58 525	60 054	60 945	62 362	63 828	64 815
6	Collective	40 575	40 708	40 679	40 187	40 524	41 200	41 469	41 659
7	*of which:* Actual individual consumption	341 850	345 776	344 780	350 296	357 618	362 445	365 039	364 673
8	**Gross capital formation**	**104 380**	**106 563**	**108 618**	**112 130**	**116 691**	**122 899**	**127 705**	**126 881**
9	Gross fixed capital formation, total	109 459	106 724	107 638	110 966	117 382	123 146	126 479	126 789
10	Dwellings	14 827	14 139	14 800	15 009	16 704	16 708	16 733	17 516
11	Other buildings and structures	31 690	30 191	30 288	31 065	35 147	37 336	37 949	37 550
12	Transport equipment	5 542	6 083	5 624	6 790	6 817	7 311	7 632	8 133
13	Other machinery and equipment	24 557	23 564	24 614	26 059	25 808	27 398	29 144	28 983
14	Cultivated assets	171	169	166	168	164	170	177	207
15	Intangible fixed assets[1]	26 351	25 771	25 688	26 140	26 957	28 169	29 154	29 116
16	Changes in inventories, acquisitions less disposals of valuables	..	..	..	..	..	..	..	..
17	Changes in inventories	-5 079	-161	980	1 164	-690	-247	1 226	92
18	Acquisitions less disposals of valuables	..	..	..	..	..	..	..	..
19	**External balance of goods and services**	**2 697**	**7 308**	**-2 668**	**-7 655**	**-11 657**	**-12 668**	**-2 227**	**5 232**
20	Exports of goods and services	61 290	75 237	73 343	71 990	80 082	90 135	93 571	86 793
21	Exports of goods	51 122	64 391	62 965	61 957	67 829	74 075	75 274	68 980
22	Exports of services	10 169	10 846	10 377	10 034	12 254	16 061	18 297	17 813
23	Imports of goods and services	58 593	67 929	76 011	79 645	91 740	102 803	95 797	81 561
24	Imports of goods	45 734	54 875	63 296	66 229	76 602	84 540	76 160	63 455
25	Imports of services	12 859	13 054	12 716	13 417	15 137	18 263	19 637	18 106
26	**Statistical discrepancy**	**0**	**0**	**0**	**0**	**0**	**0**	**0**	**0**
27	**Gross domestic product**	**489 501**	**500 354**	**491 409**	**494 957**	**503 176**	**513 876**	**531 986**	**538 446**
	AT CONSTANT PRICES, REFERENCE YEAR 2010								
28	**Final consumption expenditure**	**377 851**	**386 483**	**387 251**	**394 759**	**403 229**	**401 211**	**402 701**	**404 249**
29	Household	276 428	282 865	281 160	286 472	293 222	290 956	290 430	290 140
30	NPISH's	5 755	6 092	6 679	7 210	7 417	7 102	7 541	8 020
31	Government	95 672	97 527	99 412	101 080	102 596	103 152	104 742	106 115
32	Individual	..	..	..	..	..	..	..	..
33	Collective	40 177	40 708	40 828	40 806	41 306	41 213	41 366	41 623
34	*of which:* Actual individual consumption	337 675	345 776	346 424	353 954	361 923	359 998	361 335	362 626
35	**Gross capital formation**	**103 524**	**106 563**	**109 341**	**113 418**	**117 039**	**121 073**	**124 599**	**124 944**
36	Gross fixed capital formation, total	108 452	106 724	108 491	112 336	117 875	121 476	123 547	124 904
37	Dwellings	14 708	14 139	14 758	15 094	16 426	15 873	15 760	16 613
38	Other buildings and structures	31 543	30 191	30 047	30 902	34 575	35 945	36 235	36 039
39	Transport equipment	5 538	6 083	5 688	6 858	6 732	7 112	7 318	7 955
40	Other machinery and equipment	..	..	..	..	..	..	..	..
41	Cultivated assets	188	169	159	165	148	143	132	131
42	Intangible fixed assets[1]	26 449	25 771	25 718	26 214	27 106	27 936	28 881	28 864
43	Changes in inventories, acquisitions less disposals of valuables	..	..	..	..	..	..	..	..
44	Changes in inventories	..	..	..	..	..	..	..	..
45	Acquisitions less disposals of valuables	..	..	..	..	..	..	..	..
46	**External balance of goods and services**	**-870**	**7 308**	**3 180**	**-774**	**-2 684**	**-2 133**	**-341**	**2 421**
47	Exports of goods and services	60 233	75 237	75 052	74 985	75 556	82 576	85 005	86 142
48	Exports of goods	50 180	64 391	64 301	64 481	63 964	67 943	68 492	68 734
49	Exports of services	10 064	10 846	10 751	10 501	11 594	14 642	16 513	17 403
50	Imports of goods and services	61 102	67 929	71 872	75 760	78 240	84 709	85 345	83 721
51	Imports of goods	48 369	54 875	58 847	61 660	63 724	67 894	67 641	66 275
52	Imports of services	12 666	13 054	13 025	14 137	14 549	17 021	18 034	17 773
53	**Statistical discrepancy (including chaining residual)**	**-281**	**0**	**4**	**-154**	**-190**	**-818**	**-595**	**-311**
54	**Gross domestic product**	**480 224**	**500 354**	**499 776**	**507 248**	**517 395**	**519 334**	**526 364**	**531 303**

Note: Detailed metadata:http://metalinks.oecd.org/nav1/20180308/8a40

1. Computer software.

Source: Economic and Social Research Institute (ESRI), Cabinet Office (CAO) for Government of Japan.

Table 2. Gross domestic product, output and income approach
ISIC Rev. 4

Billion JPY

		2009	2010	2011	2012	2013	2014	2015	2016
	OUTPUT APPROACH AT CURRENT PRICES								
1	**Total gross value added at basic prices**	**488 955**	**499 136**	**488 958**	**492 361**	**500 101**	**509 927**	**527 502**	**534 292**
2	Agriculture, forestry and fishing	5 299	5 515	5 285	5 651	5 556	5 428	5 907	6 194
3	Industry, including energy	108 062	118 340	108 006	107 906	108 764	113 812	124 431	128 043
4	Manufacturing	93 721	104 239	96 639	97 663	97 799	101 394	110 223	113 337
5	Construction	25 437	23 984	24 093	24 485	26 779	28 470	29 301	29 725
6	Services	..	..	..	..	..	..	..	..
7	Distrib. trade, repairs; transp.; accommod., food serv. activ.	105 166	107 166	107 528	109 897	111 982	112 589	113 695	113 826
8	Information and communication	25 703	25 514	25 384	25 354	25 718	26 082	26 681	26 830
9	Financial and insurance activities	24 238	24 115	23 110	22 442	23 055	22 808	23 187	22 462
10	Real estate activities	59 310	59 531	59 528	59 372	59 889	60 128	60 590	61 168
11	Prof., scientif., techn. activ.; admin., support service activ.	35 898	34 940	35 682	35 546	36 513	37 144	38 354	39 256
12	Public admin.; compulsory s.s.; education; human health	76 213	76 577	77 439	78 651	78 954	80 216	82 005	83 852
13	Other service activities	23 628	23 454	22 904	23 056	22 891	23 251	23 351	22 937
14	FISIM (Financial Intermediation Services Indirectly Measured)	..	..	..	..	..	..	..	..
15	Gross value added at basic prices, excluding FISIM	488 955	499 136	488 958	492 361	500 101	509 927	527 502	534 292
16	**Taxes less subsidies on products**	**1 638**	**1 949**	**2 504**	**2 585**	**3 257**	**3 776**	**3 008**	**1 900**
17	Taxes on products	..	..	..	..	..	..	..	..
18	Subsidies on products	..	..	..	..	..	..	..	..
19	**Residual item**	**-1 092**	**-731**	**-53**	**11**	**-182**	**173**	**1 476**	**2 254**
20	**Gross domestic product at market prices**	**489 501**	**500 354**	**491 409**	**494 957**	**503 176**	**513 876**	**531 986**	**538 446**
	OUTPUT APPROACH AT CONSTANT PRICES (REF. YEAR 2010)								
21	**Total gross value added at basic prices**	**480 843**	**499 136**	**497 878**	**504 341**	**514 113**	**516 485**	**522 024**	**525 605**
22	Agriculture, forestry and fishing	5 856	5 515	5 578	5 613	5 630	5 452	5 189	4 509
23	Industry, including energy	102 607	118 340	113 801	113 930	114 562	117 757	120 101	122 728
24	Manufacturing	89 607	104 239	101 398	103 849	103 757	106 863	110 889	113 066
25	Construction	25 264	23 984	24 115	24 592	26 836	27 889	28 070	28 391
26	Services	..	..	..	..	..	..	..	..
27	Distrib. trade, repairs; transp.; accommod., food serv. activ.	104 553	107 166	107 976	110 948	113 132	111 005	110 506	109 898
28	Information and communication	25 370	25 514	25 696	25 809	26 551	26 703	27 279	27 227
29	Financial and insurance activities	23 949	24 115	23 902	24 560	26 685	26 693	27 755	27 302
30	Real estate activities	58 812	59 531	60 107	60 296	61 221	62 007	62 767	63 546
31	Prof., scientif., techn. activ.; admin., support service activ.	35 145	34 940	35 980	36 112	36 780	36 357	36 723	37 630
32	Public admin.; compulsory s.s.; education; human health	76 194	76 577	77 606	79 055	79 788	79 832	81 422	82 541
33	Other service activities	23 665	23 454	23 116	23 362	22 916	22 872	22 486	22 068
34	FISIM (Financial Intermediation Services Indirectly Measured)	..	..	..	..	..	..	..	..
35	Gross value added at basic prices, excluding FISIM	480 843	499 136	497 878	504 341	514 113	516 485	522 024	525 605
36	**Taxes less subsidies on products**	..	..	..	..	..	..	..	..
37	Taxes on products	..	..	..	..	..	..	..	..
38	Subsidies on products	..	..	..	..	..	..	..	..
39	**Residual item**	..	..	..	..	..	..	..	..
40	**Gross domestic product at market prices**	**480 224**	**500 354**	**499 776**	**507 248**	**517 395**	**519 334**	**526 364**	**531 303**
	INCOME APPROACH								
41	**Compensation of employees**	**251 424**	**251 995**	**253 319**	**253 268**	**254 404**	**258 434**	**261 950**	**268 975**
42	Agriculture, forestry and fishing	1 931	1 890	2 194	2 109	2 147	2 268	2 259	2 319
43	Industry, including energy	53 685	55 016	55 324	54 367	53 105	53 875	54 140	55 008
44	Manufacturing	49 568	51 056	51 557	50 681	49 542	50 328	50 638	51 512
45	Construction	21 867	20 421	20 070	19 773	19 738	20 263	20 480	20 727
46	Distrib. trade, repairs; transp.; accommod., food serv. activ.	60 313	62 025	62 057	62 319	63 097	63 756	63 390	65 172
47	Information and communication	10 583	11 027	10 881	10 670	10 479	11 092	11 604	11 755
48	Financial and insurance activities	10 893	10 874	10 577	10 736	10 715	10 065	10 245	10 797
49	Real estate activities	3 690	3 528	3 590	3 485	3 401	3 738	3 916	4 279
50	Prof., scientif., techn. activ.; admin., support service activ.	18 885	19 183	19 303	19 398	21 218	21 761	22 937	24 245
51	Public admin.; compulsory s.s.; education; human health	53 516	53 433	54 682	55 678	55 641	56 711	58 105	59 722
52	Other service activities	16 062	14 599	14 641	14 733	14 863	14 906	14 875	14 951
53	**Wages and salaries**	**217 014**	**217 112**	**217 647**	**216 699**	**217 341**	**220 195**	**222 560**	**228 317**
54	Agriculture, forestry and fishing	..	..	..	..	..	..	..	..
55	Industry, including energy	..	..	..	..	..	..	..	..
56	Manufacturing	..	..	..	..	..	..	..	..
57	Construction	..	..	..	..	..	..	..	..
58	Distrib. trade, repairs; transp.; accommod., food serv. activ.	..	..	..	..	..	..	..	..
59	Information and communication	..	..	..	..	..	..	..	..
60	Financial and insurance activities	..	..	..	..	..	..	..	..
61	Real estate activities	..	..	..	..	..	..	..	..
62	Prof., scientif., techn. activ.; admin., support service activ.	..	..	..	..	..	..	..	..
63	Public admin.; compulsory s.s.; education; human health	..	..	..	..	..	..	..	..
64	Other service activities	..	..	..	..	..	..	..	..
65	**Gross operating surplus and mixed income**	**207 171**	**216 559**	**205 698**	**208 745**	**215 824**	**217 532**	**227 027**	**225 260**
66	**Taxes less subsidies on production and imports**	**31 998**	**32 531**	**32 445**	**32 934**	**33 130**	**37 737**	**41 532**	**41 957**
67	Taxes on production and imports	35 464	35 969	36 146	36 105	36 568	41 010	44 826	45 210
68	Subsidies on production and imports	3 466	3 438	3 701	3 172	3 439	3 273	3 293	3 253
69	**Residual item**	**-1 092**	**-731**	**-53**	**11**	**-182**	**173**	**1 476**	**2 254**
70	**Gross domestic product**	**489 501**	**500 354**	**491 409**	**494 957**	**503 176**	**513 876**	**531 986**	**538 446**

Note: Detailed metadata:http://metalinks.oecd.org/nav1/20180308/8a40
Source: Economic and Social Research Institute (ESRI), Cabinet Office (CAO) for Government of Japan.

JAPAN

Table 3. Disposable income, saving and net lending / net borrowing

Billion JPY

		2009	2010	2011	2012	2013	2014	2015	2016
	DISPOSABLE INCOME								
1	**Gross domestic product**	**489 501**	**500 354**	**491 409**	**494 957**	**503 176**	**513 876**	**531 986**	**538 446**
2	Net primary incomes from the rest of the world	11 965	12 925	13 920	13 258	16 892	18 494	20 296	17 213
3	Primary incomes receivable from the rest of the world	16 538	17 815	18 719	18 385	23 673	27 335	30 240	27 986
4	Primary incomes payable to the rest of the world	4 573	4 890	4 799	5 127	6 781	8 842	9 945	10 773
5	**Gross national income at market prices**	**501 466**	**513 279**	**505 329**	**508 215**	**520 067**	**532 370**	**552 281**	**555 659**
6	Consumption of fixed capital	121 671	119 013	116 572	115 055	115 945	118 498	120 081	119 928
7	**Net national income at market prices**	**380 887**	**394 997**	**388 810**	**393 149**	**404 304**	**413 698**	**430 724**	**433 477**
8	Net current transfers from the rest of the world	-1 069	-850	-850	-839	-778	-1 904	-1 664	-1 922
9	Current transfers receivable from the rest of the world	2 055	1 820	1 916	2 112	2 484	2 956	3 348	2 958
10	Current transfers payable to the rest of the world	3 124	2 670	2 767	2 951	3 261	4 860	5 012	4 880
11	**Net national disposable income**	**379 818**	**394 147**	**387 960**	**392 311**	**403 526**	**411 794**	**429 060**	**431 555**
	SAVING AND NET LENDING / NET BORROWING								
12	**Net national disposable income**	**379 818**	**394 147**	**387 960**	**392 311**	**403 526**	**411 794**	**429 060**	**431 555**
13	Final consumption expenditures	382 425	386 483	385 459	390 483	398 142	403 645	406 508	406 333
14	Adj. for change in net equity of households in pension funds	-673	-572	-643	-1 127	-1 036	-583	-991	-684
15	**Saving, net**	**-2 606**	**7 664**	**2 501**	**1 828**	**5 385**	**8 149**	**22 552**	**25 222**
16	Net capital transfers from the rest of the world	-465	-434	28	-80	-744	-209	-271	-743
17	Capital transfers receivable from the rest of the world	104	78	596	477	115	47	29	54
18	Capital transfers payable to the rest of the world	570	512	568	557	859	256	300	797
19	Gross capital formation	104 380	106 563	108 618	112 130	116 691	122 899	127 705	126 881
20	Acquisitions less disposals of non-financial non-produced assets	0	0	0	0	0	0	0	0
21	Consumption of fixed capital	121 671	119 013	116 572	115 055	115 945	118 498	120 081	119 928
22	**Net lending / net borrowing**[1]	**13 128**	**18 949**	**10 430**	**4 684**	**3 713**	**3 712**	**16 134**	**19 780**
	REAL DISPOSABLE INCOME								
23	**Gross domestic product at constant prices, reference year 2010**	..	..	..	..	..	..	..	..
24	Trading gain or loss	..	..	..	..	..	..	..	..
25	**Real gross domestic income**	**484 044** e	**500 354** e	**493 910** e	**500 434** e	**508 484** e	**509 749** e	**525 155** e	**534 437** e
26	Net real primary incomes from the rest of the world	..	..	..	..	..	..	..	..
27	Real primary incomes receivable from the rest of the world	..	..	..	..	..	..	..	..
28	Real primary incomes payable to the rest of the world	..	..	..	..	..	..	..	..
29	**Real gross national income at market prices**	**495 875** e	**513 279** e	**507 901** e	**513 838** e	**525 554** e	**528 095** e	**545 190** e	**551 522** e
30	Net real current transfers from the rest of the world	..	..	..	..	..	..	..	..
31	Real current transfers receivable from the rest of the world	..	..	..	..	..	..	..	..
32	Real current transfers payable to the rest of the world	..	..	..	..	..	..	..	..
33	**Real gross national disposable income**	..	..	..	..	..	..	..	..
34	Consumption of fixed capital at constant prices	..	..	..	..	..	..	..	..
35	**Real net national income at market prices**	**376 641** e	**394 997** e	**390 789** e	**397 499** e	**408 570** e	**410 376** e	**425 193** e	**430 250** e
36	**Real net national disposable income**	**375 584** e	**394 147** e	**389 935** e	**396 651** e	**407 784** e	**408 487** e	**423 551** e	**428 342** e

Note: Detailed metadata:http://metalinks.oecd.org/nav1/20180308/a256
1.   Including a statistical discrepancy.
Source: Economic and Social Research Institute (ESRI), Cabinet Office (CAO) for Government of Japan.

Table 4. Population and employment (persons) and employment (hours worked) by industry
ISIC Rev. 4

		2009	2010	2011	2012	2013	2014	2015	2016
	POPULATION, THOUSAND PERSONS, NATIONAL CONCEPT								
1	**Total population**	**128 034.0**	**128 043.0**	**127 831.0**	**127 552.0**	**127 333.0**	**127 262.0**	**127 110.0**	**126 960.0**
2	Economically active population	..	..	..	..	..	..	..	..
3	Unemployed persons	..	..	..	..	..	..	..	..
4	Total employment	65 632.0	65 494.0	65 455.0	65 177.0	65 549.0	65 934.0	66 220.0	66 852.0
5	Employees	56 242.0	56 407.0	56 551.0	56 512.0	56 986.0	57 401.0	57 886.0	58 761.0
6	Self-employed	9 390.0	9 087.0	8 904.0	8 665.0	8 563.0	8 533.0	8 334.0	8 091.0
	TOTAL EMPLOYMENT, THOUSAND PERSONS, DOMESTIC CONCEPT								
7	Agriculture, forestry and fishing	3 173.0	3 004.0	2 908.0	2 783.0	2 707.0	2 682.0	2 660.0	2 601.0
8	Industry, including energy	11 438.0	11 338.0	11 245.0	11 080.0	10 848.0	10 849.0	10 777.0	10 787.0
9	Manufacturing	10 794.0	10 697.0	10 605.0	10 444.0	10 217.0	10 220.0	10 150.0	10 163.0
10	Construction	5 305.0	5 077.0	5 032.0	5 044.0	5 000.0	5 063.0	5 011.0	4 942.0
11	Distrib. trade, repairs; transp.; accommod., food serv. activ.	19 592.0	19 773.0	19 648.0	19 333.0	19 488.0	19 517.0	19 404.0	19 538.0
12	Information and communication	1 782.0	1 788.0	1 732.0	1 709.0	1 682.0	1 778.0	1 833.0	1 822.0
13	Financial and insurance activities	1 765.0	1 739.0	1 725.0	1 742.0	1 711.0	1 604.0	1 611.0	1 699.0
14	Real estate activities	1 005.0	995.0	1 035.0	1 012.0	974.0	994.0	1 074.0	1 099.0
15	Prof., scientif., techn. activ.; admin., support service activ.	5 044.0	4 916.0	5 010.0	5 028.0	5 379.0	5 440.0	5 605.0	5 789.0
16	Public admin.; compulsory s.s.; education; human health	10 472.0	10 798.0	11 006.0	11 300.0	11 529.0	11 752.0	12 040.0	12 313.0
17	Other service activities	6 058.0	6 067.0	6 114.0	6 146.0	6 230.0	6 258.0	6 206.0	6 264.0
18	**Total employment**	**65 632.0**	**65 494.0**	**65 455.0**	**65 177.0**	**65 549.0**	**65 934.0**	**66 220.0**	**66 852.0**
	EMPLOYEES, THOUSAND PERSONS, DOMESTIC CONCEPT								
19	Agriculture, forestry and fishing	857.0	831.0	827.0	801.0	787.0	802.0	797.0	792.0
20	Industry, including energy	10 691.0	10 625.0	10 532.0	10 362.0	10 149.0	10 113.0	10 075.0	10 156.0
21	Manufacturing	10 057.0	9 994.0	9 902.0	9 736.0	9 527.0	9 494.0	9 458.0	9 543.0
22	Construction	4 244.0	4 030.0	4 005.0	4 030.0	3 975.0	4 001.0	3 976.0	3 919.0
23	Distrib. trade, repairs; transp.; accommod., food serv. activ.	17 151.0	17 404.0	17 398.0	17 190.0	17 383.0	17 469.0	17 466.0	17 697.0
24	Information and communication	1 687.0	1 694.0	1 640.0	1 614.0	1 583.0	1 675.0	1 728.0	1 718.0
25	Financial and insurance activities	1 715.0	1 687.0	1 677.0	1 697.0	1 663.0	1 556.0	1 570.0	1 662.0
26	Real estate activities	706.0	701.0	725.0	713.0	694.0	730.0	781.0	793.0
27	Prof., scientif., techn. activ.; admin., support service activ.	4 078.0	3 998.0	4 051.0	4 049.0	4 385.0	4 467.0	4 646.0	4 823.0
28	Public admin.; compulsory s.s.; education; human health	10 102.0	10 425.0	10 645.0	10 948.0	11 171.0	11 385.0	11 658.0	11 943.0
29	Other service activities	5 012.0	5 012.0	5 050.0	5 109.0	5 195.0	5 202.0	5 189.0	5 256.0
30	**Total employees**	**56 242.0**	**56 407.0**	**56 551.0**	**56 512.0**	**56 986.0**	**57 401.0**	**57 886.0**	**58 761.0**
	SELF-EMPLOYED, THOUSAND PERSONS, DOMESTIC CONCEPT								
31	Agriculture, forestry and fishing	2 316.0	2 173.0	2 081.0	1 982.0	1 920.0	1 880.0	1 863.0	1 809.0
32	Industry, including energy	747.0	713.0	713.0	718.0	699.0	736.0	702.0	631.0
33	Manufacturing	737.0	703.0	703.0	708.0	690.0	726.0	692.0	620.0
34	Construction	1 061.0	1 047.0	1 027.0	1 014.0	1 025.0	1 062.0	1 035.0	1 023.0
35	Distrib. trade, repairs; transp.; accommod., food serv. activ.	2 441.0	2 369.0	2 250.0	2 143.0	2 105.0	2 048.0	1 938.0	1 841.0
36	Information and communication	95.0	94.0	92.0	95.0	99.0	103.0	105.0	104.0
37	Financial and insurance activities	50.0	52.0	48.0	45.0	48.0	48.0	41.0	37.0
38	Real estate activities	299.0	294.0	310.0	299.0	280.0	264.0	293.0	306.0
39	Prof., scientif., techn. activ.; admin., support service activ.	966.0	918.0	959.0	979.0	994.0	973.0	959.0	966.0
40	Public admin.; compulsory s.s.; education; human health	370.0	373.0	361.0	352.0	358.0	367.0	382.0	370.0
41	Other service activities	1 046.0	1 055.0	1 064.0	1 037.0	1 035.0	1 056.0	1 017.0	1 008.0
42	**Total self-employed**	**9 390.0**	**9 087.0**	**8 904.0**	**8 665.0**	**8 563.0**	**8 533.0**	**8 334.0**	**8 091.0**
	TOTAL EMPLOYMENT, MILLION HOURS, DOMESTIC CONCEPT								
43	Industry, including energy	..	..	..	..	..	..	..	..
44	Distrib. trade, repairs; transp.; accommod., food serv. activ.	..	..	..	..	..	..	..	..
45	Financial and insurance activities	..	..	..	..	..	..	..	..
46	Prof., scientif., techn. activ.; admin., support service activ.	..	..	..	..	..	..	..	..
47	Public admin.; compulsory s.s.; education; human health	..	..	..	..	..	..	..	..
48	**Total employment**	..	..	..	..	..	..	..	..
	EMPLOYEES, MILLION HOURS, DOMESTIC CONCEPT								
49	Industry, including energy	19 775.1	20 618.9	20 438.7	20 313.7	19 733.4	19 723.0	19 680.0	19 818.0
50	Distrib. trade, repairs; transp.; accommod., food serv. activ.	28 873.4	29 377.8	29 208.0	28 906.4	28 965.4	28 934.0	28 730.0	28 961.0
51	Financial and insurance activities	3 102.9	3 055.0	3 027.2	3 101.8	2 987.6	2 762.0	2 786.0	2 957.0
52	Prof., scientif., techn. activ.; admin., support service activ.	7 183.8	7 267.2	7 281.7	7 355.4	7 917.1	8 027.0	8 259.0	8 551.0
53	Public admin.; compulsory s.s.; education; human health	16 679.0	17 227.9	17 615.9	18 192.6	18 216.7	18 497.0	18 981.0	19 358.0
54	**Total employees**	**98 828.4**	**100 280.4**	**100 248.0**	**100 755.2**	**100 380.8**	**100 825.0**	**101 353.0**	**102 362.0**
	SELF-EMPLOYED, MILLION HOURS, DOMESTIC CONCEPT								
55	Industry, including energy	..	..	..	..	..	..	..	..
56	Distrib. trade, repairs; transp.; accommod., food serv. activ.	..	..	..	..	..	..	..	..
57	Financial and insurance activities	..	..	..	..	..	..	..	..
58	Prof., scientif., techn. activ.; admin., support service activ.	..	..	..	..	..	..	..	..
59	Public admin.; compulsory s.s.; education; human health	..	..	..	..	..	..	..	..
60	**Total self-employed**	..	..	..	..	..	..	..	..

Note: Detailed metadata:http://metalinks.oecd.org/nav1/20180308/b08c
Source: Economic and Social Research Institute (ESRI), Cabinet Office (CAO) for Government of Japan.

KOREA

Table 1. Gross domestic product, expenditure approach

Billion KRW

		2009	2010	2011	2012	2013	2014	2015	2016
	AT CURRENT PRICES								
1	**Final consumption expenditure**	**769 589**	**819 821**	**873 523**	**911 938**	**942 267**	**972 925**	**1 006 006**	**1 047 482** p
2	Household	574 794	615 228	655 109	678 097	693 861	712 682	734 369	760 320 p
3	NPISH's	20 089	21 485	24 032	29 518	33 939	35 518	36 870	38 044 p
4	Government	174 706	183 109	194 381	204 324	214 467	224 724	234 766	249 118 p
5	Individual	86 434	89 548	98 284	103 464	109 270	116 783	122 721	..
6	Collective	88 272	93 561	96 097	100 860	105 197	107 941	112 045	..
7	*of which: Actual individual consumption*	681 316	726 261	777 425	811 078	837 070	864 984	893 960	798 364 p
8	**Gross capital formation**	**327 841**	**405 188**	**439 236**	**427 029**	**416 000**	**435 078**	**452 315**	**478 284** p
9	Gross fixed capital formation, total	360 697	385 924	403 045	407 307	418 289	433 266	458 420	485 948 p
10	Dwellings	50 753	46 010	44 828	44 649	55 442	62 556	74 735	91 835 p
11	Other buildings and structures	149 400	154 609	160 840	157 051	157 664	155 778	158 414	167 150 p
12	Transport equipment	31 473	34 066	35 781	35 603	36 125	39 466	43 710	43 237 p
13	Other machinery and equipment	72 035	87 556	91 930	92 682	86 874	87 699	91 195	90 488 p
14	Cultivated assets	..	..	..	..	..	..	..	..
15	Intangible fixed assets	57 036	63 684	69 666	77 323	82 183	87 767	90 366	93 239 p
16	Changes in inventories, acquisitions less disposals of valuables	-32 856	19 264	36 191	19 722	-2 288	1 813	-6 105	-7 665 p
17	Changes in inventories	-33 269	18 333	35 301	18 781	-2 389	812	-7 360	-7 665 p
18	Acquisitions less disposals of valuables	413	931	890	941	101	1 000	1 255	0 p
19	**External balance of goods and services**	**53 979**	**40 299**	**19 922**	**38 490**	**71 178**	**78 076**	**108 883**	**111 284** p
20	Exports of goods and services	547 634	625 309	742 936	776 062	770 115	747 134	709 122	691 616 p
21	Exports of goods	479 528	549 897	666 725	690 755	687 279	658 062	621 674	605 782 p
22	Exports of services	68 107	75 412	76 211	85 308	82 836	89 072	87 448	85 835 p
23	Imports of goods and services	493 655	585 010	723 014	737 572	698 937	669 058	600 239	580 333 p
24	Imports of goods	397 129	480 813	618 071	624 344	588 411	556 152	480 498	459 014 p
25	Imports of services	96 526	104 197	104 942	113 229	110 526	112 906	119 742	121 319 p
26	**Statistical discrepancy**	**299**	**0**	**0**	**0**	**0**	**0**	**-3 079**	**371** p
27	**Gross domestic product**	**1 151 708**	**1 265 308**	**1 332 681**	**1 377 457**	**1 429 445**	**1 486 079**	**1 564 124**	**1 637 421** p
	AT CONSTANT PRICES, REFERENCE YEAR 2010								
28	**Final consumption expenditure**	**786 332**	**819 821**	**842 339**	**861 259**	**880 130**	**898 109**	**919 531**	**946 247** p
29	Household	589 467	615 228	631 984	639 782	648 429	659 239	673 721	690 613 p
30	NPISH's	20 530	21 485	23 197	28 002	31 942	33 022	33 798	34 417 p
31	Government	176 323	183 109	187 158	193 474	199 783	205 869	212 022	221 179 p
32	Individual	..	..	..	..	..	..	..	..
33	Collective	..	..	..	..	..	..	..	..
34	*of which: Actual individual consumption*	696 139 e	726 261 e	749 673 e	766 004 e	781 870 e	798 469 e	817 117 e	721 205 e
35	**Gross capital formation**	**343 840**	**405 188**	**419 283**	**409 640**	**409 154**	**430 686**	**462 114**	**486 549** p
36	Gross fixed capital formation, total	365 746	385 924	389 124	387 240	400 026	413 488	434 381	457 056 p
37	Dwellings	52 298	46 010	42 311	41 091	50 701	56 342	67 000	81 824 p
38	Other buildings and structures	155 885	154 609	151 441	145 018	145 606	142 041	144 372	152 071 p
39	Transport equipment	31 197	34 066	35 907	35 780	36 893	39 957	43 449	42 581 p
40	Other machinery and equipment	68 641	87 556	91 378	91 663	89 569	94 050	96 732	94 368 p
41	Cultivated assets	..	..	..	..	..	..	..	..
42	Intangible fixed assets	59 045	63 684	68 087	73 954	77 186	81 339	82 778	84 654 p
43	Changes in inventories, acquisitions less disposals of valuables	..	..	..	..	..	..	..	..
44	Changes in inventories	..	..	..	..	..	..	..	..
45	Acquisitions less disposals of valuables	..	..	..	..	..	..	..	..
46	**External balance of goods and services**	**55 939**	**40 299**	**51 012**	**71 549**	**92 063**	**97 859**	**82 006**	**66 987** p
47	Exports of goods and services	554 856	625 309	719 943	756 558	788 788	804 797	803 746	820 983 p
48	Exports of goods	484 518	549 897	643 816	672 052	702 111	709 759	705 633	721 002 p
49	Exports of services	70 418	75 412	76 128	84 662	86 811	95 345	98 395	100 272 p
50	Imports of goods and services	498 917	585 010	668 932	685 009	696 725	706 938	721 740	753 996 p
51	Imports of goods	403 688	480 813	565 289	576 060	583 653	586 728	590 927	612 281 p
52	Imports of services	95 029	104 197	103 643	109 174	113 402	120 734	131 458	141 846 p
53	**Statistical discrepancy (including chaining residual)**	**2 007**	**0**	**-741**	**-481**	**-515**	**319**	**3 137**	**8 482** p
54	**Gross domestic product**	**1 188 118**	**1 265 308**	**1 311 893**	**1 341 967**	**1 380 833**	**1 426 972**	**1 466 788**	**1 508 265** p

Note: Detailed metadata:http://metalinks.oecd.org/nav1/20180308/15e3

Source: Bank of Korea (BOK).

KOREA

Table 2. Gross domestic product, output and income approach
ISIC Rev. 4

Billion KRW

		2009	2010	2011	2012	2013	2014	2015	2016
	OUTPUT APPROACH AT CURRENT PRICES								
1	**Total gross value added at basic prices**	1 044 566	1 145 124	1 209 956	1 251 455	1 303 238	1 354 855	1 423 647	1 485 900 p
2	Agriculture, forestry and fishing	27 033	28 297	30 454	30 775	30 437	31 560	32 612	32 665 p
3	Industry, including energy	323 520	379 602	405 802	416 467	436 366	448 404	471 218	488 241 p
4	Manufacturing	300 037	351 771	379 521	388 010	403 657	408 510	423 652	435 937 p
5	Construction	59 610	58 634	58 587	59 959	64 251	67 267	74 522	84 681 p
6	Services	..	..	..	..	..	..	..	..
7	Distrib. trade, repairs; transp.; accommod., food serv. activ.	158 661	174 890	183 164	190 378	197 024	202 512	212 518	222 829 p
8	Information and communication	43 989	45 364	46 827	48 774	50 589	52 511	54 257	56 194 p
9	Financial and insurance activities	65 352	71 670	77 873	75 809	72 478	75 860	78 700	80 522 p
10	Real estate activities	88 208	91 042	94 716	98 924	103 527	109 549	114 619	118 153 p
11	Prof., scientif., techn. activ.; admin., support service activ.	70 188	77 950	83 277	88 828	94 758	100 937	106 944	110 289 p
12	Public admin.; compulsory s.s.; education; human health	178 719	186 560	196 507	207 232	218 227	229 471	241 066	254 161 p
13	Other service activities	29 286	31 115	32 749	34 309	35 580	36 785	37 191	38 164 p
14	FISIM (Financial Intermediation Services Indirectly Measured)	..	..	..	..	..	..	..	..
15	Gross value added at basic prices, excluding FISIM	1 044 566	1 145 124	1 209 956	1 251 455	1 303 238	1 354 855	1 423 647	1 485 900 p
16	**Taxes less subsidies on products**	107 142	120 184	122 725	126 001	126 207	131 224	140 477	151 521 p
17	Taxes on products	110 305	123 664	126 306	130 018	130 246	135 685	145 258	156 557 p
18	Subsidies on products	3 163	3 480	3 581	4 016	4 039	4 461	4 781	5 036 p
19	Residual item	..	..	..	..	..	..	..	..
20	**Gross domestic product at market prices**	1 151 708	1 265 308	1 332 681	1 377 457	1 429 445	1 486 079	1 564 124	1 637 421 p
	OUTPUT APPROACH AT CONSTANT PRICES (REF. YEAR 2010)								
21	**Total gross value added at basic prices**	1 076 430	1 145 124	1 185 403	1 213 224	1 250 079	1 290 494	1 324 279	1 359 580 p
22	Agriculture, forestry and fishing	29 576	28 297	27 745	27 507	28 358	29 378	29 251	28 414 p
23	Industry, including energy	335 953	379 602	402 646	412 531	426 403	441 138	450 062	460 914 p
24	Manufacturing	309 505	351 771	374 782	383 683	397 426	411 495	418 743	428 334 p
25	Construction	60 878	58 634	55 432	54 431	56 044	56 471	59 691	65 977 p
26	Services	..							
27	Distrib. trade, repairs; transp.; accommod., food serv. activ.	161 699	174 890	183 216	188 643	193 295	197 921	201 624	206 712 p
28	Information and communication	43 953	45 364	47 932	50 199	52 773	55 165	56 532	58 151 p
29	Financial and insurance activities	70 201	71 670	72 741	75 547	78 584	83 021	88 569	90 585 p
30	Real estate activities	89 033	91 042	93 384	93 183	94 000	97 113	98 774	99 296 p
31	Prof., scientif., techn. activ.; admin., support service activ.	73 951	77 950	80 914	83 353	87 245	91 424	95 714	97 695 p
32	Public admin.; compulsory s.s.; education; human health	181 135	186 560	189 929	195 994	200 971	206 443	211 884	218 601 p
33	Other service activities	29 957	31 115	31 466	31 973	32 683	33 106	33 000	33 445 p
34	FISIM (Financial Intermediation Services Indirectly Measured)	..	..	..	..	..	..	..	..
35	Gross value added at basic prices, excluding FISIM	1 076 430	1 145 124	1 185 403	1 213 224	1 250 079	1 290 494	1 324 279	1 359 580 p
36	**Taxes less subsidies on products**	111 675	120 184	126 490	128 708	130 627	136 455	142 688	149 067 p
37	Taxes on products	..							
38	Subsidies on products	..							
39	Residual item	13	0	0	34	127	24	-179	-382 p
40	**Gross domestic product at market prices**	1 188 118	1 265 308	1 311 893	1 341 967	1 380 833	1 426 972	1 466 788	1 508 265 p
	INCOME APPROACH								
41	**Compensation of employees**	500 935	536 350	570 367	599 309	629 400	661 406	698 570	..
42	Agriculture, forestry and fishing	3 672	3 835	4 149	4 244	4 347	4 276	4 567	..
43	Industry, including energy	134 537	150 312	163 207	174 375	182 984	192 143	200 395	..
44	Manufacturing	126 722	142 024	154 527	164 560	172 879	182 132	189 011	..
45	Construction	44 049	44 983	44 998	46 539	50 567	52 640	57 513	..
46	Distrib. trade, repairs; transp.; accommod., food serv. activ.	69 974	75 336	80 069	83 362	86 736	90 456	98 158	..
47	Information and communication	20 015	20 391	22 240	23 072	24 515	25 601	26 757	..
48	Financial and insurance activities	27 816	29 412	30 702	30 155	30 671	32 492	34 040	..
49	Real estate activities	8 518	8 984	9 753	9 476	9 419	9 839	10 733	..
50	Prof., scientif., techn. activ.; admin., support service activ.	46 423	52 343	56 282	60 542	64 026	69 028	72 532	..
51	Public admin.; compulsory s.s.; education; human health	129 914	133 821	140 736	148 500	156 815	165 394	173 928	..
52	Other service activities	16 018	16 935	18 230	19 043	19 321	19 537	19 948	..
53	**Wages and salaries**	436 257	467 508	495 153	519 229	545 166	566 998	594 920	626 550 p
54	Agriculture, forestry and fishing	..	..	..	..	..	..	..	
55	Industry, including energy	..	..	..	..	..	..	..	
56	Manufacturing	..	..	..	..	..	..	..	
57	Construction	..	..	..	..	..	..	..	
58	Distrib. trade, repairs; transp.; accommod., food serv. activ.	..	..	..	..	..	..	..	
59	Information and communication	..	..	..	..	..	..	..	
60	Financial and insurance activities	..	..	..	..	..	..	..	
61	Real estate activities	..	..	..	..	..	..	..	
62	Prof., scientif., techn. activ.; admin., support service activ.	..	..	..	..	..	..	..	
63	Public admin.; compulsory s.s.; education; human health	..	..	..	..	..	..	..	
64	Other service activities	..	..	..	..	..	..	..	
65	**Gross operating surplus and mixed income**	531 178	595 120	625 067	636 915	658 174	676 745	706 775	730 463 p
66	**Taxes less subsidies on production and imports**	119 595	133 838	137 248	141 233	141 871	147 929	158 779	170 823 p
67	Taxes on production and imports	122 907	137 470	140 963	145 398	146 075	152 559	163 707	176 017 p
68	Subsidies on production and imports	3 312	3 632	3 715	4 164	4 203	4 631	4 929	5 194 p
69	Residual item	..	..	..	..	..	..	..	..
70	**Gross domestic product**	1 151 708	1 265 308	1 332 681	1 377 457	1 429 445	1 486 079	1 564 124	1 637 421 p

Note: Detailed metadata:http://metalinks.oecd.org/nav1/20180308/15e3
Source: Bank of Korea (BOK).

KOREA

Table 3. Disposable income, saving and net lending / net borrowing

Billion KRW

		2009	2010	2011	2012	2013	2014	2015	2016
	DISPOSABLE INCOME								
1	**Gross domestic product**	**1 151 708**	**1 265 308**	**1 332 681**	**1 377 457**	**1 429 445**	**1 486 079**	**1 564 124**	**1 637 421 p**
2	Net primary incomes from the rest of the world	-2 726	1 272	7 849	14 139	10 199	4 685	4 259	1 646 p
3	Primary incomes receivable from the rest of the world	21 207	27 794	31 876	35 283	34 244	29 323	27 228	26 753 p
4	Primary incomes payable to the rest of the world	23 933	26 522	24 027	21 144	24 045	24 639	22 969	25 107 p
5	**Gross national income at market prices**	**1 148 982**	**1 266 580**	**1 340 530**	**1 391 596**	**1 439 644**	**1 490 764**	**1 568 383**	**1 639 067 p**
6	Consumption of fixed capital	221 748 e	232 133 e	252 382 e	267 390 e	279 102 e	291 307 e	305 680 e	320 714 e
7	**Net national income at market prices**	**927 234**	**1 034 447**	**1 088 148**	**1 124 206**	**1 160 543**	**1 199 457**	**1 262 703**	**1 318 352 p**
8	Net current transfers from the rest of the world	-2 472	-6 125	-5 209	-6 150	-4 547	-5 247	-5 646	-6 453 p
9	Current transfers receivable from the rest of the world	10 254	8 159	9 347	9 642	9 614	9 342	10 013	10 162 p
10	Current transfers payable to the rest of the world	12 726	14 284	14 555	15 792	14 161	14 589	15 659	16 614 p
11	**Net national disposable income**	**924 761**	**1 028 322**	**1 082 939**	**1 118 055**	**1 155 996**	**1 194 210**	**1 257 057**	**1 311 900 p**
	SAVING AND NET LENDING / NET BORROWING								
12	**Net national disposable income**	**924 761**	**1 028 322**	**1 082 939**	**1 118 055**	**1 155 996**	**1 194 210**	**1 257 057**	**1 311 900 p**
13	Final consumption expenditures	769 589	819 821	873 523	911 938	942 267	972 925	1 006 006	1 047 482 p
14	Adj. for change in net equity of households in pension funds	3 318	7 788	8 652	11 941	10 116	10 349	8 658	4 750 p
15	**Saving, net**	**155 173**	**208 501**	**209 417**	**206 117**	**213 729**	**221 285**	**251 051**	**264 417 p**
16	Net capital transfers from the rest of the world	..	..	..	..	..	..	..	..
17	Capital transfers receivable from the rest of the world	..	..	..	..	..	..	..	..
18	Capital transfers payable to the rest of the world	..	..	..	..	..	..	..	..
19	Gross capital formation	327 841	405 188	439 236	427 029	416 000	435 078	452 315	478 284 p
20	Acquisitions less disposals of non-financial non-produced assets	88	85	126	43	33	10	97	52 p
21	Consumption of fixed capital	221 748	232 133	252 382	267 390	279 102	291 307	305 680	320 714 p
22	**Net lending / net borrowing**	**48 991**	**35 374**	**22 436**	**46 431**	**76 801**	**77 505**	**104 348**	**106 434 p**
	REAL DISPOSABLE INCOME								
23	**Gross domestic product at constant prices, reference year 2010**	**1 188 118**	**1 265 308**	**1 311 893**	**1 341 967**	**1 380 833**	**1 426 972**	**1 466 788**	**1 508 265 p**
24	Trading gain or loss	-1 231 e	0 e	-31 124 e	-34 667 e	-24 019 e	-25 013 e	13 491 e	26 858 e
25	**Real gross domestic income**	**1 186 888 e**	**1 265 308 e**	**1 280 768 e**	**1 307 299 e**	**1 356 814 e**	**1 401 960 e**	**1 480 279 e**	**1 535 123 e**
26	Net real primary incomes from the rest of the world	6 119 e	1 272 e	7 543 e	13 419 e	9 681 e	4 419 e	4 031 e	1 543 e
27	Real primary incomes receivable from the rest of the world	29 462 e	27 794 e	30 634 e	33 485 e	32 504 e	27 663 e	25 769 e	25 081 e
28	Real primary incomes payable to the rest of the world	23 342 e	26 522 e	23 091 e	20 067 e	22 823 e	23 244 e	21 738 e	23 538 e
29	**Real gross national income at market prices**	**1 199 136 e**	**1 266 580 e**	**1 288 311 e**	**1 320 718 e**	**1 366 495 e**	**1 406 379 e**	**1 484 310 e**	**1 536 666 e**
30	Net real current transfers from the rest of the world	-4 194 e	-6 125 e	-5 006 e	-5 837 e	-4 316 e	-4 950 e	-5 343 e	-6 049 e
31	Real current transfers receivable from the rest of the world	8 863 e	8 159 e	8 982 e	9 151 e	9 126 e	8 813 e	9 476 e	9 527 e
32	Real current transfers payable to the rest of the world	13 056 e	14 284 e	13 988 e	14 987 e	13 441 e	13 763 e	14 819 e	15 576 e
33	**Real gross national disposable income**	**1 196 336 e**	**1 260 455 e**	**1 283 306 e**	**1 314 881 e**	**1 362 179 e**	**1 401 429 e**	**1 478 967 e**	**1 530 616 e**
34	Consumption of fixed capital at constant prices	..	..	..	..	..	..	..	..
35	**Real net national income at market prices**	**972 414 e**	**1 034 447 e**	**1 045 761 e**	**1 066 947 e**	**1 101 574 e**	**1 131 561 e**	**1 195 016 e**	**1 235 988 e**
36	**Real net national disposable income**	**969 355 e**	**1 028 322 e**	**1 040 755 e**	**1 061 110 e**	**1 097 259 e**	**1 126 611 e**	**1 189 672 e**	**1 229 939 e**

Note: Detailed metadata:http://metalinks.oecd.org/nav1/20180308/ec1a
Source: Bank of Korea (BOK).

Table 4. Population and employment (persons) and employment (hours worked) by industry
ISIC Rev. 4

		2009	2010	2011	2012	2013	2014	2015	2016
	POPULATION, THOUSAND PERSONS, NATIONAL CONCEPT								
1	**Total population**	**49 308.0**	**49 554.0**	**49 937.0**	**50 200.0**	**50 429.0**	**50 747.0**	**51 015.0**	**51 246.0**
2	Economically active population	..	..	..	..	..	..	..	..
3	Unemployed persons	..	..	..	..	..	..	..	..
4	Total employment	23 506.0	23 829.0	24 244.0	24 681.0	25 066.0	25 599.0	25 936.0	26 235.0
5	Employees	16 454.0	16 971.0	17 397.0	17 712.0	18 195.0	18 743.0	19 230.0	19 546.0
6	Self-employed	7 052.0	6 858.0	6 847.0	6 969.0	6 872.0	6 857.0	6 706.0	6 689.0
	TOTAL EMPLOYMENT, THOUSAND PERSONS, DOMESTIC CONCEPT								
7	Agriculture, forestry and fishing	1 648.2	1 566.4	1 541.7	1 528.0	1 520.1	1 452.0	1 344.9	1 286.3
8	Industry, including energy	4 026.4	4 191.7	4 254.2	4 268.3	4 362.6	4 512.8	4 680.3	4 685.3
9	Manufacturing	3 836.3	4 027.5	4 090.8	4 104.9	4 184.0	4 329.6	4 485.9	4 481.3
10	Construction	1 720.1	1 752.9	1 750.7	1 772.9	1 753.8	1 795.7	1 822.9	1 844.9
11	Distrib. trade, repairs; transp.; accommod., food serv. activ.	6 783.3	6 749.3	6 823.6	6 974.8	7 043.5	7 295.9	7 371.4	7 418.5
12	Information and communication	652.0	667.8	703.0	700.2	692.0	713.7	771.6	785.5
13	Financial and insurance activities	766.0	807.6	845.7	841.6	863.7	837.4	789.1	796.5
14	Real estate activities	500.2	516.8	486.0	485.7	485.1	507.6	534.6	570.4
15	Prof., scientif., techn. activ.; admin., support service activ.	1 787.9	1 906.0	2 047.2	2 144.3	2 195.0	2 204.6	2 296.4	2 394.6
16	Public admin.; compulsory s.s.; education; human health	3 860.8	3 911.6	3 948.2	4 094.1	4 267.3	4 457.1	4 523.5	4 690.1
17	Other service activities	1 760.6	1 758.8	1 844.0	1 870.7	1 883.2	1 822.6	1 801.7	1 763.1
18	**Total employment**	**23 505.5**	**23 828.9**	**24 244.3**	**24 680.6**	**25 066.6**	**25 599.4**	**25 936.3**	**26 235.2**
	EMPLOYEES, THOUSAND PERSONS, DOMESTIC CONCEPT								
19	Agriculture, forestry and fishing	172.7	174.5	173.4	153.3	147.3	140.3	135.2	132.5
20	Industry, including energy	3 455.6	3 594.2	3 664.9	3 703.9	3 838.3	3 999.0	4 180.9	4 169.7
21	Manufacturing	3 277.1	3 439.6	3 508.8	3 548.8	3 668.0	3 826.3	3 996.3	3 974.3
22	Construction	1 361.1	1 362.2	1 347.7	1 328.7	1 336.5	1 365.5	1 388.4	1 422.7
23	Distrib. trade, repairs; transp.; accommod., food serv. activ.	3 727.5	3 847.9	3 909.4	3 977.6	4 083.4	4 327.6	4 417.4	4 432.3
24	Information and communication	608.5	608.0	636.2	643.5	638.6	647.4	703.3	707.4
25	Financial and insurance activities	737.2	778.4	812.5	809.6	833.8	806.6	758.8	762.8
26	Real estate activities	313.4	337.9	312.2	320.8	333.6	359.0	369.1	381.8
27	Prof., scientif., techn. activ.; admin., support service activ.	1 610.6	1 723.5	1 880.2	1 958.7	2 007.6	1 986.2	2 073.5	2 178.2
28	Public admin.; compulsory s.s.; education; human health	3 422.6	3 476.7	3 543.2	3 671.8	3 805.7	3 979.3	4 063.3	4 255.8
29	Other service activities	1 044.5	1 067.1	1 117.3	1 144.2	1 169.9	1 131.6	1 139.9	1 103.3
30	**Total employees**	**16 453.7**	**16 970.6**	**17 397.1**	**17 712.1**	**18 194.7**	**18 742.5**	**19 229.8**	**19 546.4**
	SELF-EMPLOYED, THOUSAND PERSONS, DOMESTIC CONCEPT								
31	Agriculture, forestry and fishing	1 475.6	1 391.8	1 368.3	1 374.7	1 372.8	1 311.7	1 209.7	1 153.8
32	Industry, including energy	570.8	597.4	589.4	564.4	524.2	513.9	499.4	515.5
33	Manufacturing	559.2	587.9	582.0	556.1	516.0	503.3	489.6	507.1
34	Construction	359.0	390.7	402.9	444.2	417.3	430.2	434.5	422.2
35	Distrib. trade, repairs; transp.; accommod., food serv. activ.	3 055.8	2 901.4	2 914.2	2 997.2	2 960.3	2 968.2	2 953.9	2 986.2
36	Information and communication	43.5	59.7	66.8	56.7	53.5	66.3	68.3	78.2
37	Financial and insurance activities	28.9	29.2	33.2	31.9	29.8	30.8	30.3	33.7
38	Real estate activities	186.8	178.9	173.8	165.0	151.5	148.5	165.5	188.6
39	Prof., scientif., techn. activ.; admin., support service activ.	177.3	182.5	167.0	186.0	187.5	218.4	222.8	216.5
40	Public admin.; compulsory s.s.; education; human health	438.2	434.8	405.0	422.3	461.6	477.8	460.2	434.3
41	Other service activities	716.1	691.7	726.8	726.5	713.4	691.0	661.8	659.8
42	**Total self-employed**	**7 051.9**	**6 858.2**	**6 847.2**	**6 968.6**	**6 871.8**	**6 856.9**	**6 706.4**	**6 688.8**
	TOTAL EMPLOYMENT, MILLION HOURS, DOMESTIC CONCEPT								
43	Industry, including energy	..	..	..	..	..	..	..	..
44	Distrib. trade, repairs; transp.; accommod., food serv. activ.	..	..	..	..	..	..	..	..
45	Financial and insurance activities	..	..	..	..	..	..	..	..
46	Prof., scientif., techn. activ.; admin., support service activ.	..	..	..	..	..	..	..	..
47	Public admin.; compulsory s.s.; education; human health	..	..	..	..	..	..	..	..
48	**Total employment**	**50 961.2**	**51 400.5**	**51 571.2**	**51 909.0**	**52 495.2**	**52 973.2**	**53 851.4**	**54 131.9**
	EMPLOYEES, MILLION HOURS, DOMESTIC CONCEPT								
49	Industry, including energy	..	..	..	..	..	..	..	..
50	Distrib. trade, repairs; transp.; accommod., food serv. activ.	..	..	..	..	..	..	..	..
51	Financial and insurance activities	..	..	..	..	..	..	..	..
52	Prof., scientif., techn. activ.; admin., support service activ.	..	..	..	..	..	..	..	..
53	Public admin.; compulsory s.s.; education; human health	..	..	..	..	..	..	..	..
54	**Total employees**	..	..	..	..	..	..	..	..
	SELF-EMPLOYED, MILLION HOURS, DOMESTIC CONCEPT								
55	Industry, including energy	..	..	..	..	..	..	..	..
56	Distrib. trade, repairs; transp.; accommod., food serv. activ.	..	..	..	..	..	..	..	..
57	Financial and insurance activities	..	..	..	..	..	..	..	..
58	Prof., scientif., techn. activ.; admin., support service activ.	..	..	..	..	..	..	..	..
59	Public admin.; compulsory s.s.; education; human health	..	..	..	..	..	..	..	..
60	**Total self-employed**	..	..	..	..	..	..	..	..

Note: Detailed metadata:http://metalinks.oecd.org/nav1/20180308/582e
Source: Bank of Korea (BOK).

LATVIA

Table 1. Gross domestic product, expenditure approach

Million EUR (2014 LVL euro)

		2009	2010	2011	2012	2013	2014	2015	2016
	AT CURRENT PRICES								
1	**Final consumption expenditure**	**14 992**	**14 737**	**16 203**	**17 130**	**18 061**	**18 604**	**19 037**	**19 822**
2	Household	11 206	11 249	12 285	13 065	13 780	14 178	14 393	15 040
3	NPISH's	207	194	220	266	260	291	285	279
4	Government	3 580	3 295	3 698	3 799	4 022	4 136	4 358	4 502
5	Individual	1 716	1 552	1 690	1 737	1 866	1 930	2 073	2 218
6	Collective	1 864	1 743	2 008	2 062	2 156	2 206	2 285	2 284
7	*of which: Actual individual consumption*	13 129	12 994	14 195	15 068	15 906	16 398	16 752	17 538
8	**Gross capital formation**	**4 139**	**3 465**	**5 111**	**5 729**	**5 534**	**5 355**	**5 407**	**4 881**
9	Gross fixed capital formation, total	4 244	3 478	4 502	5 551	5 291	5 337	5 384	4 538
10	Dwellings	453	295	381	492	507	601	597	493
11	Other buildings and structures	2 318	1 610	1 955	2 510	2 223	2 410	2 394	1 924
12	Transport equipment	197	237	449	544	553	462	500	522
13	Other machinery and equipment	..	..	..	..	..	..	..	..
14	Cultivated assets	17	21	5	4	12	7	6	6
15	Intangible fixed assets	286	283	324	323	421	403	423	354
16	Changes in inventories, acquisitions less disposals of valuables	-105	-13	608	177	243	18	23	344
17	Changes in inventories	-105	-14	608	177	242	17	18	340
18	Acquisitions less disposals of valuables	1	1	1	1	1	1	5	4
19	**External balance of goods and services**	**-305**	**-264**	**-1 011**	**-973**	**-809**	**-341**	**-124**	**223**
20	Exports of goods and services	8 021	9 625	11 738	13 418	13 741	14 346	14 690	14 966
21	Exports of goods	5 014	6 657	8 300	9 645	9 810	10 242	10 336	10 391
22	Exports of services	3 006	2 968	3 438	3 773	3 931	4 104	4 355	4 575
23	Imports of goods and services	8 326	9 889	12 749	14 391	14 550	14 687	14 815	14 742
24	Imports of goods	6 593	8 199	10 812	12 282	12 430	12 621	12 538	12 309
25	Imports of services	1 732	1 690	1 937	2 109	2 120	2 066	2 276	2 433
26	**Statistical discrepancy**	**0**	**0**	**0**	**0**	**0**	**0**	**0**	**0**
27	**Gross domestic product**	**18 827**	**17 938**	**20 303**	**21 886**	**22 787**	**23 618**	**24 320**	**24 927**
	AT CONSTANT PRICES, REFERENCE YEAR 2010								
28	**Final consumption expenditure**	**14 708**	**14 737**	**15 176**	**15 555**	**16 223**	**16 464**	**16 853**	**17 386**
29	Household	10 925	11 249	11 568	11 900	12 525	12 680	13 016	13 459
30	NPISH's	205	194	213	253	241	262	250	244
31	Government	3 586	3 295	3 395	3 404	3 460	3 525	3 590	3 689
32	Individual	1 620	1 552	1 632	1 670	1 707	1 769	1 826	1 942
33	Collective	1 975	1 743	1 762	1 738	1 757	1 763	1 775	1 765
34	*of which: Actual individual consumption*	12 753	12 994	13 414	13 822	14 476	14 713	15 094	15 648
35	**Gross capital formation**	**4 316**	**3 465**	**5 190**	**5 143**	**4 877**	**4 442**	**4 562**	**4 570**
36	Gross fixed capital formation, total	4 335	3 478	4 314	4 935	4 637	4 640	4 617	3 926
37	Dwellings	416	295	299	341	336	369	397	305
38	Other buildings and structures	2 315	1 610	1 874	2 271	1 996	2 201	2 153	1 747
39	Transport equipment	223	237	456	498	492	406	425	460
40	Other machinery and equipment	..	..	..	..	..	..	..	..
41	Cultivated assets	24	21	4	4	10	7	5	5
42	Intangible fixed assets	299	283	296	261	332	302	308	244
43	Changes in inventories, acquisitions less disposals of valuables	..	..	..	..	..	..	..	..
44	Changes in inventories	..	..	..	..	..	..	..	..
45	Acquisitions less disposals of valuables	..	..	..	..	..	..	..	..
46	**External balance of goods and services**	**-313**	**-264**	**-1 284**	**-879**	**-798**	**-234**	**-128**	**-195**
47	Exports of goods and services	8 484	9 625	10 784	11 839	11 967	12 682	13 060	13 593
48	Exports of goods	5 448	6 657	7 402	8 284	8 280	8 767	8 828	9 122
49	Exports of services	3 002	2 968	3 382	3 538	3 678	3 908	4 247	4 495
50	Imports of goods and services	8 798	9 889	12 068	12 718	12 764	12 916	13 189	13 787
51	Imports of goods	7 088	8 199	10 196	10 742	10 819	11 046	11 213	11 706
52	Imports of services	1 691	1 690	1 872	1 976	1 943	1 863	1 970	2 074
53	**Statistical discrepancy (including chaining residual)**	**-38**	**0**	**0**	**34**	**33**	**41**	**42**	**39**
54	**Gross domestic product**	**18 674**	**17 938**	**19 083**	**19 852**	**20 335**	**20 713**	**21 328**	**21 800**

Note: Detailed metadata:http://metalinks.oecd.org/nav1/20180308/dc51
Source: Central Statistical Bureau of Latvia (CSB) via Eurostat.

LATVIA

Table 2. Gross domestic product, output and income approach
ISIC Rev. 4

Million EUR (2014 LVL euro)

		2009	2010	2011	2012	2013	2014	2015	2016
	OUTPUT APPROACH AT CURRENT PRICES								
1	**Total gross value added at basic prices**	**16 931**	**15 947**	**18 038**	**19 364**	**20 073**	**20 795**	**21 362**	**21 685**
2	Agriculture, forestry and fishing	622	707	700	716	747	789	886	854
3	Industry, including energy	2 650	2 927	3 193	3 353	3 331	3 265	3 369	3 478
4	Manufacturing	1 852	2 156	2 400	2 557	2 561	2 567	2 558	2 661
5	Construction	1 313	803	1 074	1 244	1 320	1 397	1 386	1 149
6	Services	..	..	..	..	..	..	..	..
7	Distrib. trade, repairs; transp.; accommod., food serv. activ.	4 606	4 437	4 870	5 104	5 241	5 428	5 467	5 509
8	Information and communication	714	739	783	844	898	920	977	1 056
9	Financial and insurance activities	608	539	727	806	818	943	1 003	1 081
10	Real estate activities	1 899	1 635	1 997	2 317	2 549	2 759	2 674	2 682
11	Prof., scientif., techn. activ.; admin., support service activ.	1 193	1 168	1 396	1 474	1 496	1 457	1 603	1 718
12	Public admin.; compulsory s.s.; education; human health	2 878	2 548	2 778	2 923	3 073	3 222	3 368	3 501
13	Other service activities	447	445	520	583	599	614	629	657
14	**FISIM (Financial Intermediation Services Indirectly Measured)**	..	..	..	..	..	..	..	..
15	**Gross value added at basic prices, excluding FISIM**	**16 931**	**15 947**	**18 038**	**19 364**	**20 073**	**20 795**	**21 362**	**21 685**
16	**Taxes less subsidies on products**	**1 896**	**1 991**	**2 265**	**2 522**	**2 714**	**2 823**	**2 959**	**3 241**
17	Taxes on products	1 974	2 032	2 277	2 531	2 723	2 871	3 039	3 275
18	Subsidies on products	78	41	12	9	9	48	80	34
19	**Residual item**	**0**	**0**	**0**	**0**	**0**	**0**	**0**	**0**
20	**Gross domestic product at market prices**	**18 827**	**17 938**	**20 303**	**21 886**	**22 787**	**23 618**	**24 320**	**24 927**
	OUTPUT APPROACH AT CONSTANT PRICES (REF. YEAR 2010)								
21	**Total gross value added at basic prices**	**16 713**	**15 947**	**16 967**	**17 519**	**17 839**	**18 120**	**18 572**	**18 839**
22	Agriculture, forestry and fishing	736	707	695	746	780	781	879	873
23	Industry, including energy	2 705	2 927	2 993	3 039	2 968	2 907	3 020	3 184
24	Manufacturing	1 889	2 156	2 267	2 365	2 319	2 328	2 337	2 467
25	Construction	1 221	803	1 042	1 133	1 175	1 239	1 217	998
26	Services	..	..	..	..	..	..	..	..
27	Distrib. trade, repairs; transp.; accommod., food serv. activ.	4 570	4 437	4 812	4 941	5 050	5 233	5 310	5 451
28	Information and communication	726	739	765	813	857	836	853	888
29	Financial and insurance activities	624	539	494	514	514	573	601	619
30	Real estate activities	1 694	1 635	1 646	1 703	1 790	1 815	1 840	1 844
31	Prof., scientif., techn. activ.; admin., support service activ.	1 256	1 168	1 383	1 452	1 457	1 380	1 463	1 514
32	Public admin.; compulsory s.s.; education; human health	2 736	2 548	2 626	2 619	2 678	2 770	2 815	2 887
33	Other service activities	414	445	513	563	568	557	552	564
34	**FISIM (Financial Intermediation Services Indirectly Measured)**	..	..	..	..	..	..	..	..
35	**Gross value added at basic prices, excluding FISIM**	**16 713**	**15 947**	**16 967**	**17 519**	**17 839**	**18 120**	**18 572**	**18 839**
36	**Taxes less subsidies on products**	**1 956**	**1 991**	**2 115**	**2 333**	**2 497**	**2 595**	**2 765**	**2 980**
37	Taxes on products	2 000	2 032	2 128	2 346	2 511	2 610	2 754	2 931
38	Subsidies on products	42	41	13	14	14	15	7	4
39	**Residual item**	**5**	**0**	**0**	**1**	**-1**	**-3**	**-8**	**-19**
40	**Gross domestic product at market prices**	**18 674**	**17 938**	**19 083**	**19 852**	**20 335**	**20 713**	**21 328**	**21 800**
	INCOME APPROACH								
41	**Compensation of employees**	**8 829**	**7 694**	**8 014**	**8 747**	**9 416**	**10 093**	**10 908**	**11 574**
42	Agriculture, forestry and fishing	225	223	230	238	249	306	329	353
43	Industry, including energy	1 280	1 247	1 293	1 443	1 528	1 576	1 669	1 784
44	Manufacturing	1 001	976	1 020	1 152	1 226	1 263	1 343	1 434
45	Construction	736	576	585	644	732	830	861	839
46	Distrib. trade, repairs; transp.; accommod., food serv. activ.	2 344	2 124	2 150	2 392	2 556	2 745	2 986	3 142
47	Information and communication	359	309	332	398	439	493	586	671
48	Financial and insurance activities	430	351	364	379	388	405	419	464
49	Real estate activities	255	222	233	254	263	291	297	321
50	Prof., scientif., techn. activ.; admin., support service activ.	622	578	637	714	782	843	958	1 022
51	Public admin.; compulsory s.s.; education; human health	2 306	1 836	1 947	2 021	2 170	2 298	2 444	2 594
52	Other service activities	272	228	242	263	308	305	358	384
53	**Wages and salaries**	**7 295**	**6 400**	**6 647**	**7 255**	**7 797**	**8 401**	**9 091**	**9 599**
54	Agriculture, forestry and fishing	191	188	193	199	208	257	279	298
55	Industry, including energy	1 065	1 033	1 058	1 185	1 251	1 299	1 375	1 464
56	Manufacturing	849	821	844	958	1 015	1 053	1 119	1 193
57	Construction	660	511	510	562	637	729	756	739
58	Distrib. trade, repairs; transp.; accommod., food serv. activ.	2 003	1 794	1 802	2 006	2 144	2 316	2 518	2 641
59	Information and communication	304	257	276	333	368	414	497	561
60	Financial and insurance activities	325	276	289	293	305	327	341	367
61	Real estate activities	223	191	200	220	227	253	259	277
62	Prof., scientif., techn. activ.; admin., support service activ.	533	493	546	613	672	727	829	879
63	Public admin.; compulsory s.s.; education; human health	1 765	1 463	1 569	1 622	1 727	1 823	1 934	2 049
64	Other service activities	226	193	203	222	259	256	304	325
65	**Gross operating surplus and mixed income**	**8 351**	**8 538**	**10 271**	**10 999**	**11 064**	**10 956**	**10 608**	**10 403**
66	**Taxes less subsidies on production and imports**	**1 646**	**1 706**	**2 018**	**2 140**	**2 307**	**2 569**	**2 804**	**2 949**
67	Taxes on production and imports	2 068	2 226	2 509	2 790	2 983	3 185	3 355	3 611
68	Subsidies on production and imports	422	520	491	651	676	616	551	662
69	**Residual item**	**0**	**0**	**0**	**0**	**0**	**0**	**0**	**0**
70	**Gross domestic product**	**18 827**	**17 938**	**20 303**	**21 886**	**22 787**	**23 618**	**24 320**	**24 927**

Note: Detailed metadata:http://metalinks.oecd.org/nav1/20180308/dc51
Source: Central Statistical Bureau of Latvia (CSB) via Eurostat.

Table 3. Disposable income, saving and net lending / net borrowing

Million EUR (2014 LVL euro)

		2009	2010	2011	2012	2013	2014	2015	2016
	DISPOSABLE INCOME								
1	**Gross domestic product**	**18 827**	**17 938**	**20 303**	**21 886**	**22 832**	**23 682**	**24 353**	**24 927**
2	Net primary incomes from the rest of the world	1 332	226	-6	-149	-48	-84	-137	-60
3	Primary incomes receivable from the rest of the world	1 150	944	1 109	1 253	1 224	1 174	1 318	1 398
4	Primary incomes payable to the rest of the world	-182	719	1 114	1 402	1 272	1 258	1 455	1 458
5	**Gross national income at market prices**	**20 158**	**18 163**	**20 297**	**21 737**	**22 784**	**23 597**	**24 216**	**24 867**
6	Consumption of fixed capital	4 440	4 540	4 963	5 444	5 536	5 648	5 599	5 573
7	**Net national income at market prices**	**15 718**	**13 623**	**15 335**	**16 293**	**17 247**	**17 950**	**18 617**	**19 294**
8	Net current transfers from the rest of the world	460	420	392	303	299	15	145	180
9	Current transfers receivable from the rest of the world	1 204	961	1 028	1 052	1 084	813	903	905
10	Current transfers payable to the rest of the world	743	541	636	749	785	798	758	725
11	**Net national disposable income**	**16 178**	**14 043**	**15 727**	**16 596**	**17 546**	**17 965**	**18 762**	**19 474**
	SAVING AND NET LENDING / NET BORROWING								
12	**Net national disposable income**	**16 178**	**14 043**	**15 727**	**16 596**	**17 546**	**17 965**	**18 762**	**19 474**
13	Final consumption expenditures	14 992	14 737	16 203	17 130	18 061	18 604	19 037	19 812
14	Adj. for change in net equity of households in pension funds	0	0	0	0	0	0	0	0
15	**Saving, net**	**1 186**	**-694**	**-476**	**-535**	**-515**	**-639**	**-275**	**-338**
16	Net capital transfers from the rest of the world	452	353	429	654	571	752	675	249
17	Capital transfers receivable from the rest of the world	462	364	437	660	576	756	680	262
18	Capital transfers payable to the rest of the world	11	11	8	7	5	4	5	13
19	Gross capital formation	4 139	3 465	5 111	5 729	5 579	5 419	5 440	4 891
20	Acquisitions less disposals of non-financial non-produced assets	0	1	0	1	-2	-2	0	0
21	Consumption of fixed capital	4 440	4 540	4 963	5 444	5 536	5 648	5 599	5 573
22	**Net lending / net borrowing**	**1 938**	**733**	**-195**	**-166**	**15**	**343**	**559**	**593**
	REAL DISPOSABLE INCOME								
23	**Gross domestic product at constant prices, reference year 2010**	**18 674**	**17 938**	**19 082**	**19 852**	**20 335**	**20 713**	**21 328**	**21 800**
24	Trading gain or loss	6	0	318	-26	88	-50	6	349
25	**Real gross domestic income**	**18 680**	**17 938**	**19 401**	**19 826**	**20 423**	**20 662**	**21 334**	**22 149**
26	Net real primary incomes from the rest of the world	1 321	226	-5	-135	-43	-73	-120	-53
27	Real primary incomes receivable from the rest of the world	1 141	944	1 060	1 135	1 095	1 025	1 154	1 242
28	Real primary incomes payable to the rest of the world	-180	719	1 065	1 270	1 138	1 098	1 275	1 295
29	**Real gross national income at market prices**	**20 001**	**18 163**	**19 395**	**19 692**	**20 380**	**20 589**	**21 214**	**22 095**
30	Net real current transfers from the rest of the world	457	420	375	275	267	13	127	160
31	Real current transfers receivable from the rest of the world	1 194	961	983	953	970	709	791	804
32	Real current transfers payable to the rest of the world	737	541	608	678	702	696	664	644
33	**Real gross national disposable income**	**20 458**	**18 583**	**19 770**	**19 966**	**20 648**	**20 602**	**21 341**	**22 256**
34	Consumption of fixed capital at constant prices	4 536	4 540	4 615	4 660	4 679	4 680	4 602	4 625
35	**Real net national income at market prices**	**15 596**	**13 623**	**14 653**	**14 760**	**15 428**	**15 661**	**16 309**	**17 144**
36	**Real net national disposable income**	**16 053**	**14 043**	**15 028**	**15 034**	**15 695**	**15 675**	**16 437**	**17 304**

Note: Detailed metadata:http://metalinks.oecd.org/nav1/20180308/9040
Source: Central Statistical Bureau of Latvia (CSB) via Eurostat.

LATVIA

Table 4. Population and employment (persons) and employment (hours worked) by industry
ISIC Rev. 4

		2009	2010	2011	2012	2013	2014	2015	2016
	POPULATION, THOUSAND PERSONS, NATIONAL CONCEPT								
1	**Total population**	**2 142.0**	**2 097.3**	**2 058.8**	**2 033.7**	**2 012.8**	**1 994.3**	**1 977.3**	**1 959.3**
2	Economically active population	..	..	..	..	..	..	..	..
3	Unemployed persons	..	..	..	..	..	..	..	..
4	Total employment	910.3	853.0	863.7	878.8	897.3	888.2	902.1	899.9
5	Employees	803.7	753.2	764.0	776.9	791.3	784.0	787.9	783.5
6	Self-employed	106.6	99.8	99.7	101.8	106.0	104.2	114.2	116.4
	TOTAL EMPLOYMENT, THOUSAND PERSONS, DOMESTIC CONCEPT								
7	Agriculture, forestry and fishing	76.3	66.2	68.6	68.0	67.8	65.2	69.8	67.4
8	Industry, including energy	141.7	138.4	142.2	148.0	148.9	141.4	140.6	141.0
9	Manufacturing	117.8	116.7	120.6	126.3	126.3	120.0	118.5	118.9
10	Construction	72.8	58.4	61.7	60.8	64.6	66.7	65.5	60.2
11	Distrib. trade, repairs; transp.; accommod., food serv. activ.	262.5	254.0	245.1	239.5	243.5	244.1	247.8	245.3
12	Information and communication	19.6	19.9	21.5	21.8	24.1	26.9	28.7	30.7
13	Financial and insurance activities	19.3	17.2	17.4	16.9	16.1	15.6	15.9	16.5
14	Real estate activities	21.3	19.2	19.5	20.3	21.5	22.0	22.2	22.1
15	Prof., scientif., techn. activ.; admin., support service activ.	58.5	53.6	58.6	70.3	76.6	75.0	77.7	77.5
16	Public admin.; compulsory s.s.; education; human health	191.1	178.3	182.4	184.0	183.5	179.9	179.8	181.9
17	Other service activities	40.5	38.2	39.2	39.1	42.1	39.8	40.9	43.7
18	**Total employment**	**903.7**	**843.5**	**856.2**	**868.6**	**888.6**	**876.6**	**889.0**	**886.3**
	EMPLOYEES, THOUSAND PERSONS, DOMESTIC CONCEPT								
19	Agriculture, forestry and fishing	33.6	28.2	30.6	32.1	34.0	32.8	33.8	32.7
20	Industry, including energy	133.3	130.6	133.9	139.2	140.9	133.6	131.2	131.4
21	Manufacturing	111.2	109.9	113.1	118.1	119.4	112.4	109.6	110.1
22	Construction	63.0	51.8	53.5	52.0	55.5	57.0	55.2	49.0
23	Distrib. trade, repairs; transp.; accommod., food serv. activ.	243.2	233.8	228.9	221.5	224.4	226.1	228.4	223.4
24	Information and communication	18.0	17.3	18.5	19.8	21.0	22.7	24.7	28.7
25	Financial and insurance activities	18.4	16.5	16.7	16.1	15.6	14.8	15.4	15.3
26	Real estate activities	19.8	17.6	18.4	18.4	18.7	19.0	19.5	19.1
27	Prof., scientif., techn. activ.; admin., support service activ.	50.0	45.9	51.0	61.9	64.4	61.5	62.9	63.9
28	Public admin.; compulsory s.s.; education; human health	184.8	174.2	176.7	177.1	177.5	175.6	174.0	176.8
29	Other service activities	33.3	28.4	28.9	29.1	31.0	30.2	30.4	30.1
30	**Total employees**	**797.5**	**744.3**	**757.0**	**767.3**	**783.1**	**773.0**	**775.5**	**770.5**
	SELF-EMPLOYED, THOUSAND PERSONS, DOMESTIC CONCEPT								
31	Agriculture, forestry and fishing	42.7	38.0	38.0	35.8	33.8	32.3	36.1	34.8
32	Industry, including energy	8.4	7.9	8.3	8.9	8.0	7.9	9.4	9.6
33	Manufacturing	6.6	6.9	7.5	8.2	7.0	7.6	8.9	8.9
34	Construction	9.8	6.5	8.2	8.8	9.1	9.7	10.3	11.2
35	Distrib. trade, repairs; transp.; accommod., food serv. activ.	19.3	20.3	16.3	18.0	19.1	18.0	19.4	21.9
36	Information and communication	1.6	2.6	3.1	2.0	3.1	4.2	4.0	2.0
37	Financial and insurance activities	0.9	0.7	0.8	0.8	0.5	0.8	0.6	1.2
38	Real estate activities	1.5	1.6	1.1	1.8	2.7	3.0	2.6	2.9
39	Prof., scientif., techn. activ.; admin., support service activ.	8.5	7.6	7.6	8.4	12.2	13.6	14.8	13.5
40	Public admin.; compulsory s.s.; education; human health	6.3	4.1	5.7	7.0	5.9	4.4	5.8	5.1
41	Other service activities	7.2	9.8	10.4	10.0	11.1	9.6	10.6	13.6
42	**Total self-employed**	**106.2**	**99.2**	**99.2**	**101.4**	**105.5**	**103.6**	**113.5**	**115.8**
	TOTAL EMPLOYMENT, MILLION HOURS, DOMESTIC CONCEPT								
43	Industry, including energy	273.4	270.9	281.2	289.9	290.6	279.1	268.5	272.6
44	Distrib. trade, repairs; transp.; accommod., food serv. activ.	525.9	501.1	480.6	465.7	476.4	484.6	472.3	470.1
45	Financial and insurance activities	37.6	31.7	34.3	32.8	31.3	30.5	29.1	31.9
46	Prof., scientif., techn. activ.; admin., support service activ.	113.1	100.0	110.5	130.5	141.7	136.1	141.8	140.8
47	Public admin.; compulsory s.s.; education; human health	362.9	334.4	347.1	349.3	352.4	351.9	336.9	338.0
48	**Total employment**	**1 764.3**	**1 632.3**	**1 671.3**	**1 680.2**	**1 713.1**	**1 699.3**	**1 690.6**	**1 686.2**
	EMPLOYEES, MILLION HOURS, DOMESTIC CONCEPT								
49	Industry, including energy	257.4	255.8	264.4	273.3	275.1	264.2	250.0	252.5
50	Distrib. trade, repairs; transp.; accommod., food serv. activ.	484.8	460.8	446.8	431.0	437.3	446.4	434.7	425.3
51	Financial and insurance activities	35.7	30.6	33.3	31.1	30.3	28.9	27.9	29.5
52	Prof., scientif., techn. activ.; admin., support service activ.	96.4	84.8	95.8	116.5	120.9	111.8	116.1	117.7
53	Public admin.; compulsory s.s.; education; human health	348.5	325.1	334.8	335.3	338.8	343.8	324.5	326.7
54	**Total employees**	**1 547.1**	**1 434.5**	**1 468.9**	**1 480.8**	**1 506.3**	**1 496.0**	**1 467.0**	**1 456.9**
	SELF-EMPLOYED, MILLION HOURS, DOMESTIC CONCEPT								
55	Industry, including energy	16.0	15.1	16.8	16.6	15.6	14.9	18.5	20.2
56	Distrib. trade, repairs; transp.; accommod., food serv. activ.	41.1	40.3	33.9	34.7	39.1	38.2	37.6	44.8
57	Financial and insurance activities	1.9	1.1	1.1	1.7	1.0	1.7	1.2	2.3
58	Prof., scientif., techn. activ.; admin., support service activ.	16.7	15.2	14.7	14.1	20.7	24.3	25.7	23.1
59	Public admin.; compulsory s.s.; education; human health	14.4	9.3	12.2	14.1	13.6	8.2	12.4	11.3
60	**Total self-employed**	**217.2**	**197.9**	**202.4**	**199.4**	**206.7**	**203.4**	**223.6**	**229.3**

Note: Detailed metadata:http://metalinks.oecd.org/nav1/20180308/1a67
Source: Central Statistical Bureau of Latvia (CSB) via Eurostat.

LUXEMBOURG

Table 1. Gross domestic product, expenditure approach

Million EUR (1999 LUF euro)

		2009	2010	2011	2012	2013	2014	2015	2016
	AT CURRENT PRICES								
1	**Final consumption expenditure**	**19 088**	**19 779**	**20 730**	**21 880**	**22 770**	**23 489**	**24 304**	**24 886**
2	Household	12 126	12 377	12 937	13 555	14 045	14 419	14 906	15 248
3	NPISH's	504	558	588	646	682	720	750	789
4	Government	6 458	6 844	7 205	7 679	8 043	8 350	8 648	8 849
5	Individual	3 888	4 110	4 314	4 610	4 874	5 058	5 134	5 332
6	Collective	2 570	2 735	2 891	3 069	3 169	3 292	3 514	3 517
7	*of which: Actual individual consumption*	16 518	17 045	17 838	18 811	19 600	20 197	20 789	21 368
8	**Gross capital formation**	**5 995**	**7 186**	**8 394**	**8 546**	**8 843**	**9 422**	**9 440**	**9 512**
9	Gross fixed capital formation, total	6 806	7 075	8 278	8 894	9 073	9 510	9 006	9 112
10	Dwellings	1 309	1 166	1 300	1 398	1 667	1 575	1 573	1 690
11	Other buildings and structures	3 044	2 827	3 406	2 993	3 045	3 384	3 257	3 458
12	Transport equipment	918	1 448	1 795	2 509	2 172	2 475	2 026	1 904
13	Other machinery and equipment	714	724	902	1 007	1 070	998	1 041	960
14	Cultivated assets	6	-2	-1	19	13	13	6	6
15	Intangible fixed assets	478	581	505	564	650	687	762	791
16	Changes in inventories, acquisitions less disposals of valuables	-811	111	115	-348	-230	-88	434	400
17	Changes in inventories	-326	333	96	-110	-147	22	291	391
18	Acquisitions less disposals of valuables	-485	-222	20	-239	-83	-109	144	9
19	**External balance of goods and services**	**11 894**	**13 212**	**14 041**	**13 686**	**14 887**	**17 082**	**18 358**	**18 607**
20	Exports of goods and services	60 667	70 120	76 829	82 244	88 641	104 101	116 033	117 282
21	Exports of goods	13 352	15 997	18 675	17 925	18 539	18 956	17 342	16 557
22	Exports of services	47 315	54 122	58 154	64 319	70 103	85 144	98 690	100 725
23	Imports of goods and services	48 773	56 907	62 787	68 558	73 755	87 018	97 675	98 675
24	Imports of goods	14 190	16 602	19 233	19 176	18 378	18 179	17 620	17 321
25	Imports of services	34 584	40 305	43 555	49 382	55 377	68 840	80 055	81 354
26	**Statistical discrepancy**	**0**	**0**	**0**	**0**	**0**	**0**	**0**	**0**
27	**Gross domestic product**	**36 977**	**40 178**	**43 165**	**44 112**	**46 500**	**49 993**	**52 102**	**53 005**
	AT CONSTANT PRICES, REFERENCE YEAR 2010								
28	**Final consumption expenditure**	**19 533**	**19 779**	**20 029**	**20 653**	**21 194**	**21 661**	**22 323**	**22 823**
29	Household	12 295	12 377	12 540	12 880	13 169	13 467	13 921	14 250
30	NPISH's	489	558	588	632	613	632	645	661
31	Government	6 752	6 844	6 900	7 142	7 410	7 560	7 756	7 912
32	Individual	4 139	4 110	4 091	4 215	4 428	4 500	4 514	4 668
33	Collective	2 617	2 735	2 809	2 927	2 980	3 059	3 245	3 244
34	*of which: Actual individual consumption*	16 917	17 045	17 219	17 726	18 214	18 603	19 079	19 579
35	**Gross capital formation**	**5 985**	**7 186**	**8 156**	**8 230**	**8 427**	**8 930**	**8 683**	**8 680**
36	Gross fixed capital formation, total	6 833	7 075	8 043	8 535	8 641	9 012	8 288	8 328
37	Dwellings	1 321	1 166	1 263	1 322	1 547	1 438	1 421	1 512
38	Other buildings and structures	3 064	2 827	3 312	2 834	2 833	3 099	2 954	3 107
39	Transport equipment	921	1 448	1 731	2 477	2 182	2 474	1 817	1 696
40	Other machinery and equipment	718	724	870	943	983	910	954	878
41	Cultivated assets	7	-2	-1	15	10	10	4	4
42	Intangible fixed assets	476	581	491	522	580	602	648	659
43	Changes in inventories, acquisitions less disposals of valuables	..	..	..	..	..	..	..	..
44	Changes in inventories	..	..	..	..	..	..	..	..
45	Acquisitions less disposals of valuables	-666	-222	17	-179	-79	-110	134	7
46	**External balance of goods and services**	**12 798**	**13 212**	**13 013**	**12 167**	**12 912**	**14 336**	**15 148**	**16 027**
47	Exports of goods and services	63 530	70 120	72 956	74 964	78 909	89 938	96 106	98 700
48	Exports of goods	14 112	15 997	17 500	16 464	17 383	17 865	16 718	16 243
49	Exports of services	49 414	54 122	55 456	58 527	61 555	71 981	79 047	81 949
50	Imports of goods and services	50 732	56 907	59 943	62 796	65 997	75 602	80 959	82 673
51	Imports of goods	14 907	16 602	18 276	17 686	17 327	17 356	16 829	16 892
52	Imports of services	35 826	40 305	41 667	45 120	48 669	58 076	63 742	65 337
53	**Statistical discrepancy (including chaining residual)**	**-3**	**0**	**0**	**2**	**20**	**82**	**144**	**194**
54	**Gross domestic product**	**38 314**	**40 178**	**41 198**	**41 053**	**42 553**	**45 009**	**46 297**	**47 724**

Note: Detailed metadata:http://metalinks.oecd.org/nav1/20180308/3ee8
Source: Service central de la statistique et des études économiques (STATEC) via Eurostat.

LUXEMBOURG

Table 2. Gross domestic product, output and income approach
ISIC Rev. 4

Million EUR (1999 LUF euro)

		2009	2010	2011	2012	2013	2014	2015	2016
	OUTPUT APPROACH AT CURRENT PRICES								
1	**Total gross value added at basic prices**	33 135	36 137	38 739	39 386	41 527	44 573	47 192	48 014
2	Agriculture, forestry and fishing	94	99	109	159	129	133	120	128
3	Industry, including energy	2 346	2 661	2 706	2 673	2 942	3 251	3 345	3 476
4	Manufacturing	1 768	2 106	2 133	2 103	2 272	2 489	2 530	2 681
5	Construction	1 914	1 931	2 124	2 034	2 129	2 395	2 577	2 723
6	Services	..	..	..	..	..	..	..	..
7	Distrib. trade, repairs; transp.; accommod., food serv. activ.	5 374	6 145	7 262	7 017	7 699	7 960	8 063	7 433
8	Information and communication	2 120	2 319	2 472	2 632	2 415	2 624	3 075	3 322
9	Financial and insurance activities	8 891	10 206	10 221	10 317	10 751	11 873	13 019	13 097
10	Real estate activities	2 895	2 964	3 195	3 347	3 503	3 602	3 466	3 610
11	Prof., scientif., techn. activ.; admin., support service activ.	3 560	3 568	4 020	4 119	4 359	4 782	5 340	5 865
12	Public admin.; compulsory s.s.; education; human health	5 255	5 548	5 883	6 312	6 753	7 055	7 277	7 489
13	Other service activities	686	696	748	777	848	897	909	872
14	**FISIM (Financial Intermediation Services Indirectly Measured)**	..	..	..	..	..	..	..	..
15	**Gross value added at basic prices, excluding FISIM**	33 135	36 137	38 739	39 386	41 527	44 573	47 192	48 014
16	**Taxes less subsidies on products**	3 841	4 041	4 426	4 726	4 972	5 420	4 910	4 991
17	Taxes on products	4 061	4 261	4 664	4 989	5 236	5 695	5 201	5 295
18	Subsidies on products	220	221	238	264	264	275	291	305
19	**Residual item**	0	0	0	0	0	0	0	0
20	**Gross domestic product at market prices**	36 977	40 178	43 165	44 112	46 500	49 993	52 102	53 005
	OUTPUT APPROACH AT CONSTANT PRICES (REF. YEAR 2010)								
21	**Total gross value added at basic prices**	34 402	36 137	36 843	36 533	37 862	39 954	41 143	42 092
22	Agriculture, forestry and fishing	105	99	83	104	77	86	109	104
23	Industry, including energy	2 556	2 661	2 445	2 512	2 863	3 198	3 295	3 245
24	Manufacturing	1 915	2 106	1 851	1 927	2 174	2 493	2 520	2 496
25	Construction	1 914	1 931	2 068	1 888	1 900	2 067	2 186	2 249
26	Services	..	..	..	..	..	..	..	..
27	Distrib. trade, repairs; transp.; accommod., food serv. activ.	5 612	6 145	6 609	6 183	6 616	6 786	6 646	6 208
28	Information and communication	2 017	2 319	2 522	2 679	2 406	2 583	3 192	3 955
29	Financial and insurance activities	9 412	10 206	9 721	9 432	9 668	10 316	10 559	10 692
30	Real estate activities	2 950	2 964	3 093	3 182	3 329	3 414	3 378	3 540
31	Prof., scientif., techn. activ.; admin., support service activ.	3 645	3 568	3 940	3 973	4 055	4 439	4 720	5 128
32	Public admin.; compulsory s.s.; education; human health	5 499	5 548	5 635	5 873	6 178	6 290	6 354	6 466
33	Other service activities	696	696	727	727	764	788	775	729
34	**FISIM (Financial Intermediation Services Indirectly Measured)**	..	..	..	..	..	..	..	..
35	**Gross value added at basic prices, excluding FISIM**	34 402	36 137	36 843	36 533	37 862	39 954	41 143	42 092
36	**Taxes less subsidies on products**	3 910	4 041	4 355	4 526	4 698	5 066	5 163	5 707
37	Taxes on products	4 123	4 261	4 579	4 750	4 939	5 306	5 401	5 936
38	Subsidies on products	213	221	225	224	240	240	238	237
39	**Residual item**	1	0	0	-6	-7	-10	-9	-75
40	**Gross domestic product at market prices**	38 314	40 178	41 198	41 053	42 553	45 009	46 297	47 724
	INCOME APPROACH								
41	**Compensation of employees**	19 156	19 877	20 856	21 754	22 660	23 737	25 086	26 049
42	Agriculture, forestry and fishing	31	34	36	38	38	41	43	45
43	Industry, including energy	1 967	1 965	2 007	2 013	2 030	2 046	2 103	2 129
44	Manufacturing	1 683	1 682	1 722	1 708	1 732	1 735	1 774	1 790
45	Construction	1 582	1 562	1 624	1 661	1 683	1 770	1 859	1 936
46	Distrib. trade, repairs; transp.; accommod., food serv. activ.	3 548	3 647	3 865	4 007	4 120	4 345	4 577	4 675
47	Information and communication	920	974	1 037	1 076	1 118	1 201	1 303	1 364
48	Financial and insurance activities	3 825	3 982	4 056	4 227	4 473	4 593	4 763	4 931
49	Real estate activities	86	85	96	107	116	125	143	156
50	Prof., scientif., techn. activ.; admin., support service activ.	2 469	2 616	2 804	2 964	3 126	3 326	3 738	4 096
51	Public admin.; compulsory s.s.; education; human health	4 206	4 483	4 768	5 077	5 343	5 662	5 897	6 032
52	Other service activities	523	529	563	584	613	627	661	684
53	**Wages and salaries**	16 407	17 080	17 883	18 588	19 457	20 417	21 611	22 489
54	Agriculture, forestry and fishing	27	30	32	34	34	37	37	40
55	Industry, including energy	1 659	1 674	1 720	1 729	1 750	1 785	1 821	1 847
56	Manufacturing	1 418	1 434	1 482	1 482	1 496	1 518	1 542	1 558
57	Construction	1 367	1 354	1 431	1 462	1 484	1 562	1 641	1 711
58	Distrib. trade, repairs; transp.; accommod., food serv. activ.	3 093	3 185	3 358	3 463	3 580	3 787	3 984	4 069
59	Information and communication	814	860	913	942	987	1 058	1 156	1 211
60	Financial and insurance activities	3 267	3 433	3 479	3 614	3 837	3 928	4 092	4 263
61	Real estate activities	73	77	86	96	103	111	127	139
62	Prof., scientif., techn. activ.; admin., support service activ.	2 203	2 320	2 473	2 593	2 759	2 939	3 318	3 648
63	Public admin.; compulsory s.s.; education; human health	3 437	3 674	3 889	4 141	4 381	4 655	4 849	4 953
64	Other service activities	466	473	502	515	543	555	586	609
65	**Gross operating surplus and mixed income**	13 690	15 877	17 524	17 301	18 548	20 442	21 563	21 258
66	**Taxes less subsidies on production and imports**	4 130	4 424	4 785	5 057	5 292	5 814	5 453	5 697
67	Taxes on production and imports	4 624	4 939	5 321	5 677	6 009	6 566	6 226	6 421
68	Subsidies on production and imports	494	515	536	620	718	752	773	724
69	**Residual item**	0	0	0	0	0	0	0	0
70	**Gross domestic product**	36 977	40 178	43 165	44 112	46 500	49 993	52 102	53 005

Note: Detailed metadata:http://metalinks.oecd.org/nav1/20180308/3ee8
Source: Service central de la statistique et des études économiques (STATEC) via Eurostat.

LUXEMBOURG

Table 3. Disposable income, saving and net lending / net borrowing

Million EUR (1999 LUF euro)

		2009	2010	2011	2012	2013	2014	2015	2016
	DISPOSABLE INCOME								
1	**Gross domestic product**	36 367 e	40 178	43 165	44 112	46 500	49 993	52 102	53 005
2	Net primary incomes from the rest of the world	-11 576 e	-11 199	-13 361	-13 439	-15 443	-17 641	-17 558	-16 956
3	Primary incomes receivable from the rest of the world	103 061 e	114 911	157 157	188 590	215 071	203 015	232 010	228 682
4	Primary incomes payable to the rest of the world	114 638 e	126 110	170 518	202 029	230 514	220 656	249 568	245 637
5	**Gross national income at market prices**	25 044 e	28 979	29 803	30 673	31 056	32 352	34 544	36 049
6	Consumption of fixed capital	4 632 e	4 857	5 085	5 406	5 425	5 743	6 209	6 418
7	**Net national income at market prices**	20 311 e	24 122	24 719	25 267	25 631	26 609	28 335	29 631
8	Net current transfers from the rest of the world	-315	-6	-171	-385	-63	91	494	186
9	Current transfers receivable from the rest of the world	6 248	6 715	6 846	7 033	7 424	7 823	8 385	8 493
10	Current transfers payable to the rest of the world	6 563	6 721	7 017	7 417	7 487	7 732	7 891	8 307
11	**Net national disposable income**	19 597	24 115	24 548	24 883	25 568	26 700	28 829	29 817
	SAVING AND NET LENDING / NET BORROWING								
12	**Net national disposable income**	19 597	24 115	24 548	24 883	25 568	26 700	28 829	29 817
13	Final consumption expenditures	18 915 e	19 779	20 730	21 880	22 770	23 489	24 304	24 886
14	Adj. for change in net equity of households in pension funds	-11	-10	-19	-8	-24	-6	2	2
15	**Saving, net**	498	4 325	3 799	2 994	2 775	3 205	4 527	4 934
16	Net capital transfers from the rest of the world	-186	-43	-90	-110	-91	-103	-102	-92
17	Capital transfers receivable from the rest of the world	1 033	574	188	200	361	285	34	84
18	Capital transfers payable to the rest of the world	1 219	617	278	310	452	388	136	176
19	Gross capital formation	5 521 e	7 186	8 394	8 546	8 843	9 422	9 440	9 512
20	Acquisitions less disposals of non-financial non-produced assets	782	1 148	404	439	-754	-426	595	1 495
21	Consumption of fixed capital	4 632 e	4 857	5 085	5 406	5 425	5 743	6 209	6 418
22	**Net lending / net borrowing**	-1 745	805	-5	-694	20	-152	599	253
	REAL DISPOSABLE INCOME								
23	**Gross domestic product at constant prices, reference year 2010**	38 093	39 947	40 961	40 817	42 308	44 750	46 031	47 450
24	Trading gain or loss	-1 344 e	0	575	824	1 264	1 713	1 851	1 105
25	**Real gross domestic income**	36 970 e	40 178	41 773	41 877	43 572	46 463	47 882	48 554
26	Net real primary incomes from the rest of the world	..	..	..	..	..	..	..	..
27	Real primary incomes receivable from the rest of the world	..	..	..	..	..	..	..	..
28	Real primary incomes payable to the rest of the world	..	..	..	..	..	..	..	..
29	**Real gross national income at market prices**	25 460 e	28 979	28 843	29 119	29 101	30 067	31 746	33 022
30	Net real current transfers from the rest of the world	..	..	..	..	..	..	..	..
31	Real current transfers receivable from the rest of the world	..	..	..	..	..	..	..	..
32	Real current transfers payable to the rest of the world	..	..	..	..	..	..	..	..
33	**Real gross national disposable income**	..	..	..	..	..	..	..	..
34	Consumption of fixed capital at constant prices	4 651 e	4 857	4 940	5 187	5 167	5 442	5 714	5 865
35	**Real net national income at market prices**	20 647 e	24 122	23 922	23 987	24 017	24 730	26 040	27 143
36	**Real net national disposable income**	19 922	24 115	23 756	23 622	..	..	..	..

Note: Detailed metadata:http://metalinks.oecd.org/nav1/20180308/42c4
Source: Service central de la statistique et des études économiques (STATEC) via Eurostat.

Table 4. Population and employment (persons) and employment (hours worked) by industry
ISIC Rev. 4

		2009	2010	2011	2012	2013	2014	2015	2016
	POPULATION, THOUSAND PERSONS, NATIONAL CONCEPT								
1	**Total population**	498.2	507.5	519.4	531.5	545.3	558.3	569.4	584.1
2	Economically active population	..	..	..	..	..	..	..	..
3	Unemployed persons	..	..	..	..	..	..	..	..
4	Total employment	215.0	218.3	224.2	229.6	234.2	239.6	244.7	250.2
5	Employees	196.1	199.3	204.7	210.0	214.2	219.1	223.7	228.8
6	Self-employed	18.8	19.1	19.4	19.6	20.0	20.6	21.0	21.4
	TOTAL EMPLOYMENT, THOUSAND PERSONS, DOMESTIC CONCEPT								
7	Agriculture, forestry and fishing	3.9	4.0	3.9	3.8	3.8	3.7	3.7	3.7
8	Industry, including energy	37.3	37.1	37.3	36.9	36.1	36.1	36.2	36.8
9	Manufacturing	33.0	32.7	33.1	32.6	31.9	31.8	31.8	32.3
10	Construction	38.9	39.0	39.9	40.3	40.3	40.9	41.6	42.8
11	Distrib. trade, repairs; transp.; accommod., food serv. activ.	84.3	85.4	88.1	90.1	91.3	93.3	94.6	96.0
12	Information and communication	13.7	14.1	14.8	15.1	15.6	16.2	16.7	17.3
13	Financial and insurance activities	41.2	40.9	41.3	42.1	42.3	43.3	44.5	46.0
14	Real estate activities	2.8	2.9	3.1	3.3	3.5	3.6	3.9	4.0
15	Prof., scientif., techn. activ.; admin., support service activ.	50.0	52.1	54.0	55.9	57.9	60.4	63.5	67.9
16	Public admin.; compulsory s.s.; education; human health	66.0	68.8	71.9	75.3	78.7	81.2	83.9	86.1
17	Other service activities	15.0	15.3	15.9	16.3	16.6	17.3	17.6	17.9
18	**Total employment**	353.1	359.6	370.2	379.1	386.1	396.0	406.1	418.4
	EMPLOYEES, THOUSAND PERSONS, DOMESTIC CONCEPT								
19	Agriculture, forestry and fishing	1.0	1.1	1.2	1.2	1.2	1.3	1.3	1.4
20	Industry, including energy	36.9	36.7	37.0	36.6	35.8	35.8	35.9	36.5
21	Manufacturing	32.6	32.4	32.7	32.2	31.6	31.5	31.5	32.0
22	Construction	37.9	38.2	39.0	39.5	39.4	40.1	40.7	41.9
23	Distrib. trade, repairs; transp.; accommod., food serv. activ.	78.6	80.2	83.0	85.0	86.5	88.3	89.8	91.1
24	Information and communication	13.3	13.7	14.4	14.7	15.0	15.6	16.0	16.6
25	Financial and insurance activities	41.2	40.9	41.3	42.1	42.3	43.2	44.5	46.0
26	Real estate activities	1.6	1.7	1.8	2.0	2.1	2.2	2.3	2.4
27	Prof., scientif., techn. activ.; admin., support service activ.	45.0	46.7	48.1	49.8	51.6	53.8	56.9	61.1
28	Public admin.; compulsory s.s.; education; human health	62.5	64.7	67.7	70.9	73.8	76.2	78.4	80.3
29	Other service activities	13.3	13.5	13.9	14.3	14.6	15.0	15.3	15.5
30	**Total employees**	331.4	337.4	347.4	356.0	362.4	371.5	381.0	392.7
	SELF-EMPLOYED, THOUSAND PERSONS, DOMESTIC CONCEPT								
31	Agriculture, forestry and fishing	2.9	2.8	2.7	2.6	2.5	2.4	2.4	2.3
32	Industry, including energy	0.4	0.3	0.3	0.3	0.3	0.3	0.3	0.3
33	Manufacturing	0.4	0.3	0.3	0.3	0.3	0.3	0.3	0.3
34	Construction	1.0	0.8	0.9	0.9	0.9	0.8	0.9	0.9
35	Distrib. trade, repairs; transp.; accommod., food serv. activ.	5.7	5.2	5.1	5.1	4.8	5.0	4.8	4.9
36	Information and communication	0.4	0.4	0.4	0.4	0.5	0.6	0.6	0.7
37	Financial and insurance activities	0.0	0.0	0.0	0.0	0.0	0.0	0.0	0.0
38	Real estate activities	1.2	1.2	1.3	1.3	1.4	1.4	1.6	1.7
39	Prof., scientif., techn. activ.; admin., support service activ.	5.0	5.4	5.9	6.1	6.3	6.6	6.6	6.7
40	Public admin.; compulsory s.s.; education; human health	3.4	4.1	4.2	4.4	5.0	4.9	5.5	5.8
41	Other service activities	1.7	1.8	1.9	2.0	2.0	2.3	2.4	2.4
42	**Total self-employed**	21.7	22.2	22.8	23.2	23.7	24.5	25.1	25.8
	TOTAL EMPLOYMENT, MILLION HOURS, DOMESTIC CONCEPT								
43	Industry, including energy	57.4	59.0	59.5	58.3	56.9	57.0	57.8	58.6
44	Distrib. trade, repairs; transp.; accommod., food serv. activ.	133.2	134.3	136.6	138.3	139.4	142.2	144.9	147.1
45	Financial and insurance activities	62.3	62.0	62.6	64.1	64.1	65.5	67.9	70.1
46	Prof., scientif., techn. activ.; admin., support service activ.	73.6	77.1	79.8	82.8	85.2	89.5	95.0	101.6
47	Public admin.; compulsory s.s.; education; human health	92.8	96.5	100.9	105.9	110.7	114.0	117.9	120.4
48	**Total employment**	535.5	545.3	560.8	571.8	580.1	597.2	617.7	635.8
	EMPLOYEES, MILLION HOURS, DOMESTIC CONCEPT								
49	Industry, including energy	56.7	58.4	59.0	57.8	56.5	56.6	57.3	58.2
50	Distrib. trade, repairs; transp.; accommod., food serv. activ.	124.5	126.6	129.2	131.1	132.6	135.1	138.0	140.1
51	Financial and insurance activities	62.3	61.9	62.6	64.0	64.1	65.5	67.9	70.1
52	Prof., scientif., techn. activ.; admin., support service activ.	66.4	69.3	71.6	74.1	76.4	80.2	85.6	92.0
53	Public admin.; compulsory s.s.; education; human health	88.9	91.8	96.0	100.8	104.9	108.4	111.6	113.5
54	**Total employees**	503.6	513.6	528.4	538.6	545.5	561.3	578.4	595.0
	SELF-EMPLOYED, MILLION HOURS, DOMESTIC CONCEPT								
55	Industry, including energy	0.7	0.5	0.5	0.5	0.4	0.4	0.5	0.5
56	Distrib. trade, repairs; transp.; accommod., food serv. activ.	8.7	7.7	7.5	7.2	6.8	7.0	6.9	7.0
57	Financial and insurance activities	0.0	0.0	0.0	0.0	0.0	0.0	0.0	0.0
58	Prof., scientif., techn. activ.; admin., support service activ.	7.2	7.8	8.2	8.7	8.8	9.3	9.4	9.7
59	Public admin.; compulsory s.s.; education; human health	4.0	4.7	4.9	5.2	5.8	5.6	6.3	6.9
60	**Total self-employed**	31.9	31.7	32.4	33.2	34.6	35.9	39.3	40.8

Note: Detailed metadata:http://metalinks.oecd.org/nav1/20180308/5195
Source: Service central de la statistique et des études économiques (STATEC) via Eurostat.

MEXICO

Table 1. Gross domestic product, expenditure approach

Million MXN

		2009	2010	2011	2012	2013	2014	2015	2016
	AT CURRENT PRICES								
1	**Final consumption expenditure**	**9 456 002**	**10 308 249**	**11 231 452**	**12 127 678**	**12 803 666**	**13 641 818**	**14 436 713**	**15 600 698 p**
2	Household	7 822 630	8 533 204	9 295 349	10 028 393	10 607 565	11 290 997	11 920 749	12 919 119 p
3	NPISH's	183 940	201 640	208 927	– 209 579	211 686	218 617	229 279	245 216 p
4	Government	1 449 432	1 573 405	1 727 177	1 889 705	1 984 415	2 132 204	2 286 685	2 436 363 p
5	Individual	702 161	757 510	840 513	917 161	999 616	1 059 730	1 143 781	1 206 665 p
6	Collective	747 271	815 894	886 664	972 544	984 799	1 072 475	1 142 905	1 229 699 p
7	*of which: Actual individual consumption*	8 708 731	9 492 354	10 344 788	11 155 134	11 818 867	12 569 343	13 293 809	14 371 000 p
8	**Gross capital formation**	**2 783 925**	**3 046 611**	**3 414 323**	**3 778 317**	**3 661 290**	**3 827 191**	**4 313 793**	**4 772 574 p**
9	Gross fixed capital formation, total	2 691 191	2 884 825	3 266 598	3 612 844	3 459 304	3 672 155	4 175 649	4 609 364 p
10	Dwellings	781 289	803 421	893 093	945 957	899 066	953 761	1 032 148	1 160 115 p
11	Other buildings and structures	1 065 316	1 115 478	1 221 140	1 310 404	1 221 730	1 280 884	1 334 362	1 360 660 p
12	Transport equipment	205 276	261 949	328 754	400 348	411 025	456 165	568 160	671 887 p
13	Other machinery and equipment	494 813	539 209	633 556	749 292	738 992	777 764	961 344	1 105 530 p
14	Cultivated assets	3 104	3 215	3 481	3 679	4 426	4 654	5 081	5 615 p
15	Intangible fixed assets	21 802	24 964	29 504	32 601	32 625	33 636	37 882	41 350 p
16	Changes in inventories, acquisitions less disposals of valuables[1]	92 734	161 786	147 725	165 472	201 987	155 036	138 143	163 211 p
17	Changes in inventories	92 734	161 786	147 725	165 472	201 987	155 036	138 143	163 211 p
18	Acquisitions less disposals of valuables	..	..	..	..	..	..	..	..
19	**External balance of goods and services**	**-201 631**	**-182 450**	**-204 770**	**-195 525**	**-187 769**	**-205 951**	**-378 396**	**-397 649 p**
20	Exports of goods and services	3 302 798	3 969 502	4 551 712	5 103 688	5 095 680	5 572 849	6 412 002	7 461 454 p
21	Exports of goods	3 097 840	3 773 764	4 354 657	4 888 017	4 864 480	5 290 683	6 049 914	7 003 391 p
22	Exports of services	204 958	195 738	197 055	215 671	231 200	282 166	362 087	458 063 p
23	Imports of goods and services	3 504 429	4 151 951	4 756 482	5 299 213	5 283 449	5 778 800	6 790 398	7 859 104 p
24	Imports of goods	3 164 942	3 811 952	4 365 295	4 887 216	4 872 735	5 320 075	6 272 739	7 233 047 p
25	Imports of services	339 487	340 000	391 187	411 997	410 714	458 725	517 659	626 057 p
26	**Statistical discrepancy**	**124 467**	**193 967**	**224 571**	**107 285**	**283 638**	**208 410**	**164 422**	**123 971 p**
27	**Gross domestic product**	**12 162 763**	**13 366 377**	**14 665 576**	**15 817 755**	**16 277 187**	**17 471 467**	**18 536 531**	**20 099 594 p**
	AT CONSTANT PRICES, REFERENCE YEAR 2010								
28	**Final consumption expenditure**	**9 970 671**	**10 308 249**	**10 649 426**	**10 915 474**	**11 086 447**	**11 332 908**	**11 688 982**	**12 093 806 p**
29	Household	8 240 402	8 533 204	8 827 029	9 039 265	9 212 471	9 407 092	9 728 167	10 085 471 p
30	NPISH's	191 520	201 640	201 151	199 957	188 649	191 424	193 073	198 735 p
31	Government	1 538 283	1 573 405	1 621 163	1 675 687	1 684 779	1 733 535	1 767 224	1 809 472 p
32	Individual	750 392	757 510	787 439	799 798	814 911	822 165	820 890	834 743 p
33	Collective	787 077	815 894	833 148	876 467	869 554	912 405	948 821	977 757 p
34	*of which: Actual individual consumption*	9 183 550	9 492 354	9 816 074	10 039 270	10 216 727	10 420 827	10 740 657	11 116 480 p
35	**Gross capital formation**	**2 852 996**	**3 046 611**	**3 243 348**	**3 416 551**	**3 344 372**	**3 402 733**	**3 547 730**	**3 601 842 p**
36	Gross fixed capital formation, total	2 754 977	2 884 825	3 111 218	3 264 521	3 155 138	3 251 887	3 414 026	3 451 357 p
37	Dwellings	809 011	803 421	837 015	848 324	805 566	831 284	861 698	898 150 p
38	Other buildings and structures	1 115 009	1 115 478	1 148 099	1 179 401	1 113 304	1 130 168	1 129 470	1 085 808 p
39	Transport equipment	198 044	261 949	321 188	363 059	369 446	395 487	451 032	497 179 p
40	Other machinery and equipment	492 726	539 209	617 378	679 636	693 640	712 959	754 686	761 350 p
41	Cultivated assets	3 177	3 215	3 313	3 327	3 923	3 990	4 090	4 337 p
42	Intangible fixed assets	23 225	24 964	27 563	29 552	30 160	30 894	33 318	34 421 p
43	Changes in inventories, acquisitions less disposals of valuables	..	..	..	..	..	..	..	..
44	Changes in inventories	..	..	..	..	..	..	..	..
45	Acquisitions less disposals of valuables	..	..	..	..	..	..	..	..
46	**External balance of goods and services**	**-302 946**	**-182 450**	**-109 521**	**-68 080**	**-103 581**	**-60 611**	**59 058**	**90 710 p**
47	Exports of goods and services	3 244 053	3 969 502	4 275 688	4 554 657	4 617 080	4 939 462	5 355 091	5 540 461 p
48	Exports of goods	3 034 907	3 773 764	4 086 782	4 355 911	4 410 182	4 698 154	5 053 723	5 171 373 p
49	Exports of services	208 568	195 738	189 164	199 051	207 143	241 334	300 929	367 960 p
50	Imports of goods and services	3 547 000	4 151 951	4 385 209	4 622 737	4 720 661	5 000 073	5 296 032	5 449 751 p
51	Imports of goods	3 206 280	3 811 952	4 012 641	4 251 994	4 343 107	4 597 673	4 900 198	5 036 440 p
52	Imports of services	342 258	340 000	372 981	370 504	377 278	402 184	394 676	412 302 p
53	**Statistical discrepancy (including chaining residual)**	**194 858**	**193 967**	**72 736**	**96 723**	**227 887**	**294 229**	**163 055**	**122 834 p**
54	**Gross domestic product**	**12 715 579**	**13 366 377**	**13 855 989**	**14 360 668**	**14 555 125**	**14 969 260**	**15 458 825**	**15 909 191 p**

Note: Detailed metadata:http://metalinks.oecd.org/nav1/20180308/13ff

1. Excluding *Acquisition less disposals of valuables.*

Source: Instituto Nacional de Estadistica, Geografia e Informatica (INEGI)

Table 2. Gross domestic product, output and income approach
ISIC Rev. 4

Million MXN

		2009	2010	2011	2012	2013	2014	2015	2016
	OUTPUT APPROACH AT CURRENT PRICES								
1	**Total gross value added at basic prices**	**11 658 911**	**12 824 221**	**14 160 748**	**15 334 940**	**15 642 620**	**16 567 122**	**17 463 436**	**18 841 226 p**
2	Agriculture, forestry and fishing	394 255	430 284	452 941	502 044	510 906	547 776	593 233	673 975 p
3	Industry, including energy	2 892 469	3 301 234	3 785 198	4 123 230	3 998 244	4 246 479	4 216 055	4 431 534 p
4	Manufacturing	1 848 455	2 092 725	2 264 942	2 600 047	2 592 398	2 795 184	3 187 917	3 389 492 p
5	Construction	987 136	1 025 335	1 136 737	1 219 712	1 185 596	1 256 620	1 340 718	1 462 392 p
6	Services	..	..	..	..	..	..	..	..
7	Distrib. trade, repairs; transp.; accommod., food serv. activ.	2 839 810	3 255 191	3 668 077	4 026 440	4 183 759	4 459 000	4 944 790	5 488 255 p
8	Information and communication	314 917	324 983	320 998	326 746	336 774	347 373	346 386	354 037 p
9	Financial and insurance activities	424 320	453 764	471 814	500 702	582 395	615 680	645 244	764 085 p
10	Real estate activities	1 457 988	1 545 814	1 638 733	1 714 708	1 783 300	1 872 399	1 948 748	2 033 277 p
11	Prof., scientif., techn. activ.; admin., support service activ.	811 090	837 530	912 548	993 576	1 041 206	1 086 664	1 153 835	1 238 368 p
12	Public admin.; compulsory s.s.; education; human health	1 284 330	1 383 503	1 496 675	1 632 683	1 709 808	1 813 931	1 929 341	2 032 935 p
13	Other service activities	252 595	266 582	277 027	295 099	310 632	321 200	345 086	362 370 p
14	FISIM (Financial Intermediation Services Indirectly Measured)	..	..	..	..	..	..	..	..
15	Gross value added at basic prices, excluding FISIM	11 658 911	12 824 221	14 160 748	15 334 940	15 642 620	16 567 122	17 463 436	18 841 226 p
16	**Taxes less subsidies on products**	**503 852**	**542 156**	**504 829**	**482 815**	**634 567**	**904 345**	**1 073 095**	**1 258 368 p**
17	Taxes on products	551 235	662 618	707 004	763 898	807 819	1 013 612	1 146 198	1 298 502 p
18	Subsidies on products	47 383	120 462	202 176	281 084	173 251	109 267	73 103	40 134 p
19	Residual item	..	..	..	..	..	..	..	..
20	**Gross domestic product at market prices**	**12 162 763**	**13 366 377**	**14 665 576**	**15 817 755**	**16 277 187**	**17 471 467**	**18 536 531**	**20 099 594 p**
	OUTPUT APPROACH AT CONSTANT PRICES (REF. YEAR 2010)								
21	**Total gross value added at basic prices**	**12 195 311**	**12 824 221**	**13 291 888**	**13 787 969**	**13 977 064**	**14 356 954**	**14 808 470**	**15 215 093 p**
22	Agriculture, forestry and fishing	419 816	430 284	414 090	440 412	450 454	467 484	477 164	495 153 p
23	Industry, including energy	3 115 436	3 301 234	3 383 387	3 483 737	3 491 246	3 580 471	3 603 965	3 602 705 p
24	Manufacturing	1 926 279	2 092 725	2 158 709	2 243 478	2 255 874	2 346 241	2 408 680	2 445 401 p
25	Construction	1 024 519	1 025 335	1 066 321	1 092 001	1 072 085	1 101 807	1 128 215	1 151 135 p
26	Services	..	..	..	..	..	..	..	..
27	Distrib. trade, repairs; transp.; accommod., food serv. activ.	2 968 061	3 255 191	3 471 429	3 606 398	3 675 434	3 806 843	3 979 604	4 099 840 p
28	Information and communication	325 122	324 983	337 394	377 313	392 842	411 485	478 825	570 019 p
29	Financial and insurance activities	383 832	453 764	471 919	536 635	619 083	671 070	768 887	862 492 p
30	Real estate activities	1 498 871	1 545 814	1 590 728	1 630 199	1 644 949	1 673 800	1 715 133	1 751 110 p
31	Prof., scientif., techn. activ.; admin., support service activ.	829 230	837 530	882 659	916 038	936 720	945 639	969 452	1 010 110 p
32	Public admin.; compulsory s.s.; education; human health	1 364 977	1 383 503	1 406 726	1 444 638	1 442 837	1 455 962	1 463 997	1 480 006 p
33	Other service activities	263 196	266 582	268 512	276 218	282 920	282 534	292 578	296 678 p
34	FISIM (Financial Intermediation Services Indirectly Measured)	..	..	..	..	..	..	..	..
35	Gross value added at basic prices, excluding FISIM	12 195 311	12 824 221	13 291 888	13 787 969	13 977 064	14 356 954	14 808 470	15 215 093 p
36	**Taxes less subsidies on products**	**520 354**	**542 156**	**564 140**	**572 512**	**577 826**	**612 403**	**650 800**	**695 031 p**
37	Taxes on products	641 249	662 618	687 224	700 294	701 176	729 573	766 166	807 657 p
38	Subsidies on products	119 977	120 462	123 477	127 681	124 226	120 457	120 451	119 896 p
39	**Residual item**	**-86**	**0**	**-40**	**187**	**235**	**-98**	**-445**	**-932 p**
40	**Gross domestic product at market prices**	**12 715 579**	**13 366 377**	**13 855 989**	**14 360 668**	**14 555 125**	**14 969 260**	**15 458 825**	**15 909 191 p**
	INCOME APPROACH								
41	**Compensation of employees**	**3 512 018**	**3 721 504**	**4 002 512**	**4 319 760**	**4 542 853**	**4 786 861**	**5 068 935**	**5 360 800 p**
42	Agriculture, forestry and fishing	68 299	74 529	76 315	82 644	87 476	93 631	100 922	111 283 p
43	Industry, including energy	633 886	644 761	682 114	737 610	822 276	862 272	922 552	960 571 p
44	Manufacturing	528 488	544 168	566 500	610 997	685 452	719 710	785 353	829 205 p
45	Construction	319 795	333 230	368 850	395 132	372 006	387 354	406 187	428 123 p
46	Distrib. trade, repairs; transp.; accommod., food serv. activ.	645 255	689 379	736 332	785 967	832 309	871 837	912 561	989 677 p
47	Information and communication	56 337	57 336	60 255	57 148	59 099	61 504	63 329	64 040 p
48	Financial and insurance activities	111 204	120 086	129 429	136 365	137 513	153 817	161 431	175 645 p
49	Real estate activities	28 911	29 718	31 274	32 543	36 392	37 343	39 110	39 862 p
50	Prof., scientif., techn. activ.; admin., support service activ.	392 259	413 712	451 637	490 323	520 703	544 669	569 652	600 597 p
51	Public admin.; compulsory s.s.; education; human health	1 156 704	1 252 605	1 356 021	1 481 432	1 547 402	1 641 777	1 749 680	1 841 147 p
52	Other service activities	99 369	106 147	110 286	120 595	127 678	132 655	143 511	149 854 p
53	**Wages and salaries**	..	..	..	..	..	..	..	..
54	Agriculture, forestry and fishing	..	..	..	..	..	..	..	..
55	Industry, including energy	..	..	..	..	..	..	..	..
56	Manufacturing	..	..	..	..	..	..	..	..
57	Construction	..	..	..	..	..	..	..	..
58	Distrib. trade, repairs; transp.; accommod., food serv. activ.	..	..	..	..	..	..	..	..
59	Information and communication	..	..	..	..	..	..	..	..
60	Financial and insurance activities	..	..	..	..	..	..	..	..
61	Real estate activities	..	..	..	..	..	..	..	..
62	Prof., scientif., techn. activ.; admin., support service activ.	..	..	..	..	..	..	..	..
63	Public admin.; compulsory s.s.; education; human health	..	..	..	..	..	..	..	..
64	Other service activities	..	..	..	..	..	..	..	..
65	**Gross operating surplus and mixed income**	**8 080 426**	**9 030 272**	**10 078 365**	**10 937 044**	**11 012 348**	**11 682 027**	**12 286 162**	**13 346 547 p**
66	**Taxes less subsidies on production and imports**	**570 319**	**614 602**	**584 699**	**560 950**	**721 986**	**1 002 579**	**1 181 434**	**1 392 248 p**
67	Taxes on production and imports	622 010	738 809	791 434	846 763	900 756	1 117 541	1 260 034	1 439 340 p
68	Subsidies on production and imports	51 691	124 207	206 735	285 812	178 771	114 962	78 600	47 092 p
69	**Residual item**	..	..	..	..	..	..	..	..
70	**Gross domestic product**	**12 162 763**	**13 366 377**	**14 665 576**	**15 817 755**	**16 277 187**	**17 471 467**	**18 536 531**	**20 099 594 p**

Note: Detailed metadata:http://metalinks.oecd.org/nav1/20180308/13ff

Source: Instituto Nacional de Estadistica, Geografia e Informatica (INEGI)

MEXICO

Table 3. Disposable income, saving and net lending / net borrowing

Million MXN

		2009	2010	2011	2012	2013	2014	2015	2016
	DISPOSABLE INCOME								
1	**Gross domestic product**	12 072 541	13 266 857	14 527 336	15 599 270	16 078 959	17 217 015	18 194 758	..
2	Net primary incomes from the rest of the world	-191 663	-144 146	-251 404	-327 958	-511 104	-441 426	-520 112	..
3	Primary incomes receivable from the rest of the world	92 333	135 800	130 470	172 004	144 098	149 068	128 043	..
4	Primary incomes payable to the rest of the world	283 996	279 946	381 874	499 962	655 202	590 494	648 155	
5	**Gross national income at market prices**	11 880 878	13 122 712	14 275 933	15 271 313	15 567 856	16 775 591	17 674 646	18 912 015 e
6	Consumption of fixed capital	1 461 121	1 500 520	1 614 697	1 780 070	1 835 467	1 972 505	2 252 117	2 409 783 e
7	**Net national income at market prices**	10 419 757	11 622 192	12 661 236	13 491 243	13 732 389	14 803 086	15 422 529	16 502 232 e
8	Net current transfers from the rest of the world	291 952	272 002	285 358	297 414	276 469	304 943	386 207	..
9	Current transfers receivable from the rest of the world	..	..	..	..	..	..	..	..
10	Current transfers payable to the rest of the world	..	..	..	..	..	..	..	..
11	**Net national disposable income**	10 711 709	11 894 194	12 946 594	13 788 657	14 008 858	15 108 029	15 808 736	..
	SAVING AND NET LENDING / NET BORROWING								
12	**Net national disposable income**	10 711 709	11 894 194	12 946 594	13 788 657	14 008 858	15 108 029	15 808 736	..
13	Final consumption expenditures	9 513 500	10 448 370	11 326 357	12 359 082	13 012 836	13 833 816	14 720 392	..
14	Adj. for change in net equity of households in pension funds	0	0	0	0	0	0	0	..
15	**Saving, net**	1 198 208	1 445 824	1 620 237	1 429 574	996 022	1 274 212	1 088 343	..
16	Net capital transfers from the rest of the world	0	0	0	0	0	0	0	..
17	Capital transfers receivable from the rest of the world	0	0	0	0	0	0	0	..
18	Capital transfers payable to the rest of the world	0	0	0	0	0	0	0	..
19	Gross capital formation	2 737 296	2 978 301	3 382 542	3 414 960	3 208 089	3 569 315	3 831 961	..
20	Acquisitions less disposals of non-financial non-produced assets	0	0	0	0	0	0	0	..
21	Consumption of fixed capital	1 461 121	1 500 520	1 614 697	1 780 070	1 835 467	1 972 505	2 252 117	2 409 783 e
22	**Net lending / net borrowing**	-77 967	-31 957	-147 607	-205 315	-376 600	-322 598	-491 500	..
	REAL DISPOSABLE INCOME								
23	**Gross domestic product at constant prices, reference year 2010**	12 620 904	13 266 857	13 752 823	14 253 745	14 446 754	14 857 805	15 343 726	15 790 739 p
24	Trading gain or loss	31 159 e	0 e	23 731 e	-205 690 e	-356 936 e	-336 864 e	-562 288 e	..
25	**Real gross domestic income**	12 652 063 e	13 266 857 e	13 776 554 e	14 048 055 e	14 089 818 e	14 520 941 e	14 781 437 e	..
26	Net real primary incomes from the rest of the world	-200 863 e	-144 146 e	-238 411 e	-295 345 e	-447 875 e	-372 302 e	-422 539 e	..
27	Real primary incomes receivable from the rest of the world	96 765 e	135 800 e	123 727 e	154 900 e	126 272 e	125 725 e	104 022 e	..
28	Real primary incomes payable to the rest of the world	297 629 e	279 946 e	362 139 e	450 245 e	574 146 e	498 026 e	526 562 e	..
29	**Real gross national income at market prices**	12 451 199 e	13 122 712 e	13 538 144 e	13 752 711 e	13 641 944 e	14 148 641 e	14 358 898 e	14 568 851 e
30	Net real current transfers from the rest of the world	..	..	..	..	..	..	..	..
31	Real current transfers receivable from the rest of the world	..	..	..	..	..	..	..	..
32	Real current transfers payable to the rest of the world	..	..	..	..	..	..	..	..
33	**Real gross national disposable income**	12 757 166 e	13 394 714 e	13 808 754 e	14 020 550 e	13 884 211 e	14 405 832 e	14 672 653 e	..
34	Consumption of fixed capital at constant prices	..	..	..	..	..	..	..	..
35	**Real net national income at market prices**	10 919 940 e	11 622 192 e	12 006 895 e	12 149 654 e	12 033 544 e	12 485 018 e	12 529 276 e	12 712 477 e
36	**Real net national disposable income**	11 225 906 e	11 894 194 e	12 277 506 e	12 417 492 e	12 275 811 e	12 742 209 e	12 843 031 e	..

Note: Detailed metadata:http://metalinks.oecd.org/nav1/20180308/9e7e
Source: Instituto Nacional de Estadistica, Geografia e Informatica (INEGI)

Table 4. Population and employment (persons) and employment (hours worked) by industry
ISIC Rev. 4

		2009	2010	2011	2012	2013	2014	2015	2016
	POPULATION, THOUSAND PERSONS, NATIONAL CONCEPT								
1	**Total population**	**112 853.0**	**114 256.0**	**115 683.0**	**117 054.0**	**118 395.0**	119 713.0 e	121 005.0 e	122 273.0 e
2	Economically active population	45 416.0	49 132.6	49 481.6	51 477.4	51 896.2	..	..	..
3	Unemployed persons	2 353.0	2 535.0	2 590.0	2 474.0	2 600.0			
4	Total employment	43 063.0	46 597.6	46 891.6	49 003.4	49 296.2	..	..	..
5	Employees	31 168.0	33 496.8	33 945.8	35 516.6	35 830.0			
6	Self-employed	11 895.0	13 100.9	12 945.8	13 486.8	13 466.2			
	TOTAL EMPLOYMENT, THOUSAND PERSONS, DOMESTIC CONCEPT								
7	Agriculture, forestry and fishing	..	..	..	..	..	..	..	..
8	Industry, including energy	..	..	..	..	..	..	..	..
9	Manufacturing	..	..	..	..	..	..	..	..
10	Construction	..	..	..	..	..	..	..	..
11	Distrib. trade, repairs; transp.; accommod., food serv. activ.	..	..	..	..	..	..	..	..
12	Information and communication	..	..	..	..	..	..	..	..
13	Financial and insurance activities	..	..	..	..	..	..	..	..
14	Real estate activities	..	..	..	..	..	..	..	..
15	Prof., scientif., techn. activ.; admin., support service activ.	..	..	..	..	..	..	..	..
16	Public admin.; compulsory s.s.; education; human health	..	..	..	..	..	..	..	..
17	Other service activities	..	..	..	..	..	..	..	..
18	**Total employment**	..	..	..	..	..	..	..	..
	EMPLOYEES, THOUSAND PERSONS, DOMESTIC CONCEPT								
19	Agriculture, forestry and fishing	..	..	..	..	..	..	..	..
20	Industry, including energy	..	..	..	..	..	..	..	..
21	Manufacturing	..	..	..	..	..	..	..	..
22	Construction	..	..	..	..	..	..	..	..
23	Distrib. trade, repairs; transp.; accommod., food serv. activ.	..	..	..	..	..	..	..	..
24	Information and communication	..	..	..	..	..	..	..	..
25	Financial and insurance activities	..	..	..	..	..	..	..	..
26	Real estate activities	..	..	..	..	..	..	..	..
27	Prof., scientif., techn. activ.; admin., support service activ.	..	..	..	..	..	..	..	..
28	Public admin.; compulsory s.s.; education; human health	..	..	..	..	..	..	..	..
29	Other service activities	..	..	..	..	..	..	..	..
30	**Total employees**	..	..	..	..	..	..	..	..
	SELF-EMPLOYED, THOUSAND PERSONS, DOMESTIC CONCEPT								
31	Agriculture, forestry and fishing	..	..	..	..	..	..	..	..
32	Industry, including energy	..	..	..	..	..	..	..	..
33	Manufacturing	..	..	..	..	..	..	..	..
34	Construction	..	..	..	..	..	..	..	..
35	Distrib. trade, repairs; transp.; accommod., food serv. activ.	..	..	..	..	..	..	..	..
36	Information and communication	..	..	..	..	..	..	..	..
37	Financial and insurance activities	..	..	..	..	..	..	..	..
38	Real estate activities	..	..	..	..	..	..	..	..
39	Prof., scientif., techn. activ.; admin., support service activ.	..	..	..	..	..	..	..	..
40	Public admin.; compulsory s.s.; education; human health	..	..	..	..	..	..	..	..
41	Other service activities	..	..	..	..	..	..	..	..
42	**Total self-employed**	..	..	..	..	..	..	..	..
	TOTAL EMPLOYMENT, MILLION HOURS, DOMESTIC CONCEPT								
43	Industry, including energy	..	16 605.1	17 089.2	17 504.0	18 421.9	..	..	..
44	Distrib. trade, repairs; transp.; accommod., food serv. activ.	..	33 118.4	33 564.3	34 638.6	35 362.2	..	..	..
45	Financial and insurance activities	..	991.4	946.5	1 210.6	1 153.7	..	..	..
46	Prof., scientif., techn. activ.; admin., support service activ.	..	4 893.2	5 097.3	5 291.5	5 502.3	..	..	..
47	Public admin.; compulsory s.s.; education; human health	..	11 702.9	11 710.9	12 134.9	12 201.0	..	..	..
48	**Total employment**	**89 639.3**	**99 161.6**	**99 988.6**	**103 243.4**	**105 144.6**	..	..	..
	EMPLOYEES, MILLION HOURS, DOMESTIC CONCEPT								
49	Industry, including energy	..	13 932.0	14 379.4	14 709.3	15 616.9	..	..	..
50	Distrib. trade, repairs; transp.; accommod., food serv. activ.	..	21 159.2	21 545.2	22 047.9	22 932.9	..	..	..
51	Financial and insurance activities	..	958.9	923.5	1 167.9	1 126.2	..	..	..
52	Prof., scientif., techn. activ.; admin., support service activ.	..	3 667.6	3 894.1	4 071.9	4 254.6	..	..	..
53	Public admin.; compulsory s.s.; education; human health	..	11 210.6	11 292.2	11 658.8	11 741.8	..	..	..
54	**Total employees**	**65 233.7**	**72 318.2**	**73 317.4**	**75 941.7**	**77 655.7**	..	..	..
	SELF-EMPLOYED, MILLION HOURS, DOMESTIC CONCEPT								
55	Industry, including energy	..	2 673.1	2 709.8	2 794.7	2 805.0	..	..	..
56	Distrib. trade, repairs; transp.; accommod., food serv. activ.	..	11 959.2	12 019.2	12 590.6	12 429.3	..	..	..
57	Financial and insurance activities	..	32.5	22.9	42.7	27.5	..	..	..
58	Prof., scientif., techn. activ.; admin., support service activ.	..	1 225.5	1 203.2	1 219.6	1 247.7	..	..	..
59	Public admin.; compulsory s.s.; education; human health	..	492.3	418.6	476.0	459.2	..	..	..
60	**Total self-employed**	**24 405.6**	**26 843.4**	**26 671.2**	**27 301.7**	**27 488.9**	..	..	..

Note: Detailed metadata:http://metalinks.oecd.org/nav1/20180308/2de5
Source: Instituto Nacional de Estadistica, Geografia e Informatica (INEGI)

NETHERLANDS

Table 1. Gross domestic product, expenditure approach

Million EUR (1999 NLG euro)

		2009	2010	2011	2012	2013	2014	2015	2016
	AT CURRENT PRICES								
1	**Final consumption expenditure**	**442 934**	**449 742**	**456 097**	**459 631**	**463 903**	**468 668**	**475 147**	**484 374** p
2	Household	274 318	277 194	283 456	284 265	288 086	291 027	297 688	304 703 p
3	NPISH's	5 261	5 316	5 483	5 491	5 559	5 655	5 782	5 989 p
4	Government	163 355	167 232	167 158	169 875	170 258	171 986	171 677	173 682 p
5	Individual	107 237	110 854	111 659	114 423	113 518	114 934	115 028	115 861 p
6	Collective	56 118	56 378	55 499	55 452	56 740	57 052	56 649	57 821 p
7	*of which: Actual individual consumption*	386 816	393 364	400 598	404 179	407 163	411 616	418 498	426 553 p
8	**Gross capital formation**	**129 350**	**128 957**	**131 928**	**123 587**	**119 027**	**122 455**	**136 175**	**140 919** p
9	Gross fixed capital formation, total	131 554	124 649	130 402	121 928	117 107	119 530	132 464	140 049 p
10	Dwellings	34 712	29 464	26 877	22 610	19 506	20 142	23 651	28 231 p
11	Other buildings and structures	38 974	36 793	39 615	36 137	35 717	36 024	37 543	38 109 p
12	Transport equipment	5 937	6 152	7 946	8 192	7 224	6 269	9 662	10 042 p
13	Other machinery and equipment	22 198	20 610	23 593	21 978	20 934	21 878	23 022	23 912 p
14	Cultivated assets	311	259	200	251	316	333	355	316 p
15	Intangible fixed assets	24 959	27 030	27 477	28 087	28 792	30 298	32 573	33 531 p
16	Changes in inventories, acquisitions less disposals of valuables	-2 204	4 308	1 526	1 659	1 920	2 925	3 711	870 p
17	Changes in inventories	-2 530	3 867	1 174	1 287	1 487	2 633	3 349	585 p
18	Acquisitions less disposals of valuables	326	441	352	372	433	292	362	285 p
19	**External balance of goods and services**	**45 256**	**52 813**	**54 904**	**61 946**	**69 818**	**71 885**	**72 135**	**77 348** p
20	Exports of goods and services	390 004	454 398	497 347	528 623	535 320	547 415	570 178	579 317 p
21	Exports of goods	304 198	360 296	398 744	425 408	427 390	429 655	440 240	447 927 p
22	Exports of services	85 806	94 102	98 603	103 215	107 930	117 760	129 938	131 390 p
23	Imports of goods and services	344 748	401 585	442 443	466 677	465 502	475 530	498 043	501 969 p
24	Imports of goods	250 982	300 067	333 823	354 312	352 043	353 737	361 853	364 210 p
25	Imports of services	93 766	101 518	108 620	112 365	113 459	121 793	136 190	137 759 p
26	**Statistical discrepancy**	**0**	**0**	**0**	**0**	**0**	**0**	**0**	**0**
27	**Gross domestic product**	**617 540**	**631 512**	**642 929**	**645 164**	**652 748**	**663 008**	**683 457**	**702 641** p
	AT CONSTANT PRICES, REFERENCE YEAR 2010								
28	**Final consumption expenditure**	**447 983**	**449 742**	**449 785**	**444 334**	**441 346**	**442 505**	**447 879**	**454 193** p
29	Household	277 081	277 194	277 659	274 407	271 656	272 350	277 886	282 144 p
30	NPISH's	5 359	5 316	5 308	5 295	5 236	5 279	5 392	5 537 p
31	Government	165 541	167 232	166 818	164 628	164 455	164 876	164 545	166 444 p
32	Individual	108 947	110 854	112 258	111 287	110 200	110 683	111 083	112 455 p
33	Collective	56 588	56 378	54 560	53 353	54 255	54 197	53 475	54 004 p
34	*of which: Actual individual consumption*	391 394	393 364	395 225	390 984	387 086	388 302	394 389	400 173 p
35	**Gross capital formation**	**131 042**	**128 957**	**133 421**	**125 154**	**120 251**	**124 099**	**138 041**	**142 315** p
36	Gross fixed capital formation, total	133 340	124 649	131 583	123 319	118 068	120 763	133 999	141 052 p
37	Dwellings	35 058	29 464	28 165	24 537	21 554	22 869	27 653	32 921 p
38	Other buildings and structures	39 781	36 793	39 169	35 630	34 778	34 912	36 771	37 348 p
39	Transport equipment	5 912	6 152	8 090	8 270	7 297	6 386	9 584	9 848 p
40	Other machinery and equipment	22 497	20 610	23 389	21 360	20 271	21 099	21 804	22 474 p
41	Cultivated assets	316	259	206	277	365	383	391	373 p
42	Intangible fixed assets	25 425	27 030	27 649	28 237	28 710	30 093	31 876	32 447 p
43	Changes in inventories, acquisitions less disposals of valuables	..	..	..	..	..	..	..	..
44	Changes in inventories	..	..	..	..	..	..	..	..
45	Acquisitions less disposals of valuables	..	..	..	..	..	..	..	..
46	**External balance of goods and services**	**43 718**	**52 813**	**58 812**	**65 573**	**71 895**	**76 143**	**72 465**	**76 645** p
47	Exports of goods and services	411 087	454 398	474 410	492 408	502 880	525 263	559 261	583 395 p
48	Exports of goods	323 251	360 296	375 366	388 857	396 049	408 855	431 654	453 978 p
49	Exports of services	87 734	94 102	99 044	103 601	106 988	116 908	128 298	130 111 p
50	Imports of goods and services	367 369	401 585	415 598	426 835	430 985	449 119	486 796	506 750 p
51	Imports of goods	271 493	300 067	308 916	317 683	321 664	332 349	359 279	378 150 p
52	Imports of services	95 706	101 518	106 682	109 127	109 221	116 819	127 589	128 909 p
53	**Statistical discrepancy (including chaining residual)**	**34**	**0**	**0**	**170**	**530**	**276**	**-825**	**-1 060** p
54	**Gross domestic product**	**622 777**	**631 512**	**642 018**	**635 232**	**634 023**	**643 024**	**657 561**	**672 093** p

Note: Detailed metadata:http://metalinks.oecd.org/nav1/20180308/fa85
Source: Netherlands Central Bureau of Statistics (CBS) via Eurostat.

NETHERLANDS

Table 2. Gross domestic product, output and income approach
ISIC Rev. 4

Million EUR (1999 NLG euro)

		2009	2010	2011	2012	2013	2014	2015	2016
	OUTPUT APPROACH AT CURRENT PRICES								
1	**Total gross value added at basic prices**	**553 689**	**567 757**	**579 590**	**583 832**	**588 535**	**597 414**	**614 986**	**631 032 p**
2	Agriculture, forestry and fishing	9 192	10 828	9 697	10 225	11 198	10 996	11 102	11 543 p
3	Industry, including energy	92 601	95 149	99 481	101 456	99 658	95 277	96 515	96 214 p
4	Manufacturing	65 005	67 024	69 979	69 074	66 676	68 004	73 110	76 648 p
5	Construction	33 636	30 531	30 295	27 826	26 456	27 223	28 201	29 965 p
6	Services	..	..	..	..	..	..	..	..
7	Distrib. trade, repairs; transp.; accommod., food serv. activ.	105 546	110 472	113 924	115 141	118 253	121 772	128 679	133 940 p
8	Information and communication	27 493	27 843	27 889	27 751	27 920	28 473	29 736	30 253 p
9	Financial and insurance activities	41 448	47 722	45 918	49 908	49 142	48 526	47 145	44 375 p
10	Real estate activities	33 169	31 599	33 405	29 050	31 173	34 716	35 935	37 880 p
11	Prof., scientif., techn. activ.; admin., support service activ.	76 776	75 234	78 267	78 699	79 131	83 331	89 890	95 131 p
12	Public admin.; compulsory s.s.; education; human health	119 717	123 746	125 690	128 584	130 442	131 453	131 508	134 851 p
13	Other service activities	14 111	14 633	15 024	15 192	15 162	15 647	16 275	16 880 p
14	**FISIM (Financial Intermediation Services Indirectly Measured)**	..	..	..	..	..	..	..	..
15	**Gross value added at basic prices, excluding FISIM**	**553 689**	**567 757**	**579 590**	**583 832**	**588 535**	**597 414**	**614 986**	**631 032 p**
16	**Taxes less subsidies on products**	**63 851**	**63 755**	**63 339**	**61 332**	**64 213**	**65 594**	**68 471**	**71 609 p**
17	Taxes on products	67 411	67 306	66 771	64 715	67 353	68 703	71 514	74 919 p
18	Subsidies on products	3 560	3 551	3 432	3 383	3 140	3 109	3 043	3 310 p
19	**Residual item**	**0**	**0**	**0**	**0**	**0**	**0**	**0**	**0**
20	**Gross domestic product at market prices**	**617 540**	**631 512**	**642 929**	**645 164**	**652 748**	**663 008**	**683 457**	**702 641 p**
	OUTPUT APPROACH AT CONSTANT PRICES (REF. YEAR 2010)								
21	**Total gross value added at basic prices**	**558 157**	**567 757**	**579 152**	**574 694**	**575 515**	**584 159**	**595 746**	**608 516 p**
22	Agriculture, forestry and fishing	10 819	10 828	10 674	10 541	10 595	11 052	11 222	11 436 p
23	Industry, including energy	89 618	95 149	96 139	94 979	95 957	94 566	93 028	94 088 p
24	Manufacturing	63 666	67 024	69 443	68 443	67 605	68 802	69 631	71 734 p
25	Construction	34 259	30 531	30 818	28 308	26 836	28 014	30 338	32 665 p
26	Services	..	..	..	..	..	..	..	..
27	Distrib. trade, repairs; transp.; accommod., food serv. activ.	106 221	110 472	115 245	114 878	115 335	118 647	121 743	124 827 p
28	Information and communication	27 931	27 843	28 284	28 473	29 037	30 067	31 611	32 233 p
29	Financial and insurance activities	46 397	47 722	47 165	45 717	44 650	43 436	43 232	43 008 p
30	Real estate activities	30 784	31 599	32 055	32 814	34 445	36 118	37 014	37 857 p
31	Prof., scientif., techn. activ.; admin., support service activ.	76 862	75 234	77 677	78 242	77 984	81 762	87 401	91 351 p
32	Public admin.; compulsory s.s.; education; human health	120 812	123 746	126 304	125 973	126 403	126 655	126 325	127 316 p
33	Other service activities	14 654	14 633	14 791	14 676	14 402	14 386	14 655	14 832 p
34	**FISIM (Financial Intermediation Services Indirectly Measured)**	..	..	..	..	..	..	..	..
35	**Gross value added at basic prices, excluding FISIM**	**558 157**	**567 757**	**579 152**	**574 694**	**575 515**	**584 159**	**595 746**	**608 516 p**
36	**Taxes less subsidies on products**	**64 626**	**63 755**	**62 866**	**60 548**	**58 513**	**58 903**	**61 722**	**63 453 p**
37	Taxes on products	68 118	67 306	66 495	64 165	62 087	62 461	65 335	67 220 p
38	Subsidies on products	3 495	3 551	3 629	3 624	3 588	3 562	3 587	3 756 p
39	**Residual item**	**-7**	**0**	**0**	**-11**	**-6**	**-38**	**93**	**123 p**
40	**Gross domestic product at market prices**	**622 777**	**631 512**	**642 018**	**635 232**	**634 023**	**643 024**	**657 561**	**672 093 p**
	INCOME APPROACH								
41	**Compensation of employees**	**311 679**	**310 471**	**318 040**	**322 825**	**324 595**	**327 963**	**330 060**	**339 804 p**
42	Agriculture, forestry and fishing	2 563	2 603	2 677	2 739	2 792	2 799	2 789	2 903 p
43	Industry, including energy	43 103	41 042	42 141	42 741	43 211	44 412	44 250	45 218 p
44	Manufacturing	39 125	36 912	37 771	38 285	38 555	39 645	39 493	40 478 p
45	Construction	19 115	18 765	18 786	18 660	17 277	16 652	16 262	16 599 p
46	Distrib. trade, repairs; transp.; accommod., food serv. activ.	60 461	60 724	62 806	64 182	64 446	64 763	66 113	68 435 p
47	Information and communication	14 442	13 768	14 128	14 513	14 458	14 588	15 298	15 910 p
48	Financial and insurance activities	19 126	18 987	19 306	19 383	20 503	20 512	19 409	19 430 p
49	Real estate activities	3 861	3 735	3 751	3 731	3 685	3 632	3 572	3 571 p
50	Prof., scientif., techn. activ.; admin., support service activ.	50 852	49 479	51 360	51 995	52 274	54 010	55 562	58 255 p
51	Public admin.; compulsory s.s.; education; human health	89 982	92 952	94 469	96 321	97 512	98 044	98 339	100 779 p
52	Other service activities	8 174	8 416	8 616	8 560	8 437	8 551	8 466	8 704 p
53	**Wages and salaries**	**245 616**	**246 542**	**251 715**	**253 193**	**254 034**	**253 880**	**259 619**	**267 717 p**
54	Agriculture, forestry and fishing	2 087	2 114	2 149	2 178	2 225	2 216	2 225	2 308 p
55	Industry, including energy	32 893	32 815	33 417	33 578	34 159	34 317	35 013	35 793 p
56	Manufacturing	29 763	29 589	30 011	30 187	30 602	30 681	31 289	32 063 p
57	Construction	15 241	14 881	14 813	14 568	13 570	12 813	12 622	13 018 p
58	Distrib. trade, repairs; transp.; accommod., food serv. activ.	49 015	49 270	50 738	51 283	51 324	51 362	52 994	54 764 p
59	Information and communication	11 513	11 230	11 607	11 744	11 660	11 838	12 424	13 072 p
60	Financial and insurance activities	15 280	15 138	15 238	15 258	15 586	15 041	14 829	14 683 p
61	Real estate activities	2 963	2 831	2 849	2 819	2 802	2 730	2 736	2 768 p
62	Prof., scientif., techn. activ.; admin., support service activ.	41 142	39 800	41 357	41 509	41 861	42 733	44 899	47 023 p
63	Public admin.; compulsory s.s.; education; human health	68 841	71 619	72 566	73 360	74 059	74 012	75 033	77 257 p
64	Other service activities	6 641	6 844	6 981	6 896	6 788	6 818	6 844	7 031 p
65	**Gross operating surplus and mixed income**	**247 083**	**259 005**	**263 968**	**261 721**	**263 967**	**266 358**	**283 122**	**287 137 p**
66	**Taxes less subsidies on production and imports**	**58 778**	**62 036**	**61 191**	**60 618**	**64 186**	**68 687**	**70 275**	**75 700 p**
67	Taxes on production and imports	69 966	73 329	71 871	70 513	73 439	77 597	79 003	84 876 p
68	Subsidies on production and imports	11 188	11 293	10 680	9 895	9 253	8 910	8 728	9 176 p
69	**Residual item**	**0**	**0**	**0**	**0**	**0**	**0**	**0**	**0**
70	**Gross domestic product**	**617 540**	**631 512**	**642 929**	**645 164**	**652 748**	**663 008**	**683 457**	**702 641 p**

Note: Detailed metadata:http://metalinks.oecd.org/nav1/20180308/fa85
Source: Netherlands Central Bureau of Statistics (CBS) via Eurostat.

NETHERLANDS

Table 3. Disposable income, saving and net lending / net borrowing

Million EUR (1999 NLG euro)

		2009	2010	2011	2012	2013	2014	2015	2016
	DISPOSABLE INCOME								
1	**Gross domestic product**	617 540	631 512	642 929	645 164	652 748	663 008	683 457	702 641 p
2	Net primary incomes from the rest of the world	552	5 114	11 758	13 286	9 131	-1 721	-3 847	-8 410 p
3	Primary incomes receivable from the rest of the world	172 948	224 720	247 129	232 502	233 785	258 724	228 879	208 613 p
4	Primary incomes payable to the rest of the world	172 396	219 606	235 371	219 216	224 654	260 445	232 726	217 023 p
5	**Gross national income at market prices**	618 092	636 626	654 687	658 450	661 879	661 287	679 610	694 231 p
6	Consumption of fixed capital	104 435	106 982	107 068	107 897	109 362	110 194	111 755	114 389 p
7	**Net national income at market prices**	513 657	529 644	547 619	550 553	552 517	551 093	567 855	579 842 p
8	Net current transfers from the rest of the world	-6 587	-9 256	-9 450	-9 275	-11 780	-10 632	-10 822	-7 277 p
9	Current transfers receivable from the rest of the world	10 036	10 063	10 217	10 736	10 334	11 629	12 156	11 052 p
10	Current transfers payable to the rest of the world	16 623	19 319	19 667	20 011	22 114	22 261	22 978	18 329 p
11	**Net national disposable income**	507 070	520 388	538 169	541 278	540 737	540 461	557 033	572 565 p
	SAVING AND NET LENDING / NET BORROWING								
12	**Net national disposable income**	507 070	520 388	538 169	541 278	540 737	540 461	557 033	572 565 p
13	Final consumption expenditures	442 934	449 742	456 097	459 631	463 903	468 668	475 147	484 374 p
14	Adj. for change in net equity of households in pension funds	-691	-341	-331	-345	-433	-481	-431	-413 p
15	**Saving, net**	63 445	70 305	81 741	81 302	76 401	71 312	81 455	87 778 p
16	Net capital transfers from the rest of the world	-842	-1 890	-552	-268	-562	-432	-893	-1 042 p
17	Capital transfers receivable from the rest of the world	913	896	783	780	746	723	931	847 p
18	Capital transfers payable to the rest of the world	1 755	2 786	1 335	1 048	1 308	1 155	1 824	1 889 p
19	Gross capital formation	129 350	128 957	131 928	123 587	119 027	122 455	136 175	140 919 p
20	Acquisitions less disposals of non-financial non-produced assets	-274	-703	1 328	5 877	1 092	162	33 600	596 p
21	Consumption of fixed capital	104 435	106 982	107 068	107 897	109 362	110 194	111 755	114 389 p
22	**Net lending / net borrowing**	37 962	47 143	55 001	59 467	65 082	58 457	22 542	59 610 p
	REAL DISPOSABLE INCOME								
23	**Gross domestic product at constant prices, reference year 2010**	622 777	631 512	642 018	635 232	634 023	643 024	657 561	672 093 p
24	Trading gain or loss	2 034	0	-4 358	-5 113	-4 858	-7 392	-3 129	-2 580 p
25	**Real gross domestic income**	624 811	631 512	637 660	630 119	629 165	635 631	654 432	669 512 p
26	Net real primary incomes from the rest of the world	558	5 114	11 662	12 976	8 801	-1 650	-3 684	-8 013 p
27	Real primary incomes receivable from the rest of the world	174 984	224 720	245 104	227 080	225 339	248 041	219 159	198 777 p
28	Real primary incomes payable to the rest of the world	174 426	219 606	233 442	214 104	216 537	249 691	222 843	206 791 p
29	**Real gross national income at market prices**	625 369	636 626	649 322	643 095	637 966	633 981	650 749	661 499 p
30	Net real current transfers from the rest of the world	-6 665	-9 256	-9 373	-9 059	-11 354	-10 193	-10 362	-6 934 p
31	Real current transfers receivable from the rest of the world	10 154	10 063	10 133	10 486	9 961	11 149	11 640	10 531 p
32	Real current transfers payable to the rest of the world	16 819	19 319	19 506	19 544	21 315	21 342	22 002	17 465 p
33	**Real gross national disposable income**	618 705	627 370	639 949	634 036	626 612	623 788	640 386	654 565 p
34	Consumption of fixed capital at constant prices	105 699	106 982	108 371	109 821	110 990	112 000	113 625	115 706 p
35	**Real net national income at market prices**	519 705	529 644	543 131	537 714	532 555	528 338	543 740	552 503 p
36	**Real net national disposable income**	513 040	520 388	533 759	528 655	521 201	518 145	533 377	545 569 p

Note: Detailed metadata:http://metalinks.oecd.org/nav1/20180308/69e2
Source: Netherlands Central Bureau of Statistics (CBS) via Eurostat.

Table 4. Population and employment (persons) and employment (hours worked) by industry
ISIC Rev. 4

		2009	2010	2011	2012	2013	2014	2015	2016
	POPULATION, THOUSAND PERSONS, NATIONAL CONCEPT								
1	**Total population**	16 526.0	16 612.0	16 693.0	16 752.0	16 800.0	16 863.0	16 932.0 p	17 026.0 p
2	Economically active population	..	..	..	..	..	..	..	..
3	Unemployed persons	..	..	..	..	..	..	..	..
4	Total employment	8 709.0	8 649.0	8 717.0	8 699.0	8 600.0	8 593.0	8 673.0 p	8 763.0 p
5	Employees	7 326.0	7 267.0	7 307.0	7 263.0	7 153.0	7 114.0	7 182.0 p	7 278.0 p
6	Self-employed	1 383.0	1 382.0	1 410.0	1 436.0	1 447.0	1 479.0	1 491.0 p	1 485.0 p
	TOTAL EMPLOYMENT, THOUSAND PERSONS, DOMESTIC CONCEPT								
7	Agriculture, forestry and fishing	204.0	203.0	201.0	199.0	196.0	195.0	194.0 p	195.0 p
8	Industry, including energy	885.0	863.0	857.0	848.0	835.0	830.0	832.0 p	833.0 p
9	Manufacturing	822.0	799.0	792.0	783.0	769.0	765.0	766.0 p	768.0 p
10	Construction	549.0	523.0	522.0	509.0	478.0	466.0	462.0 p	460.0 p
11	Distrib. trade, repairs; transp.; accommod., food serv. activ.	2 129.0	2 124.0	2 159.0	2 164.0	2 141.0	2 152.0	2 188.0 p	2 216.0 p
12	Information and communication	260.0	252.0	256.0	259.0	256.0	261.0	268.0 p	277.0 p
13	Financial and insurance activities	275.0	266.0	261.0	257.0	252.0	243.0	237.0 p	231.0 p
14	Real estate activities	83.0	79.0	79.0	76.0	75.0	74.0	73.0 p	73.0 p
15	Prof., scientif., techn. activ.; admin., support service activ.	1 702.0	1 653.0	1 683.0	1 685.0	1 680.0	1 719.0	1 792.0 p	1 855.0 p
16	Public admin.; compulsory s.s.; education; human health	2 381.0	2 445.0	2 457.0	2 464.0	2 448.0	2 408.0	2 387.0 p	2 384.0 p
17	Other service activities	370.0	370.0	379.0	376.0	372.0	376.0	375.0 p	377.0 p
18	**Total employment**	8 838.0	8 778.0	8 854.0	8 836.0	8 732.0	8 724.0	8 806.0 p	8 901.0 p
	EMPLOYEES, THOUSAND PERSONS, DOMESTIC CONCEPT								
19	Agriculture, forestry and fishing	100.0	98.0	98.0	97.0	96.0	95.0	94.0 p	95.0 p
20	Industry, including energy	845.0	823.0	818.0	808.0	795.0	789.0	790.0 p	792.0 p
21	Manufacturing	783.0	761.0	754.0	744.0	730.0	725.0	725.0 p	728.0 p
22	Construction	383.0	370.0	363.0	348.0	318.0	299.0	294.0 p	293.0 p
23	Distrib. trade, repairs; transp.; accommod., food serv. activ.	1 878.0	1 872.0	1 904.0	1 909.0	1 891.0	1 897.0	1 931.0 p	1 964.0 p
24	Information and communication	230.0	220.0	222.0	224.0	219.0	222.0	229.0 p	238.0 p
25	Financial and insurance activities	268.0	260.0	254.0	250.0	246.0	237.0	231.0 p	225.0 p
26	Real estate activities	73.0	69.0	68.0	65.0	63.0	63.0	62.0 p	62.0 p
27	Prof., scientif., techn. activ.; admin., support service activ.	1 290.0	1 223.0	1 240.0	1 234.0	1 223.0	1 251.0	1 320.0 p	1 385.0 p
28	Public admin.; compulsory s.s.; education; human health	2 136.0	2 207.0	2 219.0	2 212.0	2 190.0	2 150.0	2 125.0 p	2 121.0 p
29	Other service activities	253.0	254.0	258.0	252.0	243.0	242.0	240.0 p	241.0 p
30	**Total employees**	7 455.0	7 396.0	7 444.0	7 399.0	7 285.0	7 244.0	7 315.0 p	7 416.0 p
	SELF-EMPLOYED, THOUSAND PERSONS, DOMESTIC CONCEPT								
31	Agriculture, forestry and fishing	105.0	105.0	104.0	101.0	99.0	100.0	101.0 p	100.0 p
32	Industry, including energy	40.0	39.0	39.0	40.0	40.0	41.0	42.0 p	41.0 p
33	Manufacturing	39.0	38.0	39.0	39.0	39.0	40.0	40.0 p	40.0 p
34	Construction	166.0	153.0	159.0	161.0	160.0	167.0	168.0 p	167.0 p
35	Distrib. trade, repairs; transp.; accommod., food serv. activ.	251.0	252.0	255.0	254.0	249.0	255.0	257.0 p	252.0 p
36	Information and communication	31.0	31.0	34.0	36.0	37.0	39.0	39.0 p	39.0 p
37	Financial and insurance activities	7.0	6.0	6.0	6.0	6.0	6.0	6.0 p	6.0 p
38	Real estate activities	10.0	10.0	11.0	11.0	11.0	11.0	11.0 p	11.0 p
39	Prof., scientif., techn. activ.; admin., support service activ.	412.0	430.0	443.0	451.0	457.0	468.0	471.0 p	469.0 p
40	Public admin.; compulsory s.s.; education; human health	245.0	239.0	237.0	251.0	258.0	258.0	261.0 p	264.0 p
41	Other service activities	117.0	116.0	121.0	125.0	129.0	134.0	135.0 p	135.0 p
42	**Total self-employed**	1 383.0	1 382.0	1 410.0	1 436.0	1 447.0	1 479.0	1 491.0 p	1 485.0 p
	TOTAL EMPLOYMENT, MILLION HOURS, DOMESTIC CONCEPT								
43	Industry, including energy	1 405.9	1 392.4	1 389.7	1 367.1	1 360.6	1 361.5	1 354.2 p	1 363.2 p
44	Distrib. trade, repairs; transp.; accommod., food serv. activ.	2 990.9	2 976.0	3 011.0	2 985.5	2 941.3	2 963.7	2 992.0 p	3 058.6 p
45	Financial and insurance activities	420.6	408.0	402.3	394.6	388.6	378.6	369.2 p	362.4 p
46	Prof., scientif., techn. activ.; admin., support service activ.	2 235.2	2 219.7	2 276.1	2 264.5	2 268.1	2 345.8	2 444.7 p	2 558.6 p
47	Public admin.; compulsory s.s.; education; human health	3 020.9	3 060.5	3 071.0	3 076.1	3 067.0	3 053.7	3 021.1 p	3 055.2 p
48	**Total employment**	12 567.4	12 476.5	12 594.3	12 486.5	12 378.2	12 465.5	12 539.0 p	12 788.3 p
	EMPLOYEES, MILLION HOURS, DOMESTIC CONCEPT								
49	Industry, including energy	1 318.9	1 306.0	1 304.8	1 281.4	1 276.1	1 276.2	1 268.1 p	1 277.3 p
50	Distrib. trade, repairs; transp.; accommod., food serv. activ.	2 418.7	2 393.8	2 432.1	2 406.8	2 379.4	2 379.7	2 404.7 p	2 477.6 p
51	Financial and insurance activities	406.8	394.8	388.8	381.9	376.3	366.0	356.6 p	349.9 p
52	Prof., scientif., techn. activ.; admin., support service activ.	1 738.9	1 682.7	1 718.2	1 700.7	1 694.2	1 750.4	1 843.8 p	1 950.7 p
53	Public admin.; compulsory s.s.; education; human health	2 674.3	2 717.9	2 719.6	2 702.7	2 681.8	2 662.1	2 624.6 p	2 645.5 p
54	**Total employees**	10 091.5	9 982.5	10 057.2	9 923.7	9 804.0	9 819.0	9 869.3 p	10 093.0 p
	SELF-EMPLOYED, MILLION HOURS, DOMESTIC CONCEPT								
55	Industry, including energy	87.0	86.4	84.9	85.6	84.5	85.3	86.1 p	85.9 p
56	Distrib. trade, repairs; transp.; accommod., food serv. activ.	572.2	582.2	579.0	578.7	561.9	584.0	587.3 p	581.0 p
57	Financial and insurance activities	13.8	13.2	13.6	12.7	12.3	12.6	12.6 p	12.4 p
58	Prof., scientif., techn. activ.; admin., support service activ.	496.3	537.0	557.9	563.8	573.9	595.4	601.0 p	607.8 p
59	Public admin.; compulsory s.s.; education; human health	346.6	342.6	351.4	373.4	385.2	391.6	396.4 p	409.7 p
60	**Total self-employed**	2 475.9	2 494.1	2 537.2	2 562.8	2 574.2	2 646.5	2 669.7 p	2 695.4 p

Note: Detailed metadata:http://metalinks.oecd.org/nav1/20180308/da31
Source: Netherlands Central Bureau of Statistics (CBS) via Eurostat.

NEW ZEALAND

Table 1. Gross domestic product, expenditure approach

Million NZD, fiscal years

		2009	2010	2011	2012	2013	2014	2015	2016
	AT CURRENT PRICES								
1	**Final consumption expenditure**	**151 553**	**157 911**	**166 346**	**170 459**	**177 442**	**184 451**	**191 225**	**201 446 e**
2	Household	110 556	115 501	122 210	126 095	131 478	136 521	141 421	149 504 e
3	NPISH's	2 834	2 643	2 730	2 519	2 685	2 724	2 860	3 003 e
4	Government	38 163	39 767	41 406	41 845	43 279	45 206	46 944	48 938 e
5	Individual	23 985	24 754	25 809	26 327	27 232	28 531	29 454	..
6	Collective	14 178	15 013	15 597	15 518	16 047	16 675	17 490	..
7	*of which:* Actual individual consumption	137 375	142 898	150 749	154 941	161 395	167 776	173 735	183 021 e
8	**Gross capital formation**	**38 185**	**40 854**	**43 594**	**45 500**	**51 208**	**54 640**	**57 421**	**61 873 e**
9	Gross fixed capital formation, total	39 036	39 992	42 326	44 711	49 364	53 583	56 797	61 502 e
10	Dwellings	8 750	8 957	9 343	11 316	13 625	15 577	16 871	..
11	Other buildings and structures	13 116	12 028	12 662	13 157	13 346	13 856	14 432	..
12	Transport equipment	2 435	3 248	3 520	3 309	4 299	5 071	5 108	..
13	Other machinery and equipment	6 925	7 169	8 028	7 952	8 281	8 555	9 312	..
14	Cultivated assets	..	..	..	..	..	..	..	..
15	Intangible fixed assets	5 571	6 141	6 508	6 793	7 479	8 056	8 419	..
16	Changes in inventories, acquisitions less disposals of valuables	-851	862	1 268	789	1 844	1 057	624	..
17	Changes in inventories	-851	862	1 268	789	1 844	1 057	624	371 e
18	Acquisitions less disposals of valuables	0	0	0	0	0	0	..	..
19	**External balance of goods and services**	**4 512**	**4 668**	**3 301**	**1 513**	**3 674**	**1 725**	**1 785**	**696 e**
20	Exports of goods and services	55 832	61 559	64 749	62 766	67 001	67 514	70 144	70 118 e
21	Exports of goods	39 941	45 290	48 042	46 528	50 409	49 167	48 833	..
22	Exports of services	15 891	16 269	16 707	16 238	16 592	18 347	21 311	..
23	Imports of goods and services	51 320	56 891	61 448	61 253	63 327	65 789	68 359	69 422 e
24	Imports of goods	37 814	42 363	46 079	46 012	47 729	49 665	51 376	..
25	Imports of services	13 506	14 528	15 369	15 241	15 598	16 124	16 983	..
26	**Statistical discrepancy**	**0**	**0**	**0**	**0**	**0**	**1 112**	**1 324**	..
27	**Gross domestic product**	**194 250**	**203 433**	**213 241**	**217 472**	**232 324**	**241 928**	**251 755**	**265 715 e**
	AT CONSTANT PRICES, REFERENCE YEAR 2010								
28	**Final consumption expenditure**	**154 466**	**157 911**	**162 457**	**165 147**	**170 361**	**175 590 p**	**180 451 p**	**188 132 e**
29	Household	112 561	115 501	119 299	122 301	126 633	130 486 p	134 086 p	140 647 e
30	NPISH's	2 881	2 643	2 694	2 459	2 558	2 660 p	2 791 p	2 852 e
31	Government	39 026	39 767	40 464	40 385	41 169	42 443 p	43 575 p	44 650 e
32	Individual	..	..	..	..	..	..	..	..
33	Collective	..	..	..	..	..	..	..	..
34	*of which:* Actual individual consumption	140 016	142 898	147 224	150 113	154 954	159 716 p	163 946 p	170 925 e
35	**Gross capital formation**	**38 066**	**40 854**	**44 134**	**45 594**	**49 286**	**52 691 p**	**53 258 p**	**55 486 e**
36	Gross fixed capital formation, total	38 583	39 992	42 387	44 531	48 879	52 192 p	53 519 p	56 526 e
37	Dwellings	8 809	8 957	9 224	10 845	12 487	13 580 p	13 956 p	..
38	Other buildings and structures	13 192	12 028	12 229	12 473	12 459	12 577 p	12 821 p	..
39	Transport equipment	2 367	3 248	3 576	3 403	4 538	5 384 p	5 199 p	..
40	Other machinery and equipment	6 556	7 169	8 032	8 102	8 781	9 257 p	9 837 p	..
41	Cultivated assets	..	..	..	..	..	..	..	..
42	Intangible fixed assets	5 480	6 141	6 575	6 904	7 634	8 293 p	8 444 p	..
43	Changes in inventories, acquisitions less disposals of valuables	..	..	..	..	..	..	..	..
44	Changes in inventories	..	..	..	..	..	..	..	..
45	Acquisitions less disposals of valuables	..	..	..	..	..	..	..	..
46	**External balance of goods and services**	**8 844**	**4 668**	**2 337**	**3 443**	**-1 533**	**-3 708 p**	**-1 498 p**	**-4 635 e**
47	Exports of goods and services	59 870	61 559	62 968	64 882	64 897	67 662 p	71 374 p	71 911 e
48	Exports of goods	43 993	45 290	46 524	49 017	48 883	50 170 p	51 362 p	..
49	Exports of services	15 873	16 269	16 445	15 848	15 986	17 457 p	19 871 p	..
50	Imports of goods and services	51 026	56 891	60 631	61 439	66 430	71 370 p	72 872 p	76 547 e
51	Imports of goods	37 667	42 363	45 227	46 151	50 090	54 443 p	56 071 p	..
52	Imports of services	13 356	14 528	15 404	15 281	16 332	16 920 p	16 816 p	..
53	**Statistical discrepancy (including chaining residual)**	**134**	**0**	**-15**	**-49**	**60**	**284 p**	**123 p**	**448 e**
54	**Gross domestic product**	**201 510**	**203 433**	**208 912**	**214 136**	**218 174**	**224 857 p**	**232 334 p**	**239 430 e**

Note: Detailed metadata:http://metalinks.oecd.org/nav1/20180308/6670
Source: Statistics New Zealand.

NEW ZEALAND

Table 2. Gross domestic product, output and income approach
ISIC Rev. 4

Million NZD, fiscal years

		2009	2010	2011	2012	2013	2014	2015	2016
	OUTPUT APPROACH AT CURRENT PRICES								
1	**Total gross value added at basic prices**	180 018	187 437	195 345	198 990	213 031	221 683 p	..	..
2	Agriculture, forestry and fishing	15 304	17 579	17 393	15 739	19 951	15 075 p	..	..
3	Industry, including energy	26 992	28 402	29 913	30 223	31 249	34 165 p	..	..
4	Manufacturing	20 924	22 050	23 315	23 071	23 828	26 490 p	..	..
5	Construction	10 491	10 525	10 886	11 650	12 508	14 073 p	..	..
6	Services	..	..	..	..	..	..	..	..
7	Distrib. trade, repairs; transp.; accommod., food serv. activ.	29 877	31 162	32 667	33 926	36 295	39 290 p	..	..
8	Information and communication	5 901	5 841	6 113	6 176	6 434	6 637 p	..	..
9	Financial and insurance activities	11 257	10 262	11 011	11 286	12 666	13 873 p	..	..
10	Real estate activities	25 360	26 826	28 705	29 713	31 143	32 764 p	..	..
11	Prof., scientif., techn. activ.; admin., support service activ.	18 375	19 506	20 071	20 763	22 089	23 108 p	..	..
12	Public admin.; compulsory s.s.; education; human health	29 887	30 756	31 677	32 416	33 371	34 928 p	..	..
13	Other service activities	6 574	6 578	6 909	7 098	7 325	7 770 p	..	..
14	**FISIM (Financial Intermediation Services Indirectly Measured)**	..	..	..	..	..	..	..	..
15	**Gross value added at basic prices, excluding FISIM**	180 018	187 437	195 345	198 990	213 031	221 683 p	..	..
16	**Taxes less subsidies on products**	14 231	15 993	17 896	18 482	19 292	20 243 p	..	..
17	Taxes on products	14 231	15 993	17 896	18 482	19 292	20 243 p	..	..
18	Subsidies on products	..	..	..	..	..	..	..	..
19	**Residual item**	..	..	..	..	..	..	..	..
20	**Gross domestic product at market prices**	194 249	203 430	213 241	217 472	232 323	241 926 p	..	..
	OUTPUT APPROACH AT CONSTANT PRICES (REF. YEAR 2010)								
21	**Total gross value added at basic prices**	184 626	187 437	191 785	196 029	200 757	207 463	212 251	..
22	Agriculture, forestry and fishing	19 084	17 579	19 745	20 737	20 207	21 442 p	22 025 p	
23	Industry, including energy	28 122	28 402	27 813	28 155	28 372	29 109 p	29 390 p	
24	Manufacturing	21 607	22 050	22 004	22 330	22 545	22 977 p	23 317 p	
25	Construction	10 589	10 525	10 537	11 095	11 668	12 477 p	12 927 p	
26	Services	..	..	..	..	..	..	..	
27	Distrib. trade, repairs; transp.; accommod., food serv. activ.	29 584	31 162	32 090	32 742	33 711	34 972 p	35 878 p	
28	Information and communication	5 550	5 841	6 066	6 374	6 958	7 179 p	7 434 p	
29	Financial and insurance activities	10 183	10 262	10 538	10 799	11 264	11 595 p	11 959 p	
30	Real estate activities	26 328	26 826	28 077	28 758	29 365	29 985 p	30 729 p	
31	Prof., scientif., techn. activ.; admin., support service activ.	18 560	19 506	19 800	20 084	21 141	22 011 p	22 820 p	
32	Public admin.; compulsory s.s.; education; human health	30 642	30 756	30 942	31 354	31 814	32 498 p	33 024 p	
33	Other service activities	6 726	6 578	6 783	6 785	6 774	6 892 p	6 869 p	
34	**FISIM (Financial Intermediation Services Indirectly Measured)**	..	..	..	..	..	..	..	
35	**Gross value added at basic prices, excluding FISIM**	184 626	187 437	191 785	196 029	200 757	207 463	212 251	
36	**Taxes less subsidies on products**	15 744	15 993	16 263	16 687	17 165	17 869 p	18 547 p	
37	Taxes on products	15 744	15 993	16 263	16 687	17 165	17 869 p	18 547 p	
38	Subsidies on products	..	..	..	..	..	..	..	
39	**Residual item**	0	0	0	5	10	19 p	33 p	
40	**Gross domestic product at market prices**	200 370	203 430	208 048	212 721	217 932	225 351 p	230 832 p	
	INCOME APPROACH								
41	**Compensation of employees**	85 822	88 832	92 307	95 052	98 679	104 191 p	..	..
42	Agriculture, forestry and fishing	2 891	2 981	3 146	3 425	3 409	3 610 p	..	..
43	Industry, including energy	13 700	14 040	14 417	14 787	15 199	15 740 p	..	..
44	Manufacturing	11 965	12 195	12 489	12 684	13 044	13 530 p	..	..
45	Construction	5 880	6 199	6 425	6 815	7 153	7 752 p	..	..
46	Distrib. trade, repairs; transp.; accommod., food serv. activ.	17 419	17 933	18 690	19 140	20 038	21 491 p	..	..
47	Information and communication	2 397	2 456	2 636	2 661	2 696	2 660 p	..	..
48	Financial and insurance activities	4 583	4 602	4 960	5 052	5 143	5 647 p	..	..
49	Real estate activities	1 140	1 176	1 294	1 321	1 341	1 640 p	..	..
50	Prof., scientif., techn. activ.; admin., support service activ.	10 026	10 699	11 106	11 476	12 307	12 902 p	..	..
51	Public admin.; compulsory s.s.; education; human health	24 043	24 864	25 705	26 289	27 158	28 339 p	..	..
52	Other service activities	3 743	3 882	3 928	4 086	4 235	4 410 p	..	..
53	**Wages and salaries**	..	..	..	..	..	..	..	..
54	Agriculture, forestry and fishing	..	..	..	..	..	..		
55	Industry, including energy	..	..	..	..	..	..		
56	Manufacturing	..	..	..	..	..	..		
57	Construction	..	..	..	..	..	..		
58	Distrib. trade, repairs; transp.; accommod., food serv. activ.	..	..	..	..	..	..		
59	Information and communication	..	..	..	..	..	..		
60	Financial and insurance activities	..	..	..	..	..	..		
61	Real estate activities	..	..	..	..	..	..		
62	Prof., scientif., techn. activ.; admin., support service activ.	..	..	..	..	..	..		
63	Public admin.; compulsory s.s.; education; human health	..	..	..	..	..	..		
64	Other service activities	..	..	..	..	..	..		
65	**Gross operating surplus and mixed income**	85 614	89 806	93 535	94 024	103 732	106 066 p	..	..
66	**Taxes less subsidies on production and imports**	22 815	24 797	27 401	28 397	29 914	31 669 p	..	..
67	Taxes on production and imports	23 480	25 949	28 476	29 348	30 826	32 520 p	..	..
68	Subsidies on production and imports	665	1 152	1 075	951	912	851 p	..	..
69	**Residual item**	..	..	..	..	..	..	..	..
70	**Gross domestic product**	194 251	203 435	213 243	217 473	232 325	241 926 p	..	..

Note: Detailed metadata:http://metalinks.oecd.org/nav1/20180308/6670
Source: Statistics New Zealand.

NEW ZEALAND

Table 3. Disposable income, saving and net lending / net borrowing

Million NZD, fiscal years

		2009	2010	2011	2012	2013	2014	2015	2016
	DISPOSABLE INCOME								
1	**Gross domestic product**	194 251	203 434	213 241	217 473	232 324	241 927 p	251 767 p	..
2	Net primary incomes from the rest of the world	-7 963	-10 118	-9 666	-9 092	-9 518	..	..	..
3	Primary incomes receivable from the rest of the world	5 376	5 551	6 439	6 808	7 098	7 186 p	7 576 p	..
4	Primary incomes payable to the rest of the world	13 340	15 659	16 095	15 860	16 273	16 947 p	16 566 p	..
5	**Gross national income at market prices**	186 287	193 326	203 585	208 421	223 149	232 166 p	242 777 p	256 239 e
6	Consumption of fixed capital	29 995	29 977	30 280	30 990	31 930	33 348 p	35 779 p	37 763 e
7	**Net national income at market prices**	156 292	163 349	173 305	177 431	191 219	198 818 p	206 998 p	218 476 e
8	Net current transfers from the rest of the world	620	-176	-305	-401	-435	..	..	..
9	Current transfers receivable from the rest of the world	2 022	1 173	1 263	1 275	1 265	1 853 p	2 009 p	..
10	Current transfers payable to the rest of the world	1 402	1 348	1 606	1 684	1 709	2 286 p	2 624 p	..
11	**Net national disposable income**	156 912	163 174	172 962	177 022	190 775	198 385 p	206 383 p	..
	SAVING AND NET LENDING / NET BORROWING								
12	**Net national disposable income**	156 912	163 174	172 962	177 022	190 775	198 385 p	206 383 p	..
13	Final consumption expenditures	151 554	157 911	166 346	170 459	177 441	184 450 p	191 223 p	..
14	Adj. for change in net equity of households in pension funds	2 880	3 636	3 665	2 845	4 241	5 573 p	4 601 p	..
15	**Saving, net**	5 358	5 263	6 616	6 563	13 334	13 935 p	15 160 p	..
16	Net capital transfers from the rest of the world	0	18 794	871	0	0	..	..	..
17	Capital transfers receivable from the rest of the world	0	19 265	923	0	0	0 p	20 p	..
18	Capital transfers payable to the rest of the world	0	0	0	0	0	0 p	0 p	..
19	Gross capital formation	38 186	40 854	43 594	45 500	51 209	54 640 p	57 422 p	..
20	Acquisitions less disposals of non-financial non-produced assets	-17	-77	-58	1	-2	-37 p	-325 p	..
21	Consumption of fixed capital	29 995	29 977	30 280	30 990	31 930	33 348 p	35 779 p	..
22	**Net lending / net borrowing**	-2 815	13 726	-5 717	-7 949	-5 944	-8 433 p	-7 475 p	..
	REAL DISPOSABLE INCOME								
23	**Gross domestic product at constant prices, reference year 2010**	201 511	203 434	208 913	214 137	218 175	224 858 p	232 335 p	239 431 e
24	Trading gain or loss	-6 181	-1 804	-936	-3 820	2 941	3 995 p	2 128 p	..
25	**Real gross domestic income**	195 329	201 630	207 978	210 317	221 117	228 853 p	234 463 p	..
26	Net real primary incomes from the rest of the world	-8 080	-10 108	-9 502	-8 832	-8 811	-9 316 p	-8 447 p	..
27	Real primary incomes receivable from the rest of the world	5 454	5 551	6 336	6 643	6 816	6 858 p	7 118 p	..
28	Real primary incomes payable to the rest of the world	13 534	15 659	15 838	15 475	15 627	16 175 p	15 565 p	..
29	**Real gross national income at market prices**	188 997	193 326	200 337	203 366	214 284	221 585 p	228 114 p	236 985 e
30	Net real current transfers from the rest of the world	629	-175	-338	-399	-426	-413 p	-578 p	..
31	Real current transfers receivable from the rest of the world	2 051	1 173	1 243	1 244	1 215	1 769 p	1 888 p	..
32	Real current transfers payable to the rest of the world	1 422	1 348	1 580	1 643	1 641	2 182 p	2 466 p	..
33	**Real gross national disposable income**	188 210	191 337	197 132	200 830	211 036	..	..	..
34	Consumption of fixed capital at constant prices	..	..	..	..	..	..	..	..
35	**Real net national income at market prices**	158 566	163 349	170 540	173 128	183 623	189 756 p	194 496 p	202 060 e
36	**Real net national disposable income**	159 195	163 174	170 202	172 728	183 196	189 343 p	193 918 p	..

Note: Detailed metadata:http://metalinks.oecd.org/nav1/20180308/5ee1
Source: Statistics New Zealand.

NEW ZEALAND

Table 4. Population and employment (persons) and employment (hours worked) by industry
ISIC Rev. 4

		2009	2010	2011	2012	2013	2014	2015	2016
	POPULATION, THOUSAND PERSONS, NATIONAL CONCEPT								
1	**Total population**	4 318.0	4 363.0	4 393.0	4 418.0	4 460.0	4 534.0	4 623.0	4 720.0 e
2	Economically active population	..	..	..	..	..	..	..	..
3	Unemployed persons	..	..	..	..	..	..	..	..
4	Total employment	2 145.2	2 165.6	2 191.7	2 184.6	2 247.6	2 323.8	2 369.0	..
5	Employees	1 794.6	1 806.9	1 822.6	1 825.2	1 898.4	1 970.9	2 012.2	..
6	Self-employed	350.6	358.7	369.1	359.4	349.2	352.8	356.9	..
	TOTAL EMPLOYMENT, THOUSAND PERSONS, DOMESTIC CONCEPT								
7	Agriculture, forestry and fishing	139.8	148.1	148.9	146.1	145.7	141.4	147.0	..
8	Industry, including energy	271.7	274.0	276.8	270.2	274.9	284.0	289.1	..
9	Manufacturing	250.4	250.2	253.0	245.9	249.9	255.4	260.5	..
10	Construction	176.9	172.5	170.9	166.1	178.6	205.0	227.0	..
11	Distrib. trade, repairs; transp.; accommod., food serv. activ.	553.5	557.9	553.7	557.4	574.5	579.6	580.0	..
12	Information and communication	71.5	73.9	77.4	82.3	82.7	88.2	91.8	..
13	Financial and insurance activities	67.8	61.7	67.5	69.5	69.5	69.6	67.5	..
14	Real estate activities	27.2	27.2	27.0	25.9	27.9	27.5	29.1	..
15	Prof., scientif., techn. activ.; admin., support service activ.	222.2	222.0	225.8	226.0	238.2	238.6	236.2	..
16	Public admin.; compulsory s.s.; education; human health	514.2	526.9	538.5	531.5	544.7	565.5	574.8	..
17	Other service activities	91.0	94.6	98.6	101.7	101.2	112.3	112.3	..
18	**Total employment**	2 135.8	2 158.7	2 185.2	2 176.7	2 237.9	2 311.7	2 354.8	..
	EMPLOYEES, THOUSAND PERSONS, DOMESTIC CONCEPT								
19	Agriculture, forestry and fishing	81.2	84.4	81.5	80.5	84.2	82.7	92.5	..
20	Industry, including energy	248.4	249.3	252.2	244.8	248.5	259.0	262.9	..
21	Manufacturing	228.5	227.7	230.4	222.7	224.5	231.6	235.9	..
22	Construction	120.0	116.9	119.1	118.2	126.8	147.6	165.9	..
23	Distrib. trade, repairs; transp.; accommod., food serv. activ.	480.4	484.2	480.7	485.0	506.3	512.1	513.1	..
24	Information and communication	56.7	58.5	61.2	65.4	69.1	74.7	76.0	..
25	Financial and insurance activities	62.7	57.1	61.2	64.0	63.2	62.8	62.2	..
26	Real estate activities	13.5	13.9	12.7	14.3	15.2	14.9	15.0	..
27	Prof., scientif., techn. activ.; admin., support service activ.	164.6	164.8	164.3	167.0	182.6	184.0	185.1	..
28	Public admin.; compulsory s.s.; education; human health	488.8	498.9	509.1	502.2	515.7	534.4	542.7	..
29	Other service activities	72.2	74.6	76.8	78.8	80.7	90.4	88.2	..
30	**Total employees**	1 788.5	1 802.7	1 818.9	1 820.3	1 892.3	1 962.6	2 003.7	..
	SELF-EMPLOYED, THOUSAND PERSONS, DOMESTIC CONCEPT								
31	Agriculture, forestry and fishing	58.6	63.7	67.4	65.6	61.5	58.7	54.5	..
32	Industry, including energy	23.3	24.6	24.7	25.4	26.3	25.0	26.2	..
33	Manufacturing	22.0	22.5	22.6	23.2	25.4	23.8	24.6	..
34	Construction	56.9	55.5	51.8	47.9	51.8	57.4	61.1	..
35	Distrib. trade, repairs; transp.; accommod., food serv. activ.	73.1	73.7	72.9	72.4	68.2	67.5	66.9	..
36	Information and communication	14.8	15.4	16.2	16.9	13.7	13.5	15.8	..
37	Financial and insurance activities	5.1	4.5	6.3	5.5	6.3	6.8	5.3	..
38	Real estate activities	13.7	13.3	14.3	11.6	12.7	12.6	14.0	..
39	Prof., scientif., techn. activ.; admin., support service activ.	57.6	57.2	61.6	58.9	55.6	54.6	51.0	..
40	Public admin.; compulsory s.s.; education; human health	25.4	28.0	29.4	29.4	29.0	31.1	32.1	..
41	Other service activities	18.8	20.0	21.8	22.8	20.6	21.9	24.0	..
42	**Total self-employed**	347.3	355.9	366.4	356.4	345.7	349.1	350.9	..
	TOTAL EMPLOYMENT, MILLION HOURS, DOMESTIC CONCEPT								
43	Industry, including energy	510.8	531.9	537.2	523.0	536.1	564.6	563.8	..
44	Distrib. trade, repairs; transp.; accommod., food serv. activ.	945.6	959.6	968.3	964.0	1 008.1	996.1	992.7	..
45	Financial and insurance activities	119.2	115.4	121.0	127.0	125.8	124.2	120.6	..
46	Prof., scientif., techn. activ.; admin., support service activ.	372.4	376.9	379.5	380.8	402.0	394.8	396.8	..
47	Public admin.; compulsory s.s.; education; human health	817.4	835.3	830.1	842.7	878.5	896.4	906.8	..
48	**Total employment**	3 713.4	3 783.9	3 799.0	3 816.2	3 953.8	4 057.6	4 098.4	..
	EMPLOYEES, MILLION HOURS, DOMESTIC CONCEPT								
49	Industry, including energy	466.6	486.3	487.7	474.0	490.2	516.3	515.7	..
50	Distrib. trade, repairs; transp.; accommod., food serv. activ.	796.4	804.0	815.1	816.7	871.5	853.9	855.2	..
51	Financial and insurance activities	110.6	106.8	109.0	117.2	114.3	114.4	111.3	..
52	Prof., scientif., techn. activ.; admin., support service activ.	275.2	277.6	279.0	289.0	315.9	311.8	317.3	..
53	Public admin.; compulsory s.s.; education; human health	783.1	796.6	792.8	805.1	839.2	854.0	863.5	..
54	**Total employees**	3 072.9	3 120.9	3 133.4	3 180.3	3 350.1	3 437.8	3 476.3	..
	SELF-EMPLOYED, MILLION HOURS, DOMESTIC CONCEPT								
55	Industry, including energy	44.2	45.6	49.5	49.0	45.8	48.3	48.2	..
56	Distrib. trade, repairs; transp.; accommod., food serv. activ.	149.3	155.5	153.2	147.3	136.7	142.2	137.4	..
57	Financial and insurance activities	8.6	8.6	12.0	9.8	11.4	9.8	9.3	..
58	Prof., scientif., techn. activ.; admin., support service activ.	97.2	99.4	100.5	91.8	86.1	83.0	79.5	..
59	Public admin.; compulsory s.s.; education; human health	34.4	38.8	37.3	37.6	39.3	42.4	43.3	..
60	**Total self-employed**	640.5	663.0	665.7	635.9	603.7	619.8	622.2	..

Note: Detailed metadata:http://metalinks.oecd.org/nav1/20180308/4fb7
Source: Statistics New Zealand.

NORWAY

Table 1. Gross domestic product, expenditure approach

Million NOK

		2009	2010	2011	2012	2013	2014	2015	2016
	AT CURRENT PRICES								
1	**Final consumption expenditure**	**1 553 007**	**1 642 492**	**1 712 101**	**1 795 305**	**1 886 737**	**1 980 345**	**2 082 990**	**2 176 271**
2	Household	978 057	1 038 351	1 072 295	1 121 081	1 175 471	1 223 552	1 281 171	1 342 788
3	NPISH's	47 896	48 806	52 658	55 328	58 929	64 824	72 552	75 912
4	Government	527 054	555 335	587 148	618 896	652 337	691 969	729 267	757 571
5	Individual	356 057	376 133	398 517	421 214	444 612	469 797	493 834	513 641
6	Collective	170 997	179 202	188 631	197 682	207 725	222 172	235 433	243 930
7	*of which: Actual individual consumption*	1 382 010	1 463 290	1 523 470	1 597 623	1 679 012	1 758 173	1 847 557	1 932 341
8	**Gross capital formation**	**600 942**	**659 184**	**724 109**	**786 113**	**857 158**	**883 133**	**859 716**	**913 847**
9	Gross fixed capital formation, total	564 841	537 593	600 711	665 318	724 025	749 473	741 413	750 491
10	Dwellings[1]	95 311	97 973	121 474	140 290	152 301	155 517	165 708	184 829
11	Other buildings and structures[1]	255 346	235 734	257 715	299 893	336 575	358 186	346 797	343 178
12	Transport equipment	47 355	38 043	48 199	38 559	31 331	24 513	24 318	23 733
13	Other machinery and equipment	79 953	76 107	79 840	91 638	92 388	95 994	92 728	95 521
14	Cultivated assets	-24	-25	-39	15	-99	-2	37	38
15	Intangible fixed assets	86 900	89 761	93 522	94 923	111 529	115 265	111 825	103 192
16	Changes in inventories, acquisitions less disposals of valuables	36 101	121 591	123 398	120 795	133 133	133 660	118 303	163 356
17	Changes in inventories	35 746	121 206	123 019	120 450	132 826	133 327	117 955	162 991
18	Acquisitions less disposals of valuables	355	385	379	345	307	333	348	366
19	**External balance of goods and services**	**277 249**	**292 063**	**359 545**	**386 840**	**331 680**	**283 187**	**175 410**	**26 914**
20	Exports of goods and services	952 831	1 030 368	1 152 651	1 204 351	1 203 742	1 220 367	1 176 078	1 064 050
21	Exports of goods	729 867	779 203	898 294	929 002	912 144	904 516	830 913	746 425
22	Exports of services	222 964	251 165	254 357	275 349	291 598	315 851	345 165	317 625
23	Imports of goods and services	675 582	738 305	793 106	817 511	872 062	937 180	1 000 668	1 037 136
24	Imports of goods	447 933	481 693	524 020	527 441	554 220	591 265	633 574	647 831
25	Imports of services	227 649	256 612	269 086	290 070	317 842	345 915	367 094	389 305
26	**Statistical discrepancy**	..	..	..	..	..			
27	**Gross domestic product**	**2 431 198**	**2 593 739**	**2 795 755**	**2 968 258**	**3 075 575**	**3 146 665**	**3 118 116**	**3 117 032**
	AT CONSTANT PRICES, REFERENCE YEAR 2010								
28	**Final consumption expenditure**	**1 591 205**	**1 642 492**	**1 673 440**	**1 720 560**	**1 758 095**	**1 798 280**	**1 843 770**	**1 875 599**
29	Household	998 077	1 038 351	1 061 990	1 099 560	1 129 574	1 150 459	1 176 650	1 194 059
30	NPISH's	49 712	48 806	50 704	51 798	54 154	57 890	63 107	64 317
31	Government	543 515	555 335	560 745	569 475	575 038	590 311	604 300	617 238
32	Individual	367 812	376 133	378 937	386 264	389 790	395 349	400 142	409 734
33	Collective	175 701	179 202	181 810	183 191	185 232	195 026	204 422	207 700
34	*of which: Actual individual consumption*	1 415 511	1 463 290	1 491 631	1 537 428	1 573 000	1 603 112	1 639 029	1 667 581
35	**Gross capital formation**	**639 682**	**659 184**	**690 965**	**723 264**	**771 388**	**772 795**	**746 163**	**783 170**
36	Gross fixed capital formation, total	574 556	537 593	577 646	621 265	660 583	658 885	632 528	631 068
37	Dwellings[1]	99 522	97 973	114 647	127 157	133 867	131 956	136 229	148 545
38	Other buildings and structures[1]	263 044	235 734	246 538	278 867	304 592	309 747	291 725	285 841
39	Transport equipment	44 493	38 043	48 680	38 625	30 413	23 200	21 807	21 102
40	Other machinery and equipment	77 323	76 107	78 913	88 376	89 679	91 001	83 730	83 529
41	Cultivated assets	-25	-25	-38	15	-96	-4	56	56
42	Intangible fixed assets	89 990	89 761	88 907	87 609	100 523	101 058	96 606	89 100
43	Changes in inventories, acquisitions less disposals of valuables	..	..	..	..	..	..	..	..
44	Changes in inventories	..	..	..	..	..	..	..	..
45	Acquisitions less disposals of valuables	..	..	..	..	..	..	..	..
46	**External balance of goods and services**	**343 679**	**292 063**	**254 544**	**247 302**	**190 913**	**202 349**	**238 168**	**198 133**
47	Exports of goods and services	1 024 669	1 030 368	1 021 977	1 038 049	1 020 814	1 052 288	1 101 972	1 082 096
48	Exports of goods	804 517	779 203	757 319	754 839	730 437	750 798	780 017	774 411
49	Exports of services	222 907	251 165	264 657	286 580	297 026	308 930	330 858	316 248
50	Imports of goods and services	680 990	738 305	767 432	790 747	829 901	849 939	863 804	883 963
51	Imports of goods	448 112	481 693	503 146	503 916	520 974	532 866	546 360	551 325
52	Imports of services	232 793	256 612	264 286	287 163	309 562	317 746	318 038	333 280
53	**Statistical discrepancy (including chaining residual)**	**1 356**	**0**	**-1**	**-900**	**-2 074**	**-1 411**	**-1 477**	**573**
54	**Gross domestic product**	**2 575 922**	**2 593 739**	**2 618 948**	**2 690 226**	**2 718 323**	**2 772 013**	**2 826 624**	**2 857 476**

Note: Detailed metadata:http://metalinks.oecd.org/nav1/20180308/aa66

1. Dwellings includes also *Other buildings and structures*.

Source: Statistics Norway (SN).

Table 2. Gross domestic product, output and income approach
ISIC Rev. 4

Million NOK

		2009	2010	2011	2012	2013	2014	2015	2016
	OUTPUT APPROACH AT CURRENT PRICES								
1	**Total gross value added at basic prices**	2 169 915	2 310 093	2 500 701	2 659 844	2 753 459	2 814 151	2 775 506	2 758 499
2	Agriculture, forestry and fishing	31 578	40 650	37 552	33 433	40 396	45 317	47 836	66 499
3	Industry, including energy	711 551	777 821	898 895	939 170	935 954	901 398	788 961	692 852
4	Manufacturing	178 412	186 383	188 581	196 056	203 246	213 801	213 856	210 076
5	Construction	121 460	123 191	135 139	152 827	158 615	167 475	175 824	189 025
6	Services	..	..	..	..	..	..	..	..
7	Distrib. trade, repairs; transp.; accommod., food serv. activ.	324 520	340 584	346 771	365 363	380 801	400 449	412 163	410 543
8	Information and communication	86 547	94 417	97 710	102 469	107 068	109 364	112 927	117 783
9	Financial and insurance activities	97 528	97 082	94 771	117 341	131 581	137 135	139 437	145 725
10	Real estate activities	153 722	160 999	171 497	177 281	186 020	196 297	211 168	217 957
11	Prof., scientif., techn. activ.; admin., support service activ.	153 722	158 603	168 750	187 238	198 157	206 088	201 099	203 960
12	Public admin.; compulsory s.s.; education; human health	445 762	471 426	502 923	536 205	564 642	597 572	630 214	654 746
13	Other service activities	43 525	45 320	46 693	48 517	50 225	53 056	55 877	59 407
14	**FISIM (Financial Intermediation Services Indirectly Measured)**	..	..	..	..	..	..	..	..
15	**Gross value added at basic prices, excluding FISIM**	2 169 915	2 310 093	2 500 701	2 659 844	2 753 459	2 814 151	2 775 506	2 758 499
16	**Taxes less subsidies on products**	261 283	283 646	295 054	308 414	322 116	332 514	342 610	358 496
17	Taxes on products	265 362	287 420	298 693	311 903	325 891	337 295	348 528	364 881
18	Subsidies on products	4 079	3 774	3 639	3 489	3 775	4 781	5 918	6 384
19	**Residual item**	0	0	0	0	0	0	0	37
20	**Gross domestic product at market prices**	2 431 198	2 593 739	2 795 755	2 968 258	3 075 575	3 146 665	3 118 116	3 117 032
	OUTPUT APPROACH AT CONSTANT PRICES (REF. YEAR 2010)								
21	**Total gross value added at basic prices**	2 300 910	2 310 093	2 325 936	2 387 697	2 410 583	2 458 098	2 505 656	2 528 666
22	Agriculture, forestry and fishing	37 649	40 650	42 191	44 304	42 503	45 427	42 924	42 364
23	Industry, including energy	800 078	777 821	761 728	768 080	758 060	768 195	782 806	776 719
24	Manufacturing	183 145	186 383	189 646	193 632	200 159	206 165	196 543	188 239
25	Construction	126 488	123 191	126 569	135 700	137 996	140 668	143 358	149 321
26	Services	..	..	..	..	..	..	..	..
27	Distrib. trade, repairs; transp.; accommod., food serv. activ.	329 819	340 584	349 988	362 480	372 436	382 632	391 716	389 873
28	Information and communication	85 852	94 417	97 161	100 128	103 396	104 864	108 310	110 639
29	Financial and insurance activities	100 856	97 082	94 170	97 744	101 754	106 236	112 782	116 396
30	Real estate activities	158 898	160 999	166 507	171 086	176 767	179 976	186 636	188 198
31	Prof., scientif., techn. activ.; admin., support service activ.	158 537	158 603	163 169	175 087	180 236	182 435	175 030	174 840
32	Public admin.; compulsory s.s.; education; human health	459 550	471 426	478 688	488 890	494 285	503 713	516 763	529 971
33	Other service activities	45 413	45 320	45 765	46 309	47 282	48 792	49 403	51 454
34	**FISIM (Financial Intermediation Services Indirectly Measured)**	..	..	..	..	..	..	..	..
35	**Gross value added at basic prices, excluding FISIM**	2 300 910	2 310 093	2 325 936	2 387 697	2 410 583	2 458 098	2 505 656	2 528 666
36	**Taxes less subsidies on products**	275 062	283 646	293 014	302 635	308 037	314 226	321 357	329 372
37	Taxes on products	277 743	287 420	296 771	306 246	311 151	317 434	324 705	332 699
38	Subsidies on products	2 978	3 774	3 758	3 600	3 075	3 164	3 282	3 303
39	**Residual item**	-49	0	-1	-106	-297	-311	-389	-562
40	**Gross domestic product at market prices**	2 575 922	2 593 739	2 618 948	2 690 226	2 718 323	2 772 013	2 826 624	2 857 476
	INCOME APPROACH								
41	**Compensation of employees**	1 119 397	1 151 134	1 225 068	1 308 760	1 384 564	1 448 528	1 493 774	1 518 587
42	Agriculture, forestry and fishing	8 248	9 216	9 919	10 325	10 774	11 548	12 334	13 258
43	Industry, including energy	194 815	195 195	208 875	226 474	243 154	253 231	248 702	238 051
44	Manufacturing	125 827	123 504	128 582	136 534	143 521	149 136	148 058	144 468
45	Construction	80 135	81 008	87 915	97 091	104 223	109 935	115 954	122 628
46	Distrib. trade, repairs; transp.; accommod., food serv. activ.	226 851	231 123	239 904	251 886	263 703	271 879	281 944	288 071
47	Information and communication	55 571	56 635	60 505	64 352	67 182	70 743	74 011	75 162
48	Financial and insurance activities	39 146	39 555	40 355	42 285	43 501	45 482	46 494	47 535
49	Real estate activities	10 582	10 932	11 938	13 397	13 808	14 450	15 369	15 940
50	Prof., scientif., techn. activ.; admin., support service activ.	107 934	110 893	121 543	132 040	140 950	146 991	149 297	149 094
51	Public admin.; compulsory s.s.; education; human health	366 849	386 277	412 104	437 458	462 473	488 017	512 509	529 792
52	Other service activities	29 266	30 300	32 010	33 452	34 796	36 252	37 160	39 056
53	**Wages and salaries**	913 248	942 850	1 001 385	1 064 203	1 124 073	1 172 456	1 208 381	1 232 489
54	Agriculture, forestry and fishing	7 160	7 989	8 604	8 926	9 314	9 969	10 646	11 460
55	Industry, including energy	160 580	161 811	171 791	184 882	197 489	205 030	201 215	191 588
56	Manufacturing	106 194	105 085	108 962	115 172	120 709	125 074	124 059	120 152
57	Construction	67 999	68 212	73 978	81 384	87 557	92 502	97 589	103 317
58	Distrib. trade, repairs; transp.; accommod., food serv. activ.	189 173	194 275	201 451	210 774	220 595	227 743	236 423	241 814
59	Information and communication	45 300	47 153	50 050	53 022	55 246	58 341	61 017	62 101
60	Financial and insurance activities	30 698	31 721	32 905	34 013	35 139	36 586	37 503	38 445
61	Real estate activities	8 671	9 026	9 820	10 922	11 326	11 769	12 557	13 050
62	Prof., scientif., techn. activ.; admin., support service activ.	89 647	92 377	101 187	109 514	117 142	122 121	124 293	124 367
63	Public admin.; compulsory s.s.; education; human health	288 994	304 516	324 505	342 514	360 911	377 843	395 828	413 291
64	Other service activities	25 026	25 770	27 094	28 252	29 354	30 552	31 310	33 056
65	**Gross operating surplus and mixed income**	1 074 743	1 187 371	1 304 538	1 382 394	1 400 110	1 396 270	1 314 057	1 273 536
66	**Taxes less subsidies on production and imports**	237 058	255 234	266 150	277 104	290 901	301 867	310 285	324 872
67	Taxes on production and imports	286 369	307 617	319 462	332 705	348 318	361 823	374 483	392 082
68	Subsidies on production and imports	49 311	52 383	53 312	55 601	57 417	59 956	64 198	67 210
69	**Residual item**	0	0	0	0	0	0	0	37
70	**Gross domestic product**	2 431 198	2 593 739	2 795 755	2 968 258	3 075 575	3 146 665	3 118 116	3 117 032

Note: Detailed metadata:http://metalinks.oecd.org/nav1/20180308/aa66
Source: Statistics Norway (SN).

Table 3. Disposable income, saving and net lending / net borrowing

Million NOK

		2009	2010	2011	2012	2013	2014	2015	2016
	DISPOSABLE INCOME								
1	**Gross domestic product**	2 431 198	2 593 739	2 795 755	2 968 258	3 075 575	3 146 665	3 118 116	3 117 032
2	Net primary incomes from the rest of the world	13 468	27 668	26 266	24 396	32 727	99 335	129 291	149 881
3	Primary incomes receivable from the rest of the world	176 318	214 986	224 268	249 696	246 014	291 864	333 028	348 432
4	Primary incomes payable to the rest of the world	162 850	187 318	198 002	225 300	213 287	192 529	203 737	198 551
5	**Gross national income at market prices**	2 444 665	2 621 407	2 822 021	2 992 654	3 108 302	3 246 000	3 247 407	3 266 913
6	Consumption of fixed capital	396 443	413 741	437 087	460 875	484 743	522 651	555 288	572 064
7	**Net national income at market prices**	2 048 222	2 207 666	2 384 934	2 531 779	2 623 559	2 723 349	2 692 119	2 694 849
8	Net current transfers from the rest of the world	20 245	20 270	21 033	25 117	-46 703	-49 205	-55 873	-56 234
9	Current transfers receivable from the rest of the world	20 245	20 270	21 033	25 117	26 973	33 219	33 933	35 753
10	Current transfers payable to the rest of the world	..	..	..	..	73 676	82 424	89 806	91 987
11	**Net national disposable income**	2 018 377	2 171 836	2 345 023	2 492 666	2 576 856	2 674 144	2 636 246	2 638 615
	SAVING AND NET LENDING / NET BORROWING								
12	**Net national disposable income**	2 018 377	2 171 836	2 345 023	2 492 666	2 576 856	2 674 144	2 636 246	2 638 615
13	Final consumption expenditures	1 553 007	1 642 492	1 712 101	1 795 305	1 886 737	1 980 345	2 082 990	2 176 271
14	Adj. for change in net equity of households in pension funds	-1 455	-1 072	-1 189	-1 400	-2 159	-2 389	-2 348	-2 223
15	**Saving, net**	463 915	528 272	631 733	695 961	687 960	691 410	550 908	460 121
16	Net capital transfers from the rest of the world	-1 120	-1 268	-1 499	-1 279	-1 377	-1 123	-870	-822
17	Capital transfers receivable from the rest of the world	..	..	..	..	..	..	..	..
18	Capital transfers payable to the rest of the world	1 120	1 268	1 499	1 279	1 377	1 123	870	822
19	Gross capital formation	600 941	659 184	724 110	786 113	857 158	883 133	859 716	913 847
20	Acquisitions less disposals of non-financial non-produced assets	294	293	275	31	29	119	48	127
21	Consumption of fixed capital	396 443	413 741	437 087	460 875	484 743	522 651	555 288	572 064
22	**Net lending / net borrowing**	258 003	281 268	342 936	369 413	314 139	329 686	245 562	117 389
	REAL DISPOSABLE INCOME								
23	**Gross domestic product at constant prices, reference year 2010**	2 572 297	2 590 089	2 615 263	2 686 441	2 714 498	2 768 112	2 822 647	2 853 455
24	Trading gain or loss	-57 916	0	94 404	120 071	118 229	54 198	-82 745	-175 632
25	**Real gross domestic income**	2 518 006	2 593 739	2 713 353	2 810 297	2 836 551	2 826 211	2 743 880	2 681 844
26	Net real primary incomes from the rest of the world	13 949	27 668	25 492	23 098	30 184	89 219	113 773	128 955
27	Real primary incomes receivable from the rest of the world	182 614	214 986	217 658	236 408	226 895	262 141	293 058	299 785
28	Real primary incomes payable to the rest of the world	168 665	187 318	192 166	213 310	196 711	172 922	179 284	170 830
29	**Real gross national income at market prices**	2 531 954	2 621 407	2 738 845	2 833 395	2 866 735	2 915 430	2 857 653	2 810 799
30	Net real current transfers from the rest of the world	20 968	20 270	20 413	23 780	24 877	29 836	29 860	30 761
31	Real current transfers receivable from the rest of the world	20 968	20 270	20 413	23 780	24 877	29 836	29 860	30 761
32	Real current transfers payable to the rest of the world	..	..	..	..	..	..	..	..
33	**Real gross national disposable income**	2 501 043	2 585 577	2 700 110	2 796 363	2 823 662	2 871 236	2 808 486	2 762 417
34	Consumption of fixed capital at constant prices	401 042	413 741	422 027	432 321	444 304	463 421	477 163	..
35	**Real net national income at market prices**	2 121 355	2 207 666	2 314 640	2 397 046	2 419 665	2 446 005	2 369 011	2 318 605
36	**Real net national disposable income**	2 090 445	2 171 836	2 275 906	2 360 015	2 376 591	2 401 811	2 319 844	2 270 222

Note: Detailed metadata:http://metalinks.oecd.org/nav1/20180308/e341
Source: Statistics Norway (SN).

Table 4. Population and employment (persons) and employment (hours worked) by industry
ISIC Rev. 4

		2009	2010	2011	2012	2013	2014	2015	2016
	POPULATION, THOUSAND PERSONS, NATIONAL CONCEPT								
1	**Total population**	**4 829.0**	**4 889.0**	**4 953.0**	**5 019.0**	**5 080.0**	**5 137.0**	**5 191.0**	**5 236.0**
2	Economically active population	..	..	..	..	..	..	..	..
3	Unemployed persons	..	..	..	..	..	..	..	..
4	Total employment	2 605.0	2 591.0	2 630.0	2 684.0	2 713.0	2 746.0	2 757.0	2 764.0
5	Employees	2 439.0	2 431.0	2 470.0	2 524.0	2 556.0	2 591.0	2 602.0	2 609.0
6	Self-employed	166.0	160.0	160.0	161.0	157.0	154.0	155.0	155.0
	TOTAL EMPLOYMENT, THOUSAND PERSONS, DOMESTIC CONCEPT								
7	Agriculture, forestry and fishing	70.0	70.0	71.0	70.0	69.0	69.0	69.0	70.0
8	Industry, including energy	340.0	331.0	333.0	341.0	347.0	350.0	337.0	320.0
9	Manufacturing	258.0	247.0	246.0	248.0	251.0	251.0	244.0	233.0
10	Construction	190.0	187.0	194.0	205.0	211.0	216.0	221.0	228.0
11	Distrib. trade, repairs; transp.; accommod., food serv. activ.	630.0	620.0	619.0	628.0	630.0	638.0	643.0	646.0
12	Information and communication	86.0	86.0	87.0	88.0	89.0	91.0	92.0	92.0
13	Financial and insurance activities	53.0	52.0	50.0	50.0	50.0	49.0	49.0	48.0
14	Real estate activities	23.0	23.0	23.0	25.0	24.0	24.0	25.0	26.0
15	Prof., scientif., techn. activ.; admin., support service activ.	233.0	229.0	238.0	247.0	251.0	254.0	252.0	250.0
16	Public admin.; compulsory s.s.; education; human health	887.0	900.0	920.0	935.0	947.0	959.0	973.0	986.0
17	Other service activities	94.0	93.0	94.0	94.0	94.0	95.0	95.0	98.0
18	**Total employment**	**2 605.0**	**2 591.0**	**2 630.0**	**2 684.0**	**2 713.0**	**2 746.0**	**2 757.0**	**2 764.0**
	EMPLOYEES, THOUSAND PERSONS, DOMESTIC CONCEPT								
19	Agriculture, forestry and fishing	28.0	30.0	31.0	31.0	31.0	32.0	33.0	34.0
20	Industry, including energy	333.0	325.0	327.0	335.0	342.0	344.0	332.0	315.0
21	Manufacturing	252.0	241.0	240.0	243.0	245.0	246.0	239.0	228.0
22	Construction	166.0	164.0	171.0	181.0	188.0	193.0	198.0	204.0
23	Distrib. trade, repairs; transp.; accommod., food serv. activ.	596.0	588.0	586.0	595.0	598.0	607.0	613.0	615.0
24	Information and communication	82.0	82.0	83.0	85.0	86.0	88.0	89.0	88.0
25	Financial and insurance activities	53.0	51.0	50.0	50.0	49.0	49.0	48.0	48.0
26	Real estate activities	21.0	21.0	21.0	22.0	22.0	22.0	23.0	23.0
27	Prof., scientif., techn. activ.; admin., support service activ.	214.0	212.0	220.0	230.0	233.0	237.0	234.0	233.0
28	Public admin.; compulsory s.s.; education; human health	869.0	881.0	902.0	917.0	929.0	941.0	954.0	967.0
29	Other service activities	77.0	77.0	78.0	78.0	77.0	78.0	78.0	81.0
30	**Total employees**	**2 439.0**	**2 431.0**	**2 470.0**	**2 524.0**	**2 556.0**	**2 591.0**	**2 602.0**	**2 609.0**
	SELF-EMPLOYED, THOUSAND PERSONS, DOMESTIC CONCEPT								
31	Agriculture, forestry and fishing	43.0	41.0	40.0	40.0	38.0	37.0	37.0	36.0
32	Industry, including energy	6.0	5.0	6.0	6.0	5.0	5.0	5.0	5.0
33	Manufacturing	6.0	5.0	5.0	6.0	5.0	5.0	5.0	5.0
34	Construction	24.0	24.0	24.0	24.0	23.0	23.0	23.0	24.0
35	Distrib. trade, repairs; transp.; accommod., food serv. activ.	33.0	32.0	33.0	33.0	32.0	30.0	31.0	31.0
36	Information and communication	3.0	3.0	3.0	4.0	4.0	4.0	4.0	4.0
37	Financial and insurance activities	0.0	0.0	0.0	0.0	0.0	0.0	0.0	0.0
38	Real estate activities	2.0	2.0	2.0	2.0	2.0	2.0	2.0	2.0
39	Prof., scientif., techn. activ.; admin., support service activ.	18.0	17.0	17.0	18.0	17.0	17.0	18.0	17.0
40	Public admin.; compulsory s.s.; education; human health	18.0	18.0	18.0	18.0	18.0	18.0	19.0	19.0
41	Other service activities	17.0	16.0	16.0	17.0	17.0	17.0	17.0	17.0
42	**Total self-employed**	**166.0**	**160.0**	**160.0**	**161.0**	**157.0**	**154.0**	**155.0**	**155.0**
	TOTAL EMPLOYMENT, MILLION HOURS, DOMESTIC CONCEPT								
43	Industry, including energy	532.0	519.0	524.0	537.0	542.0	547.0	524.0	499.0
44	Distrib. trade, repairs; transp.; accommod., food serv. activ.	854.0	853.0	856.0	869.0	867.0	874.0	884.0	889.0
45	Financial and insurance activities	81.0	79.0	77.0	79.0	77.0	76.0	76.0	75.0
46	Prof., scientif., techn. activ.; admin., support service activ.	346.0	350.0	369.0	383.0	386.0	392.0	388.0	386.0
47	Public admin.; compulsory s.s.; education; human health	1 146.0	1 165.0	1 196.0	1 207.0	1 215.0	1 236.0	1 259.0	1 290.0
48	**Total employment**	**3 691.0**	**3 696.0**	**3 761.0**	**3 834.0**	**3 847.0**	**3 900.0**	**3 922.0**	**3 950.0**
	EMPLOYEES, MILLION HOURS, DOMESTIC CONCEPT								
49	Industry, including energy	521.0	508.0	513.0	526.0	531.0	537.0	514.0	489.0
50	Distrib. trade, repairs; transp.; accommod., food serv. activ.	795.0	796.0	799.0	811.0	811.0	820.0	830.0	834.0
51	Financial and insurance activities	81.0	79.0	77.0	79.0	76.0	76.0	75.0	75.0
52	Prof., scientif., techn. activ.; admin., support service activ.	313.0	314.0	333.0	346.0	351.0	356.0	353.0	351.0
53	Public admin.; compulsory s.s.; education; human health	1 115.0	1 135.0	1 164.0	1 176.0	1 185.0	1 204.0	1 227.0	1 258.0
54	**Total employees**	**3 377.0**	**3 384.0**	**3 454.0**	**3 524.0**	**3 546.0**	**3 602.0**	**3 621.0**	**3 648.0**
	SELF-EMPLOYED, MILLION HOURS, DOMESTIC CONCEPT								
55	Industry, including energy	11.0	11.0	11.0	11.0	11.0	10.0	10.0	10.0
56	Distrib. trade, repairs; transp.; accommod., food serv. activ.	59.0	58.0	58.0	58.0	55.0	54.0	54.0	55.0
57	Financial and insurance activities	0.0	0.0	0.0	0.0	0.0	0.0	0.0	0.0
58	Prof., scientif., techn. activ.; admin., support service activ.	33.0	36.0	36.0	36.0	36.0	36.0	36.0	36.0
59	Public admin.; compulsory s.s.; education; human health	31.0	30.0	31.0	31.0	31.0	31.0	32.0	32.0
60	**Total self-employed**	**314.0**	**312.0**	**308.0**	**309.0**	**302.0**	**298.0**	**300.0**	**302.0**

Note: Detailed metadata:http://metalinks.oecd.org/nav1/20180308/5ead
Source: Statistics Norway (SN).

Table 1. Gross domestic product, expenditure approach

Million PLN

		2009	2010	2011	2012	2013	2014	2015	2016
	AT CURRENT PRICES								
1	**Final consumption expenditure**	**1 101 662**	**1 166 136**	**1 245 885**	**1 294 568**	**1 310 124**	**1 344 723**	**1 375 381**	**1 419 174**
2	Household	832 385	875 207	948 500	987 954	995 261	1 019 428	1 038 271	1 073 596
3	NPISH's	12 566	14 593	14 551	14 469	14 454	13 205	13 215	13 746
4	Government	256 711	276 336	282 834	292 145	300 409	312 090	323 895	331 832
5	Individual	137 991	147 640	153 213	158 870	163 669	169 486	177 583	182 755
6	Collective	118 720	128 696	129 621	133 275	136 740	142 604	146 312	149 077
7	*of which: Actual individual consumption*	982 942	1 037 440	1 116 264	1 161 293	1 173 384	1 202 119	1 229 069	1 270 097
8	**Gross capital formation**	**282 306**	**308 040**	**351 592**	**342 031**	**314 498**	**350 256**	**368 330**	**364 238**
9	Gross fixed capital formation, total	294 210	293 168	324 075	322 452	311 695	339 389	361 490	335 799
10	Dwellings	47 018	45 695	47 730	51 450	48 979	52 241	45 740	56 350
11	Other buildings and structures	122 810	127 189	141 803	137 562	125 664	135 746	145 570	120 127
12	Transport equipment	23 721	24 602	26 386	24 452	25 528	29 413	33 917	29 890
13	Other machinery and equipment	80 916	76 898	89 084	87 537	89 896	97 429	110 516	102 733
14	Cultivated assets	505	475	543	511	493	568	557	528
15	Intangible fixed assets	19 240	18 309	18 529	20 940	21 135	23 992	25 190	26 171
16	Changes in inventories, acquisitions less disposals of valuables	-11 904	14 872	27 517	19 579	2 803	10 867	6 840	28 439
17	Changes in inventories	-12 096	14 666	27 332	19 376	2 633	10 696	6 669	28 315
18	Acquisitions less disposals of valuables	192	206	185	203	170	171	171	124
19	**External balance of goods and services**	**-11 760**	**-28 878**	**-30 653**	**-7 174**	**32 273**	**24 790**	**55 681**	**75 225**
20	Exports of goods and services	510 248	578 916	666 890	724 175	767 471	818 390	891 075	971 321
21	Exports of goods	412 567	471 662	545 586	590 042	625 870	663 893	720 238	774 180
22	Exports of services	97 681	107 254	121 304	134 133	141 601	154 497	170 837	197 141
23	Imports of goods and services	522 008	607 794	697 543	731 349	735 198	793 600	835 394	896 096
24	Imports of goods	445 756	515 341	600 376	624 173	627 216	677 525	710 909	761 341
25	Imports of services	76 252	92 453	97 167	107 176	107 982	116 075	124 485	134 755
26	**Statistical discrepancy**	**0**	**0**	**0**	**0**	**0**	**0**	**0**	..
27	**Gross domestic product**	**1 372 208**	**1 445 298**	**1 566 824**	**1 629 425**	**1 656 895**	**1 719 769**	**1 799 392**	**1 858 637**
	AT CONSTANT PRICES, REFERENCE YEAR 2010								
28	**Final consumption expenditure**	**1 134 116**	**1 166 136**	**1 189 158**	**1 195 179**	**1 205 040**	**1 238 585**	**1 273 874**	**1 316 723**
29	Household	853 120	875 207	903 867	911 306	914 440	937 811	966 127	1 003 343
30	NPISH's	12 894	14 593	13 951	13 378	13 245	12 100	12 218	12 786
31	Government	268 088	276 336	271 340	270 477	277 353	288 692	295 542	300 701
32	Individual	144 181	147 640	147 066	147 219	151 293	156 952	162 135	165 786
33	Collective	123 908	128 696	124 274	123 259	126 061	131 740	133 410	134 920
34	*of which: Actual individual consumption*	1 010 189	1 037 440	1 064 884	1 071 912	1 078 974	1 106 845	1 140 458	1 181 849
35	**Gross capital formation**	**281 547**	**308 040**	**347 328**	**333 887**	**314 605**	**354 908**	**372 414**	**365 177**
36	Gross fixed capital formation, total	293 294	293 168	318 872	313 203	309 858	340 950	361 853	333 217
37	Dwellings	47 721	45 695	46 236	48 604	49 051	53 150	47 060	57 926
38	Other buildings and structures	122 937	127 189	140 233	135 644	126 159	137 579	147 815	122 069
39	Transport equipment	22 606	24 602	26 362	24 041	25 259	29 513	33 306	28 400
40	Other machinery and equipment	79 914	76 898	87 746	84 912	88 741	97 202	108 802	99 033
41	Cultivated assets	499	475	530	501	494	560	554	520
42	Intangible fixed assets	19 740	18 309	17 765	19 360	19 844	22 540	23 755	24 830
43	Changes in inventories, acquisitions less disposals of valuables	..	..	..	..	..	..	..	..
44	Changes in inventories	..	..	..	..	..	..	..	..
45	Acquisitions less disposals of valuables	198	206	178	188	156	157	158	116
46	**External balance of goods and services**	**-19 563**	**-28 878**	**-18 673**	**11 721**	**40 661**	**21 630**	**31 087**	**40 720**
47	Exports of goods and services	511 997	578 916	624 428	653 053	692 775	739 018	795 877	865 895
48	Exports of goods	414 168	471 662	508 013	526 161	555 177	589 145	629 382	673 983
49	Exports of services	97 822	107 254	116 415	127 050	137 951	150 553	167 726	194 583
50	Imports of goods and services	531 560	607 794	643 101	641 332	652 114	717 388	764 790	825 175
51	Imports of goods	453 767	515 341	548 401	539 045	548 009	605 228	643 472	693 107
52	Imports of services	77 787	92 453	94 700	102 813	104 651	112 502	121 831	132 716
53	**Statistical discrepancy (including chaining residual)**	**-1 118**	**0**	**0**	**1 431**	**3 378**	**-101**	**-262**	**2 531**
54	**Gross domestic product**	**1 394 982**	**1 445 298**	**1 517 813**	**1 542 218**	**1 563 684**	**1 615 022**	**1 677 113**	**1 725 151**

Note: Detailed metadata:http://metalinks.oecd.org/nav1/20180308/4f7a
Source: Central Statistical Office of Poland via Eurostat.

Table 2. Gross domestic product, output and income approach
ISIC Rev. 4

Million PLN

		2009	2010	2011	2012	2013	2014	2015	2016
	OUTPUT APPROACH AT CURRENT PRICES								
1	**Total gross value added at basic prices**	**1 220 098**	**1 271 476**	**1 376 967**	**1 443 657**	**1 470 917**	**1 525 005**	**1 596 366**	**1 645 054**
2	Agriculture, forestry and fishing	34 101	37 085	44 371	43 413	47 618	44 939	39 630	44 231
3	Industry, including energy	304 705	313 744	347 166	369 704	365 525	386 652	417 216	436 755
4	Manufacturing	225 730	224 845	249 250	266 203	263 495	288 474	317 241	335 980
5	Construction	104 290	107 950	120 255	114 942	108 711	119 680	127 481	117 811
6	Services	..	..	..	..	..	..	..	..
7	Distrib. trade, repairs; transp.; accommod., food serv. activ.	310 009	327 183	347 720	377 034	388 180	384 544	402 401	412 099
8	Information and communication	50 126	49 571	51 759	54 923	57 078	60 144	64 483	67 097
9	Financial and insurance activities	48 694	52 684	60 315	58 128	62 660	69 043	64 917	68 222
10	Real estate activities	63 029	67 793	71 890	73 168	75 323	80 028	78 407	84 230
11	Prof., scientif., techn. activ.; admin., support service activ.	87 638	89 338	95 863	103 229	109 487	115 834	128 991	134 802
12	Public admin.; compulsory s.s.; education; human health	188 284	196 876	207 398	213 819	221 544	228 133	235 966	240 661
13	Other service activities	29 222	29 252	30 230	35 297	34 791	36 008	36 874	39 146
14	FISIM (Financial Intermediation Services Indirectly Measured)	..	..	..	..	..	..	..	..
15	Gross value added at basic prices, excluding FISIM	1 220 098	1 271 476	1 376 967	1 443 657	1 470 917	1 525 005	1 596 366	1 645 054
16	**Taxes less subsidies on products**	**152 110**	**173 822**	**189 857**	**185 768**	**185 978**	**194 764**	**203 026**	**213 583**
17	Taxes on products	157 493	178 847	194 962	189 409	190 210	197 381	204 732	215 893
18	Subsidies on products	5 383	5 025	5 105	3 641	4 232	2 617	1 706	2 310
19	**Residual item**	..	..	..	..	..	..	..	..
20	**Gross domestic product at market prices**	**1 372 208**	**1 445 298**	**1 566 824**	**1 629 425**	**1 656 895**	**1 719 769**	**1 799 392**	**1 858 637**
	OUTPUT APPROACH AT CONSTANT PRICES (REF. YEAR 2010)								
21	**Total gross value added at basic prices**	**1 228 883**	**1 271 476**	**1 335 066**	**1 357 395**	**1 377 418**	**1 422 429**	**1 474 646**	**1 516 620**
22	Agriculture, forestry and fishing	39 798	37 085	37 857	34 265	37 377	37 633	34 449	35 415
23	Industry, including energy	289 419	313 744	338 494	347 858	350 852	366 569	380 368	394 062
24	Manufacturing	206 685	224 845	242 562	250 424	251 461	271 433	290 344	302 783
25	Construction	102 877	107 950	122 486	117 633	111 703	121 757	129 551	120 196
26	Services	..	..	..	..	..	..	..	..
27	Distrib. trade, repairs; transp.; accommod., food serv. activ.	315 422	327 183	333 675	347 343	350 812	349 438	356 553	370 909
28	Information and communication	49 018	49 571	52 559	57 748	60 388	64 394	69 578	77 548
29	Financial and insurance activities	54 219	52 684	57 059	51 413	58 797	64 456	73 977	76 972
30	Real estate activities	63 547	67 793	70 670	70 789	71 277	74 921	72 818	77 169
31	Prof., scientif., techn. activ.; admin., support service activ.	89 021	89 338	93 709	98 276	102 124	106 648	117 643	122 169
32	Public admin.; compulsory s.s.; education; human health	197 415	196 876	199 104	199 398	201 263	204 740	208 934	209 625
33	Other service activities	30 176	29 252	29 453	33 269	32 132	32 830	33 130	34 808
34	FISIM (Financial Intermediation Services Indirectly Measured)	..	..	..	..	..	..	..	..
35	Gross value added at basic prices, excluding FISIM	1 228 883	1 271 476	1 335 066	1 357 395	1 377 418	1 422 429	1 474 646	1 516 620
36	**Taxes less subsidies on products**	**165 959**	**173 822**	**182 746**	**184 828**	**186 206**	**192 545**	**202 565**	**208 653**
37	Taxes on products	171 440	178 847	187 698	188 269	190 217	194 923	204 017	210 694
38	Subsidies on products	5 432	5 025	4 952	3 429	3 971	2 446	1 579	2 133
39	**Residual item**	**140**	**0**	**0**	**-6**	**59**	**47**	**-99**	**-123**
40	**Gross domestic product at market prices**	**1 394 982**	**1 445 298**	**1 517 812**	**1 542 217**	**1 563 683**	**1 615 021**	**1 677 112**	**1 725 150**
	INCOME APPROACH								
41	**Compensation of employees**	**517 207**	**547 676**	**580 533**	**606 337**	**618 838**	**646 459**	**668 171**	**706 669 p**
42	Agriculture, forestry and fishing	8 706	8 481	9 612	10 518	10 512	11 238	11 094	11 757 p
43	Industry, including energy	136 522	143 377	152 510	160 455	162 102	171 251	175 629	186 878 p
44	Manufacturing	101 347	106 474	113 910	118 869	122 336	130 981	138 095	150 340 p
45	Construction	35 654	38 522	43 236	42 284	40 748	41 392	43 076	44 991 p
46	Distrib. trade, repairs; transp.; accommod., food serv. activ.	97 846	104 459	108 883	115 930	117 751	125 738	130 809	140 074 p
47	Information and communication	16 494	17 015	18 497	19 529	20 809	20 684	23 817	26 327 p
48	Financial and insurance activities	20 486	21 180	22 167	24 253	24 607	25 117	24 484	26 463 p
49	Real estate activities	6 218	6 344	7 978	8 290	8 063	8 651	9 128	9 673 p
50	Prof., scientif., techn. activ.; admin., support service activ.	32 413	35 993	38 828	41 481	45 248	48 636	52 290	55 007 p
51	Public admin.; compulsory s.s.; education; human health	149 879	158 384	164 579	167 465	172 123	176 715	181 338	187 604 p
52	Other service activities	12 989	13 921	14 243	16 132	16 875	17 037	16 506	17 895 p
53	**Wages and salaries**	**437 731**	**462 936**	**490 388**	**506 548**	**516 978**	**540 095**	**556 845**	**590 082 p**
54	Agriculture, forestry and fishing	7 624	7 451	8 388	9 124	9 109	9 796	9 641	10 206 p
55	Industry, including energy	116 990	122 425	130 515	135 503	137 353	144 853	148 096	158 068 p
56	Manufacturing	86 881	90 893	97 410	100 309	103 627	110 696	116 473	127 259 p
57	Construction	30 459	32 387	36 269	35 597	34 140	35 064	36 591	37 954 p
58	Distrib. trade, repairs; transp.; accommod., food serv. activ.	85 205	91 025	94 736	99 807	101 421	108 426	112 145	120 424 p
59	Information and communication	14 536	14 981	16 256	16 973	18 151	17 983	20 686	22 837 p
60	Financial and insurance activities	18 209	18 826	19 758	21 325	21 679	22 220	21 562	23 402 p
61	Real estate activities	5 307	5 473	6 896	7 084	6 962	7 459	7 893	8 377 p
62	Prof., scientif., techn. activ.; admin., support service activ.	28 445	31 694	34 230	36 079	39 534	42 502	45 554	47 703 p
63	Public admin.; compulsory s.s.; education; human health	119 537	126 394	130 772	130 787	133 689	136 718	140 225	145 343 p
64	Other service activities	11 419	12 280	12 568	14 269	14 940	15 074	14 452	15 768 p
65	**Gross operating surplus and mixed income**	**699 948**	**718 983**	**790 778**	**831 084**	**849 312**	**877 474**	**922 823**	**934 532 p**
66	**Taxes less subsidies on production and imports**	**155 053**	**178 639**	**195 513**	**192 004**	**188 745**	**195 836**	**208 398**	**217 436 p**
67	Taxes on production and imports	177 631	201 179	219 163	214 257	215 201	223 234	234 001	251 576 p
68	Subsidies on production and imports	22 578	22 540	23 650	22 253	26 456	27 398	25 603	34 140 p
69	**Residual item**	..	..	..	..	..	..	..	..
70	**Gross domestic product**	**1 372 208**	**1 445 298**	**1 566 824**	**1 629 425**	**1 656 895**	**1 719 769**	**1 799 392**	**1 858 637 p**

Note: Detailed metadata:http://metalinks.oecd.org/nav1/20180308/4f7a
Source: Central Statistical Office of Poland via Eurostat.

Table 3. Disposable income, saving and net lending / net borrowing

Million PLN

		2009	2010	2011	2012	2013	2014	2015	2016
	DISPOSABLE INCOME								
1	**Gross domestic product**	1 372 208	1 445 298	1 566 824	1 629 425	1 656 895	1 719 769	1 799 392	1 858 637
2	Net primary incomes from the rest of the world	-41 190	-51 732	-56 621	-60 867	-55 564	-63 691	-65 450	-69 636
3	Primary incomes receivable from the rest of the world	31 074	34 219	36 601	39 358	43 682	43 848	43 920	54 511
4	Primary incomes payable to the rest of the world	72 264	85 951	93 222	100 225	99 246	107 539	109 370	124 147
5	**Gross national income at market prices**	1 331 017	1 393 566	1 510 204	1 568 558	1 601 331	1 656 078	1 733 942	1 789 001
6	Consumption of fixed capital	159 435	162 906	169 419	179 730	188 550	196 690	207 064	216 928
7	**Net national income at market prices**	1 171 582	1 230 660	1 340 785	1 388 828	1 412 781	1 459 388	1 526 878	1 572 073
8	Net current transfers from the rest of the world	6 335	10 714	12 656	14 384	15 090	15 626	13 189	10 966
9	Current transfers receivable from the rest of the world	28 946	31 922	34 867	41 070	41 900	41 035	42 073	40 645
10	Current transfers payable to the rest of the world	22 611	21 208	22 211	26 686	26 810	25 409	28 884	29 679
11	**Net national disposable income**	1 177 917	1 241 374	1 353 441	1 403 212	1 427 871	1 475 014	1 540 067	1 583 039
	SAVING AND NET LENDING / NET BORROWING								
12	**Net national disposable income**	1 177 917	1 241 374	1 353 441	1 403 212	1 427 871	1 475 014	1 540 067	1 583 039
13	Final consumption expenditures	1 101 662	1 166 136	1 245 885	1 294 568	1 310 124	1 344 724	1 375 382	1 419 174
14	Adj. for change in net equity of households in pension funds	0	0	0	0	0	0	0	0
15	**Saving, net**	76 255	75 238	107 556	108 644	117 747	130 290	164 685	163 865
16	Net capital transfers from the rest of the world	16 363	22 171	30 741	33 884	32 926	28 305	40 643	17 318
17	Capital transfers receivable from the rest of the world	17 604	23 970	32 657	35 998	34 661	31 546	43 297	20 434
18	Capital transfers payable to the rest of the world	1 241	1 799	1 916	2 114	1 735	3 241	2 654	3 116
19	Gross capital formation	282 306	308 040	351 592	342 031	314 498	350 256	368 330	364 238
20	Acquisitions less disposals of non-financial non-produced assets	..	-1 148	-786	-1 433	-1 416	-2 581	-2 109	1 861
21	Consumption of fixed capital	159 435	162 906	169 419	179 730	188 550	196 690	207 064	216 928
22	**Net lending / net borrowing**	-30 253	-46 577	-43 090	-18 340	26 141	7 610	46 171	32 012
	REAL DISPOSABLE INCOME								
23	**Gross domestic product at constant prices, reference year 2010**	1 394 981	1 445 297	1 517 813	1 542 218	1 563 684	1 615 022	1 677 113	1 725 151
24	Trading gain or loss	8 199	0	-10 810	-19 456	-12 480	1 126	20 511	27 783
25	**Real gross domestic income**	1 403 181	1 445 298	1 507 003	1 522 762	1 551 204	1 616 148	1 697 624	1 752 934
26	Net real primary incomes from the rest of the world	-42 120	-51 732	-54 459	-56 883	-52 020	-59 853	-61 748	-65 676
27	Real primary incomes receivable from the rest of the world	31 775	34 219	35 204	36 782	40 896	41 206	41 436	51 411
28	Real primary incomes payable to the rest of the world	73 895	85 951	89 663	93 664	92 915	101 059	103 184	117 087
29	**Real gross national income at market prices**	1 361 060	1 393 566	1 452 545	1 465 880	1 499 184	1 556 295	1 635 876	1 687 258
30	Net real current transfers from the rest of the world	6 478	10 714	12 173	13 442	14 127	14 684	12 443	10 342
31	Real current transfers receivable from the rest of the world	29 599	31 922	33 536	38 382	39 227	38 563	39 693	38 333
32	Real current transfers payable to the rest of the world	23 121	21 208	21 363	24 939	25 100	23 878	27 250	27 991
33	**Real gross national disposable income**	1 367 538	1 404 280	1 464 718	1 479 322	1 513 312	1 570 979	1 648 319	1 697 600
34	Consumption of fixed capital at constant prices	161 232	162 906	167 503	175 525	186 134	196 205	203 789	210 997
35	**Real net national income at market prices**	1 198 026	1 230 660	1 289 594	1 297 915	1 322 661	1 371 456	1 440 523	1 482 667
36	**Real net national disposable income**	1 204 504	1 241 374	1 301 767	1 311 357	1 336 789	1 386 141	1 452 966	1 493 009

Note: Detailed metadata:http://metalinks.oecd.org/nav1/20180308/0b8b
Source: Central Statistical Office of Poland via Eurostat.

POLAND

Table 4. Population and employment (persons) and employment (hours worked) by industry
ISIC Rev. 4

		2009	2010	2011	2012	2013	2014	2015	2016
	POPULATION, THOUSAND PERSONS, NATIONAL CONCEPT								
1	**Total population**	38 483.0	38 517.0	38 526.0	38 534.0	38 502.0	38 484.0	38 455.0	38 427.0
2	Economically active population	..	..	..	..	..	..	..	..
3	Unemployed persons	..	..	..	..	..	..	..	..
4	Total employment	15 868.0	15 473.0	15 563.0	15 591.0	15 568.0	15 862.0	16 084.0	16 197.0
5	Employees	12 260.0	11 918.0	12 004.0	12 100.0	12 170.0	12 475.0	12 669.0	12 841.0
6	Self-employed	3 608.0	3 555.0	3 559.0	3 491.0	3 398.0	3 387.0	3 415.0	3 356.0
	TOTAL EMPLOYMENT, THOUSAND PERSONS, DOMESTIC CONCEPT								
7	Agriculture, forestry and fishing	2 095.4	2 003.9	1 994.7	1 945.9	1 852.7	1 804.3	1 841.9	1 694.7 p
8	Industry, including energy	3 607.2	3 403.8	3 458.9	3 454.8	3 536.6	3 620.8	3 676.3	3 814.1 p
9	Manufacturing	3 044.4	2 855.9	2 892.4	2 878.8	2 941.0	3 004.8	3 093.7	3 243.8 p
10	Construction	1 280.8	1 220.7	1 246.4	1 211.2	1 144.1	1 134.2	1 156.3	1 164.2 p
11	Distrib. trade, repairs; transp.; accommod., food serv. activ.	3 536.7	3 470.3	3 470.9	3 495.0	3 460.7	3 539.2	3 608.2	3 674.1 p
12	Information and communication	316.1	299.7	298.9	315.4	332.8	360.1	374.6	362.5 p
13	Financial and insurance activities	372.1	352.7	370.6	392.6	383.1	378.4	396.5	384.6 p
14	Real estate activities	156.0	167.5	164.3	146.8	142.8	160.5	172.5	161.1 p
15	Prof., scientif., techn. activ.; admin., support service activ.	840.3	872.0	919.7	938.7	940.7	1 012.3	1 003.3	1 018.9 p
16	Public admin.; compulsory s.s.; education; human health	3 125.3	3 113.3	3 086.0	3 120.9	3 203.9	3 247.7	3 261.6	3 241.4 p
17	Other service activities	459.5	466.4	446.9	453.6	466.4	473.5	478.8	545.1 p
18	**Total employment**	15 789.4	15 370.3	15 457.3	15 474.9	15 463.8	15 731.0	15 970.0	16 060.7 p
	EMPLOYEES, THOUSAND PERSONS, DOMESTIC CONCEPT								
19	Agriculture, forestry and fishing	201.9	204.0	210.3	205.9	208.3	208.0	204.2	203.9 p
20	Industry, including energy	3 414.4	3 228.3	3 288.9	3 281.0	3 335.8	3 413.4	3 467.8	3 600.3 p
21	Manufacturing	2 857.3	2 684.2	2 727.8	2 712.8	2 750.7	2 806.0	2 894.8	3 040.5 p
22	Construction	1 008.6	941.9	970.6	940.8	868.9	869.7	900.5	875.5 p
23	Distrib. trade, repairs; transp.; accommod., food serv. activ.	2 814.3	2 753.5	2 744.3	2 794.8	2 778.8	2 865.9	2 950.4	3 015.7 p
24	Information and communication	262.8	252.9	250.6	264.5	276.4	295.3	304.6	285.0 p
25	Financial and insurance activities	320.1	305.8	317.1	342.3	330.7	322.1	342.8	337.1 p
26	Real estate activities	136.3	146.2	144.3	130.2	123.8	135.9	148.3	138.3 p
27	Prof., scientif., techn. activ.; admin., support service activ.	655.2	679.1	708.0	726.7	731.4	771.7	758.2	756.2 p
28	Public admin.; compulsory s.s.; education; human health	3 038.1	3 005.8	2 981.1	3 013.0	3 080.8	3 126.5	3 127.5	3 106.4 p
29	Other service activities	366.4	358.9	338.6	355.8	365.6	363.4	370.8	419.8 p
30	**Total employees**	12 218.1	11 876.4	11 953.8	12 055.0	12 100.5	12 371.9	12 575.1	12 738.2 p
	SELF-EMPLOYED, THOUSAND PERSONS, DOMESTIC CONCEPT								
31	Agriculture, forestry and fishing	1 893.5	1 799.9	1 784.4	1 740.0	1 644.4	1 596.3	1 637.7	1 490.8 p
32	Industry, including energy	192.8	175.5	170.0	173.8	200.8	207.4	208.5	213.8 p
33	Manufacturing	187.1	171.7	164.6	166.0	190.3	198.8	198.9	203.3 p
34	Construction	272.2	278.8	275.8	270.4	275.2	264.5	255.8	288.7 p
35	Distrib. trade, repairs; transp.; accommod., food serv. activ.	722.4	716.8	726.6	700.2	681.9	673.3	657.8	658.4 p
36	Information and communication	53.3	46.8	48.3	50.9	56.4	64.8	70.0	77.5 p
37	Financial and insurance activities	52.0	46.9	53.5	50.3	52.4	56.3	53.7	47.5 p
38	Real estate activities	19.7	21.3	20.0	16.6	19.0	24.6	24.2	22.8 p
39	Prof., scientif., techn. activ.; admin., support service activ.	185.1	192.9	211.7	212.0	209.3	240.6	245.1	262.7 p
40	Public admin.; compulsory s.s.; education; human health	87.2	107.5	104.9	107.9	123.1	121.2	134.1	135.0 p
41	Other service activities	93.1	107.5	108.3	97.8	100.8	110.1	108.0	125.3 p
42	**Total self-employed**	3 571.3	3 493.9	3 503.5	3 419.9	3 363.3	3 359.1	3 394.9	3 322.5 p
	TOTAL EMPLOYMENT, MILLION HOURS, DOMESTIC CONCEPT								
43	Industry, including energy	7 578.9	7 174.0	7 231.3	7 170.8	7 342.1	7 519.6	7 658.7	7 923.2 p
44	Distrib. trade, repairs; transp.; accommod., food serv. activ.	7 623.5	7 475.4	7 430.2	7 410.7	7 290.1	7 465.1	7 588.8	7 702.0 p
45	Financial and insurance activities	761.6	717.9	748.4	795.1	767.3	762.9	804.9	779.7 p
46	Prof., scientif., techn. activ.; admin., support service activ.	1 706.8	1 783.4	1 868.5	1 904.0	1 892.7	2 049.9	2 041.7	2 073.1 p
47	Public admin.; compulsory s.s.; education; human health	5 871.3	5 859.7	5 817.9	5 895.4	6 074.8	6 192.3	6 281.6	6 288.3 p
48	**Total employment**	32 431.4	31 490.7	31 588.5	31 544.0	31 465.0	32 112.0	32 722.7	32 930.2 p
	EMPLOYEES, MILLION HOURS, DOMESTIC CONCEPT								
49	Industry, including energy	7 117.8	6 761.4	6 836.0	6 773.3	6 887.3	7 042.4	7 174.3	7 446.2 p
50	Distrib. trade, repairs; transp.; accommod., food serv. activ.	5 894.5	5 756.2	5 703.1	5 752.6	5 695.9	5 905.5	6 067.9	6 173.8 p
51	Financial and insurance activities	647.8	621.2	636.1	689.2	661.7	650.1	693.8	679.6 p
52	Prof., scientif., techn. activ.; admin., support service activ.	1 308.9	1 369.5	1 413.7	1 451.2	1 441.3	1 535.9	1 520.4	1 513.0 p
53	Public admin.; compulsory s.s.; education; human health	5 698.5	5 648.8	5 614.0	5 680.3	5 828.7	5 959.3	6 011.9	6 020.0 p
54	**Total employees**	24 822.5	24 134.2	24 195.0	24 282.4	24 310.0	24 929.3	25 436.5	25 767.0 p
	SELF-EMPLOYED, MILLION HOURS, DOMESTIC CONCEPT								
55	Industry, including energy	461.1	412.6	395.3	397.5	454.8	477.2	484.4	477.0 p
56	Distrib. trade, repairs; transp.; accommod., food serv. activ.	1 729.0	1 719.2	1 727.1	1 658.0	1 594.2	1 559.6	1 520.9	1 528.2 p
57	Financial and insurance activities	113.7	96.8	112.3	105.9	105.6	112.8	111.1	100.1 p
58	Prof., scientif., techn. activ.; admin., support service activ.	397.9	413.9	454.8	452.8	451.4	513.9	521.3	560.1 p
59	Public admin.; compulsory s.s.; education; human health	172.8	211.0	203.9	215.1	246.1	232.9	273.4	268.3 p
60	**Total self-employed**	7 609.0	7 356.5	7 393.6	7 261.6	7 155.0	7 182.8	7 286.2	7 163.2 p

Note: Detailed metadata:http://metalinks.oecd.org/nav1/20180308/e7ef
Source: Central Statistical Office of Poland via Eurostat.

PORTUGAL

Table 1. Gross domestic product, expenditure approach

Million EUR (1999 PTE euro)

		2009	2010	2011	2012	2013	2014	2015	2016
	AT CURRENT PRICES								
1	**Final consumption expenditure**	**151 113**	**155 599**	**150 944**	**142 787**	**143 644**	**146 266**	**150 311**	**154 698** p
2	Household	110 258	115 063	112 611	108 221	107 717	110 546	114 058	117 566 p
3	NPISH's	3 251	3 266	3 351	3 389	3 426	3 514	3 669	3 769 p
4	Government	37 604	37 270	34 983	31 177	32 501	32 206	32 584	33 363 p
5	Individual	20 879	20 585	18 821	16 810	17 417	16 989	16 278	16 671 p
6	Collective	16 725	16 685	16 162	14 367	15 084	15 217	16 305	16 693 p
7	*of which: Actual individual consumption*	134 388	138 914	134 782	128 420	128 560	131 048	134 005	138 005 p
8	**Gross capital formation**	**36 478**	**37 930**	**32 764**	**26 466**	**24 914**	**26 486**	**28 452**	**28 718** p
9	Gross fixed capital formation, total	37 107	36 938	32 452	26 672	25 122	25 993	27 844	28 293 p
10	Dwellings[1]	7 114	6 500	5 750	4 967	4 194	4 287	4 401	4 596 p
11	Other buildings and structures[1]	14 347	14 540	13 291	10 104	8 989	8 697	9 443	9 284 p
12	Transport equipment	2 525	2 319	1 754	1 213	1 555	1 746	2 158	2 340 p
13	Other machinery and equipment	6 077	6 444	4 810	3 975	4 101	4 772	5 134	..
14	Cultivated assets	406	412	422	419	420	439	471	468 p
15	Intangible fixed assets	4 700	4 749	4 768	4 551	4 457	4 524	4 552	4 573 p
16	Changes in inventories, acquisitions less disposals of valuables	-629	993	312	-206	-208	493	608	425 p
17	Changes in inventories	-761	864	207	-274	-289	418	505	300 p
18	Acquisitions less disposals of valuables	132	129	105	68	81	75	103	125 p
19	**External balance of goods and services**	**-12 143**	**-13 600**	**-7 542**	**-855**	**1 711**	**327**	**1 047**	**2 078** p
20	Exports of goods and services	47 513	53 751	60 410	63 504	67 284	69 360	72 648	74 436 p
21	Exports of goods	33 603	39 021	44 471	46 833	49 270	50 415	52 341	52 816 p
22	Exports of services	13 909	14 730	15 939	16 671	18 014	18 945	20 307	21 621 p
23	Imports of goods and services	59 655	67 351	67 952	64 359	65 573	69 033	71 601	72 358 p
24	Imports of goods	51 070	58 011	58 325	55 172	56 130	58 593	60 416	60 785 p
25	Imports of services	8 585	9 339	9 627	9 187	9 443	10 441	11 185	11 573 p
26	**Statistical discrepancy**	**0**	**0**	**0**	**0**	**0**	**0**	**0**	**0** p
27	**Gross domestic product**	**175 448**	**179 930**	**176 167**	**168 398**	**170 269**	**173 079**	**179 809**	**185 494** p
	AT CONSTANT PRICES, REFERENCE YEAR 2010								
28	**Final consumption expenditure**	**153 282**	**155 599**	**149 913**	**142 446**	**140 476**	**142 800**	**145 743**	**148 296** p
29	Household	112 240	115 063	110 782	104 494	103 161	105 524	107 760	110 011 p
30	NPISH's	3 318	3 266	3 281	3 302	3 344	3 429	3 687	3 767 p
31	Government	37 765	37 270	35 847	34 671	33 983	33 829	34 266	34 473 p
32	Individual	20 833	20 585	19 504	18 992	19 018	18 233	17 563	17 733 p
33	Collective	16 932	16 685	16 336	15 675	14 971	15 586	16 670	16 708 p
34	*of which: Actual individual consumption*	136 359	138 914	133 583	126 779	125 503	127 219	129 093	131 604
35	**Gross capital formation**	**36 686**	**37 930**	**32 620**	**26 714**	**25 342**	**26 630**	**28 331**	**28 548** p
36	Gross fixed capital formation, total	37 289	36 938	32 314	26 943	25 581	26 176	27 704	28 107 p
37	Dwellings[1]	7 257	6 500	5 752	5 310	4 548	4 498	4 546	4 626 p
38	Other buildings and structures[1]	14 615	14 540	13 128	9 796	8 714	8 289	8 872	8 750 p
39	Transport equipment	2 523	2 319	1 746	1 185	1 527	1 696	2 065	2 237 p
40	Other machinery and equipment	5 981	6 444	4 776	4 077	4 232	4 906	5 297	..
41	Cultivated assets	413	412	401	389	383	393	430	432 p
42	Intangible fixed assets	4 726	4 749	4 821	4 651	4 594	4 680	4 672	4 640 p
43	Changes in inventories, acquisitions less disposals of valuables	..	..	..	..	..	..	..	..
44	Changes in inventories	..	..	..	..	..	..	..	..
45	Acquisitions less disposals of valuables	140	129	105	66	81	74	100	120 p
46	**External balance of goods and services**	**-13 379**	**-13 600**	**-5 898**	**73**	**1 457**	**-622**	**-2 231**	**-2 183** p
47	Exports of goods and services	49 078	53 751	57 533	59 492	63 648	66 409	70 484	73 606 p
48	Exports of goods	35 118	39 021	42 031	43 526	46 512	48 503	51 726	54 047 p
49	Exports of services	13 975	14 730	15 494	15 957	17 127	17 898	18 743	19 541 p
50	Imports of goods and services	62 457	67 351	63 430	59 419	62 191	67 031	72 715	75 789 p
51	Imports of goods	53 702	58 011	53 886	50 459	53 013	57 057	62 088	64 899 p
52	Imports of services	8 762	9 339	9 604	9 018	9 223	10 028	10 671	10 921 p
53	**Statistical discrepancy (including chaining residual)**	**-11**	**0**	**7**	**295**	**336**	**301**	**347**	**317** p
54	**Gross domestic product**	**176 577**	**179 930**	**176 643**	**169 527**	**167 611**	**169 108**	**172 190**	**174 978** p

Note: Detailed metadata:http://metalinks.oecd.org/nav1/20180308/10e6

1. *Other buildings and structures is included in Dwellings.*

Source: Instituto Nacional de Estatistica (INE) via Eurostat.

Table 2. Gross domestic product, output and income approach
ISIC Rev. 4

Million EUR (1999 PTE euro)

		2009	2010	2011	2012	2013	2014	2015	2016
	OUTPUT APPROACH AT CURRENT PRICES								
1	**Total gross value added at basic prices**	**155 506**	**158 326**	**154 243**	**147 362**	**149 768**	**151 365**	**156 839**	**161 141 p**
2	Agriculture, forestry and fishing	3 409	3 463	3 209	3 212	3 542	3 511	3 687	3 519 p
3	Industry, including energy	25 065	26 594	25 588	24 991	25 399	26 488	28 753	29 600 p
4	Manufacturing	19 529	20 822	19 959	19 166	19 680	20 421	21 861	22 545 p
5	Construction	9 763	9 226	8 465	7 171	6 751	6 278	6 370	6 298 p
6	Services	..	..	..	..	..	..	..	..
7	Distrib. trade, repairs; transp.; accommod., food serv. activ.	35 494	36 095	36 245	36 017	36 713	37 274	38 786	40 376 p
8	Information and communication	5 985	5 739	5 723	5 416	5 217	5 192	5 321	5 397 p
9	Financial and insurance activities	10 992	10 424	10 808	9 268	8 255	8 089	8 242	8 177 p
10	Real estate activities	15 244	16 795	16 597	17 424	18 573	18 891	19 233	19 757 p
11	Prof., scientif., techn. activ.; admin., support service activ.	11 086	11 244	10 744	9 997	10 119	10 856	11 027	11 677 p
12	Public admin.; compulsory s.s.; education; human health	34 131	34 254	32 411	29 528	30 910	30 391	30 862	31 622 p
13	Other service activities	4 338	4 491	4 455	4 338	4 288	4 395	4 558	4 718 p
14	**FISIM (Financial Intermediation Services Indirectly Measured)**	..	..	..	..	..	..	..	..
15	**Gross value added at basic prices, excluding FISIM**	**155 506**	**158 326**	**154 243**	**147 362**	**149 768**	**151 365**	**156 839**	**161 141 p**
16	**Taxes less subsidies on products**	**19 942**	**21 604**	**21 924**	**21 036**	**20 501**	**21 714**	**22 970**	**24 282 p**
17	Taxes on products	20 497	22 154	22 499	21 447	20 883	22 067	23 346	24 624 p
18	Subsidies on products	555	550	575	411	382	353	376	343 p
19	**Residual item**	**0**	**0**	**0**	**0**	**0**	**0**	**0**	**71 p**
20	**Gross domestic product at market prices**	**175 448**	**179 930**	**176 167**	**168 398**	**170 269**	**173 079**	**179 809**	**185 494 p**
	OUTPUT APPROACH AT CONSTANT PRICES (REF. YEAR 2010)								
21	**Total gross value added at basic prices**	**155 473**	**158 326**	**156 513**	**151 465**	**150 304**	**150 957**	**153 444**	**155 260 p**
22	Agriculture, forestry and fishing	3 443	3 463	3 492	3 471	3 571	3 513	3 693	3 421 p
23	Industry, including energy	25 332	26 594	26 602	25 808	25 596	26 186	27 001	27 301 p
24	Manufacturing	19 436	20 822	20 952	20 232	20 374	20 927	21 551	21 843 p
25	Construction	9 856	9 226	8 627	7 317	6 812	6 238	6 235	6 129 p
26	Services	..	..	..	..	..	..	..	..
27	Distrib. trade, repairs; transp.; accommod., food serv. activ.	34 815	36 095	35 863	35 536	36 008	36 995	37 869	39 020 p
28	Information and communication	5 954	5 739	6 060	5 818	5 694	5 634	5 644	5 667 p
29	Financial and insurance activities	10 609	10 424	10 449	9 455	8 882	8 064	7 634	7 357 p
30	Real estate activities	15 981	16 795	16 939	16 662	16 789	16 790	17 029	17 137 p
31	Prof., scientif., techn. activ.; admin., support service activ.	10 880	11 244	10 917	10 404	10 578	11 483	11 622	12 066 p
32	Public admin.; compulsory s.s.; education; human health	34 197	34 254	33 146	32 619	32 033	31 619	32 182	32 501 p
33	Other service activities	4 405	4 491	4 428	4 400	4 376	4 486	4 620	4 720 p
34	**FISIM (Financial Intermediation Services Indirectly Measured)**	..	..	..	..	..	..	..	..
35	**Gross value added at basic prices, excluding FISIM**	**155 473**	**158 326**	**156 513**	**151 465**	**150 304**	**150 957**	**153 444**	**155 260 p**
36	**Taxes less subsidies on products**	**21 100**	**21 604**	**20 129**	**18 182**	**17 513**	**18 256**	**18 811**	**19 669 p**
37	Taxes on products	21 673	22 154	20 670	18 560	17 872	18 594	19 155	19 989 p
38	Subsidies on products	574	550	541	376	356	335	341	316 p
39	**Residual item**	**4**	**0**	**0**	**-119**	**-206**	**-105**	**-66**	**50 p**
40	**Gross domestic product at market prices**	**176 577**	**179 930**	**176 643**	**169 527**	**167 611**	**169 108**	**172 190**	**174 978 p**
	INCOME APPROACH								
41	**Compensation of employees**	**83 625**	**84 842**	**81 617**	**75 305**	**76 280**	**76 472**	**78 604**	**81 929 p**
42	Agriculture, forestry and fishing	923	936	903	899	924	964	1 018	1 069 p
43	Industry, including energy	12 790	12 994	12 870	12 323	12 252	12 547	13 024	13 571 p
44	Manufacturing	11 293	11 500	11 380	10 914	10 834	11 180	11 632	12 158 p
45	Construction	6 179	6 078	5 599	4 559	4 161	3 917	4 012	4 101 p
46	Distrib. trade, repairs; transp.; accommod., food serv. activ.	18 820	19 390	18 979	17 742	17 398	17 983	18 925	19 994 p
47	Information and communication	2 460	2 553	2 586	2 488	2 603	2 558	2 734	2 853 p
48	Financial and insurance activities	4 174	4 216	4 024	4 000	4 102	3 787	3 816	3 909 p
49	Real estate activities	497	512	484	425	418	435	463	513 p
50	Prof., scientif., techn. activ.; admin., support service activ.	7 007	7 194	7 106	6 724	6 727	7 120	7 489	7 982 p
51	Public admin.; compulsory s.s.; education; human health	27 751	27 822	25 968	23 122	24 702	24 103	24 004	24 754 p
52	Other service activities	3 024	3 148	3 100	3 022	2 993	3 058	3 119	3 183 p
53	**Wages and salaries**	**65 586**	**66 260**	**63 638**	**58 783**	**59 110**	**59 585**	**61 381**	**63 988 p**
54	Agriculture, forestry and fishing	778	787	751	750	765	795	839	881 p
55	Industry, including energy	10 280	10 347	10 201	9 756	9 664	9 941	10 311	10 741 p
56	Manufacturing	9 076	9 154	9 031	8 644	8 564	8 877	9 227	9 638 p
57	Construction	5 027	4 926	4 508	3 651	3 320	3 147	3 217	3 260 p
58	Distrib. trade, repairs; transp.; accommod., food serv. activ.	15 386	15 663	15 254	14 346	14 047	14 625	15 368	16 278 p
59	Information and communication	1 978	2 012	2 020	1 960	1 966	2 028	2 174	2 262 p
60	Financial and insurance activities	3 212	3 243	3 096	3 030	3 187	2 909	2 894	2 944 p
61	Real estate activities	405	416	390	341	337	350	367	408 p
62	Prof., scientif., techn. activ.; admin., support service activ.	5 758	5 846	5 729	5 398	5 376	5 696	5 988	6 400 p
63	Public admin.; compulsory s.s.; education; human health	20 165	20 363	19 085	17 017	17 948	17 533	17 609	18 155 p
64	Other service activities	2 596	2 656	2 603	2 535	2 501	2 561	2 614	2 660 p
65	**Gross operating surplus and mixed income**	**72 250**	**74 260**	**73 231**	**72 634**	**73 454**	**74 753**	**77 355**	**78 686 p**
66	**Taxes less subsidies on production and imports**	**19 573**	**20 828**	**21 319**	**20 459**	**20 536**	**21 853**	**23 851**	**24 880 p**
67	Taxes on production and imports	22 345	23 955	24 579	23 495	23 463	24 709	26 227	27 657 p
68	Subsidies on production and imports	2 772	3 126	3 260	3 036	2 928	2 856	2 376	2 777 p
69	**Residual item**	**0**	**0**	**0**	**0**	**0**	**0**	**0**	**0 p**
70	**Gross domestic product**	**175 448**	**179 930**	**176 167**	**168 398**	**170 269**	**173 079**	**179 809**	**185 494 p**

Note: Detailed metadata:http://metalinks.oecd.org/nav1/20180308/10e6
Source: Instituto Nacional de Estatistica (INE) via Eurostat.

Table 3. Disposable income, saving and net lending / net borrowing

Million EUR (1999 PTE euro)

		2009	2010	2011	2012	2013	2014	2015	2016
	DISPOSABLE INCOME								
1	**Gross domestic product**	175 448	179 930	176 167	168 398	170 269	173 079	179 809	185 179 p
2	Net primary incomes from the rest of the world	-6 424	-6 051	-3 394	-4 081	-2 295	-2 962	-4 941	-4 006 p
3	Primary incomes receivable from the rest of the world	9 253	10 814	10 394	8 592	8 635	8 510	7 599	8 261 p
4	Primary incomes payable to the rest of the world	15 677	16 865	13 788	12 674	10 930	11 472	12 540	12 267 p
5	**Gross national income at market prices**	169 024	173 878	172 772	164 317	167 975	170 117	174 868	181 174 p
6	Consumption of fixed capital	30 098	30 965	31 429	30 552	29 884	30 324	31 013	31 340 p
7	**Net national income at market prices**	138 926	142 913	141 344	133 765	138 000	139 793	143 855	149 834 p
8	Net current transfers from the rest of the world	910	1 109	1 326	1 535	1 834	2 197	2 300	2 456 p
9	Current transfers receivable from the rest of the world	5 189	5 635	5 910	6 563	7 110	6 906	6 716	6 892 p
10	Current transfers payable to the rest of the world	4 279	4 527	4 584	5 028	5 276	4 709	4 415	4 436 p
11	**Net national disposable income**	139 836	144 022	142 670	135 300	139 924	141 990	146 156	152 290 p
	SAVING AND NET LENDING / NET BORROWING								
12	**Net national disposable income**	139 836	144 022	142 670	135 300	139 924	141 990	146 156	152 290 p
13	Final consumption expenditures	151 113	155 599	150 944	142 787	143 644	146 266	150 311	154 698 p
14	Adj. for change in net equity of households in pension funds	0	0	0	0	0	0	0	0 p
15	**Saving, net**	-11 277	-11 577	-8 275	-7 487	-3 720	-4 276	-4 155	-2 408 p
16	Net capital transfers from the rest of the world	1 955	2 385	2 431	3 339	2 635	2 101	2 131	1 715 p
17	Capital transfers receivable from the rest of the world	2 179	2 658	2 632	3 532	2 852	2 424	2 436	1 983 p
18	Capital transfers payable to the rest of the world	224	273	201	192	217	324	306	268 p
19	Gross capital formation	36 478	37 930	32 764	26 466	24 914	26 486	28 452	28 754 p
20	Acquisitions less disposals of non-financial non-produced assets	17	14	-136	-78	-61	-123	-30	28 p
21	Consumption of fixed capital	30 098	30 965	31 429	30 552	29 884	30 324	31 013	31 340 p
22	**Net lending / net borrowing**	-15 719	-16 171	-7 043	15	3 946	1 786	567	1 865 p
	REAL DISPOSABLE INCOME								
23	**Gross domestic product at constant prices, reference year 2010**	176 577	179 930	176 643	169 527	167 611	169 108	172 190	174 978 p
24	Trading gain or loss	1 149	0	-1 566	-1 177	-14	822	3 103	3 661 p
25	**Real gross domestic income**	177 726	179 930	175 077	168 350	167 597	169 930	175 293	178 639 p
26	Net real primary incomes from the rest of the world	-6 507	-6 051	-3 373	-4 080	-2 259	-2 909	-4 817	-3 864 p
27	Real primary incomes receivable from the rest of the world	9 373	10 814	10 329	8 590	8 500	8 355	7 409	7 969 p
28	Real primary incomes payable to the rest of the world	15 880	16 865	13 703	12 670	10 758	11 264	12 226	11 834 p
29	**Real gross national income at market prices**	171 219	173 878	171 704	164 270	165 338	167 021	170 476	174 775 p
30	Net real current transfers from the rest of the world	922	1 109	1 318	1 534	1 805	2 157	2 242	2 369 p
31	Real current transfers receivable from the rest of the world	5 256	5 635	5 874	6 561	6 998	6 780	6 547	6 649 p
32	Real current transfers payable to the rest of the world	4 335	4 527	4 556	5 027	5 193	4 623	4 305	4 279 p
33	**Real gross national disposable income**	172 140	174 987	173 022	165 804	167 143	169 178	172 718	177 144 p
34	Consumption of fixed capital at constant prices	30 394	30 965	31 288	31 246	30 849	30 862	31 106	31 304 p
35	**Real net national income at market prices**	140 730	142 913	140 469	133 727	135 923	137 250	140 242	144 542 p
36	**Real net national disposable income**	141 652	144 022	141 787	135 261	137 728	139 406	142 485	146 911 p

Note: Detailed metadata:http://metalinks.oecd.org/nav1/20180308/5d4f
Source: Instituto Nacional de Estatistica (INE) via Eurostat.

Table 4. Population and employment (persons) and employment (hours worked) by industry
ISIC Rev. 4

		2009	2010	2011	2012	2013	2014	2015	2016
	POPULATION, THOUSAND PERSONS, NATIONAL CONCEPT								
1	**Total population**[1]	10 568.2	10 573.1	10 557.6	10 514.8	10 457.3	10 401.1	10 358.1	10 325.5 p
2	Economically active population[1]	..	..	..	..	..	..	..	..
3	Unemployed persons								
4	Total employment	4 984.4	4 914.1	4 802.2	4 608.6	4 484.8	4 550.5	4 604.9	4 673.7 p
5	Employees	4 131.6	4 105.6	4 009.2	3 821.3	3 743.9	3 822.5	3 904.4	3 979.5 p
6	Self-employed	852.8	808.5	793.0	787.3	740.8	728.1	700.4	694.2 p
	TOTAL EMPLOYMENT, THOUSAND PERSONS, DOMESTIC CONCEPT								
7	Agriculture, forestry and fishing	571.3	543.2	527.9	537.8	509.0	485.7	458.3	451.2 p
8	Industry, including energy	811.0	790.5	776.9	748.3	734.0	748.1	770.9	786.5 p
9	Manufacturing	747.0	727.4	713.3	686.2	673.7	688.9	710.6	725.5 p
10	Construction	455.3	436.4	395.7	315.3	283.3	269.9	273.3	274.7 p
11	Distrib. trade, repairs; transp.; accommod., food serv. activ.	1 169.8	1 161.8	1 155.3	1 100.3	1 068.4	1 111.1	1 143.4	1 181.1 p
12	Information and communication	70.1	71.2	72.3	73.8	74.7	78.4	84.2	85.8 p
13	Financial and insurance activities	92.6	93.8	94.8	91.6	88.7	85.9	83.8	81.7 p
14	Real estate activities	28.3	28.2	27.4	25.4	25.3	27.0	28.1	29.7 p
15	Prof., scientif., techn. activ.; admin., support service activ.	473.0	475.9	470.1	448.8	444.9	482.1	503.1	519.5 p
16	Public admin.; compulsory s.s.; education; human health	983.7	986.1	976.1	966.9	953.1	952.2	956.6	969.9 p
17	Other service activities	286.6	284.3	280.3	273.4	268.8	272.5	274.2	270.4 p
18	**Total employment**	**4 941.7**	**4 871.3**	**4 776.7**	**4 581.4**	**4 450.2**	**4 513.0**	**4 575.8**	**4 650.5 p**
	EMPLOYEES, THOUSAND PERSONS, DOMESTIC CONCEPT								
19	Agriculture, forestry and fishing	95.1	94.5	90.2	93.1	94.9	98.5	101.2	105.1 p
20	Industry, including energy	763.1	746.0	733.3	705.0	691.8	706.0	729.0	747.2 p
21	Manufacturing	700.8	684.5	671.5	644.7	633.3	648.5	670.7	688.1 p
22	Construction	406.0	390.9	353.0	279.6	250.8	239.2	242.6	241.9 p
23	Distrib. trade, repairs; transp.; accommod., food serv. activ.	1 064.1	1 063.9	1 057.1	1 001.2	977.8	1 016.3	1 049.6	1 084.1 p
24	Information and communication	65.9	67.1	68.4	69.7	70.7	74.0	80.1	81.7 p
25	Financial and insurance activities	87.9	89.0	89.9	87.2	84.7	82.6	80.7	78.7 p
26	Real estate activities	19.0	19.4	18.6	17.1	17.5	19.1	19.3	20.4 p
27	Prof., scientif., techn. activ.; admin., support service activ.	395.2	399.5	395.6	376.1	373.5	400.0	418.6	434.3 p
28	Public admin.; compulsory s.s.; education; human health	951.7	953.6	945.2	936.5	923.5	922.7	926.0	937.6 p
29	Other service activities	243.6	242.1	233.9	229.8	225.8	228.7	229.4	226.7 p
30	**Total employees**	**4 091.7**	**4 066.2**	**3 985.3**	**3 795.3**	**3 711.1**	**3 787.0**	**3 876.3**	**3 957.7 p**
	SELF-EMPLOYED, THOUSAND PERSONS, DOMESTIC CONCEPT								
31	Agriculture, forestry and fishing	476.2	448.7	437.6	444.7	414.1	387.3	357.1	346.1 p
32	Industry, including energy	47.9	44.5	43.6	43.3	42.2	42.1	41.9	39.4 p
33	Manufacturing	46.2	42.9	41.8	41.5	40.4	40.4	39.9	37.4 p
34	Construction	49.3	45.5	42.6	35.7	32.5	30.7	30.7	32.8 p
35	Distrib. trade, repairs; transp.; accommod., food serv. activ.	105.6	97.9	98.2	99.0	90.6	94.8	93.9	97.0 p
36	Information and communication	4.3	4.0	3.9	4.1	4.0	4.4	4.1	4.0 p
37	Financial and insurance activities	4.7	4.8	4.8	4.3	4.0	3.3	3.2	3.0 p
38	Real estate activities	9.3	8.8	8.8	8.3	7.8	7.9	8.8	9.3 p
39	Prof., scientif., techn. activ.; admin., support service activ.	77.8	76.3	74.5	72.6	71.4	82.1	84.5	85.2 p
40	Public admin.; compulsory s.s.; education; human health	31.9	32.5	30.9	30.4	29.6	29.6	30.6	32.2 p
41	Other service activities	43.0	42.2	46.4	43.6	42.9	43.8	44.8	43.7 p
42	**Total self-employed**	**850.0**	**805.1**	**791.4**	**786.1**	**739.1**	**726.0**	**699.5**	**692.8 p**
	TOTAL EMPLOYMENT, MILLION HOURS, DOMESTIC CONCEPT								
43	Industry, including energy	1 502.1	1 466.1	1 436.1	1 379.1	1 358.5	1 381.1	1 417.7	1 439.6 p
44	Distrib. trade, repairs; transp.; accommod., food serv. activ.	2 419.2	2 414.3	2 351.3	2 224.7	2 160.6	2 250.2	2 308.6	2 385.4 p
45	Financial and insurance activities	149.8	153.6	154.8	150.8	148.5	144.4	139.8	137.2 p
46	Prof., scientif., techn. activ.; admin., support service activ.	939.3	951.2	922.9	876.1	873.7	938.3	978.6	1 018.7 p
47	Public admin.; compulsory s.s.; education; human health	1 832.7	1 838.3	1 801.2	1 780.9	1 773.8	1 803.5	1 815.4	1 804.3 p
48	**Total employment**	**9 325.4**	**9 205.6**	**8 916.2**	**8 471.3**	**8 273.5**	**8 425.3**	**8 579.3**	**8 671.3 p**
	EMPLOYEES, MILLION HOURS, DOMESTIC CONCEPT								
49	Industry, including energy	1 406.8	1 378.1	1 349.0	1 293.3	1 276.3	1 299.3	1 336.7	1 358.8 p
50	Distrib. trade, repairs; transp.; accommod., food serv. activ.	2 112.8	2 123.3	2 048.8	1 925.2	1 885.2	1 966.7	2 027.1	2 099.3 p
51	Financial and insurance activities	139.9	143.5	144.2	140.8	139.4	137.0	132.8	130.5 p
52	Prof., scientif., techn. activ.; admin., support service activ.	760.8	775.4	752.6	711.3	713.9	766.9	801.9	834.3 p
53	Public admin.; compulsory s.s.; education; human health	1 731.1	1 738.8	1 709.0	1 691.0	1 690.3	1 719.3	1 726.6	1 713.1 p
54	**Total employees**	**7 680.1**	**7 667.2**	**7 416.3**	**7 013.7**	**6 909.3**	**7 086.9**	**7 251.5**	**7 369.5 p**
	SELF-EMPLOYED, MILLION HOURS, DOMESTIC CONCEPT								
55	Industry, including energy	95.3	88.0	87.0	85.7	82.2	81.8	81.0	80.8 p
56	Distrib. trade, repairs; transp.; accommod., food serv. activ.	306.3	291.0	302.5	299.4	275.4	283.5	281.4	286.1 p
57	Financial and insurance activities	9.9	10.2	10.7	10.0	9.1	7.4	7.0	6.6 p
58	Prof., scientif., techn. activ.; admin., support service activ.	178.5	175.8	170.2	164.8	159.8	171.4	176.7	184.3 p
59	Public admin.; compulsory s.s.; education; human health	101.6	99.5	92.1	90.0	83.5	84.2	88.8	91.2 p
60	**Total self-employed**	**1 645.3**	**1 538.4**	**1 499.9**	**1 457.7**	**1 364.2**	**1 338.4**	**1 327.8**	**1 301.8 p**

Note: Detailed metadata:http://metalinks.oecd.org/nav1/20180308/c378
1. Data come from the Labour Force Survey and the Census on population 2001.
Source: Instituto Nacional de Estatistica (INE) via Eurostat.

SLOVAK REPUBLIC

Table 1. Gross domestic product, expenditure approach

Million EUR (2009 SKK euro)

		2009	2010	2011	2012	2013	2014	2015	2016
	AT CURRENT PRICES								
1	**Final consumption expenditure**	**51 449**	**52 331**	**53 640**	**54 817**	**55 467**	**56 751**	**58 532**	**59 995**
2	Household	37 851	38 396	39 667	40 868	41 084	41 605	42 496	43 473
3	NPISH's	690	699	710	725	730	743	746	788
4	Government	12 907	13 236	13 262	13 224	13 653	14 404	15 291	15 734
5	Individual	5 911	6 146	6 012	6 274	6 627	7 964	8 395	8 605
6	Collective	6 996	7 089	7 250	6 949	7 026	6 440	6 896	7 129
7	*of which: Actual individual consumption*	44 452	45 242	46 389	47 868	48 441	50 311	51 636	52 866
8	**Gross capital formation**	**13 524**	**16 228**	**17 633**	**15 221**	**15 563**	**16 729**	**19 096**	**18 317**
9	Gross fixed capital formation, total	13 923	14 910	16 946	15 446	15 374	15 772	18 890	17 196
10	Dwellings	1 931	1 733	1 683	1 691	2 003	1 732	1 797	1 983
11	Other buildings and structures	5 243	4 906	5 387	4 854	4 881	4 722	6 658	5 005
12	Transport equipment	1 120	1 717	1 678	1 599	1 548	2 159	2 172	2 403
13	Other machinery and equipment	3 624	3 645	6 078	5 303	4 824	5 340	6 062	5 931
14	Cultivated assets	108	204	316	286	257	170	186	214
15	Intangible fixed assets	1 118	1 937	1 249	1 251	1 536	1 218	1 420	1 206
16	Changes in inventories, acquisitions less disposals of valuables	-399	1 318	687	-225	189	957	206	1 120
17	Changes in inventories	-424	1 295	648	-246	170	937	187	1 101
18	Acquisitions less disposals of valuables	24	23	39	21	19	20	19	20
19	**External balance of goods and services**	**-949**	**-982**	**-645**	**2 666**	**3 140**	**2 608**	**1 268**	**2 842**
20	Exports of goods and services	43 286	51 585	60 066	66 473	69 586	69 889	73 348	76 792
21	Exports of goods	38 473	46 616	54 645	60 206	62 460	62 631	65 541	68 703
22	Exports of services	4 813	4 969	5 421	6 266	7 126	7 258	7 807	8 088
23	Imports of goods and services	44 235	52 567	60 712	63 807	66 446	67 281	72 080	73 950
24	Imports of goods	38 508	46 960	55 051	57 977	59 740	60 058	64 493	66 356
25	Imports of services	5 727	5 607	5 661	5 830	6 705	7 223	7 587	7 593
26	**Statistical discrepancy**	..	..	..	..	..	..	..	..
27	**Gross domestic product**	**64 023**	**67 577**	**70 627**	**72 704**	**74 170**	**76 088**	**78 896**	**81 154**
	AT CONSTANT PRICES, REFERENCE YEAR 2010								
28	**Final consumption expenditure**	**51 949**	**52 331**	**51 875**	**51 443**	**51 403**	**52 588**	**54 186**	**55 483**
29	Household	38 238	38 396	38 174	38 014	37 709	38 224	39 091	40 126
30	NPISH's	690	699	699	702	700	712	711	744
31	Government	13 021	13 236	13 003	12 724	12 999	13 672	14 414	14 641
32	Individual	6 016	6 146	5 840	5 904	6 150	7 351	7 696	7 807
33	Collective	7 004	7 089	7 163	6 816	6 842	6 269	6 666	6 782
34	*of which: Actual individual consumption*	44 945	45 242	44 713	44 620	44 556	46 272	47 484	48 662
35	**Gross capital formation**	**13 654**	**16 228**	**17 463**	**15 055**	**15 327**	**16 537**	**18 878**	**18 219**
36	Gross fixed capital formation, total	13 903	14 910	16 797	15 286	15 153	15 609	18 700	17 157
37	Dwellings	1 933	1 733	1 671	1 673	1 971	1 690	1 727	1 886
38	Other buildings and structures	5 260	4 906	5 333	4 754	4 759	4 555	6 325	4 706
39	Transport equipment	1 111	1 717	1 725	1 701	1 640	2 304	2 314	2 619
40	Other machinery and equipment	3 594	3 645	5 973	5 192	4 706	5 316	6 172	6 199
41	Cultivated assets	109	204	309	276	247	171	191	222
42	Intangible fixed assets	1 122	1 937	1 237	1 238	1 514	1 194	1 386	1 169
43	Changes in inventories, acquisitions less disposals of valuables	..	..	..	..	..	..	..	..
44	Changes in inventories	..	..	..	..	..	..	..	..
45	Acquisitions less disposals of valuables	..	..	..	..	..	..	..	..
46	**External balance of goods and services**	**-1 250**	**-982**	**144**	**4 058**	**4 952**	**4 592**	**3 592**	**5 596**
47	Exports of goods and services	44 572	51 585	57 779	63 157	67 366	69 985	74 460	79 104
48	Exports of goods	39 691	46 616	52 578	57 446	60 953	63 398	67 214	71 670
49	Exports of services	4 870	4 969	5 202	5 711	6 399	6 578	7 212	7 424
50	Imports of goods and services	45 822	52 567	57 636	59 099	62 414	65 393	70 868	73 509
51	Imports of goods	40 052	46 960	52 157	53 746	56 337	58 890	63 964	66 702
52	Imports of services	5 738	5 607	5 478	5 348	6 066	6 487	6 898	6 830
53	**Statistical discrepancy (including chaining residual)**	**-19**	**0**	**0**	**78**	**4**	**-58**	**-162**	**-260**
54	**Gross domestic product**	**64 334**	**67 577**	**69 482**	**70 634**	**71 687**	**73 658**	**76 494**	**79 037**

Note: Detailed metadata:http://metalinks.oecd.org/nav1/20180308/e79e
Source: Slovak Statistical Office via Eurostat.

SLOVAK REPUBLIC

Table 2. Gross domestic product, output and income approach
ISIC Rev. 4

Million EUR (2009 SKK euro)

		2009	2010	2011	2012	2013	2014	2015	2016
	OUTPUT APPROACH AT CURRENT PRICES								
1	**Total gross value added at basic prices**	**58 033**	**61 368**	**63 982**	**66 410**	**67 522**	**68 907**	**71 204**	**73 362**
2	Agriculture, forestry and fishing	1 936	1 727	2 160	2 351	2 685	3 072	2 672	2 697
3	Industry, including energy	14 065	16 167	17 009	17 504	17 051	18 363	18 773	19 753
4	Manufacturing	10 290	12 770	13 474	13 849	13 654	14 953	15 584	16 592
5	Construction	5 634	5 450	5 713	5 986	5 277	5 470	5 797	5 760
6	Services	..	..	..	..	..	..	..	..
7	Distrib. trade, repairs; transp.; accommod., food serv. activ.	12 576	13 146	13 681	14 004	13 927	15 050	15 602	14 808
8	Information and communication	2 748	2 752	2 833	3 120	2 879	2 816	2 962	3 087
9	Financial and insurance activities	2 249	2 469	2 687	2 710	2 706	2 862	2 915	2 662
10	Real estate activities	4 058	4 221	4 316	4 501	5 933	4 285	4 475	4 779
11	Prof., scientif., techn. activ.; admin., support service activ.	4 356	4 553	4 575	4 784	5 119	5 278	5 761	6 529
12	Public admin.; compulsory s.s.; education; human health	8 599	9 009	8 942	9 181	9 634	9 256	9 504	10 764
13	Other service activities	1 812	1 873	2 067	2 269	2 310	2 456	2 743	2 524
14	**FISIM (Financial Intermediation Services Indirectly Measured)**	..	..	..	..	..	..	..	..
15	**Gross value added at basic prices, excluding FISIM**	**58 033**	**61 368**	**63 982**	**66 410**	**67 522**	**68 907**	**71 204**	**73 362**
16	**Taxes less subsidies on products**	**5 990**	**6 209**	**6 645**	**6 293**	**6 648**	**7 180**	**7 692**	**7 792**
17	Taxes on products	6 233	6 403	6 997	6 576	6 967	7 345	7 849	7 940
18	Subsidies on products	243	194	351	283	319	164	157	148
19	**Residual item**	..	..	..	..	..	..	..	..
20	**Gross domestic product at market prices**	**64 023**	**67 577**	**70 627**	**72 704**	**74 170**	**76 088**	**78 896**	**81 154**
	OUTPUT APPROACH AT CONSTANT PRICES (REF. YEAR 2010)								
21	**Total gross value added at basic prices**	**58 314**	**61 368**	**62 899**	**64 434**	**65 168**	**66 709**	**69 056**	**71 489**
22	Agriculture, forestry and fishing	2 026	1 727	2 046	2 105	2 497	2 988	2 588	2 732
23	Industry, including energy	13 538	16 167	16 839	16 864	16 638	18 845	20 289	22 077
24	Manufacturing	10 073	12 770	13 280	13 357	13 343	15 423	17 182	19 062
25	Construction	5 787	5 450	5 741	6 091	5 350	5 497	5 654	5 580
26	Services	..	..	..	..	..	..	..	..
27	Distrib. trade, repairs; transp.; accommod., food serv. activ.	12 884	13 146	13 171	13 340	12 899	13 728	14 000	13 208
28	Information and communication	2 738	2 752	2 846	3 217	3 024	2 834	2 945	3 054
29	Financial and insurance activities	2 332	2 469	2 584	2 607	2 721	3 001	3 145	3 026
30	Real estate activities	4 212	4 221	4 453	4 640	5 939	4 098	4 155	4 370
31	Prof., scientif., techn. activ.; admin., support service activ.	4 361	4 553	4 525	4 764	5 012	5 063	5 462	6 202
32	Public admin.; compulsory s.s.; education; human health	8 724	9 009	8 677	8 649	8 930	8 373	8 425	9 307
33	Other service activities	1 836	1 873	2 018	2 175	2 181	2 235	2 412	2 110
34	**FISIM (Financial Intermediation Services Indirectly Measured)**	..	..	..	..	..	..	..	..
35	**Gross value added at basic prices, excluding FISIM**	**58 314**	**61 368**	**62 899**	**64 434**	**65 168**	**66 709**	**69 056**	**71 489**
36	**Taxes less subsidies on products**	**6 020**	**6 209**	**6 584**	**6 196**	**6 518**	**6 953**	**7 442**	**7 552**
37	Taxes on products	6 264	6 403	6 934	6 477	6 825	7 105	7 585	7 687
38	Subsidies on products	244	194	350	281	306	156	147	138
39	**Residual item**	**0**	**0**	**0**	**4**	**1**	**-3**	**-4**	**-4**
40	**Gross domestic product at market prices**	**64 334**	**67 577**	**69 482**	**70 634**	**71 687**	**73 658**	**76 494**	**79 037**
	INCOME APPROACH								
41	**Compensation of employees**	**24 064**	**24 975**	**26 112**	**26 928**	**27 481**	**28 605**	**30 332**	**31 913**
42	Agriculture, forestry and fishing	557	551	586	582	618	613	647	658
43	Industry, including energy	6 095	6 280	6 757	7 079	7 226	7 606	8 040	8 575
44	Manufacturing	5 250	5 414	5 842	6 164	6 292	6 658	7 090	7 591
45	Construction	1 376	1 423	1 403	1 373	1 343	1 332	1 393	1 445
46	Distrib. trade, repairs; transp.; accommod., food serv. activ.	5 747	6 003	6 337	6 448	6 396	6 759	7 200	7 309
47	Information and communication	905	946	1 095	1 121	1 174	1 226	1 332	1 417
48	Financial and insurance activities	806	792	845	912	862	930	970	1 020
49	Real estate activities	213	280	317	320	288	275	284	335
50	Prof., scientif., techn. activ.; admin., support service activ.	1 974	1 991	2 118	2 248	2 397	2 352	2 568	2 742
51	Public admin.; compulsory s.s.; education; human health	5 910	6 230	6 168	6 350	6 677	6 989	7 322	7 770
52	Other service activities	481	480	486	497	499	523	575	642
53	**Wages and salaries**	**18 681**	**19 283**	**20 277**	**20 900**	**21 155**	**21 935**	**23 168**	**24 527**
54	Agriculture, forestry and fishing	424	417	446	442	472	467	490	505
55	Industry, including energy	4 743	4 858	5 265	5 495	5 595	5 859	6 170	6 631
56	Manufacturing	4 090	4 185	4 553	4 786	4 871	5 129	5 440	5 864
57	Construction	1 067	1 104	1 102	1 074	1 046	1 034	1 076	1 122
58	Distrib. trade, repairs; transp.; accommod., food serv. activ.	4 456	4 650	4 959	5 048	4 979	5 238	5 565	5 680
59	Information and communication	724	751	884	900	932	973	1 053	1 130
60	Financial and insurance activities	633	620	657	717	652	711	735	772
61	Real estate activities	172	216	247	249	226	214	220	261
62	Prof., scientif., techn. activ.; admin., support service activ.	1 622	1 617	1 731	1 823	1 918	1 877	2 029	2 184
63	Public admin.; compulsory s.s.; education; human health	4 471	4 679	4 613	4 770	4 954	5 163	5 393	5 752
64	Other service activities	371	371	373	381	381	399	438	491
65	**Gross operating surplus and mixed income**	**34 254**	**36 728**	**37 942**	**39 397**	**40 000**	**40 296**	**40 935**	**41 395**
66	**Taxes less subsidies on production and imports**	**5 705**	**5 875**	**6 573**	**6 378**	**6 688**	**7 187**	**7 629**	**7 846**
67	Taxes on production and imports	6 741	6 922	7 534	7 292	7 747	8 173	8 624	8 747
68	Subsidies on production and imports	1 037	1 047	961	914	1 059	986	995	901
69	**Residual item**	..	..	..	..	..	..	..	..
70	**Gross domestic product**	**64 023**	**67 577**	**70 627**	**72 704**	**74 170**	**76 088**	**78 896**	**81 154**

Note: Detailed metadata:http://metalinks.oecd.org/nav1/20180308/e79e
Source: Slovak Statistical Office via Eurostat.

SLOVAK REPUBLIC

Table 3. Disposable income, saving and net lending / net borrowing

Million EUR (2009 SKK euro)

		2009	2010	2011	2012	2013	2014	2015	2016
	DISPOSABLE INCOME								
1	**Gross domestic product**	**64 023**	**67 577**	**70 627**	**72 704**	**74 170**	**76 088**	**78 896**	**81 154**
2	Net primary incomes from the rest of the world	-434	-1 515	-2 568	-1 394	-693	-961	-1 433	-1 145
3	Primary incomes receivable from the rest of the world	2 973	3 393	3 241	3 198	3 271	3 571	3 205	3 253
4	Primary incomes payable to the rest of the world	3 407	4 908	5 809	4 592	3 963	4 532	4 638	4 399
5	**Gross national income at market prices**	**63 589**	**66 062**	**68 059**	**71 309**	**73 477**	**75 127**	**77 463**	**80 009**
6	Consumption of fixed capital	12 856	13 348	14 089	14 641	15 314	15 641	15 901	16 119
7	**Net national income at market prices**	**50 733**	**52 714**	**53 970**	**56 668**	**58 163**	**59 486**	**61 562**	**63 890**
8	Net current transfers from the rest of the world	-802	-663	-680	-976	-1 329	-907	-628	-1 383
9	Current transfers receivable from the rest of the world	1 330	896	878	765	833	833	1 236	720
10	Current transfers payable to the rest of the world	2 131	1 559	1 559	1 742	2 163	1 740	1 864	2 103
11	**Net national disposable income**	**49 932**	**52 051**	**53 290**	**55 692**	**56 833**	**58 580**	**60 934**	**62 507**
	SAVING AND NET LENDING / NET BORROWING								
12	**Net national disposable income**	**49 932**	**52 051**	**53 290**	**55 692**	**56 833**	**58 580**	**60 934**	**62 507**
13	Final consumption expenditures	51 449	52 331	53 640	54 817	55 467	56 751	58 532	59 995
14	Adj. for change in net equity of households in pension funds	..	..	..	..	..	..	..	..
15	**Saving, net**	**-1 516**	**-279**	**-348**	**877**	**1 369**	**1 829**	**2 405**	**2 513**
16	Net capital transfers from the rest of the world	540	1 090	1 170	1 092	1 337	729	1 975	283
17	Capital transfers receivable from the rest of the world	573	1 118	1 196	1 118	1 497	959	2 304	518
18	Capital transfers payable to the rest of the world	32	28	27	26	160	230	328	235
19	Gross capital formation	13 524	16 228	17 633	15 221	15 563	16 729	19 096	18 317
20	Acquisitions less disposals of non-financial non-produced assets	2	4	3	3	189	3	322	438
21	Consumption of fixed capital	12 856	13 348	14 089	14 641	15 314	15 641	15 901	16 119
22	**Net lending / net borrowing**	**-1 646**	**-2 073**	**-2 725**	**1 386**	**2 268**	**1 467**	**863**	**160**
	REAL DISPOSABLE INCOME								
23	**Gross domestic product at constant prices, reference year 2010**	**64 334**	**67 577**	**69 482**	**70 634**	**71 687**	**73 658**	**76 494**	**79 037**
24	Trading gain or loss	310	0	-772	-1 563	-1 977	-2 091	-2 337	-2 709
25	**Real gross domestic income**	**64 644**	**67 577**	**68 711**	**69 071**	**69 710**	**71 568**	**74 157**	**76 328**
26	Net real primary incomes from the rest of the world	-438	-1 515	-2 498	-1 325	-651	-904	-1 347	-1 077
27	Real primary incomes receivable from the rest of the world	3 002	3 393	3 153	3 038	3 074	3 359	3 012	3 060
28	Real primary incomes payable to the rest of the world	3 440	4 908	5 651	4 363	3 725	4 263	4 360	4 137
29	**Real gross national income at market prices**	**64 206**	**66 062**	**66 212**	**67 746**	**69 059**	**70 664**	**72 810**	**75 251**
30	Net real current transfers from the rest of the world	-809	-663	-662	-927	-1 249	-853	-590	-1 300
31	Real current transfers receivable from the rest of the world	1 342	896	854	727	783	784	1 162	677
32	Real current transfers payable to the rest of the world	2 152	1 559	1 516	1 654	2 033	1 637	1 752	1 978
33	**Real gross national disposable income**	**63 396**	**65 399**	**65 550**	**66 819**	**67 810**	**69 811**	**72 220**	**73 950**
34	Consumption of fixed capital at constant prices	12 929	13 348	13 615	13 735	14 134	14 540	15 082	15 430
35	**Real net national income at market prices**	**51 225**	**52 714**	**52 506**	**53 837**	**54 666**	**55 952**	**57 864**	**60 090**
36	**Real net national disposable income**	**50 416**	**52 051**	**51 844**	**52 909**	**53 416**	**55 100**	**57 274**	**58 790**

Note: Detailed metadata:http://metalinks.oecd.org/nav1/20180308/66ad
Source: Slovak Statistical Office via Eurostat.

Table 4. Population and employment (persons) and employment (hours worked) by industry
ISIC Rev. 4

		2009	2010	2011	2012	2013	2014	2015	2016
	POPULATION, THOUSAND PERSONS, NATIONAL CONCEPT								
1	**Total population**	**5 417.8**	**5 430.0**	**5 398.1**	**5 406.2**	**5 413.0**	**5 418.6**	**5 422.3**	**5 430.8**
2	Economically active population	..	..	..	..	..	..	..	..
3	Unemployed persons	..	..	..	..	..	..	..	..
4	Total employment	2 365.8	2 317.5	2 315.3	2 329.0	2 329.2	2 363.1	2 424.0	2 492.1
5	Employees	1 994.7	1 947.1	1 946.8	1 968.8	1 967.1	1 999.3	2 056.6	2 107.7
6	Self-employed	371.1	370.4	368.5	360.1	362.2	363.8	367.4	384.4
	TOTAL EMPLOYMENT, THOUSAND PERSONS, DOMESTIC CONCEPT								
7	Agriculture, forestry and fishing	77.6	73.1	73.0	70.6	73.9	72.4	73.4	72.5
8	Industry, including energy	530.9	511.8	529.7	524.8	518.1	527.2	537.9	555.8
9	Manufacturing	479.6	461.5	479.8	476.5	469.5	479.1	490.7	508.8
10	Construction	187.5	183.8	177.3	171.8	166.5	164.1	163.2	166.1
11	Distrib. trade, repairs; transp.; accommod., food serv. activ.	595.4	586.2	596.8	598.9	593.5	604.3	609.0	613.5
12	Information and communication	52.4	50.2	55.4	54.7	57.0	59.3	60.9	64.2
13	Financial and insurance activities	41.3	40.1	40.6	41.8	42.4	43.9	45.7	46.3
14	Real estate activities	19.6	21.6	24.0	24.4	22.9	22.4	22.6	25.3
15	Prof., scientif., techn. activ.; admin., support service activ.	189.6	190.2	198.6	214.3	210.0	210.4	228.5	240.8
16	Public admin.; compulsory s.s.; education; human health	450.1	454.0	453.5	449.2	448.3	457.3	463.2	469.0
17	Other service activities	58.9	58.9	59.3	59.0	59.6	61.8	62.7	67.3
18	**Total employment**	**2 203.2**	**2 169.8**	**2 208.3**	**2 209.4**	**2 192.3**	**2 223.1**	**2 267.1**	**2 321.0**
	EMPLOYEES, THOUSAND PERSONS, DOMESTIC CONCEPT								
19	Agriculture, forestry and fishing	61.3	57.4	57.7	55.4	58.7	57.1	57.8	56.7
20	Industry, including energy	470.6	454.2	473.6	470.8	466.3	476.7	487.3	504.9
21	Manufacturing	420.1	404.6	424.3	423.0	418.2	429.1	440.5	458.4
22	Construction	103.0	99.3	94.7	92.1	90.1	90.3	90.2	92.6
23	Distrib. trade, repairs; transp.; accommod., food serv. activ.	478.9	472.5	487.2	493.7	492.0	509.5	518.6	525.7
24	Information and communication	43.6	41.2	46.4	45.6	47.8	50.2	51.7	54.9
25	Financial and insurance activities	34.2	32.7	33.0	33.5	33.2	33.5	34.4	34.9
26	Real estate activities	17.7	19.7	22.1	22.5	21.0	20.5	20.8	23.5
27	Prof., scientif., techn. activ.; admin., support service activ.	145.9	145.3	153.0	168.4	163.6	164.4	181.9	193.8
28	Public admin.; compulsory s.s.; education; human health	440.2	443.3	444.1	439.9	438.9	447.9	453.6	459.6
29	Other service activities	42.1	42.0	42.5	42.3	43.0	45.5	46.5	51.2
30	**Total employees**	**1 837.6**	**1 808.7**	**1 854.2**	**1 864.2**	**1 854.6**	**1 895.5**	**1 942.8**	**1 997.8**
	SELF-EMPLOYED, THOUSAND PERSONS, DOMESTIC CONCEPT								
31	Agriculture, forestry and fishing	16.3	15.7	15.4	15.2	15.3	15.3	15.6	15.8
32	Industry, including energy	60.3	57.6	56.1	54.0	51.8	50.5	50.6	50.9
33	Manufacturing	59.5	56.9	55.5	53.5	51.3	50.0	50.1	50.4
34	Construction	84.4	84.4	82.6	79.6	76.4	73.8	72.9	73.5
35	Distrib. trade, repairs; transp.; accommod., food serv. activ.	116.5	113.7	109.6	105.3	101.5	94.8	90.4	87.8
36	Information and communication	8.8	9.0	9.1	9.1	9.2	9.1	9.2	9.3
37	Financial and insurance activities	7.0	7.4	7.6	8.3	9.2	10.5	11.3	11.5
38	Real estate activities	1.9	1.9	1.9	1.9	1.9	1.9	1.8	1.8
39	Prof., scientif., techn. activ.; admin., support service activ.	43.6	44.9	45.6	45.9	46.4	46.0	46.6	47.1
40	Public admin.; compulsory s.s.; education; human health	9.9	9.7	9.4	9.3	9.4	9.4	9.6	9.4
41	Other service activities	16.8	16.9	16.9	16.7	16.6	16.3	16.2	16.1
42	**Total self-employed**	**365.6**	**361.1**	**354.1**	**345.3**	**337.6**	**327.6**	**324.3**	**323.3**
	TOTAL EMPLOYMENT, MILLION HOURS, DOMESTIC CONCEPT								
43	Industry, including energy	910.7	909.7	936.2	924.5	906.1	919.4	938.1	961.6
44	Distrib. trade, repairs; transp.; accommod., food serv. activ.	1 096.1	1 094.1	1 103.3	1 103.4	1 084.0	1 090.9	1 091.0	1 085.9
45	Financial and insurance activities	73.0	70.9	71.5	74.4	74.9	77.0	80.1	80.7
46	Prof., scientif., techn. activ.; admin., support service activ.	360.2	366.3	379.3	406.5	394.1	390.7	419.5	433.4
47	Public admin.; compulsory s.s.; education; human health	724.6	727.3	726.6	719.9	711.6	722.9	736.4	743.7
48	**Total employment**	**3 922.4**	**3 916.9**	**3 959.5**	**3 952.8**	**3 883.8**	**3 911.9**	**3 976.7**	**4 038.7**
	EMPLOYEES, MILLION HOURS, DOMESTIC CONCEPT								
49	Industry, including energy	774.2	779.5	809.6	803.1	790.4	804.7	823.0	845.8
50	Distrib. trade, repairs; transp.; accommod., food serv. activ.	831.7	834.7	853.6	861.0	852.5	876.2	884.4	884.4
51	Financial and insurance activities	57.4	55.1	55.3	56.1	54.9	54.9	56.2	56.8
52	Prof., scientif., techn. activ.; admin., support service activ.	263.0	267.5	279.1	306.1	292.8	290.1	319.5	333.6
53	Public admin.; compulsory s.s.; education; human health	704.3	707.7	707.5	700.3	691.9	702.9	715.9	723.7
54	**Total employees**	**3 093.6**	**3 100.7**	**3 160.6**	**3 171.3**	**3 127.1**	**3 177.5**	**3 248.5**	**3 312.0**
	SELF-EMPLOYED, MILLION HOURS, DOMESTIC CONCEPT								
55	Industry, including energy	136.5	130.2	126.7	121.3	115.7	114.7	115.1	115.7
56	Distrib. trade, repairs; transp.; accommod., food serv. activ.	264.4	259.4	249.7	242.4	231.6	214.8	206.6	201.6
57	Financial and insurance activities	15.6	15.8	16.2	18.3	20.0	22.1	23.9	23.8
58	Prof., scientif., techn. activ.; admin., support service activ.	97.3	98.8	100.2	100.4	101.4	100.7	100.0	99.8
59	Public admin.; compulsory s.s.; education; human health	20.3	19.6	19.1	19.6	19.8	20.0	20.5	20.1
60	**Total self-employed**	**828.7**	**816.2**	**798.9**	**781.4**	**756.8**	**734.4**	**728.2**	**726.7**

Note: Detailed metadata:http://metalinks.oecd.org/nav1/20180308/d0ef
Source: Slovak Statistical Office via Eurostat.

Table 1. Gross domestic product, expenditure approach

Million EUR (2007 SIT euro)

		2009	2010	2011	2012	2013	2014	2015	2016
	AT CURRENT PRICES								
1	**Final consumption expenditure**	**27 034**	**27 670**	**28 205**	**27 806**	**27 163**	**27 465**	**27 979**	**29 159**
2	Household	19 482	19 980	20 338	20 203	19 785	20 141	20 437	21 250
3	NPISH's	298	337	330	307	306	325	335	331
4	Government	7 255	7 353	7 537	7 296	7 073	6 999	7 207	7 578
5	Individual	4 278	4 408	4 495	4 368	4 187	4 134	4 296	4 523
6	Collective	2 977	2 945	3 042	2 928	2 886	2 866	2 911	3 055
7	*of which: Actual individual consumption*	24 057	24 724	25 163	24 878	24 278	24 600	25 068	26 104
8	**Gross capital formation**	**8 456**	**8 063**	**8 014**	**6 749**	**7 061**	**7 367**	**7 523**	**7 558**
9	Gross fixed capital formation, total	8 806	7 727	7 451	6 934	7 175	7 292	7 322	7 105
10	Dwellings	1 385	1 137	1 028	918	860	813	830	845
11	Other buildings and structures	3 509	2 853	2 349	2 296	2 263	2 650	2 477	2 046
12	Transport equipment	582	472	641	455	540	592	709	834
13	Other machinery and equipment	1 884	1 743	1 902	1 829	2 065	1 782	1 744	1 829
14	Cultivated assets	40	33	31	27	37	42	46	38
15	Intangible fixed assets	1 061	1 151	1 138	1 111	1 124	1 149	1 184	1 194
16	Changes in inventories, acquisitions less disposals of valuables	-350	336	563	-185	-114	75	201	453
17	Changes in inventories	-353	334	558	-189	-117	71	197	448
18	Acquisitions less disposals of valuables	3	2	5	3	3	4	4	5
19	**External balance of goods and services**	**676**	**520**	**677**	**1 522**	**2 015**	**2 783**	**3 335**	**3 701**
20	Exports of goods and services	20 703	23 306	25 965	26 381	27 004	28 517	29 901	31 386
21	Exports of goods	16 279	18 631	21 042	21 256	21 692	22 961	24 039	24 991
22	Exports of services	4 423	4 675	4 923	5 124	5 312	5 556	5 862	6 396
23	Imports of goods and services	20 027	22 786	25 288	24 859	24 990	25 734	26 566	27 686
24	Imports of goods	16 708	19 297	21 730	21 205	21 395	21 869	22 563	23 454
25	Imports of services	3 319	3 488	3 558	3 654	3 595	3 865	4 003	4 232
26	**Statistical discrepancy**	**0**	**0**	**0**	**0**	**0**	**0**	**0**	**0**
27	**Gross domestic product**	**36 166**	**36 252**	**36 896**	**36 076**	**36 239**	**37 615**	**38 837**	**40 418**
	AT CONSTANT PRICES, REFERENCE YEAR 2010								
28	**Final consumption expenditure**	**27 456**	**27 670**	**27 611**	**26 950**	**25 989**	**26 280**	**26 877**	**27 886**
29	Household	19 766	19 980	19 985	19 512	18 701	19 052	19 454	20 290
30	NPISH's	299	337	327	303	302	319	327	321
31	Government	7 392	7 353	7 299	7 135	6 988	6 904	7 092	7 267
32	Individual	4 377	4 408	4 461	4 387	4 261	4 226	4 364	4 478
33	Collective	3 014	2 945	2 838	2 750	2 726	2 678	2 730	2 792
34	*of which: Actual individual consumption*	24 442	24 724	24 773	24 202	23 262	23 602	24 146	25 095
35	**Gross capital formation**	**8 564**	**8 063**	**7 889**	**6 511**	**6 791**	**7 052**	**7 065**	**7 059**
36	Gross fixed capital formation, total	8 913	7 727	7 346	6 697	6 908	6 982	6 871	6 623
37	Dwellings	1 428	1 137	996	872	802	751	757	757
38	Other buildings and structures	3 592	2 853	2 268	2 181	2 111	2 448	2 266	1 843
39	Transport equipment	565	472	656	463	553	604	716	829
40	Other machinery and equipment	1 867	1 743	1 864	1 776	2 002	1 731	1 681	1 771
41	Cultivated assets	39	33	29	24	32	37	40	33
42	Intangible fixed assets	1 082	1 151	1 149	1 069	1 098	1 109	1 080	1 077
43	Changes in inventories, acquisitions less disposals of valuables	..	..	..	..	..	..	..	..
44	Changes in inventories	..	..	..	..	..	..	..	..
45	Acquisitions less disposals of valuables	..	..	..	..	..	..	..	..
46	**External balance of goods and services**	**-170**	**520**	**988**	**2 021**	**2 311**	**2 809**	**3 020**	**3 179**
47	Exports of goods and services	21 158	23 306	24 913	25 059	25 823	27 293	28 661	30 509
48	Exports of goods	16 635	18 631	20 120	20 193	20 865	22 172	23 352	24 793
49	Exports of services	4 522	4 675	4 793	4 867	4 958	5 126	5 317	5 719
50	Imports of goods and services	21 328	22 786	23 924	23 038	23 512	24 485	25 641	27 330
51	Imports of goods	17 939	19 297	20 449	19 562	20 136	20 900	21 975	23 516
52	Imports of services	3 382	3 488	3 475	3 481	3 376	3 584	3 668	3 822
53	**Statistical discrepancy (including chaining residual)**	**-41**	**0**	**0**	**32**	**20**	**17**	**13**	**15**
54	**Gross domestic product**	**35 809**	**36 252**	**36 488**	**35 514**	**35 112**	**36 158**	**36 975**	**38 139**

Note: Detailed metadata:http://metalinks.oecd.org/nav1/20180308/6534
Source: Statistical Office of the Republic of Slovenia (SORS) via Eurostat.

Table 2. Gross domestic product, output and income approach
ISIC Rev. 4

Million EUR (2007 SIT euro)

		2009	2010	2011	2012	2013	2014	2015	2016
	OUTPUT APPROACH AT CURRENT PRICES								
1	**Total gross value added at basic prices**	**31 638**	**31 583**	**32 105**	**31 299**	**31 294**	**32 515**	**33 578**	**35 009**
2	Agriculture, forestry and fishing	599	626	734	647	652	759	787	760
3	Industry, including energy	7 467	7 651	8 042	8 095	8 347	8 813	9 092	9 480
4	Manufacturing	6 188	6 367	6 730	6 762	6 953	7 439	7 751	8 136
5	Construction	2 464	2 015	1 885	1 817	1 654	1 859	1 843	1 830
6	Services	..	..	..	..	..	..	..	..
7	Distrib. trade, repairs; transp.; accommod., food serv. activ.	6 343	6 300	6 441	6 229	6 267	6 481	6 761	7 124
8	Information and communication	1 236	1 286	1 314	1 335	1 300	1 371	1 402	1 442
9	Financial and insurance activities	1 673	1 697	1 649	1 353	1 250	1 297	1 371	1 358
10	Real estate activities	2 636	2 537	2 469	2 397	2 573	2 528	2 640	2 738
11	Prof., scientif., techn. activ.; admin., support service activ.	2 871	2 990	3 021	2 962	2 982	3 195	3 315	3 482
12	Public admin.; compulsory s.s.; education; human health	5 478	5 611	5 666	5 602	5 419	5 364	5 483	5 852
13	Other service activities	872	870	885	862	851	850	885	944
14	**FISIM (Financial Intermediation Services Indirectly Measured)**	..	..	..	..	..	..	..	..
15	**Gross value added at basic prices, excluding FISIM**	31 638	31 583	32 105	31 299	31 294	32 515	33 578	35 009
16	**Taxes less subsidies on products**	**4 528**	**4 670**	**4 791**	**4 777**	**4 945**	**5 100**	**5 258**	**5 409**
17	Taxes on products	4 599	4 750	4 819	4 812	4 978	5 133	5 288	5 441
18	Subsidies on products	71	80	28	35	33	32	30	32
19	**Residual item**	0	0	0	0	0	0	0	0
20	**Gross domestic product at market prices**	**36 166**	**36 252**	**36 896**	**36 076**	**36 239**	**37 615**	**38 837**	**40 418**
	OUTPUT APPROACH AT CONSTANT PRICES (REF. YEAR 2010)								
21	**Total gross value added at basic prices**	**31 171**	**31 583**	**31 687**	**30 950**	**30 698**	**31 832**	**32 535**	**33 568**
22	Agriculture, forestry and fishing	616	626	668	613	608	705	738	723
23	Industry, including energy	7 184	7 651	7 833	7 638	7 622	7 970	8 083	8 439
24	Manufacturing	5 934	6 367	6 546	6 345	6 308	6 650	6 775	7 106
25	Construction	2 464	2 015	1 812	1 673	1 526	1 687	1 659	1 587
26	Services	..	..	..	..	..	..	..	..
27	Distrib. trade, repairs; transp.; accommod., food serv. activ.	6 223	6 300	6 408	6 146	6 141	6 337	6 656	7 019
28	Information and communication	1 244	1 286	1 287	1 283	1 292	1 355	1 446	1 450
29	Financial and insurance activities	1 706	1 697	1 632	1 561	1 514	1 492	1 452	1 495
30	Real estate activities	2 496	2 537	2 527	2 534	2 547	2 577	2 579	2 575
31	Prof., scientif., techn. activ.; admin., support service activ.	2 829	2 990	3 009	2 956	2 969	3 199	3 295	3 443
32	Public admin.; compulsory s.s.; education; human health	5 546	5 611	5 629	5 696	5 636	5 628	5 706	5 871
33	Other service activities	881	870	883	859	856	853	884	932
34	**FISIM (Financial Intermediation Services Indirectly Measured)**	..	..	..	..	..	..	..	..
35	**Gross value added at basic prices, excluding FISIM**	31 171	31 583	31 687	30 950	30 698	31 832	32 535	33 568
36	**Taxes less subsidies on products**	**4 639**	**4 670**	**4 801**	**4 562**	**4 415**	**4 347**	**4 459**	**4 592**
37	Taxes on products	4 708	4 750	4 884	4 643	4 495	4 426	4 540	4 674
38	Subsidies on products	70	80	83	85	86	85	86	85
39	**Residual item**	-1	0	0	2	-2	-21	-20	-22
40	**Gross domestic product at market prices**	**35 809**	**36 252**	**36 488**	**35 514**	**35 112**	**36 158**	**36 975**	**38 139**
	INCOME APPROACH								
41	**Compensation of employees**	**18 790**	**19 018**	**18 921**	**18 487**	**18 073**	**18 412**	**18 902**	**19 910**
42	Agriculture, forestry and fishing	123	118	111	110	104	109	114	107
43	Industry, including energy	4 599	4 683	4 792	4 832	4 833	5 004	5 151	5 426
44	Manufacturing	4 013	4 083	4 179	4 212	4 204	4 366	4 523	4 795
45	Construction	1 393	1 304	1 137	1 030	966	1 002	1 036	1 047
46	Distrib. trade, repairs; transp.; accommod., food serv. activ.	3 960	4 013	3 950	3 863	3 820	3 873	4 003	4 222
47	Information and communication	738	747	731	741	736	769	788	803
48	Financial and insurance activities	843	834	807	787	761	770	751	767
49	Real estate activities	121	127	121	116	111	121	119	126
50	Prof., scientif., techn. activ.; admin., support service activ.	1 934	2 001	2 076	1 948	1 889	1 993	2 102	2 232
51	Public admin.; compulsory s.s.; education; human health	4 536	4 641	4 666	4 546	4 355	4 278	4 335	4 651
52	Other service activities	544	551	530	514	497	492	502	529
53	**Wages and salaries**	**16 128**	**16 336**	**16 245**	**15 817**	**15 479**	**15 796**	**16 191**	**17 090**
54	Agriculture, forestry and fishing	106	102	96	94	89	94	97	92
55	Industry, including energy	3 877	3 948	4 041	4 071	4 074	4 225	4 352	4 586
56	Manufacturing	3 394	3 452	3 533	3 560	3 555	3 699	3 832	4 065
57	Construction	1 212	1 136	989	897	842	878	909	917
58	Distrib. trade, repairs; transp.; accommod., food serv. activ.	3 434	3 484	3 433	3 343	3 310	3 356	3 468	3 662
59	Information and communication	627	636	622	628	625	659	677	689
60	Financial and insurance activities	726	718	693	672	650	658	640	653
61	Real estate activities	106	113	108	103	98	108	107	112
62	Prof., scientif., techn. activ.; admin., support service activ.	1 742	1 802	1 868	1 748	1 690	1 786	1 851	2 001
63	Public admin.; compulsory s.s.; education; human health	3 825	3 914	3 929	3 812	3 663	3 600	3 649	3 913
64	Other service activities	472	482	465	451	437	433	442	464
65	**Gross operating surplus and mixed income**	**13 324**	**13 002**	**13 363**	**12 921**	**13 366**	**14 149**	**14 685**	**15 109**
66	**Taxes less subsidies on production and imports**	**4 053**	**4 232**	**4 612**	**4 668**	**4 800**	**5 055**	**5 250**	**5 399**
67	Taxes on production and imports	4 965	5 159	5 237	5 274	5 474	5 636	5 781	5 947
68	Subsidies on production and imports	912	927	625	606	674	581	531	548
69	**Residual item**	0	0	0	0	0	0	0	0
70	**Gross domestic product**	**36 166**	**36 252**	**36 896**	**36 076**	**36 239**	**37 615**	**38 837**	**40 418**

Note: Detailed metadata:http://metalinks.oecd.org/nav1/20180308/6534
Source: Statistical Office of the Republic of Slovenia (SORS) via Eurostat.

Table 3. Disposable income, saving and net lending / net borrowing

Million EUR (2007 SIT euro)

		2009	2010	2011	2012	2013	2014	2015	2016
	DISPOSABLE INCOME								
1	**Gross domestic product**	**36 166**	**36 252**	**36 896**	**36 076**	**36 239**	**37 615**	**38 837**	**40 418**
2	Net primary incomes from the rest of the world	-602	-485	-504	-561	-487	-342	-1 168	-1 129
3	Primary incomes receivable from the rest of the world	802	698	981	688	577	882	1 063	1 160
4	Primary incomes payable to the rest of the world	1 404	1 182	1 485	1 250	1 064	1 225	2 230	2 289
5	**Gross national income at market prices**	**35 564**	**35 768**	**36 392**	**35 515**	**35 753**	**37 273**	**37 669**	**39 289**
6	Consumption of fixed capital	7 064	7 212	7 391	7 663	7 724	7 794	7 999	8 152
7	**Net national income at market prices**	**28 500**	**28 555**	**29 001**	**27 851**	**28 029**	**29 479**	**29 670**	**31 137**
8	Net current transfers from the rest of the world	-416	-314	-320	-350	-373	-262	-405	-422
9	Current transfers receivable from the rest of the world	508	539	545	570	611	677	703	682
10	Current transfers payable to the rest of the world	925	853	865	920	984	939	1 109	1 104
11	**Net national disposable income**	**28 084**	**28 241**	**28 681**	**27 501**	**27 656**	**29 217**	**29 265**	**30 714**
	SAVING AND NET LENDING / NET BORROWING								
12	**Net national disposable income**	**28 084**	**28 241**	**28 681**	**27 501**	**27 656**	**29 217**	**29 265**	**30 714**
13	Final consumption expenditures	27 034	27 670	28 205	27 806	27 163	27 465	27 979	29 159
14	Adj. for change in net equity of households in pension funds	0	0	0	0	0	0	0	0
15	**Saving, net**	**1 050**	**571**	**476**	**-305**	**493**	**1 752**	**1 286**	**1 555**
16	Net capital transfers from the rest of the world	262	295	151	198	175	102	464	-278
17	Capital transfers receivable from the rest of the world	538	642	504	547	534	772	992	268
18	Capital transfers payable to the rest of the world	276	348	352	349	359	669	527	546
19	Gross capital formation	8 456	8 063	8 014	6 749	7 061	7 367	7 523	7 558
20	Acquisitions less disposals of non-financial non-produced assets	6	3	12	4	10	24	37	45
21	Consumption of fixed capital	7 064	7 212	7 391	7 663	7 724	7 794	7 999	8 152
22	**Net lending / net borrowing**	**-87**	**13**	**-8**	**804**	**1 319**	**2 257**	**2 190**	**1 826**
	REAL DISPOSABLE INCOME								
23	**Gross domestic product at constant prices, reference year 2010**	**35 809**	**36 252**	**36 488**	**35 514**	**35 112**	**36 158**	**36 975**	**38 139**
24	Trading gain or loss	899	0	-325	-573	-394	-155	162	331
25	**Real gross domestic income**	**36 708**	**36 252**	**36 163**	**34 940**	**34 717**	**36 003**	**37 137**	**38 469**
26	Net real primary incomes from the rest of the world	-611	-485	-494	-544	-466	-328	-1 116	-1 075
27	Real primary incomes receivable from the rest of the world	814	698	962	667	553	845	1 016	1 104
28	Real primary incomes payable to the rest of the world	1 425	1 182	1 456	1 210	1 019	1 172	2 133	2 179
29	**Real gross national income at market prices**	**36 097**	**35 768**	**35 669**	**34 397**	**34 251**	**35 675**	**36 020**	**37 394**
30	Net real current transfers from the rest of the world	-423	-314	-314	-339	-357	-251	-387	-402
31	Real current transfers receivable from the rest of the world	516	539	534	552	585	648	673	649
32	Real current transfers payable to the rest of the world	939	853	848	891	943	899	1 060	1 051
33	**Real gross national disposable income**	**35 674**	**35 454**	**35 355**	**34 057**	**33 894**	**35 424**	**35 633**	**36 992**
34	Consumption of fixed capital at constant prices	7 159	7 212	7 284	7 394	7 422	7 452	7 507	7 597
35	**Real net national income at market prices**	**28 927**	**28 555**	**28 425**	**26 975**	**26 852**	**28 215**	**28 371**	**29 635**
36	**Real net national disposable income**	**28 505**	**28 241**	**28 111**	**26 635**	**26 495**	**27 964**	**27 984**	**29 233**

Note: Detailed metadata:http://metalinks.oecd.org/nav1/20180308/dd70
Source: Statistical Office of the Republic of Slovenia (SORS) via Eurostat.

SLOVENIA

Table 4. Population and employment (persons) and employment (hours worked) by industry
ISIC Rev. 4

		2009	2010	2011	2012	2013	2014	2015	2016
	POPULATION, THOUSAND PERSONS, NATIONAL CONCEPT								
1	**Total population**	2 041.7	2 048.8	2 052.8	2 056.8	2 059.6	2 061.8	2 063.3	2 064.6
2	Economically active population	..	..	..	..	..	..	..	..
3	Unemployed persons	..	..	..	..	..	..	..	..
4	Total employment	982.9	964.7	950.6	944.7	934.7	938.5	941.4	967.9
5	Employees	810.6	791.2	777.3	770.0	749.9	754.2	756.6	781.6
6	Self-employed	172.3	173.4	173.3	174.7	184.9	184.3	186.4	186.3
	TOTAL EMPLOYMENT, THOUSAND PERSONS, DOMESTIC CONCEPT								
7	Agriculture, forestry and fishing	81.7	80.0	78.0	77.3	77.2	75.9	75.3	73.7
8	Industry, including energy	229.3	216.5	216.0	213.6	209.5	210.1	212.5	217.4
9	Manufacturing	208.5	195.7	195.0	192.0	188.0	188.3	190.9	196.6
10	Construction	91.3	83.0	73.2	67.7	63.0	62.3	62.6	61.9
11	Distrib. trade, repairs; transp.; accommod., food serv. activ.	212.2	207.5	202.0	199.6	197.1	196.6	200.1	205.0
12	Information and communication	24.8	25.0	25.0	25.6	26.2	26.9	27.7	28.7
13	Financial and insurance activities	25.5	25.2	24.6	24.2	23.5	22.9	22.7	22.3
14	Real estate activities	5.5	5.5	5.4	5.3	5.3	5.4	5.5	5.7
15	Prof., scientif., techn. activ.; admin., support service activ.	110.5	113.0	114.1	114.6	114.5	117.9	120.9	125.8
16	Public admin.; compulsory s.s.; education; human health	169.7	173.5	175.1	176.9	175.8	176.5	177.9	181.7
17	Other service activities	32.6	32.9	32.5	32.5	34.5	35.5	36.5	37.5
18	**Total employment**	982.9	962.1	946.0	937.2	926.7	930.0	941.6	959.7
	EMPLOYEES, THOUSAND PERSONS, DOMESTIC CONCEPT								
19	Agriculture, forestry and fishing	6.2	6.1	5.3	5.2	5.0	5.2	5.3	5.1
20	Industry, including energy	217.5	204.8	204.5	202.0	196.7	197.1	199.5	204.5
21	Manufacturing	197.3	184.7	184.2	181.4	176.3	176.5	179.1	184.8
22	Construction	77.0	69.0	59.7	54.7	50.5	50.0	50.4	49.8
23	Distrib. trade, repairs; transp.; accommod., food serv. activ.	184.9	179.9	174.5	172.2	168.0	168.0	171.3	176.6
24	Information and communication	21.8	21.6	21.5	21.8	21.9	22.0	22.4	23.0
25	Financial and insurance activities	24.2	24.0	23.3	22.9	22.3	21.8	21.6	21.2
26	Real estate activities	4.9	4.9	4.7	4.6	4.6	4.6	4.6	4.7
27	Prof., scientif., techn. activ.; admin., support service activ.	86.9	87.8	88.3	87.1	83.2	86.4	88.4	92.7
28	Public admin.; compulsory s.s.; education; human health	164.8	168.1	169.3	170.5	168.7	169.3	170.3	173.7
29	Other service activities	22.3	22.4	21.6	21.4	21.0	21.3	21.4	22.0
30	**Total employees**	810.6	788.7	772.7	762.5	741.8	745.7	755.2	773.5
	SELF-EMPLOYED, THOUSAND PERSONS, DOMESTIC CONCEPT								
31	Agriculture, forestry and fishing	75.5	73.9	72.8	72.1	72.2	70.7	69.9	68.5
32	Industry, including energy	11.7	11.6	11.5	11.6	12.9	13.0	13.0	12.9
33	Manufacturing	11.3	11.0	10.7	10.6	11.7	11.8	11.9	11.8
34	Construction	14.3	14.0	13.5	13.0	12.4	12.2	12.2	12.1
35	Distrib. trade, repairs; transp.; accommod., food serv. activ.	27.3	27.5	27.5	27.3	29.2	28.5	28.8	28.4
36	Information and communication	3.0	3.4	3.6	3.8	4.3	4.8	5.3	5.7
37	Financial and insurance activities	1.3	1.3	1.3	1.2	1.2	1.1	1.1	1.1
38	Real estate activities	0.6	0.6	0.7	0.7	0.8	0.8	0.8	0.9
39	Prof., scientif., techn. activ.; admin., support service activ.	23.5	25.2	25.7	27.5	31.3	31.5	32.5	33.1
40	Public admin.; compulsory s.s.; education; human health	4.9	5.4	5.8	6.4	7.1	7.2	7.6	8.0
41	Other service activities	10.2	10.5	10.9	11.1	13.5	14.3	15.1	15.5
42	**Total self-employed**	172.3	173.4	173.3	174.7	184.9	184.3	186.4	186.3
	TOTAL EMPLOYMENT, MILLION HOURS, DOMESTIC CONCEPT								
43	Industry, including energy	366.5	356.4	351.7	344.2	341.9	345.2	352.1	353.8
44	Distrib. trade, repairs; transp.; accommod., food serv. activ.	349.6	346.2	330.7	323.1	321.5	324.6	330.1	334.4
45	Financial and insurance activities	42.2	42.0	40.2	37.5	37.2	36.3	36.0	35.0
46	Prof., scientif., techn. activ.; admin., support service activ.	190.3	190.4	189.9	187.2	192.8	198.7	201.5	208.9
47	Public admin.; compulsory s.s.; education; human health	276.7	280.4	283.3	277.7	279.5	288.2	294.4	294.6
48	**Total employment**	1 650.0	1 616.5	1 573.4	1 541.4	1 540.6	1 564.2	1 589.2	1 599.8
	EMPLOYEES, MILLION HOURS, DOMESTIC CONCEPT								
49	Industry, including energy	345.2	335.2	331.3	324.3	319.7	321.9	328.8	330.8
50	Distrib. trade, repairs; transp.; accommod., food serv. activ.	299.4	295.9	282.2	276.6	271.7	274.0	279.5	284.4
51	Financial and insurance activities	39.8	39.6	37.9	35.5	35.2	34.3	34.1	33.1
52	Prof., scientif., techn. activ.; admin., support service activ.	144.4	143.7	143.4	140.0	137.0	141.3	143.9	149.8
53	Public admin.; compulsory s.s.; education; human health	267.5	270.6	272.9	266.9	267.4	275.2	280.6	280.3
54	**Total employees**	1 313.2	1 290.4	1 252.9	1 220.2	1 200.9	1 218.1	1 242.1	1 250.7
	SELF-EMPLOYED, MILLION HOURS, DOMESTIC CONCEPT								
55	Industry, including energy	21.3	21.2	20.4	19.8	22.2	23.3	23.3	23.0
56	Distrib. trade, repairs; transp.; accommod., food serv. activ.	50.2	50.3	48.5	46.5	49.8	50.5	50.6	49.9
57	Financial and insurance activities	2.4	2.4	2.3	2.0	2.0	2.0	1.9	1.9
58	Prof., scientif., techn. activ.; admin., support service activ.	45.9	46.7	46.6	47.2	55.8	57.3	57.7	59.2
59	Public admin.; compulsory s.s.; education; human health	9.2	9.8	10.4	10.8	12.1	13.0	13.8	14.3
60	**Total self-employed**	336.9	326.1	320.5	321.1	339.7	346.1	347.1	349.1

Note: Detailed metadata:http://metalinks.oecd.org/nav1/20180308/2def
Source: Statistical Office of the Republic of Slovenia (SORS) via Eurostat.

SPAIN

Table 1. Gross domestic product, expenditure approach

Million EUR (1999 ESP euro)

		2009	2010	2011	2012	2013	2014	2015	2016
	AT CURRENT PRICES								
1	**Final consumption expenditure**	**826 392**	**840 492**	**838 574**	**816 642**	**800 381**	**810 728**	**835 258 p**	**855 613 p**
2	Household	595 010	607 981	608 153	600 532	587 697	597 653	614 840 p	632 736 p
3	NPISH's	10 336	10 774	10 712	10 817	10 785	11 027	11 495 p	11 983 p
4	Government	221 046	221 737	219 709	205 293	201 899	202 048	208 923 p	210 894 p
5	Individual	129 195	127 658	125 425	116 863	114 447	114 081	119 628 p	121 849 p
6	Collective	91 851	94 079	94 284	88 430	87 452	87 967	89 295 p	89 045 p
7	*of which: Actual individual consumption*	734 541	746 413	744 290	728 212	712 929	722 761	745 963 p	766 568 p
8	**Gross capital formation**	**265 073**	**254 549**	**234 507**	**207 900**	**191 921**	**201 878**	**220 227 p**	**229 161 p**
9	Gross fixed capital formation, total	262 499	248 987	229 884	205 839	192 371	200 265	214 216 p	223 645 p
10	Dwellings	87 224	74 677	61 433	51 135	42 542	47 167	48 018 p	52 001 p
11	Other buildings and structures	87 164	79 868	72 617	62 124	57 026	56 014	59 698 p	59 710 p
12	Transport equipment	14 408	16 082	16 901	16 665	17 737	19 765	22 741 p	24 511 p
13	Other machinery and equipment	..	..	..	..	..	..	..	..
14	Cultivated assets	1 464	1 189	1 128	1 117	1 129	1 351	1 572 p	1 568 p
15	Intangible fixed assets	25 976	28 580	29 106	29 900	29 773	30 774	32 221 p	33 009 p
16	Changes in inventories, acquisitions less disposals of valuables	2 574	5 562	4 623	2 061	-450	1 613	6 011 p	5 516 p
17	Changes in inventories	2 574	5 562	4 623	1 825 p	-662 p	1 815 p	..	..
18	Acquisitions less disposals of valuables	..	..	..	..	..	..	..	..
19	**External balance of goods and services**	**-12 413**	**-14 106**	**-2 632**	**15 273**	**33 391**	**25 214**	**24 513 p**	**33 748 p**
20	Exports of goods and services	244 658	275 847	309 575	319 223	330 453	339 502	355 752 p	368 515 p
21	Exports of goods	163 929	190 834	215 967	224 195	235 549	239 309	250 014 p	253 901 p
22	Exports of services	80 729	85 013	93 608	95 028	94 904	100 193	105 738 p	114 614 p
23	Imports of goods and services	257 071	289 953	312 207	303 950	297 062	314 288	331 239 p	334 767 p
24	Imports of goods	205 402	238 637	260 443	253 443	249 560	261 528	272 318 p	271 325 p
25	Imports of services	51 669	51 316	51 764	50 507	47 502	52 760	58 921 p	63 442 p
26	**Statistical discrepancy**	**0**	**0**	**0**	**0**	**0**	**0 p**	**0 p**	**0 p**
27	**Gross domestic product**	**1 079 052**	**1 080 935**	**1 070 449**	**1 039 815**	**1 025 693**	**1 037 820**	**1 079 998 p**	**1 118 522 p**
	AT CONSTANT PRICES, REFERENCE YEAR 2010								
28	**Final consumption expenditure**	**835 576**	**840 492**	**825 298**	**793 731**	**771 033**	**779 185**	**800 867 p**	**820 638 p**
29	Household	606 697	607 981	593 613	572 223	554 007	562 406	579 094 p	596 099 p
30	NPISH's	10 509	10 774	10 577	10 723	10 812	11 069	11 686 p	12 546 p
31	Government	218 434	221 737	221 108	210 733	206 293	205 573	209 859 p	211 586 p
32	Individual	127 668	127 658	126 224	119 961	116 939	..	..	..
33	Collective	90 767	94 079	94 884	90 772	89 353	..	..	..
34	*of which: Actual individual consumption*	744 882	746 413	730 414	702 947	681 738	..	..	..
35	**Gross capital formation**	**264 497**	**254 549**	**236 185**	**213 630**	**203 757**	**215 540**	**234 239 p**	**241 396 p**
36	Gross fixed capital formation, total	261 722	248 987	231 713	211 764	204 466	214 052	227 985 p	235 576 p
37	Dwellings	84 459	74 677	64 765	58 087	52 157	58 034	57 432 p	59 935 p
38	Other buildings and structures	87 305	79 868	71 689	61 718	57 239	56 616	61 100 p	61 639 p
39	Transport equipment	14 492	16 082	16 809	16 731	18 636	20 820	23 717 p	24 780 p
40	Other machinery and equipment	..	..	..	..	..	..	..	..
41	Cultivated assets	1 516	1 189	1 141	1 068	1 056	1 205	1 408 p	1 402 p
42	Intangible fixed assets	26 914	28 580	28 902	29 649	29 200	30 214	31 556 p	32 413 p
43	Changes in inventories, acquisitions less disposals of valuables	..	..	..	..	..	..	..	..
44	Changes in inventories	..	..	..	..	..	..	..	..
45	Acquisitions less disposals of valuables	..	..	..	..	..	..	..	..
46	**External balance of goods and services**	**-19 089**	**-14 106**	**8 656**	**30 082**	**44 284**	**40 013**	**36 683 p**	**44 686 p**
47	Exports of goods and services	252 091	275 847	296 277	299 431	312 259	325 651	339 306 p	355 436 p
48	Exports of goods	169 821	190 834	206 043	208 586	221 884	230 107	239 081 p	246 375 p
49	Exports of services	82 191	85 013	90 234	90 841	90 251	95 428	100 097 p	108 886 p
50	Imports of goods and services	271 180	289 953	287 621	269 349	267 975	285 638	302 623 p	310 750 p
51	Imports of goods	218 105	238 637	237 782	222 824	223 554	237 952	252 437 p	255 596 p
52	Imports of services	52 892	51 316	49 839	46 517	44 324	47 597	50 094 p	54 760 p
53	**Statistical discrepancy (including chaining residual)**	**-201**	**0**	**0**	**1 365**	**2 015**	**442**	**-1 079 p**	**-950 p**
54	**Gross domestic product**	**1 080 783**	**1 080 935**	**1 070 139**	**1 038 808**	**1 021 089**	**1 035 180**	**1 070 710 p**	**1 105 770 p**

Note: Detailed metadata:http://metalinks.oecd.org/nav1/20180308/9b8c
Source: Instituto Nacional de Estadistica (INE) via Eurostat.

Table 2. Gross domestic product, output and income approach
ISIC Rev. 4

Million EUR (1999 ESP euro)

		2009	2010	2011	2012	2013	2014	2015	2016
	OUTPUT APPROACH AT CURRENT PRICES								
1	**Total gross value added at basic prices**	**1 006 093**	**989 883**	**983 670**	**953 986**	**935 616**	**944 470**	**979 874 p**	**1 014 911 p**
2	Agriculture, forestry and fishing	23 549	25 253	24 391	24 019	25 749	25 260	27 266 p	28 090 p
3	Industry, including energy	167 465	169 978	171 651	165 568	163 944	165 854	176 484 p	181 210 p
4	Manufacturing	132 507	131 436	132 447	126 036	125 681	129 683	139 300 p	144 027 p
5	Construction	106 503	87 526	73 980	63 521	53 948	53 128	54 927 p	57 005 p
6	Services	..	..	..	..	..	..	..	..
7	Distrib. trade, repairs; transp.; accommod., food serv. activ.	220 847	222 546	225 396	222 020	216 563	219 775	228 639 p	239 474 p
8	Information and communication	44 637	43 430	42 726	41 972	41 285	41 080	41 088 p	42 642 p
9	Financial and insurance activities	57 216	43 936	40 895	39 870	35 183	37 841	38 925 p	40 001 p
10	Real estate activities	89 901	100 489	106 819	110 666	113 229	112 629	110 428 p	112 112 p
11	Prof., scientif., techn. activ.; admin., support service activ.	73 116	70 971	72 678	69 502	69 200	72 934	77 962 p	83 495 p
12	Public admin.; compulsory s.s.; education; human health	183 109	185 111	184 186	176 802	177 520	177 217	184 469 p	190 247 p
13	Other service activities	39 750	40 643	40 948	40 046	38 995	38 752	39 686 p	40 635 p
14	**FISIM (Financial Intermediation Services Indirectly Measured)**	..	..	..	..	..	..	..	..
15	**Gross value added at basic prices, excluding FISIM**	**1 006 093**	**989 883**	**983 670**	**953 986**	**935 616**	**944 470**	**979 874 p**	**1 014 911 p**
16	**Taxes less subsidies on products**	**72 959**	**91 052**	**86 779**	**85 829**	**90 077**	**93 350**	**100 124 p**	**103 611 p**
17	Taxes on products	80 009	97 297	92 592	91 381	97 325	..	..	..
18	Subsidies on products	7 050	6 245	5 813	5 552	7 248	..	..	..
19	**Residual item**	**0**	**0**	**0**	**0**	**0**	**0 p**	**0 p**	**0 p**
20	**Gross domestic product at market prices**	**1 079 052**	**1 080 935**	**1 070 449**	**1 039 815**	**1 025 693**	**1 037 820**	**1 079 998 p**	**1 118 522 p**
	OUTPUT APPROACH AT CONSTANT PRICES (REF. YEAR 2010)								
21	**Total gross value added at basic prices**	**989 779**	**989 883**	**984 110**	**956 191**	**942 100**	**952 756**	**980 586 p**	**1 011 582 p**
22	Agriculture, forestry and fishing	24 724	25 253	26 373	23 821	27 051	26 727	26 080 p	27 888 p
23	Industry, including energy	164 043	169 978	169 611	161 361	155 017	158 081	166 597 p	172 519 p
24	Manufacturing	131 433	131 436	129 720	122 971	122 708	126 333	136 170 p	140 958 p
25	Construction	102 405	87 526	76 317	69 610	62 273	61 055	62 547 p	63 728 p
26	Services	..	..	..	..	..	..	..	..
27	Distrib. trade, repairs; transp.; accommod., food serv. activ.	219 167	222 546	222 235	218 121	214 473	218 133	227 937 p	236 578 p
28	Information and communication	41 787	43 430	43 358	44 036	45 485	48 855	50 628 p	53 125 p
29	Financial and insurance activities	45 425	43 936	42 892	40 400	37 536	36 211	34 216 p	33 933 p
30	Real estate activities	98 566	100 489	103 343	105 784	107 186	107 774	107 675 p	109 290 p
31	Prof., scientif., techn. activ.; admin., support service activ.	71 987	70 971	72 615	69 838	69 317	73 551	77 575 p	82 998 p
32	Public admin.; compulsory s.s.; education; human health	180 710	185 111	186 785	183 476	183 677	182 249	186 338 p	190 081 p
33	Other service activities	40 087	40 643	40 581	39 297	39 204	38 928	39 752 p	40 343 p
34	**FISIM (Financial Intermediation Services Indirectly Measured)**	..	..	..	..	..	..	..	..
35	**Gross value added at basic prices, excluding FISIM**	**989 779**	**989 883**	**984 110**	**956 191**	**942 100**	**952 756**	**980 586 p**	**1 011 582 p**
36	**Taxes less subsidies on products**	**90 995**	**91 052**	**86 029**	**82 626**	**79 085**	**82 220**	**89 295 p**	**93 212 p**
37	Taxes on products	..	..	..	..	..	..	..	..
38	Subsidies on products	..	..	..	..	..	..	..	..
39	**Residual item**	**9**	**0**	**0**	**-9**	**-96**	**204**	**829 p**	**976 p**
40	**Gross domestic product at market prices**	**1 080 783**	**1 080 935**	**1 070 139**	**1 038 808**	**1 021 089**	**1 035 180**	**1 070 710 p**	**1 105 770 p**
	INCOME APPROACH								
41	**Compensation of employees**	**549 173**	**541 475**	**530 986**	**498 790**	**485 315**	**491 643**	**517 773 p**	**532 852 p**
42	Agriculture, forestry and fishing	4 509	4 887	4 930	4 307	4 320	4 425	4 761 p	4 835 p
43	Industry, including energy	90 111	89 608	87 972	83 495	80 790	80 398	83 475 p	86 012 p
44	Manufacturing	79 784	78 340	77 045	72 356	69 848	69 354	72 260 p	74 705 p
45	Construction	54 305	46 896	39 240	31 625	27 159	26 497	28 171 p	28 194 p
46	Distrib. trade, repairs; transp.; accommod., food serv. activ.	129 054	128 055	128 721	122 772	117 626	119 986	129 286 p	134 067 p
47	Information and communication	20 403	21 086	21 792	20 752	20 423	20 748	22 003 p	22 811 p
48	Financial and insurance activities	23 113	22 862	22 380	21 232	21 465	20 174	20 042 p	19 904 p
49	Real estate activities	4 187	4 359	4 314	4 264	3 938	4 111	4 538 p	4 952 p
50	Prof., scientif., techn. activ.; admin., support service activ.	49 051	48 837	48 985	47 460	47 035	50 921	54 957 p	57 925 p
51	Public admin.; compulsory s.s.; education; human health	146 207	146 555	144 502	135 882	136 364	137 898	143 111 p	145 979 p
52	Other service activities	28 233	28 330	28 150	27 001	26 195	26 485	27 429 p	28 173 p
53	**Wages and salaries**	**436 307**	**428 707**	**420 209**	**395 377**	**384 591**	**388 992 p**	**404 207 p**	**..**
54	Agriculture, forestry and fishing	3 931	4 324	4 365	3 821	3 827	3 906 p	4 308 p	..
55	Industry, including energy	71 033	70 811	70 265	66 695	64 559	63 927 p	64 770 p	..
56	Manufacturing	62 868	62 064	61 597	57 768	55 872	55 151 p	56 124 p	..
57	Construction	43 287	37 024	30 917	24 957	21 418	20 554 p	21 690 p	..
58	Distrib. trade, repairs; transp.; accommod., food serv. activ.	104 479	102 917	102 999	99 175	94 695	96 286 p	100 960 p	..
59	Information and communication	16 229	16 732	17 334	16 534	16 070	16 323 p	17 205 p	..
60	Financial and insurance activities	17 396	17 182	16 713	15 827	15 470	14 984 p	15 019 p	..
61	Real estate activities	3 422	3 389	3 383	3 395	3 092	3 239 p	3 345 p	..
62	Prof., scientif., techn. activ.; admin., support service activ.	38 145	37 914	38 210	37 215	36 838	39 606 p	42 965 p	..
63	Public admin.; compulsory s.s.; education; human health	114 853	114 744	112 607	105 248	106 534	107 471 p	111 312 p	..
64	Other service activities	23 532	23 670	23 416	22 510	22 088	22 696 p	22 633 p	..
65	**Gross operating surplus and mixed income**	**455 145**	**445 849**	**449 346**	**446 682**	**440 354**	**441 823**	**449 136 p**	**471 020 p**
66	**Taxes less subsidies on production and imports**	**74 734**	**93 611**	**90 117**	**94 343**	**100 024**	**104 354**	**113 089 p**	**114 650 p**
67	Taxes on production and imports	93 544	111 951	108 073	109 997	116 332	..	..	..
68	Subsidies on production and imports	18 810	18 340	17 956	15 654	16 308	..	..	..
69	**Residual item**	**0**	**0**	**0**	**0**	**0**	**0 p**	**0 p**	**0 p**
70	**Gross domestic product**	**1 079 052**	**1 080 935**	**1 070 449**	**1 039 815**	**1 025 693**	**1 037 820**	**1 079 998 p**	**1 118 522 p**

Note: Detailed metadata:http://metalinks.oecd.org/nav1/20180308/9b8c
Source: Instituto Nacional de Estadistica (INE) via Eurostat.

Table 3. Disposable income, saving and net lending / net borrowing

Million EUR (1999 ESP euro)

		2009	2010	2011	2012	2013	2014	2015	2016
	DISPOSABLE INCOME								
1	**Gross domestic product**	**1 079 052**	**1 080 935**	**1 070 449**	**1 039 815**	**1 025 693**	**1 037 820**	**1 079 998**	**1 118 522**
2	Net primary incomes from the rest of the world	-19 793	-15 155	-18 559	-7 325	-5 327	-3 428	-2 291	-254
3	Primary incomes receivable from the rest of the world	51 184	52 491	52 862	49 295	50 689	53 012	53 309	52 887
4	Primary incomes payable to the rest of the world	70 977	67 646	71 421	56 620	56 016	56 440	55 600	53 141
5	**Gross national income at market prices**	**1 059 259**	**1 065 780**	**1 051 890**	**1 032 490**	**1 020 366**	**1 034 392**	**1 077 707**	**1 118 268**
6	Consumption of fixed capital	177 000	182 025	185 764	186 405	182 948	184 912	189 174	194 983
7	**Net national income at market prices**	**882 259**	**883 755**	**866 126**	**846 085**	**837 418**	**849 480**	**888 533**	**923 285**
8	Net current transfers from the rest of the world	-14 269	-12 718	-14 142	-12 583	-13 078	-11 439	-11 242	-12 347
9	Current transfers receivable from the rest of the world	12 433	13 048	12 583	12 123	12 994	12 963	13 196	13 833
10	Current transfers payable to the rest of the world	26 702	25 766	26 725	24 706	26 072	24 402	24 438	26 180
11	**Net national disposable income**	**867 990**	**871 037**	**851 984**	**833 502**	**824 340**	**838 041**	**877 291**	**910 938**
	SAVING AND NET LENDING / NET BORROWING								
12	**Net national disposable income**	**867 990**	**871 037**	**851 984**	**833 502**	**824 340**	**838 041**	**877 291**	**910 938**
13	Final consumption expenditures	826 392	840 492	838 574	816 642	800 381	810 728	835 258	855 613
14	Adj. for change in net equity of households in pension funds	0	0	0	0	0	0	0	0
15	**Saving, net**	**41 598**	**30 545**	**13 410**	**16 860**	**23 959**	**27 313**	**42 033**	**55 325**
16	Net capital transfers from the rest of the world	4 798	5 732	4 716	5 458	5 126	4 761	6 799	2 253
17	Capital transfers receivable from the rest of the world	5 634	6 497	5 437	6 212	5 786	5 007	7 072	2 536
18	Capital transfers payable to the rest of the world	836	765	721	754	660	246	273	283
19	Gross capital formation	265 073	254 549	234 507	207 900	191 921	201 878	220 227	229 161
20	Acquisitions less disposals of non-financial non-produced assets	342	-119	313	54	-1 449	-287	-273	-429
21	Consumption of fixed capital	177 000	182 025	185 764	186 405	182 948	184 912	189 174	194 983
22	**Net lending / net borrowing**	**-42 019**	**-36 128**	**-30 930**	**769**	**21 561**	**15 395**	**18 052**	**23 829**
	REAL DISPOSABLE INCOME								
23	**Gross domestic product at constant prices, reference year 2010**	**1 080 761**	**1 080 913**	**1 070 117**	**1 038 787**	**1 021 068**	**1 035 159**	**1 070 688 p**	**1 105 747 p**
24	Trading gain or loss	6 895	0	-11 260	-16 186	-13 088	-16 010	-12 939 p	-12 227 p
25	**Real gross domestic income**	**1 087 678**	**1 080 935**	**1 058 879**	**1 022 622**	**1 008 001**	**1 019 170**	**1 057 771 p**	**1 093 543 p**
26	Net real primary incomes from the rest of the world	-19 951	-15 155	-18 358	-7 204	-5 235	-3 366	-2 244 p	-248 p
27	Real primary incomes receivable from the rest of the world	51 593	52 491	52 291	48 480	49 815	52 059	52 212 p	51 706 p
28	Real primary incomes payable to the rest of the world	71 544	67 646	70 649	55 684	55 050	55 426	54 456 p	51 954 p
29	**Real gross national income at market prices**	**1 067 726**	**1 065 780**	**1 040 521**	**1 015 418**	**1 002 766**	**1 015 804**	**1 055 527 p**	**1 093 294 p**
30	Net real current transfers from the rest of the world	-14 383	-12 718	-13 989	-12 375	-12 852	-11 233	-11 011 p	-12 071 p
31	Real current transfers receivable from the rest of the world	12 532	13 048	12 447	11 923	12 770	12 730	12 924 p	13 524 p
32	Real current transfers payable to the rest of the world	26 915	25 766	26 436	24 297	25 622	23 963	23 935 p	25 595 p
33	**Real gross national disposable income**	**1 053 343**	**1 053 062**	**1 026 532**	**1 003 043**	**989 913**	**1 004 570**	**1 044 516 p**	**1 081 223 p**
34	Consumption of fixed capital at constant prices	..	..	..	..	..	..	..	..
35	**Real net national income at market prices**	**889 312**	**883 755**	**856 765**	**832 095**	**822 973**	**834 215**	**870 246 p**	**902 666 p**
36	**Real net national disposable income**	**874 928**	**871 037**	**842 776**	**819 720**	**810 121**	**822 981**	**859 236 p**	**890 595 p**

Note: Detailed metadata:http://metalinks.oecd.org/nav1/20180308/2772
Source: Instituto Nacional de Estadistica (INE) via Eurostat.

Table 4. Population and employment (persons) and employment (hours worked) by industry
ISIC Rev. 4

		2009	2010	2011	2012	2013	2014	2015	2016
	POPULATION, THOUSAND PERSONS, NATIONAL CONCEPT								
1	**Total population**	46 367.6	46 562.5	46 736.3	46 766.4	46 593.2	46 455.1 p	46 407.2 p	46 468.1 p
2	Economically active population	..	..	..	..	..	..	..	..
3	Unemployed persons	..	..	..	..	..	..	..	..
4	Total employment	19 996.1	19 655.9	19 128.3	18 371.8	17 911.2	18 070.9 p	18 521.2 p	19 025.0 p
5	Employees	17 325.9	17 063.7	16 612.1	15 847.2	15 386.3	15 565.7 p	16 006.9 p	16 486.7 p
6	Self-employed	2 670.2	2 592.2	2 516.2	2 524.6	2 524.9	2 505.2 p	2 514.3 p	2 538.3 p
	TOTAL EMPLOYMENT, THOUSAND PERSONS, DOMESTIC CONCEPT								
7	Agriculture, forestry and fishing	781.3	793.9	760.1	737.7	728.9	733.3	731.6 p	761.0 p
8	Industry, including energy	2 640.4	2 559.2	2 465.5	2 304.9	2 199.7	2 183.8	2 232.6 p	2 297.7 p
9	Manufacturing	2 408.2	2 311.2	2 217.3	2 063.4	1 963.9	1 950.2	1 997.1 p	2 059.7 p
10	Construction	1 869.5	1 630.5	1 382.5	1 149.3	1 007.6	976.1	1 040.3 p	1 051.4 p
11	Distrib. trade, repairs; transp.; accommod., food serv. activ.	5 844.4	5 761.7	5 700.0	5 479.6	5 323.6	5 400.3	5 600.1 p	5 754.4 p
12	Information and communication	475.5	470.6	478.1	459.3	450.5	455.1	480.2 p	502.7 p
13	Financial and insurance activities	407.1	402.3	389.0	380.9	369.1	361.6	356.7 p	359.1 p
14	Real estate activities	202.5	193.9	188.0	184.2	174.3	188.4	199.9 p	209.2 p
15	Prof., scientif., techn. activ.; admin., support service activ.	2 172.6	2 163.2	2 113.7	2 063.7	2 036.1	2 119.6	2 211.1 p	2 276.7 p
16	Public admin.; compulsory s.s.; education; human health	3 898.7	3 978.0	3 985.4	3 926.2	3 904.2	3 955.7	3 991.8 p	4 060.9 p
17	Other service activities	1 694.8	1 686.2	1 650.2	1 656.9	1 667.8	1 665.2	1 677.2 p	1 714.2 p
18	**Total employment**	19 986.8	19 639.5	19 112.5	18 342.6	17 861.9	18 039.2	18 521.3 p	18 987.4 p
	EMPLOYEES, THOUSAND PERSONS, DOMESTIC CONCEPT								
19	Agriculture, forestry and fishing	418.8	445.7	430.6	408.4	399.8	424.2	437.8 p	463.4 p
20	Industry, including energy	2 520.5	2 452.5	2 362.4	2 203.9	2 101.3	2 083.5	2 131.4 p	2 193.1 p
21	Manufacturing	2 289.5	2 206.1	2 116.0	1 964.2	1 866.8	1 851.7	1 897.6 p	1 956.9 p
22	Construction	1 646.0	1 417.2	1 204.4	973.8	842.6	816.1	872.4 p	888.5 p
23	Distrib. trade, repairs; transp.; accommod., food serv. activ.	4 631.0	4 576.9	4 525.8	4 308.3	4 159.2	4 243.1	4 451.9 p	4 622.9 p
24	Information and communication	449.1	448.8	453.7	435.7	427.1	429.5	452.2 p	473.2 p
25	Financial and insurance activities	381.8	376.8	362.5	353.3	341.5	333.6	325.8 p	328.9 p
26	Real estate activities	144.1	140.3	142.4	143.5	134.0	139.4	147.5 p	156.8 p
27	Prof., scientif., techn. activ.; admin., support service activ.	1 850.4	1 850.2	1 800.5	1 765.6	1 734.0	1 818.1	1 911.3 p	1 971.3 p
28	Public admin.; compulsory s.s.; education; human health	3 819.0	3 892.2	3 901.1	3 840.3	3 813.9	3 857.0	3 886.0 p	3 952.5 p
29	Other service activities	1 456.8	1 447.8	1 415.0	1 387.4	1 387.2	1 383.0	1 390.1 p	1 418.2 p
30	**Total employees**	17 317.5	17 048.4	16 598.4	15 820.2	15 340.6	15 527.3	16 006.3 p	16 468.9 p
	SELF-EMPLOYED, THOUSAND PERSONS, DOMESTIC CONCEPT								
31	Agriculture, forestry and fishing	362.5	348.2	329.5	329.3	329.0	309.1	293.8 p	297.5 p
32	Industry, including energy	119.9	106.7	103.1	101.0	98.5	100.2	101.2 p	104.6 p
33	Manufacturing	118.7	105.1	101.3	99.2	97.1	98.5	99.6 p	102.9 p
34	Construction	223.5	213.3	178.1	175.5	165.0	160.0	167.9 p	162.9 p
35	Distrib. trade, repairs; transp.; accommod., food serv. activ.	1 213.4	1 184.8	1 174.2	1 171.3	1 164.5	1 157.3	1 148.1 p	1 131.5 p
36	Information and communication	26.4	21.8	24.4	23.6	23.4	25.7	27.9 p	29.5 p
37	Financial and insurance activities	25.3	25.5	26.5	27.6	27.6	28.0	30.9 p	30.2 p
38	Real estate activities	58.4	53.6	45.6	40.7	40.3	49.0	52.4 p	52.4 p
39	Prof., scientif., techn. activ.; admin., support service activ.	322.2	313.0	313.2	298.2	302.1	301.5	299.8 p	305.4 p
40	Public admin.; compulsory s.s.; education; human health	79.7	85.8	84.3	85.9	90.3	98.8	105.7 p	108.4 p
41	Other service activities	238.0	238.4	235.2	269.5	280.6	282.2	287.1 p	296.0 p
42	**Total self-employed**	2 669.3	2 591.1	2 514.1	2 522.4	2 521.3	2 511.9	2 515.0 p	2 518.5 p
	TOTAL EMPLOYMENT, MILLION HOURS, DOMESTIC CONCEPT								
43	Industry, including energy	4 726.6	4 635.5	4 498.5	4 182.8	3 998.9	3 975.9	4 086.9 p	4 218.5 p
44	Distrib. trade, repairs; transp.; accommod., food serv. activ.	10 402.0	10 288.2	10 137.2	9 715.0	9 444.5	9 567.8	9 841.1 p	10 108.6 p
45	Financial and insurance activities	687.7	680.0	662.0	651.2	623.4	614.5	598.2 p	609.7 p
46	Prof., scientif., techn. activ.; admin., support service activ.	3 627.2	3 582.0	3 516.0	3 385.7	3 305.7	3 446.0	3 618.6 p	3 758.2 p
47	Public admin.; compulsory s.s.; education; human health	6 174.0	6 214.1	6 260.8	6 182.9	6 163.0	6 261.5	6 335.3 p	6 445.6 p
48	**Total employment**	34 370.8	33 591.3	32 787.7	31 204.4	30 249.7	30 568.9	31 477.0 p	32 304.5 p
	EMPLOYEES, MILLION HOURS, DOMESTIC CONCEPT								
49	Industry, including energy	4 486.3	4 417.8	4 282.2	3 969.8	3 790.1	3 769.0	3 875.1 p	3 997.9 p
50	Distrib. trade, repairs; transp.; accommod., food serv. activ.	7 920.5	7 828.0	7 692.6	7 281.1	6 995.7	7 107.1	7 412.8 p	7 719.1 p
51	Financial and insurance activities	642.0	629.6	609.7	599.8	572.7	561.7	543.5 p	552.3 p
52	Prof., scientif., techn. activ.; admin., support service activ.	3 027.8	2 997.9	2 931.4	2 840.3	2 732.4	2 885.7	3 058.7 p	3 170.6 p
53	Public admin.; compulsory s.s.; education; human health	6 056.3	6 088.0	6 131.9	6 057.9	6 034.6	6 116.8	6 182.0 p	6 282.1 p
54	**Total employees**	29 022.2	28 418.4	27 721.1	26 161.0	25 181.9	25 504.8	26 417.4 p	27 215.1 p
	SELF-EMPLOYED, MILLION HOURS, DOMESTIC CONCEPT								
55	Industry, including energy	240.4	217.7	216.3	213.1	208.8	206.9	211.7 p	220.6 p
56	Distrib. trade, repairs; transp.; accommod., food serv. activ.	2 481.4	2 460.2	2 444.7	2 433.9	2 448.8	2 460.7	2 428.3 p	2 389.5 p
57	Financial and insurance activities	45.8	50.3	52.3	51.4	50.7	52.8	54.7 p	57.4 p
58	Prof., scientif., techn. activ.; admin., support service activ.	599.3	584.1	584.6	545.4	573.3	560.3	559.9 p	587.6 p
59	Public admin.; compulsory s.s.; education; human health	117.7	126.1	129.0	125.0	128.4	144.8	153.3 p	163.5 p
60	**Total self-employed**	5 348.6	5 172.9	5 066.6	5 043.4	5 067.9	5 064.1	5 059.6 p	5 089.4 p

Note: Detailed metadata:http://metalinks.oecd.org/nav1/20180308/d60b
Source: Instituto Nacional de Estadistica (INE) via Eurostat.

SWEDEN

Table 1. Gross domestic product, expenditure approach

Million SEK

		2009	2010	2011	2012	2013	2014	2015	2016
	AT CURRENT PRICES								
1	**Final consumption expenditure**	**2 410 955**	**2 521 012**	**2 613 713**	**2 669 939**	**2 751 938**	**2 847 688**	**2 975 731**	**3 101 498**
2	Household	1 499 808	1 583 426	1 640 068	1 660 763	1 703 908	1 758 938	1 830 187	1 889 382
3	NPISH's	50 579	51 214	52 827	54 265	55 399	57 241	58 914	60 371
4	Government	860 568	886 372	920 818	954 911	992 631	1 031 509	1 086 630	1 151 745
5	Individual	621 862	640 002	663 514	683 657	709 536	740 256	786 808	846 547
6	Collective	238 706	246 370	257 304	271 254	283 095	291 253	299 822	305 198
7	*of which: Actual individual consumption*	2 172 249	2 274 642	2 356 409	2 398 685	2 468 843	2 556 435	2 675 909	2 796 300
8	**Gross capital formation**	**688 093**	**806 525**	**870 849**	**833 154**	**848 035**	**919 252**	**1 019 946**	**1 090 163**
9	Gross fixed capital formation, total	733 903	783 315	829 735	834 180	842 148	907 443	989 730	1 059 545
10	Dwellings	109 181	127 752	141 572	127 078	131 888	157 099	191 259	226 978
11	Other buildings and structures	182 839	184 369	184 384	204 997	201 002	214 638	219 518	231 058
12	Transport equipment	40 032	50 470	56 672	55 192	50 310	57 403	63 543	66 995
13	Other machinery and equipment	152 123	162 753	177 257	183 330	180 403	174 574	189 899	202 621
14	Cultivated assets	2 104	2 205	2 438	2 327	2 392	2 108	2 304	2 259
15	Intangible fixed assets	206 365	216 214	228 322	221 998	232 941	255 685	273 940	279 834
16	Changes in inventories, acquisitions less disposals of valuables	-45 810	23 210	41 114	-1 026	5 887	11 809	30 216	30 618
17	Changes in inventories	-46 740	22 420	40 224	-1 929	5 038	10 940	29 154	29 244
18	Acquisitions less disposals of valuables	930	790	890	903	849	869	1 062	1 374
19	**External balance of goods and services**	**189 461**	**192 457**	**172 015**	**181 707**	**169 936**	**169 900**	**204 183**	**213 141**
20	Exports of goods and services	1 461 818	1 625 716	1 706 996	1 706 915	1 651 246	1 772 883	1 913 088	1 950 148
21	Exports of goods	1 049 324	1 203 180	1 265 493	1 247 735	1 173 481	1 235 742	1 299 678	1 322 221
22	Exports of services	412 494	422 536	441 503	459 180	477 765	537 141	613 410	627 927
23	Imports of goods and services	1 272 357	1 433 259	1 534 981	1 525 208	1 481 310	1 602 983	1 708 905	1 737 007
24	Imports of goods	895 507	1 053 020	1 140 901	1 110 194	1 051 196	1 113 003	1 172 456	1 202 972
25	Imports of services	376 850	380 239	394 080	415 014	430 114	489 980	536 449	534 035
26	**Statistical discrepancy**	..	..	..	..	..	..	..	..
27	**Gross domestic product**	**3 288 509**	**3 519 994**	**3 656 577**	**3 684 800**	**3 769 909**	**3 936 840**	**4 199 860**	**4 404 802**
	AT CONSTANT PRICES, REFERENCE YEAR 2010								
28	**Final consumption expenditure**	**2 448 279**	**2 521 012**	**2 558 847**	**2 581 920**	**2 624 665**	**2 674 677**	**2 751 226**	**2 819 754**
29	Household	1 522 046	1 583 426	1 613 551	1 626 177	1 657 533	1 692 920	1 746 746	1 785 507
30	NPISH's	51 384	51 214	51 601	52 120	51 982	52 973	53 641	53 956
31	Government	874 876	886 372	893 695	903 597	915 258	929 092	951 478	980 515
32	Individual	633 617	640 002	643 077	644 135	647 489	656 872	676 129	698 717
33	Collective	241 275	246 370	250 618	259 492	267 875	272 343	275 290	281 603
34	*of which: Actual individual consumption*	2 206 994	2 274 642	2 308 229	2 322 390	2 356 702	2 402 250	2 475 874	2 538 091
35	**Gross capital formation**	**692 478**	**806 525**	**868 535**	**825 260**	**838 057**	**889 417**	**966 619**	**1 020 225**
36	Gross fixed capital formation, total	738 836	783 315	827 585	825 684	830 905	876 294	937 149	989 939
37	Dwellings	113 343	127 752	138 030	121 681	122 729	141 932	167 422	191 370
38	Other buildings and structures	188 093	184 369	177 535	192 811	187 693	197 771	201 104	210 222
39	Transport equipment	41 526	50 470	57 098	55 785	50 259	56 875	62 553	66 058
40	Other machinery and equipment	147 536	162 753	180 773	187 531	186 850	176 005	184 270	195 396
41	Cultivated assets	2 153	2 205	2 326	2 149	2 267	1 922	2 157	2 111
42	Intangible fixed assets	207 546	216 214	225 517	217 160	226 274	243 819	259 840	263 595
43	Changes in inventories, acquisitions less disposals of valuables	..	..	..	..	..	..	..	..
44	Changes in inventories		..			..			..
45	Acquisitions less disposals of valuables	941	790	864	869	585	851	..	..
46	**External balance of goods and services**	**181 409**	**192 457**	**186 399**	**195 910**	**184 279**	**178 162**	**195 529**	**200 410**
47	Exports of goods and services	1 452 278	1 625 716	1 724 907	1 741 836	1 728 378	1 819 243	1 922 661	1 985 658
48	Exports of goods	1 039 153	1 203 180	1 285 530	1 288 906	1 251 782	1 291 131	1 336 568	1 384 122
49	Exports of services	413 569	422 536	439 377	452 742	475 173	524 824	580 805	596 373
50	Imports of goods and services	1 270 869	1 433 259	1 538 508	1 545 926	1 544 099	1 641 081	1 727 132	1 785 248
51	Imports of goods	898 522	1 053 020	1 144 304	1 134 599	1 115 482	1 166 902	1 229 950	1 291 436
52	Imports of services	371 754	380 239	394 204	411 286	428 037	472 403	495 462	494 438
53	**Statistical discrepancy (including chaining residual)**	**-1 070**	**0**	**0**	**344**	**1 159**	**914**	**-939**	**-1 389**
54	**Gross domestic product**	**3 321 096**	**3 519 994**	**3 613 781**	**3 603 434**	**3 648 160**	**3 743 170**	**3 912 435**	**4 039 000**

Note: Detailed metadata:http://metalinks.oecd.org/nav1/20180308/55e7
Source: Statistics Sweden via Eurostat.

SWEDEN

Table 2. Gross domestic product, output and income approach
ISIC Rev. 4

Million SEK

		2009	2010	2011	2012	2013	2014	2015	2016
	OUTPUT APPROACH AT CURRENT PRICES								
1	**Total gross value added at basic prices**	2 887 785	3 094 787	3 222 931	3 253 975	3 333 436	3 486 881	3 719 757	3 894 261
2	Agriculture, forestry and fishing	42 602	50 271	52 549	48 384	46 230	46 804	50 509	50 590
3	Industry, including energy	610 002	712 990	724 320	694 142	687 492	703 840	696 127	723 038
4	Manufacturing	499 889	575 259	588 552	559 308	560 002	575 210	574 766	595 108
5	Construction	167 276	182 358	185 821	180 787	181 899	193 821	214 481	232 674
6	Services	..			..			..	
7	Distrib. trade, repairs; transp.; accommod., food serv. activ.	525 958	559 064	579 218	596 004	599 528	630 159	671 176	694 948
8	Information and communication	156 107	166 347	176 233	181 801	186 801	198 966	285 633	288 928
9	Financial and insurance activities	126 786	120 104	131 575	140 297	151 752	161 047	172 217	167 001
10	Real estate activities	264 004	256 087	275 367	275 591	290 967	309 368	311 291	333 815
11	Prof., scientif., techn. activ.; admin., support service activ.	282 157	310 639	333 757	344 370	365 226	386 307	416 498	446 329
12	Public admin.; compulsory s.s.; education; human health	626 512	646 294	669 327	693 972	720 469	750 297	790 431	839 648
13	Other service activities	86 381	90 633	94 764	98 627	103 072	106 272	111 394	117 290
14	**FISIM (Financial Intermediation Services Indirectly Measured)**	..	..	..	..	..	..	..	..
15	**Gross value added at basic prices, excluding FISIM**	2 887 785	3 094 787	3 222 931	3 253 975	3 333 436	3 486 881	3 719 757	3 894 261
16	**Taxes less subsidies on products**	400 724	425 207	433 646	430 825	436 473	449 959	480 103	510 541
17	Taxes on products	418 181	442 720	452 010	449 365	455 195	470 573	502 490	533 937
18	Subsidies on products	17 457	17 513	18 364	18 540	18 722	20 614	22 387	23 396
19	**Residual item**	..	..	..	..	..	..	..	..
20	**Gross domestic product at market prices**	3 288 509	3 519 994	3 656 577	3 684 800	3 769 909	3 936 840	4 199 860	4 404 802
	OUTPUT APPROACH AT CONSTANT PRICES (REF. YEAR 2010)								
21	**Total gross value added at basic prices**	2 913 193	3 094 787	3 185 944	3 182 030	3 224 732	3 310 548	3 455 368	3 559 375
22	Agriculture, forestry and fishing	53 358	50 271	50 229	50 721	50 440	51 349	53 828	54 487
23	Industry, including energy	597 891	712 990	739 137	708 797	699 032	699 525	668 051	684 452
24	Manufacturing	468 437	575 259	603 579	559 797	555 903	553 212	522 960	537 535
25	Construction	175 962	182 358	178 214	167 647	161 413	165 985	175 279	183 121
26	Services	..			..			..	
27	Distrib. trade, repairs; transp.; accommod., food serv. activ.	532 633	559 064	581 967	593 248	610 520	635 767	658 376	678 332
28	Information and communication	154 635	166 347	176 145	183 097	187 645	201 196	291 717	289 926
29	Financial and insurance activities	118 999	120 104	130 674	130 302	139 480	142 759	151 883	158 246
30	Real estate activities	268 198	256 087	264 711	275 169	286 657	301 568	309 454	324 980
31	Prof., scientif., techn. activ.; admin., support service activ.	287 549	310 639	327 755	332 171	348 111	364 619	387 071	406 604
32	Public admin.; compulsory s.s.; education; human health	639 682	646 294	645 109	647 371	646 609	652 635	664 491	679 598
33	Other service activities	87 933	90 633	92 003	92 726	93 908	95 020	98 024	101 764
34	**FISIM (Financial Intermediation Services Indirectly Measured)**	..	..	..	..	..	..	..	..
35	**Gross value added at basic prices, excluding FISIM**	2 913 193	3 094 787	3 185 944	3 182 030	3 224 732	3 310 548	3 455 368	3 559 375
36	**Taxes less subsidies on products**	407 965	425 207	427 837	421 413	423 437	432 626	457 133	479 888
37	Taxes on products	425 728	442 720	445 762	438 944	440 759	451 255	477 020	500 646
38	Subsidies on products	17 762	17 513	17 925	17 532	17 332	18 598	19 842	20 719
39	**Residual item**	-62	0	0	-9	-9	-4	-66	-263
40	**Gross domestic product at market prices**	3 321 096	3 519 994	3 613 781	3 603 434	3 648 160	3 743 170	3 912 435	4 039 000
	INCOME APPROACH								
41	**Compensation of employees**	1 552 248	1 600 603	1 692 809	1 760 363	1 813 304	1 882 976	1 967 078	2 064 902
42	Agriculture, forestry and fishing	15 826	16 580	17 036	16 930	17 607	18 281	18 394	18 850
43	Industry, including energy	280 709	281 514	296 603	300 980	301 166	306 816	299 165	304 977
44	Manufacturing	254 972	254 720	267 648	270 870	269 706	273 967	265 588	270 722
45	Construction	103 065	107 565	116 495	122 088	125 705	131 806	139 755	149 584
46	Distrib. trade, repairs; transp.; accommod., food serv. activ.	305 245	317 083	336 447	349 904	360 469	373 972	386 768	404 573
47	Information and communication	84 353	85 680	91 484	95 669	98 320	104 982	121 556	126 755
48	Financial and insurance activities	50 719	52 417	53 886	54 887	57 215	56 504	63 287	65 223
49	Real estate activities	23 321	24 133	25 703	26 810	28 279	29 254	31 401	33 673
50	Prof., scientif., techn. activ.; admin., support service activ.	175 179	185 201	203 599	215 624	224 007	234 014	248 668	265 187
51	Public admin.; compulsory s.s.; education; human health	459 243	474 022	492 830	515 960	535 877	560 162	589 286	624 619
52	Other service activities	54 588	56 408	58 726	61 511	64 659	67 185	68 798	71 461
53	**Wages and salaries**	1 307 530	1 348 429	1 423 300	1 476 496	1 517 038	1 574 530	1 642 875	1 724 000
54	Agriculture, forestry and fishing	14 172	14 954	15 588	15 551	15 876	16 484	16 609	16 994
55	Industry, including energy	235 661	236 799	248 541	252 079	251 453	255 795	249 642	254 596
56	Manufacturing	214 218	214 572	224 553	227 197	225 576	228 814	222 160	226 633
57	Construction	87 520	92 148	99 239	104 084	107 270	112 507	119 103	127 477
58	Distrib. trade, repairs; transp.; accommod., food serv. activ.	258 488	269 359	284 837	295 262	303 427	315 007	325 792	341 118
59	Information and communication	69 699	69 982	74 662	77 537	79 021	84 181	97 103	101 296
60	Financial and insurance activities	41 574	42 422	43 815	44 312	45 720	45 074	50 562	51 929
61	Real estate activities	19 718	20 321	21 607	22 489	23 610	24 390	26 118	27 933
62	Prof., scientif., techn. activ.; admin., support service activ.	145 715	153 603	168 445	177 773	183 786	191 709	203 334	216 135
63	Public admin.; compulsory s.s.; education; human health	388 632	400 860	416 831	435 209	451 871	471 962	496 074	525 989
64	Other service activities	46 351	47 981	49 735	52 200	55 004	57 421	58 538	60 533
65	**Gross operating surplus and mixed income**	1 048 878	1 198 130	1 227 029	1 175 001	1 189 265	1 265 406	1 384 810	1 423 995
66	**Taxes less subsidies on production and imports**	687 383	721 261	736 739	749 436	767 340	788 458	847 972	915 905
67	Taxes on production and imports	749 419	787 537	807 561	821 988	840 548	865 399	922 214	993 699
68	Subsidies on production and imports	62 036	66 276	70 822	72 552	73 208	76 941	74 242	77 794
69	**Residual item**	..	..			..		..	
70	**Gross domestic product**	3 288 509	3 519 994	3 656 577	3 684 800	3 769 909	3 936 840	4 199 860	4 404 802

Note: Detailed metadata:http://metalinks.oecd.org/nav1/20180308/55e7

Source: Statistics Sweden via Eurostat.

SWEDEN

Table 3. Disposable income, saving and net lending / net borrowing

Million SEK

		2009	2010	2011	2012	2013	2014	2015	2016
	DISPOSABLE INCOME								
1	**Gross domestic product**	**3 288 509**	**3 519 994**	**3 656 577**	**3 684 800**	**3 769 909**	**3 936 840**	**4 199 860**	**4 404 802**
2	Net primary incomes from the rest of the world	78 226	96 921	75 922	85 532	86 661	87 494	62 536	69 878
3	Primary incomes receivable from the rest of the world	391 413	434 318	421 289	421 725	413 608	436 714	426 148	424 794
4	Primary incomes payable to the rest of the world	313 187	337 397	345 367	336 193	326 947	349 220	363 612	354 916
5	**Gross national income at market prices**	**3 366 735**	**3 616 915**	**3 732 499**	**3 770 332**	**3 856 570**	**4 024 334**	**4 262 396**	**4 474 680**
6	Consumption of fixed capital	577 375	587 994	601 368	619 085	631 384	658 854	688 015	708 902
7	**Net national income at market prices**	**2 789 360**	**3 028 921**	**3 131 131**	**3 151 247**	**3 225 186**	**3 365 480**	**3 574 381**	**3 765 778**
8	Net current transfers from the rest of the world	-52 589	-61 307	-60 670	-62 709	-64 268	-67 529	-66 570	-56 349
9	Current transfers receivable from the rest of the world	31 311	29 258	31 535	34 895	38 212	41 340	44 070	46 901
10	Current transfers payable to the rest of the world	83 900	90 565	92 205	97 604	102 480	108 869	110 640	103 250
11	**Net national disposable income**	**2 736 771**	**2 967 614**	**3 070 461**	**3 088 538**	**3 160 918**	**3 297 951**	**3 507 811**	**3 709 429**
	SAVING AND NET LENDING / NET BORROWING								
12	Net national disposable income	2 736 771	2 967 614	3 070 461	3 088 538	3 160 918	3 297 951	3 507 811	3 709 429
13	Final consumption expenditures	2 410 955	2 521 012	2 613 713	2 669 939	2 751 938	2 847 688	2 975 731	3 101 498
14	Adj. for change in net equity of households in pension funds	12	12	10	12	16	23	30	42
15	**Saving, net**	**325 828**	**446 614**	**456 758**	**418 611**	**408 996**	**450 286**	**532 110**	**607 973**
16	Net capital transfers from the rest of the world	-3 335	-3 327	-4 153	-4 330	-4 182	-3 516	-3 786	-726
17	Capital transfers receivable from the rest of the world	2 009	1 872	1 772	1 772	1 390	1 386	1 577	2 963
18	Capital transfers payable to the rest of the world	5 344	5 199	5 925	6 102	5 572	4 902	5 363	3 689
19	Gross capital formation	688 093	806 525	870 849	833 154	848 035	919 252	1 019 946	1 090 163
20	Acquisitions less disposals of non-financial non-produced assets	818	1 489	1 853	1 444	4 924	1 908	4 316	2 061
21	Consumption of fixed capital	577 375	587 994	601 368	619 085	631 384	658 854	688 015	708 902
22	**Net lending / net borrowing**	**210 957**	**223 267**	**181 271**	**198 768**	**183 239**	**184 464**	**192 077**	**223 925**
	REAL DISPOSABLE INCOME								
23	**Gross domestic product at constant prices, reference year 2010**	**3 321 096**	**3 519 994**	**3 613 781**	**3 603 434**	**3 648 160**	**3 743 170**	**3 912 435**	**4 039 000**
24	Trading gain or loss	11 013	0	-17 207	-18 780	-21 215	-18 524	-6 015	-5 784
25	**Real gross domestic income**	**3 332 109**	**3 519 994**	**3 596 574**	**3 584 654**	**3 626 945**	**3 724 646**	**3 906 420**	**4 033 216**
26	Net real primary incomes from the rest of the world	79 263	96 921	74 676	83 207	83 375	82 778	58 167	63 983
27	Real primary incomes receivable from the rest of the world	396 602	434 318	414 376	410 263	397 923	413 175	396 373	388 959
28	Real primary incomes payable to the rest of the world	317 339	337 397	339 700	327 056	314 548	330 397	338 207	324 976
29	**Real gross national income at market prices**	**3 411 372**	**3 616 915**	**3 671 250**	**3 667 861**	**3 710 320**	**3 807 424**	**3 964 586**	**4 097 199**
30	Net real current transfers from the rest of the world	-53 286	-61 307	-59 674	-61 005	-61 831	-63 889	-61 919	-51 595
31	Real current transfers receivable from the rest of the world	31 726	29 258	31 018	33 947	36 763	39 112	40 991	42 944
32	Real current transfers payable to the rest of the world	85 012	90 565	90 692	94 951	98 594	103 001	102 910	94 540
33	**Real gross national disposable income**	**3 358 086**	**3 555 608**	**3 611 576**	**3 606 857**	**3 648 489**	**3 743 535**	**3 902 668**	**4 045 603**
34	Consumption of fixed capital at constant prices	580 623	587 994	601 589	614 775	625 237	638 093	652 364	665 707
35	**Real net national income at market prices**	**2 826 342**	**3 028 921**	**3 079 751**	**3 065 602**	**3 102 880**	**3 184 082**	**3 324 642**	**3 448 099**
36	**Real net national disposable income**	**2 773 056**	**2 967 614**	**3 020 076**	**3 004 597**	**3 041 049**	**3 120 193**	**3 262 724**	**3 396 504**

Note: Detailed metadata:http://metalinks.oecd.org/nav1/20180308/0fd8
Source: Statistics Sweden via Eurostat.

Table 4. Population and employment (persons) and employment (hours worked) by industry
ISIC Rev. 4

		2009	2010	2011	2012	2013	2014	2015	2016
	POPULATION, THOUSAND PERSONS, NATIONAL CONCEPT								
1	**Total population**	**9 298.5**	**9 378.1**	**9 449.2**	**9 519.4**	**9 600.4**	**9 696.1**	**9 799.2**	**9 923.1**
2	Economically active population	..	..	..	..	..	..	..	..
3	Unemployed persons	..	..	..	..	..	..	..	..
4	Total employment	4 498.7	4 523.7	4 625.9	4 657.1	4 704.7	4 772.3	4 797.1	4 889.1
5	Employees	4 017.8	4 028.3	4 143.8	4 170.3	4 206.5	4 279.1	4 329.0	4 437.5
6	Self-employed	480.9	495.4	482.0	486.8	498.3	493.3	468.1	451.6
	TOTAL EMPLOYMENT, THOUSAND PERSONS, DOMESTIC CONCEPT								
7	Agriculture, forestry and fishing	92.1	97.2	106.2	108.0	108.5	108.4	106.7	101.0
8	Industry, including energy	676.8	666.2	676.1	665.5	654.2	649.0	623.5	620.5
9	Manufacturing	617.0	606.8	614.4	603.0	589.8	583.2	558.0	554.6
10	Construction	294.5	301.0	315.7	321.3	324.3	332.3	341.8	354.6
11	Distrib. trade, repairs; transp.; accommod., food serv. activ.	910.5	927.3	942.5	945.4	956.1	967.4	974.0	981.0
12	Information and communication	168.9	166.6	167.7	171.3	173.1	176.4	194.4	196.0
13	Financial and insurance activities	93.9	94.1	95.6	96.2	96.0	96.1	95.4	95.9
14	Real estate activities	69.1	68.4	71.2	71.2	73.7	75.5	76.8	80.9
15	Prof., scientif., techn. activ.; admin., support service activ.	452.3	471.2	494.5	509.1	516.4	527.0	547.0	561.9
16	Public admin.; compulsory s.s.; education; human health	1 490.7	1 496.5	1 518.0	1 525.9	1 547.7	1 577.1	1 617.2	1 667.9
17	Other service activities	206.0	209.2	206.1	213.5	221.8	228.2	230.6	230.1
18	**Total employment**	**4 454.8**	**4 497.7**	**4 593.6**	**4 627.4**	**4 671.8**	**4 737.4**	**4 807.4**	**4 889.8**
	EMPLOYEES, THOUSAND PERSONS, DOMESTIC CONCEPT								
19	Agriculture, forestry and fishing	50.0	53.4	55.9	55.0	55.0	55.4	54.6	54.0
20	Industry, including energy	663.8	653.6	664.5	654.2	643.0	638.2	613.2	611.8
21	Manufacturing	604.3	594.5	603.1	592.0	578.9	572.7	548.0	545.9
22	Construction	261.6	266.4	284.7	292.6	296.1	304.9	315.1	330.4
23	Distrib. trade, repairs; transp.; accommod., food serv. activ.	857.5	874.3	893.7	901.6	913.5	926.8	935.2	946.2
24	Information and communication	159.3	157.1	158.9	162.7	164.3	168.0	186.5	188.2
25	Financial and insurance activities	93.6	93.8	95.3	95.9	95.7	95.8	95.1	95.7
26	Real estate activities	65.3	64.5	67.1	67.1	69.5	71.3	72.6	76.2
27	Prof., scientif., techn. activ.; admin., support service activ.	409.9	427.3	453.1	468.3	476.3	487.6	508.7	523.5
28	Public admin.; compulsory s.s.; education; human health	1 478.1	1 483.5	1 505.8	1 513.9	1 535.5	1 565.0	1 605.1	1 656.8
29	Other service activities	168.2	170.4	171.6	178.9	187.1	193.3	196.2	197.7
30	**Total employees**	**4 207.3**	**4 244.3**	**4 350.6**	**4 390.2**	**4 436.0**	**4 506.3**	**4 582.3**	**4 680.5**
	SELF-EMPLOYED, THOUSAND PERSONS, DOMESTIC CONCEPT								
31	Agriculture, forestry and fishing	42.1	43.8	50.3	53.0	53.5	53.0	52.1	47.0
32	Industry, including energy	13.0	12.6	11.6	11.3	11.2	10.8	10.3	8.7
33	Manufacturing	12.7	12.3	11.3	11.0	10.9	10.5	10.0	8.7
34	Construction	32.9	34.6	31.0	28.7	28.2	27.4	26.7	24.2
35	Distrib. trade, repairs; transp.; accommod., food serv. activ.	53.0	53.0	48.8	43.8	42.6	40.6	38.8	34.8
36	Information and communication	9.6	9.5	8.8	8.6	8.8	8.4	7.9	7.8
37	Financial and insurance activities	0.3	0.3	0.3	0.3	0.3	0.3	0.3	0.2
38	Real estate activities	3.8	3.9	4.1	4.1	4.2	4.2	4.2	4.7
39	Prof., scientif., techn. activ.; admin., support service activ.	42.4	43.9	41.4	40.8	40.1	39.4	38.3	38.4
40	Public admin.; compulsory s.s.; education; human health	12.6	13.0	12.2	12.0	12.2	12.1	12.1	11.1
41	Other service activities	37.8	38.8	34.5	34.6	34.7	34.9	34.4	32.4
42	**Total self-employed**	**247.5**	**253.4**	**243.0**	**237.2**	**235.8**	**231.1**	**225.1**	**209.3**
	TOTAL EMPLOYMENT, MILLION HOURS, DOMESTIC CONCEPT								
43	Industry, including energy	1 153.6	1 174.0	1 194.2	1 150.7	1 127.0	1 112.3	1 076.0	1 074.6
44	Distrib. trade, repairs; transp.; accommod., food serv. activ.	1 525.9	1 586.6	1 615.6	1 591.8	1 588.7	1 613.7	1 635.6	1 681.6
45	Financial and insurance activities	142.8	144.0	144.6	141.5	138.6	139.0	141.2	144.7
46	Prof., scientif., techn. activ.; admin., support service activ.	670.1	715.8	741.9	738.9	752.8	765.8	798.0	831.1
47	Public admin.; compulsory s.s.; education; human health	2 272.3	2 308.5	2 344.8	2 375.4	2 401.1	2 454.2	2 504.3	2 621.5
48	**Total employment**	**7 168.4**	**7 353.8**	**7 499.1**	**7 488.9**	**7 515.6**	**7 624.5**	**7 740.3**	**7 953.1**
	EMPLOYEES, MILLION HOURS, DOMESTIC CONCEPT								
49	Industry, including energy	1 131.7	1 152.5	1 171.8	1 127.3	1 104.2	1 093.3	1 056.3	1 058.8
50	Distrib. trade, repairs; transp.; accommod., food serv. activ.	1 412.9	1 474.9	1 510.3	1 499.3	1 500.2	1 525.5	1 552.3	1 610.4
51	Financial and insurance activities	142.3	143.6	144.4	141.1	138.1	138.5	140.9	144.5
52	Prof., scientif., techn. activ.; admin., support service activ.	605.4	647.4	678.2	677.6	694.7	711.1	741.8	772.0
53	Public admin.; compulsory s.s.; education; human health	2 254.0	2 290.4	2 326.4	2 354.4	2 382.8	2 437.1	2 486.6	2 604.2
54	**Total employees**	**6 707.6**	**6 885.5**	**7 047.2**	**7 051.9**	**7 093.5**	**7 201.3**	**7 329.9**	**7 574.4**
	SELF-EMPLOYED, MILLION HOURS, DOMESTIC CONCEPT								
55	Industry, including energy	21.9	21.5	22.4	23.4	22.8	19.1	19.8	15.8
56	Distrib. trade, repairs; transp.; accommod., food serv. activ.	113.0	111.7	105.2	92.5	88.5	88.2	83.4	71.2
57	Financial and insurance activities	0.5	0.4	0.3	0.4	0.5	0.5	0.3	0.2
58	Prof., scientif., techn. activ.; admin., support service activ.	64.7	68.4	63.7	61.4	58.1	54.7	56.2	59.1
59	Public admin.; compulsory s.s.; education; human health	18.3	18.1	18.4	21.1	18.3	17.1	17.7	17.3
60	**Total self-employed**	**460.9**	**468.2**	**451.9**	**437.0**	**422.2**	**423.2**	**410.4**	**378.7**

Note: Detailed metadata:http://metalinks.oecd.org/nav1/20180308/92c5
Source: Statistics Sweden via Eurostat.

SWITZERLAND

Table 1. Gross domestic product, expenditure approach

Million CHF

		2009	2010	2011	2012	2013	2014	2015	2016
	AT CURRENT PRICES								
1	**Final consumption expenditure**	**390 360**	**398 525**	**402 760**	**408 609**	**417 368**	**422 812**	**427 320**	**432 737**
2	Household	311 163	317 952	320 136	324 102	330 594	334 037	337 830 p	342 150 p
3	NPISH's	9 809	9 936	10 053	10 221	10 629	10 998	11 395 p	11 672 p
4	Government	69 388	70 637	72 571	74 286	76 146	77 777	78 094	78 915
5	Individual	33 372	34 007	34 986	36 316	37 075	38 041	38 795 p	39 321 p
6	Collective	36 015	36 630	37 585	37 970	39 070	39 737	39 300 p	39 594 p
7	*of which: Actual individual consumption*	354 345	361 895	365 175	370 639	378 298	383 075	388 020 p	393 143 p
8	**Gross capital formation**	**154 481**	**145 287**	**166 094**	**152 753**	**143 887**	**150 972**	**151 181**	**152 288**
9	Gross fixed capital formation, total	133 572	138 982	145 420	149 260	150 600	155 130	155 541	158 540
10	Dwellings	25 081	26 776	28 583	29 228	30 330	30 872	31 267 p	31 547 p
11	Other buildings and structures	25 001	25 258	25 954	27 119	28 109	29 455	29 775 p	29 701 p
12	Transport equipment	9 321	10 992	12 499	11 242	10 206	10 391	10 628 p	11 075 p
13	Other machinery and equipment	39 318	39 835	41 878	41 468	41 678	41 468	40 154 p	39 187 p
14	Cultivated assets	209	213	240	206	225	213	211 p	241 p
15	Intangible fixed assets	34 641	35 908	36 266	39 997	40 052	42 730	43 507 p	46 790 p
16	Changes in inventories, acquisitions less disposals of valuables	20 909	6 306	20 674	3 493	-6 713	-4 158	-4 360	-6 252
17	Changes in inventories	-2 303	350	3 532	203	7 551	2 630	-2 709	-8 026
18	Acquisitions less disposals of valuables	23 212	5 956	17 142	3 290	-14 264	-6 788	-1 651	1 775
19	**External balance of goods and services**	**44 372**	**65 018**	**52 402**	**65 052**	**76 922**	**75 935**	**75 234**	**73 953**
20	Exports of goods and services	337 209	389 443	406 708	419 908	459 008	417 598	406 220	433 682
21	Exports of goods	234 867	288 010	306 872	311 952	346 436	301 544	291 899	311 172
22	Exports of services	102 343	101 433	99 837	107 956	112 573	116 054	114 321	122 510
23	Imports of goods and services	292 837	324 425	354 307	354 856	382 087	341 664	330 985	359 729
24	Imports of goods	222 040	252 351	280 762	274 280	296 641	250 780	240 311	262 455
25	Imports of services	70 797	72 074	73 544	80 576	85 446	90 883	90 675	97 273
26	**Statistical discrepancy**	..	..	..	..	..	..	..	..
27	**Gross domestic product**	**589 213**	**608 831**	**621 256**	**626 414**	**638 177**	**649 718**	**653 735**	**658 978**
	AT CONSTANT PRICES, REFERENCE YEAR 2010								
28	**Final consumption expenditure**	**392 169**	**398 525**	**402 168**	**410 989**	**421 546**	**427 586**	**434 782**	**441 469**
29	Household	312 431	317 952	320 279	327 857	336 327	340 379	346 390 p	351 594 p
30	NPISH's	9 840	9 936	10 051	10 197	10 588	10 946	11 263 p	11 487 p
31	Government	69 899	70 637	71 838	72 940	74 640	76 245	77 126	78 381
32	Individual	33 630	34 007	34 612	35 601	36 291	37 215	38 231 p	39 036 p
33	Collective	36 269	36 630	37 226	37 339	38 349	39 029	38 892 p	39 341 p
34	*of which: Actual individual consumption*	355 900	361 895	364 942	373 657	383 203	388 557	395 917 p	402 160 p
35	**Gross capital formation**	**153 519**	**145 287**	**162 610**	**146 840**	**132 496**	**140 185**	**146 405**	**142 199**
36	Gross fixed capital formation, total	133 117	138 982	145 153	149 936	150 764	155 318	158 788	163 651
37	Dwellings	25 132	26 776	27 984	28 561	29 492	29 992	30 520 p	31 010 p
38	Other buildings and structures	25 145	25 258	25 366	26 334	27 090	28 393	28 808 p	28 849 p
39	Transport equipment	9 218	10 992	12 660	11 788	11 027	11 336	12 359 p	13 230 p
40	Other machinery and equipment	38 474	39 835	43 097	43 618	43 894	43 834	44 339 p	44 220 p
41	Cultivated assets	205	213	242	206	214	202	199 p	230 p
42	Intangible fixed assets	34 960	35 908	35 805	39 361	38 916	41 312	42 356 p	45 807 p
43	Changes in inventories, acquisitions less disposals of valuables	..	..	..	..	..	..	..	..
44	Changes in inventories	..	..	..	..	..	..	..	..
45	Acquisitions less disposals of valuables	26 585	5 956	16 093	2 110	-10 559	-5 520	-1 496 p	1 774 p
46	**External balance of goods and services**	**44 946**	**65 018**	**54 359**	**67 900**	**84 192**	**85 196**	**79 130**	**86 414**
47	Exports of goods and services	345 128	389 443	408 561	413 030	475 803	446 511	457 275	487 151
48	Exports of goods	244 232	288 010	309 382	306 288	364 160	329 713	338 502	358 768
49	Exports of services	100 258	101 433	99 179	106 647	111 464	115 933	117 959	127 312
50	Imports of goods and services	300 182	324 425	354 203	345 130	391 611	361 316	378 146	400 737
51	Imports of goods	232 356	252 351	275 952	260 299	303 392	267 243	274 928	291 916
52	Imports of services	67 728	72 074	78 251	85 540	88 070	94 034	103 038	108 635
53	**Statistical discrepancy (including chaining residual)**	**448**	**0**	**0**	**-364**	**-1 287**	**-418**	**233**	**-443**
54	**Gross domestic product**	**591 082**	**608 831**	**619 137**	**625 366**	**636 948**	**652 548**	**660 551**	**669 639**

Note: Detailed metadata:http://metalinks.oecd.org/nav1/20180308/f805
Source: Secrétariat d'Etat à l'économie (SECO).

Table 2. Gross domestic product, output and income approach
ISIC Rev. 4

Million CHF

		2009	2010	2011	2012	2013	2014	2015	2016
	OUTPUT APPROACH AT CURRENT PRICES								
1	**Total gross value added at basic prices**	567 995	586 333	598 926	605 344	616 923	628 321	632 777 p	638 981 p
2	Agriculture, forestry and fishing	4 440	4 256	4 332	4 127	4 422	4 684	4 255 p	4 301 p
3	Industry, including energy	122 408	126 463	130 497	129 399	130 700	130 096	129 193 p	129 869 p
4	Manufacturing	109 910	114 417	118 863	117 547	119 009	119 301	117 027 p	117 304 p
5	Construction	27 827	29 401	30 786	31 340	32 243	33 402	34 697 p	34 940 p
6	Services	..	..	..	..	..	..	..	..
7	Distrib. trade, repairs; transp.; accommod., food serv. activ.	120 054	129 009	127 323	126 434	126 411	130 334	129 506 p	129 262 p
8	Information and communication	22 891	23 839	24 017	24 418	24 819	25 501	26 344 p	26 504 p
9	Financial and insurance activities	62 975	61 148	62 033	63 010	65 090	62 419	62 110 p	59 802 p
10	Real estate activities	39 789	40 782	42 840	43 130	44 307	45 653	46 900 p	48 206 p
11	Prof., scientif., techn. activ.; admin., support service activ.	50 706	52 427	54 049	56 514	58 836	62 026	64 087 p	65 832 p
12	Public admin.; compulsory s.s.; education; human health	102 576	104 750	108 644	112 329	115 429	118 343	120 923 p	123 558 p
13	Other service activities	14 329	14 258	14 405	14 644	14 664	15 863	14 761 p	16 708 p
14	**FISIM (Financial Intermediation Services Indirectly Measured)**	..	..	..	..	..	..	..	..
15	**Gross value added at basic prices, excluding FISIM**	567 995	586 333	598 926	605 344	616 923	628 321	632 777 p	638 981 p
16	**Taxes less subsidies on products**	21 219	22 497	22 330	21 070	21 254	21 397	20 958 p	19 996 p
17	Taxes on products	33 240	34 564	35 257	35 100	35 389	35 466	35 520 p	35 199 p
18	Subsidies on products	12 022	12 066	12 927	14 029	14 135	14 068	14 562 p	15 202 p
19	**Residual item**	0	0	0	0	0	0	0	0
20	**Gross domestic product at market prices**	589 213	608 831	621 256	626 414	638 177	649 718	653 735 p	658 978 p
	OUTPUT APPROACH AT CONSTANT PRICES (REF. YEAR 2010)								
21	**Total gross value added at basic prices**	569 696	586 333	597 176	603 910	615 242	630 356	638 130 p	647 705 p
22	Agriculture, forestry and fishing	4 401	4 256	4 584	4 417	4 165	4 472	4 226 p	4 119 p
23	Industry, including energy	118 879	126 463	135 268	134 748	135 417	135 244	135 279 p	137 612 p
24	Manufacturing	106 675	114 417	123 918	122 900	123 501	124 740	125 242 p	127 444 p
25	Construction	27 554	29 401	29 596	30 024	30 586	31 375	31 417 p	31 886 p
26	Services	..	..	..	..	..	..	..	..
27	Distrib. trade, repairs; transp.; accommod., food serv. activ.	123 846	129 009	127 571	129 189	130 386	136 376	142 059 p	143 512 p
28	Information and communication	23 276	23 839	23 088	23 344	23 803	24 388	24 513 p	25 230 p
29	Financial and insurance activities	61 025	61 148	61 264	62 924	68 098	69 063	69 097 p	67 068 p
30	Real estate activities	41 182	40 782	41 389	40 319	40 301	40 580	40 700 p	41 186 p
31	Prof., scientif., techn. activ.; admin., support service activ.	51 497	52 427	53 341	55 361	56 495	59 087	60 529 p	61 788 p
32	Public admin.; compulsory s.s.; education; human health	103 674	104 750	106 806	109 157	111 593	114 390	116 423 p	119 196 p
33	Other service activities	14 478	14 258	14 270	14 344	14 232	15 133	13 780 p	15 472 p
34	**FISIM (Financial Intermediation Services Indirectly Measured)**	..	..	..	..	..	..	..	..
35	**Gross value added at basic prices, excluding FISIM**	569 696	586 333	597 176	603 910	615 242	630 356	638 130 p	647 705 p
36	**Taxes less subsidies on products**	21 384	22 497	21 961	21 465	21 713	22 198	22 425 p	21 890 p
37	Taxes on products	33 467	34 564	34 724	35 248	35 499	35 960	36 687 p	36 910 p
38	Subsidies on products	12 081	12 066	12 763	13 786	13 793	13 779	14 266 p	14 967 p
39	**Residual item**	2	0	0	-10	-7	-6	-5 p	44 p
40	**Gross domestic product at market prices**	591 082	608 831	619 137	625 366	636 948	652 548	660 551 p	669 639 p
	INCOME APPROACH								
41	**Compensation of employees**	339 199	342 558	356 011	364 931	373 632	379 388	386 525	391 670
42	Agriculture, forestry and fishing	..	..	..	..	..	..	..	..
43	Industry, including energy	..	..	..	..	..	..	..	..
44	Manufacturing	..	..	..	..	..	..	..	..
45	Construction	..	..	..	..	..	..	..	..
46	Distrib. trade, repairs; transp.; accommod., food serv. activ.	..	..	..	..	..	..	..	..
47	Information and communication	..	..	..	..	..	..	..	..
48	Financial and insurance activities	..	..	..	..	..	..	..	..
49	Real estate activities	..	..	..	..	..	..	..	..
50	Prof., scientif., techn. activ.; admin., support service activ.	..	..	..	..	..	..	..	..
51	Public admin.; compulsory s.s.; education; human health	..	..	..	..	..	..	..	..
52	Other service activities	..	..	..	..	..	..	..	..
53	**Wages and salaries**	288 393	290 451	301 640	309 249	316 154	321 346	326 853	330 693
54	Agriculture, forestry and fishing	..	..	..	..	..	..	..	..
55	Industry, including energy	..	..	..	..	..	..	..	..
56	Manufacturing	..	..	..	..	..	..	..	..
57	Construction	..	..	..	..	..	..	..	..
58	Distrib. trade, repairs; transp.; accommod., food serv. activ.	..	..	..	..	..	..	..	..
59	Information and communication	..	..	..	..	..	..	..	..
60	Financial and insurance activities	..	..	..	..	..	..	..	..
61	Real estate activities	..	..	..	..	..	..	..	..
62	Prof., scientif., techn. activ.; admin., support service activ.	..	..	..	..	..	..	..	..
63	Public admin.; compulsory s.s.; education; human health	..	..	..	..	..	..	..	..
64	Other service activities	..	..	..	..	..	..	..	..
65	**Gross operating surplus and mixed income**	230 625	245 258	244 577	242 171	244 982	250 645	247 837	248 694
66	**Taxes less subsidies on production and imports**	19 389	21 014	20 668	19 312	19 564	19 686	19 374	18 614
67	Taxes on production and imports	36 001	37 751	38 403	38 369	38 739	38 885	39 083	38 966
68	Subsidies on production and imports	16 612	16 737	17 734	19 057	19 175	19 199	19 709	20 353
69	**Residual item**	..	..	..	..	..	..	..	..
70	**Gross domestic product**	589 213	608 831	621 256	626 414	638 177	649 718	653 735	658 978

Note: Detailed metadata:http://metalinks.oecd.org/nav1/20180308/f805
Source: Secrétariat d'Etat à l'économie (SECO).

Table 3. Disposable income, saving and net lending / net borrowing

Million CHF

		2009	2010	2011	2012	2013	2014	2015	2016
	DISPOSABLE INCOME								
1	**Gross domestic product**	**589 213**	**608 831**	**621 256**	**626 414**	**638 177**	**649 718**	**653 735**	**658 978**
2	Net primary incomes from the rest of the world	11 211	35 756	7 166	14 015	13 464 p	2 796 p	16 032 p	6 138 p
3	Primary incomes receivable from the rest of the world	103 262	129 982	97 926	115 635	112 446 p	139 972 p	149 554 p	125 942 p
4	Primary incomes payable to the rest of the world	92 051	94 226	90 760	101 620	98 982	137 176	133 521	119 804
5	**Gross national income at market prices**	**600 424**	**644 587**	**628 422**	**640 429**	**651 641**	**652 515**	**669 768**	**665 115**
6	Consumption of fixed capital	125 296	125 972	128 248	129 577	133 612	136 240	135 019	136 519
7	**Net national income at market prices**	**475 128**	**518 614**	**500 174**	**510 852**	**518 030**	**516 275**	**534 748**	**528 596**
8	Net current transfers from the rest of the world	-15 383	-15 519	-13 676	-16 410	-19 385 p	-25 072 p	-21 250 p	-21 788 p
9	Current transfers receivable from the rest of the world	30 582	28 530	28 812	31 814	31 480 p	31 849 p	34 887 p	41 250 p
10	Current transfers payable to the rest of the world	45 965	44 050	42 488	48 224	50 864	56 921	56 137	63 038
11	**Net national disposable income**	**459 745**	**503 095**	**486 499**	**494 442**	**498 645**	**491 203**	**513 498**	**506 808**
	SAVING AND NET LENDING / NET BORROWING								
12	**Net national disposable income**	**459 745**	**503 095**	**486 499**	**494 442**	**498 645**	**491 203**	**513 498**	**506 808**
13	Final consumption expenditures	390 360	398 525	402 760	408 609	417 368	422 812 p	427 320 p	432 737 p
14	Adj. for change in net equity of households in pension funds	2 852	2 858	2 886	3 011	3 014	3 189 p	3 456 p	3 425 p
15	**Saving, net**	**72 237**	**107 427**	**86 624**	**88 844**	**84 290**	**71 579**	**89 634**	**77 496**
16	Net capital transfers from the rest of the world	-182	-639	-2 144	-135	-42 p	-34 p	-723 p	-179 p
17	Capital transfers receivable from the rest of the world	0	0	0	0	0 p	0 p	0 p	2 p
18	Capital transfers payable to the rest of the world	182	639	2 144	135	42	34	724	182
19	Gross capital formation	154 481	145 287	166 094	152 753	143 887	150 972 p	151 181 p	152 288 p
20	Acquisitions less disposals of non-financial non-produced assets	3 633	4 481	8 212	1 994	-919	10 328 p	13 430 p	-2 864 p
21	Consumption of fixed capital	125 296	125 972	128 248	129 577	133 612	136 240	135 019	136 519
22	**Net lending / net borrowing**	**39 237**	**82 993**	**38 422**	**63 539**	**74 891**	**46 485**	**59 320**	**64 415**
	REAL DISPOSABLE INCOME								
23	**Gross domestic product at constant prices, reference year 2010**	**588 476**	**606 146**	**616 407**	**622 608**	**634 139**	**649 670**	**657 638**	**666 686**
24	Trading gain or loss	-862	0	-2 332	-3 198	-7 975	-10 190	-4 056	-12 739
25	**Real gross domestic income**	**590 220**	**608 831**	**616 805**	**622 168**	**628 972**	**642 358**	**656 494**	**656 900**
26	Net real primary incomes from the rest of the world	11 230	35 756	7 114	13 920	13 270 p	2 765 p	16 100 p	6 118 p
27	Real primary incomes receivable from the rest of the world	103 439	129 982	97 224	114 851	110 824 p	138 387 p	150 185 p	125 545 p
28	Real primary incomes payable to the rest of the world	92 209	94 226	90 110	100 932	97 554	135 622	134 085	119 427
29	**Real gross national income at market prices**	**601 450**	**644 587**	**623 919**	**636 088**	**642 243**	**645 122**	**672 595**	**663 019**
30	Net real current transfers from the rest of the world	-15 409	-15 519	-13 578	-16 299	-19 105 p	-24 788 p	-21 340 p	-21 719 p
31	Real current transfers receivable from the rest of the world	30 635	28 530	28 606	31 598	31 026 p	31 488 p	35 034 p	41 120 p
32	Real current transfers payable to the rest of the world	46 044	44 050	42 183	47 897	50 131	56 276	56 374	62 840
33	**Real gross national disposable income**	**586 041**	**629 067**	**610 341**	**619 789**	**623 137**	**620 334**	**651 255**	**641 299**
34	Consumption of fixed capital at constant prices	..	..	..	..	..	..	..	..
35	**Real net national income at market prices**	**475 940**	**518 614**	**496 590**	**507 389**	**510 558**	**510 426**	**537 005**	**526 930**
36	**Real net national disposable income**	**460 531**	**503 095**	**483 013**	**491 090**	**491 453**	**485 638**	**515 665**	**505 210**

Note: Detailed metadata:http://metalinks.oecd.org/nav1/20180308/cbc9
Source: Secrétariat d'Etat à l'économie (SECO).

SWITZERLAND

Table 4. Population and employment (persons) and employment (hours worked) by industry
ISIC Rev. 4

		2009	2010	2011	2012	2013	2014	2015	2016
	POPULATION, THOUSAND PERSONS, NATIONAL CONCEPT								
1	**Total population**	7 774.5	7 855.7	7 912.4	7 996.9	8 089.3	8 188.6	8 282.4	8 372.4 p
2	Economically active population	..	..	..	..	..	..	..	..
3	Unemployed persons								
4	Total employment	4 268.0	4 207.6	4 298.1	4 351.4	4 393.0	4 469.0	4 538.4	4 604.4
5	Employees	3 786.9	3 725.7	3 815.1	3 869.9	3 900.7	3 978.0	4 070.3	4 135.7
6	Self-employed	481.2	481.9	482.9	481.5	492.2	491.0	468.1	468.8
	TOTAL EMPLOYMENT, THOUSAND PERSONS, DOMESTIC CONCEPT								
7	Agriculture, forestry and fishing	..	155.5	160.5	162.1	164.3	169.9	165.9	164.4
8	Industry, including energy	..	695.3	711.2	712.6	703.0	711.0	714.3	712.6
9	Manufacturing	..	654.2	668.3	669.5	660.0	666.4	668.1	665.5
10	Construction	..	310.9	318.9	324.2	327.9	333.3	336.9	337.0
11	Distrib. trade, repairs; transp.; accommod., food serv. activ.	..	1 070.6	1 079.5	1 075.4	1 078.6	1 091.1	1 096.8	1 103.3
12	Information and communication	..	130.9	136.6	141.2	147.7	154.2	155.4	157.0
13	Financial and insurance activities	..	222.9	227.9	228.9	227.5	229.5	232.3	233.7
14	Real estate activities	..	47.3	48.1	51.7	53.1	54.5	54.8	57.8
15	Prof., scientif., techn. activ.; admin., support service activ.	..	609.7	633.2	654.3	668.3	680.3	694.7	709.9
16	Public admin.; compulsory s.s.; education; human health	..	973.1	1 015.2	1 055.3	1 089.6	1 116.3	1 151.5	1 183.9
17	Other service activities	..	263.4	262.7	268.5	273.3	281.9	292.3	305.0
18	**Total employment**	4 469.1	4 479.7	4 593.8	4 674.2	4 733.2	4 822.0	4 894.9	4 964.6
	EMPLOYEES, THOUSAND PERSONS, DOMESTIC CONCEPT								
19	Agriculture, forestry and fishing	..	..	..	..	..	..	..	..
20	Industry, including energy	..	..	..	..	..	..	..	..
21	Manufacturing	..	..	..	..	..	..	..	..
22	Construction	..	..	..	..	..	..	..	..
23	Distrib. trade, repairs; transp.; accommod., food serv. activ.	..	..	..	..	..	..	..	..
24	Information and communication	..	..	..	..	..	..	..	..
25	Financial and insurance activities	..	..	..	..	..	..	..	..
26	Real estate activities	..	..	..	..	..	..	..	..
27	Prof., scientif., techn. activ.; admin., support service activ.	..	..	..	..	..	..	..	..
28	Public admin.; compulsory s.s.; education; human health	..	..	..	..	..	..	..	..
29	Other service activities	..	..	..	..	..	..	..	..
30	**Total employees**	4 086.6	3 998.4	4 112.3	4 192.6	4 241.8	4 331.1	4 425.7	4 495.4
	SELF-EMPLOYED, THOUSAND PERSONS, DOMESTIC CONCEPT								
31	Agriculture, forestry and fishing	..	..	..	..	..	..	..	..
32	Industry, including energy	..	..	..	..	..	..	..	..
33	Manufacturing	..	..	..	..	..	..	..	..
34	Construction								
35	Distrib. trade, repairs; transp.; accommod., food serv. activ.	..	..	..	..	..	..	..	..
36	Information and communication	..	..	..	..	..	..	..	..
37	Financial and insurance activities	..	..	..	..	..	..	..	..
38	Real estate activities	..	..	..	..	..	..	..	..
39	Prof., scientif., techn. activ.; admin., support service activ.	..	..	..	..	..	..	..	..
40	Public admin.; compulsory s.s.; education; human health	..	..	..	..	..	..	..	..
41	Other service activities	..	..	..	..	..	..	..	..
42	**Total self-employed**	485.3	481.3	481.5	481.5	491.4	490.9	469.2	469.2
	TOTAL EMPLOYMENT, MILLION HOURS, DOMESTIC CONCEPT								
43	Industry, including energy	..	1 237.4	1 278.1	1 265.1	1 229.5	1 249.4	1 270.9	1 265.7
44	Distrib. trade, repairs; transp.; accommod., food serv. activ.	..	1 770.3	1 792.5	1 759.8	1 745.2	1 752.3	1 797.4	1 807.1
45	Financial and insurance activities	..	393.3	407.0	400.7	389.8	393.4	401.5	405.9
46	Prof., scientif., techn. activ.; admin., support service activ.	..	556.0	572.0	599.8	608.1	615.1	638.3	663.3
47	Public admin.; compulsory s.s.; education; human health	..	1 416.9	1 464.0	1 500.3	1 540.4	1 574.4	1 632.3	1 687.8
48	**Total employment**	7 377.5 e	7 276.6	7 438.9	7 493.8	7 492.2	7 596.2	7 780.3	7 892.1
	EMPLOYEES, MILLION HOURS, DOMESTIC CONCEPT								
49	Industry, including energy	..	..	..	..	..	..	..	..
50	Distrib. trade, repairs; transp.; accommod., food serv. activ.	..	..	..	..	..	..	..	..
51	Financial and insurance activities	..	..	..	..	..	..	..	..
52	Prof., scientif., techn. activ.; admin., support service activ.	..	..	..	..	..	..	..	..
53	Public admin.; compulsory s.s.; education; human health	..	..	..	..	..	..	..	..
54	**Total employees**	..	6 385.8	6 569.8	6 641.1	6 640.6	6 772.5	6 993.2	7 105.3
	SELF-EMPLOYED, MILLION HOURS, DOMESTIC CONCEPT								
55	Industry, including energy	..	..	..	..	..	..	..	..
56	Distrib. trade, repairs; transp.; accommod., food serv. activ.	..	..	..	..	..	..	..	..
57	Financial and insurance activities	..	..	..	..	..	..	..	..
58	Prof., scientif., techn. activ.; admin., support service activ.	..	..	..	..	..	..	..	..
59	Public admin.; compulsory s.s.; education; human health	..	..	..	..	..	..	..	..
60	**Total self-employed**	..	890.7	869.1	852.7	851.6	823.6	787.1	786.8

Note: Detailed metadata:http://metalinks.oecd.org/nav1/20180308/49ad
Source: Secrétariat d'Etat à l'économie (SECO).

TURKEY

Table 1. Gross domestic product, expenditure approach

Million TRY

		2009	2010	2011	2012	2013	2014	2015	2016
	AT CURRENT PRICES								
1	**Final consumption expenditure**	**777 038**	**905 145**	**1 071 927**	**1 202 470**	**1 375 972**	**1 530 325**	**1 736 315**	..
2	Household[1]	619 462 e	731 460 e	880 852 e	979 068 e	1 120 357 e	1 242 229 e	1 411 800 e	1 560 518 e
3	NPISH's[1]	..			..				
4	Government	157 576	173 685	191 075	223 402	255 615	288 096	324 552	386 977
5	Individual	56 034 e	61 762 e	67 946 e	79 442 e	90 897 e	102 447 e	115 411 e	137 609 e
6	Collective	101 542 e	111 923 e	123 129 e	143 960 e	164 718 e	185 649 e	209 141 e	249 368 e
7	*of which: Actual individual consumption*	675 496 e	793 223 e	948 798 e	1 058 510 e	1 211 254 e	1 344 676 e	1 527 211 e	1 698 127 e
8	**Gross capital formation**	**229 998 e**	**312 888 e**	**436 035 e**	**444 282 e**	**538 810 e**	**593 577 e**	**662 710 e**	**764 662 e**
9	Gross fixed capital formation, total	223 566	288 474	391 383	428 832	516 210	590 742	694 787	764 662
10	Dwellings[2]	..	..	..	..	..	..	..	..
11	Other buildings and structures	..	..	..	..	..	..	..	..
12	Transport equipment	..	..	..	..	..	..	..	..
13	Other machinery and equipment[3]	..	..	..	..	..	..	..	..
14	Cultivated assets	..	..	..	..	..	..	..	..
15	Intangible fixed assets	..	..	..	..	..	..	..	..
16	Changes in inventories, acquisitions less disposals of valuables	..	..	..	..	..	..	..	..
17	Changes in inventories	6 432	24 414	44 651	15 451	22 600	2 835	-32 077	
18	Acquisitions less disposals of valuables	..	..	..	..	..	..	..	..
19	**External balance of goods and services**	**-7 845 e**	**-58 019 e**	**-113 484 e**	**-77 080 e**	**-105 069 e**	**-79 436 e**	**-60 992 e**	**-75 269 e**
20	Exports of goods and services	225 554	237 209	310 444	371 500	403 064	485 854	545 979	572 965
21	Exports of goods	..	..	..	..	..	..	..	..
22	Exports of services	..	..	..	..	..	..	..	..
23	Imports of goods and services	233 399	295 228	423 928	448 580	508 132	565 290	606 971	648 233
24	Imports of goods	..	..	..	..	..	..	..	..
25	Imports of services	..	..	..	..	..	..	..	..
26	**Statistical discrepancy**	..	..	..	..	..	..	..	..
27	**Gross domestic product**	**999 192**	**1 160 014**	**1 394 477**	**1 569 672**	**1 809 713**	**2 044 466**	**2 338 647**	**2 608 526**
	AT CONSTANT PRICES, REFERENCE YEAR 2010								
28	**Final consumption expenditure**	..	..	..	..	..	..	..	..
29	Household[1]	660 286 e	731 460 e	821 067 e	846 997 e	913 733 e	940 937 e	992 011 e	1 028 358 e
30	NPISH's[1]	..			..				
31	Government	170 712	173 685	175 555	187 508	202 578	208 920	217 093	237 752
32	Individual	..			..				
33	Collective	..	..	..	..	..	..	..	..
34	*of which: Actual individual consumption*	720 918 e	793 223 e	883 597 e	913 747 e	985 846 e	1 015 306 e	1 069 307 e	1 112 937 e
35	**Gross capital formation**	..	..	..	..	..	..	..	..
36	Gross fixed capital formation, total	235 458	288 474	357 253	366 917	417 693	438 991	479 751	490 532
37	Dwellings[2]	..	..	..	..	..	..	..	..
38	Other buildings and structures	..	..	..	..	..	..	..	..
39	Transport equipment	..	..	..	..	..	..	..	..
40	Other machinery and equipment[3]	..	..	..	..	..	..	..	..
41	Cultivated assets	..	..	..	..	..	..	..	..
42	Intangible fixed assets	..	..	..	..	..	..	..	..
43	Changes in inventories, acquisitions less disposals of valuables	..	..	..	..	..	..	..	..
44	Changes in inventories								
45	Acquisitions less disposals of valuables	..	..	..	..	..	..	..	..
46	**External balance of goods and services**	**-9 179 e**	**-58 019 e**	**-72 297 e**	**-29 597 e**	**-56 325 e**	**-26 035 e**	**-16 615 e**	**-39 626 e**
47	Exports of goods and services	233 320	237 209	269 110	309 185	312 504	337 989	352 511	345 926
48	Exports of goods	..	..	..	..	..	..	..	..
49	Exports of services	..	..	..	..	..	..	..	..
50	Imports of goods and services	247 065	295 228	340 790	343 170	370 746	369 423	375 762	389 840
51	Imports of goods	..	..	..	..	..	..	..	..
52	Imports of services	..	..	..	..	..	..	..	..
53	**Statistical discrepancy (including chaining residual)**	..	..	..	..	..	..	..	..
54	**Gross domestic product**	**1 069 262**	**1 160 014**	**1 288 932**	**1 350 671**	**1 465 361**	**1 541 071**	**1 634 859**	**1 686 911**

Note: Detailed metadata:http://metalinks.oecd.org/nav1/20180308/2f56

1. *Final consumption expenditure of households includes Final consumption expenditure of NPISH's.*
2. Including *Other buildings and structures.*
3. Including *Transport equipment.*

Source: State Institute of Statistics (TURKSTAT) via Eurostat.

Table 2. Gross domestic product, output and income approach
ISIC Rev. 4

Million TRY

		2009	2010	2011	2012	2013	2014	2015	2016
	OUTPUT APPROACH AT CURRENT PRICES								
1	**Total gross value added at basic prices**	891 082	1 019 911	1 226 696	1 385 413	1 585 325	1 808 190	2 060 727	2 298 896
2	Agriculture, forestry and fishing	81 234	104 704	114 838	121 693	121 709	134 725	161 448	161 305
3	Industry, including energy	184 208	214 683	275 597	302 833	355 312	410 786	461 964	511 806
4	Manufacturing	151 436	175 177	229 818	249 251	293 884	343 305	390 796	432 980
5	Construction	56 157	70 701	100 016	117 433	145 908	165 655	190 619	223 363
6	Services	..	..	..	..	..	..	..	..
7	Distrib. trade, repairs; transp.; accommod., food serv. activ.	217 369	246 209	300 455	345 988	395 050	455 449	518 557	560 899
8	Information and communication	27 162	28 516	32 323	37 763	43 158	49 404	56 072	63 445
9	Financial and insurance activities	37 459	34 122	37 763	46 114	55 726	58 817	70 003	87 063
10	Real estate activities	104 835	114 941	125 018	135 459	148 972	163 852	180 721	201 561
11	Prof., scientif., techn. activ.; admin., support service activ.	44 507	49 485	59 851	70 372	84 058	99 048	121 488	137 294
12	Public admin.; compulsory s.s.; education; human health	118 726	134 018	153 776	177 359	199 286	228 976	254 788	301 625
13	Other service activities	19 425	22 533	27 058	30 397	36 146	41 478	45 069	50 535
14	**FISIM (Financial Intermediation Services Indirectly Measured)**	..	..	..	..	..	..	..	..
15	**Gross value added at basic prices, excluding FISIM**	891 082	1 019 911	1 226 696	1 385 413	1 585 325	1 808 190	2 060 727	2 298 896
16	**Taxes less subsidies on products**	108 109	140 103	167 781	184 259	224 388	236 276	277 921	309 629
17	Taxes on products	..	..	..	..	..	..	..	..
18	Subsidies on products	..	..	..	..	..	..	..	..
19	**Residual item**	..	..	..	..	..	..	..	..
20	**Gross domestic product at market prices**	999 192	1 160 014	1 394 477	1 569 672	1 809 713	2 044 466	2 338 647	2 608 526
	OUTPUT APPROACH AT CONSTANT PRICES (REF. YEAR 2010)								
21	**Total gross value added at basic prices**	951 524	1 019 911	1 134 644	1 193 907	1 288 914	1 361 103	1 437 692	1 482 305
22	Agriculture, forestry and fishing	97 245	104 704	108 305	110 683	113 250	113 921	124 599	121 385
23	Industry, including energy	194 723	214 683	251 853	260 803	284 255	300 227	315 413	328 804
24	Manufacturing	159 837	175 177	210 253	215 005	235 021	249 347	264 061	274 199
25	Construction	60 358	70 701	88 192	95 496	108 893	114 342	119 949	126 386
26	Services	..	..	..	..	..	..	..	..
27	Distrib. trade, repairs; transp.; accommod., food serv. activ.	228 033	246 209	276 981	298 193	317 444	339 012	361 391	362 144
28	Information and communication	28 631	28 516	30 977	33 677	36 670	39 325	40 827	43 255
29	Financial and insurance activities	31 734	34 122	36 057	36 100	45 427	50 073	54 256	59 017
30	Real estate activities	110 020	114 941	120 640	125 816	129 493	132 763	135 932	140 807
31	Prof., scientif., techn. activ.; admin., support service activ.	47 428	49 485	55 649	60 317	67 835	75 084	86 659	91 159
32	Public admin.; compulsory s.s.; education; human health	132 302	134 018	140 223	145 817	154 934	162 453	165 693	174 661
33	Other service activities	21 267	22 533	25 419	26 612	28 792	30 750	30 661	31 517
34	**FISIM (Financial Intermediation Services Indirectly Measured)**	..	..	..	..	..	..	..	..
35	**Gross value added at basic prices, excluding FISIM**	951 524	1 019 911	1 134 644	1 193 907	1 288 914	1 361 103	1 437 692	1 482 305
36	**Taxes less subsidies on products**	117 532	140 103	154 288	156 793	176 398	180 102	197 388	204 854
37	Taxes on products	..	..	..	..	..	..	..	..
38	Subsidies on products	..	..	..	..	..	..	..	..
39	**Residual item**	206	0	0	-29	49	-133	-221	-248
40	**Gross domestic product at market prices**	1 069 262	1 160 014	1 288 932	1 350 671	1 465 361	1 541 071	1 634 859	1 686 911
	INCOME APPROACH								
41	**Compensation of employees**	268 996	314 231	371 489	438 578	506 359	590 558	683 729	840 205
42	Agriculture, forestry and fishing	2 421	2 890	3 531	4 493	5 136	5 797	6 648	8 325
43	Industry, including energy	61 385	72 019	85 066	100 118	116 829	137 036	159 214	195 123
44	Manufacturing	53 048	62 540	74 194	88 036	103 099	121 475	141 292	174 255
45	Construction	17 483	21 472	26 450	30 121	35 511	40 737	47 626	61 662
46	Distrib. trade, repairs; transp.; accommod., food serv. activ.	56 253	65 910	79 489	95 437	111 598	132 767	156 381	195 039
47	Information and communication	6 565	7 503	8 820	10 336	11 684	13 536	15 576	18 878
48	Financial and insurance activities	14 133	15 815	17 692	19 802	23 018	25 720	29 361	32 722
49	Real estate activities	1 531	1 693	1 843	2 089	2 435	2 895	3 464	4 498
50	Prof., scientif., techn. activ.; admin., support service activ.	15 346	18 451	22 815	28 095	33 861	41 094	50 315	66 926
51	Public admin.; compulsory s.s.; education; human health	86 921	100 280	115 939	136 511	152 706	175 074	197 097	235 762
52	Other service activities	6 956	8 199	9 844	11 577	13 581	15 901	18 047	21 270
53	**Wages and salaries**	..	..	..	..	..	..	..	..
54	Agriculture, forestry and fishing	..	..	..	..	..	..	..	..
55	Industry, including energy	..	..	..	..	..	..	..	..
56	Manufacturing	..	..	..	..	..	..	..	..
57	Construction	..	..	..	..	..	..	..	..
58	Distrib. trade, repairs; transp.; accommod., food serv. activ.	..	..	..	..	..	..	..	..
59	Information and communication	..	..	..	..	..	..	..	..
60	Financial and insurance activities	..	..	..	..	..	..	..	..
61	Real estate activities	..	..	..	..	..	..	..	..
62	Prof., scientif., techn. activ.; admin., support service activ.	..	..	..	..	..	..	..	..
63	Public admin.; compulsory s.s.; education; human health	..	..	..	..	..	..	..	..
64	Other service activities	..	..	..	..	..	..	..	..
65	**Gross operating surplus and mixed income**	621 072	701 809	851 216	941 948	1 073 758	1 220 507	1 381 988	1 474 581
66	**Taxes less subsidies on production and imports**	..	..	..	..	..	..	..	..
67	Taxes on production and imports	..	..	..	..	..	..	..	..
68	Subsidies on production and imports	..	..	..	..	..	..	..	..
69	**Residual item**	..	..	..	..	..	..	..	..
70	**Gross domestic product**	999 192	1 160 014	1 394 477	1 569 672	1 809 713	2 044 466	2 338 647	2 608 526

Note: Detailed metadata:http://metalinks.oecd.org/nav1/20180308/2f56
Source: State Institute of Statistics (TURKSTAT) via Eurostat.

Table 3. Disposable income, saving and net lending / net borrowing

Million TRY

		2009	2010	2011	2012	2013	2014	2015	2016
	DISPOSABLE INCOME								
1	**Gross domestic product**	999 192 e	1 160 014 e	1 394 477 e	1 569 672 e	1 809 713 e	2 044 466 e	2 337 530 e	..
2	Net primary incomes from the rest of the world	12 399 e	10 188 e	12 420 e	12 424 e	16 933 e	18 564 e	26 506 e	..
3	Primary incomes receivable from the rest of the world	21 162 e	17 665 e	19 761 e	22 224 e	26 289 e	28 464 e	37 619 e	..
4	Primary incomes payable to the rest of the world	8 763 e	7 477 e	7 341 e	9 800 e	9 357 e	9 900 e	11 113 e	..
5	**Gross national income at market prices**	986 793 e	1 149 826 e	1 382 057 e	1 557 248 e	1 792 780 e	2 025 902 e	2 311 023 e	..
6	Consumption of fixed capital	162 147 e	173 961 e	200 051 e	227 657 e	255 084 e	297 304 e	343 126 e	392 798 e
7	**Net national income at market prices**	824 646 e	975 865 e	1 182 006 e	1 329 591 e	1 537 696 e	1 728 598 e	1 967 897 e	..
8	Net current transfers from the rest of the world	3 680 e	2 298 e	2 995 e	2 736 e	2 731 e	3 876 e	4 179 e	..
9	Current transfers receivable from the rest of the world	977 e	1 021 e	1 469 e	1 694 e	1 801 e	1 880 e	2 527 e	..
10	Current transfers payable to the rest of the world	4 657 e	3 319 e	4 464 e	4 430 e	4 533 e	5 756 e	6 706 e	..
11	**Net national disposable income**	828 326 e	978 163 e	1 185 001 e	1 332 327 e	1 540 427 e	1 732 474 e	1 972 076 e	..
	SAVING AND NET LENDING / NET BORROWING								
12	**Net national disposable income**	828 326 e	978 163 e	1 185 001 e	1 332 327 e	1 540 427 e	1 732 474 e	1 972 076 e	..
13	Final consumption expenditures	777 038 e	905 145 e	1 071 927 e	1 202 470 e	1 375 972 e	1 530 325 e	1 736 315 e	..
14	Adj. for change in net equity of households in pension funds	0 e	0 e	0 e	0 e	0 e	0 e	0 e	..
15	**Saving, net**	51 288 e	73 018 e	113 075 e	129 858 e	164 455 e	202 149 e	235 761 e	..
16	Net capital transfers from the rest of the world	134 e	122 e	97 e	253 e	473 e	927 e	610 e	..
17	Capital transfers receivable from the rest of the world	143 e	128 e	101 e	254 e	475 e	950 e	647 e	..
18	Capital transfers payable to the rest of the world	9 e	6 e	4 e	1 e	2 e	22 e	37 e	..
19	Gross capital formation	229 998 e	312 888 e	436 035 e	444 282 e	538 810 e	593 577 e	662 613 e	..
20	Acquisitions less disposals of non-financial non-produced assets	64 e	77 e	36 e	105 e	182 e	157 e	55 e	..
21	Consumption of fixed capital	162 147 e	173 961 e	200 051 e	227 657 e	255 084 e	297 304 e	343 126 e	392 798 e
22	**Net lending / net borrowing**	-16 762 e	-66 107 e	-123 043 e	-87 126 e	-119 925 e	-95 209 e	-84 390 e	..
	REAL DISPOSABLE INCOME								
23	**Gross domestic product at constant prices, reference year 2010**	1 069 262 e	1 160 014 e	1 288 932 e	1 350 671 e	1 465 361 e	1 541 071 e	1 634 859 e	1 686 911 e
24	Trading gain or loss	..	..	..	..	..	..	..	..
25	**Real gross domestic income**	..	..	..	..	..	..	..	..
26	Net real primary incomes from the rest of the world	..	..	..	..	..	..	..	..
27	Real primary incomes receivable from the rest of the world	..	..	..	..	..	..	..	..
28	Real primary incomes payable to the rest of the world	..	..	..	..	..	..	..	..
29	**Real gross national income at market prices**	..	..	..	..	..	..	..	..
30	Net real current transfers from the rest of the world	..	..	..	..	..	..	..	..
31	Real current transfers receivable from the rest of the world	..	..	..	..	..	..	..	..
32	Real current transfers payable to the rest of the world	..	..	..	..	..	..	..	..
33	**Real gross national disposable income**	..	..	..	..	..	..	..	..
34	Consumption of fixed capital at constant prices	..	..	..	..	..	..	..	..
35	**Real net national income at market prices**	..	..	..	..	..	..	..	..
36	**Real net national disposable income**	..	..	..	..	..	..	..	..

Note: Detailed metadata:http://metalinks.oecd.org/nav1/20180308/639e
Source: State Institute of Statistics (TURKSTAT) via Eurostat.

TURKEY

Table 4. Population and employment (persons) and employment (hours worked) by industry
ISIC Rev. 4

		2009	2010	2011	2012	2013	2014	2015	2016
	POPULATION, THOUSAND PERSONS, NATIONAL CONCEPT								
1	**Total population**	72 050.0	73 003.0	73 950.0	74 898.5 e	75 774.2 e	76 619.1 e	77 439.6 e	78 247.1 e
2	Economically active population	..	..	..	..	..	..	..	..
3	Unemployed persons	..	..	..	..	..	..	..	..
4	Total employment	..	..	..	..	..	..	..	..
5	Employees	..	..	..	..	..	..	..	..
6	Self-employed	..	..	..	..	..	..	..	..
	TOTAL EMPLOYMENT, THOUSAND PERSONS, DOMESTIC CONCEPT								
7	Agriculture, forestry and fishing	..	..	..	..	..	..	..	..
8	Industry, including energy	..	..	..	..	..	..	..	..
9	Manufacturing	..	..	..	..	..	..	..	..
10	Construction	..	..	..	..	..	..	..	..
11	Distrib. trade, repairs; transp.; accommod., food serv. activ.	..	..	..	..	..	..	..	..
12	Information and communication	..	..	..	..	..	..	..	..
13	Financial and insurance activities	..	..	..	..	..	..	..	..
14	Real estate activities	..	..	..	..	..	..	..	..
15	Prof., scientif., techn. activ.; admin., support service activ.	..	..	..	..	..	..	..	..
16	Public admin.; compulsory s.s.; education; human health	..	..	..	..	..	..	..	..
17	Other service activities	..	..	..	..	..	..	..	..
18	**Total employment**	..	..	..	..	..	..	..	..
	EMPLOYEES, THOUSAND PERSONS, DOMESTIC CONCEPT								
19	Agriculture, forestry and fishing	..	..	..	..	..	..	..	..
20	Industry, including energy	..	..	..	..	..	..	..	..
21	Manufacturing	..	..	..	..	..	..	..	..
22	Construction	..	..	..	..	..	..	..	..
23	Distrib. trade, repairs; transp.; accommod., food serv. activ.	..	..	..	..	..	..	..	..
24	Information and communication	..	..	..	..	..	..	..	..
25	Financial and insurance activities	..	..	..	..	..	..	..	..
26	Real estate activities	..	..	..	..	..	..	..	..
27	Prof., scientif., techn. activ.; admin., support service activ.	..	..	..	..	..	..	..	..
28	Public admin.; compulsory s.s.; education; human health	..	..	..	..	..	..	..	..
29	Other service activities	..	..	..	..	..	..	..	..
30	**Total employees**	..	..	..	..	..	..	..	..
	SELF-EMPLOYED, THOUSAND PERSONS, DOMESTIC CONCEPT								
31	Agriculture, forestry and fishing	..	..	..	..	..	..	..	..
32	Industry, including energy	..	..	..	..	..	..	..	..
33	Manufacturing	..	..	..	..	..	..	..	..
34	Construction	..	..	..	..	..	..	..	..
35	Distrib. trade, repairs; transp.; accommod., food serv. activ.	..	..	..	..	..	..	..	..
36	Information and communication	..	..	..	..	..	..	..	..
37	Financial and insurance activities	..	..	..	..	..	..	..	..
38	Real estate activities	..	..	..	..	..	..	..	..
39	Prof., scientif., techn. activ.; admin., support service activ.	..	..	..	..	..	..	..	..
40	Public admin.; compulsory s.s.; education; human health	..	..	..	..	..	..	..	..
41	Other service activities	..	..	..	..	..	..	..	..
42	**Total self-employed**	..	..	..	..	..	..	..	..
	TOTAL EMPLOYMENT, MILLION HOURS, DOMESTIC CONCEPT								
43	Industry, including energy	..	..	..	..	..	..	..	..
44	Distrib. trade, repairs; transp.; accommod., food serv. activ.	..	..	..	..	..	..	..	..
45	Financial and insurance activities	..	..	..	..	..	..	..	..
46	Prof., scientif., techn. activ.; admin., support service activ.	..	..	..	..	..	..	..	..
47	Public admin.; compulsory s.s.; education; human health	..	..	..	..	..	..	..	..
48	**Total employment**	..	..	..	..	..	..	..	..
	EMPLOYEES, MILLION HOURS, DOMESTIC CONCEPT								
49	Industry, including energy	..	..	..	..	..	..	..	..
50	Distrib. trade, repairs; transp.; accommod., food serv. activ.	..	..	..	..	..	..	..	..
51	Financial and insurance activities	..	..	..	..	..	..	..	..
52	Prof., scientif., techn. activ.; admin., support service activ.	..	..	..	..	..	..	..	..
53	Public admin.; compulsory s.s.; education; human health	..	..	..	..	..	..	..	..
54	**Total employees**	..	..	..	..	..	..	..	..
	SELF-EMPLOYED, MILLION HOURS, DOMESTIC CONCEPT								
55	Industry, including energy	..	..	..	..	..	..	..	..
56	Distrib. trade, repairs; transp.; accommod., food serv. activ.	..	..	..	..	..	..	..	..
57	Financial and insurance activities	..	..	..	..	..	..	..	..
58	Prof., scientif., techn. activ.; admin., support service activ.	..	..	..	..	..	..	..	..
59	Public admin.; compulsory s.s.; education; human health	..	..	..	..	..	..	..	..
60	**Total self-employed**	..	..	..	..	..	..	..	..

Source: State Institute of Statistics (TURKSTAT) via Eurostat.

Table 1. Gross domestic product, expenditure approach

Million GBP

		2009	2010	2011	2012	2013	2014	2015	2016
	AT CURRENT PRICES								
1	**Final consumption expenditure**	**1 342 302**	**1 373 328**	**1 405 831**	**1 453 040**	**1 501 239**	**1 559 558**	**1 600 544**	**1 662 039**
2	Household	960 854	984 614	1 013 406	1 053 663	1 098 735	1 143 919	1 181 868	1 235 357
3	NPISH's	50 684	51 276	53 647	53 664	54 428	56 625	56 614	57 022
4	Government	330 764	337 438	338 778	345 713	348 076	359 014	362 062	369 660
5	Individual	205 848	210 597	212 508	217 274	221 294	228 672	233 707	239 551
6	Collective	124 916	126 841	126 270	128 439	126 782	130 342	128 355	130 109
7	*of which: Actual individual consumption*	1 217 386	1 246 487	1 279 561	1 324 601	1 374 457	1 429 216	1 472 189	1 531 930
8	**Gross capital formation**	**220 687**	**247 717**	**254 402**	**265 549**	**286 682**	**314 335**	**320 563**	**333 146**
9	Gross fixed capital formation, total	233 395	242 186	251 411	262 820	277 209	300 965	313 189	323 761
10	Dwellings	46 567	48 909	51 790	51 611	56 603	63 748	67 501	72 945
11	Other buildings and structures	82 990	79 747	83 837	91 628	96 534	102 610	105 970	107 947
12	Transport equipment	10 348	13 917	8 887	10 795	11 742	16 435	21 977	25 769
13	Other machinery and equipment	32 117	34 607	40 106	39 050	39 774	45 239	42 814	41 228
14	Cultivated assets	1 329	1 134	1 260	1 384	1 420	1 481	1 216	1 003
15	Intangible fixed assets	51 931	54 858	56 309	58 362	61 072	61 455	60 176	61 388
16	Changes in inventories, acquisitions less disposals of valuables	-12 708	5 531	2 991	2 729	9 473	13 370	7 374	9 385
17	Changes in inventories	-14 441	5 458	2 686	1 900	4 712	13 268	7 812	7 714
18	Acquisitions less disposals of valuables	1 733	73	305	829	4 761	102	-438	1 671
19	**External balance of goods and services**	**-33 453**	**-41 168**	**-25 171**	**-33 364**	**-35 367**	**-36 831**	**-32 370**	**-40 677**
20	Exports of goods and services	399 649	445 748	498 862	501 055	519 913	518 925	517 161	554 738
21	Exports of goods	229 107	270 196	308 171	301 621	302 169	297 306	288 770	302 067
22	Exports of services	170 542	175 552	190 691	199 434	217 744	221 619	228 391	252 671
23	Imports of goods and services	433 102	486 916	524 033	534 419	555 280	555 756	549 531	595 415
24	Imports of goods	315 521	367 376	402 950	410 308	421 952	420 428	407 396	437 562
25	Imports of services	117 581	119 540	121 083	124 111	133 328	135 328	142 135	157 853
26	**Statistical discrepancy**	**0**	**0**	**0**	**0**	**0**	**0**	**0**	**8 803**
27	**Gross domestic product**	**1 529 536**	**1 579 877**	**1 635 062**	**1 685 225**	**1 752 554**	**1 837 062**	**1 888 737**	**1 963 311**
	AT CONSTANT PRICES, REFERENCE YEAR 2010								
28	**Final consumption expenditure**	**1 365 049**	**1 373 328**	**1 366 591**	**1 387 595**	**1 406 518**	**1 437 664**	**1 467 979**	**1 504 213**
29	Household	977 567	984 614	975 121	992 558	1 011 368	1 033 151	1 061 308	1 094 107
30	NPISH's	51 667	51 276	53 345	52 338	51 569	52 360	51 932	51 869
31	Government	335 814	337 438	338 123	342 614	343 245	351 866	354 058	356 978
32	Individual	207 709	210 597	213 052	217 329	221 889	228 164	232 708	235 781
33	Collective	128 136	126 841	125 071	125 303	121 476	123 857	121 594	121 560
34	*of which: Actual individual consumption*	1 236 932	1 246 487	1 241 520	1 262 258	1 284 877	1 313 632	1 346 047	1 382 202
35	**Gross capital formation**	**217 119**	**247 717**	**253 864**	**269 640**	**297 444**	**329 893**	**343 353**	**346 535**
36	Gross fixed capital formation, total	231 698	242 186	247 432	252 562	261 189	279 706	287 465	292 596
37	Dwellings	46 622	48 909	50 845	48 952	52 158	57 057	60 311	64 114
38	Other buildings and structures	80 012	79 747	82 857	87 170	89 015	91 709	93 704	93 735
39	Transport equipment	10 391	13 917	8 624	10 515	11 429	16 596	22 359	27 034
40	Other machinery and equipment	32 451	34 607	39 350	37 726	37 794	43 832	41 093	38 360
41	Cultivated assets	1 424	1 134	1 324	1 355	1 412	1 608	1 280	1 021
42	Intangible fixed assets	52 384	54 858	55 290	56 976	58 814	58 933	57 246	57 494
43	Changes in inventories, acquisitions less disposals of valuables	..	..	..	..	..	..	..	..
44	Changes in inventories	..	..	..	..	..	..	..	..
45	Acquisitions less disposals of valuables	..	..	..	..	..	..	..	..
46	**External balance of goods and services**	**-27 778 e**	**-41 168 e**	**-17 628 e**	**-29 983 e**	**-41 877 e**	**-52 411 e**	**-55 782 e**	**-71 420 e**
47	Exports of goods and services	420 794 e	445 748 e	473 535 e	474 613 e	478 599 e	491 305 e	515 739 e	527 717 e
48	Exports of goods	242 604	270 196	288 472	283 640	280 663	289 972	306 867	304 175
49	Exports of services	178 011	175 552	185 064	191 176	198 245	201 688	209 410	222 745
50	Imports of goods and services	448 572	486 916	491 163	504 596	520 476	543 717	571 521	599 137
51	Imports of goods	327 800	367 376	372 599	381 356	391 479	408 871	424 974	444 052
52	Imports of services	120 640	119 540	118 563	123 323	129 213	135 072	146 912	155 455
53	**Statistical discrepancy (including chaining residual)**	**-839 e**	**0 e**	**-1 e**	**-682 e**	**-2 131 e**	**-4 494 e**	**-4 766 e**	**5 346 e**
54	**Gross domestic product**	**1 553 551**	**1 579 877**	**1 602 827**	**1 626 570**	**1 659 953**	**1 710 652**	**1 750 783**	**1 784 675**

Note: Detailed metadata:http://metalinks.oecd.org/nav1/20180308/ee1c
Source: Office for National Statistics (ONS) via Eurostat.

UNITED KINGDOM

Table 2. Gross domestic product, output and income approach
ISIC Rev. 4

Million GBP

		2009	2010	2011	2012	2013	2014	2015	2016
	OUTPUT APPROACH AT CURRENT PRICES								
1	**Total gross value added at basic prices**	1 392 273 e	1 422 028 e	1 458 820 e	1 505 718 e	1 564 430 e	1 638 722 e	1 684 937 e	1 749 826 e
2	Agriculture, forestry and fishing	8 424	10 417	9 973	10 170	11 457	11 743	11 196	10 545
3	Industry, including energy	198 307	203 599	209 746	214 807	227 110	229 901	235 083	244 846
4	Manufacturing	133 428	141 113	145 766	148 406	158 606	162 680	169 370	176 993
5	Construction	77 098	80 686	85 393	87 227	91 049	97 643	102 023	108 259
6	Services	..	..	..	..	..	..	..	..
7	Distrib. trade, repairs; transp.; accommod., food serv. activ.	243 819	254 233	259 290	263 739	277 383	295 253	306 080	320 440
8	Information and communication	82 745	83 319	87 818	89 541	93 983	98 539	100 652	108 114
9	Financial and insurance activities	125 924	115 673	114 128	112 870	118 035	122 358	114 267	117 143
10	Real estate activities	172 853	175 248	184 962	202 069	206 135	220 673	234 518	242 879
11	Prof., scientif., techn. activ.; admin., support service activ.	153 984	158 501	164 132	173 794	185 511	197 498	206 250	216 510
12	Public admin.; compulsory s.s.; education; human health	276 220	283 478	286 227	290 994	292 059	300 355	306 674	310 157
13	Other service activities	52 899	56 874	57 151	60 507	61 708	64 759	68 194	70 933
14	FISIM (Financial Intermediation Services Indirectly Measured)	..	..	..	..	..	..	..	..
15	Gross value added at basic prices, excluding FISIM	1 392 273	1 422 028	1 458 820	1 505 718	1 564 430	1 638 722	1 684 937	1 749 826
16	**Taxes less subsidies on products**	137 263	157 849	176 242	179 507	188 124	198 340	203 800	213 485
17	Taxes on products	143 748	164 786	182 537	186 576	194 894	205 636	212 326	222 926
18	Subsidies on products	6 485	6 937	6 295	7 069	6 770	7 296	8 526	9 441
19	**Residual item**	0	0	0	0	0	0	0	0
20	**Gross domestic product at market prices**	1 529 536	1 579 877	1 635 062	1 685 225	1 752 554	1 837 062	1 888 737	1 963 311
	OUTPUT APPROACH AT CONSTANT PRICES (REF. YEAR 2010)								
21	**Total gross value added at basic prices**	1 396 135 e	1 422 028 e	1 441 176 e	1 459 239 e	1 480 463 e	1 532 669 e	1 570 832 e	1 597 701 e
22	Agriculture, forestry and fishing	10 444	10 417	11 544	10 711	10 765	12 082	12 229	11 464
23	Industry, including energy	197 331	203 599	202 401	196 841	195 419	198 424	200 823	202 165
24	Manufacturing	134 974	141 113	144 220	142 149	140 746	144 843	144 830	145 169
25	Construction	74 347	80 686	82 461	76 783	77 899	84 871	88 646	91 508
26	Services	..	..	..	..	..	..	..	..
27	Distrib. trade, repairs; transp.; accommod., food serv. activ.	251 687	254 233	258 895	261 990	269 571	282 827	293 653	302 276
28	Information and communication	78 811	83 319	85 041	88 438	90 072	90 673	96 176	103 311
29	Financial and insurance activities	125 468	115 673	115 229	116 745	114 229	112 880	109 333	109 069
30	Real estate activities	170 553	175 248	176 130	181 909	186 061	191 749	197 073	197 283
31	Prof., scientif., techn. activ.; admin., support service activ.	149 358	158 501	167 887	177 592	187 188	201 689	212 522	221 415
32	Public admin.; compulsory s.s.; education; human health	281 372	283 478	282 519	288 836	290 689	295 356	297 285	296 804
33	Other service activities	57 582	56 874	59 067	59 667	59 085	62 808	64 171	64 258
34	FISIM (Financial Intermediation Services Indirectly Measured)	..	..	..	..	..	..	..	..
35	Gross value added at basic prices, excluding FISIM	1 396 135	1 422 028	1 441 176	1 459 239	1 480 463	1 532 669	1 570 832	1 597 701
36	**Taxes less subsidies on products**	157 735	157 849	161 650	167 096	178 906	177 347	179 396	186 210
37	Taxes on products	164 517	164 786	168 428	174 761	186 527	185 620	188 342	195 941
38	Subsidies on products	6 796	6 937	6 779	7 774	7 637	8 418	9 254	10 150
39	**Residual item**	-320	0	0	235	585	637	556	764
40	**Gross domestic product at market prices**	1 553 551	1 579 877	1 602 827	1 626 570	1 659 953	1 710 652	1 750 783	1 784 675
	INCOME APPROACH								
41	**Compensation of employees**	795 075	818 959	830 205	849 393	883 501	902 294	930 206	968 898
42	Agriculture, forestry and fishing	4 152	4 234	4 301	4 459	4 718	4 747	4 832	5 032
43	Industry, including energy	115 554	118 570	121 935	124 046	130 060	129 932	133 336	138 885
44	Manufacturing	98 795	100 172	102 788	103 813	108 859	108 410	111 015	115 635
45	Construction	44 792	45 110	46 542	47 641	49 183	50 240	50 793	52 906
46	Distrib. trade, repairs; transp.; accommod., food serv. activ.	165 096	169 338	173 033	176 254	185 349	192 476	198 478	206 734
47	Information and communication	50 128	51 350	54 086	56 733	59 491	60 232	63 178	65 807
48	Financial and insurance activities	61 289	63 500	61 022	58 830	62 390	63 809	65 721	68 454
49	Real estate activities	9 536	9 865	9 900	11 318	11 753	12 216	12 990	13 530
50	Prof., scientif., techn. activ.; admin., support service activ.	95 973	96 026	98 366	103 995	111 073	116 120	121 483	126 536
51	Public admin.; compulsory s.s.; education; human health	220 067	227 498	227 518	231 629	234 169	236 554	242 278	252 353
52	Other service activities	28 488	33 468	33 502	34 488	35 315	35 968	37 117	38 661
53	**Wages and salaries**	663 847	672 528	682 715	695 988	723 770	747 138	775 328	803 778
54	Agriculture, forestry and fishing	3 719	3 714	3 771	3 892	4 150	4 214	4 323	4 488
55	Industry, including energy	99 513	101 555	104 739	105 711	111 166	111 911	115 802	120 193
56	Manufacturing	85 085	85 775	88 426	88 538	93 147	93 474	96 480	100 139
57	Construction	38 775	39 069	40 560	41 491	42 747	44 056	44 851	46 571
58	Distrib. trade, repairs; transp.; accommod., food serv. activ.	142 065	143 078	146 385	147 422	155 752	164 143	170 558	176 968
59	Information and communication	43 113	43 535	45 894	47 780	50 296	51 342	54 341	56 386
60	Financial and insurance activities	50 244	50 277	47 519	45 268	48 246	50 207	52 332	54 181
61	Real estate activities	8 045	8 131	8 160	9 437	9 749	10 225	11 030	11 440
62	Prof., scientif., techn. activ.; admin., support service activ.	79 925	77 407	79 397	83 182	88 944	94 104	99 770	103 389
63	Public admin.; compulsory s.s.; education; human health	174 748	177 932	178 313	183 251	183 692	187 183	191 176	197 870
64	Other service activities	23 700	27 830	27 977	28 554	29 028	29 753	31 145	32 294
65	**Gross operating surplus and mixed income**	578 761	579 570	606 813	632 681	655 965	711 087	728 665	752 214
66	**Taxes less subsidies on production and imports**	155 700	181 348	198 044	203 151	213 088	223 681	229 866	239 568
67	Taxes on production and imports	168 665	193 572	209 198	214 838	224 453	235 878	243 468	255 149
68	Subsidies on production and imports	12 965	12 224	11 154	11 687	11 365	12 197	13 602	15 581
69	**Residual item**	0	0	0	0	0	0	0	2 631
70	**Gross domestic product**	1 529 536	1 579 877	1 635 062	1 685 225	1 752 554	1 837 062	1 888 737	1 963 311

Note: Detailed metadata:http://metalinks.oecd.org/nav1/20180308/ee1c
Source: Office for National Statistics (ONS) via Eurostat.

Table 3. Disposable income, saving and net lending / net borrowing

Million GBP

		2009	2010	2011	2012	2013	2014	2015	2016
	DISPOSABLE INCOME								
1	**Gross domestic product**	**1 519 459**	**1 572 439**	**1 628 274**	**1 675 044**	**1 739 563**	**1 822 480**	**1 872 714**	**1 939 637**
2	Net primary incomes from the rest of the world	5 360	20 193	19 645	-2 186	-10 341	-23 766	-25 746	-23 129
3	Primary incomes receivable from the rest of the world	179 704	178 159	204 282	174 028	160 810	142 391	133 726	143 135
4	Primary incomes payable to the rest of the world	174 344	157 966	184 637	176 214	171 151	166 157	159 472	166 264
5	**Gross national income at market prices**	**1 524 820**	**1 592 635**	**1 647 922**	**1 672 858**	**1 729 222**	**1 798 714**	**1 846 971**	**1 916 508**
6	Consumption of fixed capital	204 323	206 080	212 636	219 710	228 826	238 657	245 090	249 560
7	**Net national income at market prices**	**1 320 497**	**1 386 555**	**1 435 286**	**1 453 148**	**1 500 396**	**1 560 057**	**1 601 881**	**1 666 948**
8	Net current transfers from the rest of the world	-15 836	-20 662	-21 673	-21 913	-26 863	-25 009	-24 699	-24 349
9	Current transfers receivable from the rest of the world	16 873	15 542	14 235	16 456	19 626	19 247	19 889	20 413
10	Current transfers payable to the rest of the world	32 709	36 204	35 908	38 369	46 489	44 256	44 588	44 762
11	**Net national disposable income**	**1 304 661**	**1 365 893**	**1 413 613**	**1 431 235**	**1 473 533**	**1 535 048**	**1 577 182**	**1 642 599**
	SAVING AND NET LENDING / NET BORROWING								
12	**Net national disposable income**	**1 304 661**	**1 365 893**	**1 413 613**	**1 431 235**	**1 473 533**	**1 535 048**	**1 577 182**	**1 642 599**
13	Final consumption expenditures	1 329 939	1 363 814	1 397 112	1 442 888	1 488 161	1 541 431	1 577 526	1 630 845
14	Adj. for change in net equity of households in pension funds	0	0	0	0	0	0	0	0
15	**Saving, net**	**-25 278**	**2 079**	**16 501**	**-11 653**	**-14 628**	**-6 383**	**-344**	**11 754**
16	Net capital transfers from the rest of the world	31	-50	-576	-528	-691	-115	-903	-2 100
17	Capital transfers receivable from the rest of the world	855	1 197	1 022	729	917	1 621	915	929
18	Capital transfers payable to the rest of the world	824	1 247	1 598	1 257	1 608	1 736	1 818	3 029
19	Gross capital formation	223 875	251 218	258 222	269 490	290 640	317 272	324 976	345 818
20	Acquisitions less disposals of non-financial non-produced assets	-373	-53	-196	-361	-219	300	209	-147
21	Consumption of fixed capital	204 323	206 080	212 636	219 710	228 826	238 657	245 090	249 560
22	**Net lending / net borrowing**	**-44 426**	**-43 056**	**-29 465**	**-61 600**	**-76 914**	**-85 413**	**-81 342**	**-86 457**
	REAL DISPOSABLE INCOME								
23	**Gross domestic product at constant prices, reference year 2010**	**1 546 237**	**1 572 439**	**1 595 281**	**1 618 912**	**1 652 138**	**1 702 599**	**1 742 541**	**1 776 273**
24	Trading gain or loss	-8 936 e	0 e	-6 019 e	-3 921 e	4 295 e	12 922 e	18 885 e	..
25	**Real gross domestic income**	**1 537 301 e**	**1 572 439 e**	**1 589 262 e**	**1 614 991 e**	**1 656 433 e**	**1 715 521 e**	**1 761 426 e**	..
26	Net real primary incomes from the rest of the world	5 423 e	20 193 e	19 174 e	-2 108 e	-9 847 e	-22 371 e	-24 216 e	..
27	Real primary incomes receivable from the rest of the world	181 814 e	178 159 e	199 388 e	167 789 e	153 125 e	134 034 e	125 779 e	..
28	Real primary incomes payable to the rest of the world	176 391 e	157 966 e	180 213 e	169 896 e	162 972 e	156 405 e	149 995 e	..
29	**Real gross national income at market prices**	**1 542 725 e**	**1 592 635 e**	**1 608 439 e**	**1 612 883 e**	**1 646 586 e**	**1 693 150 e**	**1 737 213 e**	..
30	Net real current transfers from the rest of the world	-16 022 e	-20 662 e	-21 154 e	-21 127 e	-25 579 e	-23 541 e	-23 231 e	..
31	Real current transfers receivable from the rest of the world	17 071 e	15 542 e	13 894 e	15 866 e	18 688 e	18 117 e	18 707 e	..
32	Real current transfers payable to the rest of the world	33 093 e	36 204 e	35 048 e	36 993 e	44 267 e	41 659 e	41 938 e	..
33	**Real gross national disposable income**	**1 526 703 e**	**1 571 973 e**	**1 587 286 e**	**1 591 756 e**	**1 621 007 e**	**1 669 608 e**	**1 713 981 e**	..
34	Consumption of fixed capital at constant prices	203 227	206 080	208 818	211 247	214 530	220 946	224 277	224 480
35	**Real net national income at market prices**	**1 336 003 e**	**1 386 555 e**	**1 400 898 e**	**1 401 050 e**	**1 428 695 e**	**1 468 499 e**	**1 506 687 e**	..
36	**Real net national disposable income**	**1 319 981 e**	**1 365 893 e**	**1 379 744 e**	**1 379 923 e**	**1 403 116 e**	**1 444 958 e**	**1 483 456 e**	..

Note: Detailed metadata:http://metalinks.oecd.org/nav1/20180308/3c59
Source: Office for National Statistics (ONS) via Eurostat.

Table 4. Population and employment (persons) and employment (hours worked) by industry
ISIC Rev. 4

		2009	2010	2011	2012	2013	2014	2015	2016
	POPULATION, THOUSAND PERSONS, NATIONAL CONCEPT								
1	**Total population**	**62 260.0**	**62 759.0**	**63 285.0**	**63 705.0**	**64 106.0**	**64 597.0**	**65 110.0**	**65 648.0**
2	Economically active population	..	..	..	..	..	..	..	..
3	Unemployed persons	..	..	..	..	..	..	..	..
4	Total employment[1]	29 154.0	29 227.0	29 374.0	29 694.0	30 042.0	30 752.0	31 281.0	31 726.0
5	Employees	25 197.0	25 144.0	25 216.0	25 363.0	25 670.0	26 079.0	26 604.0	26 838.0
6	Self-employed	3 957.0	4 084.0	4 158.0	4 331.0	4 372.0	4 674.0	4 677.0	4 887.0
	TOTAL EMPLOYMENT, THOUSAND PERSONS, DOMESTIC CONCEPT								
7	Agriculture, forestry and fishing	390.3	416.8	410.6	410.2	374.4	434.7	397.3	407.2
8	Industry, including energy	2 852.1	2 811.1	2 819.6	2 857.0	2 839.1	2 844.1	2 880.9	2 867.5
9	Manufacturing	2 535.1	2 476.2	2 464.4	2 483.5	2 466.4	2 480.2	2 504.0	2 496.4
10	Construction	2 174.8	2 055.5	2 032.4	2 016.0	2 016.0	2 083.1	2 135.6	2 215.7
11	Distrib. trade, repairs; transp.; accommod., food serv. activ.	7 749.6	7 722.9	7 739.7	7 846.0	7 920.6	8 030.5	8 230.1	8 379.7
12	Information and communication	1 122.8	1 118.7	1 170.9	1 179.7	1 216.0	1 278.1	1 310.0	1 319.6
13	Financial and insurance activities	1 097.6	1 057.4	1 077.4	1 087.4	1 067.2	1 064.2	1 051.6	1 054.8
14	Real estate activities	424.3	432.0	425.5	448.3	480.2	490.6	509.7	501.7
15	Prof., scientif., techn. activ.; admin., support service activ.	4 245.2	4 310.3	4 388.2	4 563.4	4 681.4	4 950.5	5 128.5	5 292.7
16	Public admin.; compulsory s.s.; education; human health	7 559.6	7 748.5	7 725.0	7 699.4	7 815.1	7 846.5	7 893.0	7 903.4
17	Other service activities	1 538.1	1 553.6	1 585.4	1 586.8	1 632.2	1 730.1	1 744.5	1 783.2
18	**Total employment**	**29 154.3**	**29 226.9**	**29 374.6**	**29 694.5**	**30 042.2**	**30 752.4**	**31 281.1**	**31 725.4**
	EMPLOYEES, THOUSAND PERSONS, DOMESTIC CONCEPT								
19	Agriculture, forestry and fishing	192.9	196.6	190.7	203.4	191.4	204.8	201.1	210.6
20	Industry, including energy	2 661.8	2 610.2	2 625.2	2 635.0	2 601.3	2 620.2	2 634.9	2 622.5
21	Manufacturing	2 364.8	2 300.0	2 292.4	2 289.4	2 256.6	2 281.2	2 285.8	2 279.9
22	Construction	1 277.2	1 168.2	1 142.6	1 120.3	1 118.0	1 157.1	1 208.3	1 226.8
23	Distrib. trade, repairs; transp.; accommod., food serv. activ.	6 954.7	6 920.9	6 945.2	7 004.8	7 089.8	7 208.0	7 399.6	7 473.1
24	Information and communication	986.1	976.4	994.4	1 004.6	1 035.3	1 083.1	1 120.9	1 147.9
25	Financial and insurance activities	1 030.4	989.3	1 014.2	1 011.2	995.3	978.1	971.4	965.7
26	Real estate activities	386.0	389.5	379.1	393.0	417.2	423.0	439.0	436.7
27	Prof., scientif., techn. activ.; admin., support service activ.	3 554.7	3 579.4	3 650.1	3 751.3	3 876.0	4 055.3	4 231.7	4 370.0
28	Public admin.; compulsory s.s.; education; human health	7 048.3	7 207.3	7 172.5	7 146.5	7 236.0	7 213.3	7 240.5	7 204.5
29	Other service activities	1 105.0	1 105.7	1 102.1	1 093.2	1 109.8	1 136.1	1 156.8	1 180.2
30	**Total employees**	**25 197.1**	**25 143.3**	**25 216.0**	**25 363.3**	**25 670.2**	**26 079.0**	**26 604.2**	**26 837.9**
	SELF-EMPLOYED, THOUSAND PERSONS, DOMESTIC CONCEPT								
31	Agriculture, forestry and fishing	197.4	220.2	219.8	206.8	183.0	229.9	196.2	196.6
32	Industry, including energy	190.4	200.9	194.4	221.9	237.9	223.9	246.0	245.0
33	Manufacturing	170.3	176.2	172.0	194.1	209.8	199.1	218.2	216.6
34	Construction	897.6	887.3	889.9	895.7	898.0	926.1	927.3	988.9
35	Distrib. trade, repairs; transp.; accommod., food serv. activ.	794.9	802.0	794.5	841.3	830.8	822.5	830.5	906.6
36	Information and communication	136.7	142.4	176.5	175.0	180.7	195.1	189.1	171.6
37	Financial and insurance activities	67.2	68.1	63.2	76.2	71.9	86.0	80.2	89.1
38	Real estate activities	38.2	42.5	46.4	55.3	63.0	67.6	70.7	65.0
39	Prof., scientif., techn. activ.; admin., support service activ.	690.5	731.0	738.1	812.0	805.4	895.1	896.7	922.7
40	Public admin.; compulsory s.s.; education; human health	511.3	541.2	552.4	553.4	579.1	633.2	652.5	698.9
41	Other service activities	433.0	448.0	483.4	493.6	522.3	594.0	587.8	603.1
42	**Total self-employed**	**3 957.1**	**4 083.6**	**4 158.6**	**4 331.3**	**4 372.0**	**4 673.4**	**4 677.0**	**4 887.5**
	TOTAL EMPLOYMENT, MILLION HOURS, DOMESTIC CONCEPT								
43	Industry, including energy	5 288.4	5 274.2	5 335.9	5 398.4	5 458.9	5 433.1	5 436.9	5 444.5
44	Distrib. trade, repairs; transp.; accommod., food serv. activ.	12 333.4	12 165.7	12 235.0	12 531.4	12 777.6	12 981.2	13 219.0	13 511.0
45	Financial and insurance activities	1 926.7	1 879.0	1 963.1	1 996.8	1 950.2	1 950.6	1 866.1	1 939.6
46	Prof., scientif., techn. activ.; admin., support service activ.	7 044.5	7 081.9	7 317.1	7 713.7	7 909.2	8 348.2	8 648.9	9 033.1
47	Public admin.; compulsory s.s.; education; human health	11 257.6	11 379.6	11 440.7	11 626.4	11 844.6	11 943.0	11 890.0	11 936.6
48	**Total employment**	**47 854.7**	**47 643.9**	**48 274.9**	**49 232.5**	**50 113.9**	**51 505.6**	**51 848.0**	**53 067.8**
	EMPLOYEES, MILLION HOURS, DOMESTIC CONCEPT								
49	Industry, including energy	4 928.4	4 884.2	4 960.6	4 983.7	5 001.9	5 022.7	4 979.3	5 004.3
50	Distrib. trade, repairs; transp.; accommod., food serv. activ.	10 742.4	10 581.6	10 672.7	10 861.4	11 130.6	11 363.5	11 627.7	11 769.4
51	Financial and insurance activities	1 803.1	1 758.7	1 847.1	1 848.3	1 813.6	1 789.4	1 729.3	1 775.9
52	Prof., scientif., techn. activ.; admin., support service activ.	5 941.4	5 952.8	6 176.0	6 445.6	6 664.2	6 925.1	7 270.6	7 578.8
53	Public admin.; compulsory s.s.; education; human health	10 541.6	10 632.4	10 674.1	10 876.7	11 031.2	11 069.5	10 960.9	10 968.6
54	**Total employees**	**40 864.8**	**40 481.5**	**41 003.0**	**41 693.8**	**42 446.5**	**43 301.9**	**43 785.8**	**44 558.3**
	SELF-EMPLOYED, MILLION HOURS, DOMESTIC CONCEPT								
55	Industry, including energy	360.0	390.0	375.4	414.7	457.0	410.4	457.6	440.3
56	Distrib. trade, repairs; transp.; accommod., food serv. activ.	1 591.1	1 584.1	1 562.3	1 669.9	1 646.9	1 617.7	1 591.3	1 741.6
57	Financial and insurance activities	123.5	120.3	116.0	148.5	136.6	161.2	136.8	163.7
58	Prof., scientif., techn. activ.; admin., support service activ.	1 103.1	1 129.1	1 141.1	1 268.1	1 245.0	1 423.1	1 378.4	1 454.4
59	Public admin.; compulsory s.s.; education; human health	716.0	747.2	766.6	749.6	813.4	873.5	929.0	968.0
60	**Total self-employed**	**6 989.8**	**7 162.4**	**7 271.8**	**7 538.7**	**7 667.4**	**8 203.8**	**8 062.2**	**8 509.5**

Note: Detailed metadata:http://metalinks.oecd.org/nav1/20180308/e248
1. Total employment consists of employees, self employed, unpaid family workers and persons on a government training scheme.
Source: Office for National Statistics (ONS) via Eurostat.

Table 1. Gross domestic product, expenditure approach

Billion USD

		2009	2010	2011	2012	2013	2014	2015	2016
	AT CURRENT PRICES								
1	**Final consumption expenditure**	**12 289**	**12 724**	**13 220**	**13 595**	**13 885**	**14 426**	**14 943**	**15 479**
2	Household	9 571	9 927	10 414	10 758	11 056	11 550	12 003	12 462
3	NPISH's	276	275	275	293	305	314	329	359
4	Government	2 442	2 522	2 531	2 544	2 524	2 563	2 611	2 658
5	Individual	979	998	1 003	1 013	1 036	1 070	1 104	..
6	Collective	1 463	1 524	1 527	1 532	1 488	1 488	1 501	..
7	*of which: Actual individual consumption*	10 826	11 200	11 693	12 063	12 397	12 933	13 387	13 867 e
8	**Gross capital formation**	**2 525**	**2 753**	**2 878**	**3 126**	**3 299**	**3 511**	**3 702**	**3 667**
9	Gross fixed capital formation, total	2 673	2 691	2 836	3 064	3 206	3 433	3 590	3 632
10	Dwellings	395	385	388	442	518	568	645	705
11	Other buildings and structures	746	663	672	722	725	804	813	788
12	Transport equipment	115	175	224	262	290	321	354	335
13	Other machinery and equipment	503	519	577	632	639	669	673	656
14	Cultivated assets	..	..	..	..	..	..	..	..
15	Intangible fixed assets	731	752	784	811	837	873	908	952
16	Changes in inventories, acquisitions less disposals of valuables	-148	62	42	62	92	78	112	35
17	Changes in inventories	-148	62	42	62	92	78	112	35
18	Acquisitions less disposals of valuables	..	..	..	..	..	..	..	..
19	**External balance of goods and services**	**-395**	**-513**	**-580**	**-566**	**-492**	**-510**	**-524**	**-521**
20	Exports of goods and services	1 588	1 852	2 106	2 198	2 277	2 374	2 265	2 215
21	Exports of goods	1 065	1 280	1 467	1 526	1 563	1 618	1 497	1 446
22	Exports of services	523	573	640	672	714	756	768	769
23	Imports of goods and services	1 983	2 365	2 686	2 764	2 769	2 883	2 789	2 736
24	Imports of goods	1 590	1 950	2 245	2 306	2 301	2 396	2 291	2 224
25	Imports of services	393	415	442	458	467	487	498	512
26	**Statistical discrepancy**	..	..	..	..	..	..	..	..
27	**Gross domestic product**	**14 419**	**14 964**	**15 518**	**16 155**	**16 692**	**17 428**	**18 121**	**18 624**
	AT CONSTANT PRICES, REFERENCE YEAR 2010								
28	**Final consumption expenditure**	**12 529**	**12 724**	**12 888**	**13 019**	**13 115**	**13 412**	**13 845**	**14 181**
29	Household	9 737	9 927	10 161	10 294	10 443	10 754	11 154	11 450
30	NPISH's	273	275	272	291	298	294	297	313
31	Government	2 519	2 522	2 455	2 434	2 376	2 365	2 396	2 420
32	Individual	1 014	998	976	980	984	993	1 021	..
33	Collective	1 506	1 524	1 479	1 454	1 393	1 367	1 378	..
34	*of which: Actual individual consumption*	11 023	11 200	11 409	11 565	11 724	12 042	12 421	12 722 e
35	**Gross capital formation**	**2 513**	**2 753**	**2 832**	**3 028**	**3 148**	**3 283**	**3 434**	**3 387**
36	Gross fixed capital formation, total	2 661	2 691	2 791	2 966	3 056	3 202	3 316	3 335
37	Dwellings	393	385	385	434	485	500	552	581
38	Other buildings and structures	743	663	651	673	661	705	702	677
39	Transport equipment	110	175	219	252	275	301	327	307
40	Other machinery and equipment	500	519	567	610	613	638	638	622
41	Cultivated assets	..	..	..	..	..	..	..	..
42	Intangible fixed assets	738	752	772	790	808	834	860	907
43	Changes in inventories, acquisitions less disposals of valuables	-156	62	40	58	83	72	106	35
44	Changes in inventories	..	..	..	..	..	..	..	..
45	Acquisitions less disposals of valuables	..	..	..	..	..	..	..	..
46	**External balance of goods and services**	**-443**	**-513**	**-515**	**-503**	**-460**	**-485**	**-610**	**-653**
47	Exports of goods and services	1 655	1 852	1 979	2 047	2 118	2 209	2 218	2 210
48	Exports of goods	1 119	1 280	1 363	1 412	1 455	1 522	1 516	1 520
49	Exports of services	536	573	616	635	663	687	701	691
50	Imports of goods and services	2 098	2 365	2 494	2 550	2 578	2 694	2 827	2 863
51	Imports of goods	1 697	1 950	2 062	2 105	2 130	2 234	2 349	2 370
52	Imports of services	400	415	432	445	448	459	478	493
53	**Statistical discrepancy (including chaining residual)**	**-4**	**0**	**-1**	**-1**	**-1**	**-1**	**3**	**6**
54	**Gross domestic product**	**14 595**	**14 964**	**15 204**	**15 542**	**15 803**	**16 209**	**16 673**	**16 920**

Note: Detailed metadata:http://metalinks.oecd.org/nav1/20180308/4f76

Source: United States Department of Commerce, Bureau of Economic Analysis (BEA).

Table 2. Gross domestic product, output and income approach
ISIC Rev. 4

Billion USD

		2009	2010	2011	2012	2013	2014	2015	2016
	OUTPUT APPROACH AT CURRENT PRICES								
1	**Total gross value added at basic prices**	**13 990**	**14 510**	**15 037**	**15 648**	**16 153**	**16 833**	**17 460**	**..**
2	Agriculture, forestry and fishing	148	170	206	194	230	211	184	..
3	Industry, including energy	2 251	2 417	2 556	2 631	2 726	2 841	2 765	..
4	Manufacturing	1 703	1 806	1 883	1 957	2 006	2 070	2 142	..
5	Construction	577	542	547	584	621	672	732	..
6	Services	..	..	..	..	..	..	..	..
7	Distrib. trade, repairs; transp.; accommod., food serv. activ.	2 183	2 270	2 348	2 473	2 564	2 681	2 838	..
8	Information and communication	852	886	900	931	987	999	1 067	..
9	Financial and insurance activities	950	987	1 018	1 122	1 114	1 227	1 266	..
10	Real estate activities	1 758	1 802	1 867	1 926	1 991	2 070	2 175	..
11	Prof., scientif., techn. activ.; admin., support service activ.	1 587	1 635	1 707	1 795	1 847	1 939	2 068	..
12	Public admin.; compulsory s.s.; education; human health	3 233	3 343	3 423	3 500	3 566	3 662	3 800	..
13	Other service activities	451	459	467	492	506	533	565	..
14	**FISIM (Financial Intermediation Services Indirectly Measured)**	..	..	..	..	..	..	..	..
15	Gross value added at basic prices, excluding FISIM	13 990	14 510	15 037	15 648	16 153	16 833	17 460	..
16	**Taxes less subsidies on products**	**428**	**455**	**481**	**507**	**538**	**560**	**576**	**..**
17	Taxes on products	487	511	541	565	598	617	633	..
18	Subsidies on products	58	56	60	58	59	57	57	..
19	**Residual item**	..	..	..	..	..	..	..	..
20	**Gross domestic product at market prices**	**14 419**	**14 964**	**15 518**	**16 155**	**16 692**	**17 393**	**18 037**	**..**
	OUTPUT APPROACH AT CONSTANT PRICES (REF. YEAR 2010)								
21	**Total gross value added at basic prices**	**14 200**	**14 510**	**14 709**	**14 998**	**15 242**	**15 571**	**15 964**	**..**
22	Agriculture, forestry and fishing	168	170	161	148	177	176	181	..
23	Industry, including energy	2 314	2 417	2 442	2 484	2 544	2 599	2 637	..
24	Manufacturing	1 713	1 806	1 811	1 817	1 855	1 875	1 903	..
25	Construction	567	542	539	559	574	584	613	..
26	Services	..	..	..	..	..	..	..	..
27	Distrib. trade, repairs; transp.; accommod., food serv. activ.	2 198	2 270	2 305	2 352	2 413	2 480	2 549	..
28	Information and communication	845	886	903	933	984	998	1 082	..
29	Financial and insurance activities	987	987	996	1 048	998	1 048	1 043	..
30	Real estate activities	1 748	1 802	1 852	1 872	1 906	1 940	1 976	..
31	Prof., scientif., techn. activ.; admin., support service activ.	1 599	1 635	1 691	1 753	1 780	1 850	1 925	..
32	Public admin.; compulsory s.s.; education; human health	3 317	3 343	3 361	3 382	3 396	3 414	3 472	..
33	Other service activities	459	459	460	471	472	484	495	..
34	**FISIM (Financial Intermediation Services Indirectly Measured)**	..	..	..	..	..	..	..	..
35	Gross value added at basic prices, excluding FISIM	14 200	14 510	14 709	14 998	15 242	15 571	15 964	..
36	**Taxes less subsidies on products**	..	..	..	..	..	..	..	..
37	Taxes on products	..	..	..	..	..	..	..	..
38	Subsidies on products	..	..	..	..	..	..	..	..
39	**Residual item**	..	..	..	..	..	..	..	..
40	**Gross domestic product at market prices**	**14 595**	**14 964**	**15 204**	**15 542**	**15 803**	**16 177**	**16 597**	**..**
	INCOME APPROACH								
41	**Compensation of employees**	**7 796**	**7 969**	**8 277**	**8 619**	**8 852**	**9 267**	**9 720**	**9 992**
42	Agriculture, forestry and fishing	42	41	41	48	48	51	51	54
43	Industry, including energy	989	1 012	1 058	1 102	1 120	1 173	1 200	1 195
44	Manufacturing	836	848	883	918	929	971	1 004	1 012
45	Construction	369	345	349	367	388	423	458	487
46	Distrib. trade, repairs; transp.; accommod., food serv. activ.	1 422	1 444	1 513	1 583	1 629	1 705	1 803	1 852
47	Information and communication	399	405	433	464	484	518	553	575
48	Financial and insurance activities	549	574	607	630	640	680	714	733
49	Real estate activities	76	76	78	84	88	93	102	106
50	Prof., scientif., techn. activ.; admin., support service activ.	1 025	1 059	1 120	1 191	1 240	1 307	1 385	1 415
51	Public admin.; compulsory s.s.; education; human health	2 611	2 700	2 756	2 812	2 867	2 948	3 068	3 173
52	Other service activities	315	312	322	338	348	370	387	402
53	**Wages and salaries**	**6 260**	**6 386**	**6 641**	**6 939**	**7 126**	**7 487**	**7 871**	**8 099**
54	Agriculture, forestry and fishing	34	34	34	39	40	42	42	45
55	Industry, including energy	783	801	847	884	900	944	965	959
56	Manufacturing	661	674	707	734	746	781	807	814
57	Construction	308	286	291	305	323	350	382	408
58	Distrib. trade, repairs; transp.; accommod., food serv. activ.	1 186	1 205	1 260	1 321	1 358	1 430	1 513	1 556
59	Information and communication	330	341	364	394	412	441	474	499
60	Financial and insurance activities	466	486	513	537	546	582	611	626
61	Real estate activities	64	65	68	72	76	81	88	92
62	Prof., scientif., techn. activ.; admin., support service activ.	867	900	953	1 018	1 056	1 119	1 188	1 220
63	Public admin.; compulsory s.s.; education; human health	1 956	2 000	2 035	2 079	2 117	2 180	2 274	2 348
64	Other service activities	266	268	277	289	298	318	333	345
65	**Gross operating surplus and mixed income**	**5 580**	**5 944**	**6 237**	**6 666**	**6 862**	**7 227**	**7 458**	**7 553**
66	**Taxes less subsidies on production and imports**	**968**	**1 001**	**1 043**	**1 074**	**1 116**	**1 164**	**1 199**	**1 226**
67	Taxes on production and imports	1 026	1 057	1 103	1 132	1 175	1 222	1 256	1 288
68	Subsidies on production and imports	58	56	60	58	59	58	57	62
69	**Residual item**	75	49	-38	-203	-138	-230	-256	-147
70	**Gross domestic product**	**14 419**	**14 964**	**15 518**	**16 155**	**16 692**	**17 428**	**18 121**	**18 624**

Note: Detailed metadata:http://metalinks.oecd.org/nav1/20180308/4f76
Source: United States Department of Commerce, Bureau of Economic Analysis (BEA).

Table 3. Disposable income, saving and net lending / net borrowing

Billion USD

		2009	2010	2011	2012	2013	2014	2015	2016
	DISPOSABLE INCOME								
1	**Gross domestic product**	**14 419**	**14 964**	**15 518**	**16 155**	**16 692**	**17 428**	**18 121**	**18 624**
2	Net primary incomes from the rest of the world	151	206	247	238	244	235	205	197
3	Primary incomes receivable from the rest of the world	649	720	793	802	826	847	813	844
4	Primary incomes payable to the rest of the world	498	514	546	564	581	613	608	647
5	**Gross national income at market prices**	**14 494**	**15 121**	**15 803**	**16 596**	**17 074**	**17 892**	**18 581**	**18 969**
6	Consumption of fixed capital	2 368	2 382	2 451	2 534	2 629	2 748	2 842	2 917
7	**Net national income at market prices**	**12 126**	**12 740**	**13 352**	**14 062**	**14 445**	**15 144**	**15 740**	**16 052**
8	Net current transfers from the rest of the world	-138	-139	-148	-140	-138	-109	-131	-137
9	Current transfers receivable from the rest of the world	93	97	105	114	132	145	131	140
10	Current transfers payable to the rest of the world	231	236	253	254	270	254	262	277
11	**Net national disposable income**	**11 989**	**12 600**	**13 204**	**13 922**	**14 306**	**15 035**	**15 609**	**15 915**
	SAVING AND NET LENDING / NET BORROWING								
12	**Net national disposable income**	**11 989**	**12 600**	**13 204**	**13 922**	**14 306**	**15 035**	**15 609**	**15 915**
13	Final consumption expenditures	12 289	12 724	13 220	13 595	13 885	14 426	14 943	15 479
14	Adj. for change in net equity of households in pension funds	..	..	..	..	..	..	..	..
15	**Saving, net**	**-300**	**-124**	**-16**	**327**	**422**	**609**	**665**	**436**
16	Net capital transfers from the rest of the world	-1	-1	-2	7	-1	0	0	0
17	Capital transfers receivable from the rest of the world	0	0	0	8	0	0	0	0
18	Capital transfers payable to the rest of the world	1	1	2	1	1	0	0	0
19	Gross capital formation	2 525	2 753	2 878	3 126	3 299	3 511	3 702	3 667
20	Acquisitions less disposals of non-financial non-produced assets	0	0	0	0	0	0	0	0
21	Consumption of fixed capital	2 368	2 382	2 451	2 534	2 629	2 748	2 842	2 917
22	**Net lending / net borrowing**	**-458**	**-496**	**-445**	**-258**	**-249**	**-154**	**-195**	**-314**
	REAL DISPOSABLE INCOME								
23	**Gross domestic product at constant prices, reference year 2010**	**14 595**	**14 964**	**15 204**	**15 542**	**15 803**	**16 209**	**16 673**	**16 920**
24	Trading gain or loss	-35 e	-49 e	-13 e	155 e	123 e	223 e	355 e	301 e
25	**Real gross domestic income**	**14 560 e**	**14 915 e**	**15 191 e**	**15 697 e**	**15 926 e**	**16 432 e**	**17 028 e**	**17 221 e**
26	Net real primary incomes from the rest of the world	153 e	206 e	241 e	228 e	231 e	218 e	190 e	181 e
27	Real primary incomes receivable from the rest of the world	659 e	720 e	774 e	769 e	781 e	788 e	753 e	775 e
28	Real primary incomes payable to the rest of the world	505 e	514 e	533 e	541 e	550 e	570 e	564 e	594 e
29	**Real gross national income at market prices**	**14 713 e**	**15 121 e**	**15 432 e**	**15 925 e**	**16 157 e**	**16 650 e**	**17 217 e**	**17 402 e**
30	Net real current transfers from the rest of the world	-140 e	-139 e	-145 e	-134 e	-131 e	-101 e	-121 e	-125 e
31	Real current transfers receivable from the rest of the world	95 e	97 e	103 e	110 e	125 e	135 e	122 e	129 e
32	Real current transfers payable to the rest of the world	234 e	236 e	247 e	244 e	256 e	237 e	243 e	254 e
33	**Real gross national disposable income**	**14 573 e**	**14 982 e**	**15 287 e**	**15 791 e**	**16 026 e**	**16 549 e**	**17 096 e**	**17 277 e**
34	Consumption of fixed capital at constant prices	..	..	..	..	..	..	..	..
35	**Real net national income at market prices**	**12 309 e**	**12 740 e**	**13 039 e**	**13 494 e**	**13 669 e**	**14 093 e**	**14 584 e**	**14 726 e**
36	**Real net national disposable income**	**12 169 e**	**12 600 e**	**12 894 e**	**13 359 e**	**13 538 e**	**13 992 e**	**14 463 e**	**14 601 e**

Note: Detailed metadata:http://metalinks.oecd.org/nav1/20180308/c9fe
Source: United States Department of Commerce, Bureau of Economic Analysis (BEA).

Table 4. Population and employment (persons) and employment (hours worked) by industry
ISIC Rev. 4

		2009	2010	2011	2012	2013	2014	2015	2016
	POPULATION, THOUSAND PERSONS, NATIONAL CONCEPT								
1	**Total population**	307 240.0	309 801.0	312 114.0	314 377.0	316 569.0	318 887.0	321 173.0	323 391.0
2	Economically active population	156 448.0	156 211.0	155 930.0	157 256.0	..	..	..	..
3	Unemployed persons	14 265.0	14 825.0	13 747.0	12 506.0				
4	Total employment	142 183.0	141 386.0	142 183.0	144 750.0	146 187.0	148 507.0	151 006.0	153 588.0
5	Employees	132 354.0	131 705.0	132 734.0	135 221.0	136 777.0	139 149.0	141 498.0	143 984.0
6	Self-employed	9 829.0	9 681.0	9 449.0	9 529.0	9 408.0	9 358.0	9 508.0	9 604.0
	TOTAL EMPLOYMENT, THOUSAND PERSONS, DOMESTIC CONCEPT								
7	Agriculture, forestry and fishing	2 103.0	2 206.0	2 254.0	2 186.0	2 130.0	2 237.0	2 422.0	2 459.0
8	Industry, including energy	16 576.0	16 543.0	16 865.0	17 351.0	17 657.0	17 937.0	18 074.0	18 098.0
9	Manufacturing	14 202.0	14 081.0	14 336.0	14 686.0	14 870.0	15 102.0	15 337.0	15 410.0
10	Construction	9 702.0	9 077.0	9 039.0	8 964.0	9 271.0	9 813.0	9 935.0	10 328.0
11	Distrib. trade, repairs; transp.; accommod., food serv. activ.	35 414.0	35 183.0	35 457.0	36 129.0	36 229.0	37 036.0	37 418.0	37 864.0
12	Information and communication	5 099.0	5 054.0	5 085.0	5 063.0	5 269.0	5 459.0	5 528.0	5 699.0
13	Financial and insurance activities	6 826.0	6 605.0	6 613.0	6 786.0	6 984.0	6 958.0	7 081.0	7 241.0
14	Real estate activities	2 350.0	2 336.0	2 384.0	2 409.0	2 483.0	2 549.0	2 617.0	2 764.0
15	Prof., scientif., techn. activ.; admin., support service activ.	13 159.0	13 277.0	13 803.0	14 325.0	14 328.0	14 485.0	14 700.0	15 300.0
16	Public admin.; compulsory s.s.; education; human health	41 001.0	41 367.0	41 034.0	41 348.0	41 502.0	41 788.0	42 777.0	43 272.0
17	Other service activities	9 953.0	9 735.0	9 646.0	10 190.0	10 332.0	10 251.0	10 448.0	10 561.0
18	**Total employment**	142 183.0	141 386.0	142 183.0	144 750.0	146 185.0	148 513.0	151 000.0	153 586.0
	EMPLOYEES, THOUSAND PERSONS, DOMESTIC CONCEPT								
19	Agriculture, forestry and fishing	1 267.0	1 385.0	1 408.0	1 410.0	1 341.0	1 480.0	1 579.0	1 607.0
20	Industry, including energy	16 223.0	16 204.0	16 547.0	16 998.0	17 341.0	17 614.0	17 749.0	17 784.0
21	Manufacturing	13 881.0	13 781.0	14 060.0	14 378.0	14 597.0	14 823.0	15 051.0	15 143.0
22	Construction	8 001.0	7 378.0	7 454.0	7 446.0	7 752.0	8 218.0	8 324.0	8 700.0
23	Distrib. trade, repairs; transp.; accommod., food serv. activ.	33 814.0	33 629.0	33 914.0	34 652.0	34 833.0	35 601.0	35 893.0	36 341.0
24	Information and communication	4 817.0	4 777.0	4 849.0	4 800.0	5 015.0	5 220.0	5 257.0	5 438.0
25	Financial and insurance activities	6 564.0	6 364.0	6 389.0	6 549.0	6 763.0	6 739.0	6 850.0	6 988.0
26	Real estate activities	1 959.0	1 953.0	2 003.0	2 010.0	2 053.0	2 148.0	2 231.0	2 338.0
27	Prof., scientif., techn. activ.; admin., support service activ.	11 300.0	11 418.0	11 920.0	12 344.0	12 417.0	12 625.0	12 884.0	13 392.0
28	Public admin.; compulsory s.s.; education; human health	39 899.0	40 267.0	39 958.0	40 248.0	40 430.0	40 714.0	41 708.0	42 234.0
29	Other service activities	8 510.0	8 327.0	8 289.0	8 765.0	8 832.0	8 796.0	9 017.0	9 160.0
30	**Total employees**	132 354.0	131 705.0	132 734.0	135 221.0	136 777.0	139 155.0	141 492.0	143 982.0
	SELF-EMPLOYED, THOUSAND PERSONS, DOMESTIC CONCEPT								
31	Agriculture, forestry and fishing	836.0	821.0	846.0	776.0	789.0	757.0	843.0	852.0
32	Industry, including energy	353.0	339.0	318.0	353.0	316.0	323.0	325.0	314.0
33	Manufacturing	321.0	300.0	276.0	308.0	273.0	279.0	286.0	267.0
34	Construction	1 701.0	1 699.0	1 585.0	1 518.0	1 519.0	1 595.0	1 611.0	1 628.0
35	Distrib. trade, repairs; transp.; accommod., food serv. activ.	1 600.0	1 554.0	1 543.0	1 477.0	1 396.0	1 435.0	1 525.0	1 523.0
36	Information and communication	282.0	277.0	236.0	263.0	254.0	239.0	271.0	261.0
37	Financial and insurance activities	262.0	241.0	224.0	237.0	221.0	219.0	231.0	253.0
38	Real estate activities	391.0	383.0	381.0	399.0	430.0	401.0	386.0	426.0
39	Prof., scientif., techn. activ.; admin., support service activ.	1 859.0	1 859.0	1 883.0	1 981.0	1 911.0	1 860.0	1 816.0	1 908.0
40	Public admin.; compulsory s.s.; education; human health	1 102.0	1 100.0	1 076.0	1 100.0	1 072.0	1 074.0	1 069.0	1 038.0
41	Other service activities	1 443.0	1 408.0	1 357.0	1 425.0	1 500.0	1 455.0	1 431.0	1 401.0
42	**Total self-employed**	9 829.0	9 681.0	9 449.0	9 529.0	9 408.0	9 358.0	9 508.0	9 604.0
	TOTAL EMPLOYMENT, MILLION HOURS, DOMESTIC CONCEPT								
43	Industry, including energy	..	..	..	..	..	..	..	..
44	Distrib. trade, repairs; transp.; accommod., food serv. activ.	..	..	..	..	..	..	..	..
45	Financial and insurance activities	..	..	..	..	..	..	..	..
46	Prof., scientif., techn. activ.; admin., support service activ.	..	..	..	..	..	..	..	..
47	Public admin.; compulsory s.s.; education; human health	..	..	..	..	..	..	..	..
48	**Total employment**	242 270.0	241 652.0	245 009.0	249 863.0	253 492.0	258 564.0	264 041.0	267 472.0
	EMPLOYEES, MILLION HOURS, DOMESTIC CONCEPT								
49	Industry, including energy	25 856.0	25 910.0	26 740.0	27 354.0	27 637.0	28 210.0	28 152.0	27 846.0
50	Distrib. trade, repairs; transp.; accommod., food serv. activ.	56 493.0	56 362.0	57 815.0	59 246.0	60 172.0	61 527.0	63 127.0	63 958.0
51	Financial and insurance activities	10 428.0	10 353.0	10 519.0	10 691.0	10 693.0	10 793.0	11 112.0	11 270.0
52	Prof., scientif., techn. activ.; admin., support service activ.	26 010.0	26 405.0	27 295.0	28 106.0	29 097.0	30 147.0	30 910.0	31 549.0
53	Public admin.; compulsory s.s.; education; human health	67 517.0	68 163.0	68 202.0	69 089.0	69 748.0	70 229.0	71 354.0	72 361.0
54	**Total employees**	224 396.0	224 146.0	227 832.0	232 440.0	236 410.0	241 427.0	246 408.0	249 735.0
	SELF-EMPLOYED, MILLION HOURS, DOMESTIC CONCEPT								
55	Industry, including energy	..	..	..	..	..	..	..	..
56	Distrib. trade, repairs; transp.; accommod., food serv. activ.	..	..	..	..	..	..	..	..
57	Financial and insurance activities	..	..	..	..	..	..	..	..
58	Prof., scientif., techn. activ.; admin., support service activ.	..	..	..	..	..	..	..	..
59	Public admin.; compulsory s.s.; education; human health	..	..	..	..	..	..	..	..
60	**Total self-employed**	17 874.0	17 506.0	17 177.0	17 423.0	17 191.0	17 137.0	17 633.0	17 737.0

Note: Detailed metadata:http://metalinks.oecd.org/nav1/20180308/c35d
Source: United States Department of Commerce, Bureau of Economic Analysis (BEA).

EURO AREA

Table 1. Gross domestic product, expenditure approach

Million EUR

		2009	2010	2011	2012	2013	2014	2015	2016
	AT CURRENT PRICES								
1	**Final consumption expenditure**	**7 264 461**	**7 417 177**	**7 552 564**	**7 600 682**	**7 655 870**	**7 762 965**	**7 923 186**	**8 110 419**
2	Household	5 125 939	5 245 608	5 362 094	5 397 694	5 411 593	5 480 832	5 597 412	5 730 341
3	NPISH's	126 560	131 044	135 474	139 109	148 537	153 077	156 852	161 232
4	Government	2 011 962	2 040 525	2 054 996	2 063 877	2 095 739	2 129 055	2 168 925	2 218 846
5	Individual	1 242 198	1 264 936	1 274 691	1 280 122	1 300 212	1 330 329	1 363 154	1 397 408
6	Collective	769 764	775 590	780 305	783 756	795 527	798 729	805 773	821 441
7	*of which:* Actual individual consumption	6 494 698	6 641 587	6 772 259	6 816 924	6 860 342	6 964 239	7 117 419	7 288 982
8	**Gross capital formation**	**1 891 409**	**2 001 293**	**2 109 027**	**1 973 913**	**1 947 171**	**2 023 659**	**2 107 138**	**2 199 566**
9	Gross fixed capital formation, total	1 961 329	1 973 429	2 035 737	1 989 614	1 947 447	1 997 129	2 078 118	2 189 269
10	Dwellings	539 703	529 104	530 825	515 599	500 962	510 045	515 997	546 052
11	Other buildings and structures	537 955	516 509	537 012	515 859	500 419	496 456	500 209	505 728
12	Transport equipment	143 654	160 811	167 907	154 874	148 975	162 636	175 476	193 806
13	Other machinery and equipment	348 118	359 213	374 694	366 201	356 824	368 120	385 231	400 377
14	Cultivated assets	4 649	4 378	4 470	4 775	5 153	5 307	5 574	5 470
15	Intangible fixed assets	324 352	337 933	350 883	362 588	369 126	385 575	418 426	457 744
16	Changes in inventories, acquisitions less disposals of valuables	-69 920	27 864	73 290	-15 701	-275	26 531	29 020	10 297
17	Changes in inventories	..	..	..	..	..	..	..	..
18	Acquisitions less disposals of valuables	..	..	..	..	..	..	..	..
19	**External balance of goods and services**	**135 639**	**129 114**	**138 293**	**262 831**	**331 758**	**370 974**	**484 815**	**478 833**
20	Exports of goods and services	3 247 202	3 728 339	4 111 478	4 301 904	4 370 066	4 541 734	4 846 967	4 936 031
21	Exports of goods	2 427 920	2 837 915	3 159 010	3 283 039	3 308 632	3 388 897	3 591 342	3 637 437
22	Exports of services	819 282	890 424	952 469	1 018 866	1 061 434	1 152 837	1 255 625	1 298 594
23	Imports of goods and services	3 111 563	3 599 225	3 973 186	4 039 073	4 038 308	4 170 760	4 362 152	4 457 198
24	Imports of goods	2 326 659	2 745 191	3 073 345	3 085 346	3 042 614	3 090 381	3 163 693	3 192 168
25	Imports of services	784 904	854 033	899 840	953 728	995 694	1 080 378	1 198 459	1 265 030
26	**Statistical discrepancy**	..	..	..	..	..	..	..	..
27	**Gross domestic product**	**9 291 509**	**9 547 584**	**9 799 884**	**9 837 426**	**9 934 799**	**10 157 598**	**10 515 139**	**10 788 818**
	AT CONSTANT PRICES, REFERENCE YEAR 2010								
28	**Final consumption expenditure**	**7 360 398**	**7 417 177**	**7 412 236**	**7 343 659**	**7 316 554**	**7 375 784**	**7 500 324**	**7 647 782**
29	Household	5 206 719	5 245 608	5 241 383	5 178 280	5 137 953	5 179 904	5 274 351	5 381 907
30	NPISH's	128 177	131 044	132 222	133 805	140 638	143 395	146 067	149 396
31	Government	2 025 503	2 040 525	2 038 628	2 031 744	2 038 513	2 052 986	2 080 270	2 116 763
32	Individual	1 251 293	1 264 936	1 269 002	1 266 200	1 269 753	1 286 431	1 310 440	1 335 643
33	Collective	774 204	775 590	769 621	765 548	768 757	766 633	769 963	781 280
34	*of which:* Actual individual consumption	6 586 159	6 641 587	6 642 606	6 578 117	6 547 875	6 609 127	6 730 234	6 866 339
35	**Gross capital formation**	**1 922 372**	**2 001 293**	**2 074 401**	**1 917 293**	**1 886 460**	**1 948 580**	**2 014 444**	**2 090 023**
36	Gross fixed capital formation, total	1 980 036	1 973 429	2 003 069	1 934 485	1 886 090	1 920 998	1 983 550	2 073 763
37	Dwellings	542 731	529 104	522 924	503 506	487 194	489 294	489 667	510 520
38	Other buildings and structures	545 413	516 509	520 775	491 896	473 426	467 179	471 230	474 136
39	Transport equipment	145 157	160 811	166 190	151 987	146 707	159 158	169 569	185 999
40	Other machinery and equipment	350 458	359 213	370 700	357 150	348 411	357 110	370 028	384 284
41	Cultivated assets	4 802	4 378	4 403	4 503	4 589	4 596	4 850	4 755
42	Intangible fixed assets	329 645	337 933	346 597	354 903	358 024	371 761	398 981	432 010
43	Changes in inventories, acquisitions less disposals of valuables	..	..	..	..	..	..	..	..
44	Changes in inventories	..	..	..	..	..	..	..	..
45	Acquisitions less disposals of valuables	..	..	..	..	..	..	..	..
46	**External balance of goods and services**	**73 974**	**129 114**	**214 251**	**351 389**	**386 985**	**396 847**	**410 013**	**365 082**
47	Exports of goods and services	3 349 665	3 728 339	3 972 237	4 072 922	4 158 361	4 352 663	4 629 770	4 784 722
48	Exports of goods	2 510 693	2 837 915	3 036 724	3 094 513	3 147 864	3 264 303	3 460 161	3 572 181
49	Exports of services	838 574	890 424	935 513	978 826	1 011 145	1 089 077	1 170 142	1 212 967
50	Imports of goods and services	3 275 691	3 599 225	3 757 986	3 721 532	3 771 376	3 955 816	4 219 757	4 419 640
51	Imports of goods	2 469 551	2 745 191	2 877 852	2 815 436	2 833 689	2 949 565	3 125 733	3 263 946
52	Imports of services	805 172	854 033	880 134	907 634	940 078	1 009 072	1 096 592	1 157 655
53	**Statistical discrepancy (including chaining residual)**	**-3 893**	**0**	**0**	**2 573**	**1 800**	**-1 201**	**-3 492**	**-1 931**
54	**Gross domestic product**	**9 352 851**	**9 547 584**	**9 700 888**	**9 614 914**	**9 591 799**	**9 720 010**	**9 921 288**	**10 100 956**

Note: Detailed metadata:http://metalinks.oecd.org/nav1/20180308/59b6
Source: Statistical Office of the European Communities (Eurostat).

EURO AREA

Table 2. Gross domestic product, output and income approach
ISIC Rev. 4

Million EUR

		2009	2010	2011	2012	2013	2014	2015	2016
	OUTPUT APPROACH AT CURRENT PRICES								
1	**Total gross value added at basic prices**	8 389 775	8 593 479	8 809 934	8 843 213	8 929 292	9 123 025	9 443 181	9 680 305
2	Agriculture, forestry and fishing	128 151	140 790	147 701	148 882	156 095	152 032	153 819	151 379
3	Industry, including energy	1 557 302	1 660 941	1 725 546	1 732 551	1 738 987	1 782 543	1 899 930	1 936 550
4	Manufacturing	1 276 944	1 375 199	1 440 669	1 430 590	1 438 529	1 491 873	1 614 181	1 651 178
5	Construction	512 574	488 916	485 910	471 588	460 296	461 581	468 700	489 303
6	Services	..	..	..	..	..	..	..	..
7	Distrib. trade, repairs; transp.; accommod., food serv. activ.	1 608 600	1 627 063	1 670 650	1 664 913	1 672 502	1 720 169	1 782 677	1 831 171
8	Information and communication	398 237	397 438	406 523	408 627	408 860	418 425	433 147	451 333
9	Financial and insurance activities	433 653	447 353	438 506	445 303	444 919	458 040	464 229	454 036
10	Real estate activities	945 280	966 381	1 003 676	1 015 024	1 038 539	1 050 124	1 072 979	1 100 180
11	Prof., scientif., techn. activ.; admin., support service activ.	862 985	885 749	919 681	927 273	944 490	980 763	1 025 709	1 070 650
12	Public admin.; compulsory s.s.; education; human health	1 642 055	1 673 313	1 701 589	1 717 319	1 747 971	1 777 365	1 811 417	1 857 572
13	Other service activities	300 939	305 536	310 151	311 732	316 633	321 984	330 576	338 132
14	**FISIM (Financial Intermediation Services Indirectly Measured)**	..	..	..	..	..	..	..	..
15	**Gross value added at basic prices, excluding FISIM**	8 389 775	8 593 479	8 809 934	8 843 213	8 929 292	9 123 025	9 443 181	9 680 305
16	**Taxes less subsidies on products**	901 733	954 104	989 950	994 213	1 005 507	1 034 574	1 071 958	1 108 513
17	Taxes on products	..	..	..	..	..	..	..	..
18	Subsidies on products	..	..	..	..	..	..	..	..
19	**Residual item**	..	..	..	..	..	..	..	..
20	**Gross domestic product at market prices**	9 291 509	9 547 584	9 799 884	9 837 426	9 934 799	10 157 598	10 515 139	10 788 818
	OUTPUT APPROACH AT CONSTANT PRICES (REF. YEAR 2010)								
21	**Total gross value added at basic prices**	8 416 550	8 593 479	8 738 838	8 677 221	8 666 343	8 782 844	8 951 712	9 101 704
22	Agriculture, forestry and fishing	145 515	140 790	143 070	136 990	140 702	143 127	147 493	145 567
23	Industry, including energy	1 534 984	1 660 941	1 713 351	1 691 447	1 679 898	1 725 603	1 794 186	1 829 720
24	Manufacturing	1 255 100	1 375 199	1 442 683	1 408 980	1 405 017	1 456 766	1 527 011	1 559 876
25	Construction	510 417	488 916	473 776	450 276	433 672	429 237	430 972	437 781
26	Services	..	..	..	..	..	..	..	..
27	Distrib. trade, repairs; transp.; accommod., food serv. activ.	1 608 043	1 627 063	1 659 629	1 649 901	1 635 220	1 662 234	1 689 995	1 721 823
28	Information and communication	390 513	397 438	415 665	425 578	432 305	450 790	465 914	479 782
29	Financial and insurance activities	438 936	447 353	454 097	451 866	453 503	445 006	444 458	446 409
30	Real estate activities	961 577	966 381	981 305	984 599	1 000 044	1 004 318	1 011 812	1 021 281
31	Prof., scientif., techn. activ.; admin., support service activ.	868 119	885 749	904 975	898 233	900 942	924 973	951 234	978 782
32	Public admin.; compulsory s.s.; education; human health	1 655 688	1 673 313	1 687 776	1 687 119	1 691 035	1 698 878	1 714 910	1 737 572
33	Other service activities	305 333	305 536	305 194	301 962	300 159	300 373	303 546	306 316
34	**FISIM (Financial Intermediation Services Indirectly Measured)**	..	..	..	..	..	..	..	..
35	**Gross value added at basic prices, excluding FISIM**	8 416 550	8 593 479	8 738 838	8 677 221	8 666 343	8 782 844	8 951 712	9 101 704
36	**Taxes less subsidies on products**	936 359	954 104	962 050	938 014	926 160	937 913	969 581	998 702
37	Taxes on products	..	..	..	..	..	..	..	..
38	Subsidies on products	..	..	..	..	..	..	..	..
39	**Residual item**	-58	0	0	-321	-704	-747	-5	551
40	**Gross domestic product at market prices**	9 352 851	9 547 584	9 700 888	9 614 914	9 591 799	9 720 010	9 921 288	10 100 956
	INCOME APPROACH								
41	**Compensation of employees**	4 505 198	4 568 970	4 670 349	4 715 451	4 758 669	4 858 497	4 989 864	5 133 973
42	Agriculture, forestry and fishing	34 864	36 133	37 271	37 426	38 257	39 421	40 412	41 261
43	Industry, including energy	897 414	906 120	934 246	945 077	957 588	974 942	996 054	1 016 745
44	Manufacturing	805 642	812 799	839 191	847 062	857 933	875 020	894 145	914 045
45	Construction	292 221	282 813	279 088	270 204	261 926	262 011	265 419	270 404
46	Distrib. trade, repairs; transp.; accommod., food serv. activ.	904 547	918 423	938 084	949 997	950 708	970 818	1 003 111	1 039 445
47	Information and communication	190 453	193 005	198 775	204 295	207 287	213 209	222 878	231 130
48	Financial and insurance activities	230 316	230 146	233 360	234 716	235 328	237 220	237 820	242 613
49	Real estate activities	40 060	40 582	41 860	42 376	42 185	42 990	44 072	46 577
50	Prof., scientif., techn. activ.; admin., support service activ.	469 734	489 750	517 247	530 167	538 762	562 682	591 010	616 234
51	Public admin.; compulsory s.s.; education; human health	1 260 329	1 283 749	1 300 158	1 308 440	1 331 779	1 356 957	1 385 978	1 421 577
52	Other service activities	185 262	188 248	190 259	192 753	194 849	198 248	203 110	207 988
53	**Wages and salaries**	3 498 880	3 547 132	3 619 387	3 653 919	3 686 711	3 763 321	3 877 780	3 998 796
54	Agriculture, forestry and fishing	27 903	28 898	29 730	29 651	30 189	31 068	31 978	32 682
55	Industry, including energy	695 102	703 733	728 707	739 461	748 373	762 509	780 970	797 952
56	Manufacturing	626 635	633 831	657 680	666 690	674 076	687 225	704 860	720 872
57	Construction	232 555	225 016	221 874	215 457	209 091	209 165	212 639	217 342
58	Distrib. trade, repairs; transp.; accommod., food serv. activ.	722 349	731 928	746 880	756 665	756 564	772 959	801 980	830 797
59	Information and communication	148 587	150 682	154 572	158 785	161 039	166 240	173 870	181 568
60	Financial and insurance activities	174 031	174 797	174 716	175 865	175 491	176 117	177 432	180 225
61	Real estate activities	31 921	32 172	33 176	33 494	33 554	34 040	35 079	37 023
62	Prof., scientif., techn. activ.; admin., support service activ.	369 721	384 964	405 597	414 841	423 624	441 613	466 424	490 579
63	Public admin.; compulsory s.s.; education; human health	944 775	960 887	968 458	971 997	989 073	1 007 388	1 030 997	1 059 718
64	Other service activities	151 936	154 056	155 676	157 703	159 713	162 223	166 411	170 910
65	**Gross operating surplus and mixed income**	3 808 406	3 950 786	4 053 142	4 009 599	4 046 917	4 138 730	4 327 201	4 435 310
66	**Taxes less subsidies on production and imports**	977 905	1 027 828	1 076 392	1 112 375	1 129 213	1 160 372	1 198 074	1 219 535
67	Taxes on production and imports	..	..	..	..	..	..	..	..
68	Subsidies on production and imports	..	..	..	..	..	..	..	..
69	**Residual item**	..	..	..	..	..	..	..	..
70	**Gross domestic product**	9 291 509	9 547 584	9 799 884	9 837 426	9 934 799	10 157 598	10 515 139	10 788 818

Note: Detailed metadata:http://metalinks.oecd.org/nav1/20180308/59b6
Source: Statistical Office of the European Communities (Eurostat).

Table 3. Disposable income, saving and net lending / net borrowing

Million EUR

		2009	2010	2011	2012	2013	2014	2015	2016
	DISPOSABLE INCOME								
1	**Gross domestic product**	**9 283 778**	**9 528 825**	**9 782 693**	**9 816 104**	**9 927 384**	**10 151 029**	**10 499 442**	**10 772 870**
2	Net primary incomes from the rest of the world	..	..	..	..	..	..	..	..
3	Primary incomes receivable from the rest of the world	461 435	531 583	606 686	611 109	609 754	637 104	..	..
4	Primary incomes payable to the rest of the world	455 987	496 433	560 287	544 838	527 636	571 731	..	..
5	**Gross national income at market prices**	**9 283 183**	**9 558 552**	**9 823 504**	**9 876 906**	**10 009 580**	**10 216 279**	**10 547 440**	**10 865 421**
6	Consumption of fixed capital	1 632 497	1 672 779	1 723 374	1 765 894	1 787 080	1 815 087	1 875 293	1 921 064
7	**Net national income at market prices**	**7 650 686**	**7 885 773**	**8 100 129**	**8 111 012**	**8 222 499**	**8 401 193**	**8 672 147**	**8 944 357**
8	Net current transfers from the rest of the world	..	..	..	..	..	..	..	..
9	Current transfers receivable from the rest of the world	64 424	70 215	81 011	82 510	86 904	96 317	109 324	109 723
10	Current transfers payable to the rest of the world	191 577	203 810	212 261	218 693	231 321	238 391	246 823	248 641
11	**Net national disposable income**	**7 523 532**	**7 752 179**	**7 968 880**	**7 974 828**	**8 078 083**	**8 259 119**	**8 534 649**	**8 805 439**
	SAVING AND NET LENDING / NET BORROWING								
12	**Net national disposable income**	**7 523 532**	**7 752 179**	**7 968 880**	**7 974 828**	**8 078 083**	**8 259 119**	**8 534 649**	**8 805 439**
13	Final consumption expenditures	7 293 320	7 444 275	7 585 298	7 629 574	7 680 628	7 787 741	7 949 387	8 137 744
14	Adj. for change in net equity of households in pension funds	1	0	2	2	1	0	14	13
15	**Saving, net**	**230 213**	**307 905**	**383 584**	**345 257**	**397 456**	**471 378**	**585 276**	**667 708**
16	Net capital transfers from the rest of the world	..	..	..	..	..	..	..	..
17	Capital transfers receivable from the rest of the world	20 611	21 020	23 678	26 355	28 677	27 391	31 801	15 245
18	Capital transfers payable to the rest of the world	10 234	11 694	9 673	11 148	10 047	9 282	11 314	11 493
19	Gross capital formation	1 916 359	2 022 232	2 132 393	1 998 446	1 967 874	2 043 848	2 129 478	2 221 543
20	Acquisitions less disposals of non-financial non-produced assets	-1 875	-2 921	-595	5 972	-735	4 398	32 954	4 565
21	Consumption of fixed capital	1 632 497	1 672 779	1 723 374	1 765 894	1 787 080	1 815 087	1 875 293	1 921 064
22	**Net lending / net borrowing**	**-41 397**	**-29 302**	**-10 835**	**121 940**	**236 027**	**256 328**	**318 624**	**366 417**
	REAL DISPOSABLE INCOME								
23	**Gross domestic product at constant prices, reference year 2010**	**9 334 734**	**9 529 090**	**9 682 098**	**9 596 290**	**9 573 220**	**9 701 182**	**9 902 071**	**10 081 390**
24	Trading gain or loss	..	..	..	..	..	..	..	..
25	**Real gross domestic income**	**9 412 610**	**9 528 825**	**9 605 546**	**9 494 793**	**9 514 194**	**9 671 383**	**9 959 232**	**10 174 156**
26	Net real primary incomes from the rest of the world	5 523	35 151	45 559	64 102	78 699	62 284	..	..
27	Real primary incomes receivable from the rest of the world	467 838	531 583	595 700	591 105	584 375	607 001	..	..
28	Real primary incomes payable to the rest of the world	462 315	496 433	550 141	527 003	505 676	544 717	..	..
29	**Real gross national income at market prices**	**9 412 006**	**9 558 552**	**9 645 618**	**9 553 605**	**9 592 968**	**9 733 550**	**10 004 760**	**10 261 564**
30	Net real current transfers from the rest of the world	-128 918	-133 594	-128 873	-131 726	-138 406	-135 360	-130 424	-131 197
31	Real current transfers receivable from the rest of the world	65 318	70 215	79 544	79 809	83 287	91 766	103 699	103 625
32	Real current transfers payable to the rest of the world	194 236	203 810	208 417	211 535	221 693	227 127	234 123	234 822
33	**Real gross national disposable income**	**9 283 088**	**9 424 958**	**9 516 745**	**9 421 879**	**9 454 562**	**9 598 190**	**9 874 337**	**10 130 367**
34	Consumption of fixed capital at constant prices	..	..	..	..	..	..	..	..
35	**Real net national income at market prices**	**7 756 855**	**7 885 773**	**7 953 451**	**7 845 514**	**7 880 268**	**8 004 228**	**8 225 954**	**8 447 265**
36	**Real net national disposable income**	**7 627 937**	**7 752 179**	**7 824 578**	**7 713 788**	**7 741 862**	**7 868 868**	**8 095 530**	**8 316 068**

Note: Detailed metadata:http://metalinks.oecd.org/nav1/20180308/df2c
Source: Statistical Office of the European Communities (Eurostat).

Table 4. Population and employment (persons) and employment (hours worked) by industry
ISIC Rev. 4

		2009	2010	2011	2012	2013	2014	2015	2016
	POPULATION, THOUSAND PERSONS, NATIONAL CONCEPT								
1	**Total population**	334 120.3	334 894.0	335 722.4	336 580.7	337 297.9	338 035.7	339 049.6	340 291.4
2	Economically active population	..	..	..	..	..	..	..	..
3	Unemployed persons	..	..	..	..	..	..	..	..
4	Total employment	..	..	..	..	..	..	..	..
5	Employees	..	..	..	..	..	..	..	..
6	Self-employed	..	..	..	..	..	..	..	..
	TOTAL EMPLOYMENT, THOUSAND PERSONS, DOMESTIC CONCEPT								
7	Agriculture, forestry and fishing	5 376.0	5 303.5	5 189.5	5 129.4	5 039.0	5 041.9	4 981.0	4 958.4
8	Industry, including energy	23 878.7	23 163.7	23 127.2	22 936.8	22 631.5	22 544.5	22 596.1	22 732.0
9	Manufacturing	21 962.5	21 232.5	21 199.9	21 001.9	20 700.1	20 620.9	20 676.1	20 816.8
10	Construction	10 868.5	10 387.8	10 031.5	9 596.8	9 253.1	9 130.5	9 132.1	9 111.8
11	Distrib. trade, repairs; transp.; accommod., food serv. activ.	37 289.0	37 132.6	37 316.1	37 110.5	36 782.9	37 042.2	37 514.3	38 163.3
12	Information and communication	4 005.4	3 949.4	3 993.9	4 032.5	4 047.7	4 074.4	4 132.6	4 230.0
13	Financial and insurance activities	4 174.5	4 122.7	4 081.2	4 066.8	4 014.8	3 976.9	3 967.5	3 967.9
14	Real estate activities	1 496.2	1 490.7	1 503.5	1 504.3	1 484.0	1 487.4	1 508.5	1 537.1
15	Prof., scientif., techn. activ.; admin., support service activ.	18 061.6	18 389.0	18 894.1	19 045.5	19 130.2	19 568.5	20 110.1	20 680.4
16	Public admin.; compulsory s.s.; education; human health	35 536.1	35 891.3	35 901.7	35 896.9	36 012.5	36 363.4	36 741.6	37 208.8
17	Other service activities	10 462.9	10 475.2	10 481.0	10 543.4	10 562.9	10 633.0	10 689.1	10 803.6
18	**Total employment**	151 148.9	150 306.0	150 519.7	149 862.8	148 958.5	149 862.8	151 373.0	153 393.3
	EMPLOYEES, THOUSAND PERSONS, DOMESTIC CONCEPT								
19	Agriculture, forestry and fishing	2 023.3	2 058.3	2 050.9	2 053.0	2 046.5	2 104.4	2 139.7	2 174.3
20	Industry, including energy	22 326.3	21 683.6	21 665.9	21 504.5	21 230.0	21 166.6	21 231.0	21 377.0
21	Manufacturing	20 453.2	19 793.6	19 778.6	19 612.5	19 341.0	19 284.4	19 353.8	19 502.3
22	Construction	8 499.7	8 055.0	7 730.7	7 307.4	6 989.3	6 879.0	6 908.3	6 936.2
23	Distrib. trade, repairs; transp.; accommod., food serv. activ.	30 435.3	30 379.2	30 603.0	30 455.6	30 196.7	30 470.5	31 003.0	31 661.0
24	Information and communication	3 555.4	3 497.8	3 523.0	3 556.5	3 581.5	3 604.9	3 665.8	3 776.8
25	Financial and insurance activities	3 787.9	3 739.1	3 697.6	3 682.0	3 636.3	3 592.3	3 576.1	3 570.6
26	Real estate activities	1 178.2	1 168.2	1 182.6	1 187.0	1 181.7	1 182.2	1 195.7	1 223.5
27	Prof., scientif., techn. activ.; admin., support service activ.	14 299.8	14 554.8	14 939.6	15 022.2	15 067.6	15 474.5	15 990.9	16 539.7
28	Public admin.; compulsory s.s.; education; human health	33 562.7	33 877.0	33 852.5	33 807.6	33 900.0	34 171.8	34 481.3	34 935.5
29	Other service activities	8 758.3	8 733.1	8 713.6	8 722.1	8 728.0	8 791.9	8 834.4	8 908.9
30	**Total employees**	128 426.9	127 746.2	127 959.5	127 297.8	126 557.7	127 438.2	129 026.2	131 103.6
	SELF-EMPLOYED, THOUSAND PERSONS, DOMESTIC CONCEPT								
31	Agriculture, forestry and fishing	3 352.7	3 245.3	3 138.7	3 076.3	2 992.5	2 937.5	2 841.3	2 784.1
32	Industry, including energy	1 552.4	1 480.1	1 461.2	1 432.4	1 401.5	1 377.9	1 365.2	1 355.0
33	Manufacturing	1 509.3	1 438.9	1 421.2	1 389.4	1 359.0	1 336.5	1 322.3	1 314.4
34	Construction	2 368.7	2 332.8	2 300.8	2 289.4	2 263.8	2 251.5	2 223.8	2 175.6
35	Distrib. trade, repairs; transp.; accommod., food serv. activ.	6 853.7	6 753.4	6 713.0	6 654.9	6 586.2	6 571.6	6 511.4	6 502.3
36	Information and communication	450.0	451.6	470.8	476.1	466.1	469.5	466.8	453.2
37	Financial and insurance activities	386.6	383.5	383.6	384.8	378.5	384.6	391.4	397.4
38	Real estate activities	318.0	322.5	320.9	317.2	302.2	305.2	312.8	313.6
39	Prof., scientif., techn. activ.; admin., support service activ.	3 761.8	3 834.2	3 954.6	4 023.4	4 062.6	4 094.0	4 119.2	4 140.6
40	Public admin.; compulsory s.s.; education; human health	1 973.5	2 014.3	2 049.2	2 089.3	2 112.5	2 191.6	2 260.3	2 273.3
41	Other service activities	1 704.6	1 742.1	1 767.3	1 821.3	1 834.9	1 841.2	1 854.6	1 894.7
42	**Total self-employed**	22 722.0	22 559.7	22 560.2	22 564.9	22 400.8	22 424.6	22 346.8	22 289.7
	TOTAL EMPLOYMENT, MILLION HOURS, DOMESTIC CONCEPT								
43	Industry, including energy	38 185.2	37 778.2	37 960.1	37 104.6	36 560.9	36 535.1	36 743.7	36 996.2
44	Distrib. trade, repairs; transp.; accommod., food serv. activ.	62 356.8	62 044.3	62 027.5	61 000.0	60 004.6	60 234.3	60 768.6	61 719.1
45	Financial and insurance activities	6 762.9	6 681.2	6 629.8	6 577.8	6 457.5	6 392.0	6 382.7	6 422.1
46	Prof., scientif., techn. activ.; admin., support service activ.	28 151.5	28 792.2	29 572.6	29 442.8	29 271.2	29 965.2	30 829.0	31 704.9
47	Public admin.; compulsory s.s.; education; human health	51 055.2	51 366.3	51 458.3	51 216.0	51 124.1	51 761.3	52 274.1	52 807.4
48	**Total employment**	241 447.2	240 350.5	240 482.0	236 649.6	233 498.2	234 848.7	237 344.2	240 258.4
	EMPLOYEES, MILLION HOURS, DOMESTIC CONCEPT								
49	Industry, including energy	34 826.7	34 536.6	34 783.8	34 033.8	33 573.1	33 612.8	33 837.6	34 101.7
50	Distrib. trade, repairs; transp.; accommod., food serv. activ.	46 790.7	46 650.1	46 709.4	45 919.4	45 136.2	45 451.7	46 204.5	47 172.9
51	Financial and insurance activities	5 932.1	5 854.0	5 807.7	5 773.5	5 678.0	5 611.6	5 587.3	5 606.9
52	Prof., scientif., techn. activ.; admin., support service activ.	20 801.9	21 299.4	21 844.5	21 718.6	21 545.3	22 219.2	23 054.0	23 871.3
53	Public admin.; compulsory s.s.; education; human health	47 633.3	47 901.9	47 872.2	47 602.4	47 541.0	48 069.8	48 451.3	48 963.7
54	**Total employees**	193 006.9	192 392.0	192 565.3	189 417.3	186 985.0	188 516.4	191 113.1	194 085.8
	SELF-EMPLOYED, MILLION HOURS, DOMESTIC CONCEPT								
55	Industry, including energy	3 358.4	3 241.6	3 176.3	3 070.8	2 987.8	2 922.4	2 906.1	2 894.5
56	Distrib. trade, repairs; transp.; accommod., food serv. activ.	15 566.2	15 394.2	15 318.1	15 080.6	14 868.4	14 782.6	14 564.1	14 546.3
57	Financial and insurance activities	830.8	827.3	822.2	804.3	779.5	780.4	795.5	815.2
58	Prof., scientif., techn. activ.; admin., support service activ.	7 349.7	7 492.9	7 728.0	7 724.2	7 725.8	7 746.0	7 775.1	7 833.6
59	Public admin.; compulsory s.s.; education; human health	3 421.9	3 464.4	3 586.2	3 613.6	3 583.1	3 691.6	3 822.9	3 843.7
60	**Total self-employed**	48 440.3	47 958.5	47 916.7	47 232.3	46 513.3	46 332.3	46 231.2	46 172.6

Note: Detailed metadata:http://metalinks.oecd.org/nav1/20180308/ed46
Source: Statistical Office of the European Communities (Eurostat).

ORGANISATION FOR ECONOMIC CO-OPERATION AND DEVELOPMENT

The OECD is a unique forum where governments work together to address the economic, social and environmental challenges of globalisation. The OECD is also at the forefront of efforts to understand and to help governments respond to new developments and concerns, such as corporate governance, the information economy and the challenges of an ageing population. The Organisation provides a setting where governments can compare policy experiences, seek answers to common problems, identify good practice and work to co-ordinate domestic and international policies.

The OECD member countries are: Australia, Austria, Belgium, Canada, Chile, the Czech Republic, Denmark, Estonia, Finland, France, Germany, Greece, Hungary, Iceland, Ireland, Israel, Italy, Japan, Korea, Latvia, Luxembourg, Mexico, the Netherlands, New Zealand, Norway, Poland, Portugal, the Slovak Republic, Slovenia, Spain, Sweden, Switzerland, Turkey, the United Kingdom and the United States. The European Commission takes part in the work of the OECD.

OECD Publishing disseminates widely the results of the Organisation's statistics gathering and research on economic, social and environmental issues, as well as the conventions, guidelines and standards agreed by its members.